BARRON'S
SAT®
SUBJECT TEST IN LITERATURE
2007

3RD EDITION

Christina Myers-Shaffer, M.Ed.
Former Department Chair
Georgetown Independent School District
Georgetown, Texas

Independent Consultant and Educational Writer

BARRON'S

® SAT is a registered trademark of the College Entrance Examination Board, which was not involved in the production of, and does not endorse this book.

All inquiries should be addressed to:
Barron's Educational Series, Inc.
250 Wireless Boulevard
Hauppauge, NY 11788-3917
http://www.barronseduc.com

Library of Congress Catalog Card No. 2006040753

ISBN-13: 978-0-7641-3448-7
ISBN-10: 0-7641-3448-5

Library of Congress Cataloging-in-Publication Data

Myers-Shaffer, Christina.
    How to prepare for SAT subject test in literature / by Christina Myers-Shaffer. — 3rd ed.
        p. cm.
    Rev. ed. of: How to prepare for SAT II: Literature. 2nd ed. 2000.
    Includes bibliographical references and index.
    ISBN 0-7641-3448-5
        1. Literature—Examinations—Study guides.   2. SAT (Educationl test)—Study guides.
I. Myers-Shaffer, Christina. How to prepare for SAT II. Literature.   II. Title.

PN62.M94   2006
807.6—dc22   2006040753

PRINTED IN THE UNITED STATES OF AMERICA
9 8 7 6 5 4 3 2 1

Acknowledgments

The author gratefully acknowledges the following copyright holders for permission to reprint material used in this publication:

Page 85: From "Pied Beauty" from *Poems of Gerard Manley Hopkins* by Gerard Manley Hopkins. Reprinted with permission of Oxford University Press.

Page 120: From "Barn Burning," *Collected Stories of William Faulkner* © 1939 by William Faulkner. Reprinted by permission of Random House, Inc.

Page 218: Excerpt from *The Great Code* © 1982, 1981 by Northrop Frye. Reprinted with permission of Harcourt Brace & Company.

Page 299: "An Encounter with Honey Bees" by Lillian E. Myers © 1999 by Lillian E. Myers. Reprinted by permission of Lillian E. Myers. All rights reserved.

"Bell-tones" (page 39), "Pity the Poor Raccoon" (page 88), "Know Yourself" (page 91), "Alphabet Soup" (page 102), "Stressed and Unstressed" (pages 80–81), "Is It Euphemism or Euphony?" (page 237), and "That Sound" (page 168) by Lillian E. Myers © 1996 by Lillian E. Myers. Reprinted by permission of Lillian E. Myers. All rights reserved.

Every effort has been made to trace the copyright holders and we apologize in advance for any unintentional omissions. We would be pleased to insert the appropriate acknowledgment in any subsequent edition of this publication.

In preparing to take the SAT Subject Test in Literature, use this book for...

Review

This book reviews:

- Developing a study plan for taking the test
- The basics of literary analysis
- Basic literary terminology (definitions, uses, and effects)
- Vocabulary

Practice

This book contains:

- Two complete diagnostic tests (60 multiple-choice questions each) with answers and explanations
- Sample questions that cover each of the seven literary elements
- Three interpretive skill practice sets that cover each of the seven literary elements
- Seven complete practice tests (60 multiple-choice questions each) with answers and explanations
- Putting Essays on T.O.P. exercises in preparation for the SAT essay and the SAT Subject Test in Literature

Reference

This book is a resource for definitions and examples of literary terminology (ranging from basic to advanced) to use in:

- High school literature classes
- College literature classes
- Independent reading and study
- Study groups
- Papers analyzing prose, poetry, and drama

Advancement

This book aims to increase:

- Your skills for taking the test
- Your pleasure in reading
- Your range of reading materials
- Your reading comprehension
- Your analysis skills
- Your writing skills

Contents

Introduction

This book is a valuable tool for preparing to take the SAT Subject Test in Literature, whether you want a quick study or a complete course.

If you have limited time before the test or just want to review and practice:

1. In Part II: The Seven Literary Elements, each chapter contains the most important terms and definitions highlighted by **TERM ALERT** for quick study.

2. Also, you can go directly to the ▼ **PRACTICE QUESTIONS** ▼ that appear throughout the Literary Elements chapters. These questions illustrate and explain the concepts and types of questions that could appear on the test.

3. Finally, the book contains two diagnostic tests and seven full-length practice tests with explained answers for you to use as time allows.

If you want a complete preparation course:

In the pages that follow, you will find ideas, information, Active Thinking Exercises, and practice opportunities to help you excel on the SAT Subject Test in Literature, improve your performance on the essay portion of the SAT, and train your critical thinking skills so that you can think creatively in today's world.

To prepare for the SAT Subject Test in Literature, you need to master the following:

1. **Vocabulary.** You need to know and understand what words mean: literal definitions, implied meanings, shades of meanings, contextual definitions, historical meanings (defined by context), and the connotations certain words impart. This book provides opportunities for vocabulary development and practice using context in testing situations.

2. **Literary Terms.** Of course, you should know the definitions of major literary terms and recognize when such devices are used. You also need to understand how their use can affect the meaning of a literary work. This book provides literary terms, defined and illustrated, with practice opportunities for you to identify their uses and effects.

3. **Critical Reading Skills.** To develop critical reading skills, you need to learn how to interpret the intentional and unintentional meanings conveyed in a written work. Mastering these skills requires recognizing and understanding how seven major literary elements work together to form those meanings. This book provides Active Thinking Exercises to develop critical thinking and reading skills and (you guessed it) more practice.

Bonus: The Putting Essays on T.O.P. section helps you sharpen the writing skills you need to do well on the SAT essay requirement as you prepare for the SAT Subject Test in Literature. This section gives you opportunities to develop critical reading skills and improve your own writing.

WHY PREPARING FOR THE LITERATURE TEST IS IMPORTANT FOR YOU

Language and literature are changing and you are at the leading edge of many of the changes taking place. Each time you e-mail a friend, browse the Net, or download a new program, you are furthering the gap between how language was used in the past and how it is being used today.

Dickens and Austen were not concerned about whether their novels adapted well as made-for-TV movies. Shakespeare did not attempt to use language that would appeal to the global village of a computer-driven world. A poem, by definition, had a regular rhythm and a rhyme scheme for Tennyson; and acronyms were a clever part of the world of descriptive poetry, not ttytt (to tell you the truth) shortcuts when text-messaging a friend.

Perceptions are also changing. For example, prose and poetry are merging. The line between objectivity and subjectivity is fading, especially in the news media. The English language to some degree is losing regional differences to become more homogenized. Technology-savvy people are more willing to break the rules of language in the name of convenience and individuality than past generations. As a result, we are changing from the world of unbreakable language rules of the mid-1900s to the no-holds-barred writing of some of today's young authors.

What do these changes mean for you? Why should you be required to read and understand literature written long before you were born in language patterns that are not relevant to today's communication?

Many people would tell you that because we are a product of the past, it is only by understanding the thoughts and ideas of previous generations that we can productively move forward. True. Others would say that you are cheating yourself if you do not learn to appreciate the many worthwhile works of literature that so eloquently express the hopes, dreams, and fears of people who in many ways were similar to us. Also true. Despite these and many equally valid reasons that learning to read and understand literature of the past is worthwhile, the question, however, remains: Why do *you* need to learn the rules and elements of literature?

The answer may surprise you. Many of today's employers are seeking people who combine practical logic with the creativity needed to think outside the box. They want people who use critical thinking skills, in other words, who think actively. You might assume that thinking outside the box means that rules and conventions are no longer necessary. In reality, understanding rules and conventions is of greater importance than ever. You cannot effectively think outside the box until you know where and how far the sides of the box extend.

Critical reading can be a powerful training ground for developing critical thinking skills. Learning to recognize and use the seven literary elements (tested by the SAT Subject Test in Literature and taught in this book) will train you to look at ideas from many different perspectives. Also, the study of literature can give you experience and insight into how people think and why some events happen as they do, an advantage in any age.

PART I

PREPARING FOR THE LITERATURE TEST

College Entrance Examinations

SAT Subject Test in Literature

Hints and Helps for the Literature Test

Diagnostic Test I

College Entrance Examinations

The College Board, headquartered in Princeton, New Jersey, administers the SAT Program. The two main categories of tests that make up the SAT Program are the SAT and the SAT Subject Tests. The results of these tests are used by educational counselors, student-placement personnel, and scholarship committees, among others, to assist students in their postsecondary academic careers.

SAT REASONING TEST

As its name implies, the SAT measures your mathematical and verbal reasoning abilities. The results of the SAT provide a comparative measure of your preparation and abilities to those of other students. Your score is used in conjunction with your high school grades, activities, class rank, and other factors (depending upon the requirements of the particular institution) to provide you and a wide range of academic professionals with a picture of how you have done, an idea of how you are doing, and most significantly a basis for projection of how you are likely to do in a postsecondary setting.

SAT SUBJECT TESTS

The Subject Tests that you need to take will be determined by such factors as the requirements of the postsecondary institution to which you are planning to apply and what subject areas are likely to be significant to your personal academic plan. Your academic counselor should be able to assist you in these areas. As with the SAT, the SAT Subject Tests are used in conjunction with many other factors for admission (both to postsecondary institutions and to programs within those schools), for predicting future performance, for placing students within programs, and for guiding them in their academic choices.

THE COLLEGE BOARD

Students can ask questions and request materials concerning the SAT Program by writing to

College Board SAT Program
P.O. Box 6200
Princeton, NJ 08541-6200

or by calling 609-771-7600. You can find the College Board online at http://www.collegeboard.com.

SAT Subject Test in Literature

The SAT Subject Test in Literature is one of the Subject Tests (Achievement Tests) administered by the College Board.

THE LITERATURE TEST FORMAT

As with most of the SAT Subject Tests, the Literature Subject Test is entirely multiple-choice, expected to take about one hour to administer.

Here are some of the key features concerning the structure and content of the Literature Subject Test.

The Literature Test:

- Attempts to measure your skills in reading literature
- Contains from six to eight reading selections
- Asks about 60 multiple-choice questions based on those reading selections
- Requires extended verbal abilities, particularly in reading comprehension and figurative language
- Contains selections from English and American prose, poetry, and drama written during the Renaissance through the twentieth century (Some selections other than English or American, but written in English, and some selections other than prose, poetry, or drama might be included.)
- Asks from four to twelve questions per selection
- Asks questions about meaning, form, narrative voice, tone, character, use of language, and meaning(s) in context
- Requires a knowledge of basic literary terminology
- Includes selections that are complete short works or excerpts from longer works

The individual selections might be, for example, taken from nineteenth-century American prose, sixteenth-century English drama, twentieth-century poetry written in English by a South African, and so forth. The percentage distributions shown in the graphs on the next page, however, represent averages and may—or may not—be reflected in any given test. (The slanted lines represent variable numbers. For example, a test may contain 40 to 50 percent selections from English literature.)

The Literature Test does *not*

- Include test questions about literary periods, authors' biographies, or literary criticism
- Require preknowledge of selections on the test
- Require you to study a specified reading list

After each selection on the Literature Test, you will find the year the work was first published. Knowing the date of publication can help you better understand the context of the work.

THE SELECTIONS ON THE LITERATURE TEST

SOURCE: 0 10 20 30 40 50 60 70 80 90 100 %

English |||||||||||||||||||////

American |||||||||||||||||||////

Other   ////

CENTURY: 0 10 20 30 40 50 60 70 80 90 100 %

16th–17th |||||||||||||

18th–19th |||||||||||||

20th |||||||||||||||||

GENRE: 0 10 20 30 40 50 60 70 80 90 100 %

Prose |||||||||||||||||||//

Poetry |||||||||||||||||||//

Drama   ////

Hints and Helps for the Literature Test

Read the following list of Hints and Helps to begin your preparation for the Literature Test.

1. PRACTICE ACTIVE THINKING EXERCISES.

You can use critical reading practice as a way to develop critical thinking skills. This book is designed to give you that practice. At the heart of literature, you will find seven literary elements. In addition to diagnostic tests, practice sets, and full-length practice tests, the chapters that follow explain the seven literary elements (tested by the SAT) with definitions and examples. Then, at the end of each of the seven literary element chapters in Part II, you will find Active Thinking Exercises to help you master these skills. Here is how:

Step 1. ▶Focus◀

Have you ever finished reading something and cannot remember a thing you just read? A divided mind wastes time and leads to mistakes. To focus is to shut out the world (your surroundings and any off-the-subject thinking) so your mind is totally concentrated on the reading selections and what they mean. In the following Active Thinking Exercises, you will get to investigate different focus techniques to find what works best for you.

Step 2. My Own Words (MOW).

In searching for the meaning of a literary selection, a good way to begin is to express the subject and the writer's main points in your own words. MOWing teaches you to paraphrase and summarize, two time-honored techniques that really work.

Step 3. Break It Down (BID).

Yes, you need to look for facts and details in the literary selections on the test. But when you BID, you see meaning in the facts and details. You will be working with them from the seven different literary perspectives tested by the SAT. Learning to BID is where the action is.

Step 4. Test Taker to Test Maker (TT→TM).

When your mind shifts from test taker to test maker, your thinking moves outside the box and views literature with new understanding. You will be guided on how to identify what elements in any given literary selection would make test questions, and you will learn different ways those questions could be asked.

▶Focus◀, MOW, BID, and TT→TM. Do you see what these four exercises have in common? They all challenge you to think actively with greater attention, comprehension, and confidence.

2. STUDY THE TEST TO STUDY FOR THE TEST.

Become familiar with the following:

(a) Test Questions

The SAT Subject Test in Literature consists of about 60 multiple-choice questions, with five answer choices (A through E) for each question. The question stem might be worded in two ways:

1. As a question, such as "What is the meaning of 'establishment' as it is used in line 2?"
2. As an incomplete sentence, such as "The vehicle of the metaphor in line 3 is"

There are three different kinds of multiple-choice questions that may appear on the test:

1. Regular multiple-choice questions

What is the speaker's attitude? (Question stem)
(A) Angry (A through E answer choices)
(B) Raucous
(C) Profane
(D) Morbid
(E) Defensive

Someone once compared the regular multiple-choice question to a series of five true-false questions, because essentially you are examining each answer choice to see if it is true or false. Usually, the true answer choice is the correct one. In these questions, however, you may encounter more than one answer choice that is to some degree true or correct, in which case you would select the answer choice that is best.

2. NOT, LEAST, or EXCEPT questions

All the following appear in lines 1–4 EXCEPT
(A) personification
(B) simile
(C) metaphor
(D) paradox
(E) apostrophe

Which of the following is the LEAST accurate description of the dog in line 12?
(A) Fierce
(B) Friendly
(C) Fiendish
(D) Fiery
(E) Furious

Which of the following uses of language does NOT appear in lines 1–4?
(A) Personification
(B) Simile
(C) Metaphor
(D) Paradox
(E) Apostrophe

Some test questions might contain the words EXCEPT, LEAST, or NOT. In these questions, you are looking for the response that does not apply to the situation or that is inappropriate to the question stem—just the opposite of a regular multiple-choice question.

3. Roman numeral questions

In this passage, the rose is

   I. an emblem

   II. a vehicle for metaphor

   III. an allegorical representation

   (A) I only

   (B) II only

   (C) I and III only

   (D) II and III only

   (E) I, II, and III

In these questions, you will be given several words, phrases, or clauses that are labeled with Roman numerals. The answer choices allow you to select either individual ideas or combinations of ideas as possible correct answer choices.

The practice tests in this book will provide you with opportunities to work with each of these three different types of multiple-choice questions. Here are a few tips to keep in mind:

- Read through all the answer choices—do not stop when you reach the "correct" answer. Reason: Answer Choice B, for example, may indeed be "correct"; however, in multiple-choice questions you may be looking for the answer that is most accurate among more than one "correct" answer. You may later find that Answer Choice E is a better answer than B!
- After you read through all the answer choices, eliminate those that are clearly not the correct answer choice.
- Compare the answer choices that are left, taking close note of key words in the question stem, including requirements such as "What is the effect…"
- Some testing authorities recommend that if you cannot decide on a final answer, continue with the next question, then return if time allows.
- Keep in mind that
  1. You get one point for each correct answer.
  2. You lose one-fourth of one point for each wrong answer.
  3. Omitted questions and questions for which you mark more than one answer choice are not counted.

(b) Basic Literary Terms and Related Vocabulary

The SAT Subject Test tests your knowledge of basic literary terms.

TERM ALERT Not everyone agrees on which literary terms are "basic." There are some terms, however, that you really should know, terms that either have appeared on previous tests or may reasonably be tested on the SAT Subject Test.

TERM ALERT will point out these important literary terms, give you definitions, examples, and opportunities to practice dealing with the terms in SAT-type questions.

Beyond basic definitions (such as that a simile is a comparison using "like" or "as"), you need to be able to recognize when the concepts behind the literary terms are being used and the effects their uses create.

For example, you should be able to recognize that "The woman felt like a small child whose pet dog was missing" contains a simile that in context might make the woman seem in a state of panic, hurt, and fear with perhaps implied elements of emotional immaturity. A resulting test question might ask the following:

> In the line, "The woman felt like a small child whose pet dog was missing," comparing the woman to a child who lost her pet has the effect of
> (A) condemning her anger
> (B) making the woman seem unstable
> (C) limiting her options for response
> (D) emphasizing a sense of worry
> (E) reinforcing a sense of disillusionment

If the woman has just lost something of great value to her, the answer might be D (losing a pet can cause worry); however, you cannot be sure without the context. What if the paragraph from which this sentence is taken is describing in detail the woman having hallucinations of friends who had left her life thirty years earlier? A woman feeling "like a small child whose pet dog was missing" in these circumstances would perhaps make her seem more "unstable" (B).

(c) Other Literary Concepts and Related Vocabulary

You do *not* need to memorize advanced literary terms for taking the literature test. This book, however, does include definitions and illustrations of some advanced literary terms that you can use for analyzing selections and improving your work in your literature classes. Also, understanding how these concepts are used and the effects they create, even if you do not remember the terms themselves, can help increase your reading perception. The practice questions included with the concepts behind the terms will help you prepare for the test.

(d) Extensive, General Vocabulary

The importance of enlarging your vocabulary cannot be overstated. Students have made incorrect answer choices on questions they might have otherwise answered correctly because they did not understand the meaning of a word used in the question stem or answer choices.

Perhaps the most direct and effective way to increase your vocabulary is to adopt a sense of language awareness when you read. Just memorizing words and meanings may have little lasting value. On the other hand, as you are reading works of literature, class assignments, magazine articles, or even the daily newspaper, make note of new words as they are used in context. By associating the words with how they are used, you can increase your vocabulary in a meaningful way. Begin looking for opportunities to use these words in your own class work and personal writings.

3. LEARN TO USE CONTEXT.

About sixty percent of the selections on the SAT Subject Test in Literature are taken from works written before 1900. How can you, as a modern reader, learn to understand the meanings of words and how they are used in a poem written, for example, in 1780?

First, the literary elements or perspectives are universal and can apply to any literature, regardless of time and place. Master them and you will be on your way to understanding what you are reading.

Second, like spotting clues in an Agatha Christie mystery, developing context skills can help you bridge the gap between the past and the present. To provide you with opportunities to develop context skills, this study guide emphasizes pre-1900 literature. It provides the names of authors and titles of the works from which the selections are taken, and the exercises emphasize ways you can develop the context skills you need to understand them. These skills will help your reading comprehension regardless of when or where the selection was written. You should not let nonstandardized spellings, obsolete words, regional diction, or culturally based expressions confuse you. Use context.

TERM ALERT You should know this term: **context**

Definition: Context refers to the information that comes before or after a given word, phrase, sentence, or paragraph and helps the reader understand the exact or intended meaning. Generally, the reader studies the context to find clues to meaning.

Sometimes the writer will provide you with clues to meaning. The following examples illustrate some of the more direct types of context clues.

CONTEXT CLUE:	EXAMPLE:
1. definition	Some older churches contain feretories, shrines used to house relics of saints.
2. example	There are some members of the lily family that we eat every day, for example, garlic.
3. restatement	"She won't need your help anymore, Wally. In other words, get out and don't come back."
4. comparison	An oriel is like a large bay window with attitude.
5. contrast	Unlike the silk flowers in the hall, origami is made with paper.
6. synonym	He sent in troops to quash, or subdue, the rioting crowd.
7. detail	Frontogenesis occurred over central Texas last night. Cold air from the north collided with warm Gulf air to produce thunderstorms.

How do you determine the meaning, however, when the writer does not give you any direct clues? If you are determining the meaning of an individual word, you can look for prefixes and suffixes and examine the root or base of the word. Another way is to look at the part of speech. What function does the mystery word serve in the sentence?

One of the most valuable techniques you can use for determining meaning from context, in general, is making inferences.

TERM ALERT You should know this term: **inference**

Definition: To make an inference from context is to draw a conclusion or make an assumption based on the evidence within the text. For example, what can you infer from this sentence?

> **Rosemarie threw aside the freshly picked daffodils as she ran to rescue her child from the oncoming eighteen-wheeler.**

We can infer that it is springtime (when daffodils bloom) and that Rosemarie and the child are along a highway.

Inference is especially helpful when a word has multiple meanings:

> **Elizabeth loved spinning wool from her own sheep. Many evenings would find her with her *distaff* in one hand and her spindle in the other.**

We can infer that the distaff is a piece of equipment used to spin wool and that Elizabeth probably lives on a farm.

> **The genetic disorder once again appeared in the *distaff* side of the family. None of the men showed any symptoms.**

We can assume that the women are showing the symptoms.

> **He would do only what he considered "men's work." *Distaff* was totally out of the question for his weekend's activities.**

We can infer that he will not do what he considers "women's work."

▼PRACTICE QUESTION▼

These lines come from *Wuthering Heights* by Emily Brontë:

> But his [Earnshaw's] self-love would endure no further torment—
> I heard, and not altogether disapprovingly, a manual check given to
> her saucy tongue—The little wretch [Catherine] had done her utmost
> Line   to hurt her cousin's sensitive though uncultivated feelings, and a
> (5)   physical argument was the only mode he had of balancing the
> account, and repaying its effects on the inflicter.

The "manual check" probably was
(A) Catherine suddenly becoming silent
(B) Earnshaw scolding Catherine
(C) Catherine abruptly holding her tongue
(D) Catherine holding her hand over her mouth
(E) Earnshaw slapping Catherine

Explanation: What evidence is in this selection? Catherine and Earnshaw (cousins) are fighting. She hurt his feelings. The "manual check" has made the argument physical. The narrator "heard" the "manual check," which was applied to Catherine's "saucy tongue" (mouth). The only conclusion that can be drawn from this evidence is that he slapped her.

Correct Answer: **E**

Begin using context clues as you respond to the practice questions throughout this book. Also, you will learn more about context in Literary Element #7, Meanings of Words, Phrases, and Lines in Context (Meanings in Context).

4. PLAN TO SUCCEED.

Prepare yourself when you study.

Begin with a positive attitude toward reading and understanding literature. Realize that the critical reading and thinking skills you develop in preparing for this test can help you in other subjects and areas in life. This study is worth the effort.

Because critical reading is a skill, it requires practice over time. Pace yourself and set goals. Practice on a regular basis is probably the most effective way to prepare your mind to think critically for the test.

Take good care of yourself; eat correctly, and exercise your body as well as your mind. Concentrate totally when you are studying, but get adequate rest and relaxation at intervals, as well. Add variety to your test preparation. Sometimes study alone. At other times you might want to join friends or a study group to discuss the literary element chapters or quiz each other over terms and definitions. Do what works the best for you.

Prepare yourself for the day of the test.

Prepare for the test day by planning comfortable clothes, assembling any materials you need, getting a good night's sleep, and eating a proper diet.

Be sure to confirm the day, time, and location of the test and allow yourself time the night before to review terms and concepts.

During the test, listen to all verbal directions and read all written instructions carefully. Pace yourself. Do not struggle over any one question. Move on; then return to unanswered questions after answering all those with certain answers.

▶ Focus ◀ Periodically check the number of the question you are answering against the number on the answer sheet to be sure you are answering in the correct space.

Finally, be quiet, calm, and relaxed. After you have trained your mind to think critically, the test becomes just another opportunity to use your critical reading skills.

Conclusion

At this point, you should have a plan, understand the structure of the test, and be ready to develop your active thinking and context skills. Now it is time to see where your strengths and weaknesses are with Diagnostic Test I.

Diagnostic Test I: Literature

The purpose of the following Diagnostic Test is to

1.   Introduce you to the format and structure of the test
2.   Acquaint you with the types of questions that may be asked
3.   Illustrate and explain the content of questions that are based on interpretive thinking skills
4.   Help you identify your strengths—and your weaknesses—in critical reading and the seven major literary elements

Diagnostic Test I is not intended to be an easy test. It will present you with an opportunity to use evaluative skills over a wide range of literary devices, including symbolism and connotative word meanings. Some of the test is written to provide you with examples and experience in dealing with questions in which shades of meaning, minute details, and subtle distinctions make selecting the correct answer difficult.

You need to know that you need to know. Do not be concerned about any questions that you miss; the answers are explained after the test and the concepts behind the questions are explained later in the book.

To take this test, remove the answer sheet (see page 15) to record your answers. Allow yourself one hour (using a timer or clock to time yourself).

Be sure to read all directions carefully.

Remember: You may *not* use other papers, books, or reference materials of any kind.

After you complete the test, use the Answer Key (see page 27) to check your answers and to determine your raw score. Then use the Analysis: Diagnostic Test I (see page 30) to help you evaluate your answer choices.

ANSWER SHEET FOR DIAGNOSTIC TEST I

1. Ⓐ Ⓑ Ⓒ Ⓓ Ⓔ
2. Ⓐ Ⓑ Ⓒ Ⓓ Ⓔ
3. Ⓐ Ⓑ Ⓒ Ⓓ Ⓔ
4. Ⓐ Ⓑ Ⓒ Ⓓ Ⓔ
5. Ⓐ Ⓑ Ⓒ Ⓓ Ⓔ
6. Ⓐ Ⓑ Ⓒ Ⓓ Ⓔ
7. Ⓐ Ⓑ Ⓒ Ⓓ Ⓔ
8. Ⓐ Ⓑ Ⓒ Ⓓ Ⓔ
9. Ⓐ Ⓑ Ⓒ Ⓓ Ⓔ
10. Ⓐ Ⓑ Ⓒ Ⓓ Ⓔ
11. Ⓐ Ⓑ Ⓒ Ⓓ Ⓔ
12. Ⓐ Ⓑ Ⓒ Ⓓ Ⓔ
13. Ⓐ Ⓑ Ⓒ Ⓓ Ⓔ
14. Ⓐ Ⓑ Ⓒ Ⓓ Ⓔ
15. Ⓐ Ⓑ Ⓒ Ⓓ Ⓔ
16. Ⓐ Ⓑ Ⓒ Ⓓ Ⓔ
17. Ⓐ Ⓑ Ⓒ Ⓓ Ⓔ
18. Ⓐ Ⓑ Ⓒ Ⓓ Ⓔ
19. Ⓐ Ⓑ Ⓒ Ⓓ Ⓔ
20. Ⓐ Ⓑ Ⓒ Ⓓ Ⓔ

21. Ⓐ Ⓑ Ⓒ Ⓓ Ⓔ
22. Ⓐ Ⓑ Ⓒ Ⓓ Ⓔ
23. Ⓐ Ⓑ Ⓒ Ⓓ Ⓔ
24. Ⓐ Ⓑ Ⓒ Ⓓ Ⓔ
25. Ⓐ Ⓑ Ⓒ Ⓓ Ⓔ
26. Ⓐ Ⓑ Ⓒ Ⓓ Ⓔ
27. Ⓐ Ⓑ Ⓒ Ⓓ Ⓔ
28. Ⓐ Ⓑ Ⓒ Ⓓ Ⓔ
29. Ⓐ Ⓑ Ⓒ Ⓓ Ⓔ
30. Ⓐ Ⓑ Ⓒ Ⓓ Ⓔ
31. Ⓐ Ⓑ Ⓒ Ⓓ Ⓔ
32. Ⓐ Ⓑ Ⓒ Ⓓ Ⓔ
33. Ⓐ Ⓑ Ⓒ Ⓓ Ⓔ
34. Ⓐ Ⓑ Ⓒ Ⓓ Ⓔ
35. Ⓐ Ⓑ Ⓒ Ⓓ Ⓔ
36. Ⓐ Ⓑ Ⓒ Ⓓ Ⓔ
37. Ⓐ Ⓑ Ⓒ Ⓓ Ⓔ
38. Ⓐ Ⓑ Ⓒ Ⓓ Ⓔ
39. Ⓐ Ⓑ Ⓒ Ⓓ Ⓔ
40. Ⓐ Ⓑ Ⓒ Ⓓ Ⓔ

41. Ⓐ Ⓑ Ⓒ Ⓓ Ⓔ
42. Ⓐ Ⓑ Ⓒ Ⓓ Ⓔ
43. Ⓐ Ⓑ Ⓒ Ⓓ Ⓔ
44. Ⓐ Ⓑ Ⓒ Ⓓ Ⓔ
45. Ⓐ Ⓑ Ⓒ Ⓓ Ⓔ
46. Ⓐ Ⓑ Ⓒ Ⓓ Ⓔ
47. Ⓐ Ⓑ Ⓒ Ⓓ Ⓔ
48. Ⓐ Ⓑ Ⓒ Ⓓ Ⓔ
49. Ⓐ Ⓑ Ⓒ Ⓓ Ⓔ
50. Ⓐ Ⓑ Ⓒ Ⓓ Ⓔ
51. Ⓐ Ⓑ Ⓒ Ⓓ Ⓔ
52. Ⓐ Ⓑ Ⓒ Ⓓ Ⓔ
53. Ⓐ Ⓑ Ⓒ Ⓓ Ⓔ
54. Ⓐ Ⓑ Ⓒ Ⓓ Ⓔ
55. Ⓐ Ⓑ Ⓒ Ⓓ Ⓔ
56. Ⓐ Ⓑ Ⓒ Ⓓ Ⓔ
57. Ⓐ Ⓑ Ⓒ Ⓓ Ⓔ
58. Ⓐ Ⓑ Ⓒ Ⓓ Ⓔ
59. Ⓐ Ⓑ Ⓒ Ⓓ Ⓔ
60. Ⓐ Ⓑ Ⓒ Ⓓ Ⓔ

Diagnostic Test I

> <u>Directions</u>: The following questions test your understanding of several literary selections. Read each passage or poem and the questions that follow it. Select the best answer choice for each question by blackening the matching oval on your answer sheet. **Special attention should be given to questions containing the following words: EXCEPT, LEAST, NOT.**

<u>Questions 1–10</u> are based on the following passage.

All eyes were now turned on the country lad, standing at the door, in his worn three-cornered hat, grey coat, leather breeches,
Line and blue yarn stockings, leaning on an
(5) oaken cudgel, and bearing a wallet on his back.

Robin replied to the courteous innkeeper, with such an assumption of confidence as befitted the Major's relative. "My honest
(10) friend," he said, "I shall make it a point to patronize your house on some occasion, when"—here he could not help lowering his voice—"when I may have more than a parchment threepence in my pocket. My
(15) present business," continued he, speaking with lofty confidence, "is merely to inquire my way to the dwelling of my kinsman, Major Molineux."

There was a sudden and general
(20) movement in the room, which Robin interpreted as expressing the eagerness of each individual to become his guide. But the innkeeper turned his eyes to a written paper on the wall, which he read, or seemed to
(25) read, with occasional recurrences to the young man's figure.

"What have we here?" said he, breaking his speech into little dry fragments. " 'Left the house of the subscriber, bounden
(30) servant, Hezekiah Mudge,—had on, when he went away, grey coat, leather breeches, master's third-best hat. One pound currency reward to whosoever shall lodge him in any jail of the province.' Better trudge, boy,
(35) better trudge!"

Robin had begun to draw his hand towards the lighter end of the oak cudgel,
but a strange hostility in every countenance induced him to relinquish his purpose of
(40) breaking the courteous innkeeper's head. As he turned to leave the room, he encountered a sneering glance from the bold-featured personage whom he had before noticed; and no sooner was he
(45) beyond the door, than he heard a general laugh, in which the innkeeper's voice might be distinguished, like the dropping of small stones into a kettle.

My Kinsman, Major Molineux
by Nathaniel Hawthorne

1. The "wallet" that Robin bears on his back in line 5 probably refers to his
   (A) money bag
   (B) pocketbook
   (C) knapsack
   (D) billfold
   (E) jacket decal

2. Of the literary devices listed below, which is used in lines 46–48 to describe the innkeeper's voice?
   (A) Metaphor
   (B) Personification
   (C) Paradox
   (D) Simile
   (E) Apostrophe

3. That the innkeeper "seemed to read" the paper (line 24) implies that
   (A) he is illiterate
   (B) he is fabricating the paper's contents
   (C) he has the notice memorized
   (D) he feels reticent about reading it aloud
   (E) he is eager to warn the boy of danger

4. How does contrast of Robin's appearance to his attitude contribute to the tone of this selection?
   (A) It uses direct threat to create a hostile tone.
   (B) It incorporates humility to create an impertinent tone.
   (C) It includes paradox to create an aggressive tone.
   (D) It emphasizes hyperbole to create a retaliatory tone.
   (E) It uses situational irony to create a comic tone.

5. The tone of "My honest friend" (line 9) in the context in which it is said sounds
   (A) conciliatory
   (B) condescending
   (C) impatient
   (D) polite
   (E) kind

6. Robin "could not help lowering his voice" (line 12) probably because he
   (A) wants the innkeeper to realize his honest intentions
   (B) does not want to appear too affluent
   (C) is ashamed of his lack of money
   (D) feels intimidated by the others in the room
   (E) fears the others would rob him

7. The sarcastic tone in lines 40 is the result of
   (A) paradox
   (B) hyperbole
   (C) verbal irony
   (D) alliteration
   (E) symbolism

8. The description of the innkeeper's speech in line 28 is
   (A) an allusion
   (B) a simile
   (C) a recurrent theme
   (D) personification
   (E) a metaphor

9. The innkeeper's use of the word "trudge" in line 35 is intended as
   (A) harsh reality for a threatening effect
   (B) verbal irony for a comic effect
   (C) situational irony for a tragic effect
   (D) overstatement of the boy's condition
   (E) a parody of the traveling genre

10. In the context of the selection, how can "cudgel" (lines 5 and 37) be defined?
   I. A walking stick
   II. A weapon
   III. A type of cane
   (A) I only
   (B) II only
   (C) III only
   (D) I and II only
   (E) I, II, and III

Questions 11–19 are based on the following poem.

Proof to No Purpose

You see this gentle stream, that glides,
Shoved on, by quick-succeeding tides:
Try if this sober stream you can
Line Follow to th' wilder ocean,
(5) And see, if there it keeps unspent
In that congesting element.
Next, from that world of waters, then
By pores and caverns back again
Induct that inadultrate same
(10) Stream to the spring from whence it came.
This with a wonder when ye do,
An easy, and else easier too:
Then may ye recollect the grains
Of my particular remains,
(15) After a thousand lusters hurled,
By ruffling winds, about the world.

by Robert Herrick

11. The central denotative theme of the poem addresses the subject of
   (A) water cycles
   (B) how oceans are formed
   (C) seasons and weather of the world
   (D) life cycles
   (E) the instabilities of life

12. As seen in lines 3 and 5, the speaker's attitude toward the silent auditor seems to be somewhat
    (A) mocking
    (B) challenging
    (C) loving
    (D) deferential
    (E) churlish

13. Within the context of this poem, the speaker's "remains" in line 14 can be seen as his
    I. work left to be done
    II. remnant of material possessions
    III. dead body
    IV. surviving writings
    (A) I only
    (B) II only
    (C) II, III, and IV only
    (D) II and III only
    (E) III and IV only

14. As the word is used in line 14, "particular" describes the speaker's "remains" as all the following EXCEPT
    (A) apart from others
    (B) personal
    (C) special rather than general
    (D) precise
    (E) considered separately

15. What is the outcome of the speaker's use of the phrase "unspent/In that congesting element" (lines 5–6)?
    (A) The use influences the reader to regard the stream as lost forever in the ocean.
    (B) The use creates a sense of nature's economy.
    (C) The use establishes an alliterative pattern with line 7.
    (D) The use contradicts the return of the stream to its source in line 10.
    (E) The use makes the stream seem like an exhausted person in an overcrowded situation.

16. Figuratively, the stream represents
    (A) part of the water cycle
    (B) the source for the ocean
    (C) people in a state of innocence
    (D) literary works
    (E) the natural elements of life

17. Of the literary devices listed below, which is used in line 3?
    (A) Parody
    (B) Allusion
    (C) Personification
    (D) Apostrophe
    (E) Assonance

18. The octosyllabic construction of the poem (eight syllables per line) contributes to its
    (A) sense of conformity
    (B) hypnotic effect
    (C) cyclical tone
    (D) tone of urgency
    (E) regulated imagery

19. In the poem's title, "to No Purpose" means
    (A) irrelevant
    (B) unresolved
    (C) without design
    (D) untalented
    (E) misdirected

Questions 20–26 are based on the following passage.

SETTING: *Morning-room in Algernon's flat in Half-Moon Street.*
The room is luxuriously and artistically furnished.

LADY BRACKNELL It really makes no matter, Algernon. I had some crumpets with Lady Harbury, who seems to me to be living entirely for pleasure now.

Line

(5) ALGERNON I hear her hair turned quite gold from grief.

LADY BRACKNELL It certainly has changed its color. From what cause I, of course, cannot say.

(10) ALGERNON *crosses and hands tea.*

Thank you. I've quite a treat for you tonight, Algernon. I am going to send you down with Mary Farquhar. She is such a nice woman, and so attentive to her

(15) husband. It's delightful to watch them.

ALGERNON I am afraid, Aunt Augusta, I shall have to give up the pleasure of dining with you tonight after all.

LADY BRACKNELL [*frowning*]   I hope not,
(20)   Algernon. It would put my table completely
out. Your uncle would have to dine upstairs.
Fortunately he is accustomed to that.

ALGERNON   It is a great bore, and, I need
hardly say, a terrible disappointment to me,
(25)   but the fact is I have just had a telegram to
say that my poor friend Bunbury is very ill
again. [*Exchanges glances with Jack*] They
seem to think I should be with him.

LADY BRACKNELL   It is very strange. This
(30)   Mr. Bunbury seems to suffer from
curiously bad health.

ALGERNON   Yes; poor Bunbury is a
dreadful invalid.

LADY BRACKNELL   Well, I must say,
(35)   Algernon, that I think it is high time that Mr.
Bunbury made up his mind whether he was
going to live or to die. This shilly-shallying
with the question is absurd. Nor do I in any
way approve of the modern sympathy with
(40)   invalids. I consider it morbid. Illness of any
kind is hardly a thing to be encouraged in
others. Health is the primary duty of life. I
am always telling that to your poor uncle,
but he never seems to take much notice...as
(45)   far as any improvement in his ailments
goes. I should be much obliged if you
would ask Mr. Bunbury, from me, to be
kind enough not to have a relapse on
Saturday, for I rely on you to arrange my
(50)   music for me. It is my last reception, and
one wants something that will encourage
conversation, particularly at the end of the
season when everyone has practically said
whatever they had to say, which, in most
(55)   cases, was probably not much.

The Importance of Being Earnest
by Oscar Wilde

20. Lady Bracknell's attitude can be seen as
   (A) anxious
   (B) opinionated
   (C) sympathetic
   (D) encouraging
   (E) resentful

21. Lady Bracknell's air of authoritative conde-
scension is ironic because
   I. she knows it is "at the end of the season"
   and everyone has had his or her say,
   which is not much (lines 52–55)
   II. Algernon as well as Algernon's uncle do
   not seem to respect or obey her orders
   III. she is unable to determine the cause of
   Lady Harbury's change in hair color
   (A) I only
   (B) II only
   (C) III only
   (D) I and II only
   (E) I, II, and III

22. What does the stage direction [*Exchanges
glances with* Jack] in line 27 tell you about
Algernon's character?
   (A) He is far more worried about Bunbury
   than he wants his aunt to know.
   (B) He is not really worried about Bunbury,
   but still feels it is his duty to go.
   (C) He is sincere about not wanting to miss
   dining with his aunt.
   (D) He may not be telling the truth about
   Bunbury.
   (E) He does not want to appear ungrateful to
   his aunt.

23. Based on the speaker's tone, how should
Algernon's use of verbal irony in lines 5–6 be
regarded?
   (A) A mean-spirited hatred
   (B) A childish rambling
   (C) A witty repartee
   (D) A titillating discourse
   (E) A ludicrous burlesque

24. Lady Bracknell's comments throughout the
passage reveal her to be
   (A) pious
   (B) obsequious
   (C) indecisive
   (D) sympathetic
   (E) pompous

25. The stage direction [*Exchanges glances with Jack*] in line 27 indicates that Jack might be Algernon's
    (A) confidant
    (B) villain
    (C) protagonist
    (D) antagonist
    (E) *vers libre*

26. The expressions "shilly-shallying" (line 37), "modern sympathy" (line 39), and "primary duty" (line 42) produce which of these effects?
    (A) They strengthen Lady Bracknell's argument, making it obvious that in a contest of wills she would win.
    (B) They underscore Lady Bracknell's opinion that good health is the decided result of attitude.
    (C) They suggest that to be ill is to lack sympathy for others.
    (D) They provide a contrast to Algernon's obvious deep concern for his ill friend.
    (E) They imply motivation on Lady Bracknell's part to help people overcome their illnesses.

Questions 27–35 are based on the following poem.

My Friend, the Things That Do Attain

My friend, the things that do attain
The happy life be these, I find:
The riches left, not got with pain;
The fruitful ground; the quiet mind;
(5) The equal friend; no grudge, no strife;
No charge of rule, nor governance;
Without disease, the healthy life;
The household of continuance;

The mean diet, no dainty fare;
(10) Wisdom joined with simpleness;
The night dischargéd of all care,
Where wine the wit may not oppress:

The faithful wife, without debate;
Such sleeps as may beguile the night;
(15) Content thyself with thine estate,
Neither wish death, nor fear his might.

by Henry Howard, Earl of Surrey

27. The central theme of the poem is the
    (A) resplendent nature of a happy life
    (B) finding a happy life in "the mean estate"
    (C) self-denial necessary to pursue a happy life
    (D) contrast of a sumptuous life against a meager existence
    (E) beguiling nature of "the rich estate"

28. How does the personification of death affect the meaning in line 16?
    (A) The inevitability of death is emphasized.
    (B) The ultimate end of both friend and speaker are revealed.
    (C) Death becomes the friend of the poet.
    (D) Pain (line 3), disease (line 7), and wine (line 12) all play into death's hands.
    (E) Death, as someone not to be feared, is less threatening than an abstract concept.

29. Which of the following statements summarizes the relationship of lines 1–2 to the rest of the poem?
    (A) They establish the rhyme pattern.
    (B) They set a pattern of contrasts.
    (C) They introduce the topic.
    (D) They reveal an attitude of covetousness.
    (E) They reinforce a sense of tension.

30. Another way of saying "The household of continuance" (line 8) is
    (A) an unbroken home
    (B) family wealth
    (C) genetically based good health
    (D) a large inheritance
    (E) a family estate

31. In the poem's context, "pain" (line 3) can be thought of as all the following EXCEPT
    (A) physical hurt
    (B) punishment
    (C) mental anguish
    (D) expiation
    (E) penalty

32. "Wisdom joined with simpleness" (line 10) is a(n)
    - (A) metaphor for a simple life
    - (B) metrical accent within the stanza
    - (C) paradox to emphasize that a simple life is wise
    - (D) hyperbole to emphasize the great value of simplicity
    - (E) ironic point of departure within the theme

33. The attitude of "I" (line 2) to "My friend" (line 1) can be seen as
    - (A) conciliatory
    - (B) impatient
    - (C) didactic
    - (D) critical
    - (E) impersonal

34. The word "beguile," as it is used in line 14, conveys which of the following ideas?
    - I. Pass the time pleasingly
    - II. Relieve weariness in
    - III. Deceive or cheat
    - (A) I only
    - (B) II only
    - (C) III only
    - (D) I and II only
    - (E) I, II, and III

35. Line 6 refers to
    - (A) the peace that comes from not charging items, thus reducing debt
    - (B) not engaging in attacks and warlike behavior
    - (C) avoiding political activities
    - (D) not taking on the responsibilities of being in control or in a position of authority
    - (E) resistance to rules and forms of government

Questions 36–44 are based on the following passage.

Mrs. Stuart, having just returned from Italy, affected the artistic, and the new applicant found her with a Roman scarf
Line about her head, a rosary like a string of
(5) small cannon balls at her side, and azure draperies which became her as well as they did the sea-green furniture of her marine boudoir, where unwary walkers tripped over coral and shells, grew sea-sick looking
(10) at pictures of tempestuous billows engulfing every sort of craft, from a man-of-war to a hencoop with a ghostly young lady clinging to it with one hand, and had their appetites effectually taken away by a choice
(15) collection of water-bugs and snakes in a glass globe, that looked like a jar of mixed pickles in a state of agitation.

Madame was intent on a water-color copy of Turner's "Rain, Wind, and Hail," that
(20) pleasing work which was sold upsidedown and no one found it out. Motioning Christie to a seat she finished some delicate sloppy process before speaking. In that little pause Christie examined her, and the impression
(25) then received was afterward confirmed.

Mrs. Stuart possessed some beauty and chose to think herself a queen of society. She assumed majestic manners in public and could not entirely divest herself of them in
(30) private, which often produced comic effects. Zenobia troubled about fish-sauce, or Aspasia indignant at the price of eggs will give some idea of this lady when she condescended to the cares of housekeeping.

(35) Presently she looked up and inspected the girl as if a new servant were no more than a new bonnet, a necessary article to be ordered home for examination. Christie presented her recommendation, made her
(40) modest little speech, and awaited her doom.

Mrs. Stuart read, listened, and then demanded with queenly brevity:

"Your name?"

"Christie Devon."

(45) "Too long; I should prefer to call you Jane as I am accustomed to the name."

"As you please, ma'am."

"Your age?"

"Twenty-one."

(50) "You are an American?"

"Yes, ma'am."

Mrs. Stuart gazed into space a moment, then delivered the following address with impressive solemnity.

(55)   "I wish a capable, intelligent, honest, neat, well-conducted person who knows her place and keeps it. The work is light, as there are but two in the family. I am very particular and so is Mr. Stuart. I pay two

(60) dollars and a half, allow one afternoon out, one service on Sunday, and no followers. My table-girl must understand her duties thoroughly, be extremely neat, and always wear white aprons."

(65)   "I think I can suit you, ma'am, when I have learned the ways of the house," meekly replied Christie.

"Work"
by Louisa May Alcott

36. The primary effect of the curtness of the dialogue in lines 43–51 is
(A) confusion over who said what
(B) stream-of-consciousness narration
(C) an omniscient point of view
(D) an overbearing tone
(E) a melodramatic style

37. That Mrs. Stuart "gazed into space" in line 52 implies that
(A) she has a memory problem
(B) what follows is a memorized speech given often
(C) she is searching for just the right words
(D) Christie has impressed her deeply
(E) what follows is an expression of her true feelings

38. The first paragraph includes all the following except
(A) personification
(B) simile
(C) mixed sensory imagery
(D) hyperbole
(E) verbal irony

39. That Christie formed an early impression of Mrs. Stuart that was "afterward confirmed" (line 25) implies that Christie's modest (line 40) and meek (line 67) demeanor may be
(A) a sincere gesture
(B) a frank appraisal
(C) not efficacious
(D) an affectation
(E) an unfeigned response

40. The tone of lines 45–46 can be considered
(A) patronizing
(B) accusatory
(C) sycophant
(D) passive
(E) responsive

41. The underlying potential conflict presented in this selection is based on
(A) nationality
(B) age
(C) taste
(D) education
(E) class distinction

42. The narrator's attitude toward Mrs. Stuart, Christie, and their encounter seems to be
(A) deeply bitter
(B) mostly bewildered
(C) lachrymal
(D) regretful
(E) somewhat amused

43. The tone of the first and second paragraphs is
(A) mocking, comic, and censorious
(B) comic, sporting, and encouraging
(C) foreboding, resentful, and challenging
(D) solemn, respectful, and comforting
(E) provocative, energetic, and engaging

44. Mrs. Stuart's attitude toward herself can best be described as
(A) perceptive
(B) self-delusional
(C) superficial
(D) psychotic
(E) self-deprecatory

Questions 45–54 are based on the following poem.

That Time of Year

That time of year thou mayst in me behold
When yellow leaves, or none, or few, do
hang
Upon those boughs which shake against the
cold,
Bare ruined choirs, where late the sweet
birds sang.

Line

(5) In me thou see'st the twilight of such day
As after sunset fadeth in the west;
Which by and by black night doth take away,
Death's second self, that seals up all in rest.
In me thou see'st the glowing of such fire,

(10) That on the ashes of his youth doth lie,
As the deathbed whereon it must expire,
Consumed with that which it was nourished
by.
This thou perceiv'st, which makes thy love
more strong,
To love that well which thou must leave ere
long.

by William Shakespeare

45. Lines 5, 9, and 13 contain changes in
    (A) internal rhyme
    (B) voice
    (C) end rhyme scheme
    (D) rhythm
    (E) scansion

46. The progression of "ruined" (line 4) to
    "fadeth" (line 6) to "expire" (line 11) can be
    seen as
    (A) a resistance to death
    (B) a progression of life to death
    (C) love transcending death
    (D) the instability of life
    (E) fear of death

47. The poem's subject is
    (A) dead trees
    (B) sunsets
    (C) dying fires
    (D) making love grow stronger
    (E) approaching death

48. In lines 1–4, the speaker compares the coming
    of winter to
    (A) a winter landscape
    (B) a leafless tree
    (C) a time when birds leave
    (D) his own period of old age
    (E) his inability to engage in youthful activity

49. In lines 5–8, the speaker uses twilight as a
    (A) symbol of depression
    (B) metaphor for approaching death
    (C) personification of death
    (D) representation of his state of mind
    (E) transitional device

50. Of the following literary identifications, which
    best describes the ashes as they are used in
    lines 9–12?
    I. A metaphor for life that is spent
    II. The termination of the sunset
    III. A symbol of youth
    (A) I only
    (B) II only
    (C) III only
    (D) I and II only
    (E) I, II, and III

51. What is the speaker's tone in lines 1–4?
    (A) Arrogant
    (B) Ironic
    (C) Shocked
    (D) Lonely
    (E) Encouraged

52. What is the effect of the progression from
    "yellow leaves" to "none" to "few" in line 2?
    (A) It emphasizes the lateness of the season.
    (B) It shows that the speaker's vision is not
        clear.
    (C) It represents unfulfilled dreams.
    (D) It implies human uncertainties about life
        and death.
    (E) It contrasts the "ruined choirs" in line 4.

53. Lines 13–14 relate to the rest of the poem in which of the following ways?
    (A) They summarize the point that when death is near, love should intensify.
    (B) They intensify the sadness of the autumn, sunset, and dying fires.
    (C) They reinforce the sense of struggle for life.
    (D) They introduce love as an answer for old age and death.
    (E) They serve to change both subject and attitude.

54. How does the personification of sleep in line 8 affect the meaning?
    (A) Sleep becomes a friend offering rest and solace.
    (B) The comparison to a sunset is intensified.
    (C) The speaker reinforces his struggle for life.
    (D) Sleep is made more threatening as a reflection or shadow of death.
    (E) Sleep resists death and makes night less threatening.

Questions 55–60 are based on the following passage.

[Passage from George Washington's Farewell Address delivered to his cabinet on September 17, 1796]

The unity of government which constitutes you one people is also now dear to you. It is justly so, for it is a main pillar in the
Line edifice of your real independence, the
(5) support of your tranquility at home, your peace abroad, of your safety, of your prosperity, of that very liberty which you so highly prize.
    But as it is easy to foresee that from
(10) different causes and from different quarters much pains will be taken, many artifices employed, to weaken in your minds the conviction of this truth, as this is the point in your political fortress against which the
(15) batteries of internal and external enemies will be most constantly and actively (though often covertly and insidiously) directed, it is of infinite moment that you should properly estimate the immense value of your national

(20) union to your collective and individual happiness....
    The name of American, which belongs to you in your national capacity, must always exalt the just pride of patriotism more than
(25) any appellation derived from local discriminations. With slight shades of difference, you have the same religion, manners, habits, and political principles. You have in a common cause fought and
(30) triumphed together. The independence and liberty you possess are the work of joint councils and joint efforts, of common dangers, sufferings, and successes.

55. "The unity of government which constitutes you one people is also now dear to you. It is justly so, for it is a main pillar in the edifice of your real independence, the support of your tranquility at home" (lines 1–5). Of the following statements concerning Washington's comment, all are correct EXCEPT which statement?
    (A) They are aphoristic.
    (B) They state a conclusion.
    (C) They serve to establish the tone.
    (D) They establish distance between speaker and subject.
    (E) They contain metaphorical language.

56. In this selection, the speaker's tone can be considered
    (A) paternal and patriotic
    (B) patronizing and discouraging
    (C) intensely ironic
    (D) enthusiastically optimistic
    (E) disappointed

57. The "truth" described in lines 12–13 probably is that
    (A) tranquility, peace, and safety are highly prized
    (B) some people may try to undermine truth
    (C) happiness is of immense value
    (D) various interest groups try to weaken government unity
    (E) independence depends upon unity of government

58. Of the statements that follow, which is the best description of the relationship between the first paragraph and the second?
    (A) The second paragraph simply reiterates the main point of the first paragraph.
    (B) The second paragraph creates a sense of emotional tension.
    (C) Both paragraphs serve to support a change in public policy.
    (D) The point of the first paragraph renders moot the main idea of the second paragraph.
    (E) The second paragraph introduces an optimistic tone.

59. What organizational pattern does the speaker use to persuade his audience?
    (A) Classification
    (B) Process analysis
    (C) Conclusion-premise relationship
    (D) Spondaic stress
    (E) Metrical scan

60. What is the literary function of the phrase "political fortress" in line 14?
    (A) Metaphor for a system of beliefs under attack
    (B) Reference to independence
    (C) Hyperbole for truth
    (D) Literary allusion to governmental systems
    (E) Affective fallacy

ANSWER KEY: DIAGNOSTIC TEST I

Step 1. Score Your Test

- Use the following table to score your test.
- *Compare* your answers with the correct answers in the table:
- ✓ Place a check in the "Right" column for those questions you answered correctly.
- ✓ Place a check in the "Wrong" column for those questions you answered incorrectly.
- If you omitted answering a question, leave both columns blank.

Step 2. Analyze Your Test Results

- *Read* the portions of the "Analysis: Diagnostic Test I" (analysis follows the scoring table) that apply first to those questions you missed.
- *Scan* the rest of the analysis for those questions you answered correctly. This analysis provides the correct answer, identifies the literary element tested by each question, and briefly discusses the answer choice(s).

Step 3. Learn from Your Test Results

- *Circle* the question number on the Answer Key Table for each of the questions you answered incorrectly. Which literary elements were these questions testing?

  Obviously, many of the questions are actually testing more than one literary element. Consequently, these identifications serve only as a guide to pinpoint "problem" areas.
- *Review* the seven literary elements.

ANSWER KEY: DIAGNOSTIC TEST I

| SCORING | | | LITERARY ELEMENT TESTED | | | | | | |
RIGHT	WRONG	ANSWER	1	2	3	4	5	6	7
		1. C							*
		2. D						*	
		3. B							*
		4. E				*			
		5. B				*			
		6. C					*		
		7. C						*	
		8. E						*	
		9. B						*	
		10. E							*
		11. D	*						
		12. B			*				

ANSWER KEY: DIAGNOSTIC TEST I

| SCORING | | | LITERARY ELEMENT TESTED | | | | | | |
RIGHT	WRONG	ANSWER	1	2	3	4	5	6	7
		13. C						*	
		14. D							*
		15. E						*	
		16. D						*	
		17. C						*	
		18. C				*			
		19. A							*
		20. B			*				
		21. B						*	
		22. D					*		
		23. C				*			
		24. E					*		
		25. A					*		
		26. B							*
		27. B	*						
		28. E						*	
		29. C		*					
		30. A							*
		31. D							*
		32. C						*	
		33. C			*				
		34. D							*
		35. D							*
		36. D				*			
		37. B			*				
		38. A						*	
		39. D			*				
		40. A				*			

ANSWER KEY: DIAGNOSTIC TEST I

SCORING		ANSWER	LITERARY ELEMENT TESTED						
RIGHT	WRONG		1	2	3	4	5	6	7
		41. E	*						
		42. E			*				
		43. A				*			
		44. B			*				
		45. C		*					
		46. B		*					
		47. E	*						
		48. D						*	
		49. B						*	
		50. A						*	
		51. D				*			
		52. D							*
		53. A		*					
		54. D						*	
		55. D						*	
		56. A				*			
		57. E							*
		58. B		*					
		59. C		*					
		60. A						*	

TO OBTAIN YOUR RAW SCORE:

_____ divided by 4 = _____
Total wrong   Score W

_____ minus _____ = _____
Total right   Score W   Score R

HOW DID YOU DO?

55–60 = Excellent
44–54 = Very Good
35–43 = Above Average
23–34 = Average
15–22 = Below Average

Round Score R to the nearest whole number for the raw score.

ANALYSIS: DIAGNOSTIC TEST I

> **NOTE:** The scope and definition of each of the literary elements sometimes can differ among the literary critics. As a result, the rationale behind what constitutes a correct or an incorrect answer also may differ. Many of the questions in Diagnostic Test I are testing your skills in more than one literary element. Also, each answer analysis might be viewed from more than one perspective. Consequently, this analysis should be used as only a part of your study program.

1. **C** Element 7 (meanings in context) If you are unaware that a knapsack used to carry food and clothing was sometimes called a "wallet," you can still find the correct answer by eliminating obviously incorrect answers. The description of Robin's clothing indicates a time before the use of jacket decals. Pocketbook refers to a handbag or purse. Billfolds are generally carried in concealed locations. Even an inexperienced traveler would know not to sling a money bag across his back.

2. **D** Element 6 (use of language) ". . . like the dropping of small stones into a kettle" is a comparison using "like," a simile.

3. **B** Element 7 (meanings in context) If the notice really described the boy, would these men deliberately allow "One pound currency" to walk out of the room? Their laughter once the "country lad" who put on airs leaves the room supports the idea that the innkeeper made up the description as a joke.

4. **E** Element 4 (tone) The irony of Robin's situation is so amusing that the men enjoy a joke at his expense.

5. **B** Element 4 (tone) What in other contexts might be a form of polite address sounds patronizing or condescending when said with "an assumption of confidence" (line 8).

6. **C** Element 5 (character) Clues to Robin's attitudes are found in his "assumption of confidence" (line 8), his "speaking with lofty confidence" (line 16), his expectation of one day doing business there (line 11), and his supposition that his position will influence the others to guide him. He feels important and would probably be ashamed to reveal his lack of money.

7. **C** Element 6 (use of language) The "courteous" innkeeper has just threatened the boy with possible arrest and insulted his sense of superiority. From Robin's perspective, he is no longer "courteous."

8. **E** Element 6 (use of language) His speech is being described as "little dry fragments," in an implied comparison of something heard to something seen, tasted, or felt. Some would view this metaphor as an example of synaesthesia (a mixture of sensory images).

9. **B** Element 6 (use of language) To trudge is to walk in a weary manner. The innkeeper is threatening the boy with possible arrest as a runaway servant, a situation calling for rapid flight, not slow walking.

10. **E** Element 1 (meanings in context) Usually, a cudgel refers only to a rather short weapon. Context shows that this cudgel, however, is long enough to lean upon and, consequently, could be and probably was used as a walking stick or cane.

11. **D** Element 1 (meaning) Although you might be tempted to select answer A because the first twelve lines do, indeed, contain an eloquent (but incomplete) description of the earth's water cycle, this answer is inadequate because the question stem asks about the *central* theme—the one that is the structural support for the entire poem. Seasonal aspects and weather of the world are mentioned, but the central theme is reflected in the last four lines that reveal that lines 1–12 are being used with the cycles of life—answer D.

12. **B** Element 3 (narrative voice) The poem evidences the speaker as one who is trying to make a point. First, he uses the water cycle analogy to establish what would seem to be a rather straightforward metaphor. Notice, however, the tone in which he addresses the silent auditor, particularly in lines 3 and 5: "Try if…you can…And see…." Couple this tone with the forceful use of "Then" in line 13 when he says "Then may ye recollect the grains/Of my particular remains" [emphasis added] and you will discover a speaker whose attitude is challenging (B). What do you think has caused this attitude?

13. **C** Element 6 (use of language) Obviously, the "remains" of the speaker can be seen as his dead body (III), the "grains" of which he challenges the silent auditor to "recollect." Also, an argument might be made that upon the speaker's death, his remnant of material possessions (II) would be left to be recollected (brought together); however, on a highly figurative level, the "remains" can be seen as the speaker's surviving writings (IV) that are "particular" (personal) and that the silent auditor would "recollect" (recall or remember) after "a thousand lusters" (fame or renown) "hurled by ruffling winds" (disturbing or rippling air that bears trends or information).

14. **D** Element 7 (meanings in context) Answers A through E are all definitions of "particular"; consequently, context is essential to determining which meaning is not applicable to this situation. A major clue is in the description of the stream that flows into and becomes part of the ocean, but then returns to the springs from which it originated. Likewise, the speaker suggests that the silent auditor "recollect" (implying a gathering again) his "particular remains"—those that are separated from those mixed in the "world of waters" (line 7) or "about the world" (line 16). This association of ideas supports selection of definitions that reflect this sense of individualism: apart from others (A), personal (B), special rather than general (C), and considered separately (E). Precise (D) does not conform to the established association.

15. **E** Element 6 (use of language) The word "spent" means to be exhausted or without energy. To be "unspent," then, would mean to have energy. The speaker contends that the silent auditor should "see, if there it [the stream] keeps unspent"—remains full of energy—"in that congesting [overcrowded] element" of the ocean. This subtle personification renders the stream to seem like an exhausted person in an overcrowded situation (E).

16. **D** Element 6 (use of language) On a literal level, the stream flows as a source for the ocean. On a figurative level, the root of its meaning can be found in the last four lines of the poem in which the speaker establishes two levels of meaning: (1) based on the life cycle of the human body and (2) based on his personal literary works ("particular remains") and their recollection. Using this second level as a basis, the stream can be seen as literary works (perhaps the personal works of the speaker) that gently flow into the "wilder ocean" (line 4) of the world's body of literary conventions

and criticisms where it (line 5) becomes exhausted "In that congesting [overcrowded] element" (line 6). Eventually, it returns to the "spring from whence it came" (inspiration?—line 10).

17. **C** Element 6 (use of language) Personification is giving human attributes to nonhumans: "sober stream." Also, the repeated initial consonant(s) is an example of alliteration.

18. **C** Element 4 (tone) The speaker uses several literary devices (including alliteration, assonance, regular rhythm and rhyme, diction, and octosyllabic construction) to project the smooth, cyclical tones that extend to support the imagery of the poem's figurative meaning—answer C.

19. **A** Element 7 (meanings in context) The phrase "to the purpose" means something is relevant or pertinent (as: Is that remark to the purpose?). Consequently, "to no purpose" would be something that is irrelevant. What do you think is the significance of the title to the poem's literal and to its figurative meanings?

20. **B** Element 3 (narrative voice) Lady Bracknell has very distinct opinions (B). Notice her opinions about Lady Harbury, about Algernon's reason not to dine with her, about Mr. Bunbury's illness, and about her reception guests.

21. **B** Element 6 (use of language) Irony, in this case, involves the difference between the way Lady Bracknell views herself and the way she is viewed by those around her. She obviously has an air of authority (note that she does not hesitate even to order people to be healthy) and a sense of condescension (note her air of superiority over her reception guests). But do those around her respect her opinions or orders? Algernon refuses her invitation to dine and his uncle does not heed her advice.

22. **D** Element 5 (character) In determining motivation and character, context is extremely important. How sincere is Algernon about his "sick" friend? Clues can be found in Lady Bracknell's comments that Bunbury's illness is "very strange" (line 29), that he suffers from *curiously* bad health" (line 30—emphasis added), and that he brushes with death frequently (lines 36–38)… perhaps Algernon is not telling the truth.

23. **C** Element 4 (tone) In answering this question, the first step is to determine what is ironic in Algernon's statement. Verbal irony occurs when the speaker's meaning is different from what he or she says, usually revealing the speaker's attitude or opinion on the subject. One can assume that Lady Harbury has been through a traumatic event

(causing her grief or what would normally be expected to cause her grief). In such circumstances, a person's hair generally does not turn gold from grief. Also, note that Lady Bracknell points out that Lady Harbury "seems to me to be living entirely for pleasure now," so Algernon is aware that Lady Harbury is not really grieving at all. His comment that "her hair has turned quite gold from grief" really means that grief had nothing to do with her hair turning gold. Although his comment, when coupled with that of Lady Bracknell, is suggestive that Lady Harbury is acting in a way unbecoming a person in grief, his observation is by no means titillating (exciting) or burlesque (an amusing imitation of a literary work). Does anything in his dialogue indicate that he hates her (A)? Does he ramble on about it? No, he simply makes this witty reply (C), then drops the subject.

24. **E** Element 5 (character) A pompous character is one who is self-important (an exaggerated sense of her own importance). This trait can be seen in Lady Bracknell's attempts to control others: She tells Algernon "I am going to send you down with Mary Farquhar" (lines 12–13). She is willing to make her husband dine upstairs to balance her table. She even commands sick people to control their illnesses for her convenience and to facilitate her dinner party plans.

25. **A** Element 5 (character) A confidant (A) is someone in a play who acts to establish the character of someone else by being a sounding board, by reacting with the other character, or by some other means revealing the personality of the more dominant or main character. In this case, Jack simply being there to exchange glances gives the reader/viewer clues into Algernon's personality and motives.

26. **B** Element 7 (meanings in context) Nothing in the selection supports the idea that Lady Bracknell's strong will prevails over that of others—except perhaps over Algernon's uncle at dinner. Neither is "deep concern" on the part of Algernon established. Although Lady Bracknell may be motivated to help Algernon's uncle be healthy, these strongly connotative words do reveal that Lady Bracknell believes people should not encourage illness in others by expressing sympathy, but rather invalids should make health a duty and simply decide to be well (B). Lack of sympathy on the part of ill people is not discussed.

27. **B** Element 1 (meaning) The structure of this poem helps to define its central idea: first, the writer sets forth his topic—these are the "things" that make a happy life. He then lists those things, all of which are found in a simple, humble lifestyle, or in other words, "the mean estate" (B).

28. **E** Element 6 (use of language) Personification is the attributing of human qualities to inanimate objects or abstract ideas. The unknown and abstract can be very frightening; however, by encouraging the reader to think of death in human terms is to make it less fearful, less threatening. Be aware, though, that context is *very* important in recognizing the effects of personification or of any literary use of language. The context of this poem allows the personification of death to render death less threatening, but the context of another work might mean that such personification would turn death into a monster.

29. **C** Element 2 (form) In this particular poem, the complete rhyme scheme or pattern cannot be determined from just the first two lines—the rhyme pattern of the entire poem needs to be examined. Neither covetousness (D) nor contrast (B) are revealed here, and tension also is not an element (E). The first two lines do, however, introduce the topic (C).

30. **A** Element 7 (meanings in context) The central idea of the poem is that a simple, humble life can be very happy; therefore, wealth (B), an inheritance (D), and an estate (E) are in antithesis to the speaker's main point. Although no inherited diseases or illnesses would make for a happy situation, a household (home, family, and the affairs of the home) of continuance (an unbroken succession) would be a home not broken (by anger or separation).

31. **D** Element 7 (meanings in context) (A), (B), (C), and (E) can all be associated with pain; but expiation (D) is a condition of having made reparation or amends for wrongdoing and, as such, could be considered a *release from pain* of guilt.

32. **C** Element 6 (use of language) Being "simple" is often viewed as the opposite of being "wise." Here the concepts of simpleness and wisdom are used in a paradox to point out that simpleness (from the perspective of simplicity in living) can, in fact, be quite wise.

33. **C** Element 3 (narrative voice) A conciliatory attitude (A) has connotations of winning over or placating, implying that some division has taken place. Yet there is no indication in this poem of any separation between the two people in thought, emotion,

or action having taken place, except the difference of opinion concerning lifestyles *implied* by the poet's sense of need to write this poem expounding the benefits of a simple lifestyle. Neither does the speaker seem impatient (B) or impersonal (E). Although he may be somewhat critical (again, by implication) of the high stress life of wealth, his attitude mostly is didactic (C) as he wants to instruct his friend—to teach him about the pursuit of happiness.

34. **D** Element 7 (meanings in context) In a "night discharged of all care" (line 11) the time would be passed pleasingly (I) and would relieve weariness (II), but would not deceive or cheat (III).

35. **D** Element 7 (meanings in context) A "charge" is a responsibility or duty when in a position of "rule" or in a position of governance (control and the exercise of authority). A simple life, then, would mean avoiding the "headaches at the top"—positions of responsibility.

36. **D** Element 4 (tone) As the mistress of the house, the "queenly" Mrs. Stuart sets the tone of the interview. She "demanded" answers with what the narrator calls "queenly brevity."

37. **B** Element 3 (narrative voice) The narrator emphasizes Mrs. Stuart's casual attitude toward the interview (line 37) and presents the process as if it has become a ritual for her.

38. **A** Element 6 (use of language) The paragraph contains similes ("like a string"; "like a jar"), mixed sensory imagery ("a jar of mixed pickles in a state of agitation"), hyperbole ("every sort of craft"), and verbal irony (a "choice" collection of snakes—in a bedroom!). It does not, however, contain personification (human characteristics given to an inanimate object, animal, or abstract idea).

39. **D** Element 3 (narrative voice) Christie is bold enough to "examine" her new employer, perceptive enough to form correct impressions even after a brief examination, and intelligent enough to make a "modest little speech" before she "awaited her doom." Christie is giving answers in the demeanor she believes Mrs. Stuart is seeking.

40. **A** Element 4 (tone) A person's name is an integral part of her individuality. Not to be viewed as an individual person in this circumstance is demeaning and patronizing.

41. **E** Element 1 (meaning) Although Christie's age and nationality are mentioned and Mrs. Stuart's lack of taste is evident, the wide gap between servant and mistress is emphasized by Mrs. Stuart's insulting words and attitude.

42. **E** Element 3 (narrative voice) The narrator describes Mrs. Stuart as "comic," Christie as someone awaiting "her doom," and she details their encounter in a comic tone.

43. **A** Element 4 (tone) The narrator mocks the taste of her marine boudoir, silently laughs at reactions of "unwary walkers," and censors her "affected" sense of art.

44. **B** Element 3 (narrative voice) The narrator does not describe Mrs. Stuart as a society leader, but that she "think[s] herself a queen of society" who "assumed majestic manners in public and could not entirely divest herself of them in private."

45. **C** Element 2 (form) This 14-line, iambic pentameter poem's end rhyme scheme is in the tradition of the English (sometimes called Shakespearean) sonnet. Consequently, the end rhyme pattern changes in lines 5, 9, and 13:

line	1	behold	a
line	2	hang	b
line	3	cold	a
line	4	sang	b
line	5	day	c
line	6	west	d
line	7	away	c
line	8	rest	d
line	9	fire	e
line	10	lie	f
line	11	expire	e
line	12	by	f
line	13	strong	g
line	14	long	g

Note: Once you have identified a poem as a sonnet, the end rhyme scheme *sometimes* can be a clue to meaning and structure. English sonnets can be identified by an abab cdcd efef gg rhyme scheme. The structure is a vehicle for a step-by-step progression of ideas that is either summarized or reversed by the final couplet. If, on the other hand, the sonnet's rhyme scheme divides it into two parts, often with an abbaabba cdecde rhyme scheme, then the sonnet is Italian (sometimes called Petrarchan). In an Italian sonnet, you can anticipate that the first eight lines will contain either a statement or a question that will be answered, explored, or somehow addressed in the last six lines. Also, you might look for the two sections to provide a contrast of ideas.

English Sonnet   Italian Sonnet

English Sonnet		Italian Sonnet	
a		a	
b		b	
a		b	
b		a	makes a
		a	statement or
c		b	asks a question
d	progression	b	
c	of ideas	a	
d			
		(sometimes contrasts ideas)	
e			
f		c	
e		d	
f		e	explores
		c	concept or
g	summary or	d	answers
g	reversal	e	question

Not all sonnets are in this form; however, identification of the rhyme scheme can provide clues to help you answer questions about the poem's meaning and structure. Question 46 and its analysis exemplify finding the progression of ideas leading to the summary or reversal in an English sonnet.

46. **B** Element 2 (form) This poem is a sequence of three metaphors comparing old age and approaching death to a season of the year (when things are still there but "ruined"), to the end of a day (a briefer period, when light "fadeth"), and to the dying down of a fire (that can be extinguished in a brief moment, when the life of the fire "expire[s]").

47. **E** Element 1 (meaning) This poem is primarily about old age and death. Trees, sunsets, and fires are used as vehicles within the poem.

48. **D** Element 6 (use of language) We are to "behold" "in me" (the speaker) "That time of year." How can a time of year be seen in a person? This poem is built upon a conventional metaphor that has been used many times in literature and in the popular culture:

    spring = birth and youth
    summer = prime of life
    fall = retirement and "golden years"
    winter = old age and death

Forms of this metaphor can be found in poetry, in music (note Frank Sinatra singing "It Was a Very Good Year"), and even in expressions such as "a May-December romance."

49. **B** Element 6 (use of language) The metaphor here is an implied comparison: the speaker's approaching death is like the twilight after sunset—a time

just before death comes in line 8. Sunrise and sunset representing life and death is another conventional metaphor commonly found in literature (note the song "Sunrise, Sunset").

50. **A** Element 6 (use of language) The reader sees in the speaker the "fire" (line 9) that lies on the "ashes of his youth" (line 10); consequently, if the fire is his life, the ashes are what remains of the life that is spent or gone.

51. **D** Element 4 (tone) The leaves of summer have yellowed, fallen, and no doubt blown away (line 2) and the birds with their sweet songs are gone (line 4), leaving the tree (representing the speaker) alone—shaking against the cold (line 3).

52. **D** Element 7 (meanings in context) The speaker wants the reader to "behold" (line 1) in him the "time of year" (line 1)—obviously the late fall of life. But in this request, he must also look at himself. At first he sees how late in the season it is (the trees have "yellow leaves"). Then he observes "or none," suggesting an emotional sense of loss. Yet he adds "or few" leaves "do hang." Why? Is he not yet ready to face completely "bare" limbs (line 4)? This suggests human uncertainties about life and death on the part of the speaker.

53. **A** Element 2 (form) This final couplet makes the point of the poem—the summary concept that when someone is old and dying, like a tree in winter (lines 1–4), the sun about to set (lines 5–8), and a fire going out (lines 9–12), this condition should "make thy love more strong" (line 13).

54. **D** Element 6 (use of language) The personification (the giving of human qualities) to sleep "that seals up all in rest" (line 8) makes sleep more threatening as "Death's second self" (line 8).

55. **D** Element 6 (use of language) Washington makes an implied comparison (a metaphor) in these lines, likening unity of government to a support pillar and likening real independence to an edifice or large building. In so doing, he states a conclusion: real independence requires unity of government (B). He states a principle (unity of government is a main support of real independence) in a concise, somewhat aphoristic manner (A). The rather impassioned, definitely persuasive tone (C) is established in part by the use of "dear" and "It is justly so." These lines do not, however, establish distance between speaker and subject (D). On the contrary, use of the word "also" implies that unity of government was "dear" to the speaker some time ago.

56. **A** Element 4 (tone) The speaker's fatherly (paternal) concern for the well-being of his fellow-Americans can be seen in the second paragraph where he expresses concern that you "should properly estimate the immense value of your national union to your collective and individual happiness...." The patriotic tone is throughout, particularly in the third paragraph in which he directly addresses "the just pride of patriotism."

57. **E** Element 7 (meanings in context) The "truth" that "different causes" will try "to weaken in your minds" is that "unity of government... is a main pillar in the edifice of your real independence"—independence depends upon unity of government (E).

58. **B** Element 2 (form) The first paragraph makes the reader emotionally care about government unity by associating it with such connotatively charged words as "peace... safety...prosperity." Then the second paragraph poses a threat to "that very liberty which you so highly prize," a threat of artifices (tricks), a threat of minds weakened to "truth," a threat of "batteries of internal and external enemies...." Making the reader care, then posing a threat creates a sense of emotional tension.

59. **C** Element 2 (form) Of the four forms or types of composition (narration, description, exposition, and argumentation), this portion of Washington's speech is mostly argumentative; his purpose is to convince his listeners of the truth of his proposition. Writers can include the elements of several methods of organization in argumentation; however, argumentation generally has at its core the examination of a possible relationship between a conclusion and a premise (evidence from which the conclusion can be drawn.) One conclusion-premise relationship in this passage is:

Conclusion: "The unity of government...is dear to you."

Premise: [because it makes possible] "your real independence...your tranquility at home, your peace abroad...."

Do you see any other conclusions and premises?

60. **A** Element 6 (use of language) The speaker uses a military metaphor (an implied comparison) to describe the threats against the "truth" of governmental unity. He describes their systems of beliefs as a "political fortress" and the tricks and attempts on the part of the "internal and external enemies" to destroy those beliefs as "batteries" (tactical military weapons).

PART II

THE SEVEN LITERARY ELEMENTS

Understanding Prose, Poetry, and Drama

An Introduction to the Seven Literary Elements

Literary Elements
  Number One: MEANING
  Number Two: FORM
  Number Three: NARRATIVE VOICE
  Number Four: TONE
  Number Five: CHARACTER
  Number Six: USE OF LANGUAGE
  Number Seven: MEANING(S) IN
                          CONTEXT

Understanding Prose, Poetry, and Drama

The SAT Subject Test in Literature consists of about 45 to 50 percent poetry, 45 to 50 percent prose, and 0 to 10 percent drama.

PROSE

Prose is expression (whether written or spoken) that does not have a regular rhythmic pattern. Prose does have rhythm, but its rhythm lacks any sustained regularity and is not meant to be scanned.

POETRY

Poetry is expression that is written in verse, often with some form of regular rhythm. The basis of poetic expression is a heightened sense of perception or consciousness.

A poem can look like prose, and prose can contain poetic elements.

Do all poems have regular rhythm? No. Do all poems take verse form? No. As a result, prose and poetry can be seen as two levels or planes, each going in opposite directions, but partially overlapping at their common ends.

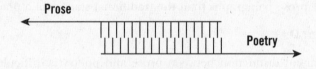

▼PRACTICE QUESTION▼

BELL-TONES

Bells have been ringing and marking time in my life. Bells to come
for and bells to go by. Bells to ring and bells to hear. Easy bell-tones
turn to clattering bells ringing, finally becoming muted into many soft
Line   death knells.
(5)   I started with Tinker Bell, then listened to school bells between
playing in fields of bluebells. Happy bells ringing; proms, parties,
and dancing, playing happily and listening to the ringing of sleigh
bells. Church bells comforting and confirming and wedding bells
promising our love Always; such joy, bluebonnets and baby bonnets,
(10)   with happy baby bells on baby booties.
     Dinner bells called me; laundry bells startled me; cake timers
beckoned me; liberty bells stirred me; jingle bells amused me until all
the bells jangled and wrangled metallic as door bells and telephone
bells ringing in pairs demanded me.
(15)   Then bells rang for help...time to get up, time to sleep, time to eat,
time to leave, time to escape danger, time to come and time to go.
Bells marked the hours and the times of my life. Now the beautiful

bluebells in fields are calling me once again, mute bells singing soft notes as Church bells sound in blissful bell-tones, while we are
(20)   waiting for the joyful ringing rapture of the Resurrection.

by L. E. Myers

Where would you place this poem on the diagram?

All the following can be said about this poem EXCEPT
(A) it contains personification
(B) the sound of the poem reflects its meaning
(C) ringing bells are symbolic of life's major events
(D) it consists of traditional stanzas
(E) it contains repetition of initial consonants

Explanation: In this question, you are looking for the one answer choice that is false. The poem does contain personification ("bluebells … calling me"). Also, the meaning is reflected and intensified by elements of rhythm (sound) throughout the work, such as the back-and-forth bell-like movement in "time to sleep, time to eat, time to leave…." The ringing bells represent (are symbolic of) major events from birth (baby booties) to death ("soft death knells"). The initial consonant *b* is repeated throughout, with *r* and *p* also repeated in places. Such a sound device is called alliteration. The stanzas, however, look more like prose paragraphs than the traditional stanzas of a poem.

Correct Answer: **D**

Obviously, a clear-cut distinction between prose and poetry is difficult to establish; you need to be constantly alert to the poet's use of prose techniques and the prose writer's borrowing of poetic devices.

The following lists summarize some of the key distinguishing features of prose and poetry.

Poetry has (or can have)

- imaginative elements
- significance and levels of meaning
- a regularity of rhythm
- intensity
- unity
- poetic diction ("poetic" language [such as archaisms, epithets, and periphrases used by eighteenth-century poets] once used by English writers, but no longer used except perhaps to create irony)
- poetic license (liberties poets take in varying from standardized diction, rhyme, spelling, syntax, and mechanics)
- sense impressions and heightened consciousness
- concrete language
- versification (meter, rhyme, and stanza forms)
- sentences divided into lines (verse-lines/lineation)

- stanzas
- bound speech
- sound patterning
- syntactic deployment
- both meaning and sound

Prose has (or can have)

- rhythmic patterns (but not regular or sustained) called *prose rhythm*
- consciously shaped writing
- logical grammatical order
- connected (not listed) ideas
- levels of diction
- "style"
- Rhetorical accent (When the accent is determined by the intent or meaning, for example, "She gave the keys to <u>you</u>?" implies that the speaker is surprised at who is the recipient of the keys. Compare: "She <u>gave</u> the keys to you?" questions whether she really did give the keys or "<u>She</u> gave the keys to you?" questions who actually gave the keys.)
- Modes or types of formal organization (These "formal" organizations can range from loosely structured everyday discourse through carefully structured exposition.)
- A primary function: to communicate information
- Sentences
- Paragraphs

▼PRACTICE QUESTION▼

Next, read these lines taken from Edgar Allan Poe's "The Man in the Crowd."

> As I endeavored, during the brief minute of my original survey, to
> form some analysis of the meaning conveyed, there arose confusedly
> and paradoxically within my mind, the ideas of vast mental power,
> Line of acution, of penuriousness, of avarice, of coolness, of malice, of
> (5) blood-thirstiness, of triumph, of merriment, of excessive terror, of
> intense—of extreme despair. I felt singularly aroused, startled,
> fascinated.

How does the narrator create a prose rhythm that mirrors his thoughts?
(A) Paradoxical diction
(B) Stream-of-consciousness analogies
(C) Parallel syntax
(D) Use of abstract over concrete diction
(E) Poetic diction

Explanation: Notice the rhythm of his building mental confusion. He has "ideas of vast mental power, of caution, of…of…of…of…of…of…of intense—of extreme despair."

Correct Answer: **C**

DRAMA

Drama is a story intended to be acted out on a stage. Some critics include pantomime (silent acting), but others specify that drama requires dialogue. Drama does require a plot, a setting, and characters.

Obviously, elements of drama can be found in prose fiction and in narrative poetry. The dramatist can also, however, incorporate elements of prose and poetry within the development of the drama. Take the use of poetic forms in drama as an example. In Elizabethan drama, Marlowe's lower-class characters speak in prose, but the "Good and Bad Angels" speak in blank verse. Of William Shakespeare's plays, a large number are written in blank verse. Shakespeare used poetic elements throughout his dramas to create moods, to project character, to develop plot, and even to signal the mechanical elements of the play.

▼Practice Question▼

A striking example is in Shakespeare's *The Tragedy of Julius Caesar.*

> Act V Scene V
>
> MARCUS BRUTUS. Hence! I will follow.
>   [*Exeunt* CLITUS, DARDANIUS, *and* VOLUMNIUS.]
>   I prithee, Strato, stay thou by the lord:
>   Thou art a fellow of a good respect;
>   Thy life hath had some smatch of honour in it:
>   Hold, then, my sword, and turn away thy face,
>   While I do run upon it. Wilt thou, Strato?
>
> STRATO. Give me your hand first: fare you well, my lord.
>
> MARCUS BRUTUS.
>   Farewell, good Strato.—Caesar, now be still:
>   I kill'd not thee with half so good a will.
>   [*He runs on his sword, and dies.*]

The last words of Marcus Brutus before his suicide are structurally dramatized through the use of
(A) heroic couplet
(B) archaic words
(C) direct address
(D) melodrama
(E) name-dropping

Explanation: Shakespeare ingeniously uses couplets to cue entrances and to close scenes. In this case, he rhymes "still" with "will" to further the dramatic effect of the moment when the struggle between Caesar and Marcus Brutus ends. The two rhyming lines are written in iambic pentameter, making them an example of heroic couplet.

Correct Answer: **A**

HOW LANGUAGE SAVED A NATION

English prose is the result of the courage and farsighted thinking of a young hero named Alfred the Great, the ninth-century King of Wessex. In the 870s, the Danes were vigorously attacking the English-speaking kingdoms. Should they have war, there would not have been any English-speaking kingdoms left. The English language was in danger of extinction. King Alfred managed to push back the Danes from Wessex, but he knew that without the help of the Englishmen surrounding Wessex, the treaty the Danes had signed would not save them. What could he do?

In a brilliant move to unify the kingdoms against the Danes, King Alfred consolidated the people on the basis of their "Englishness," with the English language at the heart of their new awareness of national identity. In a sense, King Alfred used the English language to establish and at the same time save a nation. Once the people were united against the Danes, Alfred moved boldly ahead. He replaced Latin with English, had English chronicles written to give the people a sense of history, established a standardized English writing system, and earned for himself the title of "founder of English prose" by writing (in a.d. 887) the first example of completed English prose (*Handbook*).

The Danes were a threat to the English-speaking people and their language as a nation, and Latin was a threat to English prose within the nation. Obviously, Alfred's promotion of English over Latin as an impetus for national unity did much to help English prose in its struggling stages. Even after English prose became more prevalent, however, its forms and syntax were significantly influenced by Latin.

Here is the point: Do not make assumptions. Just because a selection is prose does not mean it cannot contain poetic and dramatic elements. Dialogue in a drama can be written in poetic form, and poetry, too, can borrow from prose and drama.

With this point in mind, you are ready to learn about the seven literary elements.

AN INTRODUCTION TO THE SEVEN LITERARY ELEMENTS

Interpretive skills involve learning to examine and analyze the literary elements that work together in a selection. What are these literary elements? Meaning; Form; Narrative Voice; Tone; Character; Use of Language; and Meanings of Sentences, Lines, Phrases, and Words in Context, hereinafter called Meaning(s) in Context.

One of the purposes of this book is to help you identify and explicate (explain in detail) each of these seven literary elements when they are at work in literary selections.

Begin by taking an overview approach to the seven literary elements. Scan the following questions. They will give you an idea of the information you will be seeking when you analyze a literary selection.

Meaning

- What is the work about—its theme?
- What effect or impression does the work have on the reader?
- What is the argument or summary of the work?
- What is the writer's intent?

Form

- How has the writer organized the literary work to achieve the effect or to express the meaning?
- How is the work structured or planned—as prose or as verse? As topics or as scenes? As a long narrative or as several short stories or episodes?
- Into what genre—type or category—could the work be placed?
- What method of organization or pattern of development is used within the structure of the work?

Narrative Voice

- Who is telling the story?
- How is the speaker or narrator characterized (his or her character revealed)? By action or by description? Expressed or implied?
- From what perspective is the story told? By a person outside the story or by someone actually involved in the narrative?
- Is the speaker, the one telling the story, and the writer of the work the same person?
- If the writer and the speaker are two different individuals, are their attitudes toward the subject, the events, and the readers the same or different?

Tone

- What is the writer's attitude toward the material, subject, or theme?
- What is the speaker's attitude (if different from the writer) toward the material, subject, or theme? Toward the reader?
- Is the tone playful? Serious? Angry? Formal? Pleading? Joyful?
- What is the atmosphere of the work (the way in which the mood, setting, and feeling blend together to convey the prevailing tone)?

Character

- Who are the people in the work?
- How do dialogue (what he or she says) and action (what he or she does) reveal a character's personality traits?
- Is there a principal character?
- What is the character's motivation?
- Is the character's personality revealed directly by the speaker telling the reader or indirectly by the character's own words and deeds, requiring the reader to come to conclusions about the character based on dialogue and action?

Use of Language

- Does the selection include any imagery (the use of sensory images to represent someone or something)?
- What figures of speech does the writer use, and what effect do they have on the meaning of the selection?
- How does the writer use diction—word choice—to convey meaning?

Meaning(s) in Context

- What is the effect of the sentences, lines, phrases, and words as they are used in the selection?
- Did the writer intend the words used to convey the meanings normally assigned to those words (the connotations)?
- Did the writer intend that some words would imply additional, associated meanings for the reader (connotations)?
- What is the significance of those implications to the meaning of the selection and the intent of the writer?
- How does the use of denotation, connotation, and syntax (how the words are structured and grouped to create meaningful thought units) relate to the style of the selection?
- Does the language of the selection include any elements of propaganda?

THE LITERARY ELEMENTS—WORKING TOGETHER FOR UNITY

Have you ever tasted a well-made sweet-and-sour sauce? You can identify the sweet taste. You can identify the sour taste. Yet these two identifiable tastes join together and unify the sauce to produce a unique blend that is a flavor of its own. Much in the same way, each of the literary elements can be identified individually; however, they also join together to unify the writing and to produce a blend that is unique to that particular work.

How are the literary elements interrelated?

1. Shared concepts and functions

Writers can use one literary element to affect or produce another. For example, a writer might have a character be habitually sarcastic to everyone. Sarcasm is a *Use of Language* in which the words mean the exact opposite of what the speaker means, such as telling someone who made a dreadful mistake, "You really used your brains this time!" Of course, being sarcastic would reveal elements of the person's *Character* and project the character's attitude, producing a *Tone*.

▼PRACTICE QUESTION▼

To further illustrate how the elements share concepts and functions, read these lines taken from John Donne's "The Legacy."

> When last I died, and dear, I die
> As often as from thee I go,
> Though it be but an hour ago
> —And Lovers' hours be full eternity—

Answer the following question and see if you can identify what literary elements are being tested.

Lines 1–4 are structured as elements

(A) in antithesis

(B) that overstate the case

(C) that understate the case

(D) of a narrative poem

(E) of a riddle

Explanation: These lines contain an exaggeration or hyperbole. The speaker claims to die every time he leaves his lover. The speaker is using hyperbole, which is a *Use of Language,* to introduce his theme, a combination of *Meaning* and *Form.* Is the speaker (*Character*) sincere? Only context might show. The remainder of the poem works around the idea of figurative death (another *Use of Language*).

Correct Answer: **B**

2. Shared definitions

Defining the literary elements is sometimes difficult because they share so many concepts and functions. The good news is that you can use the exercises that follow to become familiar with each of the literary elements (how they are commonly defined and work together) as they relate to answering SAT-type comprehension questions.

Literary Element Number One: Meaning

In any given literary selection, what is the writer's purpose? What is the speaker's point? Can you take the words at face value? The answers to these and similar questions are at the heart of a work's meaning.

IMPORTANT CONCEPT #1: THE WRITER'S PURPOSE

Concept Explained:

The purpose of writing is communication. Whether the literary selection is in the form of prose, poetry, or drama, the writer is communicating. That communication, that purpose on the part of the writer, forms an important part of the meaning of the work. One of the first steps in determining meaning is to identify the writer's purpose. There are four types of writing based on its purpose or function:

TERM ALERT You should know this term: **The descriptive or expressive purpose**

Definition: In description, the prose writer, poet, or dramatist attempts to "paint a picture with words." Description can be factual (describing, for example, the color and dimensions of an object) or impressionistic (such as expressing what love feels like). Although descriptive or expressive writing may make extended use of descriptive adjectives and be characterized by powerful action verbs, it is not necessarily "wordy." A tightly written work that makes use of carefully chosen figurative language can be *very* expressive.

▼PRACTICE QUESTION▼

Notice the rich textures of meaning in these four lines from a poem by Percy Bysshe Shelley:

> From thy nest every rafter
> Will rot, and thine eagle home
> Leave thee naked to laughter,
> When leaves fall and cold winds come.

The speaker's description of the silent auditor's future is NOT
(A) extreme
(B) pessimistic
(C) contemptuous
(D) dangerous
(E) optimistic

Explanation: A *silent auditor* is addressed by the speaker, but does not respond to the speaker. In this poem, the silent auditor is being compared to a young eagle whose nest falls from rotted rafters, leaving him or her naked and subject to the contemptuous disgrace of laughter and the dangers of cold.

Correct Answer: **E**

TERM ALERT You should know this term: **The expository or informative purpose**

Definition: Exposition explains something. This book is expository: the purpose of this work is to explain about the major literary elements and to inform about the SAT Subject Test in Literature as it relates to those literary elements. Most instructional textbooks are written with an expository purpose. The expository writer includes ideas and facts about the focus subject. Encyclopedias, newspapers, and business reports are all written to inform the reader.

▼PRACTICE QUESTION▼

Read the boxed selection on page 43 titled "How Language Saved a Nation."

The speaker's main purpose in the selection is to
(A) inform readers about how Alfred used English prose politically
(B) make Alfred the Great famous
(C) give Alfred the Great the credit due him
(D) inform readers about English prose
(E) explain how *Handbook* came to be the first English prose

Explanation: In looking for a main purpose, examine the selection as a whole. What is it all about? Alfred used English prose to save England from the Danes. Answers B, C, and E are true, but too narrow to be the main purpose. Answer D is too general.

Correct Answer: **A**

TERM ALERT You should know this term: **The narrative purpose**

Definition: A narrator tells a story. The story may focus on an incident or brief episode (as in an anecdote), the story might chronicle a hero's adventurous relationship to the history of a nation (as in an epic poem), or it might follow the history of a family's generations (as in a saga). An important element of narration is time—events unfolding through time.

▼PRACTICE QUESTION▼

This passage is taken from Anne Royall's account of her visit to "Peal's Museum" in 1826.

> The first object of my inquiry was the mammoth skeleton, but I was greatly disappointed in its appearance.... I beheld it without surprise or emotion.... I could not forbear smiling at a gentleman who, like
> Line myself, had formed extravagant notions of the mammoth. He
> (5) stooped under the rail in order to examine it minutely, and scraping a part of the skeleton with his pen-knife, swore "it was nothing but wood," saying to his friend, that he was cheated out of his money; they both retired displeased.

The anecdote within the passage is used mainly
(A) in antithesis
(B) as hyperbole
(C) to contrast the speaker's view
(D) as a revelation of the characters of people
(E) to reinforce the speaker's point

Explanation: Although the anecdote (a little story, in this case used within a larger account) provides some descriptive detail and reveals how people can react in a situation, the speaker identifies herself with the gentleman ("who, like myself"). The result is a reinforcement of her point. She is not alone in her opinion.

Correct Answer: **E**

TERM ALERT You should know this term: **The argumentative and/or persuasive purpose**

A writer or speaker uses argumentation to convince readers or hearers of the truth (or falsehood) of a proposition. The purpose of persuasive writing, however, is to convince the reader or hearer that some action must be taken. The writer's purpose might simply be to convince you that what he or she is saying is true, such as that the spotted owl is an endangered species. But the writer's purpose may also include persuading you to take some action, such as pressuring your local representative to support legislation that would set aside protected habitats for the spotted owl. Expository or informative writing focuses on the subject; persuasion focuses on the reader or listener.

▼PRACTICE QUESTION▼

This selection is taken from a speech made by Abby Kelley Foster.

> My friends, I feel that in throwing out this idea, I have done what
> was left for me to do. But I did not rise to make a speech—my life
> has been my speech. For fourteen years I have advocated this cause
> by my daily life. Bloody feet, sisters, have worn smooth the path by
> (5) which you have come up hither. You will not need to speak when
> you speak by your everyday life. Oh, how truly does Webster say,
> action, action is eloquence! Let us, then, when we go home, go not
> to complain, but to work. Do not go home to complain of the men,
> but go and make greater exertions than ever to discharge your
> (10) everyday duties.

Line (5) and (10) appear to the left of the quoted text.

The speaker's central call to action can be summarized as which of the following?
(A) Put your money where your mouth is.
(B) The early bird catches the worm.
(C) A stitch in time saves nine.
(D) A picture is worth a thousand words.
(E) Don't just talk the talk, but walk the walk.

Explanation: "Do not go home to complain …, but go and make greater exertions…." This speech aims to convince, to persuade the hearers to action.

Correct Answer: **E**

Although a literary selection may be identified as predominantly one of these four types of composition, seldom is a work exclusively one type. Generally, the writer uses elements of the other three types to aid in the development of the main purpose. For instance, description is frequently used in narration; describing details about oppressive heat, black water, and clinging leeches helps the narrator tell his or her story of convicts escaping a swamp-bound prison camp. An expository writer, aiming to "tell the facts," can narrate an anecdote (an episode or event) to help the reader better understand the information; and political writers often incorporate illustrative narration in their persuasive speeches.

IMPORTANT CONCEPT #2: THE EFFECTS OF A WORK

Concept Explained:

Determining the meaning of a work also involves looking at its *effect*. The emotional impact, the impression the work leaves on the reader, is part of its effect. Skillful writers will plan a certain effect—perhaps feelings of anger, aversion, joyful laughter—by careful use of the literary elements and the techniques available to the writer within those elements. Sometimes an effect happens unintentionally, without the writer's deliberate plan or even conscious knowledge. Meaning is a two-sided concept. On one side you have the writer, someone with a topic to discuss, a point to make, an agenda to fulfill. When you look for the purpose in a work, you are looking at the writer's intent. On the other side of meaning is the reader, someone who often comes to the work without pre-knowledge of the writer's intent, but someone who does generally have some preconceived thoughts or opinions. For the reader, the focus is on the work itself and what effect the work has on him or her.

▼**PRACTICE QUESTION**▼

THE FLY
An Anacreontic

Busy, curious, thirsty fly,
Gently drink, and drink as I;
Freely welcome to my cup,
Line Could'st thou sip, and sip it up;
(5) Make the most of life you may,
Life is short and wears away.
Just alike, both mine and thine,
Hasten quick to their decline;
Thine's a summer, mine's no more,
(10) Though repeated to threescore;
Threescore summers when they're gone,
Will appear as short as one.

by William Oldys

The focus of this poem is
(A) the speaker's fondness for a fly
(B) a fly drinking from the speaker's cup
(C) the fly's impending death
(D) the relative brevity of life
(E) the speaker's impending death

Explanation: Each of the above five answer choices correctly addresses some level of meaning in this poem. The best description of the poem's focus, however, is the answer choice that summarizes the speaker's intent or main point. Why does the speaker fondly welcome the fly to drink from his cup (A and B)? Because the fly's life is short (C). Why does the speaker care that the fly's life is short? Because the speaker's life also seems short (E). What is the <u>effect</u> (emotional impact) of this comparison on the poem's meaning? It establishes, in relation to the life cycle, a similarity between the speaker and the fly: that whether life lasts a summer or threescore summers, life is relatively short.

Correct Answer: **D**

IMPORTANT CONCEPT #3: LEVELS OF MEANING

Concept Explained:

Another way to determine the meaning of a literary selection is to look for different levels of meaning. Some levels of meaning are

1. The literal meaning

This level of meaning is based on taking the work at its "face value"—without examining any figurative levels.

2. The allegorical meaning

At the allegorical level, particularly in narrative works, each object, person, place, and event represents something else, with the characters of the narrative personifying abstract qualities. An entire work may be allegorical (as, for example, in *Pilgrim's Progress* in which the man named Christian meets Mr. Worldly Wiseman—a story in which people and places represent the qualities after which they are named) or a literary selection may have or incorporate a few allegorical elements.

3. The symbolic meaning

Symbols have dual meanings, the literal or face value meaning and a representative meaning—the symbol stands for something else. "Old Glory, Mother, and apple pie" are symbols of down-home American patriotism. A symbol represents something else, but in a less structured way than an allegory.

4. The figurative meaning

At the figurative level the writer strives for a special meaning other than the standard or literal meaning of the words. These special meanings are brought about by the use of tropes. Some tropes include simile (a comparison using "like" or "as"—lips as red as a rose) and metaphor (an implied comparison—rose-red lips).

▼PRACTICE QUESTIONS▼

DARK HOUSE

Dark house, by which once more I stand
Here in the long unlovely street,
Doors, where my heart was used to beat
So quickly, waiting for a hand,

Line

(5) A hand that can be clasped no more—
Behold me, for I cannot sleep,
And like a guilty thing I creep
At earliest morning to the door.

He is not here; but far away
(10) The noise of life begins again,
And ghastly thro' the drizzling rain
On the bald street breaks the blank day.

by Alfred, Lord Tennyson

The condition of the speaker is that he
(A) has been evicted
(B) has insomnia
(C) is insane
(D) is dreaming
(E) is unemployed

As used in this poem, the "dark house" represents
(A) nightmares
(B) ghosts
(C) abandonment and loneliness
(D) grief and death
(E) urban decay

The description in line 7 implies
(A) the speaker is subhuman
(B) avoidance of the law
(C) secrecy and shame
(D) the house is haunted
(E) a need for confession

Explanation: The speaker literally cannot sleep in line 6. The house is a "dark house" because the speaker can no longer clasp the hand of the one who lived there (lines 4–5), making the place a symbol of the speaker's grief over the probable death of his friend. Also, line 7 compares the speaker to "a guilty thing" that creeps, a very emotional comparison that implies a sense of secrecy and shame. As readers, we cannot help but wonder why he feels this way. Does he feel somehow responsible for the person's death? Does he feel guilty because he is alive and his friend is not? Perhaps he is ashamed to show such emotion openly? Had they argued and not had opportunity to restore fellowship?

Correct Answers: **B, D, C**

IMPORTANT CONCEPT #4: THE PARTS VERSUS THE WORK AS A WHOLE

Concept Explained:

A literary selection is made up of parts. These parts may be external structure (such as chapters in a novel, stanzas in a poem, or acts and scenes in a play) or they may be internal (such as plot in a narrative). Each of these parts can have meaning independent of or contributing to the meaning of the work as a whole. Sometimes the meaning of a selection is the sum of its parts—sometimes the meaning can be determined by a key portion of the work. In a testing situation, you may be asked to determine the meaning of an entire selection—or of just a portion of that selection. You may be asked to identify how the meaning of each part contributes to the whole, or how it contrasts that meaning.

▼PRACTICE QUESTIONS▼

Reexamine Shakespeare's sonnet that you worked with in Diagnostic Test I. Notice that the silent auditor of this poem, the person being addressed by the speaker, appears to be the object of his love.

> That time of year thou mayst in me behold
> When yellow leaves, or none, or few, do hang
> Upon those boughs which shake against the cold,
> Bare ruined choirs, where late the sweet birds sang. — Line
> In me thou see'st the twilight of such day — (5)
> As after sunset fadeth in the west;
> Which by and by black night doth take away,
> Death's second self, that seals up all in rest.
> In me thou see'st the glowing of such fire,
> That on the ashes of his youth doth lie, — (10)
> As the deathbed whereon it must expire,
> Consumed with that which it was nourished by.
> This thou perceiv'st, which makes thy love more strong,
> To love that well which thou must leave ere long.

In lines 1–4, the speaker's purpose is to
(A) confess he is growing older
(B) predict the weather
(C) hint at health problems
(D) protest the coming cold
(E) describe a fall scene

In lines 5–8, the speaker makes death seem
(A) frightening
(B) longed for
(C) beautiful
(D) fading
(E) inevitable

In lines 9–12, the speaker deals with

(A) the fiery passions of youth

(B) youth and eventually life being gone

(C) the fires of love being extinguished

(D) deathbed arrangements

(E) burning wood

The silent auditor's love is "more strong" (line 13) because

(A) the speaker must leave in the fall

(B) the silent auditor has sleeping sickness

(C) the speaker has suffered burns

(D) the speaker is dying

(E) the silent auditor is trapped with an aging lover

Explanation: The speaker compares growing old and dying to the approach of winter (lines 1–4), the end of a day (lines 5–9), and a dying fire (lines 9–12). However, each comparison reveals a slightly different side to his meaning. First, he confesses that he is growing older (line 1). Next, he says that death is inevitable (line 8). Finally, the speaker deals with the fact that he is no longer young—his youth is burned up ashes. Taken all together, three parts of the poem tell us that the speaker is dying. The speaker's point? Love me now while you can (the final couplet).

Correct Answers: **A, E, B, D**

IMPORTANT CONCEPT #5: THE SUBJECT AND MAIN IDEA

Concept Explained:

The meaning of a work also includes the statement of its topic, theme, or thesis.

TERM ALERT You should know this term: **topic**

Definition: The topic is the subject of a work, usually expressed as a word or short phrase. Examples include war, love, business, and children. Some very popular topics are survival, children raised by animals, UFO invasions and abductions, lost pets, the end of the world, and good versus evil.

▼PRACTICE QUESTION▼

These lines are taken from a speech made by Frances Willard in 1876.

> Longer ago than I shall tell, my father returned one night to the
> far-off Wisconsin home where I was reared, and, sitting by my
> mother's chair, with a child's attentive ear I listened to their words. He
> Line told us of the news that day that had brought about Neal Dow, and
> (5) the great fight for prohibition down in Maine, and then he said: "I
> wonder if poor, rum-cursed Wisconsin will ever get a law like that!"
> And mother rocked awhile in silence, in the dear old chair I love, and
> then she gently said: "Yes, Josiah, there'll be such a law all over the
> land some day, when women vote."

(10)   My father had never heard her say as much before. He was a
great conservative; so he looked tremendously astonished, and replied
in his keen, sarcastic voice: "And pray, how will you arrange it so that
women shall vote?" Mother's chair went to and fro a little faster for a
minute, and then, looking not into his face, but into the flickering flame
(15)   of the grate, she slowly answered: "Well, I say to you, as the Apostle
Paul said to his jailor: 'You have put us into prison, we being Romans,
and you must come and take us out.'"
         That was a seed-thought in a girl's brain and heart. Years passed
on, in which nothing more was said upon the dangerous theme. My
(20)   brother grew to manhood, and soon after he was twenty-one years old
he went with Father to vote.

What is the main subject of this passage?
(A) Parenthood
(B) Growing up
(C) Prohibition
(D) Interpersonal relationships
(E) Women's suffrage

Explanation: Both Prohibition and women's suffrage are subjects here, but which one
is the *main* subject? Paragraph 1: Prohibition laws will come when women vote. Paragraph 2: A confrontation occurs over women voting. Paragraph 3: A young girl watches
men go off to vote.

Correct Answer: E

TERM ALERT You should know this term: **theme**

Definition: The **theme** summarizes or asserts to the reader some main point, doctrine, or generalization about life, love, religion, the condition of the world, and so forth. Occasionally,
the writer will directly state the theme, but more often it is implied.

In some prose fiction, the theme can be seen as the "moral of the story." To cite an
instance, *Aesop's Fables* are noted for the concise nature of their theme statements. Also,
theme is referred to as "the message" of the story. The narrative, then, exemplifies or makes
concrete an otherwise abstract idea.

▼PRACTICE QUESTION▼

What is "the dangerous theme" in the last paragraph?
(A) Voters must enact Prohibition laws in Wisconsin.
(B) Mother should become involved in the Prohibition movement.
(C) Mother should arrange for women's suffrage.
(D) Father must vote for Prohibition laws in Wisconsin.
(E) Men must give women the right to vote.

Explanation: First, establish why the theme is dangerous. The danger is revealed in the
mother's response to her husband's question about how she would "arrange it so that
women shall vote." Her answer is an allusion to Paul, the Apostle, who questioned his

jailors' right to incarcerate him, a Roman citizen. The context makes the reference clear. They violated his innate rights by putting him in jail just as, in the context of the mother's opinion, men had violated women's innate right to vote. The jailors must grant Paul's freedom from jail; men must grant women their freedom to vote.

Correct Answer: **E**

TERM ALERT You should know this term: **thesis**

Definition: The theme, the central idea of the work, is also called the **thesis** in nonfiction prose. The thesis refers to the writer's position on the subject. The thesis may be directly stated or may be implied; it might lead off the first paragraph of the selection or the author might "build" his or her main points to a concluding thesis. How a thesis is developed relates directly to the writer's purpose (descriptive, informative, narrative, or argumentative/persuasive).

▼PRACTICE QUESTION▼

This passage is taken from Samuel Johnson's *The Rambler*, No 4.

> I remember a remark made by Scaliger upon Pontanus, that all his writings are filled with the same images; and that if you take from him his lilies and his roses, his satyrs and his dryads, he will have
> Line nothing left that can be called poetry. In like manner almost all the
> (5) fictions of the last age will vanish, if you deprive them of a hermit and a wood, a battle and a shipwreck.

The speaker's main point is that
(A) the writings of Scaliger are critical
(B) the errors of Pontanus include overuse of certain images
(C) fictions of the last age are difficult to understand
(D) past writers have overused conventional characters and images
(E) poetry and fiction depend on conventional characters and images

Explanation: Conventional characters and images, such as those mentioned in the selection, are those that recur in various literary forms. Even if you do not know what a satyr or dryad might be, you can tell his point from "lilies and his roses." The overuse of them can make the character or image become expected and stereotypical. Although answers A and B are in the passage, these statements are too narrow for the theme statement. The speaker generalizes to say that past writers (represented by Pontanus and those of the "last age") filled their poetry and fictions with conventional characters (represented by hermits) and images (represented by lilies and roses).

Correct Answer: **D**

IMPORTANT CONCEPT #6: THE DRAMATIC HOOK

Concept Explained:

In drama written for television and movies, the main idea (the literal meaning) is a summary statement called a "hook." In *Close Encounters of the Third Kind,* the hook is aliens telepathically contacting humans, with the narrative culminating in an actual encounter. Hooks may revolve around any number of topics, ranging from social issues to famous personalities. But to find the meaning in literary drama, the hook serves only as a starting point. The action, setting, and character work with the plot to establish meaning in drama.

At the center of literary drama and its meaning is conflict. This conflict (the good guys versus the bad guys, the obstacles to overcome, the love of winning, and so forth) will naturally affect the meaning of the play.

The meaning often results from how the characters deal with the conflict. For instance, think about a play in which the hook is two ghetto-born brothers who each must face and deal with a legacy of abuse and poverty. One brother strives for immediate gratification by joining street gangs and drug dealers, eventually being killed by an overdose of drugs. The other brother exercises self-discipline and works his way through college to become a successful businessman and father. At this point the meaning might be that the way to overcome a life of abuse and poverty is through perseverance and self-discipline. What if, however, the play continues and the successful brother returns to the ghetto to do community-service work and is killed by a senseless, drive-by shooting? Now meaning is being affected not by how the characters deal with the conflict but by how the setting and forces within the plot structure work together with the conflict to overcome the characters. In this case the meaning changes to be a very pessimistic view that regardless of the struggle, the forces of poverty and abuse cannot be overcome (an example of dramatic irony).

When trying to find meaning in a dramatic selection, remember that a play is intended to be performed. Consequently, you should first find the hook, then look for the deeper meaning.

▼PRACTICE QUESTION▼

This passage is taken from Oliver Goldsmith's play *She Stoops to Conquer,* written in 1773.

Act I

Scene.—A Chamber in an old-fashioned House

Enter Mrs. Hardcastle and Mr. Hardcastle.

Mrs. Hardcastle. I vow, Mr. Hardcastle, you're very particular. Is there a creature in the whole country, but ourselves, that does not take a trip to town now and then, to rub off the rust a little? There's
Line the two Miss Hoggs, and our neighbour, Mrs. Grigsby, go to take a
(5) month's polishing every winter.

Hardcastle. Ay, and bring back vanity and affectation to last them the whole year. I wonder why London cannot keep its own fools at home. In my time, the follies of the town crept slowly among us, but now they travel faster than a stage-coach. Its fopperies come down,
(10) not only as inside passengers, but in the very basket.

Mrs. Hardcastle. Ay, your times were fine times, indeed; you have been telling us of *them* for many a long year. Here we live in an old rumbling mansion, that looks for all the world like an inn, but that we never see company. Our best visitors are old Mrs. Oddfish, the
(15) curate's wife, and little Cripplegate, the lame dancing-master: And

all our entertainment your old stories of Prince Eugene and the Duke
of Marlborough. I hate such old-fashioned trumpery.

    Hardcastle. And I love it. I love every thing that's old: old friends,
old times, old manners, old books, old wine; and, I believe, Dorothy
(20) [*taking her hand*], you'll own I have been pretty fond of an old wife.

The main idea of the discussion between Hardcastle and his wife is
(A) visiting neighbors
(B) vanity
(C) resistance to change
(D) gossip with neighbors
(E) growing older

Explanation: What are they talking about? She hates things that are "old-fashioned" and
wants "to rub off the rust a little," to remove the old and expose a fresh, new surface.
He resists such change; he loves the old.

Correct Answer: **C**

IMPORTANT CONCEPT #7: CONVENTIONAL MOTIFS AND THEMES

Concept Explained:

Different periods of literary history have brought with them identifiable motifs and
themes, as well as conventions and traditions. You do not need to memorize period motifs
and conventions for the SAT Subject Test in Literature, but being aware that motifs and conventions exist can help you understand the meaning of a selection.

A *motif* is a figure or element that recurs in literary works; the *theme* of a work is its main
idea or concept, which often is a moral or aims to teach a lesson in life. Some common motifs
include the following:

Loathly Lady motif—an ugly girl turns out to be a beautiful woman, the ugly duckling
  becomes a beautiful swan (closely related to the Cinderella motif).
  Possible theme: Do not judge a book by its cover.

Ubi sunt motif—the motif of mourning a lost past (sometimes used in lyric poetry); these
  poems often include the question, "Where are…?" (Latin: *Ubi sunt*), such as, "Where are
  the carefree days of youth?"
  Possible theme: The good old days were better than today.

Magic spell motif—music makes the girl fall in love; an apple causes a princess to fall asleep.
  Possible theme: Good triumphs over evil.

Star-crossed lovers—a boy and girl fall in love, but are doomed to tragedy because their families are feuding (*Romeo and Juliet*, the Hatfields and McCoys, and *West Side Story*).
  Possible theme: Senseless hatred can cause the innocent to suffer.

Motifs may include a sense of formula. You can expect the princess to awaken when kissed
by her prince, the frog to become a prince when kissed by the beautiful girl.

▼**PRACTICE QUESTION**▼

Here is Edmund Waller's "Song: Go, lovely rose!" written in 1645.

>   Go, lovely rose!
>   Tell her that wastes her time and me
>   That now she knows,
> Line When I resemble her to thee
> (5)   How sweet and fair she seems to be.
>
>   Tell her that's young,
>   And shuns to have her graces spied,
>   That hadst thou sprung
>   In deserts, where no men abide,
> (10)   Thou must have uncommended died.
>
>   Small is the worth
>   Of beauty from the light retired;
>   Bid her come forth,
>   Suffer herself to be desired,
> (15)   And not blush so to be admired.
>
>   Then die! That she
>   The common fate of all things rare
>   May read in thee;
>   How small a part of time they share
> (20)   That are so wondrous sweet and fair!

The theme of this poem is best stated as
(A) his love is as beautiful as a rose
(B) life is short; enjoy it while you are young
(C) beauty unseen is not beauty
(D) the speaker is angry with his love
(E) roses should grow in gardens, not deserts

Explanation:

Stanza 1: The speaker establishes that his love is wasting time (line 2), but he thinks she is as sweet as a rose.

Stanza 2: She is like a rose hidden in the desert.

Stanza 3: She should get over being shy.

Stanza 4: Here is the point: Like the rose, she will die after "how small a part of time…." The theme of this poem relates to its *carpe diem* motif, which means "seize the day" because of the brevity of life.

The key to finding the correct answer? Context, of course!

Correct Answer: **B**

Here is Shakespeare's "Hark, Hark! The Lark."

> Hark, hark! the lark at heaven's gate sings,
> And Phoebus 'gins arise,
> His steeds to water at those springs
> On chaliced flowers that lies:
> And winking Mary-buds begin
> To ope their golden eyes:
> With every thing that pretty is,
> My lady sweet, arise!
> Arise, arise!

Line (5) [lines labeled: Line at line 4, (5) at line 5]

The speaker's aim in this poem is
(A) for his love to wake up
(B) for the hearer to water the steeds and Mary-buds
(C) for his love to sing with him
(D) for the hearer to recognize true beauty
(E) for his love to pick flowers for a chalice

Explanation: In the wake-up motif, one lover urges the other to awaken. Often this motif is used in an *aubade*, a song at dawn. In this poem, the speaker calls his lady to arise because the birds are singing and the flowers are blooming—everything is pretty to see.

Correct Answer: **A**

ACTIVE THINKING EXERCISES FOR MEANING

STEP 1. ▶FOCUS◀

To think actively on the test, you need to focus your attention. You want to think clearly, with sharp definition. One way to attain this type of concentration when you are reading is to know beforehand what you are looking for in the passage. This knowledge gives your reading purpose.

▼**EXERCISE**▼

Turn to Interpretive Skill Practice Set A on page 331.

1. Read the first selection, then answer question #1 on page 335, Questions About Meaning. (Selection First Method)
2. For the second selection, read question #2 on page 335 *first*, then read the selection and answer the question. (Question First Method)

Now, try these methods alternately with the next three selections. The answers are on page 355. How did you do? Continue with the Questions About Meaning in Practice Sets B and C, if you wish.

Does reading the questions before you read the selection help you to focus better? To experiment in a test-length situation, turn to Practice Test One on page 359.

3. Use the Selection First Method for the *Middlemarch* selection and then the poem "A Bed of Forget-Me-Nots."

4. Use the Question First Method for *The Pilot*. Repeat this method for the poem "Come Down, O Maid."

Try to determine which method is most effective for you as an individual. Also, consider whether one method may work better for poems and the other for prose. Continue working with these methods to complete the test. How did you do?

STEP 2. MOW (MY OWN WORDS)

Putting a selection into My Own Words helps establish the context, identify the main idea, and discern the speaker's purpose.

MOWing can be done on three levels:

Level 1.   Generalize the whole.

What is the subject, purpose, and main idea?

Level 2.   Examine each stanza or paragraph.

What is the speaker's point in each stanza or paragraph, and how do the stanzas or paragraphs relate to each other?

Level 3.   Examine each line or sentence.

What does each line or sentence mean?

MOWing uses versions of two major techniques:

TECHNIQUE 1: SUMMARIZING

When you summarize, you condense the facts and ideas of a selection. You express the main idea and any major support for that idea clearly and concisely. A summary is short. A statement of the theme is a type of summary.

TECHNIQUE 2: PARAPHRASING

To paraphrase is to take the ideas of a line or sentence and reword them, putting them in your own words.

Obviously, you can determine the main idea of a passage (summarize) without understanding what every word in every line means. Sometimes, however, you need to paraphrase to discern accurately the author's real meaning.

▼PRACTICE QUESTION▼

Read the following poem written by Walt Whitman.

A Noiseless Patient Spider

A noiseless patient spider,
I marked where on a little promontory it stood isolated,
Marked how to explore the vacant vast surrounding,
Line   It launched forth filament, filament, filament, out of itself,
(5)   Ever unreeling them, ever tirelessly speeding them.

And you O my soul where you stand,
Surrounded, detached, in measureless oceans of space,
Ceaselessly musing, venturing, throwing, seeking the
spheres to connect them,
(10)   Till the bridge you will need be formed, till the ductile
anchor hold,
Till the gossamer thread you fling catch somewhere,
O my soul.

What is the subject of this poem?
(A) A spider
(B) Space
(C) The work ethic
(D) Anchoring of the soul
(E) Building bridges

Explanation: At first glance, the subject is a spider—on a literal level. But is a spider *really* the poet's subject, or is a spider the means he uses to approach another, more abstract subject?

Try using summary and paraphrase to discover the answer.

Paraphrase (put into your own words) lines 1–2: _____
_____

Paraphrase line 3: _____
_____

Paraphrase lines 4–5: _____
_____

Write one sentence that *summarizes* lines 1–5: _____
_____

Paraphrase lines 6–7: _____
_____

Paraphrase line 8: _____
_____

Paraphrase lines 9–10: _____
_____

Write a sentence that *summarizes* lines 6–10: _____
_____

Compare your response with this one:

Lines 1–2: The speaker saw a spider standing alone on a promontory.

Line 3: The spider checked out its surroundings.

Lines 4–5: It spun a web.

Summary of lines 1–5: The speaker watched a spider spin a web.

Lines 6–7: The speaker's soul is standing detached in space.

Line 8: His soul is checking out his surroundings.

Lines 9–10: His soul is seeking to become attached to something.

Summary of lines 6–10: The speaker's soul, like the spider, is detached and is seeking to be attached.

Now, based on the paraphrase and summary, what is the subject? It can be expressed many ways: anchoring of the soul, isolation, the soul.

Based on the paraphrase, the theme is a product of a structural metaphor (an implied comparison). In the first stanza, the speaker describes how a spider is isolated in space, spinning a web. In the second stanza, he describes how the soul is isolated in space, attempting to fling "the gossamer thread"—to become attached (like a spider spinning its web).

One way the theme, then, might be expressed is that the soul, like a spider, is isolated and detached, trying to make connections with its surroundings.

Correct Answer: **D**

STEP 3. BID (BREAK IT DOWN)

When you **BID**, you Break It Down, examining the specific elements at work in a selection.

To **BID** using Literary Element #1: Meaning, first review the seven Important Concepts and the Term Alerts for this chapter.

▼EXERCISE▼

Match the following terms with their definitions.

1. descriptive purpose	A. the subject of a work
2. expressive purpose	B. meant to inform the reader
3. expository purpose	C. the writer's main point in nonfiction
4. informative purpose	D. impressionistic description
5. narrative purpose	E. factual description
6. argumentative purpose	F. tells a story
7. persuasive purpose	G. meant to explain something
8. topic	H. written to convince readers of a truth
9. theme	I. written to motivate readers
10. thesis	J. summarizes the main point

Correct Answers:
1. **E**   2. **D**   3. **G**   4. **B**   5. **F**   6. **H**   7. **I**   8. **A**   9. **J**   10. **C**

Next, determine if each of the following statements is true or false based on the seven Important Concepts for Meaning.

1. Most literary works are written exclusively with one purpose.
2. The effects of a work include its emotional impact on the reader.
3. A work can have more than one meaning.
4. Meaning relates only to a work in its entirety.
5. A theme or thesis must be directly expressed in the work.
6. In drama, meaning often results from how characters deal with conflict.
7. By definition, a theme must be unique.

Correct Answers:
1. **F**   2. **T**   3. **T**   4. **F**   5. **F**   6. **T**   7. **F**

Finally, consider these questions. If you are looking for the meaning of a selection,

1. What is the writer's purpose?
2. What is the topic or subject?
3. What is the thesis or theme?
4. What does any given paragraph or stanza mean literally?
5. Are there any other levels of meaning?
6. In a drama, how does the conflict relate to the meaning?
7. Have you seen or heard this theme before?

Correct Answers: (will vary with the selections being read)

▼PRACTICE QUESTIONS▼

Here is a passage taken from Charles Lamb's "A Bachelor's Complaint of the Behaviour of Married People." Answer the five questions that follow the selection.

As a single man, I have spent a good deal of my time in noting down the infirmities of Married People, to consol myself for those superior pleasures, which they tell me I have lost by remaining as I am.

Line   I cannot say that the quarrels of men and their wives ever made
(5)   any great impression upon me, or had much tendency to strengthen in me those anti-social resolutions, which I took up long ago upon more substantial considerations. What oftenest offends me at the houses of married persons where I visit, is an error of quite a different description; it is that they are too loving.

(10)   Not too loving neither: that does not explain my meaning. Besides, why should that offend me? The very act of separating themselves from the rest of the world, to have the fuller enjoyment of each other's society, implies that they prefer one another to all the world.

(15)   But what I complain of is, that they carry this preference so undisguisedly, they perk it up in the faces of us single people so shamelessly, you cannot be in their company a moment without

(20) being made to feel, by some indirect hint or open avowal, that you are not the object of this preference. Now there are some things which give no offence, while implied or taken for granted merely, but expressed, there is much offence in them.

If a man were to accost the first homely-featured or plain-dressed young woman of his acquaintance, and tell her bluntly, that she was not handsome or rich enough for him, and he could not marry her,

(25) he would deserve to be kicked for his ill manners; yet no less is implied in the fact, that having access and opportunity of putting the question to her, he has never yet thought fit to do it. The young woman understands this as clearly as if it were put into words; but no reasonable young woman would think of making this the ground

(30) of a quarrel. Just as little right have a married couple to tell me by speeches, and looks that are scarce less plain than speeches, that I am not the happy man—the lady's choice. It is enough that I know I am not: I do not want this perpetual reminding.

1. Of the following representative pairs of words, which mirrors the writer's sense of "no offence" versus "much offence" (lines 20–21) ?
   (A) "single" … "married" (lines 1–2)
   (B) "reasonable" … "quarrel" (lines 29–30)
   (C) "implied" … "expressed" (lines 20–21)
   (D) "too loving" … "not too loving" (lines 9–10)
   (E) "speeches" … "looks" (line 31)

2. Line 11 contains which of the following?
   (A) Analytical question
   (B) Rhetorical question
   (C) Ironic question
   (D) Deliberative rhetoric
   (E) Symbolic rhetoric

3. The effect of the speaker correcting himself in line 10 is to
   (A) show himself to be unlearned
   (B) acknowledge a genuine error
   (C) explain faulty thinking
   (D) rhetorically shift to an argumentative tone
   (E) present the major premise of a syllogism

4. In the second paragraph, the speaker would have the reader believe that
   (A) his being single is an accident
   (B) he is distressed over quarrels in married couples
   (C) his being single was a thought-out decision
   (D) the houses of married couples offend him
   (E) visiting married couples is an error

5. What is the main idea of the passage?
   (A) Married couples love too much.
   (B) Married couples make singles feel rejected.
   (C) Singles are unhappy.
   (D) Married couples are an enigma.
   (E) Married couples are generally quarrelsome.

Answers and Explanations:

1. **C** Reread lines 20–21 for the obvious answer.
2. **B** A rhetorical question does not require an answer; it serves to make a point.
3. **D** The speaker provides the subject and some background information in the first two paragraphs. By the third paragraph, however, he begins to explain his position and to attempt to win his reader over to his point of view.
4. **C** The speaker's choice to be single was made based on "substantial considerations" (line 7).
5. **B** The speaker directly states "what I complain of is" in the fourth paragraph.

STEP 4: TT→TM (MOVE FROM TEST TAKER TO TEST MAKER)

To this point, you have been engaging in active reading techniques designed to increase your understanding of what you read. Active reading, however, is somewhat limited to the thinking of the author of the selection and the test maker.

Active Thinking is unlimited. You begin with active reading techniques, then go beyond the thinking of others to develop your own original ideas, thinking outside the box.

There is no mystery to Active Thinking. As you learn to apply active reading techniques to prepare for the SAT test, you can begin to use those techniques in other subjects and life. Ultimately, when faced with a challenge and no obvious solution is in sight, the student who engages in Active Thinking asks the question, "How else can I do this?"

Take the first step outside the box by thinking about how test makers write questions on the meaning of a selection.

You have learned that an entire selection can have meaning. Looking at the passage from Lamb's essay, practice Question 5 deals with his overall meaning. A paragraph or stanza can also have meaning. Do you notice something attention-getting in the third paragraph? Lamb refers to his own meaning. Can you turn that line into a test question?

Begin by thinking of ways to word the question stem, then how to word the correct answer. Finally, include incorrect answers.

_____

_____

(A) _____

(B) _____

(C) _____

(D) _____

(E) _____

How did you do? There are several ways you could approach this question: Why does "too loving" NOT explain the speaker's meaning? What does the speaker really mean by "too loving"? Did you find a different approach?

Here is something to think about:

Of course, test questions can simply ask, "What is the speaker's purpose?" or "What is the speaker's theme in the passage?" Sometimes, however, the questions are more challenging and combine literary elements. Again, look at the Lamb essay and Question 3. Did you realize that this question concerns meaning? The correct answer is D. The speaker deliberately corrects himself as if actually talking to us rather than writing a carefully constructed essay. Why? So that he can *argue* his point: the argumentative purpose.

Finally, break free of the box altogether with this exercise:

Look for meaning as it is used in a literary context in the world around you:

1. Watch a movie and look for the dramatic hook.
2. In your reading assignment for history or science class, try to identify the author's topic and thesis statement.
3. Listen to several conversations either in person or on television. As each person is speaking, try to identify his or her purpose and main point. What does he or she mean by what was just said? Can you take what was said literally (at face value) or is there some other level of meaning?

Think about this idea: Does a speaker's body language and facial expressions contribute to meaning? What happens when physical expression does not match the words spoken?

MEANING IN CONCLUSION

Actually, meaning does not conclude at this point. Meaning provides the foundation for the other six literary elements. Consequently, you will be seeing a lot more about meaning in the chapters that follow.

Literary Element Number Two: Form

LINES WRITTEN IN RIDICULE OF CERTAIN POEMS

Wheresoe'er I turn my view,
All is strange, yet nothing new;
Endless labor all along,
Line Endless labor to be wrong;
(5) Phrase that time has flung away,
Uncouth words in disarray,
Tricked in antique ruff and bonnet,
Ode, and elegy, and sonnet.

by Samuel Johnson

Ode…elegy…sonnet—their misuse in poorly executed works led Samuel Johnson to write these critical lines "Phrase that time has flung away" and "Uncouth words." Yet, when well written, these forms of literary expression can stir emotions from deep within the reader or hearer.

Meaning might be called the "what?" (as in "What is the writer trying to say?") in a literary selection, and form can be called the "how?" ("How does he or she say it?"). Form includes many different patterns of development or methods of organization that can be used for self-expression, providing information, persuasion, and entertainment. Some forms of writing, of course, communicate certain meanings better than others.

IMPORTANT CONCEPT #1: SEQUENCE PATTERNS

Concept Explained:

As you identify and study the form of a literary selection, give attention to *sequence* or *order* of presentation. Here are some of the most common ways writers sequence their work:

1. Chronological sequence—tells what happened according to time
2. Climactic order—arranged from the least important to the most important
3. Deductive order—arrangement based on deductive reasoning (from the general to the specific)
4. Inductive order—arrangement based on inductive reasoning (from the specific to the general)
5. Problem-solving sequence—presents a problem, then suggests or explains the solution
6. Spatial sequence—describes a location
7. Topical order—presents ideas by topics
8. Mixed order—arrangement that is a blend of patterns

▼PRACTICE QUESTION▼

Susanna Moodie wrote the following selection.

As the sun rose above the horizon, all these matter-of-fact circumstances were gradually forgotten and merged in the surpassing grandeur of the scene that rose majestically before me.

Line
(5)

The previous day had been dark and stormy, and a heavy fog had concealed the mountain chain, which forms the stupendous background to this sublime view, entirely from our sight. As the clouds rolled away from their grey, bald brows, and cast into denser shadow the vast forest belt that girdled them round, they loomed out like mighty giants—Titans of the earth, in all their rugged and awful

(10)

beauty—a thrill of wonder and delight pervaded my mind. The spectacle floated dimly on my sight—my eyes were blinded with tears—blinded by the excess of beauty. I turned to the right and to the left. I looked up and down the glorious river; never had I beheld so many striking objects blended into one mighty whole! Nature had

(15)

lavished all her noblest features in producing that enchanting scene.

Structurally, this passage is
(A) climactic and deductive
(B) climactic and spatial
(C) spatial and topical
(D) spatial and inductive
(E) chronological and spatial

Explanation: The speaker describes scenes (spatially) as she sees them (chronologically).

Correct Answer: **E**

IMPORTANT CONCEPT #2: ORGANIZING PRINCIPLES

Concept Explained:

Once the overall sequence pattern is established, the writer generally must organize his or her thoughts within that pattern. The chart on page 71 provides you with the basic organizing principles most commonly used in literature.

Here is a selection taken from Thackeray's *Vanity Fair:*

> What is there in a pair of pink cheeks and blue eyes forsooth?
> These dear Moralists ask, and hint wisely that the gifts of genius, the
> accomplishments of the mind, ... and so forth, are far more valuable
> Line   endowments for a female, than those fugitive charms which a few
> (5)   years will inevitably tarnish. It is quite edifying to hear women
> speculate upon the worthlessness and the duration of beauty.
> But though virtue is a much finer thing, and those hapless
> creatures who suffer the misfortune of good looks ought to be
> continually put in mind of the fate which awaits them....

The organizational pattern used by the narrator to make his main point is best
described as

(A) cause and effect
(B) definition
(C) process analysis
(D) analysis and classification
(E) comparison and contrast

Explanation: Do you see the organizational clue? The comparative degree: "more valuable," "much finer."

Correct Answer: **E**

ORGANIZING PRINCIPLES

BASIC ORGANIZATION PRINCIPLE:	DEFINITION:	EXAMPLE:
Analogy	Comparisons using the known to explain or clarify the unknown	Fried frog legs (the unknown) taste a lot like fried chicken (the known).
Cause and Effect (Causal Analysis)	Establishing a relation between outcomes and the reasons behind them	She fired him (effect) because he drank on the job (cause).
Comparison/Contrast	Pointing out similarities and differences of subjects	His management style is bold, like Kennedy's (comparison), but less organized (contrast).
Definition	Clarifying by using synonyms or by pointing out uniqueness within a general class	Mucilage, liquid glue, (synonym) was used to hold the inlaid pieces of the mosaic— a picture (general class) that's made of inlaid pieces (unique feature).
Description	Using words to convey sensory impressions or abstract concepts	The temperature was –32°F (objective description), with a frigid wind blowing blankets of snow over the ice (subjective description).
Analysis and Classification (Division)	Dividing a subject into parts (analysis) or grouping information by class	The elements of Earth's crust are mostly oxygen and silicon (analysis). Gold, silver, and copper, which are all found in the ground, have been known to man for many years (classification).
Example	Using illustrations to clarify, explain, or prove a point	A case in point is this column of this summary.
Induction	Reasoning that arrives at a general principle or draws a conclusion from the facts or examples	He was late for supper, late for our wedding, and even a late delivery when he was born (examples)—that man is habitually late (conclusion)!
Deduction	Reasoning that uses a syllogism (two premises and a conclusion)	Premise 1: When it rains more than 5 inches, the river floods. Premise 2: It has rained 6 inches. Conclusion: The river is overflowing its banks.
Narration	Telling what happened or is happening in chronological order (recounting events or telling a story)	I walked to the refrigerator, opened the door, pulled out the turkey, and spilled an open carton of milk.
Process (Analysis)	Explaining how something happened or happens (works)—sometimes instructional in purpose	First, cream the sugar and butter. Next, add eggs and milk; then blend in the sugar, flour, and baking powder. Finally, pour into the cake pan and bake at 350° for 50 minutes.

An Introduction to Genre

Genre is the product of a work's sequence pattern, organization of thought, subject, and/or structure (parts).

The College Board has specified that the SAT Subject Test in Literature will include selections from three major genre groups: **prose**, **poetry**, and **drama**. Under these three "umbrella" genres you will find many other genres. In preparing for the SAT Subject Test in Literature, you may need to be able to identify the major characteristics of the main genres.

IMPORTANT CONCEPT #3: PROSE NONFICTION

Concept Explained:

Generally, the main nonfiction genres include the following:

1. Genre: Essay
Characteristics:

- Defined as a brief prose composition
- Restricted topics
- Purpose: discussion or persuasion
- Often contains a thesis statement
- Addressed to general audience
- Two types:
    a. Formal essay—serious tone, scholarly, organized
    b. Informal essay—intimate tone, everyday topics, humor, less structure

2. Genre: Biography
Characteristics:

- Defined as the story of a person's life as told or recorded by another
- Word first used by Dryden (1683) and defined as "the history of particular men's lives"

3. Genre: Autobiography
Characteristics:

- Defined as the story of one's own life
- Subtypes of autobiography:
    a. **Diaries**—an intimate account of day-to-day life, including thoughts
    b. **Journals**—chronological logs of day-to-day events (also, some scholarly periodicals such as *The Journal of Medicine*)
    c. **Letters**—notes and epistles; correspondence from one person to another
    d. **Memoirs**—recollections that center around certain other people or events in the life of the writer
    e. **Confessions**—autobiographical recollections of matters that are normally held private

Autobiographies and memoirs are written to be published, whereas diaries, journals, and letters are more personal, with (in the case of letters especially) perhaps only a few people at most reading them.

4. Genre: Criticism

Characteristics:

- Defined as studies that analyze and comment upon works of art and literature
- Rhetoric and diction—the subject of critics in Renaissance England

5. Genre: Informational Text

Characteristics:

- Factual
- Structured by topical outline (if subject allows)
- Can include extensive use of example, analogy, and description, but most organizing principles can be used effectively

An instructional text is a type of informational text aimed at teaching. Sometimes these types rely heavily on process analysis for the purpose of the reader following instructions.

▼PRACTICE QUESTION▼

Of course, you should be able to distinguish between a biography and an autobiography, a letter and a diary, for example. However, the selections on the test are generally short. As a result, the nonfiction genres could be tested indirectly, focusing on their characteristics, especially as they relate to the writer's purpose.

Lord Chesterfield wrote these lines:

> If you would particularly gain the affection and friendship of
> particular people, whether men or women, endeavor to find out their
> predominant excellency, if they have one, and their prevailing
> Line   weakness, which everybody has; and do justice to the one, and
> (5)   something more than justice to the other. Men have various objects
> in which they may excel or at least would be thought to excel; and,
> though they love to hear justice done to them, where they know that
> they excel, yet they are most and best flattered upon those points
> where they wish to excel, and yet are doubtful whether they do or
> (10)   not. As for example: Cardinal Richelieu, who was ...

The speaker probably intends the text to be
(A) instructional
(B) biographical
(C) confessional
(D) a formal essay
(E) a humorous essay

Explanation: Beyond just giving information, the speaker instructs, using directives and an example. An interesting note: Lord Chesterfield wrote these words in a letter to his son, making the work *both* informational (instructional) and autobiographical (a letter). He wants to teach his son, so he writes him a letter.

Correct Answer: **A**

IMPORTANT CONCEPT #4: PROSE FICTION (STRUCTURE)

Concept Explained:

Fiction is an imaginative literary narrative that can be in the form of prose, poetry, or drama. Most prose fiction falls into one of several types based primarily on length. The novel is an extended prose narrative. A novelette generally consists of about 15,000 to 50,000 words, the short story only from 500 (in the short-short story) to 15,000 words. An anecdote is a narrative of a single episode (an incident). It is very popular among magazine article writers as an attention-getting device to introduce their subjects. Also, political speech writers use the anecdote to enliven what might be otherwise dull, issue-based speeches; and, if the narrative is about someone with whom the audience can identify, they use the anecdote as a means of persuasion.

TERM ALERT You should know this term: **setting**

Definition: The setting is the time and place of the story, as well as the socioeconomic background of the characters.

TERM ALERT You should know this term: **plot**

Definition: A plot is a summary of the action of the story, including the words and deeds of the characters.

But what precipitates this action? Why does the reader care about the words and deeds of the characters? Conflict. The motivating, driving force that involves both characters and (if written well) involves the readers in the narrative is **conflict**. Conflict makes readers care. Conflict means opposition: person versus person, person versus group, person versus environment, person versus nature, or person versus self. Generally, when reading a narrative, the reader begins to anticipate the conflicts in the plot, selects a side that he or she thinks is right, evaluates the characters to see which side each is on, identifies which character(s) he or she wants to win, and eventually may even begin to identify with that character. The plot, then, with conflict as its driving force, provides unity for the work as a whole.

TERM ALERT You should know this term: **narrative plot line**

Definition: In its simplest, most predictable form, a narrative plot looks like this:

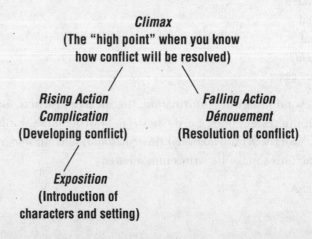

Climax
(The "high point" when you know
how conflict will be resolved)

**Rising Action
Complication**
(Developing conflict)

**Falling Action
Dénouement**
(Resolution of conflict)

Exposition
(Introduction of
characters and setting)

How can the plotline for a narrative be summarized? In a stereotypical romance it might go like this: Jasmine is a beautiful, single professional woman on vacation in Hawaii (*Exposition*). She meets Roberto, the dark, handsome, rich sugar baron who sweeps her off her feet until Susan, Jasmine's rival for Roberto's affections, causes a misunderstanding that makes Roberto doubt Jasmine's love (*Complication*—developing conflict that obviously is the longest part of the narrative). Roberto discovers Susan's treachery while Jasmine is headed in a taxi to the airport to leave his life forever (*Climax*—the reader knows how this is going to end). Roberto races to the airport and reconciles with Jasmine just in time to live happily ever after (*Dénouement*). Some genres have very predictable plotlines and are sometimes called formula plots. They consist of variations on the same plotline story after story.

▼PRACTICE QUESTIONS▼

This selection comes from Poe's "The Man of the Crowd."

With my brow to the glass, I was thus occupied in scrutinizing the
mob, when suddenly there came into view a countenance (that of a
decrepit old man, some sixty-five or seventy years of age,)—a
Line countenance which at once arrested and absorbed my whole
(5) attention, on account of the absolute idiosyncrasy of its expression.
Any thing even remotely resembling that expression I had never seen
before. I well remember that my first thought, upon beholding it, was
that Retszch, had he viewed it, would have greatly preferred it to his
own pictural incarnations of the fiend. As I endeavored, during the
(10) brief minute of my original survey, to form some analysis of the
meaning conveyed, there arose confusedly and paradoxically within
my mind, the ideas of vast mental power, of caution, of
penuriousness, of avarice, of coolness, of malice, of blood-thirstiness,
of triumph, of merriment, of excessive terror, of intense—of extreme
(15) despair. I felt singularly aroused, startled, fascinated. "How wild a
history," I said to myself, "is written within that bosom!" Then came a
craving desire to keep the man in view—to know more of him.
Hurriedly putting on an overcoat, and seizing my hat and cane, I
made my way into the street, and pushed through the crowd in the
(20) direction which I had seen him take; for he had already
disappeared. With some little difficulty I at length came within sight
of him, approached, and followed him closely, yet cautiously, so as
not to attract his attention.

Where is the speaker when he first sees the man?
(A) In the street
(B) In a crowd of people
(C) Walking from building to building
(D) Inside a building looking out
(E) On a subway train

As presented, this portion of the narrative is best described as
(A) the exposition
(B) the exposition and rising action
(C) the rising action and climax
(D) the climax and falling action
(E) the falling action and dénouement

The speaker's actions can be summarized as
(A) preempting the man's authority
(B) following the man
(C) violating the man's privacy
(D) harassing the man
(E) stalking the man

Explanation: His "brow to the glass" (line 1) shows that he is looking out the window. He then makes his way "into the street" (setting). Although the privacy issue is a tempting answer, actually the speaker is stalking the man by *covertly* following him (plot). Finally, this paragraph as it is presented (out of context) is a description of exposition (the man and his circumstance introduced) and the rising action (the speaker follows him amid increasing inner turmoil).

Correct Answers: **D, B, E**

IMPORTANT CONCEPT #5: PROSE FICTION (EFFECTS)

Concept Explained:

Sometimes writers will depart from the usual plot structure in order to achieve a specific effect. In fact, most plots (whether traditonal or those that are departures from the usual) will aim to create some effect. Five significant examples (but by no means an exhaustive list) of effects that are the result of plot are the following:

1. Tragedy

In a tragic narrative, humans do not and cannot overcome inevitable failure, although they may demonstrate grace and courage along the way.

2. Comedy

A comic effect is produced when the plot leads the characters into amusing situations, ridiculous complications, and a happy ending.

3. Satire

A narrative is satiric when it makes a subject look ridiculous. The subjects being derided can range from an individual to society.

4. Romance

A romantic narrative (called a *prose romance*) has clear distinctions between the "good guys and the bad guys," an adventurous plot, and events that occasionally demand that the reader believe the otherwise unbelievable.

5. Realism

A realistic narrative is in contrast to the romance. It tries to mirror real life, not present life as the reader thinks or wishes it could be. In realism, the leading characters are not necessarily beautiful or handsome, rich or talented. The plot revolves around events that people face every day in a real world.

In narrative fiction, the writer uses **genre** (a narrative identified by structure, technique, and subject matter) to achieve a tragic, comedic, satiric, romantic, realistic, or some other effect. The genres available to writers are numerous.

▼Practice Question▼

As a genre, an entire narrative might be a tragedy, comedy, satire, and so forth, depending on how the plot unfolds. In an excerpt, however, you can sometimes detect the elements of these effects as they are being developed.

To illustrate, return to the Poe selection to answer this question:

> This selection contains elements that are best described as
> (A) tragic and realistic
> (B) comic and romantic
> (C) satiric and tragic
> (D) romantic and realistic
> (E) realistic and satiric

Explanation: The plot has adventurous elements, but no clear distinction between the "good guys and the bad guys." Who is the hero? The man is compared to Retzsch's representations of a fiend. The speaker is an obsessed stalker, such as one might hear about on the evening news. Is failure inevitable? Perhaps not, but the elements are in place for a tragic ending.

Correct Answer: **A**

IMPORTANT CONCEPT # 6: PROSE FICTION (SUBJECT)

Concept Explained:

You are probably familiar with many of the genres that are based on the subject of the work. Some of them include the following:

- Detective—Also called crime stories, murder mysteries, and "whodunits," the plot focuses on solving a crime, often murder.
- Psychological—Plot tells not only what happens, but also why it happens, concentrating on motivation.
- Problem—Plot centers on solving a problem.
- Novels of
  a. Sensibility—Plot focuses on emotion.
  b. Character—Plot focuses on character.
  c. Manners—Plot focuses on a social class.
  d. Incident—Plot focuses on episodes.
  e. The Soil—Plot focuses on rural regional struggle to survive.
- Sociological—A type of problem novel, it purports to have the solutions for specified problems in society.
- Propaganda—Plot is subordinated to the role of a vehicle to put forth a particular doctrine.
- Western—"Dime novels" are set in the American West.

- Gothic—Plot centers on ghostly castles, medieval settings, and romantic knights bound by chivalry.
- Epistolary—Plot is carried out through a series of letters between or among the characters.
- Science Fiction—Plot centers on science fantasy, such as time machines, aliens, or mutants.
- Suspense—Also called "edge-of-your-seat" stories, the plot keeps the reader in a somewhat sustained sense of suspense or anticipation.
- Utopia—Plot depends upon a fictional, perfect world. (Contrasted with *dystopia* in which the fictional world is far less than perfect, as in Orwell's *1984*.)

You can add to this list shorter narratives that rely on their subjects for genre identification:

1. The *tale* that centers on an outcome—As a result of this focus, the tale may not be as tightly structured as some of the other short narrative genres. Look to O'Henry for some example tales.

2. The *tall tale* that centers on the exaggerated feats of (generally) American heroes—Examples include such characters as Paul Bunyan and Davy Crockett (although some tall tales have been written in other countries).

3. The *fable* that centers on a moral—The moral is often expressed in an *epigram* put forth by the writer or one of the characters at the end. Examples include the famous fables of Aesop.

4. The *folktale* that is a narrative that originally was transmitted orally—Elements of the folktale are commonly found in tall tales and fables.

5. The *parable* that teaches a lesson by using very tightly structured allegory—As pointed out by Professors William Harmon and the late C. Hugh Holman of the University of North Carolina at Chapel Hill in *A Handbook to Literature* (Macmillan Publishing Company, 1992), the most famous parables are those of Jesus Christ. (Examples include the "Prodigal Son," the "Parable of the Sowers," and the "Parable of the Workers.")

6. The *legend* that relates the life of the hero—people whose lives are of legendary proportions.

7. The *myth* that once was believed to be true but is now accepted as fiction—these stories are generally of anonymous origin and include supernatural elements.

▼PRACTICE QUESTION▼

Identifying genre based on a work's subject is generally easy. If the plot involves little green men from Mars, you can be fairly sure it is science fiction. That same narrative, however, may contain within it some detective work on the part of the characters, a Western setting, and suspenseful moments when characters attempt to solve the problem and examine their psychological responses to aliens coming to Earth, with the story ending with a statement of sociological propaganda that if we all lived in peace, we could have a Utopian world. So, if you owned a bookstore, in which genre section would you shelve such a story?

Again, return to Poe's "The Man in the Crowd."

This selection can be described as all the following EXCEPT

(A) suspenseful
(B) psychological
(C) utopian
(D) tragic
(E) realistic

Explanation: Notice that the speaker not only tells us that he follows the man, but also tells us in detail his thinking when he sees and follows him. By the end of the paragraph, the reader is asking, "What happens next?" in anticipation of what follows. This description is not, however, of a perfect world.

Correct Answer: **C**

IMPORTANT CONCEPT #7: POETRY (RHYTHM)

Concept Explained:

Unlike prose, most poems have a regular rhythm.

ERM ALERT You should know this term: **rhythm**

Definition: Rhythm is a variation of stressed and unstressed sounds that has some type of regular pattern. Generally, the stressed sounds or syllables (accents) recur regularly and, almost as a natural consequence, cause grouping of the stressed sounds into units. These groupings of accented and unaccented syllables are fundamental to the driving beat of hard rock, the toe-tapping cadence of a Texas two-step, and the slow rhythm of the blues. Rhythm can directly affect people's moods and perhaps their perceptions.

Notice the strong regularity of this rap-style work:

> So you gotta take a test
> And you wanna do your best
> Work hard'n you'll be knowin'
> That to college you'll be goin'

ERM ALERT You should know this term: **iambic pentameter**

Definition: Iambic pentameter is a very popular rhythm in English and American poetry. It consists of five units (meters) of unstressed, then stressed syllables in one line of poetry. How can you tell if a poem is written in iambic pentameter?

The study of the rhythms and sounds of poetry is called **prosody**; the system used to describe rhythm is called **scansion**. When you **scan** a line of poetry, you first identify which kind of **foot** is being used. A foot is the unit formed by a strong stress or accent and the weak stress(es) or unaccented syllable(s) that accompany it. You identify the type or kind of foot that is being used as you "walk" along the individual line.

To illustrate, *scan* the first stanza of "The Wife of Usher's Well."

> There lived a wife at Usher's Well,
> And a wealthy wife was she;
> She had three stout and stalwart sons,
> And sent them o'er the sea.

The first step in scanning is to determine the accented or stressed sounds. This is done by placing an accent mark over each stressed syllable. (Remember: You are finding the "beat" of the poem.)

```
     /        /        /        /
There lived a wife at Usher's Well,
              /       /        /
     And a wealthy wife was she;
     /         /          /        /
She had three stout and stalwart sons,
              /        /        /
     And sent them o'er the sea.
```

Next, identify the unstressed syllables by placing an X over each.

```
  X    /  X  /  X   /  X     /
There lived a wife at Usher's Well,
     X X   / X    / X   /
     And a wealthy wife was she;
 X   /  X    /  X    /  X    /
She had three stout and stalwart sons,
     X   /  X   /  X    /
     And sent them o'er the sea.
```

Now look for a pattern. In this poem, there seems to be a pattern of an unstressed syllable followed by a stressed syllable. Divide the groups of unstressed and stressed syllables into *feet* by using a slash mark (called a *virgule.*)

```
  X     /   X   /   X   /   X     /
There lived / a wife / at Ush / er's Well,
     X X   /   X   /   X   /
     And a weal / thy wife / was she;
 X    /    X    /    X   /    X    /
She had / three stout / and stal / wart sons,
     X   /    X    /   X   /
     And sent / them o'er / the sea.
```

You have now identified iambic foot. There are many different kinds of feet, but the most common to English poetry are illustrated by L. E. Myers in the following five stanzas called "Stressed and Unstressed":

"Stressed and Unstressed"

Iambic foot (X /) unstressed, stressed

```
X  / X  /X  /  X   /
Iambic is a line of verse,
     X   / X   /   X    /
     That first is weak, then strong.
```

X   / X   / X / X   /

If this light rhyme you do rehearse,

        X   / X / X   /

        You're sure to do no wrong.

Anapestic foot (X X /) unstressed, unstressed, stressed

X X   / X X / X X   / X X /

With two weak and a strong we will learn anapest,

     X X / X   X   / X X /

     As we take this small verse right along.

X X   / X   X   / XX / XX   /

Feel the beat, mark the stress, anapest is the best,

      X X / X   X / X X /

      With a rhythm that can be a song.

Trochaic foot (/ X) stressed, unstressed

  /   X   /   X   / X / X

Strong then weak should bring no terror—

     /   X / X / X

     Verse that is trochaic.

/ X   /   X   / X / X

Up then down—you will not error—

     / X / X / X

     Never be prosaic!

Dactylic foot (/ X X) stressed, unstressed, unstressed

/ X   X   / X X / X   X   / X X

He could write verses like Alfred, Lord Tennyson,

     / X X / X   X   / X X / X X

     Dactylic foot that could march clear to Dennison.

/ X   X   / X X   /   X X / X X

Rhythms he kept and to rhyme he was dutiful—

     /   X X / X X /   X X / XX

     That's why his work was so strong and so beautiful.

Spondaic foot (/ /) stressed, stressed

X   / X / X / X /

When two successive syllables

     X / X X   / X X / X /

     with equal strong stresses occur in verse,

/   /   / X/ /

Strong, strong, spondaic foot

     / X   / X /

     comes to mind at first.

After determining the type of foot, you need to identify the **meter**. Meter refers to how many feet are *in each line*.

Traditionally: one foot   = monometer
two feet   = dimeter
three feet = trimeter
four feet   = tetrameter
five feet   **= pentameter**
six feet   = hexameter
seven feet = heptameter
eight feet = octameter

Scan these two lines from Anne Bradstreet's "The Author to Her Book."

Thou ill-form'd offspring of my feeble brain,
Who after birth did'st by my side remain,

Obviously, the lines are iambic. Now, count the number of feet to determine the meter.

Thou ill-/form'd off/spring of /my fee/ble brain, (5)
Who af/ter birth/dids't by/my side/remain, (5)

The lines are iambic pentameter.

Look at the first line of "The Wife of Usher's Well":

There lived / a wife / at Ush / er's Well,

There are four feet in this line: tetrameter.

Consequently, the *meter* or *metrical pattern* of line one is iambic tetrameter. Notice the metrical patterns of the entire stanza:

Iambic tetrameter—There lived/ a wife/ at Ush/er's Well,
Iambic trimeter—and a weal/thy wife/ was she;
Iambic tetrameter—She had/ three stout/ and stal/wart sons,
Iambic trimeter—and sent/ them o'er/ the sea.

Because iambic and anapestic meters end on a high stress, they are often referred to as the *rising meters* or rhythms, whereas dactylic and trochaic are *falling meters* or rhythms. The meter used, the metrical pattern, can directly affect the mood, the tone, and/or the meaning of a poem. For example, the metrical pattern can contribute to a *comic effect*:

I DO NOT LOVE THEE, DR. FELL

I do not love thee, Dr. Fell,
The reason why I cannot tell;
But this I know, and know full well,
I do not love thee, Dr. Fell.

by Tom Brown

▼PRACTICE QUESTION▼

You should be able to identify iambic pentameter in a testing situation. Although you may not need to know less frequently used metrical patterns, you should be able to recognize when the rhythm and changes in the rhythm affect the meaning of a poem.

Here is Tennyson's "Break, Break, Break."

> Break, break, break,
>   On thy cold gray stones, O Sea!
> And I would that my tongue could utter
>   The thoughts that arise in me.
>
> Line
> (5) O well for the fisherman's boy,
>   that he shouts with his sister at play!
> O well for the sailor lad,
>   That he sings in his boat on the bay!
> And the stately ships go on
> (10)   To their haven under the hill;
> But O for the touch of a vanished hand,
>   And the sound of a voice that is still!
>
> Break, break, break,
>   At the foot of thy crags, O Sea!
> (15) But the tender grace of a day that is dead
>   Will never come back to me.

The contrast in rhythm of the first line of the last stanza to the rhythm of the second stanza serves to

(A) accentuate the harshness of the speaker's mood about his position in life
(B) change the poem's emphasis from the speaker to the sea
(C) weaken the speaker's argument
(D) heighten the impact of the sea's danger
(E) reinforce that the sea represents normal life

Explanation: "Break, break, break" makes a strong spondaic foot that sounds harsh and reflects the speaker's feelings of "a day that is dead." In contrast, the second stanza trips along like the children playing.

Correct Answer: **A**

▼PRACTICE QUESTION▼

You probably do not need to memorize the new terms given concerning the Lovelace selection that follows, but do consider the concepts they represent.

Examine Richard Lovelace's "Going to the Wars" to see how he used rhythm to affect meaning. What follows is one way this poem could be scanned. Note that some poems are scanned differently by different critics. For example, the very first line might also be scanned:

/ X /   / X / X /
Tell me not (Sweet) I am unkind.

Going to the Wars

```
        X   /  X    /  X  /  X  /
1.  Tell me not (Sweet) I am unkind,

         X    /  X    /  X /
2.     That from the nunnery

      X  /  X     /  X  / X    /
3.  Of thy chaste breast, and quiet mind,

         X   /  X   /  X /
4.     To war and arms I fly.


          /  X X   /  X   /  X   /
5.  True; a new mistress now I chase,

          X   /  X  / X   /
6.     The first foe in the field;

      X    /  X  /  X  /  X   /
7.  And with a stronger faith embrace

          X   /  X  /  X  /
8.     A sword, a horse, a shield.


       X   /  X / X / X  /
9.  Yet this inconstancy is such,

         X   /  X   /  X  /
10.    As you too shall adore;

      X  /  X  /  X    /  X  /
11. I could not love thee (Dear) so much,

          X  / X   /  X    /
12.    Loved I not honour more.
```

Lines 1, 3, 5, 7, 9, and 11 are iambic tetrameter; lines 2, 4, 6, 8, 10, and 12 are iambic trimeter. Each line ends with a strong stress, called a **masculine ending**. (A line that ends with a weak stress is a **feminine ending**.)

Notice the natural pauses in both thought and reading at the ends of lines 1, 3, and 4 in the first stanza, lines 5, 6, and 8 in the second, and lines 9, 10, 11, and 12 in the third stanza. Lines such as these are called **end-stopped**. On the other hand, examine how the lack of natural pause at the end of line 2 pulls the reader to line 3. This movement of thought and rhythm is called a run-on line. Line 7 also is a **run-on line** (called *enjambement* in French). Can you spot any significant departures or breaks in the rhythm of this poem? Look at line 5. The poet uses two devices that break the rhythm; the semicolon is a clue to a very strong, lengthy pause—a *caesura*. Also, the usual iambic foot has been inverted to create a trochee (trochaic foot). Such a dramatic change in an otherwise predictable rhythm is a definite clue to a shift in thought—a change in meaning.

The speaker uses a break in tempo in line 5 to suggest that he
(A) is conceding the point to his mistress
(B) is angry because he must go to war
(C) is shifting from a defensive to an offensive position
(D) resents the position in which war places him
(E) realizes his mistake

Explanation: Have you ever argued a position using a negative drone of words until you break the tension with "Yes! I feel this way because . . ."? Were you able to "feel" the startled response such a shift makes?

In the first stanza the speaker is being defensive—he is "not...unkind" (line 1). But the second stanza's change in rhythm, his abrupt "True; a new mistress now I chase," (line 5) marks a dramatic and somewhat startling shift in the tone of his position: Yes! I must leave...I have an honorable reason to go. (Also startling: "a new mistress")

Correct Answer: C

Before leaving this poem, look at line 8. Can you see any subtle differences between this line and the last lines of the first and last stanzas (lines 4 and 12)—differences that might contribute to meaning?

RM ALERT You should know this term: **sprung rhythm**

Definition: Gerard Manley Hopkins coined the term "sprung rhythm." He liked it because it produces a rhythm that sounds like natural speech rhythms. There are complex rules for the stresses of poems written in sprung rhythm. Simply stated, each foot begins with a stressed syllable, and the numbers of syllables in a foot varies from one foot to the next.

▼PRACTICE QUESTION▼

Pied Beauty

Glory be to God for dappled things—
For skies of couple-color as a brindled cow;
For rose-moles all in stipple upon trout that swim;
Line Fresh-firecoal chestnut-falls; finches' wings;
(5) Landscape plotted and pieced—fold, fallow, and plow;
And all trades, their gear and tackle and trim.
All things counter, original, spare, strange;
Whatever is fickle, freckled (who knows how?)
With swift, slow; sweet, sour; adazzle, dim;
(10) He fathers-forth whose beauty is past change:
Praise him.
by Gerard Manley Hopkins

The rhythm of this poem emphasizes
(A) a fiery nature
(B) natural landscapes
(C) propriety
(D) percussion
(E) irregularity

Explanation: Line 1 establishes the subject: dappled (variegated, spotted) things, things that are irregular. The rest of the poem expounds upon this subject. Likewise, the sprung rhythm is irregular.

Correct Answer: E

IMPORTANT CONCEPT #8: POETRY (RHYME SCHEME)

Concept Explained:

Poems often rhyme; the rhymes can form patterns; and the patterns can affect the meaning.

TERM ALERT You should know this term: **rhyme**

Definition: Rhyme is when two or more words have a sound in common or echo one another.

The degree to which words rhyme is affected, of course, by pronunciation. You should be aware that pronunciations have changed in time, pronunciations differ nationally between American English and British English, and pronunciations differ regionally. Essentially, the argument is summarized by "Did you pick a 'tomato' (long *a*) or 'tomawto' from your garden?" and "Is your mother's sister your 'aunt' (pronounced as *ant*) or your 'awnt'"? Differences can be subtle, as in *quinine* (American *kwi-nin* with long *i* in both syllables, British *kwin-en* with short *i* in the first syllable and long *e* in the last) or striking, as in *clerk* (American pronunciation usually rhyming with *work*, British pronunciation usually rhyming with *lark*), used by John Donne in "And though fowl now be scarce, yet there are clerks, / The sky not falling, think we may have larks."

Here are some of the major rhyme forms and how they are used.

End rhymes   are when the rhyming words fall at the ends of two or more lines of verse:

> But were some child of yours alive that *time*,
> You should live twice—in it, and in *my rhyme*.

Echo verse   employs a form of end rhyme used commonly in the 1500s and 1600s in which the closing syllables of a line are repeated to form the next line:

The Echo

> About the tow'r an' churchyard wall,
> Out nearly overright our door,
> A tongue ov wind did always call
> Whatever we did call avore.
> The vaice did mock our neames, our cheers,
> Our merry laughs, our hands' loud claps,
> An' mother's call "Come, come my dears"
> —*my dears*;
> Or "Do as I do bid, bad chaps"
> —bad chaps.

by William Barnes

In some echo poems, the echo's repeated syllables serve to answer a question posed in the previous line:

> For the Candidate
> Echo! How can I show my support
> to devote it?
> Vote it.

Internal rhymes are two or more rhyming words within a line of verse: *As the rain goes down the drain.* . . .

Masculine rhyme is rhyme of a single stressed syllable that generally is forceful: look, cook; sing, bring; sob, rob; sweet, treat.

Feminine (or *double*) *rhyme* is rhyme of a stressed then unstressed syllable and, as a result, is softer than masculine rhyme: looking, cooking; feature, creature.

Compound rhyme is rhyme of both pairs of compound components: fish broth, dishcloth; corkscrew, pork stew.

Triple rhyme is rhyme of a stressed followed by two unstressed syllables:

>   /   /
> bacteria, diptheria. (Take note of the way rhyme blends with rhythm for a pleasing
>   / XXX   / XXX
> effect in such words as "mandatory" and "obligatory.")

Perfect rhyme (also called true or pure rhyme) is an exact alignment of sounds, whereas *imperfect rhyme* (also called partial, slant, or half rhyme) is only a close alignment: *afternoon, broom.*

Eye rhymes (also called **visual rhyme**) look like they should rhyme (and at one time perhaps did) but do not, such as *horse, worse* or *move, love.*

Rime riche (also called *identical rhyme*) consists of words that sound the same but have different spellings and meanings (homonyms): seas, sees; hare, hair; their, there; heart, hart. Rime riche is sometimes identified as one of the many ways writers can make a "play on words," and *rime riche* lies at the heart of a pun.

Notice Shakespeare's use of *rime riche* as an internal rhyme in these lines from *The Rape of Lucrece*:

> That for his prey to pray he doth begin,
> As if the heavens should countenance his sin.

Historical rhymes are words that once rhymed, but because of pronunciation shifts no longer rhyme: *tea* once rhymed with *day*.

Forced rhymes are those that are "invented" by the poet. Along with eye rhyme and imperfect rhyme, forced rhymes are examples of *poetic license*—when a poet departs from the usual use of rhyme, diction, syntax, and other such conventions.

▼**PRACTICE QUESTION**▼

PITY THE POOR RACCOON

Pity the poor raccoon.
He could run fast 'cause he stayed slim and trim;
But one day right at noon he heard a loon's tune
Line   That bedazzled and mystified him.
(5)   "What's that sound?" he bemused, for he felt quite amused
'Til a hound heard the sound when Raccoon left the ground.
He was trapped! He was cornered! But he wasn't forlornered.
The hound saw a flash and his teeth he did gnash
For the prey he had treed just turned tail and fleed.

by L. E. Myers

The rhymes used contribute to the poem's
(A) defensive tone
(B) comic tone
(C) serious tone
(D) austere tone
(E) sentimental tone

Explanation: Notice the pairing of "cornered" with "forlornered" and of "treed" with "fleed." The poem's subject and rhymes combine to produce a comic tone.

Correct Answer: **B**

TERM ALERT You should know this term: **rhyme scheme**

Definition: After you have identified the poet's use of rhyme, you can then work out the *rhyme scheme* or pattern of the end rhyme of each line.

To illustrate determining the rhyme scheme of a poem examine, line by line, Robert Browning's "Meeting at Night":

Line 1:   **The gray sea and the long black land;**
The line ends with the word "*land*" and is assigned the letter **a**.

Line 2:   **And the yellow half-moon large and low;**
Because "*low*" does not rhyme with "*land*," it is given the letter **b**.

Line 3:   **And the startled little waves that leap**
"*Leap*" does not rhyme with "*low*" or "*land*," so it is given the letter **c**.

Line 4:   **In fiery ringlets from their sleep,**
"*Sleep*" and "*leap*" do rhyme; therefore, "*leap*" is given the letter **c**, also.

Line 5:   **As I gain the cove with pushing prow,**
Line 5 picks up the rhyme of line 2 ("*prow*" and "*low*"—eye-rhyme) and is consequently labeled **b**.

Line 6:   **And quench its speed i' the slushy sand.**
This last line of the first stanza ends with *sand,* rhyming with line 1. This line is given the letter **a.**

The rhyme scheme, then, of the first stanza is **a b c c b a.**

Now look at the second stanza.

Line 7:   **Then a mile of warm sea-scented beach;**
Because "*beach*" does not rhyme with "*land*" (the **a** rhyme), with "*low*" (the **b** rhyme), or with "*leap*" (the **c** rhyme), line 7 is given the letter **d.**

Line 8:   **Three fields to cross till a farm appears;**
"*Appears*" does not rhyme with any of the previous lines, so it is also given a new letter, **e.**

Line 9:   **A tap at the pane, the quick sharp scratch**
Again, "*scratch*" does not rhyme with any other line, so it is given the letter **f.**

Line 10:   **And blue spurt of a lighted match,**
Return to a rhyme with "*scratch*" and give the line the letter **f.**

Line 11:   **And a voice less loud, through its joys and fears,**
"*Fears*" and "*appears*" (line 8) rhyme so line 11 is given an **e.**

Line 12:   **Than the two hearts beating each to each!**
The final line of the second stanza picks up the rhyme of line 7 ("*beach*" and "*each*") and is assigned the letter **d.**

The rhyme scheme of the last stanza is **d e f f e d.**

The rhyme scheme, then, of "Meeting at Night" is as follows:

First stanza		Second stanza	
…land	**a**	…beach	**d**
…low	**b**	…appears	**e**
…leap	**c**	…scratch	**f**
…sleep	**c**	…match	**f**
…prow	**b**	…fears	**e**
…sand	**a**	…each	**d**

What effect does an ***abccba deffed*** rhyme scheme have on the reader (or listener)? Because the third and fourth lines of each stanza introduce rhyme to the poem's structure (form), the reader pauses (perhaps even imperceptibly) or may have a sense of anticipation of a new direction that will either complement or contrast with the first two lines. In the pattern of "Meeting at Night," however, a new direction is *not* taken as you return in the fifth line to rhyme with the second line and in the last line of the stanza to rhyme with the first line.

▼PRACTICE QUESTION▼

What are some of the possible effects of the rhyme scheme of "Meeting at Night"? Emphasis…unity of thought…perhaps using the rhyme scheme to contribute to the tone. Subliminally, the cyclical nature of the rhyme scheme may give the reader a sense of movement and expectation—an expectation that is fulfilled—that is emotionally satisfying in the first stanza when the speaker comes ashore and the last stanza when he is reunited with the one waiting for him. This sense of movement, expectation, and fulfillment that results from the rhythm, rhyme, and meaning of the poem can form the basis for a test question.

> In this poem, the relationship of lines 1–4 to lines 5–6 and of lines 7–10 to lines 11–12 reflect the speaker's progression from
> (A) danger to safety
> (B) understanding to fear
> (C) resistance to acceptance
> (D) challenge to attainment
> (E) communication to noncommunication

Explanation: Notice in lines 1–4 that the speaker is in a challenging situation: at sea surrounded by "startled little waves that leap in fiery ringlets"; however, he "gain[s] the cove" and makes it ashore in lines 5–6. This progression from challenge to attainment is mirrored in the second stanza as he is challenged to cross the beach and fields and to gain the attention of the one lighting the match in lines 7–10, then attains reunion in lines 11–12.

Correct Answer: **D**

TIP

How do you determine the rhyme scheme in a poem when the pronunciations of one or more of the end-line words are unfamiliar to you because of regionalisms or changes in pronunciation over time or when the rhyme is imperfect? Here is a stanza from Shakespeare's "The Phoenix and the Turtle":

> Let the priest in surplice white
>   That defunctive music can,
>   Be the death-divining swan,
> Lest the requiem lack his right.

"White," "can," "swan," and "right"—what seems to be an *abca* rhyme scheme: When you look at the next two stanzas, however, the rhyme scheme appears to be somewhat different. (Because the rhyme schemes of individual stanzas are being compared, each stanza will begin with "a" for the first line.)

And thou treble-dated crow,	a
That thy sable gender makest	b
With the breath thou givest and takest,	b
'Mongst our mourners shalt thou go.	a
Here the anthem doth commence:	a
Love and constancy is dead;	b
Phoenix and the turtle fled	b
In a mutual flame from hence.	a

You might surmise, based on the context of the rhyme scheme of the other stanzas, that the poet intends "can" and "swan" to rhyme for an **abba** pattern. When dealing with possible historical rhyme, eye rhyme, or imperfect rhyme, you need to look first at the context (the established rhyme scheme of the poem—a process called **correspondence**) and then at the meanings of the line in which the rhyme appears. **Caution:** A poet may break from the established rhyme pattern for a specific *effect*, such as a shift in meaning, a contrast, or simply an attention-getting device.

IMPORTANT CONCEPT #9: POETRY (PHYSICAL FORM)

Concept Explained:

The physical form of a poem is the product of its rhyme scheme, rhythm, and physical appearance.

TERM ALERT You should know this term: **free verse**

Definition: Free verse is just that—free of a regular meter. Also called "open form" or *vers libre*, free verse is characterized by short, irregular lines, no rhyme pattern, and a dependence on the effective and more intense use of pauses, words selected not only for meaning but for how that meaning is intensified by their position in the poem.

▼PRACTICE QUESTION▼

Of course, you might be asked to identify free verse when you see it; however, you should also be able to identify how this form can affect meaning.

Notice the use of free verse in "Know Yourself" by L. E. Myers:

KNOW YOURSELF

There is a
truth
with us
Line   and in us.
(5)   Is this the truth?

There is a
lie
with us,
but not in us.
(10)   Is this the truth?

The meaning of this poem is based on
(A) a pun
(B) repetition
(C) a contrast
(D) sentence structure
(E) its brevity

Explanation: Notice the physical isolation of "truth" in the first stanza and "lie" in the second, placing an emphasis on their contrast of meanings.

Correct Answer: **C**

TERM ALERT You should know this term: **blank verse**

Definition: Blank verse is written in iambic pentameter, but with no rhyme pattern. It is the major verse form used by Shakespeare in his plays. In blank verse, divisions are referred to as **verse paragraphs** (although the verse paragraph can also be in free verse).

▼PRACTICE QUESTION▼

Here is an excerpt from William Wordsworth's rather lengthy "Lines Composed a Few Miles above Tintern Abbey on Revisiting the Banks of the Wye During A Tour, July 13, 1798."

> Five years have passed; five summers, with the length
> Of five long winters! and again I hear
> These waters, rolling from their mountain-springs
> With a soft inland murmur, Once again
> Do I behold these steep and lofty cliffs,
> That on a wild secluded scene impress
> Thoughts of more deep seclusion; and connect
> The landscape with the quiet of the sky.

Line (5)

The lack of rhyme in this poem emphasizes
(A) movement
(B) false impressions
(C) quietness
(D) grand thinking
(E) seclusion

Explanation: Notice the iambic pentameter rhythm and lack of punctuation at the ends of the lines. As a result, the reader is pulled from one line to the next, like time passes and water rolls. If the lines had been written in *qualitative verse* (with measurable rhythm, but also with an identifiable rhyme scheme), the emphasis on movement would have been diminished.

Correct Answer: **A**

TERM ALERT You should know this term: **stanza**

Definition: A stanza consists of lines that are grouped together in a poem because of the rhythm, rhyme scheme, and/or meaning.

TERM ALERT You should know this term: **couplet**

Definition: A couplet consists of two grouped lines that rhyme.

TERM ALERT You should know this term: **heroic couplet**

Definition: Heroic couplets are written in iambic pentameter.
   NOTE: A test question may require you to look at a particular stanza or identify the relationship of one stanza to another. You should be able to recognize when a couplet is heroic and to look for ways the form of the stanzas affects the poem's meaning.

This chart gives you a sampling of stanza forms. Notice that most are written in iambic pentameter.

STANZA:	NO. OF LINES:	METER:	RHYME SCHEME:
Ballad	4	lines 1 and 3 iambic tetrameter	abcb
		lines 2 and 4 iambic trimeter	
Elegiac	4	iambic pentameter	abab
Terza Rima	3	iambic pentameter	aba, bcb, cdc, ded,...
Rhyme Royal	7	iambic pentameter	ababbcc
Ottava Rima	8	iambic pentameter	abababcc
Spenserian	9	lines 1–8 iambic pentameter	ababbcbcc
		line 9 iambic hexameter (an Alexandrine)	

Other terms referring to the number of lines in a stanza include these:

tristich (triplet, tercet)	— three lines
quatrain	— four lines
quintain (quintet, cinquain)	— five lines
sextain (sestet)	— six lines
heptastich	— seven lines
octave	— eight lines

IMPORTANT CONCEPT #10: POETRY (MODES AND GENRES)

Concept Explained:

Poems can be grouped by modes, the prevailing method by which the writer treats the subject of the poem.

Two important ways a writer can convey his or her subject are the following:

1. Telling a story

TERM ALERT You should know this term: **narrative mode**

Definition: A poem can simply tell us a story with or without a recognizable narrator. If the narrative includes dialogue, it has elements of the dramatic mode.

2. Expressing feelings or ideas

TERM ALERT You should know this term: **lyric mode**

Definition: In the lyric mode, the poem is reflective, at times even introspective, with the speaker discussing an experience or expounding upon an idea.

A. Lyric poems historically include poems that were meant to be sung, so the strong rhythms of some lyric poems are the result of musical origins.

B. Lyric poems can be based on an image or groups of images to convey the speaker's thoughts and emotions, usually without telling a story.

C. Some lyric poems are meant to explore a subject, discuss a theme, or prove a point, without strong rhythms or predominant use of the subtle language of imagery.

TERM ALERT You should know this term: **dramatic monologue**

Definition:

A persona (someone who is not the poet) unintentionally reveals his or her character by expressing a poem in dramatic circumstances. There may or may not be a silent auditor—the person to whom the monologue is being addressed.

▼PRACTICE QUESTION▼

Notice some of the literary elements at work in this small excerpt from Tennyson's "Ulysses." Written in the first person, the speaker is Odysseus (Ulysses), a Greek hero of the Trojan War and the king of Ithaca.

ULYSSES

It little profits that an idle king,
By this still hearth, among these barren crags,
Matched with an agéd wife, I mete and dole
Line Unequal laws unto a savage race,
(5) That hoard, and sleep, and feed, and know not me.
I cannot rest from travel; I will drink
Life to the lees. All times I have enjoyed
Greatly, have suffered greatly, both with those
That loved me, and alone; on shore, and when
(10) Through scudding drifts the rainy Hyades
Vexed the dim sea. I am become a name;
For always roaming with a hungry heart
Much have I seen and known—cities of men
And manners, climates, councils, governments
(15) Myself not least, but honored of them all—
And drunk delight of battle with my peers,
Far on the ringing plains of windy Troy.
I am a part of all that I have met;
Yet all experience is an arch wherethrough
(20) Gleams that untravelled world, whose margin fades
For ever and for ever when I move.

In the poem "Ulysses," the speaker reveals that he
(A) does not frequently leave his responsibilities as king
(B) considers himself an adventurer
(C) is not well liked among his people
(D) shuns battle and confrontation
(E) deeply respects his subjects

Explanation: Look for how the speaker's character is revealed. He "cannot rest from travel" and views experience as "an arch where through/Gleams that untravelled world...."

Correct Answer: **B**

TERM ALERT You should know this term: **elegy**

Definition: An elegy is a lament over the death of someone.

▼PRACTICE QUESTION▼

Read the first stanza of Thomas Gray's "Elegy Written in a Country Churchyard." Notice his use of the elegiac stanza (four lines of iambic pentameter with an abab rhyme scheme).

> The curfew tolls the knell of parting day,
> The lowing herd wind slowly o'er the lea,
> The plowman homeward plods his weary way,
> And leaves the world to darkness and to me.

In the context of the poem, the emphasis is on
(A) curfew
(B) fear
(C) work
(D) loneliness
(E) nature

Explanation: In addition to recognizing an elegy, you need to look for its main element: grief. In this stanza, curfew means people are getting off the streets, the day is parting, the cattle and plowman are going home, and the speaker is alone in the dark—grieving.

Correct Answer: **D**

TERM ALERT You should know this term: **ode**

Definition: An ode is a complex, serious, long lyric poem. Odes are very unified with just one theme handled in an extremely dignified manner. The purpose of many odes is to eulogize someone or something.

▼PRACTICE QUESTION▼

Here is "Ode on Solitude" by Alexander Pope.

> Happy the man, whose wish and care
>   A few paternal acres bound,
> Content to breathe his native air,
>   In his own ground.
>
> (5) Whose herds with milk, whose fields with bread,
>   Whose flocks supply him with attire,
> Whose trees in summer yield him shade,
>   In winter fire.
>
> Blest, who can unconcern'dly find
> (10)   Hours, days, and years slide soft away,
> In health of body, peace of mind,
>   Quiet by day,
>
> Sound sleep by night; study and ease,
>   Together mixed; sweet recreation;
> (15) And innocence, which most does please
>   With meditation.
>
> Thus let me live, unseen, unknown,
>   Thus unlamented let me die,
> Steal from the world, and not a stone
> (20)   Tell where I lie.

Line (5) (10) (15) (20)

The theme of this poem revolves mainly around

(A) life
(B) self-sufficiency
(C) a solitary, natural life
(D) the balance of nature
(E) innocence

Explanation: What is the theme? The final stanza provides the answer: To be happy (line 1), live a solitary, natural life, and die alone (last stanza). What is the subject of this theme? A solitary, natural life.

Correct Answer: **C**

TERM ALERT You should know this term: **sonnet**

Definition: A sonnet is a 14-line poem written in iambic pentameter. You should be able to identify a given poem as a sonnet. Be aware (for questions over meaning) that there are three main types of sonnet:

1. The **Italian (Petrarchan) sonnet** consists of eight lines (in an abba abba rhyme scheme) that ask a question or present a statement that is answered or somehow addressed by the concluding six lines.

▼Practice Question▼

Notice Wordsworth's use of the sonnet form in "Nuns Fret Not."

Line X / X / X / X / X /

Nuns fret not at their convent's narrow room;	a
And hermits are contented with their cells;	b
And students with their pensive citadels;	b
Maids at the wheel, the weaver at his loom,	a
(5) Sit blithe and happy; bees that soar for bloom,	a
High as the highest Peak of Furness-fells,	b
Will murmur by the hour in foxglove bells:	b
In truth the prison, into which we doom	a
Ourselves, no prison is: and hence for me,	c
(10) In sundry moods, 'twas pastime to be bound	d
Within the Sonnet's scanty plot of ground;	d
Pleased if some Souls (for such there needs must be)	c
Who have felt the weight of too much liberty,	c
Should find brief solace there, as I have found.	d

The main point of this poem is
(A) the sonnet form is beneficial
(B) a call to abandon what imprisons us
(C) we all sit in our own prisons
(D) we should break free from the sonnet
(E) life is made of choices

Explanation: First, in lines 1–9, Wordsworth tells the reader that some "imprison" themselves by choice (nuns, hermits, students)—hence if by choice, then they are not really in prison (lines 8–9). He concludes in lines 10–14 that the "prison" of the sonnet (the confines of structure required to write in this form) is actually a "solace" from "the weight of too much liberty,"—poems lacking the tight structure of a sonnet.

Correct Answer: **A**

2. The **English (Shakespearean) sonnet** consists of three quatrains (four lines each) concluding with a couplet in an abab cdcd efef gg rhyme scheme. You can expect the final couplet either to summarize the theme variations in the first three quatrains or to be epigrammatic.

▼Practice Question▼

An example from Shakespeare:

X / X / X / X / X /

Why is my verse so barren of new pride,	a
So far from variation or quick change?	b
Why, with the time, do I not glance aside	a
Line To newfound methods and to compounds strange?	b
(5) Why write I still all one, ever the same,	c
And keep invention in a noted weed,	d
That every word doth almost tell my name,	c

Showing their birth, and where they did proceed?	d
O, know, sweet love, I always write of you,	e
(10) And you and love are still my argument;	f
So all my best is dressing old words new,	e
Spending again what is already spent:	f
For as the sun is daily new and old,	g
So is my love still telling what is told.	g

The poem's subject is
(A) the speaker's pride
(B) undying love
(C) new inventions
(D) a lovers' argument
(E) the speaker's love poetry

Explanation: Lines 1–4 ask why the speaker does not try new methods of verse. (Notice the connotative implications of the first line: "Why is my verse so barren of *new pride*,"— Does he consider trying new forms of verse a means of pride?) Lines 5–8 ask why he still writes the same—to the extent that his work is easily identified as his. (Consider: These questions may be *rhetorical*, in other words, he may not expect a reply, but may be using the interrogative to emphasize his point. The rhetorical question will be discussed in more detail in a later section.) Lines 9–12 imply that there are only so many ways to describe his love. The concluding couplet is slightly aphoristic as he likens the sun, which is old yet is seen new each day, to how he expresses his love. This poem is about the poetry he writes for his "sweet love."

Correct Answer: **E**

3. The **Spenserian sonnet** consists of the three quatrains being linked by a continuing rhyme scheme, namely abab bcbc cdcd ee.

▼PRACTICE QUESTION▼

LIKE AS A HUNTSMAN AFTER WEARY CHASE

X / X / X / X / X /	
Like as a huntsman after weary chase,	a
Seeing the game from him escaped away,	b
Sits down to rest him in some shady place,	a
Line With panting hounds beguiléd of their prey:	b
(5) So, after long pursuit and vain assay,	b
When I all weary had the chase forsook,	c
The gentle deer returned the self-same way,	b
Thinking to quench her thirst at the next brook:	c
There she, beholding me with milder look,	c
(10) Sought not to fly, but fearless still did bide;	d
Till I in hand her yet half trembling took,	c
And with her own good-will her firmly tied.	d
Strange thing, meseemed, to see a beast so wild,	e
So goodly won with her own will beguiled.	e

by Edmund Spenser

What is the "Strange thing" in line 13?

(A) The huntsman

(B) An ironic circumstance

(C) The brutality of hunting

(D) Dogs hunting a deer

(E) The "gentle deer"

Explanation: Lines 1–4: The hunter rests from chasing a deer. Lines 5–8: The deer returns to drink. Lines 9–12: She allows the hunter to catch her. Lines 13–14 point out the irony of the situation.

Correct Answer: **B**

ERM ALERT You should know this term: **haiku**

Definition: A haiku is a single-stanza, three-line, (originally Japanese) lyric poem of 17 syllables. The subject is generally impressionistic of a scene in nature or a natural object:

Line 1 with five syllables
Line 2 with seven syllables
Line 3 with five syllables

▼PRACTICE QUESTION▼

Haiku

Hear their sad refrain
To capture sense with a sound.
Doves before the rain.

by C. Myers-Shaffer

The sound in line 2 refers to

(A) sadness

(B) doves cooing

(C) rain falling

(D) hearing impairment

(E) acute hearing

Explanation: This haiku deals with the sad sound that doves make just before the rain begins to fall. Their sound captures the mood of the speaker.

Correct Answer: **B**

TERM ALERT You should know this term: **ballad**

Definition: Ballads are narrative songs that may be sung or simply recited. The subjects are usually courage or love. They sometimes contain repetition of words or phrases for effect (a refrain), and consist of four-line stanzas in an abcb defe rhyme scheme. Generally, a ballad is in iambic foot.

▼PRACTICE QUESTION▼

For an example of the literary ballad, read these first four stanzas of Coleridge's *The Rime of the Ancient Mariner*, Part I.

> It is an ancient Mariner
> And he stoppeth one of three.
> "By thy long gray beard and glittering eye,
> Now wherefore stopp'st thou me?
>
> (5) The Bridegroom's doors are opened wide,
> And I am next of kin;
> The guests are met, the feast is set:
> May'st hear the merry din."
>
> He holds him with his skinny hand,
> (10) "There was a ship," quoth he.
> "Hold off! unhand me, gray-beard loon!"
> Eftsoons his hand dropt he.
>
> He holds him with his glittering eye—
> The Wedding-Guest stood still,
> (15) And listens like a three years' child:
> The Mariner hath his will.

Line markers: (5), (10), (15)

Why does the wedding guest listen to the mariner?
(A) The mariner physically restrains him.
(B) The wedding guest does not stop.
(C) The wedding was called off.
(D) The mariner restrains him by his will.
(E) The mariner follows him to the wedding.

Explanation: Notice the narrative elements in this poem. We have an unknown narrator and two principal characters (the mariner and the wedding guest), a conversation, and the beginning of conflict. At first the mariner held the guest with his "skinny hand"; however, "Eftsoons his hand dropt he./He holds him with his glittering eye— … The Mariner hath his will."

Correct Answer: **D**

TERM ALERT You should know this term: **parody**

Definition: A parody is a comic or satiric imitation of a more serious work. It generally ridicules a work, an author, or a style.

▼PRACTICE QUESTION▼

A parody can be fun to write, especially when the original poem has a very pronounced rhythm or mood. Edgar Allan Poe's "The Raven" has such a distinctive rhythm pattern that it works well in parody. Here is the first stanza of the original poem:

Once upon a midnight dreary, while I pondered, weak and weary,
Over many a quaint and curious volume of forgotten lore,
While I nodded, nearly napping, suddenly there came a tapping,
Line   As of some one gently rapping, rapping at my chamber door.
(5)   "'Tis some visitor," I muttered, "tapping at my chamber door—
            Only this and nothing more."

Here is a parody of the preceding stanza:

Once upon a schoolday dreary, while I studied, weak and weary,
Over many a quaint and curious volume of literature,
Feeling grisly, grim and grumbling, suddenly there came a rumbling,
Line   A gruesome gripping kind of rumbling, rumbling that was premature.
(5)   "'Tis my stomach," then I muttered, "rumbling here so premature—
            Candy bars will be the cure."

The main point of the parody is to ridicule
  I. "The Raven"
 II. Poe
III. narrative poetry
 IV. literary study
(A) I only
(B) II only
(C) III only
(D) I, III, and IV only
(E) I, II, III, and IV

Explanation: The parody obviously is capitalizing on the style and mode of "The Raven" (I and III). The speaker of the parody is a weary student studying literature for a class or test. To select such a famous work to bewail studying "quaint and curious ... literature" also mocks literary study. The author of the original work is not in focus.

Correct Answer: **D**

'ERM ALERT You should know this term: **limerick**

Definition: A limerick is a nonsense verse usually written in five anapestic lines with trimeter (lines 1, 3, 5) and dimeter (lines 2, 4) rhythm and an aabba scheme.

```
    X X   /  X X   /  X X  /
    I sat next/ to the Duch/ess at tea.         a
    X X    / X X   /   X  X   /
    It was just/ as I thought/ it would be:     a
        X   /  X X   / X X
        Her rumblings ab/dominal                 b
```

```
          X   / X X   / X X
          Were simply phe/nomenal                              b
   Line   X  /   X X    / X X   /
   (5)    And ev/eryone thought/ it was me.                    a
```

TERM ALERT You should know this term: **epigram**

Definition: Epigrams are short poems that are characteristically witty with a twist in the thought at the end. An epigram, however, can also be defined as simply a clever saying used for a variety of purposes, including to eulogize, to compliment, or to satirize.

This anonymous Latin epigram sums up the point:

> Three things must epigrams, like bees, have all,
> A sting, and honey, and a body small.

TERM ALERT You should know this term: **epitaph**

Definition: An epitaph is generally a poem intended for a tombstone (or as if for carving on a tombstone). The epitaph may be lengthy or short (an epigram), serious or comic:

MY OWN EPITAPH

> Life is a jest; and all things show it.
> I thought so once; but now I know it.

> by John Gay

William Blake wrote an epitaph in which he compares his subject to an epigram:

HER WHOLE LIFE IS AN EPIGRAM

> Her whole life is an epigram: smack, smooth & neatly penned,
> Platted quite neat to catch applause, with a sliding noose at the end.

TERM ALERT You should know this term: **concrete poetry**

Definition: Concrete poems are highly graphic, modern poems that are also graphic art.

▼PRACTICE QUESTION▼

```
              A
              l
               p h a
              b
                et
            Soup
```

A Bowl Can Do Each Friend Good
Hot In January—Knowing Life's
Mean, Nasty—Only Please
Quick—Run Straight To
Universal Values With
Xtra Yummy Zoups
(-oops-)

> by L. E. Myers

Notice how the shape of this poem relates to its subject.

The meaning of this poem revolves around
(A) friends
(B) a conflict
(C) the nastiness of life
(D) an ironic situation
(E) mistakes

Explanation: Hot soup is traditionally viewed as a comfort food and an economical food to feed the hungry, such as in a "soup kitchen." Alphabet soup has been enjoyed by generations. Structuring the poem by placing the alphabet in sequence, then contrasting that traditional structure with a deliberate departure from traditional spelling (Xtra Yummy Zoups) to maintain the alphabetical sequence creates irony. This structural irony mirrors the irony in the poem's meaning: When life gets mean and nasty, the speaker goes to "Universal Values" (hot food that is traditionally thought to bring comfort) only to find by the bottom of the bowl that some breaks with tradition have to be made. The comfort food of tradition sometimes is not enough (-oops-).

Correct Answer: **D**

IMPORTANT CONCEPT #11: DRAMA (STRUCTURE)

Concept Explained:

The structure of a typical stage play (whether a tragedy or a comedy) looks like this:

1. Exposition, introduction, or status quo

During the opening of the play the setting is established and the audience meets the main characters. Sometimes the story begins in the conflict; sometimes you only get clues of the conflict to come. In the movie *E. T.*, the exposition introduces the audience to a mother and her children in an average American home setting and endears the viewer to a gentle, supernatural, slightly comical alien who just wants to "phone home."

2. Conflict or exciting force

The **conflict** is the point at which you recognize a threat to something and/or to someone. Obstacles are placed in the way of the protagonist (the main character). Called the **exciting force**, these obstacles set into motion the rising action in the play. Being able to identify the exciting force in the structure of a drama is very important because it gives the characters motivation for their words and deeds and it gives the audience motivation to care.

Note: In preparing to answer test questions about the conflict (exciting force) in a story, you need to identify it from two perspectives: (1) in general terms, such as "The exciting force is rebellion," and (2) in specific terms, such as "Joe is rebelling against conforming to the values of his friends." For example, in the film *E. T.* the exciting force is a chase. More specifically, government agents discover the possible existence of an alien and the chase begins as they try to capture E. T.

3. Rising action or complication

Once the exciting force has set the action in motion, the struggle builds dramatic tension toward a confrontation. This stage in the dramatic structure consists of a series of emotional highs and lows, with each high gaining intensity. The conflict becomes more complicated.

How? In the movie *E. T.*, the alien is hunted by government authorities and barely escapes as the pursuers close in on the children and the alien they are hiding.

4. Climax, crisis, or turning point

Then it happens—the inevitable moment of confrontation. This is the point of *climax*—the turning point in the plot—the point at which there is a reversal from rising action to falling action.

Be aware that the word "climax" actually has more than one usage in literary analysis. "Climax" is a synonym for crisis when you are determining the structure of a story or a drama, but climax can also refer to the point of highest intensity for the reader or audience—a point that might come before or after the crisis. In the case of *E. T.*, the emotional climax or point of highest intensity might be when the alien "dies." The structural climax (crisis or turning point), however, might be when the alien revives, because it is at this point that his "fortunes" have reversed. Although more near misses ensue, you know that somehow he will make it.

5. Falling action

Briefer than rising action, the falling action may still have some suspenseful moments, but for the most part gives the reader or audience a sense of completion, with the various unsettled issues at work within the plot reaching some state of resolution. In *E. T.*, there is one last race to the spaceship and a moment for farewells to be said.

6. Resolution or Dénouement

The hero has won or lost; issues are resolved; order is restored. The alien goes home.

Structure also includes techniques and devices that create various effects. Here are just a few:

Foreshadowing: Hints at the future that can build anticipation and tension in the audience. In the movie *Back to the Future*, foreshadowing is very cleverly used in a psychologically reversed way as events in the present "foreshadow" events in the past.

Flashbacks: Descriptions or enactments of past events for the purpose of clarifying the situation, usually as it relates to the conflict.

Intrigue: A scheme designed by one of the characters, the success of which depends on another character's innocence or ignorance of the situation. The usual result is a complication in the plot.

In medias res: The first scene opening in the middle of the action.

Suspense: Establishing caring on the part of the viewers for one or more of the characters, then presenting events that create a sense of uncertainty concerning what will happen to them.

Double plots: Especially evident in Elizabethan drama—use of a *subplot* or second plotline weaving in and out of the main plot.

Surprise: Once the audience has a sense of expectation, events happen that are not expected.

Reversal: Also called *peripety*—when the main character either fails or succeeds.

Discovery: When the main character finally realizes the reality of the situation.

Monologue: When an actor delivers a speech in the presence of other characters who listen, but do not speak.

Dramatic conventions: The elements of a play that the audience knows merely represent reality, but is willing to accept them as real for the sake of the story: actors representing the characters of the story, the stage set representing a real location in time and space, suspended time or jumps forward or backward in time, Italians in Italy speaking English, and other such conventions.

The aside: When an actor speaks directly to the audience, however, the rest of the actors on stage supposedly cannot hear him or her.

Soliloquy: When an actor delivers a speech when he or she is alone, expressing thoughts.

Complications: Causing conflict by introducing new characters, information, or events.

Scenes: Portions of an act, sometimes triggered by the clearing of the stage for the next scene. Some types of scenes include *relief scenes* that allow the audience to relax briefly in the tension of the drama and *balcony scenes.* (Remember *Romeo and Juliet?*)

NOTE: Comic relief scenes are widely used in English drama. Be aware that sometimes their purpose is to ease tension, but they also can add a sense of poignant sadness. Such a scene could lead to test questions about character, meaning, or tone.

▼PRACTICE QUESTIONS▼

Here are a few lines from Shakespeare's *The Tempest.*

	Miranda.	Sir, are not you my father?
	Prospero.	Thy mother was a piece of virtue, and
		She said thou wast my daughter; and thy father
Line		Was Duke of Milan; and his only heir
(5)		A princess—no worse issued.
	Miranda.	O the heavens!
		What foul play had we that we came from thence?
		Or blessed was't we did?
	Prospero.	Both, both, my girl!
(10)		By foul play, as thou say'st, were we heaved thence,
		But blessedly holp hither.
	Miranda.	O, my heart bleeds
		To think o' th' teen that I have turned you to,
		Which is from my remembrance! Please you, farther.
(15)	Prospero.	My brother and thy uncle, called Antonio—
		I pray thee mark me—that a brother should
		Be so perfidious!—he whom next thyself
		Of all the world I loved, and to him put
		The manage of my state, as at that time
(20)		Through all the signories it was the first
		And Prospero the prime duke, being so reputed

In dignity, and for the liberal arts
Without a parallel: those being all my study,
The government I cast upon my brother
(25) And to my state grew stranger, being transported
And rapt in secret studies. Thy false uncle—
Dost thou attend me?

Who are Prospero and Miranda?
(A) Duke of Milan and his daughter, a princess
(B) The uncle of the Duke and his niece
(C) Antonio's uncle and his daughter, a princess
(D) Antonio's nephew and his daughter
(E) A signory and his niece

The situation of the drama is that
(A) Prospero is telling a story about the Duke of Milan
(B) Prospero identifies himself as a servant of a prime duke and princess
(C) Prospero reveals his true identity and circumstances
(D) Prospero and Antonio are co-rulers of Milan
(E) Prospero declares Antonio to be Miranda's father

The point in the plot is best described as part of the
(A) conflict
(B) rising action
(C) climax
(D) falling action
(E) resolution

Explanation: In speaking to Miranda, Prospero says she is his daughter, a princess, and that he was the Duke of Milan (lines 1–5). The key to understanding the situation in this selection is to realize that Prospero shifts in lines 3–4 from first to third person, but is still referring to himself. From that point on, he is revealing who he is and how he came to be in his current circumstances. Obviously, his struggle with his brother provides conflict for the story.

Correct Answers: **A, C, A**

IMPORTANT CONCEPT #12: VALIDITY AND LOGICAL FALLACIES

Concept Explained:

Be alert to the validity of the reasoning of a writer or speaker. Some things that are written are not valid; some things that are written are not true. You need to be able to distinguish the following:

1. Valid arguments (logical conclusions based on true premises) from logical fallacies (errors in reasoning caused by false premises or illogical consequences)
2. Whether the invalidity of the faulty thinking is intentional or unintentional
3. Whether the valid or invalid argument is the voice of the speaker or the voice of the writer and whether they agree

Voice will be discussed in a later chapter, but at this point you need to be able to identify some of the more common logical fallacies you may encounter in literary selections. Whether they be persuasive speeches, powerful short stories, or expressive poems, logical fallacies are sometimes hidden (intentionally or unintentionally) within literary works. These fallacies might serve the purpose of the writer or they may simply reveal faulty thinking on his or her part. The presence of logical reasoning is form contributing to, shaping, and developing meaning.

When you are asked a question about the meaning in a selection, you need to be alert to any logical fallacies or any flaws in form (misuses of organizing principles) that can affect the meaning.

The checklist on page 108 will give you some examples of ambiguous thinking and mis-representations of the facts that are based on or can lead to logical fallacies.

HERE IS THE POINT: Be sure you carefully consider whether any given point or idea is based on fact or opinion. Are the facts being misused? Is the opinion valid?

▼PRACTICE QUESTION▼

This passage is taken from Emily Brontë's *Wuthering Heights*.

> He [Earnshaw] afterwards gathered the books and hurled them on the fire. I read in his countenance what anguish it was to offer that sacrifice to spleen—I fancied that as they consumed, he recalled the pleasure they had already imparted; and the triumph and ever-increasing pleasure he had anticipated from them—and I fancied, I guessed the incitement to his secret studies, also. He had been content with daily labour and rough animal enjoyments, till Catherine crossed his path—Shame at her scorn, and hope of her approval were his first prompters to higher pursuits; and instead of guarding him from one, and winning him the other, his endeavours to raise himself had produced just the contrary result.

The narrator's assessment of Earnshaw's motivation is probably based on
(A) careful analysis
(B) the opinions of others
(C) conjecture
(D) shared confidences
(E) trained observations

Explanation: There is no evidence of analysis, consultations with others, or training in observation on the part of the narrator. He does, however, confess to conjecture in "I fancied, I guessed." Only learning more about the unknown narrator, the other characters, and his relationship to them, in this case will help you determine whether his opinions could be valid. This question, however, illustrates the first step in establishing the validity of any point being made: Is the point an opinion or a statement of fact?

Correct Answer: **C**

A Validity Checklist

When reading a selection, look for the following:

- Consistency of thought
- Fairness
- Ambiguous thinking, such as

  1. Statements that have more than one meaning, for example, "Several beautiful paintings are being hung in the lobby. Yours will be hung in the back office." (Regional dialects can sometimes be the source of these miscommunications.)

  2. Misuse of personification, such as, "The company will have to take better care of its employees for me to work there." (People within companies make policies to take care of people.)

  3. Statements that are inappropriate in their context (as a woman is shopping and the clerk says, "That dress does *wonders* for your shape"). Note that when such statements are made intentionally, they can create a form of verbal irony or can be sarcasm.

  4. Changing meanings of words (Alice: He certainly is calm and collected about raising money for his rent. Jayne: He's collected, all right, from Moris, and Jules, and from me!)

  5. Assumptions that if something is true of the whole, then it is also true of the parts or that something true of the parts can be generalized to the whole. For example, "The Pizza Dilly is a great pizza place, so we will get the pizza we ordered delivered on time." (Even "great" places can have an occasional late delivery.) The pizza has extra of my favorite cheese, so it will be delicious. (What if the crust is burned?)

- Misrepresentations of the facts (distortions), such as

  1. Assuming a premise is true without proof
  2. Taking words out of context
  3. Exaggerating a statement out of context
  4. Diverting attention from the real issue by introducing a false issue
  5. Calling names or attacking the credibility of a person
  6. Making generalizations based on assumptions or on too little evidence
  7. Asking a "loaded question" that by simply answering implies guilt ("Have you stopped stealing from your neighbor?")
  8. Establishing double standards through connotatively charged words (Why is one person called "thrifty" or "frugal" whereas another is called "cheap" or "tight" with money, when both exhibit the same spending habits?)
  9. Comparing dissimilar things as though they are similar
  10. Omitting facts or ignoring alternatives
  11. Presenting coincidence as a cause-and-effect relationship
  12. Attempting to influence the reader through a sense of pity, ignorance, fear, expertise, or some other emotion, all based on false or misleading information
  13. Stereotyping
  14. Oversimplifying

- Remember:

  a. Sometimes faulty reasoning is for the purpose of misleading the reader.
  b. Sometimes these errors in reasoning, however, are made by people within a story or by a speaker other than the writer—thus revealing character.

ACTIVE THINKING EXERCISES FOR FORM

STEP 1. ▸FOCUS◂

Another method that will help you focus on a given selection is to begin asking your own questions: What is the subject? What is the point? Who is involved? As you read the passage, underline names; put checkmarks or exclamation marks in the margins next to important points.

▼EXERCISE▼

Turn again to the Interpretive Skill Practice Sets that begin on page 330. Using the specified five selections, answer the Questions About Form on page 336. As you read each selection,

1. underline key names,

2. put checkmarks or exclamation marks at key points, and

3. in the poems, put a slash mark (/) where one sentence ends and another begins. Notice that sentences end midline in some poems.

Develop your own method for marking selections. Just remember that time is important. Do not linger too long making notes.

Now, turn to Practice Sets B and C and the questions for Form. This time, in addition to marking the selections, as you read each question, quickly strike through all answers that you know are incorrect. This method will increase your focus and decrease possible confusion.

Finally, turn to Practice Test 2 on page 373 and practice using these techniques as you read the selections and take the test:

1. Look for the subject and the main point.

2. Underline names; mark key points; divide sentences in poems.

3. Strike through obviously incorrect answer choices.

How did you do?

STEP 2. MOW (MY OWN WORDS)

▼PRACTICE QUESTIONS▼

Read the following poem, "Early Affection" by George Moses Horton.

> I lov'd thee from the earliest dawn,
>   When first I saw thy beauty's ray,
>   And will, until life's eve comes on,
> Line   And beauty's blossom fades away;
> (5)   And when all things go well with thee,
>   With smiles and tears remember me.
>
>   I'll love thee when thy morn is past,
>   And wheedling gallantry is o'er,
>   When youth is lost in ages blast,

(10)   And beauty can ascend no more,
         And when life's journey ends with thee,
         O, then look back and think of me.

         I'll love thee with a smile or frown,
          'Mid sorrow's gloom or pleasure's light,
(15)   And when the chain of life runs down,
          Pursue thy last eternal flight,
         When thou hast spread thy wing to flee,
         Still, still, a moment wait for me.

         I'll love thee for those sparkling eyes,
(20)   To which my fondness was betray'd,
         Bearing the tincture of the skies,
          To glow when other beauties fade,
         And when they sink too low to see,
         Reflect an azure beam on me.

On the lines below, write a paraphrase for each stanza.

Stanza 1: _____

_____

Concluding couplet:

Stanza 2: _____

_____

Concluding couplet:

Stanza 3: _____

_____

Concluding couplet:

Stanza 4: _____

_____

Concluding couplet:

With your paraphrase to guide you, answer the following questions:

1. What is the subject? _____

2. What is the speaker's purpose? _____

3. Summarize the main idea (one sentence): _____

_____

Armed with this analysis, answer the following questions. Most of them relate to form. Some, however, require you to use your context skills to determine the answers.

1. The meaning of "wheedling gallantry" (line 8) can be seen in the paraphrase
   (A) flattering attention
   (B) brave action
   (C) coaxing boldness
   (D) amorous intrigue
   (E) polite attention

2. The descriptive contrast of sunrise in the first stanza to sunset in the last describes
   (A) the speaker's lifespan
   (B) the duration of their acquaintance
   (C) the lover's lifespan
   (D) the duration of his interest
   (E) the duration of his love's interest

3. The concluding couplet of each stanza structurally
   (A) reinforces the extent of the speaker's love
   (B) negates the previous four lines
   (C) serves to instruct the lover
   (D) shifts attention from the speaker's lover to himself
   (E) implies that his love is not reciprocated

4. By considering the poem in its entirety, the reader can conclude that
   (A) the lover is about to die
   (B) the speaker's love is based on more than beauty
   (C) the speaker is about to die
   (D) the speaker's love is based on beauty alone
   (E) the speaker's intent is uncertain

5. The third stanza implies that the speaker
   (A) is angry
   (B) expects his lover to outlive him
   (C) and his lover are angry with each other
   (D) expects love to survive death
   (E) is frustrated

6. Death is metaphorically compared to all the following EXCEPT
   (A) a blossom
   (B) a run-down clock
   (C) a last flight
   (D) a journey's end
   (E) an evening

7. The object of the poet's affection probably
   (A) is an older woman
   (B) has blue eyes
   (C) is near death
   (D) has green eyes
   (E) is uncomely

8. The speaker's purpose is best described as
   (A) descriptive
   (B) expository
   (C) narrative
   (D) persuasive
   (E) informative

9. The alliterative repetition of "still" (palilogy) in line 18 emphasizes
   (A) the lack of structure
   (B) a dual meaning
   (C) a mixed metaphor
   (D) symbolic rhetoric
   (E) the rhythmic pattern

10. The structural theme of this poem can best be described as
    (A) chronological sequence
    (B) climactic order
    (C) narrative description
    (D) definitive analysis
    (E) causal analysis

11. The title "Early Affection" would be ironic only if the poem's sentiment is
    (A) a sincere expression of lasting love
    (B) a vehicle expressing love's enduring nature
    (C) a literary allusion
    (D) a summary of life's events
    (E) hyperbole expressing love's early enthusiasm

Answers and Explanations:

1. **A** By definition, "gallantry" can mean any of the answer choices, but "wheedling" can mean "flattering" (A) or "coaxing" (C). Again, turn to context: Lines 10–11 establish lost beauty that no longer gathers "flattering attention," answer choice A.

2. **B** This one is tricky. "Earliest dawn" (line 1) and the lover's eyes fading would support C, "the lover's lifespan," or with line 18 perhaps even A, "the speaker's lifespan." However, a lifespan is from the beginning to the end of one's life. "The earliest dawn" is defined by the speaker in line 2 as when he first saw his lover, not when his physical life began. The sunrise and sunset are the duration of their acquaintance, from first meeting, until parted by death.

3. **D** ". . . remember me . . . think of me . . . wait for me . . . reflect . . . on me."

4. **B** Every stanza speaks to love beyond beauty: "beauty's blossom fades away" (line 4), "beauty can ascend no more" (line 10), "frown . . . sorrow's gloom" (lines 13–14), "other beauties fade" (line 22).

5. **D** Read the question carefully. To imply is to hint or suggest, but not to express directly. He speaks directly to love "with a smile or frown" in line 13. The subject shifts to death in line 15, an "eternal flight" for which he wants her to "wait for me" (line 18), implying love beyond death.

6. **A** The metaphors: death compared to a run-down clock (line 15), a last flight (line 16), a journey's end (line 11), and an evening (lines 3, 23).

7. **B** . . . those sparkling eyes . . . Bearing the tincture of the skies" (lines 19–21).

8. **D** The speaker loves her unto death and attempts to persuade her to love him, too.

9. **B** This poem is very structured (A) and the repetition of "still" creates a pause that disrupts the rhythmic pattern (E). No metaphors or symbols appear isolated in this line, but in context, the deliberate pause in line 18 dramatically emphasizes the dual meaning of "still": The speaker wants his lover to "Pursue thy last eternal flight (line 16) . . . Still [Yet], still [quietly], a moment wait for me."

10. **E** Although the dawn, morning, and sunset imagery hints at chronological sequence, each stanza repeats the same structural pattern: "I lov'd thee/I'll love thee," followed by the poet expounding upon the extent of his love (cause), concluding with a statement of the desired effect.

11. **E** The poem expresses love so great it extends beyond beauty and even life. "Early Affection" as a title seems an understatement, unless the entire poem is examining the exaggerated claims of new love. In such a case, the title would be ironic.

STEP 3. BID (BREAK IT DOWN)

First review some of the important concepts and terms that relate to a literary work's form.

▼**EXERCISE**▼

Match the following terms with their definitions.

1. plot A. involves having sounds in common

2. climax B. rhythm with five units in a line

3. rising action C. the introduction of characters and setting

4. exposition D. 14 lines of iambic pentameter

5. setting E. narrative song

6. rhythm F. a summary of a story

7. pentameter G. when conflict develops in a story

8. rhyme H. patterns of stressed and unstressed sounds

9. sprung rhythm I. the "high point" of a story

10. blank verse J. iambic pentameter, no rhyme scheme

11. free verse K. no rhyme pattern, no regular rhythm

12. heroic couplets L. time and place of a story

13. stanza M. lines grouped together in a poem

14. ballad N. two rhymed lines in iambic pentameter

15. sonnet O. an irregular rhythm

Correct Answers:

1. **F** 2. **I** 3. **G** 4. **C** 5. **L** 6. **H** 7. **B** 8. **A** 9. **O** 10. **J** 11. **K**
12. **N** 13. **M** 14. **E** 15. **D**

Next, determine if each of these statements is true or false.

1. Writers must select one order of presentation and present their ideas only in that sequence.
2. Inductive reasoning generalizes from specific ideas.
3. Essays are always serious or scholarly.
4. Both biography and autobiography recount life's experiences.
5. Anecdotes usually involve the narrative of a single incident.
6. Realistic narratives are usually amusing.
7. Humans in tragic narratives usually end in failure.
8. Rhythm and rhyme affect sound, but not meaning.
9. You cannot determine rhyme scheme if the pronunciations have changed over time.
10. Historically, lyric poems were meant to be sung.
11. In concrete poetry, shape reflects meaning.
12. Valid arguments result from the misuse of organizing principles.

Correct Answers:

1. **F** 2. **T** 3. **F** 4. **T** 5. **T** 6. **F** 7. **T** 8. **F** 9. **F** 10. **T** 11. **T** 12. **F**

Finally, consider these questions. If you are looking at the form of a selection:

1. What sequence and what organizing principles within that sequence is the writer using?
2. How would you describe the predominant genre?
3. In a narrative, what is the plot?
4. In a poem, what is the rhythm and rhyme scheme?
5. Are there any areas of ambiguous thinking or misrepresentations of the facts?

Correct Answers: (will vary with the selections being read)

▼PRACTICE QUESTIONS▼

Here is a passage taken from William Wordsworth's "Preface" to *Lyrical Ballads*. Most of the questions that follow deal with meaning and the effects of the work's form. Also, you will find some questions covering meanings of words in context and uses of language. These questions aim to direct your thinking for the literary element chapters that follow.

> Several of my friends are anxious for the success of these poems from a belief, that,
> if the view with which they were composed were indeed realized, a class of poetry
> would be produced, well adapted to interest mankind permanently, and not
> Line unimportant in the multiplicity, and in the quality of its moral relations: and on this
> (5) account they have advised me to prefix a systematic defence of the theory, upon
> which the poems were written. But I was unwilling to undertake the task, because I
> knew that on this occasion the reader would look coldly upon my arguments, since I
> might be suspected of having been principally influenced by the selfish and foolish

(10) hope of *reasoning* him into an approbation of these particular poems: and I was still more unwilling to undertake the task, because, adequately to display my opinions, and fully to enforce my arguments, would require a space wholly disproportionate to the nature of a preface. For to treat the subject with the clearness and coherence, of which I believe it susceptible, it would be necessary to give a full account of the present state of the public taste in this country, and to determine how far this taste is

(15) healthy or depraved; which, again, could not be determined, without pointing out, in what manner language and the human mind act and react on each other, and without retracing the revolutions, not of literature alone, but likewise of society itself. I have therefore altogether declined to enter regularly upon this defence; yet I am sensible, that there would be some impropriety in abruptly obtruding upon the public,

(20) without a few words of introduction, poems so materially different from those, upon which general approbation is at present bestowed.

1. Why does the writer finally decide to write a "few words of introduction?"
   (A) He does not want to be misunderstood.
   (B) His friends have convinced him.
   (C) Every poetic work must have an introduction.
   (D) His poems do not fit popular preconceptions.
   (E) He wants to convince readers that his poems are well written.

2. By telling readers of his friends' opinions and advice concerning his poems, the speaker
   (A) makes his work seem less important
   (B) emphasizes his own general popularity
   (C) makes his work seem more important
   (D) reveals his lack of self-esteem
   (E) conceals the true nature of his motives

3. This passage contains all the following EXCEPT elements that are
   (A) autobiographical
   (B) informational
   (C) formal
   (D) biographical
   (E) critical

4. The writer declines to write a defense (line 6) because it would be
   (A) too lengthy for a preface
   (B) too difficult to write
   (C) unjustifiable to his friend
   (D) selfish to use the space
   (E) too sentimental

5. The writer suspects his readers would "look coldly" (line 7) upon his arguments as
   (A) incongruent
   (B) self-sufficient
   (C) self-serving
   (D) unreasonable
   (E) unimportant

6. If the speaker had written a "systematic defence" (British spelling), it would have included discussion of all the following EXCEPT
   (A) public tastes
   (B) interaction of mind and language
   (C) the need for friends
   (D) literary changes
   (E) societal changes

7. The "general approbation" (line 21) refers to
   (A) public malaise
   (B) public disapproval
   (C) public approval
   (D) military honors
   (E) hypercriticism

8. As described in lines 14–17, his "systematic defence" might NOT include
   (A) analogy
   (B) analysis and classification
   (C) description
   (D) narration
   (E) cause and effect

9. The use of "not unimportant" in lines 3–4 is a rhetorical example of
   (A) hyperbole, an exaggeration used to increase importance
   (B) litotes, a negative affirmation used to increase importance
   (C) meiosis, an understatement used to decrease importance
   (D) paradox, a self-contradictory statement used to make a point
   (E) apophasis, a pretended denial used to indict

10. For the "subject" to be "susceptible," as used in lines 12–13, it would be which of the following?
   I. Subject to influence from others
   II. Capable of clearness and coherence
   III. Emotionally sensitive
   (A) I only
   (B) II only
   (C) III only
   (D) II and III only
   (E) I, II, and III

Answers and Explanations:

1. **D** His poems are "materially different" (line 20) from those generally accepted.

2. **C** Connotative word choices, such as "anxious for the success" (line 1), and references to producing a new "class of poetry" (line 2) that would "interest mankind" (line 3), work together to convey a sense of importance.

3. **D** The speaker is telling his own story; it is not being told by someone else.

4. **A** It would "require a space . . . disproportionate ..." (line 11).

5. **C** Notice lines 8–9: "the selfish and foolish hope."

6. **C** Lines 14–17 describe a possible defense, one involving "public taste . . . in what manner language and the human mind act and react on each other . . . and . . . revolutions . . . of literature . . . society. . . ." Friends are not mentioned.

7. **C** Approbation refers to approval.

8. **A** He would describe the present state of public taste, analyze and classify its health, determine the cause-and-effect relationships of language and mind, and narrate the changes made in literature and society.

9. **B** By definition, "not unimportant" is an example of litotes.

10 **B** Context shows the speaker's intent is "clearness and coherence" (line 12).

▼EXERCISE▼

Below is Samuel Daniel's "Time, Cruel Time" (circa 1600). Using X to mark unstressed and / to mark stressed syllables, scan the poem. Then use a letter at the end of each line to determine the rhyme scheme.

> Time, cruel Time, come and subdue that brow,
>
> Which conquers all but thee; and thee too stays,
>
> As if she were exempt from scythe or bow,
>
> From love or years, unsubject to decays.
>
> (5) Or art thou grown in league with those fair eyes,
>
> That they may help thee to consume our days?
>
> Or dost thou spare her for her cruelties,
>
> Being merciless like thee, that no man weighs?
>
> And yet thou see'st thy power she disobeys;
>
> (10) Cares not for thee, but lets thee waste in vain;
>
> And prodigal of hours and years betrays
>
> Beauty and Youth to Opinion and Disdain.
>
> Yet spare her, Time, let her exempted be;
>
> She may become more kind to thee or me.

Line (5) and (10) markers appear to the left.

The poem's genre is _____ because _____.

Based on the rhyme scheme, what two lines *may* have rhymed historically (1600), but do not rhyme today? _____

What is the rhyme of the last two lines called? _____

Discussion: Review pages 79–91 over rhythm and rhyme scheme. This poem is a sonnet because it is fourteen lines written in iambic pentameter. The rhyme scheme indicates that the poet probably intended lines 5 and 7 to correspond or rhyme. The concluding two lines of the poem form a couplet.

STEP 4. TT → TM (TEST TAKER TO TEST MAKER)

Look at some of the ways test questions over form are written.

A regular multiple-choice question requires one correct answer and four incorrect ones. Of the incorrect choices, one or more might also be acceptable, but the correct answer (when compared) is the better or best choice. Some of the answers will be incorrect to varying degrees, and one might be just plain silly.

Look again at the Wordsworth selection. As pointed out in Question 4, one reason he declines to write a systematic defense is that it would "require a space . . . disproportionate to . . . a preface." He gives another reason, however, in lines 8–9: he might be "suspected of . . . the selfish and foolish hope of *reasoning* him [the reader] into an approbation of these particular poems. . . ."

You can write a multiple-choice question about this reason.

First, paraphrase it. How could the reason be expressed more simply?

_____

_____

Next, put the idea into a question. Here is one possibility: Why would a systematic defense make the speaker seem "selfish and foolish?"

Now you need to word the correct answer: A systematic defense would make the speaker seem "selfish and foolish" because

_____

_____

Finally, think of some incorrect answers. Make the correct answer choice C.

According to the speaker, a systematic defense might make him seem "selfish and foolish" because

(A) _____

(B) _____

(C) _____

(D) _____

(E) _____

More about types of questions:

Look again at Questions 3, 8, and 10 concerning the Wordsworth selection. EXCEPT, NOT, and Roman Numeral Questions are used when just one correct answer is too restrictive. By asking you to identify the one element that Wordsworth does not use in his preface, the question is impressing on you that he is using and blending together four others. The same idea is behind Question 8.

In the case of the Roman numerals in Question 10, only II is correct; however, the *possibility* exists for more than one answer to be correct.

Advertising for products and political advertising are wonderful areas to practice identifying the misuses of the organizing principles listed on page 71 and to spot logical fallacies discussed in the Validity Checklist on page 108. For example, are the lower numbers of cases of heart disease in a given country *really* the result of eating certain foods, as growers and producers would have you believe? Could there be other causes of this healthy effect? Can we generalize to say that if people everywhere would eat the same food, we would all enjoy the same health benefits? Examine the advertising around you and try to spot at least one logical fallacy. Then ask yourself this question: What would have to be done to turn this idea into a valid argument?

FORM IN CONCLUSION

A writer's intended meaning determines what form the work will take, and the form of a work can enhance or destroy its meaning: a reciprocal relationship.

Literary Element Number Three: Narrative Voice

Separating the literary elements into neat compartments is difficult. Some literary elements are so interrelated that critics and teachers differ widely on how to define and apply them. A good example is voice and tone. Among the varied elements of voice that follow, you can see how voice and tone relate to each other.

Defining elements that contribute to the voice of a literary work include the following:

1. The narrator's or nonnarrative speaker's attitude toward the reader and subject (therefore projecting a tone)
2. The sense the reader gets of the writer's presence
3. The sense the reader gets of a writer's presence when the narrator's (or speaker's) attitude and the writer's attitude toward the subject differ (in which case the voice may disagree with the tone)
4. The point of view from which a selection is narrated
5. The persona (mask-voice) of the writer (expressing a tone)
6. A characteristic of a writer's style
7. The thoughts of a poet to himself or to a reader
8. The thoughts of a character in a poem
9. A writer's style characterized by using active voice (as in, "I threw the ball") or passive voice ("The ball was thrown to me") to project his or her point of view

IMPORTANT CONCEPT #1: POINT OF VIEW

Concept Explained:

The first step in determining narrative voice is to decide what point of view is being used. In other words, who is telling the story, how does that person relate to the action of the plot, and how much does he or she know about what is going on in the story and in the minds of the characters?

Pretend that the "world" of a story is represented by this illustration:

The world of the NARRATIVE	The world outside the NARRATIVE

The place, time, characters, and events of the story all exist within "the world of the narrative." The "world outside the narrative" is where the readers exist. The narrator, then, stands between the reader and the story; and his or her aim is to tell the reader a story, to describe the characters and events as they move around within the confines of the world of the narrative while the reader watches and listens.

TERM ALERT You should know this term: **limited omniscient point of view**

Definition: In the limited omniscient point of view (also called third-person limited point of view), the narrator tells the story using third-person pronouns (he, she, they, him, her, them) and is evidenced by such narrative constructions as "He said this or that" or "She walked to the fireplace." The third-person narrator is telling the story from outside the world of the characters. Also, the narrator is able to tell the reader the thoughts, opinions, motives, and inner feelings of *only one* of the characters in the story, someone who often is the main character or protagonist. Suppose the major characters are Pam, Bob, and Sue, with Sue being the main character. The following illustration places Sue at the focus point in the narrative world:

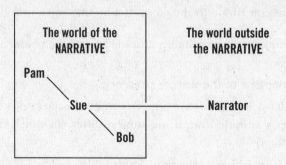

The narrator, who is not a character in the story, tells the reader what Bob and Pam do and say (generally as these elements relate to Sue), but more importantly he or she tells *about* Sue—her consciousness—to the point that the reader can understand Sue or perhaps even relate to her. The reader learns (through the narrator sharing Sue's thoughts, opinions, and feelings with the reader) how Sue is dealing with the relationships and events that affect her and how she perceives the world around her. The reader sees the other characters through Sue's eyes.

Sometimes the narrator, reveals the main character's thoughts through **stream of consciousness** techniques, the flow of thoughts that people experience, thoughts that range from the unintelligible to the very rational and well articulated. One such technique is the *interior monologue* in which the main character's thoughts are reported as they occur—often in vague terms with sometimes (but not always) illogical order and a lack of grammatical clarity.

Both James Joyce and William Faulkner used stream-of-consciousness techniques in their writings. Here is a sample from Faulkner's short story "Barn Burning."

> They were running a middle buster now, his brother holding the
> plow straight while he handled the reins, and walking beside the
> straining mule, the rich black soil shearing cool and damp against
> his bare ankles, he thought *Maybe this is the end of it. Maybe even*
> *that twenty bushels that seems hard to have to pay for just a rug will*
> *be a cheap price for him to stop forever and always from being*
> *what he used to be;* thinking, dreaming now, so that his brother had
> to speak sharply to him to mind the mule:
> *Maybe he even won't collect the twenty bushels. Maybe it will all*
> *add up and balance and vanish—corn, rug, fire; the terror and grief,*
> *the being pulled two ways like between two teams of horses—gone,*
> *done with for ever and ever.*

Line

(5)

(10)

ERM ALERT You should know this term: **omniscient point of view**

Definition: In the omniscient or third-person unlimited point of view, the narrator knows everything about everyone in every situation and feels free to reveal this information at will to the reader.

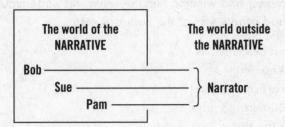

The reader no longer needs to rely upon Sue's observations; the narrator can directly reveal the thoughts, motives, and actions of Pam and Bob.

ERM ALERT You should know this term: **first-person point of view**

Definition: The first-person narrator might be the main character, one of the minor characters, or simply an observer. Written in the first-person "I," the readers can easily identify with the person telling the story and eventually become "a part" of the narrative. But when the narrator is also one of the characters, the reader is *limited* in his or her view of the narrative world (in others words, the world of the characters in the story) to one as seen by an active participant in that world. This view, however, is one that generally has a heightened sense of both realism and sometimes (but not always) credibility.

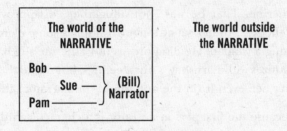

▼PRACTICE QUESTIONS▼

Examine again this selection taken from *Wuthering Heights.*

> But his self-love would endure no further torment—I heard, and not
> altogether disapprovingly, a manual check given to her saucy
> tongue—The little wretch had done her utmost to hurt her cousin's
> Line sensitive though uncultivated feelings, and a physical argument was
> (5) the only mode he had of balancing the account, and repaying its
> effects on the inflicter.
> He [Earnshaw] afterwards gathered the books and hurled them on
> the fire. I read in his countenance what anguish it was to offer that
> sacrifice to spleen—I fancied that as they consumed, he recalled the
> (10) pleasure they had already imparted; and the triumph and ever-

increasing pleasure he had anticipated from them—and I fancied, I guessed the incitement to his secret studies, also. He had been content with daily labour and rough animal enjoyments, till Catherine crossed his path—Shame at her scorn, and hope of her approval

(15) were his first prompters to higher pursuits; and instead of guarding him from one, and winning him the other, his endeavours to raise himself had produced just the contrary result.

The narrator is best described as
(A) unlimited in knowledge
(B) able to read Earnshaw's mind
(C) able to read Catherine's mind
(D) a character in the story
(E) an observer outside the story

Which of the following pairs LEAST effectively describes the contrast of the narrator's attitude toward Catherine and Earnshaw?
(A) censorious, understanding
(B) angry, approving
(C) disapproving, sympathetic
(D) disapprobative, pitying
(E) critical, sensitive

Explanation: This account is obviously written in the first person ("I"). He is in the scene, observing the countenance of Earnshaw, which means the narrator is a character in the story. What are his attitudes? All five answers are possible (a LEAST question), but the subtle elements of B make it the least effective contrast. The speaker does not show real anger toward Catherine. That he was "not altogether" disapproving when she was slapped ("manual check … to her saucy tongue") implies some element of disapproval over Earnshaw hitting a woman. He disapproves of Catherine's behavior (calling her a wretch) and sympathizes with Earnshaw's hurt feelings, but not to the point of complete approval of slapping her, even if (in the opinion of the narrator) she deserves it.

Here is the point: Because the first-person narrator is a character in the story, he cannot project an attitude based on really knowing what Catherine and Earnshaw are thinking, as a third-person unlimited or even third-person limited narrator might have done.

Correct Answers : **D, B**

IMPORTANT CONCEPT #2: CHARACTERIZATION OF THE NARRATOR

Concept Explained:

The point of view tells you whether the narrator is in the story or out of the story and to some degree how much he or she knows about the thinking of the characters. The narrator can also be characterized in three major areas:

1. Is the narrator self-conscious or self-effacing?

The self-conscious narrator deliberately allows the reader to know that the work is a fictional account or goes so far as to point out the elements of narration at work.

▼PRACTICE QUESTION▼

Read as an example this first paragraph of *The Posthumous Papers of the Pickwick Club* by Charles Dickens:

> The first ray of light which illumines the gloom, and converts into a
> dazzling brilliancy that obscurity in which the earlier history of the
> public career of the immortal Pickwick would appear to be involved,
> Line is derived from the perusal of the following entry in the Transactions
> (5) of the Pickwick Club, which the editor of these papers feels the
> highest pleasure in laying before his readers, as a proof of the
> careful attention, indefatigable assiduity, and nice discrimination,
> with which his search among the multifarious documents confided to
> him has been conducted.

The narrator's attitude toward his work is somewhat
(A) self-confident
(B) self-condemning
(C) belligerent
(D) uncaring
(E) relaxed

Explanation: The narrator describes himself as "the editor of these papers" in the third person and describes his work as done with "careful attention, indefatigable assiduity, and nice discrimination." He *knows* that his work is done well. He has a self-confident attitude.

Correct Answer: **A**

▼PRACTICE QUESTION▼

Also, note the first paragraph of *Oliver Twist*, how the narrator refers to the writing process:

> Among other public buildings in a certain town, which for many
> reasons it will be prudent to refrain from mentioning, and to which I
> will assign no fictitious name, there is one anciently common to most
> Line towns, great or small: to wit, a workhouse; and in this workhouse
> (5) was born: on a day and date which I need not trouble myself to
> repeat, inasmuch as it can be of no possible consequence to the
> reader, in this stage of the business at all events: the item of
> mortality whose name is prefixed to the head of this chapter.

These paragraphs are found near the end of *Oliver Twist*, in which the narrator talks of "this tale" and describes his writing of the conclusion:

> The fortunes of those who have figured in this tale are nearly
> closed. The little that remains to their historian to relate, is told in few
> and simple words.
>
> ... ...
>
> Line And now, the hand that traces these words, falters, as it
> (5) approaches the conclusion of its task: and would weave, for a little
> longer space, the thread of these adventures.

(10)

(15)

(20)

I would fain linger yet with a few of those among whom I have so long moved, and share their happiness by endeavouring to depict it. I would show Rose Maylie in all the bloom and grace of early womanhood, shedding on her secluded path in life such soft and gentle light, as fell on all who trod it with her, and shone into their hearts. I would paint her the life and joy of the fireside circle and the lively summer group; I would follow her through the sultry fields at noon, and hear the low tones of her sweet voice in the moonlit evening walk; I would watch her in all her goodness and charity abroad, and the smiling untiring discharge of domestic duties at home; I would paint her and her dead sister's child happy in their mutual love, and passing whole hours together in picturing the friends whom they had so sadly lost; I would summon before me, once again, those joyous little faces that clustered round her knee, and listen to their merry prattle; I would recall the tones of that clear laugh, and conjure up the sympathising tear that glistened in the soft blue eye. These, and a thousand looks and smiles, and turns of thought and speech—I would fain recall them every one.

What is the narrator's attitude toward Rose Maylie?
(A) Passionate
(B) Affectionate
(C) Amorous
(D) Zealous
(E) Dispassionate

Explanation: The narrator's affectionate attitude toward Rose Maylie is obvious in his choice of description. She was "the life and joy of the . . . summer group," one of "goodness and charity," and so forth.

Correct Answer: **B**

At the other extreme, you are almost totally unaware of the existence of the self-effacing author because when the author is self-effacing, the story is told objectively. Scenes are described, dialogue spoken, and action conveyed, but the author fades into the background, out of sight.

2. Is the narrator reliable or unreliable?

Although the reader may have a tendency to believe that the narrator is *always* credible and correct in his or her opinions, sometimes the narrator has an erroneous understanding of the situation. Take, as an example, works in which the narrator is the main character and the reader must rely upon his or her perspective. In such cases, the main character, through whose eyes the reader sees the world of the story, may have a distorted view of things—is perhaps naive, too self-confident, mentally unstable, or even immature. Such a narrator is characterized as **unreliable** or **fallible**. An example is Huck Finn in *The Adventures of Huckleberry Finn*.

3. Is the narrator intrusive or unintrusive?

In addition, a narrator can be characterized as either **intrusive** or as **unintrusive** (objective, impersonal). As the name implies, the intrusive narrator gives opinions concerning the words and deeds, the personalities and motives, and the events and circumstances at work in the story. Sometimes these comments will even take the form of an essay that engages in "editorializing," and his or her comments are generally regarded as truthful or reliable.

▼PRACTICE QUESTION▼

Notice how the narrator interjects his opinions in this excerpt from *Oliver Twist*:

> Although I am not disposed to maintain that the being born in a
> workhouse, is in itself the most fortunate and enviable circumstance
> that can possibly befall a human being, I do mean to say that in this
> particular instance, it was the best thing for Oliver Twist that could
> (5) by possibility have occurred. The fact is, that there was considerable
> difficulty in inducing Oliver to take upon himself the office of
> respiration,—a troublesome practice, but one which custom has
> rendered necessary to our easy existence; and for some time he lay
> gasping on a little flock mattress, rather unequally poised between
> (10) this world and the next: the balance being decidedly in favour of the
> latter. Now, if, during this brief period, Oliver had been surrounded
> by careful grandmothers, anxious aunts, experienced nurses, and
> doctors of profound wisdom, he would most inevitably and
> indubitably have been killed in no time. There being nobody by,
> (15) however, but a pauper old woman, who was rendered rather misty
> by an unwonted allowance of beer; and a parish surgeon who did
> such matters by contract; Oliver and Nature fought out the point
> between them. The result was, that, after a few struggles, Oliver
> breathed, sneezed, and proceeded to advertise to the inmates of the
> (20) workhouse the fact of a new burden having been imposed upon the
> parish, by setting up as loud a cry as could reasonably have been
> expected from a male infant who had not been possessed of that
> very useful appendage, a voice, for a much longer space of time
> than three minutes and a quarter.

Based on his general attitude, the narrator's opinion of life is
(A) respectful
(B) pessimistic
(C) optimistic
(D) sanguine
(E) zealous

Explanation: The narrator describes in a somewhat sarcastic tone the struggle between Nature and a newborn child, a struggle that the child wins, only to become "a new burden . . . on the parish"—a pessimistic attitude.

Correct Answer: **B**

The unintrusive narrator is quite the opposite of the intrusive; he or she reports without personal comment the words and deeds of the characters in the context of the events of the story. Is there such a thing as a totally unintrusive narrator? Possibly not. The connotative values of word choices alone reflect a certain degree of personal opinion; however, when the narrator refrains from direct statements of opinion and at least attempts the straightforward telling of the story, the reader can (perhaps with reservation) *characterize* the narrator as unintrusive.

Of course, you should be able to identify when a narrator is intruding his or her opinions into the story. However, also focus on what those opinions and attitudes are and how they affect the telling of the story.

TO SUMMARIZE: The narrator of a story can openly let you know he or she is telling the story (or not), be someone you can trust (or not), and give you his or her opinions (or not). All three of these characteristics of the narrator will affect how you view that person's attitude.

IMPORTANT CONCEPT #3: THE NARRATOR VERSUS THE AUTHOR

Concept Explained:

Some readers mistakenly assume that the writer and the narrator are the same. Sometimes the author and narrator are the same, but at other times they are two distinctly different voices. When the narrative is in the first person, with a character being the one telling the story as the narrator or speaker, identifying the voice of the writer as different from that of the narrator can be difficult.

The story world can be used to illustrate on a very basic level and to build, step-by-step, a basis for this distinction. Suppose the story is a first-person narrative actually being told by the person who is living the events. This autobiographical story is told live as the events happen—as a news reporter does at the scene of an ongoing news story. The present tense adds a tone of excitement. The story might include elements of stream-of-consciousness writing, also. Here is an excerpt of Elaine's account of being trapped in a burning building:

> I hope this microphone is still working and I'm still on the air...
>   I am looking at the locked door. I can almost see how hot it must be! If I try to touch it, I'll get burned. The fire is raging on the other
> Line side. Jayne is screaming for someone to unlock the door. Smoke is
> (5)   choking me—my eyes are smarting with thick black fumes that blanket
>   my head. I hear Roel calling my name....

"I" (Elaine) is the narrator, the main character, and (because this is an autobiographical story), the author.

The world of the NARRATIVE		The world outside the story
	Jayne	
Elaine the narrator, CHARACTER, and author	Roel	

Now look at the difference a simple change in verb tense can make. Once again suppose this is a real-life event that happens to Elaine; however, rather than telling the story as it happens, she waits until the fire trucks leave and writes her story for broadcast much later—perhaps the next day:

Line

(5)

> I tried the microphone, but it wouldn't work. I looked at the locked door. I could almost see how hot it must have been. If I had tried to touch it, I would have gotten burned. The fire was raging on the other side. Jayne was screaming for someone to unlock the door. Smoke was choking me—my eyes smarted with the thick fumes that blanketed my head. I heard Roel calling my name.

The main character is still Elaine, but what about the narrator and author? In the first account, the narrator and author are Elaine *as she lived the experience*. In the second account, the author is Elaine *after the experience*, taking the role of a narrator telling about herself as a character at a previous time.

A story can be told by a participant from his or her perspective while it is happening; however, as soon as time elapses, the story can be retold only as an account in which the participant has a dual role: first as the person who was in the story and second as the narrator who is now outside the world (the time and place) in which the events occurred.

Where should Elaine appear on the illustration in her role as narrator? Who is telling the story?

The world of the NARRATIVE	The world outside the story
Jayne	
Elaine the CHARACTER	Elaine the author and narrator (remembering the events)
Roel	

Now that a distinction has been established between the character and the author/narrator in a first-person account, the illustration can be taken one step further. Suppose that Sally Smith, as an author, wrote the account of the events of the fire, placing Elaine Brown as a major character in the story. Elaine Brown is the main character narrating the story (written in the first person); however, Sally Smith is the author:

The world of the NARRATIVE	The world outside the story
Jayne	
Elaine Brown the CHARACTER and narrator	Sally Smith the author
Roel	

Because the story is in first person, you might easily assume that when the character/narrator tells us that "I thought this or I did ..." that these words are the thoughts and actions of the writer of the story, but this is clearly not the case. Because Sally Smith (author) is writing the words and actions of Elaine Brown (character), those words and actions (whether in past or present tense) are those of a character in the story and may or may not reflect Sally Smith's opinions, even though they are written in the first person. The narrator and the author are two different voices. This forms the basis for distinguishing *between the narrator (speaker) and the writer*.

▼PRACTICE QUESTION▼

Sometimes the speaker and the author can arguably be viewed as the same voice. For example, in Charles Dickens's *David Copperfield* (a story that Dickens based on some of his own life experiences and in which he expresses many of his own personal views), Dickens has written in the first person:

DAVID COPPERFIELD
by
Charles Dickens
I Am Born.

Whether I shall turn out to be the hero of my own life, or whether that station will be held by anybody else, these pages must show. To begin my life with the beginning of my life, I record that I was born
Line (as I have been informed and believe) on a Friday, at twelve o'clock
(5) at night. It was remarked that the clock began to strike, and I began to cry, simultaneously.

In consideration of the day and hour of my birth, it was declared by the nurse, and by some sage women in the neighbourhood who had taken a lively interest in me several months before there was
(10) any possibility of our becoming personally acquainted, first, that I was destined to be unlucky in life; and secondly, that I was privileged to see ghosts and spirits; both these gifts inevitably attaching, as they believed, to all unlucky infants of either gender, born towards the small hours on a Friday night.
(15) I need say nothing here, on the first head, because nothing can show better than my history whether that prediction was verified or falsified by the result. On the second branch of the question, I will only remark, that unless I ran through that part of my inheritance while I was still a baby, I have not come into it yet. But I do not at all
(20) complain of having been kept out of this property; and if anybody else should be in the present enjoyment of it, he is heartily welcome to keep it.

The autobiographical elements of this story probably make David's attitude toward superstition

(A) in antithesis of Dickens's opinion
(B) unnecessary to the story
(C) indefensible
(D) a betrayal of trust
(E) a reflection of the author's view

Explanation: In this story Dickens is the author, David is the main character, and David is the narrator who tells the story using the first-person pronoun "I" as if he is the author. David is Dickens's **persona**: in other words, he is a character who narrates the story for the author. As Dickens's persona, David the narrator and Dickens the author have the same voice.

Correct Answer: **E**

In other situations, however, the narrator and author do not share the same attitude, as illustrated by Swift's "A Modest Proposal" and discussed in more detail in the next Important Concept.

IMPORTANT CONCEPT #4: THE ATTITUDE OF THE SPEAKER

Concept Explained:

Speakers in nonnarrative works also project an attitude. Just as with narrators, sometimes the speaker and author share the same opinions, sometimes not.

▼Practice Question▼

Read carefully the following excerpt from "A Modest Proposal," written in 1729 by Jonathan Swift at a time when landowners were turning deaf ears to the suffering of homeless Irish who were victims of a three-year drought.

> It is a melancholy object to those who walk through this great
> town or travel in the country, when they see the streets, the roads,
> and cabin doors, crowded with beggars of the female sex, followed
> by three, four, or six children, all in rags and importuning every
> (5) passenger for an alms. These mothers, instead of being able to work
> for their honest livelihood, are forced to employ all their time in
> strolling to beg sustenance for their helpless infants, who, as they
> grow up, either turn thieves for want of work, or leave their dear
> native country to fight for the Pretender in Spain, or sell themselves
> (10) to the Barbados.
> I think it is agreed by all parties that this prodigious number of
> children in the arms, or on the backs, or at the heels of their
> mothers, and frequently of their fathers, is in the present deplorable
> state of the kingdom a very great additional grievance; and
> (15) therefore whoever could find out a fair, cheap, and easy method of
> making these children sound, useful members of the commonwealth
> would deserve so well of the public as to have his statue set up for a
> preserver of the nation.
> But my intention is very far from being confined to provide only for
> (20) the children of professed beggars; it is of much greater extent, and
> shall take in the whole number of infants at a certain age who are
> born of parents in effect as little able to support them as those who
> demand our charity in the streets.
> As to my own part, having turned my thoughts for many years
> (25) upon this important subject, and maturely weighed the several
> schemes of other projectors, I have always found them grossly
> mistaken in their computation. It is true, a child just dropped from its
> dam may be supported by her milk for a solar year, with little other
> nourishment; at most not above the value of two shillings, which the
> (30) mother may certainly get, or the value in scraps, by her lawful
> occupation of begging; and it is exactly at one year that I propose
> to provide for them in such a manner as instead of being a charge

The word "Line" appears at the left of line 4.

(35)
upon their parents or the parish,...they shall on the contrary contribute to the feeding, and partly to the clothing, of many thousands.

* * *

(40)
I am assured by our merchants that a boy or a girl before twelve years old is no salable commodity; and even when they come to this age they will not yield above three pounds, or three pound and half a crown at most on the Exchange; which cannot turn to account either to the parents or the kingdom, the charge of nutriment and rags having been at least four times that value.

I shall now therefore humbly propose my own thoughts, which I hope will not be liable to the least objection.

(45)
I have been assured by a very knowing American of my acquaintance in London, that a young healthy child well nursed is at a year old a most delicious, nourishing, and wholesome food, whether stewed, roasted, baked, or boiled; and I make no doubt that it will equally serve in a fricassee or a ragout....

Of the attitudes listed, which is the attitude of the speaker toward his readers?

(A) Overbearing self-confidence
(B) Aggressive hostility
(C) Confident conviction
(D) Feigned sincerity
(E) Ribald frivolity

Explanation: Swift is the author; "I" is the speaker. Does this speaker, however, represent Swift's true opinions? Obviously not. Note the shocking nature of the speaker's proposal, particularly when he exposes his "plan" for turning children into a food source in the last paragraph of the excerpt, a totally alien concept to any civilized people. The writer might have directly said, "You are allowing these children to starve and to be treated like animals," but would such direct words have had the attention-getting effect and the same shame-producing impact that his proposal elicits? In the case of "A Modest Proposal," the author and the speaker do not share the same voice.

Correct Answer: **D**

TERM ALERT You should know this term: **satire**

Definition: In general, satire makes a subject look ridiculous in order to make a point. The previous essay is a satire because Swift uses wit to censor or criticize society, with the aim toward reform. In satire, the writer's attitude often is one of condemnation or contempt.

TERM ALERT You should know this term: **persona**

Definition: A persona is a narrator, speaker, or implied author created by the real writer as a "mask" to tell the story and/or express opinions in the first person. The attitude of the persona may or may not be the same as that of the author. The speaker in "A Modest Proposal" is Swift's persona.

A **naive narrator** is a character who narrates in the first person as if he or she is the author, but whose opinions, actions, or thoughts are so naive or so obtuse (as in this case) that they ironically make the point of the author. If the naive narrator is a child whose simplicity of thought could conceivably end in tragedy, however, the result might be pathos rather than irony.

To summarize, there can be different voices heard in a literary work: the writer and/or the speaker/narrator. For example, in the *Sherlock Holmes* mysteries of Sir Arthur Conan Doyle, you will find

1. Doyle—the writer
2. Dr. Watson—the speaker/narrator, a character in the story, and *persona* for Doyle
3. Holmes—the main character

```
┌──────────────────────────────────┐
│  The world of the    The world outside
│  NARRATIVE           the story
│
│  Watson
│  CHARACTER
│  narrator            Sir Arthur Conan Doyle
│            Holmes         Author
│       main CHARACTER
└──────────────────────────────────┘
```

When reading a passage from one of these mysteries, a relevant question might be (if, for example, the passage is Watson speaking), is this the voice of Dr. Watson, the persona for Doyle (the writer) speaking? (FYI: When the author creates a fictional character who writes the story or book, the device is called the **putative author**.)

HERE IS THE POINT: Sometimes the speaker and the author are not of the same opinion, even when the work is written in the first person.

IMPORTANT CONCEPT #5: MECHANICAL VOICES

Concept Explained:

Generally speaking, the narrative point of view, the roles of the writer, the narrator (or speaker in a nonnarrative work), the style of writing, and so forth blend together to project attitude(s) toward the reader. There are, however, some mechanical elements of literary forms that writers can use to create a sense of the speaker's attitude and writer's presence.

1. Voice in narrative poetry has many of the same considerations as in its narrative prose form; however, voice in lyric poetry has some significant differences. As proposed by T. S. Eliot, voice in poetry encompasses three different perspectives: (a) the silent contemplations of the poet, (b) the meaning conveyed from the poet to the reader/hearer, and (c) the role of the persona that the poet uses in the poem.

Lyric poems are nonnarrative works that express the speaker's feelings, state of mind, thoughts, and other expressions, and are written generally in the first person. The usage of the first person "I" in the lyric poem does not necessarily mean that the poet is the speaker (just as the first person narrator of a story is not always the author).

Perhaps recognition of the lyric speaker can best be illustrated by looking again at a type of lyric poem called the **dramatic monologue**. The characteristics of the dramatic monologue are

a. A persona (called the lyric speaker and *not* referring to the poet) who expresses the lyric at some dramatic moment or in a situation

b. A one-sided conversation in which the clues in the lyric reveal that this poem is part of a conversation addressed *to* someone, but only the lyric of the (persona) speaker can be heard—the other people in the one-sided conversation are *silent* auditors

c. Revelation of the lyric speaker's character (usually unintentional) through what he or she says

▼PRACTICE QUESTIONS▼

Read this often referenced dramatic monologue by Robert Browning called "My Last Duchess." The lyric speaker is *not* Browning, but rather a sixth-century Italian duke named Alfonso II. He was married to a fourteen-year-old girl who died when she was just seventeen. Her death has been described as "suspicious"; however, Duke Alfonso went on to negotiate an arrangement to marry a member of Austrian royalty. He used an agent for these negotiations; that agent is the silent auditor to whom this lyric poem is addressed:

MY LAST DUCHESS

That's my last Duchess painted on the wall,
Looking as if she were alive. I call
That piece a wonder, now: Fra` Pandolf's hands
Line   Worked busily a day, and there she stands.
(5)   Will't please you sit and look at her? I said
"Fra` Pandolf" by design, for never read
Strangers like you that pictured countenance,
The depth and passion of its earnest glance,
But to myself they turned (since none puts by
(10)   The curtain I have drawn for you, but I)
And seemed as they would ask me, if they durst,
How such a glance came there; so, not the first
Are you to turn and ask thus. Sir, 'twas not
Her husband's presence only, called that spot
(15)   Of joy into the Duchess' cheek: perhaps
Fra` Pandolf chanced to say "Her mantle laps
Over my lady's wrist too much," or "Paint
Must never hope to reproduce the faint
Half-flush that dies along her throat": such stuff
(20)   Was courtesy, she thought, and cause enough
For calling up that spot of joy. She had
A heart—how shall I say?—too soon made glad,
Too easily impressed; she liked whate'er
She looked on, and her looks went everywhere.
(25)   Sir, 'twas all one! My favor at her breast,
The dropping of the daylight in the West,

The bough of cherries some officious fool
Broke in the orchard for her, the white mule
She rode with round the terrace—all and each
(30) Would draw from her alike the approving speech,
Or blush, at least. She thanked men,—good! but thanked
Somehow—I know not how—as if she ranked
My gift of a nine-hundred-years-old name
With anybody's gift. Who'd stoop to blame
(35) This sort of trifling? Even had you skill
In speech—which I have not—to make your will
Quite clear to such an one, and say, "Just this
Or that in you disgust me; here you miss,
Or there exceed the mark"—and if she let
(40) Herself be lessoned so, nor plainly set
Her wits to yours, forsooth, and made excuse,
—E'en then would be some stooping; and I choose
Never to stoop. Oh sir, she smiled, no doubt,
Whene'er I passed her; but who passed without
(45) Much the same smile? This grew; I gave commands
Then all smiles stopped together. There she stands
As if alive. Will't please you rise? We'll meet
The company below, then I repeat,
The Count your master's known munificence
(50) Is ample warrant that no just pretense
Of mine for dowry will be disallowed;
Though his fair daughter's self, as I avowed
At starting, is my object. Nay, we'll go
Together down, sir. Notice Neptune, though,
(55) Taming a sea-horse, thought a rarity,
Which Claus of Innsbruck cast in bronze for me!

by Robert Browning

Now, examine the poem to answer the following questions:

a. Can you *distinguish between the speaker and the writer?*

The form(a dramatic monologue) dictates this distinction: the poet (Browning) has used a persona, a lyric speaker in the person of the duke.

b. What in the poem reveals the speaker's attitude?

Some lines are obvious; however, look for the more subtle hints at his character, for example, notice how easily he glides from the painting of his late wife to discussing another work of art—the bronze statue (lines 54–56).

c. Are there any clues to what Browning's attitude toward the duke might be?

Be sure to look for clues arising from the choice of words he had the duke speak or from the elements of character Browning (the poet) chose to have this lyric speaker reveal.

d. Finally, what role does the silent auditor serve here?

Notice lines 1, 5–7, 12–13, 35–41 (Is "you" referring specifically to the silent auditor—the marriage agent to whom he is speaking?), and 51–52.

In lines 21–45, the attitude of the speaker toward his late wife is best described as
(A) magnanimous
(B) indulgent
(C) meddlesome
(D) lenient
(E) petty

Why did the speaker never voice his objections to his wife?
(A) bashfulness
(B) shame
(C) pride
(D) insolence
(E) humility

The poet presents the speaker as a man who is
(A) grieving
(B) cold-blooded
(C) fickle
(D) dignified
(E) vulnerable

Explanation: The duke resented that his wife had the same youthful smile for everyone and everything that pleased her, including him. He wanted her to smile and blush only for himself. His pettiness went so far as to criticize the excitement she felt over such innocent things as a sunset (line 26) and riding her mule (line 28). He did not tell her so that she could amend her actions, because to do so would be "stooping; and I choose/Never to stoop" (lines 42–43), projecting his attitude of pride. What is the poet's attitude toward this man? Condemning. Browning presents him as unreasonable, filled with pride, and capable of murdering a young girl (lines 45–47), then going on without regret to negotiate marriage to yet another (lines 47–53), in other words, a cold-blooded killer.

Correct Answers: **E, C, B**

2. Can a drama have a narrative voice? Critics and teachers vary on the subject. On one hand, plays have no narrator, no one to intervene between the audience and the events and conversations being acted out on stage and no true sense of the author's presence. From this view, narrative voice is not an element of drama. The opposing view would contend that you can catch glimpses of the writer, even in drama, from time to time.

How can you determine the voice in a drama? Trying to establish the point of view is fruitless: the point of view refers to who is telling the story (first or third person). Because in a drama the characters act out their own stories, the narrative is not "narrated" and as a result is not first person or third person. There generally is a main character; however, you do not see the world of the play through his or her eyes except for the few clues you may gather from the main character's words.

In order to determine the narrative voice, in a play, some look to the dramatist's use of dramatic conventions, especially the use of the chorus, the choral-character, the prologue, and the epilogue.

The **chorus**, for example, originally was composed of singers (and dancers) but eventually underwent a progression of forms until it came to be editorial-type comments, foreshadowing, and points for plot development recited between acts by a single actor in Elizabethan drama.

▼PRACTICE QUESTION▼

Here is the chorus from the Prologue before Act I Scene I of *Romeo and Juliet.*

> ACT I PROLOGUE
> [*Enter*] CHORUS
> CHORUS.
>
> Two households, both alike in dignity,
> In fair Verona, where we lay our scene,
> From ancient grudge break to new mutiny,
> Where civil blood makes civil hands unclean.
> From forth the fatal loins of these two foes
> A pair of star-crost lovers take their life;
> Whose misadventured piteous overthrows
> Doth with their death bury their parents' strife.
> The fearful passage of their death-mark'd love,
> And the continuance of their parents' rage,
> Which, but their children's end, naught could remove,
> Is now the two hours' traffic of our stage;
> The which if you with patient ears attend,
> What here shall miss, our toil shall strive to mend. [*Exit*]

Line (5) ... (10) *(marginal line numbers)*

Notice the role of the chorus:

- It sets the scene (line 2).
- It foreshadows the ending (line 7).
- It tells the length of the play (line 12).
- It gives the cause of the tragedy (lines 1, 3).
- It promises more detail (lines 13–14).
- It editorializes through use of connotatively charged words ("grudge," "mutiny," "unclean," and "piteous").
- It directly addresses the tragedy of the story (lines 10–11).

The attitude projected by the chorus toward the lovers is best described as
(A) sympathetic
(B) lenient
(C) callous
(D) matter-of-fact
(E) inclement

Explanation: Although the lines do seem somewhat matter-of-fact, the connotations of some lines reveal sympathy for the lovers. The are "star-crost," their "overthrows" are "misadventured" and "piteous," and their "parents' rage" could be removed only by "their children's end."

Correct Answer: **A**

3. Another mechanical voice writers use is grammatical voice.

You are probably familiar with active voice and passive voice: When the subject does the action in a sentence or in the condition named by the verb, the voice of the verb is active. (I threw a ball.) When the subject receives the action, the voice of the verb is passive. (The ball was thrown by me.) Passive voice constructions are made with the past participle and a form of the verb *to be*: was thrown. Much of the writing done in English is in the active voice, and the occasional shift to passive voice can be very effective, particularly when emphasis is to be placed on the object, as in "The difficult test was passed by the student" (emphasis is on the test) or when the actors are not known, as in "Many books have been written this year" (Who wrote the books?).

Largely an element of a writer's style, overuse of the passive voice can affect the tone of a narrative and, as a result, might influence the reader's perception.

▼PRACTICE QUESTIONS▼

Compare these two versions of the same paragraph:

VERSION ONE:

The ball was hit by Jim, but it was immediately caught by the outfielder. Roars were heard from the crowd. Tears streaming down his face were awkwardly wiped away by Jim's gloved hand. The truth was finally realized by him: the championship game was lost.

VERSION TWO:

Jim hit the ball, but the outfielder caught it immediately. The crowd roared. Jim's gloved hand awkwardly wiped away the tears streaming down his face. He finally realized the truth: the championship game was lost.

In Version One, the narrator probably views the scene as
(A) merely a game
(B) active, loud, and sentimental
(C) the loss of a man's dream
(D) unexciting and regrettable
(E) just another part of sports

In Version Two, the narrator probably views the scene as
(A) merely a game
(B) active, loud, and sentimental
(C) the loss of a man's dream
(D) unexciting and regrettable
(E) just another part of sports

Explanation: In Version One, attention is on our descriptive senses: seeing the ball being hit, hearing the roar, seeing tears flow (emotionally centered). In Version Two, the attention is on Jim, the outfielder, and the crowd (people-centered).

Correct Answers: **B, C**

In a narrative, the use of active voice helps to intensify the action (a function of tone) and hold the reader's attention, but overuse of the passive voice misdirects attention away from Jim—the main subject of the sample narrative. Controlled use of passive voice can be useful: the shift from active to passive in the last sentence of Version Two effectively serves to catch the reader's attention that something is different (in this case a significant point is being made). In narrative writing, as this example illustrates, use of active and passive voice has significant implications on the reader's perceptions of tone and meaning.

ACTIVE THINKING EXERCISES FOR (NARRATIVE) VOICE

STEP 1. ▸FOCUS◂

Conventional advice: Prepare study places that are pleasant, well lighted, and conducive to concentrated study without distractions. So true. For many people, a quiet place helps them focus their concentration. If you have the luxury of a quiet study place—great! But in the real world, there is noise. Do not become so dependent on quiet, perfect conditions that you fall apart when things happen.

On the other hand, some people thrive on chaos and at the very least need a radio on in the background to concentrate. The "I can hear a pin drop" quiet of a strict testing situation can become uncomfortable and actually break their concentration.

One of your focus goals should be to learn to concentrate, to focus your attention when you study and when you take the test. Developing and practicing techniques to help you focus will also help you overcome test nerves. Learning to focus will prevent you from reading the test selections mechanically, only to find that when you begin to answer the questions, you do not understand or remember what you just read.

You already practiced a few ideas in the previous chapters. Here is another to add to your list.

▼EXERCISE▼

The "Me and My Shadow" method

To focus your attention, learn to talk to yourself internally as you read. Develop a mental relationship with what you read. To illustrate, below is a selection from *The Pickwick Papers*. As you read, here are some things you might think about that will help you crowd out of your mind distracting, nonhelpful thoughts:

THE PICKWICK PAPERS
by
Charles Dickens

"My secret was out; and my only struggle now, was for liberty
and freedom. I gained my feet before a hand was on me, threw
myself among my assailants, and cleared my way with my strong
Line   arm as if I bore a hatchet in my hand, and hewed them down before
(5)   me. I gained the door, dropped over the banisters, and in an instant
was in the street.

First paragraph: What secret? He must be a prisoner. Must be in great shape to drop over a banister.

"Straight and swift I ran, and no one dared to stop me. I heard
the noise of feet behind, and redoubled my speed.... When I woke I
found myself here—here in this gray cell where the sun-light seldom
(10)   comes, and the moon steals in, in rays which only serve to show the
dark shadows about me, and that silent figure in its old corner.

> When I lie awake, I can sometimes hear strange shrieks and cries
> from distant parts of this large place. What they are, I know not; but
> they neither come from that pale form, nor does it regard them. For
> (10) from the first shades of dusk 'till the earliest light of morning, it still
> stands motionless in the same place, listening to the music of my iron
> chain, and watching my gambols on my straw bed."

Second paragraph: Being chased. What happened? Did someone knock him out? What silent figure? How long is he in there? What could it be?

> At the end of the manuscript, was written, in another hand, this
> note:—

Single line paragraph: Quote marks ended. First two paragraphs must be what was written in manuscript.

Last paragraph: (Your turn—What thoughts cross your mind as you read this paragraph?)

_____

_____

_____

> (15)   [The unhappy man whose ravings are recorded above, was a
> melancholy instance of the baneful results of energies misdirected in
> early life, and excesses prolonged until their consequences could
> never be repaired....It is only matter of wonder to those who were
> acquainted with the vices of his early career, that his passions, when
> (20) no longer controlled by reason, did not lead him to the commission
> of still more frightful deeds.]

This method may be too time consuming to use on the entire test. When you sit down and begin the first selection, however, it may help your mind settle down and concentrate on the task at hand.

In this selection, part of a manuscript is written in the first person, followed by a commentary (the "note") written in the third person by someone else in reference to the writer of the manuscript. A question concerning the narrator's attitude would probably be referring to the writer of the commentary. Be aware, however, that there is yet a third voice. Although this limited excerpt reveals very little about his or her attitude, the existence of this person needs to be recognized: Who is the voice that says, "At the end of the manuscript, was written, in another hand, this note:"?

▼Practice Questions▼

While you have the Dickens selection before you, stop for a moment and look at how narrative voice is used.

The attitude of the speaker "I" in the first two paragraphs is
(A) optimistically exuberant
(B) angrily resistant
(C) intensely forlorn
(D) respectfully submissive
(E) earnestly imploring

What is the attitude of the commentator toward the "unhappy man" in the last paragraph?

(A) Judgmental
(B) Sympathetic
(C) Hostile
(D) Defensive
(E) Compassionate

Explanation: The imprisoned man is without sunlight, surrounded by shadows, listening to shrieks and cries, and watching a "silent figure." He is forlorn, in a miserable condition. The commentator makes a stern judgment about him: His early life was "misdirected" and he believes it is a "wonder" that the prisoner did not come to worse.

Correct Answers: **C, A**

▼Exercise▼

Turn to the Interpretive Skill Practice Sets A, B, and C beginning on page 330. Using the "Me and My Shadow" method, answer the questions about narrative voice in Set A. Check your answers using the key on page 355. How did you do? Continue the method with Sets B and C, if you wish.

Turn to Practice Test Three on page 387. Use the "Me and My Shadow" method for the *first selection only*, then continue the test using your other focus techniques. Once again, score your test. How did you do?

STEP 2. MOW (MY OWN WORDS)

Here is a selection from Jane Austen's *Northanger Abby*:

(1) At the end of the first dance, Captain Tilney came towards them again, and, much to Catherine's dissatisfaction, pulled his brother away. (2) They retired whispering together; and, though her
Line delicate sensibility did not take immediate alarm, and lay it down as
(5) fact, that Captain Tilney must have heard some malevolent misrepresentation of her, which he now hastened to communicate to his brother, in the hope of separating them for ever, she could not have her partner conveyed from her sight without very uneasy sensations. (3) Her suspense was of full five minutes' duration; and
(10) she was beginning to think it a very long quarter of an hour, when they both returned and an explanation was given, by Henry's requesting to know, if she thought her friend, Miss Thorpe, would have any objection to dancing, as his brother would be most happy to be introduced to her. (4) Catherine, without hesitation, replied,
(15) that she was very sure Miss Thorpe did not mean to dance at all. (5) The cruel reply was passed on to the other, and he immediately walked away.

(6) "Your brother will not mind it I know," said she, "because I heard him say before, that he hated dancing; but it was very good-
(20) natured in him to think of it. (7) I suppose he saw Isabella sitting down and fancied she might wish for a partner, but he is quite mistaken, for she would not dance upon any account in the world."

(8) Henry smiled, and said, "How very little trouble it can give you to understand the motive of other people's actions."

(25)   (9) "Why?—What do you mean?"

(10) "With you, it is not, How is such a one likely to be influenced? (11) What is the inducement most likely to act upon such a person's feelings, age, situation, and probable habits of life considered?—but, how should *I* be influenced, what would be *my*

(30)   inducement in acting so and so?"

(12) "I do not understand you."

(13) "Then we are on very unequal terms, for I understand you perfectly well."

(14) "Me?—yes I cannot speak well enough to be unintelligible."

(35)   (15) "Bravo?—an excellent satire on modern language."

Paraphrase each sentence:

1. _____

2. _____

3. _____

4. _____

5. _____

6. _____

7. _____

8. _____

9. _____

10. _____

11. _____

12. _____

13. _____

14. _____

15. _____

What is the subject? _____

What is the narrator's purpose? _____

Summarize the main idea of sentences 1–5: (one sentence) _____

_____

Summarize the main idea of sentences 8–15: _____

_____

Keep this analysis handy. You will be using it to BID in step 3.

STEP 3. BID (BREAK IT DOWN)

First, review what you have learned about voice by completing the following.

▼EXERCISE▼

Match the following terms with their definitions.

1. point of view	A. knows everyone's mind
2. limited omniscient	B. first or third person
3. omniscient	C. knows only one character's mind
4. first person	D. the writer's mask
5. persona	E. my story

Correct Answers:

1. **B**   2. **C**   3 **A**   4. **E**   5. **D**

Next, determine if each of the following statements is true or false.

1. Nonnarrative speakers cannot have a voice.

2. Limited omniscient point of view is in the first person.

3. A self-conscious narrator lets readers know that he or she is writing the story.

4. An intrusive narrator keeps to the facts and never injects an opinion.

5. If the story is told in the first person, the narrator always is the author.

6. A satire uses wit to censor society so people will change.

7. A dramatic monologue often is told by a persona.

8. Dramatists have no means to project their voice because a drama usually does not have a narrator.

9. Voice is also a part of grammar.

10. A dramatic monologue is the voice of the writer.

Correct Answers:

1. **F**   2. **F**   3. **T**   4. **F**   5. **F**   6. **T**   7. **T**   8. **F**   9. **T**   10. **F**

Finally, consider these three important questions. If you are looking for the voice in a selection, ask the following:

1. From what point of view is this story being told?

2. Who is speaking? Possible answers:

   a. The narrator or speaker

   b. The writer

   c. A character

3. Is the narrator/speaker credible?

Correct Answers: (will vary with the selection being read)

▼PRACTICE QUESTIONS▼

Look again at the selection by Jane Austen in the MOW step, then answer the following nine questions that deal with voice and its consequences.

1. The narrator of this passage is using
   (A) third-person unlimited point of view
   (B) third-person limited point of view
   (C) first-person point of view
   (D) stream-of-consciousness techniques
   (E) first-person omniscient point of view

2. The narrator of this passage is best characterized as somewhat
   (A) intrusive
   (B) self-conscious
   (C) unintrusive
   (D) unreliable
   (E) fallible

3. The narrator denies that Catherine took "immediate alarm, and lay it down as fact" concerning "some malevolent misrepresentation of her" (sentence 2). What is the probable intended effect?
   (A) To reinforce that Catherine really is misunderstood
   (B) To influence readers to suspect Catherine really is alarmed with paranoid speculations
   (C) To reveal the unreliable nature of the narrator
   (D) To make the narrator seem infatuated with Catherine
   (E) To suggest that Catherine is the heroine in a burlesque

4. Contextually, the tone of "her delicate sensibility" (sentence 2) is
   (A) sarcastic
   (B) understanding
   (C) nostalgic
   (D) indignant
   (E) deferential

5. Of the following, which is the LEAST accurate definition of "habits of life" as used in sentence 11?
   (A) Costume or dress
   (B) Disposition
   (C) Usual ways or practices

   (D) Customs
   (E) Addictions

6. The two uses of "understand you" (sentences 12–13) are reflected in which of the following?
   (A) To see with the eyes versus to see with the mind
   (B) Unspoken, implied meaning versus expressed meaning
   (C) To comprehend your words versus to discern your character
   (D) Uninformed versus informed meaning
   (E) Auditory problems versus attention deficit disorder

7. The exchange of dialogue in sentences 12–15 can best be described as
   (A) good-natured banter
   (B) japing
   (C) pleasantries
   (D) repartee
   (E) joking

8. In what way can "I cannot speak well enough to be unintelligible" (sentence 14) be considered satire?
   (A) It reveals that Catherine lacks the classical scholarship needed to be understood.
   (B) It stresses the importance of erudition.
   (C) It derides the paradox of being recondite as a measure of eloquence.
   (D) It highlights Catherine's intellectualism.
   (E) It mocks pedantry.

9. The ridicule found in Catherine's remark in sentence 14 is aimed at
   (A) modern language
   (B) satires
   (C) herself
   (D) Isabella
   (E) erudite speakers

Answers and Explanations:

1. **B** Within the confines of this short excerpt, the narrator reveals to us the inner thoughts of only one character: Catherine.

2. **A** The narrator injects his or her opinions. For example, Catherine's reply was "cruel."

3. **B** Generally, the purpose of apophasis (making a point by denying it) is to introduce and plant the suggestion in the mind of the reader or listener that the idea is true.

4. **A** "Delicate sensibility" is in contrast to someone who would make a cruel reply and jump to the conclusion that a simple, private conversation must be about her and "malevolent" in nature. This contrast makes the tone of the description seem sarcastic.

5. **A** The conversation relates to elements of character, not costumes. You may have been tempted with "addictions" as an answer choice because of the negative connotations associated with today's drug culture. The word "addiction," however, as it relates to "habits of life" can properly refer to a sense of devotion or habit, including good habits.

6. **C** The discussion between Catherine and Henry revolves around elements of character.

7. **D** Catherine and Henry respond to each other in quick, witty replies.

8. **C** A satire points out or ridicules stupidities, vices, unjust situations, and so forth. Many devices can be used to make a satiric poem, such as verbal irony, paradox, a sarcastic tone. In this case, Henry labels Catherine's sarcastic comment as a satire on modern language. Catherine points out a paradox that being unintelligible or recondite (use of language beyond the ordinary or language that is obscure) is in relationship to speaking well.

9. **E** Although Henry credits Catherine with a satire on modern language, the context of the discussion is about character. That to speak well (with erudition or scholarly learning) is linked to being unintelligible is a ridicule of erudite speakers.

STEP 4. TT → TM (TEST TAKER TO TEST MAKER)

One obvious way to question voice is "The narrator's attitude is ..." followed by a list of adjectives that relate to attitudes, such as the following:

assertive	dictatorial
boisterous	dilatory
bravado	insolent
callous	irascible
censorious	irrational
churlish	optimistic
complaisant	petty
condescending	petulant
derisive	sanctimonious
derogatory	sanguinary

Questions about voice, as you have already experienced, can come from several other directions, including identifying the point of view used and deciding on the identity of the narrator or speaker. Test questions also could ask you to determine just how involved the narrator is with the characters and events of the story. In addition, some structural elements can make good questions, such as when the point of view shifts from third person to first person or when the story shifts in verb tense from, for example, the past to the present. All these elements and many more can affect the voice of a literary work.

Some of these types of questions can be fun to write. Examine this little poem and see where analysis will take you.

Epitaph in Bookish Style

The Body
of
Benjamin Franklin
Line
(5)
(Like the cover of an old book
Its contents torn out
And stript of its lettering and gilding)
Lies here, food for worms.
But the work shall not be lost.
(10)
For it will (as he believed) appear once more
In a new and more elegant edition
Revised and corrected
by
The Author.

Printer

1. Define the form: An epitaph is a short poem intended for a tombstone.

2. Identify the subject: Ben Franklin's dead body

3. Who is speaking? Probably Franklin

Now, paraphrase:

Lines 1–4 and line 8: _____

_____

Lines 5–7: _____

_____

Lines 9–14: _____

_____

Next, turn this analysis into a question over voice. This time, we will give you the answer choices; you provide the question.

Question: _____
(A) fearful
(B) unacceptable
(C) mournful
(D) optimistic
(E) ominous

Correct Answer: **D**

(Possible question: What is the speaker's attitude toward death?)

This poem gives you an opportunity to look at another type of question that is important: the contrast question. Think about the contrast of the two ideas at work here: Franklin's dead body eaten by worms versus life in a new body "more elegant" and "Revised and corrected."

This time you provide the correct answer and one incorrect answer.

The central contrast in this poem is reflected in all the following EXCEPT
(A) old, new
(B) _____, _____
(C) contents torn out, appear once more
(D) _____, _____
(E) stript, Revised

Correct Answer: **B**

For your incorrect answer, you should look for words that represent the contrast. For your correct answer, look for words that do not represent the contrast, such as "old book," "the work."

Extend your thinking with this question: Franklin's poem is an example of shaped verse (lines are shaped to fit the meaning). How does the shape of his "Epitaph" fit its meaning?

NARRATIVE VOICE IN CONCLUSION

The nonnarrative speaker, the narrator, and the writer all have attitudes. The secret to identifying the voice in a work is first to establish clearly who is speaking and what that person is saying. You can then determine the person's attitude. In its broadest sense, voice involves the writing style, the writer's purpose, and the form of the work as it affects our understanding of the speaker's, writer's, or narrator's attitude. This element does not end here, however. The attitudes expressed in a work also give it a tone, the next literary element.

Literary Element Number Four: Tone

Defining elements of tone include the following:

1. The narrator's or speaker's attitude toward the reader and subject
2. The writer's attitude toward the reader and subject
3. A device to develop mood and atmosphere
4. The musical elements (rhyme and rhythm) in literature
5. How a literary selection is supposed to be read aloud, hence, "tone of voice"

Do any of these defining elements sound familiar? Voice and tone are so interrelated that even critics and teachers have difficulty separating and defining them.

Perhaps the best way for you to understand narrative voice and tone in preparation for the test is to concentrate not on separating tone from voice, but rather to focus on their relationship to each other.

One workable relationship is to view tone as a product of voice.

First, identify the voice. Is it the voice of the writer or of a persona (mask) for the writer? If the voice is of a narrator, from what point of view is he or she telling the story? Can the narrator's opinions be trusted? What is the attitude of the speaker or narrator? The writer? How would you characterize the narrator?

Second, determine the tone (of voice). How does the attitude projected by the speaker, narrator, or writer sound? In other words, the attitude of the speaker can cause his or her words to have a certain tone about them.

Example: **He has a dogmatic attitude (voice). It makes him sound overbearing (tone).**

When trying to describe the tone (of voice) used, generally such descriptors as happy, sad, ironic, abstruse, sincere, playful, straightforward, formal, informal, serious, and condescending are used. Usually the tone is described as, for example, "He has a somber tone of voice." In other words, tone answers the question, "How does the literary speaker 'sound' to the listener?" The tone (of voice) sometimes will reveal information about the speaker's opinion of the intelligence and sensitivity of the reader or listener. For example, an adult might use a condescending tone of voice with a child. Even an apology can be turned into further hostility through the tone used. "I beg your pardon" can be sincere words of regret or they can be sarcastically spoken.

IMPORTANT CONCEPT #1: ELEMENTS THAT CONTRIBUTE TO TONE

Concept Explained:

Elements that contribute to making the tone of a work are

1. The speaker or narrator

The speaker has an attitude toward the subject. *How* he or she expresses that attitude projects a tone. If the speaker's attitude is, for example, condemning of those who hunt for sport, his or her tone when describing a hunting scene might influence the readers to regard the act as grisly or morbid. The narrative voice is condemning; the tone is morbid. In contrast, if the speaker's attitude is admiring of hunters, his or her tone when describing a hunting scene might make the act appear adventurous or necessary (for food or protection). The narrative voice is admiring; the tone is exciting.

2. The author

The author also has an attitude toward the subject. How the author expresses that attitude, however, depends upon the relationship of the speaker or narrator to the writer. If the speaker is the author's persona expressing his or her own views, the tone is more likely that expressed by the speaker. When the speaker speaks and acts *in contrast* to the views of the author, this discrepancy or difference in voice creates an ironic tone. Swift's "A Modest Proposal" is an example.

3. The theme or subject

Some themes or subjects carry with them intrinsic elements of tone. For instance, death usually has an unhappy tone and birth generally a happy tone. You should not assume, however, that a work about death is always in a negative tone: The tone is a product of many elements that work together, including the author's intent.

▼Practice Questions▼

Look at this poem written in the mid-1600s.

PEACE

My soul, there is a country
    Far beyond the stars,
Where stands a wingèd sentry
Line   All skilful in the wars;
(5) There above noise, and danger
    Sweet peace sits crowned with smiles,
And one born in a manger
    Commands the beauteous files;
He is thy gracious friend,
(10) And (O, my Soul, awake!)
Did in pure love descend
    To die here for thy sake.
If thou canst get but thither,
    There grows the flower of peace,
(15) The rose that cannot wither,
    Thy fortress, and thy ease;
Leave then thy foolish ranges,
    For none can thee secure,
But one, who never changes,
(20) Thy God, thy life, thy cure.

by Henry Vaughan

The speaker of this poem is
(A) a disembodied spirit
(B) in a dream
(C) in a state of self-contemplation
(D) in astral projection
(E) in a nightmare

The central contrast can be summarized as
(A) waking and sleeping
(B) friends and enemies
(C) love and hate
(D) war and peace
(E) silence and noise

The speaker's
(A) negative attitude toward death sounds discouraging
(B) boisterous attitude toward war sounds dangerous
(C) irascible attitude toward peace sounds contradictory
(D) complaisant attitude toward love sounds tranquil
(E) positive attitude toward peace sounds hopeful

The speaker's attitude toward his own soul gives the poem a sense of
(A) urgency
(B) remorse
(C) ominousness
(D) belligerence
(E) condescendence

Explanation: Lines 1 and 10 tell us that the speaker is talking to his own soul or spiritual self in a state of self-contemplation. What is he thinking? First, he meditates upon a "country /Far beyond the stars." The country has a sentry, "skilful in the wars"—military imagery. The country is "above noise, and danger" (line 5) where there is peace. Lines 7–12 contain a biblical allusion. (We will discuss allusion in more detail in a later chapter.) Context, then, pinpoints a country where the speaker will find his fortress (a symbol of protection from war). The references to "foolish ranges" (line 17) that cannot be secured here in this life again add to the war imagery. The speaker is contrasting war below with the peace above. Of course, such a positive attitude would be hopeful.

There is yet another attitude at work in this poem: the attitude of the speaker toward his own soul. He begins with a rather matter-of-fact tone of self-address in line 1, but he commands his soul to "awake!" in line 10 and to "Leave" in line 17. In conjunction with the hint of uncertainty of "If thou canst get but thither" in line 13, his commanding attitude gives a sense of urgency to the tone of the entire poem.

A concluding thought: Who is the speaker? Is he Vaughan, the poet? Perhaps. However, line 10 commands his soul to "awake!" Is his soul asleep (in death)? Consider this possibility: What if the speaker is a persona for Vaughan? If so, how would you describe him? Could he be someone dying on the field of battle?

Correct Answers: **C, D, E, A**

4. The characters

The characters in a work (what they say and do) and how they are characterized (what is said about them) can significantly influence the tone of a work. The individual temperaments of the characters, how they act and react, what they say and how they say it are all important elements of tone.

▼PRACTICE QUESTIONS▼

Here is an excerpt of dialogue from *The Old Curiosity Shop* by Charles Dickens.

"I can't see anything but the curtain of the bed," said Brass, applying his eye to the keyhole of the door. "Is he a strong man, Mr. Richard [Dick Swiveller]?"

Line   "Very," answered Dick.

(5)   "It would be an extremely unpleasant circumstance if he was to bounce out suddenly," said Brass. "Hallo there! Hallo, hallo!"

While Mr. Brass, with his eye curiously twisted into the keyhole, uttered these sounds as a means of attracting the lodger's attention, and while Miss Brass plied the hand-bell, Mr. Swiveller put his stool

(10)   close against the wall by the side of the door, and mounting on the top and standing bolt upright, began a violent battery with the ruler upon the upper panels of the door.

Suddenly the door was unlocked on the inside and flung violently open. Miss Sally dived into her own bedroom; Mr. Brass, who was not

(15)   remarkable for personal courage, ran into the next street, and finding that nobody followed him, armed with a poker or other offensive weapon, put his hands in his pockets, walked very slowly all at once, and whistled.

Meanwhile Mr. Swiveller, on the top of the stool, drew himself into

(20)   as flat a shape as possible against the wall and looked, not unconcernedly, down upon the single gentleman, who appeared at the door growling and cursing in a very awful manner, and, with the boots in his hand, seemed to have an intention of hurling them downstairs. This idea, however, he abandoned, and he was turning

(25)   into his room again, still growling vengefully, when his eyes met those of the watchful Richard.

"Have you been making that horrible noise?" said the single gentleman.

"I have been helping, sir," returned Dick, keeping his eye upon him.

(30)   "How dare you then," said the lodger. "Eh?"

To this, Dick made no other reply than by inquiring whether the lodger held it to be consistent with the conduct and character of a gentleman to go to sleep for six-and-twenty hours at a stretch, and whether the peace of an amiable and virtuous family was to weigh as

(35)   nothing in the balance.

"Is my peace nothing?" said the single gentleman.

"Yes, sir, indeed," returned Dick, yielding, "but an equal quantity of slumber was never got out of one bed and bedstead, and if you're going to sleep in that way, you must pay for a double-bedded room."

Dick's attitude toward the cost basis of renting a bed is best described as
(A) illogical
(B) reasonable
(C) thoughtful
(D) intuitive
(E) cogent

The incident about the price of a bed has a
(A) fanatic sense
(B) comic tone
(C) preoccupied sense
(D) sagacious tone
(E) tragic tone

Explanation: First, examine the situation. Dick Swiveller, Miss Brass, and Mr. Brass are trying to get the single gentleman's attention. When he opens the door, Miss Brass "dived into her own bedroom," Mr. Brass runs away, then pretends nothing is wrong, and Dick flattens himself against the wall, perhaps instinctively to hide. This *Three Stooges*–type scene is obviously meant to be amusing.

In this context, we have Dick confronting the single gentleman with his complaint. Implied in the scene is that the stranger is a lodger who is paying rent for a single bed. We, at this point, learn Dick's mission in disturbing the man. He objects that the lodger slept for twenty-six hours straight and contends that the bed got so much use that the stranger should "pay for a double-bedded room." Such reasoning is illogical and contributes to the comic tone.

Correct Answers: **A, B**

5. The use of language and meaning of the language in context

How words are used in a selection, the connotations, the figurative language, all contribute directly to setting the tone.

▼PRACTICE QUESTION▼

For example, look at how the meanings of the language in context sets the tone in this excerpt from a communication sent by Benjamin Franklin to Lord Kames of England in April of 1767.

> But America, an immense territory, favored by nature with all advantages of climate, soil, great navigable rivers and lakes, etc., must become a great country, populous and mighty; and will, in a
> Line less time than is generally conceived, be able to shake off any
> (5) shackles that may be imposed on her, and perhaps place them on the imposers. In the meantime, every act of oppression will sour their tempers, lessen greatly, if not annihilate, the profits of your commerce with them, and hasten their final revolt; for the seeds of liberty are universally sown there, and nothing can eradicate them.

Franklin's tone implies all the following EXCEPT
(A) confidence
(B) nerve
(C) rashness
(D) a threat
(E) dauntlessness

Explanation: The context of the communication is the growing resistance of the American colonists to British rule. First, Franklin describes America as "immense ... favored by nature ... a great country, populous and mighty"—in other words, a formidable nation. Then he introduces the element of time and uses figurative language to say that "any shackles ... imposed" on America may eventually be placed "on the imposers"—a very connotatively harsh metaphor that compares Britain's relationship to America as enslavement, and that the slaves may turn and enslave their masters. He then points out that "oppression" might even "annihilate, the profits of your commerce"—a threat to Britain's financial base in America. Again, he links the element of time ("hasten") to the impending "final revolt." He concludes the excerpt with another powerful metaphor comparing liberty to sown seeds that cannot be eradicated (another strongly connotative word).

In the context of the excerpt, what is Franklin's (the speaker's) attitude? Disapproving, unintimidated, one of warning. What is his tone (in what manner does he convey this attitude)? In a threatening tone ... a bold tone ... an uncompromising tone ... a confident tone.

Correct answer: **C**

6. The sound of the language

The rhythm and rhyme also affect the tone of a work, just as they affect the tone of music. This element of language has been referred to as its *tone color* and has been compared to the timbre in music. Just as certain musical selections can make people want to dance and others can give listeners the "blues," the sounds of literary selections (even in prose) can bring to the reader or listener certain tones.

▼Practice Question▼

Taylor uses rhythm, rhyme, alliteration, and other sound devices to contribute to the tone with this excerpt from "Upon a Spider Catching a Fly":

> Thou sorrow, venom elf:
> Is this thy play,
> To spin a web out of thyself
> To catch a fly?
> For why?
>
> I saw a pettish wasp
> Fall foul therein,
> Whom yet thy whorl-pins did not clasp
> Lest he should fling
> His sting.
> ...
> by Edward Taylor

Line
(5)

(10)

The use of couplets and short lines to conclude each stanza makes the speaker sound

(A) rowdy

(B) roguish

(C) cunning

(D) unrestrained

(E) playful

Explanation: His subject is a spider. He observes that a spider spins webs to catch flies, but the spider does not tackle a wasp because of the sting. The speaker may have a very serious meaning behind this observation; however, the sound of the verses (particularly the couplets) is incongruent with a serious attitude. They create a playful tone.

Correct Answer: **E**

7. The setting

TERM ALERT You should know this term: **setting**

Definition: Setting in a literary selection refers to

- Geographical location: Location includes area or region, the general locale, descriptions of architecture, flora and fauna, floor plans, furniture arrangements, weather conditions, and so forth.
- Time: The time may refer to a historical period, time of day, season of the year, projection into the future, period of life (such as the time of "mid-life crisis"), or even a nonexistent time (used extensively in the science fiction genre).
- Socioeconomic conditions: These conditions are revealed, generally, on two different levels: First, there are those conditions and circumstances that relate directly to the characters, including their occupations, family lives, lifestyles, and social interactions. Second, there is the larger society that surrounds and affects the microcosm of the characters. This larger societal structure includes its predominant mores and the general social and work environments.

Although setting is generally associated with narrative writing, some aspects of setting, particularly those of socioeconomic conditions, can affect the tone even in nonnarrative works.

The effects on tone of some settings are dramatic and easy to identify: the romantic tone of a deserted island, the frightening tone of a lonely graveyard on a stormy night, the harsh tone of an inner city ghetto, the warm tone of a family gathering on Christmas Eve. Some, however, are more subtle, changing, or perhaps even unexpected, as when the romantic island becomes a place of fear and hardship when food and water supplies dwindle or when the harsh tone of the inner city ghetto changes to a warm, caring tone as residents join together to overcome their adversities.

IMPORTANT CONCEPT #2: SHADES OF TONE

Concept Explained:

Tone also relates to emotional responses on the part of the writer, characters, narrator/speaker, and to a limited degree, the readers.

TERM ALERT You should know this term: **mood**

Definition: **Mood** refers to an emotional state, especially as projected by the characters in the work: "Joyce is in a foul mood" or "Eric is in a happy mood." Moods, of course, can change (as can many of the other elements of tone) within the work. As the attitude of the author toward the subject is revealed, his or her mood might be seen as self-righteous, defiant, proud, noble, or even reactionary, to name a few. When the author's voice is different from that of the main character or the speaker, the mood might differ from the tone (of voice) used by the author. For example, the mood of the speaker in "A Modest Proposal" (on pages 129–130) could be described as helpful, conciliatory, and serious, but the tone of the author (Swift) is satiric, whose mood (quite possibly) was angry and indignant when he put pen to paper.

Also, attitude and tone can be projected by the mood of the verb used.

Indicative mood is used for making statements or questioning fact (or probable fact).

> **The book is on the desk.**
> **I think that he is here.**
> **Do you own a car?**

The indicative mood is generally neutral; the tone of the speaker's attitude must be determined by other elements, such as connotative word choice.

Imperative mood is used to make direct requests or commands and requires the use of a simple form of the verb. Usually, the subject of the verb is the unspoken "you" or an indefinite pronoun.

> **(You) Stop jumping on the bed.**
> **(Everybody) Follow the path through the woods.**
> **(Somebody) Please help me!**

Because the speaker is making a request or command of someone, the imperative mood of the verb obviously affects the tone of the speaker's words. The verb choice plus the context determine varying degrees of urgency of the request, as well as the speaker's purpose. Does the request have an instructional tone? Is the tone of the command authoritative?

Subjunctive mood is used to make conditional statements of possibility, hypothesis, speculation, wishes, and so forth.

Present subjunctive uses present tense, first- and second-person singular:

> **Should *I be* home to meet him?**
> **The teacher demands that *he stay* late tomorrow.**

Past subjunctive uses the simple past tense. The verb "to be," however, requires "were" regardless of the number (singular, plural) or person (first, second, or third):

> **If *I were* to stay, I might eat too much.**
> **I wish that *he were* here for the holidays.**

A conditional statement can powerfully affect the tone in a variety of ways. It can imply that there is an element of doubt about the situation in question:

> **If Elizabeth were to have left this morning, surely Justin would have told me.**

The subjunctive might suppose that a change in certain conditions would lead to different results:

> **If they were to leave, Georgia Ann would become hysterical.**
> **Unless we were to have a flat tire, we'll be there by seven.**

Longings of the heart, unfulfilled dreams, wishes, suggestions, and indirect requests can all be conveyed using the subjective.

> **If I were a rich woman, I would buy that car.**
> **We recommend that the applicant complete the form quickly because the firm is requesting that her follow-up interview be scheduled for this afternoon.**

Notice the use of "that" in these constructions.

Some uses of the subjunctive mood are so commonplace that they have become cliché. For example: Be that as it may. Far be it from me. If I were in your shoes. So be it.

▼PRACTICE QUESTION▼

These lines are taken from Frances S. Osgood's "To Labor Is to Pray."

> Work,—and pure slumbers shall wait on thy pillow;
> Work,—thou shalt ride o'er Care's coming billow;
> Lie not down 'neath Woe's weeping Willow,
> Work with a stout heart and resolute will!

How does the mood relate to the tone of these lines?
(A) Use of the indicative mood creates a formal tone.
(B) Use of the subjunctive mood creates a stressful tone.
(C) Use of the subjunctive creates a wishful tone.
(D) Use of the imperative mood creates an uncertain tone.
(E) Use of the imperative mood creates an urgent tone.

Explanation: These lines are a series of commands with an understood subject. In this case, the commands add a sense of urgency.

Correct Answer: **E**

TERM ALERT You should know this term: **feeling**

Definition: **Feeling** has been defined as an intellectual state: the attitude of the author toward his subject on an intellectual rather than on an emotional basis. Conversationally, this might be approached with the question, "What is your *feeling* on the subject?" to which the respondent would express his or her views.

TERM ALERT You should know this term: **atmosphere**

Definition: The setting, the tone (of voice) of the author and speaker, the emotional moods of the author, the speaker, and/or the characters, and the feelings of the author blend together to give the work its **atmosphere**—that prevailing and pervasive ambience that gives the reader the basis for expectation.

Atmosphere is often described using such terms as "mysterious," "romantic," "gloomy," "horrifying," "intellectual," and other expressions depicting these types of effects. When movie critics label a motion picture as a "feel-good movie," they are referring to its atmosphere.

What follows is Edgar Allan Poe's "The Raven" in its entirety. Teachers, critics, and anthology editors for generations have pointed to "The Raven" as an American classic because of its distinctive use of rhythm, rhyme, and alliterative elements that contribute to its tone.

First, read the poem for enjoyment. Notice the use of internal rhyme: "dreary" and "weary"; "napping," "tapping," and "rapping"; "remember," "December," and "ember"; "morrow," "sorrow," and "borrow." In the third stanza, listen to the effects of "silken, sad, uncertain rustling." But how do these elements work together to give the poem its atmosphere? How would you describe the atmosphere of "The Raven?"

THE RAVEN

Stanza:

1 Once upon a midnight dreary, while I pondered, weak and weary,
    Over many a quaint and curious volume of forgotten lore,
While I nodded, nearly napping, suddenly there came a tapping,
    As of some one gently rapping, rapping at my chamber door.
"'Tis some visitor," I muttered, "tapping at my chamber door—
    Only this and nothing more."

2 Ah, distinctly I remember it was in the bleak December,
    And each separate dying ember wrought its ghost upon the floor.
Eagerly I wished the morrow; vainly I had sought to borrow
    From my books surcease of sorrow—sorrow for the lost Lenore,
For the rare and radiant maiden whom the angels name Lenore—
    Nameless *here* for evermore.

3 And the silken, sad, uncertain rustling of each purple curtain
    Thrilled me—filled me with fantastic terrors never felt before;
So that now, to still the beating of my heart, I stood repeating,
    "'Tis some visitor entreating entrance at my chamber door—
Some late visitor entreating entrance at my chamber door—
    This it is and nothing more."

4 Presently my soul grew stronger: hesitating then no longer,
    "Sir," said I, "or Madam, truly your forgiveness I implore;
But the fact is I was napping, and so gently you came rapping,
    And so faintly you came tapping, tapping at my chamber door,
That I scarce was sure I heard you"—here I opened wide the door—
    Darkness there and nothing more.

5 Deep into that darkness peering, long I stood there, wondering, fearing,
    Doubting, dreaming dreams no mortal ever dared to dream before;
But the silence was unbroken, and the stillness gave no token,
    And the only word there spoken was the whispered word "Lenore!"
This I whispered, and an echo murmured back the word "Lenore!"
    Merely this and nothing more.

6   Back into the chamber turning, all my soul within me burning,
        Soon again I heard a tapping, somewhat louder than before.
     "Surely," said I, "surely that is something at my window lattice;
        Let me see, then, what thereat is, and this mystery explore—
     Let my heart be still a moment and this mystery explore—
        'Tis the wind and nothing more."

7   Open here I flung the shutter, when, with many a flirt and flutter,
        In there stepped a stately Raven of the saintly days of yore.
     Not the least obeisance made he, not a minute stopped or stayed he,
        But with mien of lord or lady perched above my chamber door—
     Perched upon a bust of Pallas just above my chamber door—
        Perched and sat, and nothing more.

8   Then, this ebony bird beguiling my sad fancy into smiling
        By the grave and stern decorum of the countenance it wore,
     "Though thy crest be shorn and shaven, thou," I said, "art sure no craven,
        Ghastly, grim, and ancient Raven, wandering from the nightly shore:
     Tell me what thy lordly name is on the night's Plutonian shore!"
        Quoth the Raven, "Nevermore."

9   Much I marveled this ungainly fowl to hear discourse so plainly,
        Though its answer little meaning, little relevancy bore;
     For we cannot help agreeing that no living human being
        Ever yet was blessed with seeing bird above his chamber door—
     Bird or beast upon the sculptured bust above his chamber door—
        With such name as "Nevermore."

10   But the Raven, sitting lonely on the placid bust, spoke only
        That one word, as if his soul in that one word he did outpour.
     Nothing further then he uttered, not a feather then he fluttered;
        Till I scarcely more than muttered, "Other friends have flown before:
     On the morrow he will leave me, as my hopes have flown before."
        Then the bird said, "Nevermore."

11   Startled at the stillness broken by reply so aptly spoken,
        "Doubtless," said I, "what it utters is its only stock and store,
     Caught from some unhappy master whom unmerciful Disaster
        Followed fast and followed faster till his songs one burden bore,
     Till the dirges of his hope that melancholy burden bore
        Of 'Never—nevermore.'"

12   But the Raven still beguiling my sad fancy into smiling,
        Straight I wheeled a cushioned seat in front of bird and bust and door;
     Then, upon the velvet sinking, I betook myself to linking
        Fancy unto fancy, thinking what this ominous bird of yore,
     What this grim, ungainly, ghastly, gaunt, and ominous bird of yore
        Meant in croaking "Nevermore."

13   This I sat engaged in guessing, but no syllable expressing
        To the fowl, whose fiery eyes now burned into my bosom's core;
     This and more I sat divining, with my head at ease reclining
        On the cushion's velvet lining that the lamplight gloated o'er,
     But whose velvet-violet lining with the lamplight gloating o'er,
        She shall press, ah, nevermore!

14   Then, methought, the air grew denser, perfumed from an unseen censer
        Swung by seraphim whose foot-falls tinkled on the tufted floor.
     "Wretch," I cried, "thy God hath lent thee—by these angels he hath sent thee
        Respite—respite and nepenthe from thy memories of Lenore!
     Quaff, oh quaff this kind nepenthe, and forget this lost Lenore!"
        Quoth the Raven, "Nevermore."

15   "Prophet!" said I, "thing of evil! prophet still, if bird or devil!
        Whether Tempter sent, or whether tempest tossed thee here ashore,
     Desolate yet all undaunted, on this desert land enchanted—
        On this home by Horror haunted—tell me truly, I implore:
     Is there—is there balm in Gilead?—tell me—tell me, I implore!"
        Quoth the Raven, "Nevermore."

16   "Prophet!" said I, "thing of evil—prophet still, if bird or devil!
        By that Heaven that bends above us, by that God we both adore,
     Tell this soul with sorrow laden if, within the distant Aidenn,
        It shall clasp a sainted maiden whom the angels name Lenore:
     Clasp a rare and radiant maiden whom the angels name Lenore!"
        Quoth the Raven, "Nevermore."

17   "Be that word our sign of parting, bird or fiend!" I shrieked, upstarting:
        "Get thee back into the tempest and the Night's Plutonian shore!
     Leave no black plume as a token of that lie thy soul hath spoken!
        Leave my loneliness unbroken! quit the bust above my door!
     Take thy beak from out my heart, and take thy form from off my door!"
        Quoth the Raven, "Nevermore."

18   And the Raven, never flitting, still is sitting, *still* is sitting
        On the pallid bust of Pallas just above my chamber door;
     And his eyes have all the seeming of a demon's that is dreaming,
        And the lamp-light o'er him streaming throws his shadow on the floor;
     And my soul from out that shadow that lies floating on the floor
        Shall be lifted—nevermore!

                                                        by Edgar Allan Poe

   Now examine the poem for some of the elements of tone (of voice) and narrative voice
that have been discussed. These questions can help you prepare for the types of questions
about voice, tone, and atmosphere that might appear on the SAT Subject Test in Literature.

   1. "I" can best be described as _____

   _____.

2. The attitude of "I" toward Lenore is best described as _____

_____.

3. The attitude of "I" toward the raven changes from _____ to

_____ in the poem.

4. The attitude of the author toward the speaker is best described as _____

_____.

5. The attitude of "I" toward the unknown visitor is best described as _____

_____ in Stanza 4.

6. What changes in tone are introduced in the twelfth stanza? _____

_____

7. How does the theme influence the tone? _____

_____

8. How does the setting influence the tone? _____

_____

9. The speaker's tone suggests that the raven is _____

_____.

10. The tone of the speaker in the second stanza is best described as _____.

11. The tone of the speaker in the eighth stanza is best described as _____.

12. The tone of the speaker in the fifteenth stanza is best described as _____.

13. The tone of the speaker in the last stanza is best described as _____.

14. What is the tone of the entire poem? _____

Finally, look at the structural elements as they relate to tone and atmosphere.

1. Examine the rhyme scheme. What is its effect on the atmosphere? _____

_____

2. Examine the rhythm. How does it affect the atmosphere? _____

_____

3. Alliteration and assonance refer to the repetition of consonant and vowel sounds, respectively. How does the use of alliteration and assonance affect the atmosphere of this work? _____

Keep these answers to use later in the chapter.

IMPORTANT CONCEPT #3: STYLE

Concept Explained:

Style is how the writer uses the literary elements to express his or her attitude.

Although a writer may try to emulate another author's style, like snowflakes, no two writers' styles are *exactly* alike. The labels readers place on a particular writer's style can be based on a wide range of factors. For example, you might associate the style of a writer with his or her purpose (a scientific style, a journalistic style, a didactic style). Sometimes a writer consistently works in the same genre and one comes to describe his or her style based on that genre (a romantic style or a swashbuckler style). If a writer tries to emulate the work of a particular literary period, school, or favorite writer, you might label the style accordingly (a Shakespearean style, a New Formalism style). Also, readers tend to label the style of a writer based on their overall impression of the "sense" they get of elements that are generally consistent throughout that particular author's work. You might label his or her writing style as imaginative (or unimaginative), exciting (or dull), sensitive (or insensitive). Once a writer has established a recognizable style, readers tend to examine each of his or her new works to see how it measures against their perception of his or her style. Readers then talk about whether the new work is consistent with or is a departure from the writer's "style."

▼PRACTICE QUESTIONS▼

THE BERLIN CRISIS
by
John F. Kennedy

Seven weeks ago tonight I returned from Europe to report on my meeting with Premier Khrushchev and the others. His grim warnings about the future of the world, his aide-mémoire on Berlin, his
Line subsequent speeches and threats which he and his agents have
(5) launched, and the increase in the Soviet military budget that he has announced have all prompted a series of decisions by the administration and a series of consultations with the members of the NATO organization. In Berlin, as you recall, he intends to bring to an end, through a stroke of the pen, first our legal rights to be in
(10) West Berlin and secondly our ability to make good on our commitment to the two million free people of that city. That we cannot permit...

West Berlin is 110 miles within the area which the Soviets now dominate—which is immediately controlled by the so-called East
(15) German regime.... We are there as a result of our victory over Nazi Germany—and our basic rights to be there deriving from that victory include both our presence in West Berlin and the enjoyment of access across East Germany. These rights have been repeatedly confirmed and recognized in special agreements with the Soviet
(20) Union. Berlin is not a part of East Germany but a separate territory under the control of the allied powers. Thus our rights there are clear and deep-rooted. But in addition to those rights is our commitment to sustain—and defend, if need be—the opportunity for more than two

(25) million people to determine their own future and choose their own way of life.

Thus, our presence in West Berlin, and our access thereto, cannot be ended by any act of the Soviet government. The NATO shield was long ago extended to cover West Berlin—and we have given our word that an attack in that city will be regarded as an attack upon (30) us all.

For West Berlin—lying exposed 110 miles inside East Germany, surrounded by Soviet troops and close to Soviet supply lines—has many roles. It is more than a showcase of liberty, a symbol, an island of freedom in a Communist sea. It is even more than a link (35) with the Free World, a beacon of hope behind the Iron Curtain, an escape hatch for refugees.

West Berlin is all of that. But above all it has now become— as never before—the great testing place of Western courage and will, a focal point where our solemn commitments stretching back over the (40) years since 1945 and Soviet ambitions now meet in basic confrontation.

It would be a mistake for others to look upon Berlin, because of its location, as a tempting target. The United States is there; the United Kingdom and France are there; the pledge of NATO is there—and (45) the people of Berlin are there. It is as secure, in that sense, as the rest of us—for we cannot separate its safety from our own....

We do not want to fight, but we have fought before. And others in earlier times have made the same dangerous mistake of assuming that the West was too selfish and too soft and too divided to resist (50) invasions of freedom in other lands. Those who threaten to unleash the forces of war on a dispute over West Berlin should recall the words of the ancient philosopher: "A man who causes fear cannot be free from fear."...

So long as the Communists insist that they are preparing to end by (55) themselves unilaterally our rights in West Berlin and our commitments to its people, we must be prepared to defend those rights and those commitments. We will at all times be ready to talk, if talk will help. But we must also be ready to resist with force, if force is used upon us. Either alone would fail. Together, they can serve the cause of (60) freedom and peace...

Thus, in the days and months ahead, I shall not hesitate to ask the Congress for additional measures or exercise any of the executive powers that I possess to meet this threat to peace. Everything essential to the security of freedom must be done; and if that should (65) require more men, or more taxes, or more controls, or other new powers, I shall not hesitate to ask them. The measures proposed today will be constantly studied and altered as necessary. But while we will not let panic shape our policy, neither will we permit timidity to direct our program.

Answer these questions:

1. What is the subject? _____

2. What is the resulting tone? _____

3. What is Kennedy's attitude toward the subject? _____

4. What is the resulting tone? _____

5. What is his message to
   a. the world community? _____
   b. the Communist powers? _____
   c. the American people? _____

6. What is the tone of his message to
   a. the world community? _____
   b. the Communist powers? _____
   c. the American people? _____

7. How would you describe his style? _____

First, the reader should look at how the subject affects the tone of this speech. The subject? The threat of war. The resulting tone? Serious, urgent, grave.

Next, look at the speaker's attitude toward the subject and his attitude toward his listeners to see how the tone is affected. His attitude toward the subject? America is justified in resisting the threats made against West Berlin. The resulting tone? Confident, resolved.

The president has essentially three groups of listeners to this speech: the world community (who are poised, listening to see what America and the American president will do), Communist powers (particularly Premier Khrushchev), and the American people. To the world community he points out that he recognizes West Berlin as "the great testing place of Western courage and will"—a matter of "commitment"; however, he also forms psychological alliance with much of the free world. To the Communists and Khrushchev he sends the message: "We have fought before." To the American people he gives assurances ("We will at all times be ready to talk, if talk will help"); he prepares Americans for the possibility of war ("But we must also be ready to resist with force, if force is used upon us") and for the sacrifices that might be ahead ("more men…more taxes…more controls…"). His attitude toward his listeners? He seems to view the world community as both spectators and (particularly NATO, the United Kingdom, and France) as allies, the Communist regime as a threat, and the American people as needing to know where they stand. The resulting tone? Responsible (to the world community), brave, unflinching (to the Communist aggressors), forthright (to the American people).

Because he is speaking to three different audiences—three groups of listeners—he uses elements of style to facilitate his message, to communicate three distinct messages to three different groups without ever addressing his remarks directly to any one of them. President Kennedy uses several stylistic devices to accomplish this: two will be examined here.

In comparing the first and second paragraphs, the speaker's style

(A) remains constant

(B) shifts slightly to suit his audience and purpose

(C) becomes more formal

(D) loses focus

(E) becomes didactic

Explanation: Notice in the first paragraph the sentence "His grim warnings…have all prompted a series of decisions…." The syntax of this sentence cannot be closed until almost the end of the sentence. Use of this style in the first paragraph establishes a formal tone in which he introduces the gravity of his topic to all three audiences simultaneously. In the second paragraph, however, he changes (particularly in the first and second sentences) to a more loosely joined construction that could have a period before the end of the sentence and still be complete in terms of syntax. The more relaxed style helps to shift the focus as he explains to the world community in a more conversational tone why America is justified in its position in West Berlin. His subtle use of syntax helps to change the tone.

Correct Answer: **B**

Also, most of the speech is written in a style using subordinate phrases, clauses, and conjunctions that establish relationships (often cause and effect). At precise times, however, he quite effectively changes to a style using no subordination or conjunctions other than perhaps *and* between sentences). For example, notice the effect of his use of both styles in this paragraph:

> It would be a mistake for others to look upon Berlin, because of its location, as a tempting target. The United States is there; the United Kingdom and France are there; the pledge of NATO is there—and
> Line the people of Berlin are there. It is as secure, in that sense, as the
> (5)   rest of us—for we cannot separate its safety from our own….

As you can see, the speaker in this speech uses *subtle* changes in his use of stylistic elements to alter his tone to convey the message to the intended audiences more effectively.

Based upon the speaker's tone, the listener should consider Soviet intentions to be
(A) amusing and trivial
(B) aggressive and threatening
(C) committed and respectable
(D) uncontrollable and unstoppable
(E) inevitable and ambitious

Of the following statements, all are true of the context of this speech except that the
(A) message is intended to inform the American people
(B) speaker is unintimidated
(C) purpose is to state America's position in the conflict
(D) last two paragraphs suggest that peaceful resolutions are possible
(E) tone is mocking

When the speaker says, "We do not want to fight, but we have fought before," his tone can be described as
(A) disinterested
(B) disrespectful
(C) intrepid
(D) offensive
(E) pusillanimous

Correct Answers: **B, E,** and **C**

▼PRACTICE QUESTIONS▼

IVANHOE
by
Sir Walter Scott

In that pleasant district of merry England which is watered by the
river Don, there extended in ancient times a large forest, covering
the greater part of the beautiful hills and valleys which lie between
Line   Sheffield and the pleasant town of Doncaster. The remains of this
(5)   extensive wood are still to be seen at the noble seats of Wentworth,
of Wharncliffe Park, and around Rotherham. Here haunted of yore
the fabulous Dragon of Wantley; here were fought many of the most
desperate battles during the Civil Wars of the Roses; and here also
flourished in ancient times those bands of gallant outlaws whose
(10)   deeds have been rendered so popular in English song.

Such being our chief scene, the date of our story refers to a
period towards the end of the reign of Richard I., when his return
from his long captivity had become an event rather wished than
hoped for by his despairing subjects, who were in the meantime
(15)   subjected to every species of subordinate oppression. The nobles,
whose power had become exorbitant during the reign of Stephen,
and whom the prudence of Henry the Second had scarce reduced
into some degree of subjection to the crown, had now resumed their
ancient license in its utmost extent; despising the feeble interference
(20)   of the English Council of State, fortifying their castles, increasing the
number of their dependants, reducing all around them to a state of
vassalage, and striving by every means in their power to place
themselves each at the head of such forces as might enable him to
make a figure in the national convulsions which appeared to be
(25)   impending.

The situation of the inferior gentry, or franklins, as they were
called, who, by the law and spirit of the English constitution, were
entitled to hold themselves independent of feudal tyranny, became
now unusually precarious. If, as was most generally the case, they
(30)   placed themselves under the protection of any of the petty kings in
their vicinity, accepted of feudal offices in his household, or bound
themselves, by mutual treaties of alliance and protection, to support
him in his enterprises, they might indeed purchase temporary repose;
but it must be with the sacrifice of that independence which was so
(35)   dear to every English bosom, and at the certain hazard of being
involved as a party in whatever rash expedition the ambition of their
protector might lead him to undertake. On the other hand, such and
so multiplied were the means of vexation and oppression possessed
by the great barons, that they never wanted the pretext, and seldom
(40)   the will, to harass and pursue, even to the very edge of destruction,
any of their less powerful neighbours who attempted to separate
themselves from their authority, and to trust for their protection,

during the dangers of the times, to their own inoffensive conduct and
to the laws of the land.

(45)   A circumstance which greatly tended to enhance the tyranny of the
nobility and the sufferings of the inferior classes arose from the
consequences of the Conquest by Duke William of Normandy. Four
generations had not sufficed to blend the hostile blood of the
Normans and Anglo-Saxons, or to unite, by common language and
(50) mutual interests, two hostile races, one of which still felt the elation of
triumph, while the other groaned under all the consequences of
defeat. The power had been completely placed in the hands of the
Norman nobility by the event of the battle of Hastings, and it had
been used, as our histories assure us, with no moderate hand. The
(55) whole race of Saxon princes and nobles had been extirpated or
disinherited, with few or no exceptions; nor were the numbers great
who possessed land in the country of their fathers, even as
proprietors of the second or of yet inferior classes. The royal policy
had long been to weaken, by every means, legal or illegal, the
(60) strength of a part of the population which was justly considered as
nourishing the most inveterate antipathy to their victor. All the
monarchs of the Norman race had shown the most marked
predilection for their Norman subjects; the laws of the chase, and
many others, equally unknown to the milder and more free spirit of
(65) the Saxon constitution, had been fixed upon the necks of the
subjugated inhabitants, to add weight, as it were, to the feudal
chains with which they were loaded. At court, and in the castles of
the great nobles, where the pomp and state of a court was
emulated, Norman-French was the only language employed; in
(70) courts of law, the pleadings and judgments were delivered in the
same tongue. In short, French was the language of honour, of
chivalry, and even of justice, while the far more manly and
expressive Anglo-Saxon was abandoned to the use of rustics and
hinds, who knew no other. Still, however, the necessary intercourse
(75) between the lords of the soil, and those oppressed inferior beings by
whom that soil was cultivated, occasioned the gradual formation of a
dialect, compounded betwixt the French and the Anglo-Saxon, in
which they could render themselves mutually intelligible to each
other; and from this necessity arose by degrees the structure of our
(80) present English language, in which the speech of the victors and the
vanquished have been so happily blended together; and which has
since been so richly improved by importations from the classical
languages, and from those spoken by the southern nations of
Europe.

(85)   This state of things I have thought it necessary to premise for the
information of the general reader, who might be apt to forget that,
although no great historical events, such as war or insurrection, mark
the existence of the Anglo-Saxon as a separate people subsequent
to the reign of William the Second, yet the great national distinctions
(90) betwixt them and their conquerors, the recollection of what they had

(95) formerly been, and to what they were now reduced, continued, down to the reign of Edward the Third, to keep open the wounds which the Conquest had inflicted, and to maintain a line of separation betwixt the descendants of the victor Normans and the vanquished Saxons.

What is the setting? _____

Describe the social conditions: _____

What is the narrator's opinion of the social conditions? _____

_____

That opinion makes the tone of the selection seem _____

The tone of the first paragraph
(A) is unnecessary to the story
(B) contrasts to the second paragraph
(C) is continued in the second paragraph
(D) conflicts with the narrator's point
(E) is critical

The overall style of this selection relies heavily upon
(A) lively dialogue
(B) figurative language
(C) romance
(D) connotative word choices
(E) journalistic technique

Explanation: This first-person narrative excerpt is setting the scene for the story. The scene is England "toward the end of the reign of Richard I" when nobles had "exorbitant" power over the people. Such social conditions create a tone that is serious. What is the narrator's tone of voice regarding the subject? He does not refrain from connotative word choices that *editorialize*—revealing his opinion of the conditions in England at the time: outlaws described as "gallant," "despairing subjects," "oppression," "despising the feeble interference of the English Council of State," "reducing all around them to a state of vassalage" (the position of a vassal being subservient to the feudal lord). The resulting tone? a condemnatory tone toward the nobles. (Also, the speaker refers to the position of the independence of franklins, the inferior gentry, as "now unusually precarious"—giving the reader a sense of anticipation of trouble ahead.) This condemnatory tone is extended to include the speaker's opinion of the Norman-French in racial terms. In this regard, the speaker describes, in a rather patriotic tone, the Saxon constitution as "milder and more free spent" and the Anglo-Saxon tongue as "more manly and expressive," as compared to Norman-French.

The narrator has invested significant effort in establishing the tone of the setting in its historical context, giving the reader reason to *anticipate* that the focus of the narrative is on, not exclusively the characters, but also on how the events of the time and place (as they are historically significant) affect the lives of the characters and how, in turn, the lives of the characters may (or may fail to) affect historical events and outcomes.

In examining the style of the narrative, you will find that the writer uses some figurative language, but relies heavily upon connotative word choices, particularly in the contrast of the tone established in the first paragraph (the tone projected by the description of a beautiful place of fabulous events) with the following paragraphs (the tone projected by introduction of a blight imposed upon that beautiful place by hated conquerors).

Correct Answers: **B, D**

▼PRACTICE QUESTION▼

Now read the following excerpt from *The Scarlet Letter* by Nathaniel Hawthorne:

> The Grass Plot before the jail, in Prison Lane, on a certain summer morning, not less than two centuries ago, was occupied by a pretty large number of the inhabitants of Boston; all with their eyes intently
> Line fastened on the iron-clamped oaken door. Amongst any other
> (5) population, or at a later period in the history of New England, the grim rigidity that petrified the bearded physiognomies of these good people would have augured some awful business in hand. It could have betokened nothing short of the anticipated execution of some noted culprit, on whom the sentence of a legal tribunal had but
> (10) confirmed the verdict of public sentiment. But, in that early severity of the Puritan character, an inference of this kind could not so indubitably be drawn. It might be that a sluggish bond-servant, or an undutiful child, whom his parents had given over to the civil authority, was to be corrected at the whipping-post. It might be, that
> (15) an Antinomian, a Quaker, or other heterodox religionist, was to be scourged out of the town, or an idle and vagrant Indian, whom the white man's fire-water had made riotous about the streets, was to be driven with stripes into the shadow of the forest. It might be, too, that a witch, like old Mistress Hibbins, the bitter-tempered widow of
> (20) the magistrate, was to die upon the gallows. In either case, there was very much the same solemnity of demeanour on the part of the spectators; as befitted a people amongst whom religion and law were almost identical, and in whose character both were so thoroughly interfused, that the mildest and the severest acts of
> (25) public discipline were alike made venerable and awful. Meagre, indeed, and cold, was the sympathy that a transgressor might look for, from such bystanders at the scaffold. On the other hand, a penalty which, in our days, would infer a degree of mocking infamy and ridicule, might then be invested with almost as stern a dignity as
> (30) the punishment of death itself.

Which of the pairs of adjectives below identifies the tone of the passage?
(A) Lively and sporting
(B) Solemn and entreating
(C) Resentful and challenging
(D) Ominous and foreboding
(E) Respectful and encouraging

Explanation: The use of structure is important to the tone of this work. The narrator reveals the character of the people first by comparison and contrast: morbid preoccupation with the jail by another people would have been precipitated by "the anticipated execution of some noted culprit," but these people—*these* people would be drawn to the jail for a glimpse of the punishment of someone for any of a number of much lesser crimes. The list of things they deem worthy of such punishment defines the values and character of this group of people.

"Their eyes intently fastened on the iron-clamped oaken door" causes us to picture a silent, grim mob staring to see the criminal's fate. The list of crimes and the consequences that might have been the cause of the people's interest in the jail makes the reader picture horrific scenes of whippings, scourgings, and hangings. Use of such descriptive words as "Meagre, indeed, and cold, was the sympathy" and "the grim rigidity that petrified the bearded physiognomies" makes the reader picture stony faces inflicting pain in an unyielding manner. What is Hawthorne's style in this excerpt? He *makes the reader picture the scene* using a blend of structural and connotative devices including character revelation. The result is a distinctive tone or atmosphere.

Correct Answer **D**

IMPORTANT CONCEPT #4: SOUND EFFECTS

Concept Explained:

One element that has significant impact on the tone of a work is the sound of the language.

One needs to look no further than the limerick to probe the effect of rhythm and rhyme on tone. Meaning is at the root of a limerick's humorous impact (its funny tone), but the impact of the rhythm and rhyme scheme on its tone cannot be denied:

THERE WAS A YOUNG FELLOW NAMED HALL

There was a young fellow named Hall,
Who fell in the spring in the fall;
'Twould have been a sad thing
If he'd died in the spring,
But he didn't—he died in the fall.

Line
(5)

Anon.

Also look to nursery rhymes for tones set by rhythm and rhyme. These musical rhythms and easy-to-complete rhymes create a wide range of tones (ranging from comforting to scary) that captivate children's attention:

I HAD A LITTLE NUT TREE

I had a little nut tree,
Nothing would it bear
But a silver nutmeg
And a golden pear;
The King of Spain's daughter
Came to visit me,
And all for the sake
Of my little nut tree.

Line
(5)

▼**PRACTICE QUESTION**▼

Here is "That Sound," written by L. E. Myers.

What fun camping out—
  Wild animals all about.
Then it gets dark
  In the National Park.

Line

(5)   And after all are fed,
  You're tired and ready for bed.
The tents are all in a row
  And into bed you all go.

(10)   You hear that sound
  And out of bed you bound.
It's still quite early—
  Only about four-thirty.

That sound came from who-o-o
(15)   Just in time to scare you.
A quivering sound that's eerie;
  The dark makes you leery.

The others hear it, too—
  That same sound that scared you.
(20)   Please try to identify
  That strange and scary cry.

The tone of this poem is NOT the result of
(A) figurative language
(B) the subject
(C) the intended audience
(D) style
(E) rhyme scheme

Explanation: Obviously intended to entertain children, this riddle poem (describing campers encountering an owl) uses a style appropriate to the audience (simple words and sentence structure), as well as an uncomplicated rhyme scheme that keeps the emphasis on the subject –a mysterious sound in the woods.

Correct Answer: **A**

In songs, ballads, and other styles of poetry set to music, the tone is influenced greatly by the arrangement of the music itself. Examples include the emotional impact of rhythm and blues, the playful tone of the English children's ballad, "The Fox Went Out on a Chilly Night," the agitated tone in some rap music, the humorous tone in country and western's "Tennessee Bird Walk," the hauntingly sad tone of Patsy Cline singing "I Fall to Pieces," the serious tone of a tragic opera, the inspiring tone of a gospel song, and the reverent tone of a hymn like "Amazing Grace."

Poems not intended to be sung, however, can also rely on verbal and musical elements to project a tone. There is more to the "sound" of a poem as it relates to the tone it projects than just rhythm and rhyme. Tone in a poem is also a product of *sound effects* (their uses and tonal qualities). Here are a few of the more commonly found sound effects:

ERM ALERT You should know this term: **onomatopoeia**

Definition: Onomatopoeia refers to words, lines, and passages whose sound, size, movement, and overall effect denote the sense or meaning. The sounds work together to carry the meaning. Tennyson's *The Princess* ("Come Down, O Maid"—1847):

> "...The moan of doves in immemorial elms,
> And murmuring of innumerable bees."

Notice how, in this first stanza of a poem written by Robert Burns in the late eighteenth century, the sounds work together to carry its meaning and to establish the tone:

AFTON WATER

> Flow gently, sweet Afton, among thy green braes,
> Flow gently, I'll sing thee a song in thy praise;
> My Mary's asleep by thy murmuring stream,
> Flow gently, sweet Afton, disturb not her dream.

by Robert Burns

The sounds here seem to have a "feel" about them that relates to the meaning and results in a tone.

Phonic echo devices

There are three major devices in which sound repeats or "echoes":

ERM ALERT You should know this term: **alliteration**

Definition: Alliteration occurs when the initial consonant or consonant cluster sounds in stressed syllables are repeated (generally in successive or closely associated stressed syllables).

> Lo, how I hold mine arms abroad,
> Thee to receive ready yspread!

In its more extreme form, alliteration becomes the tongue twister "Peter Piper picked a peck of pickled peppers" and "She sells sea-shells by the sea-shore." Alliteration is used by the broadcast media as an attention-getting device, by advertisers to help a slogan stay in the consumer's mind, and by writers in general to lighten material that might otherwise be dry or boring. For example, a newspaper might use "The Top Ten Terrific Tomatoes to Try This Time for Your Texas Territory" to head a variety and region chart for growing tomatoes in Texas. A jingle for a new car wash named "Curly Carl's" that is in competition with "Sudsy Sam" might be

> Curly Carl can keep your car,
> Scrubbed, sparkling like a star.
> No scuffs, no scum, no scrapes, no scratches,
> So Sudsy Sam still tries to match us.

Once again, the sounds have a "feel" that relates to the meaning and results in a tone.

TERM ALERT You should know this term: **assonance**

Definition: Assonance occurs when the same (or similar) vowel sounds are repeated in nearby words (usually in stressed syllables). Unlike rhyme, which has similarity of both vowel and final consonant sounds (for example, "book" and "took"), assonance repeats only the vowel sounds and ends with different consonant sounds. Notice the use of elements of rhyme, alliteration ("w"), and assonance in this anonymous ballad:

HELEN OF KIRCONNELL

I wish I were where Helen lies,
Night and day on me she cries;
O that I were where Helen lies
On fair Kirconnell lea!

"I" and "night" both contain the long i sound. This assonance is emphasized in the rhyme of "lies" with "cries." You also may find assonance a popular substitution for end rhyme, especially in the ballad form:

His hounds they lie downe at his *feete*,
So well they can their master *keepe*.

TERM ALERT You should know this term: **consonance**

Definition: Consonance occurs when final consonant sounds of stressed syllables are repeated but the preceding vowels are different. Consonance is often used in conjunction with alliteration (as in *reader* and *rider*); however, initial alliteration is not always a factor (as in *learn*, *torn*). The aural appeal can be heard in George Wither's use of consonance in the last stanza of "Shall I Wasting in Despair" in which *d, r, v, l,* and *t* are repeated:

Great, or good, or kind, or fair,
I will ne'er the more despair,
If she love me, this believe,
I will die, ere she shall grieve.
If she slight me when I woo,
I can scorn, and let her go.
For, if she be not for me,
What care I for whom she be?

(Note also that the basis for "eye rhyme" often is consonance: *gone, stone.*)

TERM ALERT You should know these terms: **cacophony** and **dissonance**

Definition: Both terms refer to harshness of sounds that produce an unpleasant or unsettling tone. A sound has dissonance when it is harsh, inharmonious, or discordant with the sounds and rhythm that surround it. A sound has cacophony when it is simply harsh in and of itself, regardless of the sounds and rhythms that surround it. Cacophony is often an accident; dissonance, on the other hand (discordance with surrounding sounds and rhythms), can be very deliberate.

Note the conscious use of dissonance in "Broken-Down Car":

> A budget bruised, bent blistered broken relic needin' fixin'.
> Dented dimpled dinges from fender benders galore—grief over
> > grime and time.

> Line   Courage: There goes cash on four tires.
> (5)   Frame and bumpers lookin' good—not me still under hood.

> Clank...grind...bang...grime grating against metal and skin.
> Squirting oil and squirming torso—pain.

> Start and stop motor again—not a gain, sorry mess
> Headin' for the Junk-heap next, I guess.

by C. Myers-Shaffer

Cacophony, harsh sounds (words) that are unpleasant in and of themselves, can result from many things, such as too many unvoiced plosives in a poem. Some poets feel that overuse of *s* or *sh* sounds have a cacophonic effect and consequently try to avoid them.

TERM ALERT You should know this term: **euphony**

Definition: Euphony refers to sounds that are pleasing and easy to pronounce, producing a pleasant tone. Sounds exhibiting euphony (the opposite of cacophony) generally contain more vowel sounds. Poetry exhibiting euphony tends also to avoid difficult-to-pronounce sound combinations and to stress sound patterns that include repetitions.

In determining the euphony of a selection, its sense of a pleasing tone, do not overlook the part meaning sometimes contributes to that sense of pleasantness. One poem that many consider "pleasant" to the tongue and ear is "The Raven," although the tone is very disquieting.

▼PRACTICE QUESTIONS▼

Return to "The Raven" and your analysis beginning on page 155 to answer these questions.

The mood of the poem is best described as
(A) sad, yet hopeful
(B) a reflection of the speaker's grief
(C) influenced by Lenore's return
(D) constant throughout the work
(E) based on the role of the bird

The atmosphere of much of the poem is
(A) relaxed
(B) artificial
(C) desperate
(D) homey
(E) celebrative

Stanza 5, lines 1–2, contain all the following EXCEPT
(A) alliteration
(B) assonance
(C) consonance
(D) internal rhyme
(E) dissonance

The significance of the onomatopoeia in Stanza 11, line 1, is that it
(A) breaks the mood established in Stanza 10
(B) begins a new alliterative pattern
(C) simply starts a new thought
(D) reinforces the mood of Stanza 10
(E) stresses the relationship of bird and man

The repetitive elements of each stanza's final line contribute LEAST to
(A) a sense of the meaning
(B) the atmosphere
(C) the overall tone
(D) character development
(E) a distinctive style

Correct Answers: **B, C, E, A, D**

ACTIVE THINKING EXERCISES FOR TONE

STEP 1. ▸FOCUS◂

Another method to focus your thinking is to develop a relationship with what you are reading and the questions that follow the selection.

▼EXERCISE▼

When you are reading a selection, focus on any ideas or relationships that seem familiar to help you establish a relationship with what you are reading.

Turn once again to Practice Set A on Page 331. As you read the selection, do you see any ideas that you have experienced? For example, have you ever received a letter or note from someone you did not know, or have you ever been uncertain of a letter's contents? How did you feel just before you opened it? Have you ever experienced news so shocking that you had to sit down or so surprising that you could not say a word?

Now, turn to page 337 and answer the first question about tone. Continue practicing this method for selections 2–5 of Set A.

▼EXERCISE▼

What follows is a speed method to allow you to answer as many questions correctly as possible in the shortest amount of time. Turn to Practice Set B selections on page 340. You should be familiar with the selections by now, but do skim through them to refresh your memory. Now go to the Questions About Tone on page 344. Look through the questions and answer those that you can answer quickly without any further reading or effort, then return to the more difficult ones. The idea behind this exercise is to answer those questions first that require the least amount of time. Continue with Practice Set C.

▼**EXERCISE**▼

Turn to Practice Test Four on page 401.

Use this test to experiment with ways to increase your speed and to develop a relationship to the writer's ideas (when possible).

1. Skim the questions for each selection, read the passage (marking key spots), then return to the questions to answer all those you can answer immediately.

2. Return to each unanswered question one at a time. Cross off obviously incorrect answers, reducing the number of possible answers.

3. Reread as necessary the portions of the selection that apply.

STEP 2. MOW (MY OWN WORDS)

Here is John Scott's "I Hate That Drum's Discordant Sound."

> I hate that drum's discordant sound,
> Parading round, and round, and round:
> To thoughtless youth it pleasure yields,
> And lures from cities and from fields,

Line

(5)
> To sell their liberty for charms
> Of tawdry lace, and glittering arms;
> And when Ambition's voice commands,
> To march, and fight, and fall, in foreign lands.

> I hate that drum's discordant sound,

(10)
> Parading round, and round, and round:
> To me it talks of ravaged plains,
> And burning towns, and ruined swains,
> And mangled limbs, and dying groans,
> The widows' tears, and orphans' moans;

(15)
> And all that Misery's hand bestows,
> To fill the catalogue of human woes.

MOW this poem by answering these questions and paraphrasing its key points.

What is the subject? _____

What is the speaker's purpose? _____

What is the main point of lines 1-2 and 9-10? _____

_____

Paraphrase what the drum's sound means to youth in lines 3-8: _____

_____

_____

Paraphrase what the drum's sound means to the speaker in lines 10-17: _____

_____

_____

Summarize the main idea (one sentence): _____

_____

▼PRACTICE QUESTIONS▼

With this analysis in mind, answer the following questions:

1. The speaker sees the drum's sound as symbolic of all the following EXCEPT
   (A) national pride
   (B) death
   (C) destruction of property
   (D) wounded men
   (E) grief

2. Lines 2 and 8 both contain which of the following?
   (A) Iambic pentameter rhythm
   (B) Internal rhyme
   (C) Hyperbole
   (D) Alliteration
   (E) Puns

3. This poem as a whole can be considered onomatopoeic because
   (A) the subject is music
   (B) colloquial expressions make the meaning more intense
   (C) connotative word choices reinforce the poem's meaning
   (D) combined use of rhythm and phonic echo devices reflect the poem's meaning and tone
   (E) the syntax of the poem includes balanced sentence elements

4. Structurally, the poet uses repetition in lines 1-2 and 9-10 to
   (A) parody previous military works
   (B) exaggerate the role of rhythm in war
   (C) make the poem sound less combative
   (D) reinforce the paradoxical elements of war
   (E) introduce and sustain the seemingly endless rhythm of war

5. Why does the speaker consider the drum "discordant" (line 1)?
   (A) He dislikes the lengths of military parades (line 2).
   (B) The drum seems pleasant (line 3) but leads to woes (line 16).
   (C) The drum both "lures" (line 4) and "talks" (line 11).
   (D) He blames wars on military music.
   (E) The drum's sound represents patriotism.

Answers and Explanations:

1. **A** The poet associates drum sounds with death (dying groans, line 13), destruction of property (burning towns, line 12), wounded men (mangled limbs, line 13), and grief (line 14). Although drum marches may elicit national pride, the speaker only alludes to such marches as "pleasure" in line 3.

2. **D** Alliteration is used in lines 2 and 8: the repetition of *r* and *f* sounds.

3. **D** The correct answer choice defines onomatopoeia.

4. **E** Although war's rhythms are accentuated in this poem (B), you need to keep the work as a whole in mind. What is the speaker's main point? The even meter, phonic sound devices, and repetitive structures, including lines 1-2 and 9-10, support a constant tone that reflects the speaker's view of the relentless nature of war.

5. **B** Discordant refers to incompatibility and disagreement, so the correct answer choice would point out a contrast.

STEP 3. BID (BREAK IT DOWN)

▼EXERCISE▼

Begin to **BID** by matching the following terms with their definitions.

1. mood	A. repeated final consonant sounds
2. feeling	B. an intellectual state
3. atmosphere	C. an emotional state
4. onomatopoeia	D. pleasant to pronounce
5. alliteration	E. repeated vowel sounds
6. assonance	F. tongue twisters
7. consonance	G. harsh with sounds around it
8. cacophony	H. harsh regardless of sounds around it
9. dissonance	I. the prevailing ambience
10. euphony	J. words imitate sounds

Correct Answers:

1. **C**   2. **B**   3. **I**   4. **J**   5. **F**   6. **E**   7. **A**   8. **G**   9. **H**   10. **D**

Next, determine if each of the following statements is true or false.

1. Voice and tone are unrelated concepts.
2. Setting includes geographical location, time, and socio-economic conditions.
3. A writer's style includes the voice and tone.
4. The subject of a work generally does not contribute to its tone.
5. The tone of a work can be affected by the sound of the language used.

Correct Answers:

1. **F**   2. **T**   3. **T**   4. **F**   5. **T**

Finally, consider these questions. If you are looking for the tone of a selection:

1. Who is the speaker?
2. What tone (of voice) do you hear in the work as a whole?
3. Can you describe the writer's style?
4. What elements (such as characters and setting) are contributing to the tone?
5. Do rhythm, rhyme, or other sound effects contribute to the tone of this work?

Correct Answers: (will vary with the selection being read)

▼PRACTICE QUESTIONS▼

Here is a poem called "Day, in Melting Purple Dying" written by Maria Brooks.

Day, in melting purple dying;
Blossoms, all around me sighing;
Fragrance, from the lilies straying;
Line   Zephyr, with my ringlets playing;
(5)   Ye but waken my distress;
I am sick of loneliness!

Thou, to whom I love to hearken,
Come, ere night around me darken;
Though thy softness but deceive me,
(10)   Say thou'rt true, and I'll believe thee;
Veil, if ill, thy soul's intent,
Let me think it innocent!

Save thy toiling, spare thy treasure;
All I ask is friendship's pleasure;
(15)   Let the shining ore lie darkling,—
Bring no gem in luster sparkling;
Gifts and gold are naught to me,
I would only look on thee!

Tell to thee the high-wrought feeling,
(20)   Ecstasy but in revealing;
Paint to thee the deep sensation,
Rapture in participation;
Yet but torture, if comprest
In a lone, unfriended breast.

(25)   Absent still! Ah! come and bless me!
Let these eyes again caress thee,
Once in caution, I could fly thee;
Now, I nothing could deny thee.
In a look if death there be,
(30)   Come, and I will gaze on thee!

1. The use of "Absent still! Ah!" in line 25
   (A) renders the speaker's emotion more intense
   (B) illustrates the speaker's lack of communicative skills
   (C) suggests a silent auditor
   (D) implies no one is really coming
   (E) introduces a new thought

2. The speaker's feelings toward her absent friend in the second stanza project a sense of
   (A) bewilderment
   (B) uncertainty
   (C) incredulity
   (D) fickleness
   (E) indecision

3. The tone of the second stanza makes the speaker seem
   (A) accusatory
   (B) innocent
   (C) desperate
   (D) reticent
   (E) retiring

4. Which of the following stanzas reveals a change in the speaker's attitude toward her friend?
   (A) Stanza 1
   (B) Stanza 2
   (C) Stanza 3
   (D) Stanza 4
   (E) Stanza 5

5. What is the result of the loss of the established rhyme scheme in the last stanza?
   (A) It reinforces the sense of desperation revealed in the speaker.
   (B) It suggests a change in emphasis.
   (C) It destroys the poem's unity.
   (D) It reflects a progression of thought in the speaker.
   (E) It emphasizes the faithlessness of her friend.

Answers and Explanations:

1. **A** The absent, silent auditor is established in the second stanza. There is no suggestion that the auditor will never come, but the use of the stark "Ah!" is an emotional release that intensifies the moment.

2. **B** Is her friend deceiving her (line 9)? Is the soul's intent "ill" (line 11)? Although willing to accept her friend regardless, these questions reveal the uncertainty in her mind.

3. **C** She is willing to believe deception and is wanting her friend to conceal ill intents from her so that she will not be "sick of loneliness." Friendship at any cost makes her seem desperate.

4. **E** Lines 27-28: She changed from cautious rejection to desperate longing for her friend.

5. **A** The couplets of the previous stanzas give a sense of measure and regularity. The couplets abandoned to six rhymed lines in the last stanza mirror the speaker's desperate abandon of caution (line 27) and willingness to die (line 29) for companionship.

STEP 4. TT → TM (TEST TAKER TO TEST MAKER)

Life is full of changes. Sometimes these changes are caused by certain events, or the events could be coincidental. We tend, however, to associate points of change with "landmark events."

In written works, too, you will often find changes in plot, characters, point of view, tone, and so forth. Recognizing when a change happens is important and provides a perfect subject for a test question.

Return one more time to "The Raven" on page 155 and look at the last line of each stanza. Do you see a change at any point?

One major change occurs between Stanzas 7 and 8. In the first seven stanzas, the last line is either thought or uttered by the speaker. Beginning in Stanza 8, the bird dominates the line, except for Stanza 13 and the final stanza when the speaker uses the line to summarize his situation.

This chapter concentrates on the tone of the poem, so aim at writing a question about how this change is a landmark that affects the tone.

What attitude is the speaker projecting in the first seven stanzas? _____

_____

Possible answers: denial, grief, a little "whistling in the dark" bravado, but all in a general sense about the loss of Lenore.

How does this attitude change? _____

_____

One possible change: Progressively with each stanza, the bird replaces Lenore as the speaker's center of attention and, by the end of the poem, becomes a symbol of his overpowering grief over Lenore. The bird's single word answer increases in meaning and intensifies the speaker's mood or emotional state.

Based on the last lines of Stanzas 1-7, the tone, then, could be described as sad, lonely, disappointed. The last lines of Stanzas 8-12, however, shift to mysterious (What is this strange bird?) and puzzling (meant to be solved).

Here is the question. You write one correct and four incorrect answer choices. Do not use the adjectives already given. Make E the correct answer.

The last lines in Stanzas 7 and 8 mark a shift in tone from

(A) _____ to _____

(B) _____ to _____

(C) _____ to _____

(D) _____ to _____

(E) _____ to _____

TONE IN CONCLUSION

The tones used by a speaker or writer greatly influence our perception of any given work. Tone also applies to the characters within a narrative, affecting interaction among characters, as well as how readers view each character. Consequently, the time is here to move on to Literary Element #5, Character.

Literary Element Number Five: Character

A character is a person (or a being given the characteristics of a person) who appears in, acts and/or speaks in, narrates, or is referred to in a literary work.

ERM ALERT You should know this term: **characterization**

Definition: Characterization includes the methods used to portray a person or being (a character). To characterize someone or something is to describe any distinguishing traits or features present, including moral qualities.

IMPORTANT CONCEPT #1: DISTINCTIVE TRAITS

Concept Explained:

One basis for characterization is the revelation of the character's *identifying traits*, the mental and ethical (including moral) traits (qualities or characteristics) of the individual. A person's temperament, disposition, and distinctive personal and social traits can be viewed as a function of his or her (1) attitudes, (2) emotional states, (3) response mechanisms, and (4) intrinsic values. All these elements combine to make an individual's personality.

1. Attitudes

A character's attitudes are his or her mental positions or feelings with regard to self, other people, objects, or a subject. Conversation often includes talk about a person's attitude as being "good" or "bad," as being "productive" or "unproductive," as being "responsive" or "unresponsive," and the list goes on. Evidently, there are many degrees of productivity and responsiveness; however, people frequently tend to make generalizations that polarize their perceptions of a person's attitude to either the "positive" or the "negative."

When test questions ask you to identify a character's:

viewpoint	feeling	bearing
opinion	conclusion	position
posture	mien	assumption
presumption	impression	judgment
demeanor	notion	standpoint
stance	idea	appearance
sentiment	pose	

(to name a few), they may be asking you to identify his or her attitude.

How can an attitude be described? Some possibilities include:

positive (attitudes):	negative (attitudes):
productive	unproductive
responsive	unresponsive
good	bad
kind	unkind
soft	firm
helpful	helpless

lenient	strict
inspired	uninspired
godly	irreverent
constructive	destructive
forgiving	unforgiving
happy	sad

▼PRACTICE QUESTION▼

The following passage is taken from Nathaniel Hawthorne's *The Blithdale Romance*.

"Angry with you, child? What a silly idea!" exclaimed Zenobia, laughing. "No, indeed! But, my dear Priscilla, you are getting to be so very pretty that you absolutely need a duenna; and, as I am

(Line)

(5) older than you, and have had my own little experience of life, and think myself exceedingly sage, I intend to fill the place of a maiden aunt. Every day, I shall give you a lecture, a quarter of an hour in length, on the morals, manners, and proprieties of social life. When our pastoral shall be quite played out, Priscilla, my worldly wisdom may stand you in good stead."

(10) "I am afraid you are angry with me!" repeated Priscilla, sadly; for, while she seemed as impressible as wax, the girl often showed a persistency in her own ideas as stubborn as it was gentle.

"Dear me, what can I say to the child!" cried Zenobia, in a tone of humorous vexation. "Well, well; since you insist on my being

(15) angry, come to my room, this moment, and let me beat you!"

Zenobia bade Hollingsworth good night very sweetly, and nodded to me with a smile. But, just as she turned aside with Priscila, into the dimness of the porch, I caught another glance at her countenance. It would have made the fortune of a tragic actress, could she have

(20) borrowed it for the moment when she fumbles in her bosom for the concealed dagger or the exceedingly sharp bodkin, or mingles the ratsbane in her lover's bowl of wine or her rival's cup of tea. Not that I in the least anticipated any such catastrophe—it being a remarkable truth that custom has in no one point a greater sway

(25) than over our modes of wreaking our wild passions. And besides, had we been in Italy, instead of New England, it was hardly yet a crisis for the dagger or the bowl.

It often amazed me, however, that Hollingsworth should show himself so recklessly tender towards Priscilla, and never once seem to

(30) think of the effect which it might have upon her heart. But the man, as I have endeavored to explain, was thrown completely off his moral balance, and quite bewildered as to his personal relations, by his great excrescence of a philanthropic scheme. I used to see, or fancy, indications that he was not altogether obtuse to Zenobia's

(35) influence as a woman. No doubt, however, he had a still more exquisite enjoyment of Priscilla's silent sympathy with his purposes, so unalloyed with criticism, and therefore more grateful than any

intellectual approbation, which always involves a possible reserve of
latent censure. A man—poet, prophet, or whatever he may be—
(40)   readily persuades himself of his right to all the worship that is
voluntarily tendered. In requital of so rich benefits as he was to
confer upon mankind, it would have been hard to deny
Hollingsworth the simple solace of a young girl's heart, which he
held in his hand, and smelled to, like a rosebud. But what if, while
(45)   pressing out its fragrance, he should crush the tender rosebud in his
grasp!
    As for Zenobia, I saw no occasion to give myself any trouble.
With her native strength, and her experience of the world, she could
not be supposed to need any help of mine. Nevertheless, I was
(50)   really generous enough to feel some little interest likewise for
Zenobia. With all her faults (which might have been a great many
besides the abundance that I knew of), she possessed noble traits,
and a heart which must, at least, have been valuable while new.
And she seemed ready to fling it away as uncalculatingly as Priscilla
(55)   herself. I could not but suspect that, if merely at play with
Hollingsworth, she was sporting with a power which she did not full
estimate. Or, if in earnest, it might chance, between Zenobia's
passionate force and his dark, self-delusive egotism, to turn out such
earnest as would develop itself in some sufficiently tragic
(60)   catastrophe, though the dagger and the bowl should go for nothing
in it.

The narrator characterizes Priscilla as
(A) psychologically unbalanced
(B) a clever little actress
(C) simpleminded
(D) naïve and unsophisticated
(E) stubborn and self-centered

Explanation: Be sure to read all the answer choices. Priscilla is stubborn; however, there
are no indications that she is self-centered. She is naïve (she gave her heart "like a
rosebud" in an implied state of worship) and so unsophisticated that Zenobia presumes
she needs someone worldly to teach her.

Correct Answer: **D**

ERM ALERT You should know this term: **climate**

Definition: A group of people (such as a family or community), a nation, or a literary work
can have a prevailing attitude. Sometimes this is referred to as the "climate"—the political
climate might be referred to as liberal or conservative; the intellectual climate might be
referred to as decaying; the moral climate as strict; the climate of opinion as going against
a particular stance; the climate of the stock market as "bullish." A prevailing attitude or
climate can also sometimes be identified in a literary work.

▼PRACTICE QUESTIONS▼

Using the Hawthorne passage, answer the following questions:

The "dagger and the bowl" come to represent in the passage
(A) tragic acting
(B) suicidal tendencies
(C) homicidal jealousy
(D) a drunken rage
(E) martyrdom

The general climate of this passage serves to
(A) make philanthropy seem selfish
(B) foreshadow trouble
(C) cast a shadow on the value of experience
(D) reveal the best in the characters
(E) conceal true motives

Explanation: In classical literature, a romantic triangle often ends with murder committed by violence (symbolized by a dagger) or poison (symbolized by the bowl). The general climate of the passage is a product of the words and actions of the characters and the observations of the narrator. Three people are living together. One is a young, impressionable girl who worships the much older man, who has a "self-delusive egotism." The third character is an experienced woman (with many faults) who is "ready to fling" her heart at the man. Such conditions would naturally produce a climate that is emotionally stressful. Add to this mix the repeated allusions to the dagger and bowl and an element of danger is injected into the scene. This climate hints at future trouble. Notice: Both times the narrator mentions dagger and bowl, he denies that he really believes that a "tragic catastrophe" will actually happen; however, the fact that he does mention them plants the idea in the reader's mind.

Correct Answers: **C, B**

2. Emotions

The emotions of a character are his or her intense feelings. These emotions may include states of excitement, emotional attachment or dissociation, stability or instability, emotional insulation, emotionalism, and degrees of emotional appeal.

Fundamental to the examination of a character's emotions is the degree to which the individual exhibits feelings or lack of feelings. Sometimes a character has emotions that are reflected in almost all he or she says, does, or thinks. But these emotions, as with attitudes, can polarize to the "positive" or to the "negative." Generally, the following emotions are regarded as "positive" because they are rooted in feelings:

affection	warmheartedness	vehemence
passion	sentiment	gusto
sensitivity	fervor	zeal
sympathy	ardor	responsiveness
tenderness	cordiality	demonstrativeness

But even "positives" can be "too much":

mawkishness	insipidity
sentimentality	melodrama
"mush"	emotionalism
"wearing one's heart on one's sleeve"	

At the other extreme are those emotions connotatively regarded as "negative" because of their lack of feeling:

soulessness	callousness
emotionlessness	hardness
heartlessness	hardheartedness
frigidity	obduracy
cold-heartedness	imperviousness
cold-bloodedness	apathy
untouchability	listlessness
unresponsiveness	lethargy
unimpressionability	indifference

The role of hope and of its opposite, hopelessness, on character development and revelation should not be underestimated. Hope is a powerful motivating force as seen in last-minute plays that win the championship game or in acts of heroism that save lives or win wars; and being in a state of hopelessness can be equally powerful, as seen in lives that have lost meaning, ending in suicides or unfulfilled dreams.

What words are connotative of a character's sense of hope?

expectation	reliance	assurance
trust	assumption	dreams
confidence	optimism	faith

Are all hopes justified? Is the character deluding himself or herself? Consider such words as

bubble	fool's paradise	pipe dream

Words connotative of hopelessness:

impossibility	disappointment	cynical
despair	defeated	gloominess
desperation	pessimistic	irrevocability
despondent	irretrievable	incorrigible
forlorn	incurable	disconsolate

Another term you may encounter when examining a character's emotional state is *disposition*. "Emotional state" is connotative of that person's feelings *at a particular time*—his or her emotional state may be happy today, unhappy tomorrow. In contrast, a character's disposition is connotative of his or her feelings as well as *natural attitudes toward life* that are somewhat consistent throughout his or her life. Although we may say that George, for example, might be unhappy today, he generally has a "happy disposition," outlook on life, or temperament.

▼PRACTICE QUESTION▼

Return to the Hawthorne passage to answer this question.

According to the narrator, the greatest influence on how people express extreme emotion is
(A) the law
(B) a sense of duty
(C) social convention
(D) habit
(E) fear

Explanation: "—it being a remarkable truth that custom has in no one point a greater sway than over our modes of wreaking our wild passions." (fourth paragraph)

Correct Answer: **C**

3. Response mechanisms

How does the character respond physically and emotionally to life? character traits that are revealed by the character's response to the world about him or her can, as with attitudes and emotions, be discussed by examining the extremes.

- To what degree does the character exhibit signs of stress when put under pressure? These character traits include, for example, agitation, perturbation, trepidation, fury, frenzy, excitation, exhilaration, or explosion. In contrast, the character might react with dispassion, even-temperedness, impassiveness, nonchalance, composure, serenity, self-confidence, offhandedness, placidity, or staidness.
- How nervous does the character become? A nervous character is agitated, unnerved, unstrung, demoralized, or shaken. In the opposite case, the character is steady, calm, unflinching, steel-nerved, or relaxed.
- Is the character patient or impatient? Tolerant or intolerant? Resigned or anxious?

Other character traits that are revealed by a character's response mechanisms include these:

honest (dishonest)	rejoicing (lamenting)
fight (flight)	happy (sad)
brave (cowardly)	cheerful (solemn)
courageous (fearful)	contented (discontented)
wise (foolish)	social (unsocial)
faithful (unfaithful)	hospitable (inhospitable)
rash (cautious)	companionable (secluded)
pleasant (unpleasant)	courteous (discourteous)
witty (dull)	forgiving (unforgiving,
humorous (boring)	revengeful, retaliatory)
pitying (pitiless)	giving (taking, envious,
regretful (glad)	jealous, resentful)

▼**PRACTICE QUESTION**▼

Return again to the Hawthorne passage.

Context suggests that in the third paragraph, Zenobia's choice of words
(A) marks the beginning of a joke
(B) makes her seem like a child abuser
(C) reveals her true intentions
(D) renders her role as the "maiden aunt" unbelievable
(E) conceals, yet ironically reveals, her genuine reactions

Explanation: Of course, Zenobia is joking. The next paragraph, however, reveals that she also is dealing with jealousy concealed by her joking tone, but revealed by choice of humor. She is responding with jealousy toward the girl.

Correct Answer: **E**

4. Intrinsic values

Character traits can also arise from examining the character's intrinsic values: those traits that result from the value judgments made in the heart of the person—what is really important (or not important) to him or her. At their core are fundamental concepts: home, family, country, religion, fellowman, self, and other value-type concepts.

How the reader perceives the character traits that are part of the character's intrinsic values is largely a product of the attitudes, emotions, and response mechanisms the character has exhibited in word and deed within the selection. These perceptions can lead to generalizations about what kind of person he or she is. Are these generalizations always accurate statements of that person's intrinsic values? Perhaps not, but nonetheless, these conclusions are often reached.

Based on the character traits revealed by a character's attitudes, emotions, and response mechanisms in a literary selection, the reader may conclude that the character is trustworthy, a criminal, a proud man, a humble boy, a fastidious girl, an honorable woman, a shallow person, a devil—or a saint. Once the reader has generalized the exhibited traits of character to mean that the person is "honorable" or "moral" or "shallow," the reader then tends to assume that this person will most likely exhibit the characteristics of "honor" or of "morality" or of "shallowness" in most situations because, the reader assumes, these characteristics arise from the person's intrinsic value system.

▼**PRACTICE QUESTION**▼

In the Hawthorne passage, Hollingsworth is portrayed as
(A) dangerous
(B) generous
(C) moral
(D) obsequious
(E) unpretentious

Explanation: Look for clues to his intrinsic values. Normally, an act of philanthropy is associated with a generous heart. In Hollingsworth's case, his "philanthropic scheme" is an "excrescence," contextually meaning an abnormal outgrowth that, according to the narrator, has made Hollingsworth "thrown completely of his moral balance." Also, he is capable of emotionally crushing a person "like a rosebud" (Priscilla), and he is a "power" with a "dark, self-delusive egotism." We can conclude from these statements that he is a potentially dangerous man.

Correct Answer: **A**

IMPORTANT CONCEPT #2: METHODS OF CHARACTERIZATION

Concept Explained:

Characterization—Character development in a story—can be accomplished through many different methods or techniques.

1. Disclosure of character through stereotyping

This method of characterization involves identifying a character with a group about which you have certain cultural assumptions (stereotypes). If a character is, as an illustration, a West Texas cowboy who is visiting Boston for the first time, the reader might make certain assumptions concerning his dress, speech, and character traits that are based on stereotypical conceptions.

Look again at the last paragraph in the Hawthorne passage. The narrator describes Zenobia as an experienced woman who still has some "noble traits" (a derogatory stereotype). He also hints at her heart condition (symbolic of kindness) as "valuable when new," alluding to the stereotype of "a heart of gold."

2. Disclosure of character through exposition

Sometimes the author or narrator will simply tell the reader about the character. These explanatory messages might include descriptions of the person's background, motivating forces, personality traits, relationships, and physical characteristics. Generally, a person tends to accept these characterizations as truthful and accurate until proven to be otherwise by the character's own words, revealed thoughts, and actions.

▼PRACTICE QUESTION▼

An example of characterization through exposition can be seen in this paragraph taken from the early nineteenth-century American short story "Rip Van Winkle" by Washington Irving:

The great error in Rip's composition was an insuperable aversion to all kinds of profitable labor. It could not be from the want of assiduity or perseverance; for he would sit on a wet rock, with a rod
Line as long and heavy as a Tartar's lance, and fish all day without a
(5) murmur, even though he should not be encouraged by a single nibble. He would carry a fowling-piece on his shoulder for hours together, trudging through woods and swamps, and up hill and down dale, to shoot a few squirrels or wild pigeons. He would never refuse to assist a neighbor even in the roughest toil, and was a
(10) foremost man at all country frolics for husking Indian corn, or building stone fences; the women of the village, too, used to employ him to run their errands, and to do such little odd jobs as their less obliging husbands would not do for them. In a word, Rip was ready to attend to anybody's business but his own; but as to doing family
(15) duty, and keeping his farm in order, he found it impossible.

What irony does the speaker use to characterize Rip Van Winkle?

(A) Rip liked to fish.

(B) Rip worked for his family, but not others.

(C) Rip would work for others, but not for his own family.

(D) Rip refused to help neighbors.

(E) Rip had a kind nature and conciliatory disposition.

Explanation: In this case, the narrator uses examples to disclose Rip's character. The contradictory nature of Rip's behavior produces irony and insight into his character.

Correct Answer: **C**

▼PRACTICE QUESTION▼

At about the same time Irving was writing in America, Jane Austen (a writer of the Romantic Period) was in England writing this characterization in her novel of manners *Persuasion*:

> Vanity was the beginning and the end of Sir Walter Elliot's character; vanity of person and of situation. He had been remarkably handsome in his youth; and, at fifty-four, was still a very
> Line fine man. Few women could think more of their personal appearance
> (5) than he did; nor could the valet of any new made lord be more delighted with the place he held in society. He considered the blessing of beauty as inferior only to the blessing of a baronetcy; and the Sir Walter Elliot, who united these gifts, was the constant object of his warmest respect and devotion.
> (10) His good looks and his rank had one fair claim on his attachment; since to them he must have owed a wife of very superior character to any thing deserved by his own. Lady Elliot had been an excellent woman, sensible and amiable; whose judgement and conduct, if they might be pardoned the youthful infatuation which made her Lady
> (15) Elliot, had never required indulgence afterwards.—She had humoured, or softened, or concealed his failings, and promoted his real respectability for seventeen years; and though not the very happiest being in the world herself, had found enough in her duties, her friends, and her children, to attach her to life, and make it no
> (20) matter of indifference to her when she was called on to quit them.

Lady Elliot's character is largely

(A) silly

(B) infatuated

(C) disrespectful

(D) vain

(E) pragmatic

Explanation: The narrator tells us that Lady Elliot is sensible and did not indulge herself once married. Even though she married a man with failings, she grounded herself in her duties, friends, and children (a practical response to life).

Correct Answer: **E**

3. Disclosure of character through the character's actions

What does the character do at times of crisis? How does he or she react to conflict? To everyday situations? To extraordinary situations?

You can learn a great deal about a character from the way in which he or she reacts in different circumstances and situations.

▼PRACTICE QUESTION▼

Here is an excerpt from Jane Austen's *Persuasion*.

> Something occurred, however, to give her a different duty. Mary,
> often a little unwell, and always thinking a great deal of her own
> complaints, and always in the habit of claiming Anne when any thing
> Line was the matter, was indisposed; and foreseeing that she should not
> (5) have a day's health all the autumn, entreated, or rather required her,
> for it was hardly entreaty, to come to Uppercross Cottage, and bear
> her company as long as she should want her, instead of going to
> Bath.

Mary's treatment of Anne is best described as

(A) virtuous
(B) self-abnegatory
(C) selfish
(D) magnanimous
(E) impersonal

Explanation: By changing the word choice from "entreated" to "or rather required" and by describing her "habit of claiming Anne," the narrator portrays a character used to self-indulgence and attention, regardless of the feelings of others.

Correct Answer: **C**

4. Disclosure of character through the character's words

You also can deduce a great deal about a character's personality from his or her own words. Sometimes a character will reveal significant hidden aspects of his or her personality from words spoken in an unguarded moment or during a heated argument.

▼PRACTICE QUESTION▼

Here is a conversation that takes place in *Persuasion*.

> 'Oh! he talks of you,' cried Charles, 'in such terms,'—Mary
> interrupted him. 'I declare, Charles, I never heard him mention Anne
> twice all the time I was there. I declare, Anne, he never talks of you
> Line at all.'
> (5) 'No,' admitted Charles, 'I do not know that he ever does, in a
> general way—but however, it is a very clear thing that he admires
> you exceedingly.—His head is full of some books that he is reading
> upon your recommendation, and he wants to talk to you about them;
> he has found out something or other in one of them which he thinks—
> (10) Oh! I cannot pretend to remember it, but it was something very fine—
> I overheard him telling Henrietta all about it—and then "Miss Elliot"

(15) was spoken of in the highest terms!—No Mary, I declare it was so, I heard it myself, and you were in the other room.—"Elegance, sweetness, beauty," Oh! there was no end of Miss Elliot's charms.'

(15) 'And I am sure,' cried Mary warmly, 'it was very little to his credit, if he did. Miss Harville only died last June. Such a heart is very little worth having; is it, Lady Russell? I am sure you will agree with me.'

'I must see Captain Benwick before I decide,' said Lady Russell, smiling. . . .

(20) 'Oh! as to being Anne's acquaintance,' said Mary, 'I think he is rather my acquaintance, for I have been seeing him every day this last fortnight.'

'Well, as your joint acquaintance, then, I shall be very happy to see Captain Benwick.'

(25) 'You will not find any thing very agreeable in him, I assure you, ma'am. He is one of the dullest young men that ever lived. He has walked with me, sometimes, from one end of the sands to the other, without saying a word. He is not at all a well-bred young man. I am sure you will not like him.'

(30) 'There we differ, Mary,' said Anne. 'I think Lady Russell would like him. I think she would be so much pleased with his mind, that she would very soon see no deficiency in his manner.'

Mary's reaction to Charles reveals she is

(A) plaintive
(B) exuberant
(C) genial
(D) competitive
(E) jocular

Explanation: Her petty attitude in claiming Benwick as her acquaintance and not Anne's, yet defaming his character, reveals a self-centered, competitive nature. In her view, he is *her* friend, not Anne's; he sees *her* every day, but never mentions Anne.

Correct Answer: **D**

5. Disclosure of character through the character's thoughts

A character's own thoughts (through such devices as interior monologue and stream of consciousness) can be a rich source for insight into motivation and character; however, be alert for elements of self-delusion on the part of the character. Also, be aware of the role that *perception* plays in thought. A character's perception includes the following:

• Awareness of the environment through his or her physical senses
• Realizations of events, activities, and conversations
• Insight into the deeper meanings of the words and events that occur
• Comprehension of the significance of these words and events

A character's thoughts can be penetrating, discerning, and discriminating or they can be shallow, undiscerning, and indiscriminating.

In the context of the situation, is the person sagacious and shrewd? Sensible? Sensitive? Knowing? Discriminative? Or is his or her thinking shallow? Insincere? Insensitive? Indiscriminative?

▼**PRACTICE QUESTION**▼

Again, examine an excerpt from *Persuasion*.

> . . . He had been engaged to Captain Harville's sister, and was
> now mourning her loss. They had been a year or two waiting for
> fortune and promotion. Fortune came, his prize-money as lieutenant
> being great,—promotion, too, came at *last*; but Fanny Harville did not
> live to know it. She had died the preceding summer, while he was at
> sea. Captain Wentworth believed it impossible for man to be more
> attached to woman than poor Benwick had been to Fanny Harville,
> or to be more deeply afflicted under the dreadful change. . . . The
> sympathy and good-will excited towards Captain Benwick was very
> great.
>
> 'And yet,' said Anne to herself, as they now moved forward to
> meet the party, 'he has not, perhaps, a more sorrowing heart than I
> have. I cannot believe his prospects so blighted for ever. He is
> younger than I am; younger in feeling, if not in fact; younger as a
> man. He will rally again, and be happy with another.'

Line (5) ... (10) ... (15) (margin line numbers)

Anne views Captain Benwick's situation with

(A) optimism
(B) Pollyannaism
(C) aggravation
(D) palliation
(E) drollness

Explanation: Anne reveals a sense of optimism that he will "rally again"; however, she is not optimistic to the extreme of a Pollyanna. FYI: Pollyanna is the name of the heroine of a book by Eleanor Porter. The name has come to represent an excessively optimistic person.

Correct Answer: **A**

6. Disclosure of character through the words of others

A lot can be learned about a character by "listening in" on what other characters have to say about him or her.

▼**PRACTICE QUESTION**▼

In this excerpt, the reader learns something of the character of Captain Wentworth (in *Persuasion*):

> 'Miss Elliot,' said he [Captain Harville], speaking rather low, 'you
> have done a good deed in making that poor fellow talk so much. I
> wish he could have such company oftener. It is bad for him, I know,
> to be shut up as he is; but what can we do? we cannot part.'
> 'No,' said Anne, 'that I can easily believe to be impossible; but in
> time perhaps—we know what time does in every case of affliction,
> and you must remember, Captain Harville, that your friend may yet
> be called a young mourner—Only last summer, I understand.'
> 'Ay, true enough,' (with a deep sigh) 'only June.'

Line (5) (margin line numbers)

(10)   'And not known to him, perhaps, so soon.'

'Not till the first week in August, when he came home from the Cape,—just made into the *Grappler*. I was at Plymouth, dreading to hear of him; he sent in letters, but the *Grappler* was under orders for Portsmouth. There the news must follow him, but who was to tell it? (15)   not I. I would as soon have been run up to the yard-arm. Nobody could do it, but that good fellow, (pointing to Captain Wentworth). The *Laconia* had come into Plymouth the week before; no danger of her being sent to sea again. He stood his chance for the rest—wrote up for leave of absence, but without waiting the return, travelled (20)   night and day till he got to Portsmouth, rowed off to the *Grappler* that instant, and never left the poor fellow for a week; that's what he did, and nobody else could have saved poor James. You may think, Miss Elliot, whether he is dear to us!'

Harville sees Wentworth's character as a(n)

(A) chivalrous rival
(B) self-abasing knight
(C) unpardonable tyrant
(D) magnanimous hero
(E) diabolic fiend

Explanation: First, Wentworth accomplished a job Harville would not do: telling James that his fiancée is dead. Secondly, he rushed to be with James through the first week of grief ("nobody else could have saved poor James"). He acted the role of a hero in Harville's eyes: noble, honorable, generous.

Correct Answer: **D**

Use caution, however, in accepting the words of other characters—be sure to examine their motives (and the possibility of differences in their perceptions) for how their personal interests might affect their words about the character in question.

7. Disclosure of character through the use of setting

The setting can to varying degrees be a factor in determining character.

An example might be a story set in a remote area of the Rocky Mountains. A group of people are on a back-to-nature excursion. Encounters with hardships that are a natural possibility in such a setting (a flash flood, a member falling and becoming injured, an attack by wild animals, running out of food, or becoming lost) can bring out in the characters' personalities tendencies toward bravery or cowardice, stamina or weakness, selflessness or selfishness, and other traits.

In real life, people are constantly affected by their environment—the settings around them. Likewise, the setting can affect characters in literature.

Shakespeare's *Julius Caesar*

Act I Scene II

The same. A hall in Caesar's *palace.*

Thunder and lightning, Enter Julius Caesar, *in his nightgown.*

	Julius Caesar.	Nor heaven nor earth have been at peace to-night:
[This sets the atmosphere and permits you	→	Thrice hath Calphurnia in her sleep cried out,
to know it is a threatening situation for Caesar.]		"Help, ho! they murder Caesar!"—Who's within?

Enter a Servant.

Servant.   My lord?

Julius Caesar.	Go bid the priests do present sacrifice,
[Here you learn Caesar is superstitious, believing →	And bring me their opinions of success.
the priests can give him insight into his chances	
for success.]	

8. Disclosure of character through the humours

From the period of Elizabethan literature, the *humours* were used by various writers to describe the temperaments of characters, with the word "humour" (British spelling) referring to a person's mood. For example, we might say, "He's in good humor [American spelling] today!" (See chart.)

THE FOUR HUMOURS

The concept of humours is based on early theories of physiology: there are (according to old theories of cosmology) four elements in the universe. The humours need to be in balance because if any one humour predominates, it can lead to sickness and disease and can affect personality. The following chart summarizes these theories.

Element	Characteristic	Humour	Personality*
earth	cold, dry	black bile	melancholic—depressed, gloomy, gluttonous, sentimental
air	hot, moist	blood	sanguine—cheerful, hopeful, amorous
fire	hot, dry	yellow bile	choleric—angry vengeful, impatient
water	cold, moist	phlegm	phlegmatic—stoic, apathetic, impassive, dull, cowardly

* A person was said to be of a sanguine personality, for example, if that humour was predominant. A well-balanced person has all four humours in balance.

▼PRACTICE QUESTION▼

Jane Austen, for example, refers to his "sanguine temper" in this description of Captain Wentworth in *Persuasion*:

> Captain Wentworth had no fortune. He had been lucky in his
> profession, but spending freely, what had come freely, had realized
> nothing. But, he was confident that he should soon be rich;—full of
> Line life and ardour, he knew that he should soon have a ship, and soon
> (5) be on a station that would lead to every thing he wanted. He had
> always been lucky; he knew he should be so still.—Such confidence,
> powerful in its own warmth, and bewitching in the wit which often
> expressed it, must have been enough for Anne; but Lady Russell saw
> it differently.— His *sanguine temper, and fearlessness of mind,
> (10) operated very differently on her. She saw in it but an aggravation of
> the evil. It only added a dangerous character to himself. He was
> brilliant, he was headstrong.—Lady Russell had little taste for wit; and
> of any thing approaching to imprudence a horror. She deprecated
> the connection in every light.

Captain Wentworth is characterized as having what personality type?

(A) Sentimental
(B) Hopeful
(C) Vengeful
(D) Apathetic
(E) Cowardly

Explanation: See note at bottom of humours chart.

Correct Answer: **B**

9. Disclosure of character through eliciting reader responses

As pointed out by novelist Kit Reed in *Mastering Fiction Writing*, writers sometimes "become" the characters in their stories, just as actors may "become" the characters that they are portraying. This is a very interesting and useful perspective for the reader of literature as well as for the writer. The reader also brings his or her own experience to the work and, to greatly varying degrees, becomes the characters.

TERM ALERT You should know this term: **empathy**

Definition: When readers empathize with a character, they experience a sense of participation in the story or situation, often based on vivid descriptions of experiences common to both the reader and the character.

▼PRACTICE QUESTION▼

Here is the first stanza of John Keats's "The Eve of St. Agnes."

> St. Agnes' Eve—Ah, bitter chill it was!
> The owl, for all his feathers, was a-cold;
> The hare limped trembling through the frozen grass,
> And silent was the flock in woolly fold:
> Numb were the Beadsman's fingers, while he told
> His rosary, and while his frosted breath,
> Like pious incense from a censer old,
> Seemed taking flight for heaven, without a death,
> Past the sweet Virgin's picture, while his prayer he saith.

Line (5)

To empathize with the Beadsman would be to

(A) participate in a rosary
(B) vicariously feel the cold
(C) outline his actions
(D) meditate on cold weather
(E) become emotionally detached

Explanation: The vivid descriptions of the cold, especially the Beadsman's cold fingers and breath, make the scene seem real for the reader.

Correct Answer: **B**

The reader's *sympathy* in this context includes a sense of emotional agreement (empathy).

In "Lord Randal," the anonymous fifteenth-century ballad, the reader can certainly feel pity and grief both for the poisoned child and for his mother; however, the reader generally does not identify with them or feel what they are feeling, although the emotion of the last stanza is very moving:

> "O I fear ye are poisond, Lord Randal, my son!
> O I fear ye are poisond, my handsome young man!"
> "O yes! I am poisond; mother, make my bed soon,
> For I'm sick at the heart, and I fain wald lie down."

(Note: "Make my bed soon" is an expression said to refer to making a coffin—a bed for the sleep of death, with *bed* also referring to the grave.)

Of course, the character can also elicit feelings of antipathy from the reader—aversion, dislike, distrust, disassociation, and as a result, distance from the reader.

TERM ALERT You should know this term: **pathos**

Definition: Modern slang would probably call many scenes of pathos real "tearjerkers," but pathos does occur when a passage (or scene) captures the heart of the reader or audience with intense feelings of sorrow and pity.

▼PRACTICE QUESTION▼

The Old Curiosity Shop by Charles Dickens:

The old man looked from face to face, and his lips moved; but no sound came from them in reply.

"If we were knit together then," pursued the younger brother,
Line "what will be the bond between us now! And even," he added in an
(5) altered voice, "even if what I dread to name has come to pass—even if that be so, or is to be—still, dear brother, we are not apart, and have that comfort in our great affliction."

By little and little, the old man had drawn back towards the inner chamber, while these words were spoken. He pointed there, as he
(10) replied, with trembling lips.

"You plot among you to wean my heart from her. You never will do that—never while I have life. I have no relative or friend but her—I never had—I never will have. She is all in all to me. It is too late to part us now."

(15) Waving them off with his hand, and calling softly to her as he went, he stole into the room. They who were left behind drew close together, and after a few whispered words followed him. They moved so gently, that their footsteps made no noise; but there were sobs from among the group, and sounds of grief and mourning.

(20) For she was dead. There, upon her little bed, she lay at rest. The solemn stillness was no marvel now.

Her couch was dressed with here and there some winter berries and green leaves, gathered in a spot she had been used to favour. "When I die, put near me something that has loved the light, and
(25) had the sky above it always." Those were her words.

The old man held one languid arm in his, and had the small hand tight folded to his breast, for warmth. It was the hand she had stretched out to him with her last smile—the hand that had led him on through all their wanderings. Ever and anon he pressed it to his lips;
(30) then hugged it to his breast again, murmuring that it was warmer now; and as he said it he looked, in agony, to those who stood around, as if imploring them to help her.

But she was dead, and past all help, or need of it.

Holding the dead girl's hand serves to
(A) make the scene macabre
(B) add a bitter tone to the scene
(C) introduce an element of insanity
(D) instill a sense of unreality to the situation
(E) intensify the sense of the old man's grief

Explanation: Pathos, fundamentally, is a response from the heart of the individual, yet pathos or the lack of pathos is also often a reflection of society and the norms and cultures of the age. Dickens and the readers of his day lived in a world without television, action news reports, and big-screen movie theaters. As a result, stage productions, concerts, and reading were major outlets for the feelings and interests of the people. The readers of *The Old Curiosity Shop* during the period when it was first written reacted strongly to Little Nell's death. According to one historian, a reader wrote in his diary that he had never read such painful words, and another reader threw his copy of the book out a train window in his grief. Writers of the time record that American readers were also deeply affected—a crowd of concerned people gathered at a New York pier to shout questions at an arriving ship concerning Little Nell's fate. These reactions show that they had become personally involved with the character Little Nell as if she were a real person.

Correct Answer: **E**

IMPORTANT CONCEPT #3: CHARACTER DEVELOPMENT

Concept Explained:

Character development is when a character's character traits are revealed as the story unfolds or when a character's character traits change within the narrative.

Whether a person can change personality, disposition, or other like elements of character is questionable, but changes of attitude, emotional states, and some response mechanisms are common and necessary to making a character seem real to the reader. Such changes can be the critical turning point of the story.

Character development, as already mentioned, must be *credible*—rooted in probability. A few areas that are considered pivotal to establishing the probability of a character's development include the following:

1. Did the character have sufficient motivation to change?

For the reader to be convinced that a character really has changed, he or she must also be convinced that there is some reason to change: directly stated, character change often is seen as a cause-and-effect relationship. To see the effect (the change) without seeing the cause or without being convinced that what is being presented as the cause is sufficient motivation (reason) for the change, weakens the credibility of the work.

2. Was there sufficient time (in terms of "story time") for the character change to be realistic and probable?

People can suddenly change, but unless the reader is thoroughly convinced of the motivation, abrupt changes leave the reader with an uneasy sense of incredulity. Of course, a writer is faced with the problem of translating "real time" (two hours for a movie, three to four hours to read an average novel, for example) into "story time" that may involve days, weeks, years, or generations. There are some techniques available to the writer to give the reader a sense of protracted time, such as weaving subplots in and out of the main story or changing points of view. Regardless of the methods used, the reader needs to be convinced that the character who has changed or who is changing has a realistic amount of time in which to make these changes.

3. Has the reader been given adequate information about the character to make the change seem believable?

A story, because of the physical confines of the medium, is a "slice of life." Even in stories that follow a character from birth to death, only certain amounts of the details of that life can be presented. Consequently, filling in the reader on the parts not chronicled in detail is important to establishing the credibility of a character change.

TERM ALERT You should know this term: **flashback**

Definition: One method to give readers more detail is the use of **flashback**, such as dream sequences, recollections by a character, and other means in which past events are recounted. Sometimes the flashback can be almost the entire story. For example, the story might begin with the main character awaiting sentencing after a jury trial. He sits "remembering" the events that led to that point, and then the story concludes with the judge's pronouncement of sentence.

TERM ALERT You should know this term: **foreshadowing**

Definition: Another means a writer can use to achieve credibility for change is the effective use of **foreshadowing**, a means of preparing the reader or audience for upcoming events. Foreshadowing devices include the clues in a mystery or a prevailing atmosphere, among others.

▼PRACTICE QUESTIONS▼

Read the following selection from William Makepeace Thackeray's *Vanity Fair*.

When Rebecca saw the two magnificent Cashmere shawls which Joseph Sedley had brought home to his sister, she said, with perfect truth, "that it must be delightful to have a brother," and easily got
Line the pity of the tender-hearted Amelia, for being alone in the world,
(5) an orphan without friends or kindred.

"Not alone," said Amelia; "you know, Rebecca, I shall always be your friend, and love you as a sister—indeed I will."

"Ah, but to have parents, as you have—kind, rich, affectionate parents, who give you everything you ask for; and their love, which
(10) is more precious than all! My poor papa could give me nothing, and I had but two frocks in all the world! And then, to have a brother, a dear brother! Oh, how you must love him!"

Amelia laughed.

"What! *don't* you love him? You, who say you love everybody?"
(15) "Yes, of course, I do—only—"

"Only what?"

"Only Joseph doesn't seem to care much whether I love him or not.

He gave me two fingers to shake when he arrived after ten years'
(20) absence! He is very kind and good, but he scarcely ever speaks to me; I think he loves his pipe a great deal better than his"—but here Amelia checked herself, for why should she speak ill of her brother? "He was very kind to me as a child," she added; "I was but five years old when he went away."
(25) "Isn't he very rich?" said Rebecca. "They say all Indian nabobs are enormously rich."

"I believe he has a very large income."

"And is your sister-in-law a nice pretty woman?"

"La! Joseph is not married," said Amelia, laughing again.

(30)   Perhaps she had mentioned the fact already to Rebecca, but that young lady did not appear to have remembered it; indeed, vowed and protested that she expected to see a number of Amelia's nephews and nieces. She was quite disappointed that Mr. Sedley was not married; she was sure Amelia had said he was, and she

(35) doted so on little children.

      "I think you must have had enough of them at Chiswick," said Amelia, rather wondering at the sudden tenderness on her friend's part; and indeed in later days Miss Sharp would never have committed herself so far as to advance opinions, the untruth of which

(40) would have been so easily detected. But we must remember that she is but nineteen as yet, unused to the art of deceiving, poor innocent creature! And making her own experience in her own person. The meaning of the above series of queries, as translated in the heart of this ingenious young woman, was simply this:—"If Mr. Joseph Sedley

(45) is rich and unmarried, why should I not marry him? I have only a fortnight, to be sure, but there is no harm in trying."

Rebecca can be characterized as all the following EXCEPT
(A) perceptive
(B) sophisticated
(C) clever
(D) artful
(E) opportunistic

The narrator's comment that Rebecca is "unused to the art of deceiving" (line 41) probably
(A) betrays a kindness of spirit in Rebecca
(B) sarcastically foreshadows Rebecca's future conduct
(C) provides a basis for her friendship
(D) reduces her to a thief
(E) reinforces Amelia's good opinion of her

Rebecca's character is best summarized as
(A) opportunistic
(B) unresponsive
(C) indifferent
(D) disconsolate
(E) antagonistic

Amelia's feelings toward her brother are NOT the result of
(A) his absence
(B) the gifts he sends her
(C) his kindness as a child
(D) his being single
(E) his coldness toward her

Explanation: Amelia Sedley and Rebecca Sharp are the main characters in this excerpt; however, a third character, Joseph Sedley (Amelia's brother), is also mentioned.

From the context, you can gather several clues about each person's identity as a character and insight into his or her personality.

Amelia Sedley: 1. wealthy, 2. both parents alive, 3. has a brother named Joseph, 4. "tender-hearted," 5. perhaps naïve, 6. five years old when brother left + 10 years he was away = 15 years old, 7. claims to love her brother, 8. feels hurt because of her brother's actions and demeanor, 9. loyal to family and friends, 10. misinterprets Rebecca's conduct, except perhaps at an intuitive level, 11. affectionate.

Rebecca Sharp: 1. now an orphan, 2. poor heritage, 3. knew her father, 4. implications of being manipulative, 5. interested in wealth, 6. nineteen years old, 7. inexperienced at deception, but learning—foreshadowing trouble ahead, 8. intends to try to marry the rich Mr. Joseph Sedley, 9. has little time to implement her plans, 10. has no friends except Amelia.

Joseph Sedley: 1. just returned from India, 2. wealthy, 3. smokes a pipe, 4. has been away for ten years, 5. single, 6. brought presents for his sister, 7. was kind as a child, but has changed and is reserved with his sister now.

Correct Answers: **B, B, A, D**

IMPORTANT CONCEPT #4: SPECIAL CHARACTERS

Concept Explained:

In literary discussion, the word "character" carries with it several meanings beyond those already discussed. Some of these special characters are listed below.

1. The *character* is a brief, very descriptive essay that focuses on a person who embodies a particular virtue, vice, or character trait. The *character sketch* is a short essay that focuses on a person, describing all aspects of his or her personality.

2. The *character of places and things* refers to the essential quality found there. For example: "That wonderful country restaurant on the corner has a lot of character." "His essay is *characterized* by a somber tone that conflicts with the trivial nature of the subject."

3. The *conventional roles of characters* in a narrative include the following:

ERM ALERT You should know these terms: **hero(ine)** or **protagonist**

Definition: The leading male (female) character, who generally exhibits superior qualities or who simply is the main character.

ERM ALERT You should know these terms: **villain(ess)** or **antagonist**

Definition: A character who is often characterized as evil and in opposition to the protagonist.

ERM ALERT You should know this term: **superhero(ine)**

Definition: A larger-than-life, usually supernatural, hero(ine).

ERM ALERT You should know these terms: **antihero(ine)** and **tragic hero**

Definition: An antihero(ine) is a protagonist who is more ordinary than a traditional hero(ine) or one who is somewhat villainous. A *tragic hero* has a flaw in his character that causes his defeat, even though he was originally of a noble family (tragic genre).

TERM ALERT You should know the following terms of other character roles:

a. **flat character:** two-dimensional, described without details necessary to view the character as an individual

b. **round character:** three-dimensional, complex, as lifelike as possible

c. **stock character:** one used frequently in certain literary forms, such as Prince Charming in fairy tales

d. **type character:** represents the characteristics of a particular class or group of people, but still unpredictable and individualized

e. **stereotype character:** predictable, repeated without variation from one story to the next, lacks originality

4. Some *dramatic characters* are defined by how they reveal their thoughts.

TERM ALERT You should know the following terms and definitions:

a. A *confidant*—generally a friend, who "draws out" the person into talking about private matters

b. A *foil*—a contrasting character, who through that very contrast causes the viewer to see more clearly the personality of another character

c. An *aside*—in which a character directly addresses the audience

d. A *soliloquy*—in which a character, alone on stage, delivers a speech that reveals his or her thoughts

▼PRACTICE QUESTIONS▼

These words are taken from Benjamin Franklin's *Autobiography.*

> It was about this time I conceiv'd the bold and arduous project of arriving at moral perfection. I wish'd to live without committing any fault at any time; I would conquer all that either natural inclination,
> Line custom, or company might lead me into. As I knew, or thought I
> (5) knew, what was right and wrong, I did not see why I might not always do the one and avoid the other. But I soon found I had undertaken a task of more difficulty than I had imagined. While my care was employ'd in guarding against one fault, I was often surprised by another; habit took the advantage of inattention;
> (10) inclination was sometimes too strong for reason. I concluded, at length, that the mere speculative conviction that it was our interest to be completely virtuous, was not sufficient to prevent our slipping; and that the contrary habits must be broken, and good ones acquired and established, before we can have any dependence on a
> (15) steady, uniform rectitude of conduct. For this purpose I therefore contrived the following method.

This passage can best be characterized as
(A) comic, with a silly tone
(B) tragic, with a circumspective tone
(C) farcical, with a careless tone
(D) melodramatic, with a dogmatic tone
(E) serious, with a pragmatic tone

"A Descent into the Maelström" by Edgar Allan Poe:

> As the old man spoke, I became aware of a loud and gradually
> increasing sound, like the moaning of a vast herd of buffaloes upon
> an American prairie; and at the same moment I perceived that what
> Line seamen term the *chopping* character of the ocean beneath us, was
> (5) rapidly changing into a current which set to the eastward.

The *chopping* character of the ocean refers to which of the following?
  I. The nature of its sound
 II. The nature of its movement
III. The nature of its changes
(A) I only
(B) II only
(C) III only
(D) I and II only
(E) I, II, and III

Return to Poe's "A Man of the Crowd" on page 75 to answer the next question.

Based on the passage, the narrator is best described as
(A) the antagonist
(B) a villain
(C) the protagonist
(D) a superhero
(E) an antihero

These lines come from Anthony Trollope's *The Warden*:

> Do we not all know some reverend, all but sacred, personage
> before whom our tongue ceases to be loud, and our step to be
> elastic? But were we once to see him stretch himself beneath the
> Line bedclothes, yawn widely, and bury his face upon his pillow, we
> (5) could chatter before him as glibly as before a doctor or a lawyer.

The narrator's underlying premise is based on
(A) boring aspects of flat characters
(B) the unpredictability of round characters
(C) the predictability of type characters
(D) the sensible aspects of stereotyping people
(E) the fallacy of stereotyping people

Explanation: These four examples illustrate some of the ways "special characters" can work within literary selections. Franklin's serious (though unsuccessful) first attempt at self-improvement is followed by a sensible idea: making a plan. The *chopping* character of Poe's water refers to its up-and-down movement. It then changes in character to become a current. Poe's narrator in "A Man of the Crowd" is clearly the main character or protagonist; however, an excellent case could be made to label him an antihero because of his somewhat peculiar behavior. Trollope's narrator first gives a stereotypical description of a person held in high esteem (people use hushed tones and subdued movements when in his or her presence), then points out that such a person is human; the basis for the sterotype is not grounded in reality.

Correct Answers: **E, B, C, E**

ACTIVE THINKING EXERCISES FOR CHARACTER

STEP 1. ▸FOCUS◂

The SAT Subject Test in Literature has a sixty-minute time limit to answer approximately sixty to sixty-three questions over six to eight passages. Speed counts.

Obviously, you need to think clearly to think quickly; therefore, you may need to spend a little longer getting started on the first selection. Once you have begun, however, you may want to establish some sort of pacing or rhythm so that you answer all the questions you feel sure about before returning to those questions that you left unanswered.

Familiarity speeds your thinking. This book gives you lots of practice in working with the literary elements. In addition, simply having a consciousness about them in everyday life will help make them a natural part of your thinking processes. Everyone around you, for example, is a character and has character. Becoming sensitive to the elements of character will help you in your other studies and everyday life, in addition to the literature test.

To begin, simplify the elements you have studied so far:

1. *Meaning:* What is the subject? What is the point?
2. *Form: Prose?* Fiction or nonfiction? Genre? How organized?
     Poetry? Free, blank, or qualitative? How organized?
     Drama? Tragic or comic? How organized?
3. *(Narrative) Voice:* Point of view? Attitude of narrator or speaker?
4. *Tone:* Sound of attitude(s)? Writer's attitude? Atmosphere of work?
5. *Character:* Identity? Motivation? Personality?
     Nonnarrative work: how characterized?

▼EXERCISE▼

Turn to Interpretive Skill Practice Set A on page 331 and *without close reading* try to identify the five literary elements in each:

Selection One.

1 *Meaning:* Subject? A letter. Point? Breach of marriage lawsuit
2. *Form:* Prose, fiction, dialogue, letter
3. *(Narrative) Voice:* third-person narrator, unintrusive
4. *Tone:* Men in shock; threatening letter

5. *Characters:* All characters in mute astonishment, afraid to speak. Then Pickwick in denial, shock; Weller, alarmed; Winkle, "confiding females"; Snodgrass, musing about combination; Mrs. Bardele, wants money; Tupman, trembling voice.

Now, answer the question about character for Selection One on page 337.

Selection Two.

1. *Meaning:* Subject: fans. Point? Training women to use fans like men use swords
2. *Form:* Prose; nonfiction; letter within essay; satire? (letter); speaker presents letter to readers
3. *(Narrative) Voice:* Essay and letter in first person; speaker in essay views letter as diversionary; writer of letter views women's fans as weapons
4. *Tone:* Speaker in essay sounds amused; writer of letter sounds sarcastic
5. *Characters:* Speaker, writer of letter; speaker wants to be noncommittal; writer of letter wants to make a point

Answer the question over character for Selection Two.

Now, you try it.

Selection Three.

1 *Meaning:* _____
2. *Form:* _____
3. *(Narrative) Voice:* _____
4. *Tone:* _____
5. *Characters:* _____

Answer the question over character for Selection Three.

Selection Four.

Meaning: _____

Form: _____

(Narrative) Voice: _____

Tone: _____

Characters: _____

Answer the question over character for Selection Four.

For additional practice, continue this activity for Selection Five and Practice Sets B and C.

▼**EXERCISE**▼

If you can intuitively spot basic literary elements the first time you read through a selection, you will more likely be able to answer complex questions without breaking your mental rhythm or decreasing your speed. Your goal is to make identifying basic elements second nature. You can practice on your own by identifying the basic meaning, form, (narrative) voice, tone, and character of such communications as

- a front-page newspaper article
- an editorial
- a magazine article
- a short section in a history textbook
- a scene between commercial breaks of a television sitcom, movie, or talk show
- a randomly selected poem
- a page from a novel or short story

Here is the point: The more you practice, the keener your literary senses will become.

▼EXERCISE▼

Turn to Practice Test Five on page 415.

By this point, you should be developing a set of test-taking strategies that are comfortable and work for you as an individual. Take a moment to review them before taking Practice Test Five.

STEP 2. MOW (MY OWN WORDS)

When you **MOW** the following selection, look especially at the characters involved, their situations, attitudes, and actions.

This selection is taken from George Eliot's *Middlemarch*.

Dorothea's native strength of will was no longer all converted into resolute submission. She had a great yearning to be at Lowick, and was simply determined to go, not feeling bound to tell all her

Line reasons. But every one around her disapproved. Sir James was much
(5) pained, and offered that they should all migrate to Cheltenham for a few months with the sacred ark, otherwise called a cradle: at that period a man could hardly know what to propose if Cheltenham were rejected.

The Dowager Lady Chettam, just returned from a visit to her
(10) daughter in town, wished, at least, that Mrs. Vigo should be written to, and invited to accept the office of companion to Mrs. Casaubon: it was not credible that Dorothea as a young widow would think of living alone in the house at Lowick. Mrs. Vigo had been reader and secretary to royal personages, and in point of knowledge and
(15) sentiments even Dorothea could have nothing to object to her.

Mrs. Cadwallader said, privately, "You will certainly go mad in that house alone, my dear. You will see visions. We have all got to exert ourselves a little to keep sane, and call things by the same names as other people call them by. To be sure, for younger sons
(20) and women who have no money, it is a sort of provision to go mad: they are taken care of then. But you must not run into that. I daresay you are a little bored here with our good dowager; but think what a bore you might become yourself to your fellow-creatures if you were always playing tragedy queen and taking things sublimely. Sitting
(25) alone in that library at Lowick you may fancy yourself ruling the weather; you must get a few people round you who wouldn't believe you if you told them. That is a good lowering medicine."

Paraphrase the following:

Paragraph 1: _____

_____

Paragraph 2: _____

_____

Paragraph 3: _____

_____

What is the subject? _____

_____

Summarize the main idea (in one sentence): _____

_____

Keep this analysis for **BID**ing in Step 3.

STEP 3. BID (BREAK IT DOWN)

As usual, begin to BID by reviewing the basics of this chapter's focus element.

▼EXERCISE▼

Match the following terms with their definitions.

1. characterization	A. main character
2. climate	B. Superman or Wonder Woman
3. flashback	C. methods to portray someone
4. foreshadowing	D. recounting past events
5. protagonist	E. a prevailing attitude
6. antagonist	F. opposes main character
7. superhero	G. hints at the future

Correct Answers:
1. **C**   2. **E**   3. **D**   4. **G**   5. **A**   6. **F**   7. **B**

Next, determine if each of the following statements is true or false.

1. A character's attitudes can be based on assumption.

2. An attitude can be positive or negative.

3. Emotions of a character are almost always considered positive.

4. Characters sometimes respond to their circumstances.

5. A stereotype involves making assumptions.

6. Empathy can include plots that are "tearjerkers."

7. Characters frequently change personality.

8. To seem real, character changes need motivation, time, and detail.

9. Stock characters generally are three-dimensional and complex.

10. A foil provides a contrast to allow you to see someone else's character more clearly.

Correct Answers:
1. **T** 2. **T** 3. **F** 4. **T** 5. **T** 6. **F** 7. **F** 8. **T** 9. **F** 10. **T**

Finally, consider these questions. If you are looking at character:

1. Who are the characters? (names, ages, occupations)
2. What role does each play? (protagonist, antagonist, or other)
3. What are their personalities?
4. Do you see any character changes?
5. How would you characterize the work itself?

Correct Answers: (will vary with selection)

▼EXERCISE▼

Using the selection from *Middlemarch* and your **MOW** analysis from Step 2, answer the following mixture of questions. Notice that many of them are asking about elements of character, yet the word "character" is never used.

1. Based on the first paragraph, Sir James perhaps
   (A) is in ill health
   (B) is contemptuous of Dorothea
   (C) enjoyed traveling with his family
   (D) is overly enamored with a baby
   (E) dislikes Dorothea

2. That Dorothea does not feel "bound to tell all her reasons" (line 3) implies that
   (A) she gave no explanation
   (B) she does not understand herself
   (C) her reasons are simple and silly
   (D) she has reasons that are personal
   (E) she does not trust Sir James

3. The reasoning in the second paragraph and the tone of "even Dorothea" (line 15) probably reflect the attitude of
   (A) the narrator
   (B) Mrs. Vigo
   (C) Mrs. Casaubon
   (D) Dowager Lady Chettam
   (E) Sir James

4. Based on contextual clues, the reader can conclude that Dorothea
   (A) is insane
   (B) resists change
   (C) is wealthy
   (D) lacks resolve
   (E) dislikes Dowager Lady Chettam

5. Mrs. Cadwallader's choice of words in the last paragraph results in
   (A) making her seem intuitive
   (B) giving the selection a tragic tone
   (C) giving the selection a romantic tone
   (D) making Dorothea seem already insane
   (E) making the widow's grief seem contrived

6. The first paragraph indicates in Dorothy
   (A) a love for Lowick over Cheltenham
   (B) a return from submission to strength of will
   (C) a tendency to disapprove
   (D) a disagreeable nature
   (E) animosity toward Sir James

7. The reference to Mrs. Vigo's "sentiments" in line 15 indicates that she is
   (A) maudlin
   (B) opinionated
   (C) private and contemplative
   (D) emotional and unreasoning
   (E) intelligent and perceptive

Answers and Explanations:

1. **D** The narrator's tongue-in-cheek reference to the cradle as "the sacred ark" is sarcastic in tone and implies answer choice D.

2. **D** By elimination, Dorothea may have given an explanation, just not "all" her reasons (A), which suggests that she does have reasons (B) and that they may be complex rather than simple (C).

3. **D** Dowager Lady Chettam wants Dorothea to engage Mrs. Vigo; therefore, the attitude and reasons described probably reflect Dowager Lady Chettam's thinking.

4. **C** Titles, friends, money for a paid companion (Mrs. Vigo), no need to seek employment, and the contrast made between Dorothea and "women who have no money" all imply wealth.

5. **E** She might seem intuitive except for the nature of her arguments. That a widow would be "playing tragedy queen" implies manipulation and is consistent with the suggestion that poor widows can get care by going mad.

6. **B** Directly expressed in line 1, her strength of will returned.

7. **E** Although sentiment includes opinion and complex feelings, context does not support the extremes of answer choices A, B, or D. Clearly, Mrs. Vigo is being described as an intelligent, perceptive companion.

STEP 4. TT → TM (TEST TAKER TO TEST MAKER)

Determining people's characters (personalities, motivations, and so forth) is an important communication skill inside the classroom or out, whether reading about people or observing them in action.

A practical method for becoming sensitive to elements of character is to develop a personality or character profile, much like investigators do to find missing people.

▼EXERCISE▼

Select a character from a novel or history and develop a character profile on that person. Using this chapter to guide you, list every aspect of his or her character that you can support with evidence.

If you were going to cast this person in a drama, what role would he or she play? (protagonist, antagonist, or other)?

Finally, a *foil* is a contrasting character, whose personality and actions help us see the main character more clearly. Describe the personality of someone who would be a foil for your focus character.

▼**EXERCISE**▼

Using the *Middlemarch* selection, what key points would describe Dorothea's character? Select one and write a test question based on that point.

CHARACTER IN CONCLUSION

Character concludes the first five literary elements that, to a great degree, deal with a selection as a whole: what is the work's meaning, form, overall voice, and tone, and how is it characterized? There are details within these elements, of course, but understanding how they work in the big picture is an important step in critical reading. The next two elements, in contrast, deal almost exclusively with details, where understanding can hinge on a single word.

Literary Element Number Six: Use of Language

You are traveling in the American Midwest and open the newspaper to learn about the area. There are the grocery store ads: This week's featured item in the bakery—apple pie.

A crust, cooked apples, cinnamon.

You can see it in your mind's eye now: hot apple pie, rich pastry crust that flakes apart when your fork hits it. Steam rises from the slice and softly brushes your cheek as the slice is lifted from the rest of the pie—and it smells *so-o-o* good. You begin to breathe deeper: Aromas of hot cinnamon and vanilla and baked apples swirl around your head. Maybe add a thick slice of American cheese that melts down into the apples and sauce. No, better yet— a big scoop of rich vanilla ice cream that melts and makes a creamy, thick sauce all around the chunks of steamy apples, mixing with the cinnamon in great big swirls of flavor. Your mouth waters in anticipation of that first bite. After all, it's your duty to eat a slice of fresh-baked apple pie, because what represents America better than the flag, Mom, and apple pie?

Welcome to the world of **imagery**.

ERM ALERT You should know this term: **imagery**

Definition: Roughly defined, imagery—the use of images—refers to the mental pictures you get as a result of words.

An image can be **literal**, a standard meaning like the mental picture of apples and cinnamon baked in a pastry crust for an apple pie, or it can be **figurative**, like the American love of country associated with apple pie. Imagery can refer to visual pictures that come to mind, or it can also include all the sensual qualities (kinesthetic/motion, auditory/hearing, thermal/heat, tactile/touch, gustatory/taste, and olfactory/smell). Imagery can also refer to abstract, nonsensual qualities, such as love, hate, peace, fear, and other emotions.

ERM ALERT You should know this term: **image**

Definition: An **image**, then, consists of the mental representations that certain words and certain uses of language produce.

Imagery is a collection of images. Look at the collection of images used in the preceding apple pie illustration. You see the pie (visual), smell the pie (olfactory), feel the steam (tactile), and taste the pie (gustatory). When one sense is described by terms usually associated with another sense, such a mixture of sensory images is called **synaesthesia**: "a red-hot candy." Imagery can also take on patterns as the images are used throughout a work or can be seen as **image-clusters** (recurring groupings of images) that can actually affect the tone of a work.

To summarize: Words create images in people's minds, some of which are literal and some of which are figurative.

ERM ALERT You should know these terms: **figure of speech**
figurative language

Definition: A figure of speech is the result of using language in such a way that a figurative, rather than literal, meaning is conveyed. A figure of speech can change the meanings of words or change the way words are used without changing the meanings. Figurative language, then, is based on using figures of speech.

IMPORTANT CONCEPT #1: FIGURES OF SPEECH BASED ON ANALOGY

Concept Explained:

Analogy, which has its origin in mathematics, involves explaining the unknown and unfamiliar by drawing comparisons to the known and familiar.

When in mathematics you figure $\frac{a}{b} = \frac{c}{d}$, *a* (an analogue) is to *b* in the same relationship as *c* (another analogue) is to *d*; therefore, although *a* and *c* are not necessarily identical, they are similar because *a* has the same relationship to *b* that *c* has to *d*.

Analogies are drawn to explain, to describe, to argue, and to justify; however, whatever the purpose in making the comparison, at the root of analogy are two distinct units of thought: the **vehicle** and the **tenor**.

The tenor is the subject or idea you are trying to explain, and the vehicle is the means by which you explain it. If you try to describe a zebra by comparing it to a horse with stripes, the zebra is the tenor and the horse is the vehicle. Likewise, if you wanted to explain some abstract concept, such as rage, you might compare it to a consuming fire: Tenor? Rage. Vehicle? Fire.

TERM ALERT You should know this term: **simile**

Definition: **Simile** is a comparison using "like" or "as." A person who has never tasted buffalo meat might ask someone who just ate a buffalo burger, "What does it taste *like*?" The answer, "It tastes *like* a very strong beef burger," is a simile.

Similes are characterized by their directness, as in the opening couplet of Henry Constable's sixteenth-century poem:

HOPE, LIKE THE HYENA

Hope, like the hyena, coming to be old,
Alters his shape, is turned into despair.

The speaker compares hope that is delayed ("old") to a hyena that changes shape like hope changes into despair. What is the tenor? Hope. Its vehicle? The hyena.

▼PRACTICE QUESTIONS▼

Sometimes the simile is sustained for an entire stanza or even an entire poem. Here is the first stanza of Thomas Lodge's "Love in My Bosom."

> Love in my bosom like a bee
>   Doth suck his sweet;
> Now with his wings he plays with me,
>   Now with his feet.
> (5) Within mine eyes he makes his nest,
> His bed amidst my tender breast;
> My kisses are his daily feast,
> And yet he robs me of my rest.
>   Ah, wanton, will ye?

The speaker compares love to a

(A) bosom
(B) bee
(C) wing
(D) kiss
(E) bed

The simile in this poem makes love seem

(A) dangerous
(B) annoying
(C) delightful
(D) thrilling
(E) burdensome

Explanation: "Love…like a bee" (line 1): This bee of love is playful, rests in the speaker's eyes and heart (emotions), and ultimately "robs" the speaker of his rest.

Correct Answers: B, B

TERM ALERT You should know this term: **metaphor**

Definition: **Metaphor**, unlike the direct nature of the simile, is an *implied* comparison: rosy-red lips (tenor—lips; vehicle—a red rose).

▼PRACTICE QUESTIONS▼

Thomas Nashe's sixteenth-century "Adieu, Farewell Earth's Bliss":

> Beauty is but a flower
> Which wrinkles will devour;
> Brightness falls from the air,
> (Line) Queens have died young and fair,
> (5) Dust hath closed Helen's eye.
> I am sick, I must die.
>   Lord, have mercy on us!

"A flower" in line 1 is used as a vehicle to describe

(A) brightness
(B) queens
(C) beauty
(D) Helen
(E) wrinkles

"A flower" in line 1 relates to
(A) time
(B) love
(C) personality
(D) appearance
(E) royalty

An important approach to understanding any use of language is to determine the *effects* of its use.

Comparing beauty to a flower in line 1 has the effect of
(A) emphasizing the natural elements of beauty
(B) making beauty seem fragile
(C) elevating beauty to a higher symbolic level
(D) limiting beauty to natural elements
(E) exaggerating beauty's impact

Explanation: "Beauty is...a flower" (line 1); beauty, as it relates to a flower, is based on appearance because "wrinkles will devour" it, as opposed to inner beauty. In the third question, context will help you select answer B (the correct answer) over A (an answer that may seem to be correct): use of "but" in the sense of "nothing more than" or "merely" and the clear reference to a flower's fragility in line 2—"wrinkles will devour."

Correct Answers: **C, D, B**

▼PRACTICE QUESTION▼

At other times the metaphor (like simile) can be a **controlling image**. A controlling image is an image that runs throughout a work. Shakespeare's "Sonnet 97":

> How like a winter hath my absence been
> From thee, the pleasure of the fleeting year!
> What freezings have I felt, what dark days seen!
> What old December's bareness everywhere!
>
> (5) And yet this time removed was summer's time,
> The teeming autumn, big with rich increase,
> Bearing the wanton burden of the prime,
> Like widowed wombs after their lords' decease:
> Yet this abundant issue seemed to me
> (10) But hope of orphans and unfathered fruit;
> For summer and his pleasures wait on thee,
> And, thou away, the very birds are mute.
> Or, if they sing, 'tis with so dull a cheer,
> That leaves look pale, dreading the winter's near.

The controlling image compares
(A) winter to widowed wombs
(B) pleasure to the fleeting year
(C) autumn to abundant issue
(D) absence to summer's time
(E) absence to the winter season

Explanation: The first simile is presented in line 1: his absence has been "like a winter." A different simile appears in line 8; however, he returns to the winter image by line 11, using "For" to establish a causal relationship and ending with "winter's near."

Correct Answer: **E**

▼PRACTICE QUESTION▼

Sometimes a tenor will have more than one vehicle: "His attitude was ice-cold, rock-hard, and knife-sharp." Anthony Munday uses more than twenty vehicles in "I Serve a Mistress":

> I serve a mistress whiter than the snow,
>   Straighter than cedar, brighter than the glass,
> Finer in trip and swifter than the roe,
>   More pleasant than the field of flowering grass;
> More gladsome to my withering joys that fade,
> Than winter's sun or summer's cooling shade.
>
> Sweeter than swelling grape of ripest wine,
>   Softer than feathers of the fairest swan,
> Smoother than jet, more stately than the pine,
>   Fresher than poplar, smaller than my span,
> Clearer than beauty's fiery pointed beam,
> Or icy crust of crystal's frozen stream.
>
> Yet is she curster than the bear by kind,
>   And harder-hearted than the agèd oak,
> More glib than oil, more fickle than the wind,
>   Stiffer than steel, no sooner bent but broke.
> Lo! thus my service is a lasting sore;
> Yet will I serve, although I die therefore.

Line (5), (10), (15) marked in margin.

The change in imagery in this poem describes
(A) mental instability
(B) seasonal changes
(C) primeval hatred
(D) a love-hate relationship
(E) a reversal of fortune

Explanation: Notice the change in vehicles in the last stanza from how wonderful she is to how horrible, to the point of making his "service ... a lasting sore."

Correct Answer: **D**

Note: **Mixed metaphors** are the result of a blend of incongruous vehicles for the same tenor. Mixed metaphors can be effectively used, but when poorly done, a mixed metaphor can produce undesirable effects: "She watched the eagle sail the sea of air currents with egg-beater movements and calypso rhythms." Comparing the air currents (the tenor) to the sea (the vehicle) is a common metaphor: however, this poor bird's flight (the tenor) is being compared to three very incongruous vehicles: a ship ("sail"), an eggbeater ("egg-beater movements"), and dance music ("calypso rhythms"). You may find mixed metaphors in prose narratives, such as "She sailed into the room and clawed through the books on the tables."

▼PRACTICE QUESTION▼

A *conceit* is a very intricate parallel drawn between two otherwise *dissimilar* concepts or things:

ELEGY

My prime of youth is but a frost of cares,
My feast of joy is but a dish of pain,
My crop of corn is but a field of tares,
And all my good is but vain hope of gain;
The day is past, and yet I saw no sun,
And now I live, and now my life is done.

Line
(5)

by Chidiock Tichborne

The speaker sees his life as
(A) comic
(B) too short
(C) tragic
(D) too long
(E) too busy

Explanation: Youth is generally associated with spring's warmth, not fall's frost; joy is not associated with pain; tares have invaded his corn crop (the product of his work is worthless); even his good was only "vain hope." His life is about over—a day without sun. What a tragic situation!

Correct Answer: C

Note: In your reading, you also may find some use of metaphor in which the tenor is not directly named but only implied. These sophisticated comparisons are called **implicit metaphors** and you must rely on context for meaning. In a work about a young woman's growing affection for a young man, a descriptive line might read "The bud drowned in the seas of distrust and envy." The *bud* is a vehicle for an implied tenor that can only be determined by the situation: undeveloped love. In contrast, the second metaphor at work here has directly stated tenors (distrust and envy) for its vehicle (seas).

Also, a metaphor can "die." **Dead metaphors** are those that are so commonplace that the reader no longer perceives the fact that the vehicle and tenor do not match: "pig-headed attitude," "the skin of one's teeth," "the core of the subject," "to set your heart on...," "the long arm of the law."

When metaphors are extended into narrative form in which the actual story and its elements (actions, places, people, and things) represent elements outside the story, often with the characters and events representing ideas, the work is called an **allegory**. John Bunyan's *Pilgrim's Progress* is a famous allegory in which the journey of "Christian" (a character in the story) from the City of Destruction to the Celestial City allegorizes the Christian doctrine of salvation.

TERM ALERT You should know this term: **personification**

Definition: In personification inanimate objects, animals, or abstract ideas are given human characteristics.

▼PRACTICE QUESTIONS▼

In the third stanza of "The Aged Lover Renounceth Love" (Lord Thomas Vaux's sixteenth-century work), age and "lusty life" are both personified:

> For age with stealing steps
> Hath clawed me with his crutch,
> And lusty life away she leaps
> As there had been none such.

Age is given the human characteristics of walking with a crutch. Lusty life—youth—is given the human characteristic of leaping.

In a testing situation, you may be asked to identify that the object or idea is being personified. Tests also may include questions concerning the effects of the personification:

"Lusty life," as a character in lines 3–4, of the above stanza seems
(A) uncaring
(B) happy
(C) athletic
(D) an illusion
(E) deceptive

The personification of "age" in lines 1–2 emphasizes
(A) that no one escapes age
(B) the speaker's acceptance of age
(C) universal carnality
(D) age's feeble condition
(E) age's furtive nature

Explanation: The lusty life of youth does not even look back; age has used stealth, coming on the speaker unexpectedly.

Correct Answers: **A, E**

▼PRACTICE QUESTION▼

In Sir Phillip Sidney's sixteenth-century poem "Loving in Truth," he personifies Invention, Nature, and Study:

> Loving in truth, and fain in verse my love to show,
> That she, dear she, might take some pleasure of my pain,
> Pleasure might cause her read, reading might make her know,
> Line Knowledge might pity win, and pity grace obtain,
> (5) I sought fit words to paint the blackest face of woe,
> Studying inventions fine, her wits to entertain,
> Oft turning others' leaves, to see if thence would flow
> Some fresh and fruitful showers upon my sunburnt brain.
> But words came halting forth, wanting Invention's stay;
> (10) Invention, Nature's child, fled step-dame Study's blows;
> And others' feet still seemed but strangers in my way.
> Thus great with child to speak, and helpless in my throes,
> Biting my truant pen, beating myself for spite:
> "Fool," said my Muse to me, "look in thy heart and write."

The effect of personifying Invention, Nature, and Study (lines 9–10) is to

(A) contrast the natural to the artificial

(B) emphasize love

(C) imitate other poets

(D) confirm his love for his auditor

(E) compare his work to that of others

Explanation: What is the *effect* of this personification? The first four lines set up the situation: The speaker wants to write a poem that will show the woman he loves how much he loves her. Lines 5–8 outline that he studied "inventions" and "others' leaves" (other poets' writings) for ideas, but his brain is "sunburnt"—what today might be called "writer's block" or "burnout." Lines 9–10 (the lines that contain the personification) reveal that although he wanted "Invention" (originality) which is "Nature's child" (unlearned, natural) to stay, it "fled" from "step-dame Study's blows." Line 11 confirms that copying the style of others' works did not help him. He compares himself to a pregnant woman in line 12, his message wants so to be delivered; he is desperate by line 13. But line 14 makes his point: originality must come from within.

Within this context, what is the *effect* of personifying Invention and Nature? One possible effect is to make originality, as "Nature's child" seem innocent (as a child), nonthreatening and desirable. The personification of Study, on the other hand, heightens the perception that the speaker has lost his fresh approach (perhaps) to imitation of others' works (a "step-dame" relationship to Invention in contrast to Invention as "Nature's child"—a natural relationship). The effect of the personification of Invention, Nature, and Study is to emphasize that writing a poem is a natural process from within rather than an artificial process.

Correct Answer: **A**

NOTE: Reification is a means of describing abstract ideas as if they were concrete things, sometimes using metaphor (for example, "Life is a flowing stream"), sometimes personifying the abstraction (as in, "Love wonders the lonely paths in my heart"). The effect, regardless of the type of analogy used, is to give the reader a sense of tangible reality for otherwise difficult-to-explain ideas.

NOTE: Do not confuse personification (figurative language in which human characteristics are given to inanimate objects or abstract ideas) with *anthropomorphism*, which is presenting a nonhuman (such as an animal or mythical god) as a human. The rabbit who declares he is "late" in *Alice in Wonderland* is an anthropomorphism; the rabbit described by the hunter as "a worthy opponent who planned his strategy well, laughing at my clumsiness and disdaining the sophistication of my weapons" is being personified.

TERM ALERT You should know this term: **allusion**

Definition: **Allusion** is a direct or indirect reference in a literary work to some person, place, thing, or event outside the work, or to some other literary work.

There are several different kinds of allusion. **Topical allusions** are based on current events and serve a significant role in the comedy routines of late-night television talk show hosts. **Personal allusions** are references to events, facts, and other information in the writer's own life. Obviously, the significance of many topical and personal allusions are lost to readers of later generations. **Allusions to historical events and personages, other works** (the writers, the works themselves, or the styles of the works), and **documented information**, however, have a sense of timelessness, although realizing the full significance may require a broad base of knowledge on the part of the reader.

▼PRACTICE QUESTIONS▼

You will not be tested over obscure allusions; however, you are expected to be familiar with allusions that are considered part of the common knowledge of British and American cultures. For example, you should know that there is a rabbit that talks in *Alice in Wonderland*.

Some allusions are popular among writers and are used over the centuries. The Trojan War, its characters and circumstances, has remained a rich source of allusion for both prose and poetry for many generations. These two stanzas from Thomas Nashe's "Adieu, Farewell Earth's Bliss" (1592) are characteristic:

> Beauty is but a flower
> Which wrinkles will devour,
> Brightness falls from the air,
> Queens have died young and fair,

Line
(5)
(allusion) →
> Dust hath closed Helen's eye.
> I am sick, I must die.
>   Lord, have mercy on us!

> Strength stoops unto the grave,

(allusion) →
> Worms feed on Hector brave,

(10)
> Swords may not fight with fate,
> Earth still holds ope her gate.
> Come! come! the bells do cry.
> I am sick, I must die.
>   Lord, have mercy on us!

In line 5, "Helen" is presented as
(A) a woman who became ill and died
(B) famous for growing flowers
(C) a woman symbolic of beauty
(D) the speaker's lover
(E) the victim of a dust storm

Explanation: The allusion to Helen as beautiful and Hector as brave has been used so extensively as to become traditional "types" of beauty and bravery.

Correct Answer: **C**

A common source for allusion that might be tested is the systems of Greek and Roman mythology. For example, Matthew Arnold's "Memorial Verses," for the day that William Wordsworth died (April 27, 1850):

> When Byron's eyes were shut in death,
> We bowed our head and held our breath.
> He taught us little; but our soul

Line
> Had *felt* him like the thunder's roll.

(5)
> With shivering heart the strife we saw
> Of passion with eternal law;
> And yet with reverential awe
> We watched the fount of fiery life

(allusion) →
> Which served for that Titanic strife.

The allusion in the last line ("Titanic strife") serves to
(A) confound the issue
(B) emphasize the size of the strife
(C) reinforce the speaker's trauma
(D) contrast the "fiery life"
(E) diminish the size of the strife

Explanation: The Titans of Greek myth were known for their enormous size and strength. *The Titanic,* a ship that sank when it hit an iceberg in 1912, was notable at the time for its large size.

Correct Answer: **B**

The Bible is another source of literary allusion that might be tested because of its prevalence in terms of numbers of references in English and American literature. In 1611, England's King James the First sponsored an English translation from the Greek "New Testament" and Hebrew "Old Testament." The King James Version, also called the Authorized Version, is the most popular English Bible and a best seller yet today.

Professor Northrup Frye of the University of Toronto makes this very strong statement in *The Great Code* (published in 1982, 1981, Harcourt Brace Jovanovich, Publishers): "I soon realized that a student of English literature who does not know the Bible does not understand a good deal of what is going on in what he reads: the most conscientious student will be continually misconstruing the implications, even the meaning." Although not all writers did use or are using the Bible as a source for allusions, a significant number of important works of English and American literature indisputably include biblical references and allusions that range from occasional biblical references to literature in which the very structures of the works themselves rely on the readers' knowledge of the Bible for understanding the writers' meanings.

Based on Judeo-Christian traditions, the English-speaking culture assimilated many of the principles, values, and teachings of the Bible. As a result, both religious and secular writings oftentimes reflect these influences. Some biblical phrases and concepts often used include:

- The apple of my eye
- A Judas
- A prophet has no honor in his own country
- The salt of the earth
- Hiding your light under a bushel
- Man does not live by bread alone
- Turning water into wine
- Walking on water
- Casting the first stone
- My brother's keeper
- A house divided cannot stand
- Standing against a Goliath
- Forty years in the wilderness
- Being thrown to the lions
- Being thrown into the fiery furnace
- Trying to pass a camel through the eye of a needle
- The patience of Job

- Wisdom of Solomon
- A coat of many colors
- A leopard changing its spots

This list could go on and on. After years of usage in secular writing, readers, speakers, and writers may not recognize that these phrases and concepts are found in the Bible.

One significant factor that separates the Bible from other works is the pervasiveness of the Bible's influence. It has affected to varying degrees a people's belief system and, as a result, influenced history with a major impact on literature.

▼PRACTICE QUESTIONS▼

LEAVE ME, O LOVE

Leave me, O Love, which reachest but to dust,
And thou, my mind, aspire to higher things;
Grow rich in that which never taketh rust:
Whatever fades but fading pleasure brings.
    Draw in thy beams, and humble all thy might
To that sweet yoke where lasting freedoms be;
Which breaks the clouds and opens forth the light
That doth both shine and give us sight to see.
    O take fast hold; let that light be thy guide
In this small course which birth draws out to death,
And think how evil becometh him to slide,
Who seeketh heav'n, and comes of heav'nly breath.
    Then farewell, world, thy uttermost I see;
Eternal Love, maintain thy life in me.

Line
(5)

(10)

by Sir Philip Sidney

This poem does NOT include
(A) sonnet form
(B) biblical allusion
(C) metaphor
(D) allusion to current events
(E) a concluding couplet

The central contrast is seen in which of the following?
(A) Love (line 1) and Eternal Love (line 14)
(B) mind (line 2) and world (line 13)
(C) Grow rich (line 3) and evil (line 11)
(D) birth (line 10) and farewell (line 13)
(E) clouds (line 7) and light (line 7)

Explanation: This poem is fourteen lines written in iambic pentameter (a sonnet) with a concluding couplet. Seeking Heaven and Eternal Love is a frequently used biblical allusion. In the context of this poem, "Love, which reachest but to dust" obviously is finite, carnal, and earthbound in contrast to Eternal Love.

Correct Answers: **D, A**

▼Practice Questions▼

Prose writers, too, within the Judeo-Christian tradition of England and America rely heavily on the Bible as a source for literary allusion. For example, most Americans are familiar with Patrick Henry's most famous speech in which he challenged, "Give me liberty, or give me death!" Notice his use of biblical allusion (highlighted by arrows) in these excerpts from the speech:

LIBERTY OR DEATH
by
Patrick Henry

Mr. President, it is natural to man to indulge
in the illusions of hope. We are apt to shut our
eyes against a painful truth and listen to the
Line   song of that siren, till she transforms us into
(5)   beasts. Is this the part of wise men, engaged in
a great and arduous struggle for liberty? Are we
disposed to be of the number of those, who,
→ having eyes, see not, and having ears, hear not,
the things which so nearly concern their
(10)   temporal salvation? For my part, whatever
anguish of spirit it may cost, I am willing to
know the whole truth, to know the worst and to
provide for it.
    I have but one lamp by which my feet are
(15)   guided, and that is the lamp of experience. I
know of no way of judging of the future but by
the past. And judging by the past, I wish to know
what there has been in the conduct of the
British ministry for the last ten years to justify
(20)   those hopes with which gentlemen have been
pleased to solace themselves and the House? Is
it that insidious smile with which our petition
has been lately received? Trust it not, sir; it will
prove a snare to your feet. Suffer not yourselves
(25) → to be betrayed with a kiss. Ask yourselves how
this gracious reception of our petition comports
with these warlike preparations which cover our
waters and darken our land. Are fleets and
armies necessary to a work of love and
(30)   reconciliation? Have we shown ourselves so
unwilling to be reconciled that force must be
called in to win back our love? Let us not
deceive ourselves, sir. These are the
implements of war and subjugation, the last
(35)   arguments to which kings resort....If we wish to
be free—if we mean to preserve inviolate those
inestimable privileges for which we have been

(40)   so long contending—if we mean not basely to
        abandon the noble struggle in which we have
        been so long engaged, and which we have
        pledged ourselves never to abandon until the
        glorious object of our contest shall be obtained,
        we must fight! I repeat it, sir, we must fight! An
→   appeal to arms and to the God of Hosts is all
(45)   that is left us!

                    * * *

        It is in vain, sir, to extenuate the matter.
→   Gentlemen may cry, peace, peace!—but there
        is no peace. The war is actually begun! The next
        gale that sweeps from the north will bring to our
(50)   ears the clash of resounding arms! Our brethren
        are already in the field! Why stand we here idle?
        What is it that gentlemen wish? What would they
        have? Is life so dear, or peace so sweet, as to
        be purchased at the price of chains and slavery?
(55)   Forbid it, Almighty God! I know not what course
        others may take, but as for me: *Give me liberty,
        or give me death!*

Having eyes, but not seeing, and ears, but not hearing, refers to
  I. being deaf and mute
 II. understanding
III. attitudes
 IV. being deaf and blind
(A) I only
(B) II only
(C) IV only
(D) II and III only
(E) I, II, III, and IV

Being "betrayed with a kiss" (line 25) is an allusion to
(A) the murder of Caesar by Mark Anthony
(B) the suicide of Cleopatra
(C) Hitler's death orders during World War II
(D) warnings that the "British are coming!"
(E) Judas identifying Jesus Christ to Roman soldiers

"An appeal to arms and to the God of Hosts" (line 44) is to
(A) watch and listen
(B) recruit men and be hospitable
(C) fight and pray
(D) challenge and capitulate
(E) carry and enlist

According to the speaker, the gentlemen who cry peace are

(A) mistaken

(B) peacemakers

(C) reliable

(D) true prophets

(E) politicians

Explanation: In this often-referenced biblical allusion, those who have eyes (physically to see), but do not see (spiritual discernment) and who have ears to listen with, but do not hear the message lack understanding because of their attitudes. A modern key to understanding this allusion is the expression "Oh, I see!" when we finally understand something or "I hear you" said when we understand and are in agreement. In contrast, people sometimes say, "I hear you talking" to indicate that they understand what is being said, but do not agree with it (by implication, the hearer views what is being said as simply "talk"). Based on the account of Judas Iscariot kissing Jesus on the cheek to identify him to Roman soldiers, "betrayed by a kiss" is a traditional symbol of betrayal by those once thought to be friends. Also, the name "Judas" is a related symbol. To call someone a "Judas" is to accuse the person of betrayal. "An appeal to arms" or weapons is to fight. The men who cry peace are mistaken because "The war is actually begun!"

Correct Answers: **D, E, C, A**

TERM ALERT You should know this term: **metonymy**

Definition Metonymy occurs when a closely associated name of an object is used in place of a word, such as referring to a king as "the ring giver" or "the crown," or to his position of authority as "the throne." In the United States, people often refer to the executive branch of the federal government or to the president as "the White House."

▼PRACTICE QUESTION▼

James Shirley uses metonymy in this seventeenth-century poem "The Glories of Our Blood and State":

> The glories of our blood and state
> Are shadows, not substantial things;
> There is no armour against fate;
> Death lays his icy hand on kings:
> Sceptre and crown
> Must tumble down,
> And in the dust be equal made
> With the poor crooked scythe and spade.

(Line (5) metonymy → "Sceptre and crown"; metonymy → "With the poor crooked scythe and spade.")

"Scythe and spade" in the last line contextually refers to

(A) damaged equipment

(B) death

(C) farm implements

(D) the working man

(E) fate

"Sceptre and crown" is a metonymy for the king, and "scythe and spade" is a metonymy for the working man.

Correct Answer: **D**

ERM ALERT You should know this term: **synecdoche**

Definition: In a **synecdoche**, the name of a part represents the whole or the name of the whole represents the part. Workers may be referred to as "hands." A country's "ears and eyes" are its spies. A "roof over your head" is a home, and a musical producer might refer to the lead singer as "the voice."

NOTE: Antonomasia is a figure of speech used extensively in politics. In antonomasia, a proper name is used to represent an idea. For example, "Watergate" refers to an entire network of events during the 1970s. Sometimes the antonomasia is a person's name, as when western movie enthusiasts say, "There aren't any John Waynes in movies anymore"—John Wayne representing (a type of) the rugged, "all-male" western hero who exhibits certain expected characteristics.

TERM ALERT You should know this term: **epithet**

Definition: An **epithet** is an adjective, noun, or noun phrase describing a particular characteristic of a person or thing. An epithet might be to describe a puzzle as a "brain-twister," a home as a "sanctuary from the storm," or an admired leader as a "shining beacon of light." An epithet is often used as a substitution for a proper name, such as when, in referring to Elvis Presley, tabloid headlines read "The King of Rock'n'Roll Spotted in White House Tour Group." Note that the epithet is not restricted to just the negative name-calling normally associated with the term.

▼PRACTICE QUESTION▼

This selection is found in *The Pilot* by James Fenimore Cooper.

> "No man—I speak not of women, who cannot be supposed so well
> versed in human nature—but no man who has reached the time of life
> that entitles him to be called by that name, can consort with these
> Line disorganizers, who would destroy everything that is sacred—these
> (5) levellers who would pull down the great to exalt the little—these
> Jacobins, who—who—"
> "Nay, sir, if you are at a loss for opprobrious epithets," said
> Katherine, with provoking coolness, "call on Mr. Christopher Dillon
> for assistance; he waits your pleasure at the door."

The best understanding of "opprobrious epithets" as used in the passage is
(A) high-sounding praise
(B) contemptuous names
(C) burdensome directives
(D) convenient titles
(E) harsh orders

Explanation: By definition and supported by context, to be opprobrious is to be contemptuous in an abusive or shameful manner. An epithet refers to, in this context, negative name-calling.

Correct Answer: **B**

TERM ALERT You should know this term: **symbol**

Definition: A **symbol** (in contrast to metaphor that serves to illustrate) is a type of image that begins with some objective thing that calls to mind a second level of meaning that oftentimes embodies abstract concepts, that in turn elicit from the reader a range of emotions.

▼PRACTICE QUESTION▼

Here is the third stanza of "The Canonization," by John Donne.

> Call us what you will, we are made such by love.
>   Call her one, me another fly,
>   We're tapers too, and at our own cost die;
>   And we in us find th'eagle and the dove.
>   The phoenix riddle hath more wit
>   By us; we two, being one, are it.
> So to one neutral thing both sexes fit,
>   We die and rise the same, and prove
>   Mysterious by this love.

Line → (line 4)
(5)

The eagle and dove could represent which of the following in this context?
 I. Strength
 II. Purity
 III. Peace
 IV. National pride
(A) I only
(B) II only
(C) III only
(D) I, II, and III only
(E) I, II, III, and IV

Explanation: Generally, symbols depend for their associated meanings on the context of the literary work in which they are used. A deeper analysis would be needed to explore the levels of meaning of "th' eagle and the dove" in this poem; however, traditionally an eagle symbolizes strength and the dove represents purity and peace. The eagle is a symbol of America, but within the context of this stanza, national pride does not fit.

Correct Answer: **D**

UNIVERSAL SYMBOLS

SYMBOL	MEANING LEVEL ONE	MEANING LEVEL TWO	*POSSIBLE EMOTIONS
1. National flag	Cloth with pattern	Represents country	Pride, patriotism
2. Sea	Large body of water	Represents countless people	Fear of invasion, pity on the masses
3. Red rose	Flower	Represents love	Sentimentalism, special person
4. Purple	Color	Represents royalty	Respect, honor
5. Wedding ring	Gold band worn on left hand	Represents a state of being married	Fidelity, loyalty
6. Longhorned steer	Steer with long, curved horns	Represents football team at a Texas school	School loyalty and rivalry
7. *Yellow	Color	Represents cowardice and fear	Shame, dishonor
		also	
		Slow down	Caution
		and	
		Homecoming, reunion (ribbons)	Support, honor, and happiness
		and survival, winning	Pride, courage, hope

* Notice that the same symbol can have both negative or positive connotations depending on usage or context.

IMPORTANT CONCEPT #2: FIGURES OF SPEECH BASED ON RHETORIC

Concept Explained:

In its broadest sense, rhetoric is use of language for the purpose of persuading the readers or hearers.

ERM ALERT You should know this term: **rhetorical question**

Definition: Rhetorical questions are those asked, not for the purpose of eliciting an expressed answer, but rather for their rhetorical effect: an emphasis of the speaker's point.

▼PRACTICE QUESTIONS▼

In this excerpt from James Madison's June 6, 1788, speech, Madison (who favored a federal constitution) is arguing against a speech made the previous day by Patrick Henry in which Henry spoke against ratification:

> I must confess I have not been able to find his usual consistency in the gentleman's argument on this occasion. He informs us that the people of the country are at perfect repose; that is, every man
>
> Line enjoys the fruits of his labor peaceably and securely, and that
> (5) everything is in perfect tranquility and safety. I wish sincerely that this were true. If this be their happy situation, why has every state acknowledged the contrary? Why were deputies from all the states sent to the general convention? Why have complaints of national and individual distresses been echoed and reechoed throughout the
> (10) continent? Why has our general government been so shamefully disgraced and our Constitution violated? Wherefore have laws been made to authorize a change, and wherefore are we now assembled here? A federal government is formed for the protection of its individual members. Ours has attacked itself with impunity. Its authority has been disobeyed and despised.

The effect of the speaker's series of rhetorical questions is to
(A) cast doubt on another speaker's argument
(B) reinforce the other speaker's ideas
(C) reveal a certain gullibility
(D) give grounds for an act of war
(E) attest to the lack of need for action

Madison amplifies which of the following?
(A) "usual consistency" (lines 1–2)
(B) "perfect repose" (line 3)
(C) "their happy situation" (line 6)
(D) "complaints" (line 8)
(E) "authorize a change" (line 12)

Madison uses repetition to
(A) keep an even tone
(B) keep from revealing his anger
(C) emphasize his point
(D) reveal his anger
(E) take attention from Henry

Explanation: Madison uses three different rhetorical devices in the passage:

1. He uses rhetorical questions to cast doubts on Henry's argument. "If" (line 6) what he says is true, then "why" (lines 8–16) does the evidence not support it?

2. He amplifies "perfect repose" in lines 4–7. Amplification occurs when a word, concept, point, or idea is defined or explained, then is followed by even more explanation. Amplification is rhetorically effective to emphasize the importance of an idea, clarify it, and help the reader retain the idea.

3. He uses a form of repetition (called palilogy) when he keeps repeating "Why...? Why ...?" in lines 6–10. Generally, such repetition serves to emphasize. In this case, it creates an emotionally driving tone of doubt.

Correct Answers **A, B, C**

Note: **Apophasis** occurs when the speaker makes a point by pretending to deny it. For instance, "If I did not know you are an honest person, I would think you took that money," or "I would have to conclude your participation in this plan was with knowledge and pre-meditation, were it not for our long years of friendship and trust."

'ERM ALERT You should know this term: **anachronism**

Definition: **Anachronism** refers to violations of time and space in which an event or person is placed in the wrong time. When these violations appear in movies and television, viewers include them in a broad category of cinematic error called "bloopers." Examples of anachro-nistic-type bloopers are when the soldiers defend the fort against an Indian attack in 1855 by setting up a Gatling gun (not invented until 1861) or when Geronimo (not born until 1829) attacks a fort in 1820. Such anachronisms can be found in prose, poetry, and drama.

▼Practice Question▼

Here are some lines from Shakespeare's *Julius Caesar*.

> MARCUS BRUTUS. Alas, good Cassius, do not think of him:
> If he love Caesar, all that he can do
> Is to himself,—take thought, and die for
>   Caesar:
>
> Line
> (5)
> And that were much he should; for he is
>   given
> To sports, to wildness, and much company.
>
> TREBONIUS. There is no fear in him; let him not die;
> For he will live, and laugh at this hereafter.
>
> [*Clock strikes.*]
>
> (10) MARCUS BRUTUS. Peace! count the clock.
>
> CASSIUS. The clock hath stricken three.
>
> TREBONIUS. 'Tis time to part.

An anachronism occurs when
(A) sports is mentioned
(B) Caesar has already died
(C) the clock strikes
(D) Brutus counts the clock
(E) Cassius has already died

Explanation: A clock that can strike the hour? In Caesar's Rome?

Correct Answer: **C**

Note: **Litotes** is a favorite of Anglo-Saxon writing. In litotes, a sense of understatement is achieved through negative affirmation (the negative of the opposite), which actually confirms or increases the importance of what is being discussed:

LITOTES	MEANING
not bad	good
not fat	thin
not least	great
not unbecoming	appropriate
not the smartest	stupid

TERM ALERT You should know this term: **hyperbole** (overstatement or exaggeration)

Definition: Hyperbole can be especially comic: Texans, as a case in point, are noted for their use of hyperbole, exaggeration, in a state where "the men are braver, the sky is bluer, the steaks are bigger, and the women are prettier than anywhere else in the world."

▼PRACTICE QUESTION▼

Read this first stanza of Andrew Marvell's "To His Coy Mistress":

TO HIS COY MISTRESS

→Had we but world enough, and time,
This coyness, Lady, were no crime.
We would sit down, and think which way
To walk, and pass our long love's day.

(5) Thou by the Indian Ganges' side
Should'st rubies find: I by the tide
Of Humber would complain. I would
→Love you ten years before the Flood:
And you should if you please refuse

(10) →Till the conversion of the Jews.
My vegetable love should grow
→Vaster than empires, and more slow.
→And hundred years should go to praise
Thine eyes, and on thy forehead gaze.

(15) →Two hundred to adore each breast:
→But thirty thousand to the rest.
An age at least to every part,
And the last age should show your heart.
For, Lady, you deserve this state;

(20) Nor would I love at lower rate.

by Andrew Marvell

The speaker's use of hyperbole is intended to create a sense of

(A) absurdity
(B) sincerity
(C) irony
(D) urgency
(E) affirmation

Explanation: The speaker exaggerates a period of endless time in order to emphasize time's brevity in reality. This overstatement creates an urgent tone.

Correct Answer: **D**

NOTE: Meiosis, or understatement, treats a serious subject as though it is much less important than it is. Often meiosis projects a derogatory manner; however, context may dictate any number of effects, such as irony.

This example is from *Oliver Twist* by Dickens.

> The fact is, that there was considerable difficulty in inducing Oliver to take upon himself the office of respiration,—a troublesome practice, but one which custom has rendered necessary to our easy existence;...

TERM ALERT You should know this term: **paradox**

Definition: Paradox is a statement that seems to contradict itself, yet is actually true. Statements of paradox occur in conversations in everyday life: a couple may look at a pug-faced dog in a store window and exclaim, "He's so ugly he's cute!"

▼PRACTICE QUESTION▼

The second stanza of Chidiock Tichborne's sixteenth-century "Elegy" is built upon paradoxical relationships:

> My tale was heard and yet it was not told,
>   My fruit is fallen and yet my leaves are green,
> My youth is spent and yet I am not old,
> I saw the world and yet I was not seen;
>   My thread is cut and yet it is not spun,
>   And now I live, and now my life is done.

Line
(5)

Which of the following words best summarizes the speaker's view of his life?

(A) Confused
(B) Inconsequential
(C) Unfulfilled
(D) Imitative
(E) Immutable

Explanation: How can a tale be heard, but not told? A youth gone, but the person not be old? In this stanza, viewed apart from the rest of the poem, the speaker is expressing dissatisfaction over a life that is unfulfilled. Perhaps an event has happened to make him believe his "life" is over even if his biological life continues.

Correct Answer: **C**

TERM ALERT You should know this term: **oxymoron**

Definition: An **oxymoron** occurs when words, terms, or expressions appear to be self-contradicting: bittersweet, a dry martini, sweet-and-sour, love-hate relationships, passive resistance, jumbo shrimp, or a kind ogre.

Sometimes you will find passages in which the speaker makes extensive use of oxymorons, as Romeo's speech in *Romeo and Juliet* (Act I Scene I) "loving-hate" and "cold fires." More often, though, the oxymoron will be used with more restraint, primarily for the contradictory effect that produces such feelings as an emphasized sense of confusion, frustration, or determination (to name a few). Context, once again, is a prime determinant of the effect.

▼PRACTICE QUESTION▼

The fourth stanza of Sir Thomas Wyatt's "Marvel No More" ends with an oxymoron.

> Play who that can that part:
>   Needs must in me appear
> How fortune, overthwart,
>   Doth cause my mourning cheer.

The oxymoron in the last line is based on
(A) rhyme scheme
(B) a play on words
(C) a reversal of thought
(D) sentimentality
(E) an allusion to coffee

Explanation: Morning/mourning is a play on words (pun).

Correct Answer: B

TERM ALERT You should know this term: **irony**

Definition: Irony is a concept that involves opposites. The many types of irony form two distinct categories: **situational** or **dramatic irony**, in which the result following a sequence of events is the opposite of what is expected, and **verbal irony**, in which the speaker uses words that express the opposite of what is actually meant.

Ironic situations are a mainstay of popular comedy. The acting comedy of Lucille Ball, for example, relied heavily on situational irony as a source of humor. Often Lucy, who wanted to be part of her husband's nightclub act, would devise a plan to be part of the show. Rather than achieving her expected results, however, her plans usually ended with Lucy locked in a closet, hanging from a balcony, or in some other embarrassing situation.

Occasionally, a situation is ironic when someone who intends harm against another becomes the victim of his or her own plan, for instance, when the angry teenager is splashing paint on his neighbor's car, but an unexpected wind causes the paint to blow back on his own parked car, ruining the finish. Sometimes, if the person's attitudes or motives are unjustified and he or she becomes the victim of an ironic situation, he or she is said to have "gotten what he deserves."

Situational irony can be sad or even poignant, as when parents secure weapons to protect their children from danger, only to have a child injured or killed by one of those same weapons. On very subtle levels, situations can be intrinsically ironic, such as when the undeserving, cowardly, or lazy are rewarded while the deserving, brave, or industrious are punished.

Sometimes irony results from making false assumptions, and the very presence of an ironic outcome might lead you to examine the validity of the assumptions you have made.

▼PRACTICE QUESTIONS▼

The following paragraph comes from Samuel Johnson's "On Self-love and Indolence."

> It seems generally believed, that, as the eye cannot see itself, the
> mind has no faculties by which it can contemplate its own state, and
> that therefore we have not means of becoming acquainted with our
> Line   real characters; an opinion which, like innumerable other postulates,
> (5)   an inquirer finds himself inclined to admit upon very little evidence,
> because it affords a ready solution of many difficulties. It will explain
> why the greatest abilities frequently fail to promote the happiness of
> those who possess them; why those who can distinguish with the
> utmost nicety the boundaries of vice and virtue, suffer them to be
> (10)   confounded in their own conduct; why the active and vigilant resign
> their affairs implicitly to the management of others; and why the
> cautious and fearful make hourly approaches toward ruin, without
> one sigh of solicitude or struggle for escape.

The speaker's main point revolves around the ironic situation that
(A) "the eye cannot see itself"
(B) "the mind [cannot]...contemplate its own state"
(C) "the greatest abilities...fail to promote...happiness"
(D) "the active and vigilant resign their affairs...to others"
(E) "the cautious and fearful make hourly approaches toward ruin"

In line 1, "...as the eye cannot see itself" is
  I. the vehicle in an ironic simile
 II. a comparison of conditions
III. the tenor in an ironic metaphor
(A) I only
(B) II only
(C) III only
(D) I and II only
(E) I, II, and III

Explanation: This paragraph contains all the ironies listed in the first question and more; however, the central irony is B. Answer choice A serves only to introduce it, and all the other ironies illustrate it. In "...as the eye cannot see itself," use of "as" makes it a simile, not a metaphor. Its tenor is that the mind cannot "contemplate its own state." Both the eye and the mind are in the ironic condition of not being able to apply their primary functions to themselves.

Correct Answer: **B, D**

Verbal irony occurs when the speaker says the opposite of what he or she means. How can you tell that verbal irony is at work in a statement? One clue is through the speaker's "ironic" tone of voice and through facial expression. The effect of the irony is a product of the speaker's intent.

For instance, a married couple plans to meet another couple at a restaurant for dinner. The wife arrives first, as usual for this couple. The other couple arrives and asks about her overdue husband. "He'll be here in a moment, I'm sure," she says with a laugh and wink. "Steve is *never* late!" Obviously from her tone, body language, and emphasis on <u>never</u>, Steve generally <u>is</u> late (a knowledge that, by implication, is shared by the other couple); however, his wife is not distressed but rather views this as a comical part of Steve's personality. But what if her attitude is different—perhaps critical because Steve's habitual tardiness had caused the couple serious social, business, and family problems? "He'll be here in a moment, I'm *sure*," she says through clenched teeth, her gaze rolling toward the ceiling in disdain. "*Steve* is *never* late!" The tone is hostile; the intent is critical. When the intent of the irony is to criticize by use of praise, the form is called **sarcasm**. (The sarcastic tone of Robert Browning's "Soliloquy of the Spanish Cloister" is an oft-cited example, as is Swift's "A Modest Proposal.")

Verbal irony, although sometimes described as "tongue in cheek," is not always sarcastic in tone or intent. The irony may be the result of **understatement**, also called **meiosis**, ("I think we have a little water in the basement"—when the basement contains a 3-foot-deep flood), in which the irony intensifies the meaning of what is said; the result of **overstatement**, also known as **hyperbole** ("This pimple outshines a neon sign!"), in which the irony lessens the importance of the meaning of what is said; or the result of **contradiction in context** (such as describing a cruel, uncaring person in terms that are endearing).

▼PRACTICE QUESTIONS▼

The following paragraph comes from Thackeray's *Vanity Fair*.

> "We don't care a fig for her," writes some unknown correspondent
> with a pretty little hand-writing and a pink seal to her note. "She is
> fade and insipid," and adds some more kind remarks in this strain,
> Line which I should never have repeated at all, but that they are in truth
> (5) prodigiously complimentary to the young lady whom they concern.

Which of the literary devices listed below is used to describe the remarks of the "unknown correspondent"?
(A) Situational irony
(B) Metaphoric prose
(C) Paradoxical amplification
(D) Verbal irony
(E) Personification

The situational irony presented by this narrator can best be seen in which of the following?
(A) "*fade* and insipid...prodigiously complimentary"
(B) "don't care a fig...more kind remarks"
(C) "unknown correspondent...the young lady"
(D) "kind remarks...repeated"
(E) "pretty little hand-writing and a pink seal"

Explanation: "*Fade* and insipid" are, in this context, insulting rather than kind remarks. This paragraph provides examples of both verbal and situational irony. To call insults "kind" is verbally ironic, and it is an ironic situation when insults reveal jealousy and become a compliment.

Correct Answers: **D, A**

IMPORTANT CONCEPT #3: FIGURES OF SPEECH BASED ON SYNTAX

Concept Explained:

Syntax refers to how words are arranged into patterns. A few of the more common figures of speech that depend on syntax are summarized in the chart on page 234.

What effects can you expect from the use of figures of speech based on syntax? Figures such as antithesis and apostrophe can, depending on context, project a formal tone or render the work more or less emotional. Hyperbatons and hypallages can add a sense of confusion, particularly when the speaker is portraying a state of mental anxiety, as an example. Sleights of "and" can be witty, provocative, or disruptive, again based on context. Of course, the chart on page 234 is only a partial list of the many effects syntax-based figures can have in a work.

ERM ALERT You should know this term: **antithesis**

Definition: Refer to the chart on page 234. Also, return to the "Elegy" by Chidioch Tichborne on page 229. This conceit consists of a series of ideas that are antithetical (in antithesis to one another).

ERM ALERT You should know this term: **apostrophe**

Definition: Refer to the chart on page 234.

IMPORTANT CONCEPT #4: DICTION

Concept Explained:

Syntax refers to the arrangement of words into patterns; diction refers to the word choices being arranged into those patterns.

ERM ALERT You should know this term: **diction**

Definition: Diction will be discussed in greater detail in the next chapter, but as a use of language, diction (defined as word choice) plays an obvious role, particularly in imagery and figures of speech. Sometimes the change of a single word can make—or destroy—the tone or the meaning of a selection, hence a writer's diction is generally aimed at producing a desired effect, an effect that may go beyond the literal meaning of the word choice.

To some degree, diction can be viewed as isolated word choices. For example, a **malapropism** is the use of a word that is inappropriate for the context, but that resembles a word that is appropriate. The effect, of course, of using the incorrect word can be amusing or it can be embarrassing when the error in word choice is unintentional. Richard Brinsley Sheridan's Mrs. Malaprop in *The Rivals* (1775) is the character whose constant misuse of

FIGURES OF SPEECH BASED ON SYNTAX

FIGURE OF SPEECH	CHARACTERISTIC SYNTACTICAL STRUCTURE	EXAMPLES
1. **Antithesis**	Balance of contrasting terms with parallel grammatical structure	O, change thy thought, that I may change my mind!
2. **Apostrophe**	Direct address to an auditor (called **invocation** if to a muse)	My pen, take pain a little space. To follow that which doth me chase.
3. Hyperbaton	Transposition or rearrangement of normal sentence order	Which when she entered, although the younger except, none could attain, fixed the smile for the rest....
4. Hypallage	An epithet or qualifier placed next to less proximate of a group of nouns	"the Gypsy's wondering curse" for "the wondering Gypsy's curse"
5. Sleight of "and"	Tropes that use co-ordinating conjunctions For example, the zeugma:	
	• Same grammatical relation, but different idiomatic use	• He will pay Jane her due and her rent.
	• Two different verbs	• He bussed the table in the restaurant and the children to school.
	• Subject-verb agreement problem	• You or she is going to have to leave.

words, such as "a progeny of learning," gave rise to the expression "malapropism." In the case of Mrs. Malaprop, she was trying to display mastery of a large vocabulary.

▼Practice Question▼

Romeo and Juliet, Act II Scene III

NURSE. By my troth, it is well said;—'for himself to mar,' quoth a'?— Gentlemen, can any of you tell me where I may find the young Romeo?

Line (5) ROMEO. I can tell you; but young Romeo will be older when you have found him than he was when you sought him: I am the youngest of that name, for fault of a worse.

NURSE. You say well.

MERCUTIO.   Yea, is the worst well? very well took, i'faith;
              wisely, wisely.

NURSE.   If you be he, sir, I desire some confidence with you.

BENVOLIO.   She will indite him to some supper.

(10) MERCUTIO.   A bawd, a bawd, a bawd! So-ho!

As used in the selection, which of the following contains misuses of diction?
(A) Nurse: troth; Romeo: worse
(B) Nurse: confidence; Benvolio: indite
(C) Benvolio: indite; Mercutio: bawd
(D) Nurse: quoth; Mercutio: i'faith
(E) Romeo: fault; Mercutio: worst well

Explanation: The first malapropism is the nurse's use of "confidence" where she most likely means "conference." The effect this malapropism has on Benvolio is to cause him to mock her by deliberately using a malapropism: "indite" for "invite."

Correct Answer: **B**

TERM ALERT You should know this term: **pun**

Definition: A pun is a word choice that is referred to as a "play on words"—two words have the same sound but very different meanings.

Puns rely, of course, on context for their witty overtones because context gives significance to *both* meanings.

▼PRACTICE QUESTION▼

An often quoted pun appears in *Romeo and Juliet*, Act III Scene I when Mercutio is wounded:

ROMEO.   Courage, man; the hurt cannot be much.

MERCUTIO. No, 'tis not so deep as a well, nor so wide as a church-
          door; but 'tis enough, 'twill serve: ask for me to-morrow,
          and you shall find me a grave man.

Which of the following words is used as a pun in this passage?
(A) Courage
(B) Hurt
(C) Well
(D) Serve
(E) Grave

Explanation: What is the pun at work here? "Grave" can refer either to a "serious" man (as, indeed, his wound is a serious situation) and to a man in his grave.

Correct Answer: **E**

▼PRACTICE QUESTION▼

Here is a stanza from John Donne's "A Hymn to God the Father."

> I have a sin of fear, that when I have spun
> My last thread, I shall perish on the shore;
> But swear by Thy self, that at my death Thy Son
> Shall shine as he shines now, and heretofore;
> Line   And, having done that, Thou hast done;
> (5)   I fear no more.

Which of the following words is used as a pun in this stanza?
(A) Fear
(B) Spun
(C) Thread
(D) Shore
(E) Son

Explanation: A very obvious pun "Son" and "sun." (Keep in mind that the pun as a literary device can be very serious.) There is another pun at work throughout this poem. Hint: Look again at the poet's name.

Line 5: "And, having done that, Thou hast done;…"

Correct Answer: **E**

Diction also refers to the level of words used: vocabulary that is high, plain, or low. As you study diction and its effect on literature, you will find that many different descriptive systems have been developed to try to identify the different levels of diction that writers and speakers use:

1. Diction can be described by dialect.

Dialects are the speech patterns (including diction, grammatical constructions, and accents) of a defined geographical region or group.

Generally, this descriptive system identifies *Standard English* as the speech used by the mainstream professionals of the age in question.

Standard English can be formal, general, or informal in level. For example, general English often includes the use of the **vernacular**, the jargon of the person's profession or the diction that is specific to the region. Informal English is marked by colloquial expressions, slang, and clipped words that are sometimes drawn from nonstandard usage.

Nonstandard English consists of colloquial expressions, slang, and clipped words plus diction that is characteristically considered "nonstandard," such as *ain't.* The grammatical constructions of Nonstandard English do not conform to the rules of Standard, particularly in the use of pronouns and subject-verb agreement, or to the rules of standardized spelling. Keep in mind, however, that words and constructions considered Nonstandard today may well have been considered Standard (or vice versa) in a previous period. Because the pronoun "they" was once considered to be a singular pronoun, "If a person laughs, they must be happy" would be considered a Standard usage. Even double negatives and "ain't" were once a part of Standard English.

2. Diction can be described by purpose.

The purpose of language is communication. Consider the use of technical terms, so useful and appropriate for instructing or enlightening professionals in a given field, (terms that become an "-ese" as in "educationese" or "doctorese" to the untrained layperson). Oftentimes the reader or hearer will respond to technical language with the plea "Can you put that in plain English?"

3. Diction can be described by tone.

The diction of communication can give the work a formal or an informal tone. Formal writing depends upon diction that is higher level vocabulary, whereas informal writing engages casual diction, such as the **colloquial expressions, idiomatic diction** (based on tradition rather than on logic, for instance, "call off," "get on," or "set about"), and **slang** (vernacular language) of everyday speech.

ᴛERM ALERT You should know this term: **euphemism**

Definition: Some choices of words are considered offensive to readers. Consequently, writers sometimes replace those words with inoffensive synonyms called euphemisms. What is considered offensive diction, of course, is based on the culture of the age when the work is being written.

Do not confuse euphemism with euphony. Both affect the tone of a work, but euphemism is based on the meaning of a word and euphony relates to the sound. This little poem may help you differentiate the two literary terms:

IS IT EUPHEMISM OR EUPHONY?

Is it euphemism or euphony?
    The answer has evaded me.
Euphemism, they say, is to render
    A harsh word into one kind and tender.
(5) We don't say "leg"; we say a "limb."
    Don't call him "skinny," instead say "trim."
But when a poem has euphony,
    It simply "sounds" pleasant to you and me.
Now all your doubts should flee when you see:
(10)   Is it euphemism or euphony?

by L. E. Myers

ACTIVE THINKING EXERCISES FOR USE OF LANGUAGE

STEP 1. ▸FOCUS◂

Sometimes you can spot signal words and mechanical elements that will help you focus. They can appear in the selections or in the questions. When you see them, they will alert you to a wide variety of ideas that will help you concentrate specifically on answering the questions at hand.

▼EXERCISE▼

Turn to the Practice Sets on page 330. For each selection:

1. Familiarize yourself with the selection by identifying any mechanical elements, such as letters, dates, poetry forms, genre, major characters, and so forth.

2. Read the question about Use of Language and circle any key words in the question, including line numbers.

3. Return to the selection and circled lines/words that relate to answering the question.

4. Answer the question.

Continue this activity to develop a marking system that works for you.

Finally, turn to Practice Test Six beginning on page 429 to gain experience on a full-length test:

1. Make note of any mechanical elements or key words in the selection.

2. Circle signal words in the questions.

3. Read the selection; circle key words that relate to answering the question.

4. Answer the question, if possible. Skip it if you are not sure of the answer.

5. Go back to unanswered questions as time allows.

Repeat 1–4 for each selection until you have completed the test. How did you do?

STEP 2. MOW (MY OWN WORDS)

This poem was written by John Cleveland "To the Memory of Ben Jonson."

The Muse's fairest light in no dark time,
The wonder of a learnéd age; the line
Which none can pass; the most proportioned wit,—
To nature, the best judge of what was fit;
(5) The deepest, plainest, highest, clearest pen;
The voice most echoed by consenting men;
The soul which answered best to all well said
By others, and which most requital made;
Tuned to the highest key of ancient Rome,
(10) Returning all her music with his own;
In whom, with nature, study claimed a part,
And yet who to himself owed all his art:
Here lies Ben Jonson! every age will look
With sorrow here, with wonder on his book.

The word "Line" appears at line 4, and "(5)" and "(10)" mark lines 5 and 10.

To begin **MOW**ing this poem, first identify its form: fourteen lines of iambic pentameter—a sonnet. The subject? Ben Jonson. The speaker's purpose? To eulogize Jonson's death. These first steps are somewhat universal in MOWing any selection. When you MOW a sonnet, however, your next steps will depend upon how the particular sonnet you are working with is structured. You need to break the sonnet into units of thought. Some are four lines/four lines/four lines/concluding couplet. Some are six lines/six lines/two lines.

Usually, but not always, the concluding couplet will make the speaker's main point. Consequently, beginning with the last two lines can sometimes be a quick path to understanding. In this sonnet, line 13 is bluntly stated. Also, every age is sorrowful over his death. Now, try to discover the relationship of the first twelve lines to the concluding couplet.

Read lines 1–12. How do they relate to lines 13–14?

_____

_____

Possible answer: They tell us why every age is sorrowful over his death.

Next, paraphrase each unit of thought:

Lines 1–2: _____

Lines 2–3:_____

Line 4: _____

Line 5: _____

Line 6: _____

Lines 7–8:_____

Lines 9–10:_____

Lines 11–12:_____

TERM ALERT You should know this term: **argument**

Definition: An argument is the thesis of a poem. The prose summary, sometimes written by the poet, that explains the meaning of a lengthy poem is also called an argument. A third definition of argument is the plot summary of a play.

Summarize the main idea in one sentence: _____

_____

▼PRACTICE QUESTIONS▼

Using your analysis to guide you, answer the following questions. (Poem is on page 238.)

1. Based on its subject and form, this poem is best described as a(n)
   (A) literary ballad
   (B) elegiac sonnet
   (C) regular ode
   (D) literary epitaph
   (E) satiric complaint

2. Lines 11–12 address Jonson's
   (A) skill as a painter
   (B) academic career
   (C) nature paintings
   (D) originality
   (E) library or den

3. The hyperbole found in this poem is mostly achieved through the use of
   (A) superfluity
   (B) redundancy
   (C) diminution
   (D) depreciation
   (E) superlatives

4. Line 5, the "pen" figuratively represents which of the following?
   (A) Ben Jonson
   (B) Jonson's literary style
   (C) The quill writing instrument of his day
   (D) A writing instrument that uses ink
   (E) Jonson's style of script

5. In line 1, "no dark time" is a litotes (negative affirmation) probably referring to
   (A) a time of mysterious, not easily understood writings
   (B) the Dark Ages
   (C) the speaker's loss of sight
   (D) an age enlightened by inspired knowledge
   (E) the gloomy, disheartening nature of death

6. Which of the following most closely reflects the subject of line 6?
   (A) The lack of acquiescence
   (B) Elocution
   (C) Repeated words and ideas
   (D) Hollow ideas
   (E) Ventriloquism

7. The "line / Which none can pass" in lines 2–3 probably refers to which of the following?
   I. A point of conformity
   II. A succession of great intellectuals
   III. Intellectual achievement
   (A) I only
   (B) II only
   (C) III only
   (D) I and II only
   (E) I, II, and III

8. In lines 9–10, the speaker uses a musical metaphor to
   (A) accentuate the extent of Jonson's originality
   (B) describe Jonson's superb singing voice
   (C) extol the intellectualism of Rome
   (D) praise Jonson's speaking voice
   (E) build upon the imagery begun in line 6

Answers and Explanations:

1. **B** "Here lies Ben Jonson!" (line 13) makes this an elegy. It is fourteen lines written in iambic pentameter (sonnet form).

2. **D** As defined by context, art can include creativity (original thinking and production). This idea is supported by the idea that study (of other's work) claimed part of him "And yet…," a qualifying conjunction meaning "nevertheless."

3. **E** The superlatives include "fairest" (line 1), "most proportioned" (line 3), "best" (line 4), four superlatives in line 5, "best" (line 7).

4. **B** Jonson, not his writing instruments or penmanship, is the subject, eliminating C, D, and E. Does this line praise Jonson or his style? The choice of adjectives points to his literary style.

5. **D** Notice the appositive in line 2: "the wonder of a learnéd age."

6. **C** Lines 4–10 deal with Jonson's interaction with others. He could judge what was fit (line 4), could answer well (line 7), and could improve upon the ancients (line 10). In this context, others would echo or repeat his ideas and expressions.

7. **C** The "line" in this context obviously is a point of excellence set by Jonson that no one else can go beyond. His, according to the speaker, is the best wit, literary style, intellect, and character.

8. **A** The implied tenor of the metaphor is the literary achievement of Rome. Jonson returned Rome's music and added his own.

STEP 3. BID (BREAK IT DOWN)

To BID for the uses of language possible in a selection is much more than just memorizing definitions. Consequently, the following exercise is designed to give you rapid-fire practice in identifying figurative language in action.

Thou ill-form'd offspring of my feeble brain,
Who after birth did'st by my side remain,

> (from "The Author to Her Book"
> by Anne Bradstreet)

1. The emotional relationship of the speaker to her book is revealed through use of which of the following?
   I. Apostrophe
   II. Mother-child imagery
   III. Personification
   (A) I only
   (B) II only
   (C) III only
   (D) II and III only
   (E) I, II, and III

At thy return my blushing was not small,
My rambling brat (in print) should mother call,

> (from "The Author to Her Book"
> by Anne Bradstreet)

2. Negative affirmation (litotes) means that the speaker
   (A) has rosacea
   (B) wore too much makeup
   (C) was greatly embarrassed
   (D) was not very angry
   (E) was not very embarrassed

Heavy they roll their fleecy world along;
And the sky saddens with the gathered storm.

> (from "Winter Scenes" by James Thomson)

3. The first line contains which of the following?
   (A) Simile
   (B) Metaphor
   (C) Personification
   (D) Allusion
   (E) Metonymy

4. The second line contains which of the following?
   (A) Simile
   (B) Metaphor
   (C) Personification
   (D) Allusion
   (E) Metonymy

But truly I imagine it falleth out with these poet-whippers, as with some good women, who often are sick, but in faith they cannot tell where.

> (from "An Apology for Poetry"
> by Sir Philip Sidney)

5. The simile compares
   (A) poet-whippers to women with unspecified illnesses
   (B) poet-whippers to poet-lovers
   (C) women with real illnesses to poet-whippers
   (D) poetry to sick women
   (E) falling poet-whippers to faithful women

It is the strangest and yet the fittest thing in the jumble of human vicissitudes, that he, out of so many millions,
Line
(5) unlooked for, unselected by any intelligible process that could be based upon his genuine qualities, unknown to those who chose him, and unsuspected of what endowments may adapt him for his tremendous responsibility, should have
(10) found the way open for him to fling his lank personality into the chair of state—where, I presume, it was his first impulse to throw his legs on the council-table, and tell the Cabinet Ministers a story. There is
(15) no describing his lengthy awkwardness, nor the uncouthness of his movement; and yet it seemed as if I had been in the habit of seeing him daily, and had shaken hands with him a thousand times
(20) in some village street; so true was he to the aspect pattern of the American,...

> (from an essay on Abraham Lincoln
> by Nathaniel Hawthorne)

6. The metonymy in this selection is

_____.

It represents
(A) the White House
(B) a thronelike piece of furniture
(C) the first American-made product
(D) the president's bed
(E) the presidency

7. The hyperbole in this selection is

_____.

It serves to make Lincoln seem
(A) common and uncivilized
(B) a traveler
(C) more accessible
(D) noncommunicative
(E) unresponsive

line
(1) A good that never satisfies the mind,
(2) A beauty fading like the April flowers,
     * * *
(7) A treasury which bankrupt time
    devours,
(8) A knowledge than grave ignorance
    more blind,
     * * *
(13) Are the strange ends we toil for here
     below,
(14) Till wisest death make us our errors
     know.

        (from "Sonnet" by William Drummond)

8 Lines 1 and 8 contain elements that are
(A) in direct address
(B) in antithesis
(C) exaggerations
(D) spoonerisms
(E) colloquial

9. That knowledge can be more blind than igno-
rance (line 8) is
(A) ironic
(B) understatement
(C) euphonic
(D) grand style
(E) hyperbole

10. In view of the concluding couplet, "grave" in
line 8 can be seen as a(n)
(A) pun
(B) ambiguity
(C) euphemism
(D) personification
(E) poetic diction

Life! we've been long together
Through pleasant and through cloudy weather,

        (from "Life" by A. L. Barbauld)

11. The direct address to "Life" as the silent
auditor is an example of
(A) antithesis
(B) analogy
(C) apostrophe
(D) anthropomorphism
(E) aphorism

12. Weather, representing events and conditions in
life, serves as a
(A) symbol
(B) metaphor
(C) simile
(D) pun
(E) synecdoche

Exert thy voice, sweet harbinger of spring!
This moment is thy time to sing,
        * * *
Muse, thy promise now fulfill!
Sweet, oh! sweet, still sweeter yet....

        (from "To the Nightingale" by Anne Finch)

13. Directly addressing the nightingale, then
directly addressing a "Muse" is a change from
(A) antithesis to apostrophe
(B) verbal irony to situational irony
(C) litotes to hyperbole
(D) apostrophe to invocation
(E) hyperbole to meiosis

It was now full night-fall, and a thick humid fog hung over the city, soon ending in a settled and heavy rain. This
Line change of weather had an odd effect
(5) upon the crowd, the whole of which was at once put into new commotion, and overshadowed by a world of umbrellas. The waver, the jostle, and the hum increased in a tenfold degree. For my
(10) own part I did not much regard the rain— the lurking of an old fever in my system rendering the moisture somewhat too dangerously pleasant. Tying a handkerchief about my mouth, I kept on.

(from "The Man of the Crowd"
by Edgar Allan Poe)

14. The phrase "dangerously pleasant" is which of the following?
    I. An oxymoron
    II. Descriptive of a situational irony
    III. A controlling image
    (A) I only
    (B) II only
    (C) III only
    (D) I and II only
    (E) I, II, and III

15. The "world of umbrellas" is an example of which of the following?
    (A) Simile
    (B) Caricature
    (C) Allegory
    (D) Personification
    (E) Hyperbole

16. "waver...jostle...hum" appeal to which of the following senses?
    (A) Visual, kinesthetic, auditory
    (B) Olfactory, tactile, kinesthetic
    (C) Kinesthetic, visual, auditory
    (D) Kinesthetic and auditory
    (E) Visual and auditory

Even if literature were of no other use to the fair sex than to supply them with employment, I should think the time
Line dedicated to the cultivation of their minds
(5) well bestowed: they are surely better occupied when they are reading or writing than when coquetting or gaming, losing their fortunes or their characters. You despise the writings of women—you
(10) think that they might have made a better use of the pen than to write plays, and poetry, and romances. Considering that the pen was to women a new instrument, I think they have made at least as good
(15) a use of it as learned men did of the needle some centuries ago, when they set themselves to determine how many spirits could stand upon its point, and were ready to tear one another to pieces
(20) in the discussion of this sublime question...You say that the experiments we have made do not encourage us to proceed,...Did you expect that the fruits of good cultivation should appear before
(25) the seed was sown?—You triumphantly enumerate the disadvantages to which women...are liable....and after pointing out all these causes for the inferiority of women in knowledge, you ask for a list
(30) of the inventions and discoveries of those who, by your own statement of the question, have not been allowed opportunities for observation. With the insulting injustice of an Egyptian task-
(35) master, you demand the work, and deny the necessary materials.

(from "Letters to Literary Ladies"
by Maria Edgeworth)

17. The "fair sex" (line 2) is used as a(n)
    (A) epithet
    (B) metonymy
    (C) symbol
    (D) amplification
    (E) rhetorical device

18. "Egyptian task-master" (line 34) alludes to when the Children of Israel were slaves in Egypt and were required to make brick without straw.

This allusion does NOT serve to
(A) make women appear as victims
(B) emphasize the suffering of women seeking education
(C) convey a sense of indignation
(D) illustrate the irony of the situation
(E) define the parameters of the issue

19. The speaker uses an agricultural metaphor to describe which of the following?
(A) Women's education and writing
(B) Women's employment
(C) Coquetting and gaming
(D) The laws and customs of society
(E) Experiments in women's rights

20. "This sublime question" (lines 20–21) is an example of _____.
Its tone sounds
(A) affable
(B) altruistic
(C) malevolent
(D) sarcastic
(E) obtuse

21. Which of the following maxims best summarizes the central irony in this passage?
(A) What goes around comes around.
(B) A woman cannot win for losing.
(C) You can lead a horse to water, but you cannot make it drink.
(D) Pride goes before a fall.
(E) A woman's work is never done.

...Had his daughters, had his wife, been educated to feel their responsibilities, they would have taken
Line their rights, and he would have been a
(5) happy and contented man, and would not have been reduced to the mere machine for calculating and getting money that he now is.

My friends,... For fourteen years I have
(10) advocated this cause by my daily life. Bloody feet, sisters, have worn smooth the path by which you have come up hither. You will not need to speak when you speak by your everyday life.

(a speech by Abby Kelley Foster)

22. The speaker uses the metaphoric phrase "the mere machine for calculating and getting money" as a(n)
(A) simile that simply compares man to a machine
(B) epithet that describes man's ultimate purpose
(C) epithet that implies the dehumanization of man
(D) anachronism that violates the time of the speaker
(E) hyperbole that exaggerates man's role

23. In context, the figuratively descriptive adjective "bloody" connotes
(A) domestic physical abuse
(B) cruel wrongs suffered
(C) lack of protections for women
(D) lack of proper shoes
(E) a lengthy struggle

24. What is the rhetorical effect of calling the listeners "sisters"?
(A) It identifies them as part of a female religious order.
(B) It designates the audience as a family reunion.
(C) It emotionally bonds the listeners together.
(D) It alienates men.
(E) It contrasts with "daughters" and "his wife."

Correct Answers:
1. **E** 2. **C** 3. **B** 4. **C** 5. **A** 6. "chair of state," **E** 7. "shaken hands a thousand times," **C** 8. **B** 9. **A** 10. **A** 11. **C** 12. **B** 13. **D** 14. **E** 15. **E** 16. **A** 17. **A** 18. **E** 19. **A** 20. verbal irony, **D** 21. **B** 22. **C** 23. **B** 24. **C**

STEP 4. TT→TM (TEST TAKER TO TEST MAKER)

How would you write test questions over figurative language? Here is a selection from Poe's "A Descent into the Maelström":

> Line
> (5) "It could not have been more than two minutes afterwards until we suddenly felt the waves subside, and were enveloped in foam. The boat made a sharp half turn to larboard, and then shot off in its new direction like a thunderbolt. At the same moment the roaring noise of the water was completely drowned in a kind of shrill shriek—such a sound as you might imagine given out by the water-pipes of many thousand steam-vessels, letting off their steam all together. We were now in the belt of
> (10) surf that always surrounds the whirl; and I thought, of course, that another moment would plunge us into the abyss—down which we could only see indistinctly on account of the amazing velocity with which we were borne along. The boat did not seem to sink into the water at all, but to skim like an airbubble upon the surface of the surge. Her starboard side was next the whirl, and on the larboard arose the world of ocean
> (15) we had left. It stood like a huge writhing wall between us and the horizon."

1. First, what figurative language does Poe use? Seek and find four similes. (Circle them in the paragraph.)
2. Also, look at this sentence:

> At the same moment the roaring noise of the water was completely drowned in a kind of shrill shriek—

In the context of the paragraph, there are four different figures of speech used in this sentence. What are they?
a._____
b._____
c._____
d._____

Answers and Explanations:

1. Similes: Like a thunderbolt; a sound as…water-pipes of many thousand steam-vessels; like an air-whirl; like a huge writhing wall.
2. The sentence contains a fascinating blend of images. On the surface, each word has a meaning that seems literal. Roaring is a loud noise; noises can be drowned or muffled by other noises. However, in the context of a very figure-laden description of a whirlpool with an "abyss" and a "huge writhing wall" of water, this line takes on powerfully figurative meaning.

For the sound of water to be "drowned" becomes contradictory (paradoxical); that it would be overpowered by yet more water is ironic. The noise is roaring, metaphorically comparing it to a wild beast capable of "writhing." This image, combined with the sound being drowned and the new sound being a "shrill shriek" (like a person might make), makes this sentence intensify the sense of fear and danger. Figures of speech used: irony, paradox, personification, metaphor.

Of course, you could ask an identification question: "like a thunderbolt" is... (B) a simile. Or you could ask about what the similes mean in the sentence:

The figurative language used in the first two similes are meant to describe
(A) direction
(B) visual impact
(C) direction and sound
(D) the water and steam vessels
(E) speed and sound

Correct Answer: **E**

Instead, move to the next level and write a question about the effects of the similes used.

Select one of the four similes and list two to three *effects* created by it. For example, the simile "like a huge writhing wall" makes the water seem beastlike.

Finally, write your question. You can give one correct effect and two or three incorrect or some other combination. You can even list all correctly identified effects.

The simile, "_____," has which of the following effects?
I. _____
II. _____
III. _____
IV. _____
(A) I only
(B) II only
(C) III only
(D) _____
    (a combination, such as I and III only)
(E) I, II, III, (and IV, if needed)

What is your correct answer?

USE OF LANGUAGE IN CONCLUSION

This chapter dealt with images that go beyond the written page and the figures of speech used to create those images. The last literary element will take a magnifying glass to look at the sentences, lines, phrases, and words as they relate to the context of the work.

Literary Element Number Seven: Meaning(s) in Context

Some questions on the literature test deal with the meanings of words, phrases, lines, or sentences as they are used in context (the ideas and information that come before or after the words in question).

IMPORTANT CONCEPT #1: DENOTATION

TERM ALERT You should know this term: **denotation**

Definition: Denotation is the basic or literal meaning or meanings of a word.

You need to develop your sight vocabulary to include as many words as possible. However, often you can use context to determine the intended meaning for words that have more than one denotation (literal meaning). For example, the verb "cover" has more than twenty definitions in some unabridged dictionaries. When a writer has a character decide to "cover" a bill on her desk, only context can tell you whether "cover" means she is protecting this bill from damage by children playing with water pistols nearby, hiding the amount of the bill from the prying eyes of another worker, or deciding to pay the bill herself rather than letting the company pay for it. Writers actually can use confusion over denotation as a tool in character or plot development when, for instance, one character overhears part of a conversation and draws conclusions based on misunderstanding the speaker's denotation. If he hears that she is going to "cover" something, he may assume she is hiding some activity, when she actually is trying to find time to attend and report on an event, such as to "cover" the local ball game for the newspaper.

Writers also can use the multiple denotative meanings of words to construct figures of speech, such as metaphors.

▼PRACTICE QUESTIONS▼

"The Author to Her Book" is by Anne Bradstreet (1612–1672).

> Thou ill-form'd offspring of my feeble brain,
> Who after birth did'st by my side remain,
> Till snatcht from thence by friends, less wise then true
Line Who thee abroad, expos'd to publick view,
(5) Made thee in raggs, halting to th' press to trudge,
> Where errors were not lessened (all may judg).
> At thy return my blushing was not small,
> My rambling brat (in print) should mother call,
> I cast thee by as one unfit for light,
(10) Thy Visage was so irksome in my sight;
> Yet being mine own, at length affection would
> Thy blemishes amend, if so I could:
> I wash'd thy face, but more defects I saw,
> And rubbing off a spot, still made a flaw.

(15)   I stretcht thy joynts to make thee even feet,
Yet still thou run'st more hobling then is meet;
In better dress to trim thee was my mind,
But nought save home-spun Cloth, i'th' house I find.
In this array, 'mongst Vulgars mayst thou roam,

(20)   In Criticks hands, beware thou dost not come;
And take thy way where yet thou art not known,
If for thy Father askt, say, thou hadst none:
And for thy Mother, she alas is poor,
Which caus'd her thus to send thee out of door.

The word "blemishes" in line 12 contextually means which of the following?

(A) Deformities

(B) Stains

(C) Pimples

(D) Disfigurements

(E) Errors

Explanation: All five answer choices are denotations (literal definitions) of "blemishes." How is the word used in *this* selection? What is the context? A metaphor in which the author compares her book to a crippled child. Her friends gave her book to the public (lines 4–5), "Where errors were not lessened…" (line 6). Upon return of the book, she "cast" it by for a while (line 9) and then tried to correct its errors.

Correct Answer: **E**

Line 15 probably refers to

(A) physical therapy

(B) rehabilitation

(C) rhythm

(D) illusion

(E) allusion

Explanation: In her structural metaphor, she compares her book to a crippled child. "Feet" can be stretched on a child literally in physical therapy; however, in a book of verse (the real subject of the poem), she is stretching the poetic "feet" of rhythm. Notice that this poem consists of couplets written in iambic pentameter (heroic couplets).

Correct Answer: **C**

Lack of precision in day-to-day conversations has resulted in confusion over words that are similar both in their individual meanings and in their shades of meaning. The words <u>assure</u>, <u>ensure</u>, and <u>insure</u> are examples. These three words tend to be used interchangeably, yet each has its own meaning:

<u>Assure</u> means to give a promise to a person— "Let me assure you that I'll be there on time."

<u>Ensure</u> means to make sure— "Your participation will ensure the success of the program."

<u>Insure</u> means to protect with insurance— "I must insure the house against flood damage."

TERM ALERT You should know these terms: **specific** versus **general words**; **concrete** versus **abstract words**

Definitions: Another element of denotation (the literal meanings of words) involves diction (the writer's or speaker's choice of words): the degree to which the words used are **specific** or **general**, and **concrete** or **abstract**.

1. General words denote a group or class: <u>cat</u>
2. Specific words denote members of a group or class: <u>Siamese</u>, <u>tabby</u>
3. Concrete words denote people and things that are perceived by the five senses: <u>a warm coat</u>
4. Abstract words denote concepts and ideas: <u>pride</u>, <u>responsibility</u>

Concrete words are easily defined; abstract words, however, often defy universally accepted definitions because they cannot be measured or described by physical senses. The more specific and concrete the diction used, the easier it is to establish the meanings. Look at this series of five statements. Which statement contains the most easily defined underlined word?

1. "I like having <u>protection</u> around."
2. "I like having an <u>animal</u> around."
3. "I like having a <u>dog</u> around."
4. "I like having a <u>Great Dane</u> around."
5. "I like having my dog <u>Killer</u> around."

In the first statement, <u>protection</u> is very abstract as an idea and very general. It might refer to a barbed wire fence, to bodyguards, to bolted, steel doors, to a weapon or any number of other means of protection. The second sentence is far more concrete (animals can be seen, felt), but still is rather ambiguous, rather general. The third sentence begins to give a more specific, concrete picture—obviously this person likes having some type of dog around. What breed? Sentence four gives an even more concrete picture; however, the fifth sentence, in which there is a particular dog—named "Killer"—is both concrete and specific.

▼PRACTICE QUESTIONS▼

This selection comes from Sir Philip Sidney's "An Apology for Poetry," in which he attempts to explain the significance of the abstract world of poetry.

> But truly I imagine it falleth out with these poet-whippers, as with
> some good women, who often are sick, but in faith they cannot tell
> where. So the name of poetry is odious to them, but neither his
> Line cause nor effects, neither the sum that contains him nor the
> (5) particularities descending from him, give any fast handle to their
> carping dispraise.
> Since then poetry is of all human learning the most ancient and of
> most fatherly antiquity, as from whence other learnings have taken
> their beginnings, since it is so universal that no learned nation doth
> (10) despise it, nor no barbarous nation is without it; since both Roman
> and Greek gave divine names unto it, the one of *prophesying*, the
> other of *making*, and that indeed that name of *making* is fit for him,
> considering that whereas other arts retain themselves within their
> subject, and receive, as it were, their being from it, the poet only
> (15) bringeth his own stuff, and doth not learn a conceit out of a matter,

(15) but maketh matter for a conceit; since neither his description nor his end containeth any evil, the thing described cannot be evil; since his effects be so good as to teach goodness and to delight the learners; since therein (namely in moral doctrine, the chief of all knowledges) he doth not only far pass the historian, but, for instructing, is well-

(20) nigh comparable to the philosopher, and, for moving, leaves him behind him; since the Holy Scripture ... hath whole parts in it poetical...; since all his kinds are not only in their united forms but in their severed dissections fully commendable; I think (and think I think rightly) the laurel crown appointed for triumphing captains doth

(25) worthily (of all other learnings) honor the poet's triumph.

1. What is the poet "moving" in line 20?
   (A) Philosophers' opinions
   (B) Historians' facts
   (C) Knowledge
   (D) Doctrines
   (E) Emotions

2. As used in lines 5–6, "any fast handle to their carping dispraise" could be paraphrased to mean
   (A) help in understanding poetry
   (B) solid reason for censure
   (C) misunderstandings of the issue
   (D) reasonable clues to faithfulness
   (E) a cause and effect of poetry

3. The phrase "carping dispraise" is somewhat
   (A) paradoxical
   (B) redundant
   (C) anachronistic
   (D) analytical
   (E) flattering

4. As used in lines 15–16, "matter" versus "conceit" can be thought as
   (A) what is important versus imaginations or fancy
   (B) substance versus self-flattery
   (C) a document versus figure of speech
   (D) what occupies space versus fanciful expression
   (E) what is spoken or written versus an idea or understanding

Answers and Explanations:

1. **E** The speaker establishes a contrast as he builds to his main point that poetry surpasses "all other learnings" (line 25). He claims that the poet is "comparable to the philosopher" (line 20) for "instructing," but "leaves him behind" for "moving" (a play on words). Philosophers can instruct in ideas, attitudes, opinions, facts; however, "moving" speaks to our emotions, an abstract concept. Today, we might say, "That story is moving" when the outcome "touches" our hearts or stirs emotions within us.

2. **B.** "Fast" as an adjective can be meant to be firm or solid, with "dispraise" meaning "censure."

3. **B** Both "to carp" and "to dispraise" mean "to censure."

4. **E** "Matter" and "conceit" could mean any of the answer choices, but only E is supported by the context. In contrast to "other arts," poetry is the expression (written or spoken) of the poet's ideas or thoughts (expressions of the abstract).

IMPORTANT CONCEPT #2: SYNTAX

ᴇRM Aʟᴇʀᴛ You should know this term: **syntax**

Definition: Diction is the choice of words used; syntax is their arrangement into patterns. Understanding syntax can provide context for understanding the meaning.

NOTE: You need to know grammar and basic punctuation. The literature test might require you to identify the subject or main verb of a sentence, recognize a pronoun-antecedent relationship, and so forth. Often, you must understand word functions to understand fully the meaning of a selection.

▼PRACTICE QUESTION▼

The following stanza is taken from "Day, in Melting Purple Dying" by Maria Brooks.

> Tell to thee the high-wrought feeling,
> Ecstasy but in revealing;
> Paint to thee the deep sensation,
> Line Rapture in participation;
> (5) Yet but torture, if comprest
> In a lone, unfriended breast.

In the context of line 2, "but" is
(A) a conjunction meaning *exact*
(B) an adverb meaning *merely*
(C) a conjunction meaning *that*
(D) an adverb meaning *only*
(E) a conjunction meaning *however*

Explanation: Context will help you determine the answer. Lines 2–4 reveal that the speaker's "sensation" is "rapture in participation." In other words, if she tells the auditor of her feelings (line 1), "rapture"; if she does not, the result is "torture" (line 5). Her feelings are "Ecstasy but [or only] in revealing."

Correct Answer: **D**

Syntax also involves the **function** these words and groups of words serve within the sentence: **subject, verb, object, modifier, connective, complement, preposition,** and **absolute**.

In English, the most common sequence pattern is subject-verb-object. Other common sequence patterns include subject-verb-modifier/complement

Very often, but not always, the subject will appear before the verb. Exceptions include such constructions as "There are three mice in the room" in which the subject, "mice," comes after the verb "are." Verbs can be transitive and be followed by an object, intransitive and not be followed by an object, or linking and used to connect a complement (an adjective or noun) to the subject. Objects can be direct receivers of action (He threw the <u>ball</u>) or indirect receivers of action (He threw me the ball). *Complements* follow linking verbs.

Modifiers describe or limit, with adjectives and adverbs usually appearing before the word(s) they modify, with phrase and clause modifiers usually coming after—although exceptions to the generalization abound. Connectives include coordinating conjunctions that connect words that are in similar functions (such as two subjects: "Jane and John went home"), subordinating connectives that connect a subordinate clause to a main clause ("I can't continue <u>unless</u> you stop eating"), and transitional connectives ("There will be a test on Monday. <u>As a result</u>, she will not assign any further homework.")

Prepositions both connect and show a relationship of the word that follows to another word, quite often one that precedes ("The ball rolled <u>under</u> the table"—<u>under</u> tells where the ball rolled). Absolutes are not grammatically related to anything; they just "feel right" and somehow help the sentence ("<u>No</u>, I can't!" or "<u>For crying out loud</u>, do you expect him to believe her?").

Here are four different types of sentences:

1. The loose, common, or cumulative sentence

The loose or common sentence is the most used sentence structure in the English language. It generally is written in one of three basic patterns, each of which can be expanded by coordinating similar structures into the sentence or by modifying parts of or the entire sentence with more information:

Subject	Transitive Verb	Object
The car	hit	a tree.

Subject	Intransitive Verb	
Susan	cried.	

Subject	Linking Verb	Complement
Roger	was	a student.
The dog	is	happy.
The book	is	there.

Once the independent clause is written, modifiers are placed after the subject and verb. For example: I will hire him, despite his lack of references.

Effect: As the most common sentence structure used, there is a sense of met expectation (comfortable style caused by familiarity). The writing tends to be "choppy" if most of the sentences contain little coordination or modification. Too much elaboration, however, results in a difficult, wordy style.

2. The periodic or climactic sentence

In contrast to the loose sentence in which the subject often appears early in the sentence, in the periodic sentence the subject and its verb come much later, and serve as a climactic statement to a series of subordinate clauses or phrases. For example: Despite his lack of references, I will hire him. The rhetorical benefits of building to the main point can clearly be seen:

> Reaching deep within herself for some type of consolation, some small reflection of the pride and dignity that had once been the fighting edge of her courage, some reassurance that all was not lost, the *destitute woman opened the courtroom door.*

The defining element of a periodic sentence is that you must read to the end of the sentence to find the complete subject and verb (the independent clause).

Effect: The rhetorical buildup to the main point is dramatic.

3. The parallel sentence

Parallel sentences consist of a series of phrases, main clauses, or subordinate clauses:

The mother was *always laughing at his jokes, crying over his heartbreaks, and justifying his faults.*

The children laughed; the dog yelped; the young girl cried.

You should always remember *which key unlocks the chain, which chain binds the heart, and which heart breaks for you.*

Effect: The parallel sentence appeals to the reader's sense of logic in sequencing similar ideas or items and provides a sense of rhythm to the writing.

4. The balanced sentence

The balanced sentence is a type of parallel construction in which two major sentence elements that contrast with one another are balanced between a coordinating conjunction:

The river's ravishes stunned the older onlookers, *but* the water's pull mesmerized the younger ones.

Working on the project satisfied his sense of justice, *but* destroyed his sense of independence.

Effect: The balanced sentence, as a type of parallel sentence, provides a sense of rhythm to the sentence, but also provides emphasis or contrast—an element of logic.

▼PRACTICE QUESTION▼

Return to Sidney's essay to answer this question (page 249).

Based on syntax, the speaker's conclusion that poets deserve the laurel crown is based upon how many proofs?

(A) 7
(B) 8
(C) 9
(D) 10
(E) 11

Explanation: The speaker uses eight dependent clauses, each beginning with "since," to support his conclusion.

Correct Answer: **B**

▼PRACTICE QUESTIONS▼

The introductory paragraph of *A Tale of Two Cities* by Charles Dickens further illustrates the point:

> It was the best of times, it was the worst of times, it was the age of wisdom, it was the age of foolishness, it was the epoch of belief, it was the epoch of incredulity, it was the season of Light, it was the
>
> Line season of Darkness, it was the spring of hope, it was the winter of
>
> (5) despair, we had everything before us, we had nothing before us, we were all going direct to Heaven, we were all going direct the other way —in short, the period was so far like the present period, that some of its noisiest authorities insisted on its being received, for good or for evil, in the superlative degree of comparison only.

Structurally, lines 1–7 contain elements that are which of the following?
  I. Allusive
 II. Antithetical
III Paradoxical
(A) I only
(B) II only
(C) III only
(D) II and III only
(E) I, II, and III

In line 7, "in short" is significant because it
(A) marks a change in structure
(B) is a misuse of an absolute
(C) negates the speaker's meaning
(D) contrasts times and periods
(E) balances two opposing elements

What is the effect of the change in the subject pronoun in line 5?
(A) It has no real effect.
(B) It emphasizes superiority of the narrator's times.
(C) It shifts the tone from impersonal to personal.
(D) It affects the characterization of the narrator.
(E) It diminishes the sense of connection to the times.

Explanation: The bulk of the paragraph consists of a series of main clauses that are structured as loose or common sentences using a very simple, plain, easy-to-understand level of diction. This gives the reader a comfortable, nonthreatening beginning. Although so many short sentences would normally be "choppy," they have been joined together **mechanically** with commas (representing "and") and have been joined together **structurally** with parallel sentence construction.

	We had:	It was:	the best of times
	everything before us		the worst of times
	nothing before us		the age of wisdom
Line			the age of foolishness
(5)			the epoch of belief
	We were:		the epoch of incredulity
	all going direct to Heaven		the season of Light
	all going direct the other way		the season of Darkness
			the spring of hope
(10)			the winter of despair

The result is a rhythm that literally pulls the reader along, far outweighing any staccato effect the short, loose sentences might have otherwise produced.

Next, examine the contents of the syntactical structure used in the excerpt. "It was" is the subject-verb for the first ten independent clauses. The subject-verb changes to "We had" and "We were" respectively in the final four independent clauses. What is the effect of this change? One possible effect is that the momentum builds with a series of paradoxical statements with "it"—a neutral, *third-person* pronoun—as the subject. The change to "we"—a *first-person* pronoun—is startling; it jars the reader from any "lull" the otherwise comfortable rhythm might have given. Notice also how the paradoxes change from "time;" "ages," "epochs," "seasons," "spring...winter," to "everything … nothing <u>before us</u>" and to the promise, "We were all going direct to Heaven" countered by the threat, "We were all going direct the other way." The syntactical structure makes the reader comfortable, appeals to our sense of logic through parallel sentence structure, then gains the reader's attention first with a change in pronoun usage, followed by the abrupt break in syntax with the use of an absolute: "in short." What is the significance of the use of this absolute to the meaning of the paragraph? It divides the paragraph structurally into two parts: The first part is a series of paradoxical relationships of a period that at first seems impersonal, but eventually comes to be on a more personal level as it relates to the "we" of the story. The second part summarizes that these paradoxes of that period are "like the present period"—a meaning that personally involves the reader.

Correct Answers: **D, A, C**

▼PRACTICE QUESTION▼

What sentence structures does Shakespeare use in his "Sonnet 64" and how do they affect meaning?

> When I have seen by Time's fell hand defaced
> The rich proud cost of outworn buried age;
> When sometime lofty towers I see down razed,
> And brass eternal slave to mortal rage;
> (5) When I have seen the hungry ocean gain
> Advantage on the kingdom of the shore,
> And the firm soil win of the watery main,
> Increasing store with loss, and loss with store;
> When I have seen such interchange of state,
> (10) Or state itself confounded to decay,
> Ruin hath taught me thus to ruminate,
> That Time will come and take my love away.
> This thought is as a death, which cannot choose
> But weep to have that which it fears to lose.

Line and (5), (10) are marginal line markers.

by William Shakespeare

Lines 1–11 consist mostly of
(A) simple sentences
(B) subordinate clauses
(C) balanced sentences
(D) absolutes
(E) subject-verb constructions

Explanation: The first sentence is lines 1 through 12. Notice the parallel constructions:

Line 1 "When I have seen…"
Line 3 "When sometime lofty towers I see…"
Line 5 "When I have seen…"
Line 9 "When I have seen…"

These are subordinate clauses—so where are the subject and the verb of the sentence? They do not appear until line 11: "Ruin hath taught." Lines 1 through 12 consist of a periodic sentence in which the speaker "builds" to his point. This heightens the impact, then, of the meaning of the concluding couplet that is a loose sentence, in structural contrast to the preceding periodic sentence.

Correct Answer: **B**

NOTE: Another element of syntax that is helpful to determining meaning is the **transitional marker**. Transitional markers are relationship words—words that somehow establish some type of meaning between the words that appear before the marker to those that follow. Naturally, these include that large group called the **conjunction**. Most readers are aware that <u>and</u> signals combining relationships or addition, whereas <u>but</u> signals an exception. Some transitional markers carry obvious meaning, others have more subtle shades of meaning that although they may be similar, are not exactly the same:

<u>Thus</u> involves how, why, or to what extent something is done and suggests results.
<u>Thence</u> implies a forward progression from a specified point in space or time.
<u>Also</u> is a marker for additional information.

<u>Moreover</u> indicates an excess beyond that designated previously.

<u>Nevertheless</u> means despite the circumstances.

<u>However</u> marks relationships of manner, degree, or exception.

▼PRACTICE QUESTION▼

As these few illustrations show, the transitional marker can affect meaning. To demonstrate, read this first stanza of "Oft, in the Stilly Night" by Thomas Moore. How would the meaning of the last four lines change if the speaker had used "Thence" rather than "Thus" in line 11?

> Oft, in the stilly night,
>   Ere Slumber's chain has bound me,
> Fond Memory brings the light
>   Of other days around me;
> (5)   The smiles, the tears,
>   Of boyhood's years,
> The words of love then spoken;
>   The eyes that shone,
>   Now dimmed and gone,
> (10) The cheerful hearts now broken!
> Thus, in the stilly night,
>   Ere Slumber's chain hath bound me,
> Sad Memory brings the light
>   Of other days around me.

In line 11, "Thus" points the reader to

(A) the element of time at work

(B) a degree of intensity of the speaker's emotion

(C) in what manner the speaker's night is spent

(D) new information concerning the speaker

(E) emotion beyond that previously expressed

Explanation: "Thus" generally marks a reason, a method, or what has happened.

Correct Answer: **C**

TERM ALERT You should know this term: **aphorism**

Definition: An aphorism is a pointed or concise statement of principle. Also called *maxims*, these statements combine denotation and syntax to achieve concise expression.

> **Examples: To the victor belong the spoils.**
> **To err is human, to forgive, divine.**
> **An apple doesn't fall far from the tree.**
> **The proof of the pudding is in the eating.**

TERM ALERT You should know this term: **cliché**

Definition: A cliché is an expression that, although once considered clever, has been overused.

Examples: **Don't put the cart before the horse.**
To make a long story short ...
Fingers on the pulse of ...
Not worth a plugged nickel
Don't rock the boat.

Sometimes an aphorism can also be considered a cliché.

▼PRACTICE QUESTION▼

This selection is from Samuel Johnson's "The Rambler, No 4."

> These books are written chiefly to the young, the ignorant, and the
> idle, to whom they serve as lectures of conduct, and introduction into
> life. They are the entertainment of minds unfurnished with ideas, and
> Line   therefore easily susceptible of impressions; not fixed by principles, and
> (5)   therefore easily following the current of fancy; not informed by
> experience, and consequently open to every false suggestion and
> partial account.

These lines exhibit a sense that is
(A) apologetic
(B) apathetic
(C) apocalyptic
(D) aphoristic
(E) apostrophic

Explanation: Look at the sentence structure. They ("These books") are the entertainment of minds unfurnished with ideas, and therefore easily susceptible of impressions. They ("These books") are the entertainment of minds not fixed by principles, and therefore easily following the current of fancy. They ("These books") are the entertainment of minds not informed by experience, and consequently open to every false suggestion and partial account. Each of these constructions could stand as a one-sentence statement of principle.

Correct Answer: **D**

TERM ALERT You should know this term: **idiom**

Definition: An idiom is an expression that does not make sense on a literal level, such as "to hang around" or "to fall off the wagon."

▼PRACTICE QUESTION▼

> As far as the eye could reach, a line of white buildings extended
> along the bank, their background formed by the purple hue of the
> dense, interminable forest.
>
> (from Susanna Moodie's "A Visit to Grosse Isle")

"As far as the eye could reach" is best described as which of the following?

I. A maxim

II. An aphorism

III. An idiom

IV. A cliché

(A) I only

(B) II only

(C) III only

(D) III and IV only

(E) I, II, III, and IV

Explanation: How far can an eye reach? This idiom has been well used over generations.

Correct Answer: **D**

NOTE: At this point, take a moment to think about what you have learned about meanings of words, phrases, lines, and sentences. Use the following questions to review.

▼Practice Questions▼

Here is John Donne's "The Legacy."

> When last I died, and, dear, I die
> 　As often as from thee I go,
> 　Though it be but an hour ago
> —And lovers' hours be full eternity—
> (5)　I can remember yet, that I
> 　Something did say, and something did bestow;
> Though I be dead, which sent me, I might be
> Mine own executor, and legacy.
> 　I heard me say, "Tell her anon,
> (10)　That myself," that is you, not I,
> 　"Did kill me," and when I felt me die,
> I bid me send my heart, when I was gone;
> But I alas! could there find none;
> 　When I had ripp'd, and search'd where hearts should be
> (15)　It kill'd me again, that I who still was true
> In life, in my last will should cozen you.
>
> Yet I found something like a heart,
> 　But colors it and corners had;
> 　It was not good, it was not bad,
> (20)　It was entire to none, and few had part;
> As good as could be made by art
> 　It seemed, and therefore for our loss be sad.
> I meant to send that heart instead of mine,
> But O! no man could hold it, for 'twas thine.

1. Of the following definitions and illustrative phrases, which best reflects the meaning of "corners" as used in line 18?
   (A) Geometric angles
   (B) Critical points
   (C) Secret places
   (D) Shortest routes
   (E) Awkward positions

2. That the speaker intended to "send" his heart but "could there find none" in the second stanza is
   (A) sarcastic rhetoric
   (B) symbolic of the nature of love
   (C) a structural pun describing discouragement
   (D) a parody of the first stanza
   (E) the vehicle for the legacy

3. The theme of the poem is mostly developed by
   (A) narrative accounts
   (B) paradoxical relationships
   (C) love lyrics
   (D) comparison and contrast
   (E) legal analogies

4. In line 24, "no man could hold it, for 'twas thine" projects an attitude of
   (A) congeniality
   (B) intimacy
   (C) devotion
   (D) isolation
   (E) disillusionment

5. What is the intended "legacy" in line 8?
   (A) "my heart" (line 12)
   (B) "executor" (line 8)
   (C) "Eternity" (line 4)
   (D) "something like a heart" (line 17)
   (E) "art" (line 21)

6. The central irony of the poem can be seen in which of the following lines?
   (A) Line 4
   (B) Line 9
   (C) Line 14
   (D) Line 17
   (E) Line 24

Answers and Explanations

1. **C** They are secret places (the corners of the heart and mind) rather than geometric angles (the corners of the room), critical points (to turn a corner), shortest routes (to cut corners), or awkward positions (backed into a corner). Hint: When reading this poem, explore the figurative meanings of "heart" and "death."

2. **C** The speaker lost his heart (line 13), which also can mean that he "lost heart," an expression meaning discouragement.

3. **B** Some of the paradoxical elements in this poem include the following: an hour equals an eternity; a dead person being his own executor and legacy; the speaker finding his lover's heart in his own body. The seemingly contradictory concepts rely upon the figurative meanings of death and the heart.

4. **E** Look closely at the poet's description of his lover's heart: "something like a heart" (line 17), "not good...not bad" (line 19), and particularly note the description in lines 20–21. The speaker has taken a revealing look at his lover to find that "our loss be sad" (line 22). He feels disillusionment.

5. **A** The speaker, on a figurative level, plans upon death to send his legacy or heart to his lover (line 12).

6. **E** After a killing inner search of his own feelings or heart in the second stanza, he finds that he has already lost his heart to his lover and has lost heart in the process. As we read the third stanza, however, he does find and describe a heart that is less than perfect. Does it belong to him? Are his feelings less deep than those implied in the first stanza? No. Ironically, it belongs to his lover.

IMPORTANT CONCEPT #3: CONNOTATION

TERM ALERT You should know this term: **connotation**

Definition: Denotations are the literal meanings of words; *connotations* are their emotional meanings. Sometimes *associations* result from a person's own nonverbal experiences. Such associations can be very powerful. A particular song might be associated with a first love. Certain foods can remind you of a person, an enjoyable vacation, or a particular place. Events in your life may be brought to mind when you hear a name, smell a fragrance, or experience a familiar feeling. Such associations can be positive or negative, but seldom without some type of emotional response.

Similarly, words can gain connotative meaning for a person through his or her personal experiences. These connotations might be negative or positive, sad or happy, discouraging or encouraging—reflecting any number of emotional responses. Connotative meanings also can be universal (shared by most people) or shared by some group (such as a nation, an organization, a race, a religion, or a profession or trade).

Words, then, can stir emotions and can cause a person to make certain associations. A writer can elicit emotions from his or her readers simply by selecting connotatively charged words. This translates into tremendous power—power to influence beyond the effects of denotation.

Public speakers use connotatively charged words as rhetorical devices to persuade their listeners. Story writers use connotation to create an emotional bond between the readers and a character (or to elicit some other response from readers).

▼PRACTICE QUESTION▼

These words are taken from George Eliot's *Silas Marner*.

> 'Well, my meaning is this, Marner,' said Godfrey, determined to
> come to the point. 'Mrs Cass and I, you know, have no children—
> nobody to be the better for our good home and everything else we
> Line have—more than enough for ourselves. And we should like to have
> (5) somebody in the place of a daughter to us—we should like to have
> Eppie, and treat her in every way as our own child. It'ud be a great
> comfort to you in your old age, I hope, to see her fortune made in
> that way, after you've been at the trouble of bringing her up so well.
> And it's right you should have every reward for that. And Eppie, I'm
> (10) sure, will always love you and be grateful to you: she'd come and
> see you very often, and we should all be on the look-out to do
> everything we could towards making you comfortable.'
> A plain man like Godfrey Cass, speaking under some
> embarrassment, necessarily blunders on words that are coarser than
> (15) his intentions, and that are likely to fall gratingly on susceptible
> feelings. While he had been speaking, Eppie had quietly passed her
> arm behind Silas's head, and let her hand rest against it caressingly:
> she felt him trembling violently. He was silent for some moments
> when Mr Cass had ended—powerless under the conflict of emotions,
> (20) all alike painful. Eppie's heart was swelling at the sense that her

father was in distress; and she was just going to lean down and speak to him, when one struggling dread at last gained the mastery over every other in Silas, and he said, faintly—'Eppie, my child, speak. I won't stand in your way. Thank Mr and Mrs Cass.'

"Susceptible feelings," as used in the second paragraph, connotes
(A) that Cass is feeling very emotional
(B) that Marner would agree to anything
(C) Eppie's insignificant role in Marner's life
(D) a vulnerability in Marner
(E) that Marner felt anger at Cass's manner

Explanation: To be susceptible denotes feelings that are easily affected and sensitive. Susceptible feelings, as a result, connote a sense that Marner is vulnerable at this point.

Correct Answer: **D**

▼PRACTICE QUESTIONS▼

Nonnarrative prose writers also use connotative word choices to project or intensify meaning. Here are a few lines from a letter written by Lord Chesterfield to his son.

> But there is no living in the world without a complaisant indulgence for people's weaknesses, and innocent, though ridiculous vanities.

The speaker's use of "complaisant" in this context connotes a sense of
(A) annoyance and resentment
(B) smugness and condescension
(C) rivalry and contention
(D) obedience and yielding
(E) compunction and regret

Explanation: "Complaisant" denotes having pleasing manners. Its connotative meaning is associated with a patronizing, condescending attitude *in this context*. The speaker indulges the "ridiculous vanities" and weaknesses of others, making him seem smug.

Correct Answer: **B**

Poets, too, use connotative language. Return to "The Author to Her Book" by Anne Bradstreet on pages 247–248 to answer this question.

Using the more specific word "Vulgars" (line 19) rather than the more general "common people" has which of these effects?
(A) Connotatively emphasizes that the work lacks refinement
(B) Illustrates the speaker's sense of drama
(C) Varies the tone of the poem
(D) Insults the readers of her work
(E) Reinforces the reader's sense of sympathy for the child

Explanation: Although synonyms by definition, "Vulgars" carries with it a connotation emphasizing that only those without culture or refinement would appreciate her work.

Correct Answer: **A**

This brief overview of connotative language might be summarized with the following illustration:

<u>Positive connotation</u>   <u>Neutral</u>
an antique   an old chair

<u>Negative connotation</u>
junk

IMPORTANT CONCEPT #4: IMPLICATIONS

TERM ALERT You should know this term: **implication**

Definition: **Implication** and **inference** are two easily confused words that have related meanings. An *implication* is an involvement or indication that is made indirectly by association; an *inference* is a conclusion drawn from facts or premises. The speaker implies (hints at, suggests) some idea from which the hearer or reader infers (receives, draws) a conclusion.

Do you see any implications in these lines from Joseph Conrad's "An Outpost of Progress?"

> **He had charge of a small clay storehouse with a dried-grass roof, and pretended to keep a correct account of beads, cotton cloth, red kerchiefs, brass wire, and other trade goods it contained.**

What are the implications in the statement that he "pretended to keep a correct account?" The obvious answer is that although he led others to believe the accounts were accurate, they were not; and he knew that they were not. This much can be learned from the implications of "pretended." From these implications, can an inference be made concerning <u>why</u> he did this? Perhaps he did not have the ability to keep accurate books and as a result tried to cover careless and perhaps unintended errors. Maybe he deliberately misled others to cover embezzlement or to harm them financially.

You can discover whether these conclusions are accurate only if the context reveals more information.

Implications can be subtle or they can be easily seen. Often implications are the product of connotative word choices. Although the verbs "authenticate," "confirm," "corroborate," "substantiate," "validate," and "verify," for example, all mean to establish the truth of a situation or some information, each word choice carries with it a distinctive connotation that can imply a greater meaning in a given context.

You might *authenticate* someone's signature, proving it to be real; a traveler can *confirm* a hotel reservation, assuring the manager that he will be there by a certain time and proving his intentions by prepaying the bill; a witness might *corroborate* a defendant's alibi by swearing to have been with her at the time in question; fingerprints at a crime scene can *substantiate* the prosecution's theory that a defendant was there; city parking lot rules require patrons to *validate* their parking tickets, proving they were in the designated office or store; and a researcher might *verify* a project's conclusions by duplicating a key experiment several times and comparing the results.

> "Can you authenticate that this is a genuine Monet?" Andre paused, waiting for Joseph to answer. Finally, he repeated the question, sounding out each syllable of "authenticate" as if Joseph might not understand the meaning of the word.

That Andre expected Joseph to authenticate the painting implies that
(A) Andre is an art expert
(B) Joseph forged the painting
(C) Andre does not believe Joseph owns the painting
(D) Joseph should have documentation to prove Monet painted it
(E) Joseph is an art expert

Explanation: At first glance, you might select E as the correct answer choice. However, that Andre decided "Joseph might not understand the meaning of the word" implies that Joseph is not an art expert, although Andre does expect him to have some type of proof that the painting is genuine.

Correct Answer: **D**

> "Can you corroborate that this is a genuine Monet?" Andre paused, waiting for Joseph to answer. Joseph looked nervously at his partner, Norton, then resettled his gaze on his feet. "Can you corroborate that this is a genuine Monet?" Andre repeated impatiently.

That Andre asked Joseph to corroborate that the painting is genuine implies that
(A) Norton and Joseph are fighting
(B) Norton has already claimed the painting is a Monet
(C) Norton is the sole owner of the painting
(D) Joseph is covering for his partner
(E) the painting is a forgery

Explanation: Indeed, Norton's reluctance to answer may mean that the painting is a forgery; however, within the limits of the context, use of "corroborate," together with Joseph's look toward Norton, strengthens the implication that Norton has already claimed the painting is genuine. One person is being asked to confirm the word of another.

Correct Answer: **B**

IMPORTANT CONCEPT #5: POETIC SYNTAX

Concept Explained:

Poetic syntax includes language that speaks to the reader's emotions and a use of syntax that focuses on its effect over its conformity to rules. Some literary scholars cite this freedom in the use of syntax as a major line drawn between prose and poetry. How do poets use syntax? A few notable ways include:

1. Words that are normally assigned one function are used in an unusual function in a syntactical structure. For example, <u>was</u> normally functions as a verb and <u>lifetime</u> as a noun. The poet might assign <u>was</u> to the role of subject and use <u>lifetime</u> as a verb.

> <u>Was</u> is a lifetime ago...
> And she has <u>lifetimed</u> her existence away.

2. Inversion of normal syntactical patterns, called *anastrophe*, such as placing the modifier after rather than before the word it modifies:

> This <u>Hermit good</u> lives in that wood
> Which slopes down to the sea. [emphasis added]

Or placing the predicate modifier first in the sentence:

> <u>Silent</u> is the house: all are laid asleep. [emphasis added]

What would be the normal syntactical pattern for this structure?

> With olives ripe the sauces
> Were flavored, without exception.

3. Repetition of syntactical patterns:

> MY MIND TO ME A KINGDOM IS
>
> Some have too much, yet still do crave;
> I little have, and seek no more.
> They are but poor, though much they have,
> And I am rich with little store.
> <u>They poor, I rich; they beg, I give;</u>
> <u>Thy lack, I leave; they pine, I live.</u>

> [emphasis added]

> by Sir Edward Dyer   (fifth stanza)

▼Practice Questions▼

You probably can easily spot poetic syntax in a selection. The real challenge in dealing with poetic syntax (particularly anastrophe) is deciding what the speaker is saying. Look at these lines taken from Alexander Pope's "An Essay on Criticism."

> A perfect judge will read each work of wit
> With the same spirit that its author writ:
> Survey the whole, nor seek slight faults to find
> Line   Where Nature moves, and rapture warms the mind;
> (5)   Nor lose, for that malignant dull delight,
> The generous pleasure to be charmed with wit.
> But in such lays as neither ebb nor flow,
> Correctly cold, and regularly low,
> That, shunning faults, one quiet tenor keep,
> (10)   We cannot blame indeed—but we may sleep.
> In wit, as nature, what affects our hearts
> Is not the exactness of peculiar parts;
> 'Tis not a lip, or eye, we beauty call,
> But the joint force and full result of all.

(15) Thus when we view some well-proportioned dome
(The world's just wonder, and even thine, O Rome!),
No single parts unequally surprise,
All comes united to the admiring eyes:
No monstrous height, or breadth, or length appear;
(20) The whole at once is bold and regular.

1. The speaker sees the pleasures of being "charmed with wit" (line 6)
   (A) as a result of "shunning faults"
   (B) as a reason to keep "quiet tenor"
   (C) as greater than enjoying finding "slight faults" (line 3)
   (D) as an unworthy goal compared to seeking faults
   (E) as a shallow endeavor, putting him to "sleep"

2. "We cannot blame" whom in line 10?
   (A) Judges
   (B) Nature
   (C) Wit
   (D) Authors
   (E) Rome

3. Lines 7–9 describe
   (A) an author sacrificing technical precision for wit
   (B) judges justly demanding precise writing
   (C) the role of nature's "ebb" and "flow"
   (D) an author sacrificing wit for technical precision
   (E) the character of the perfect judge

4. A "perfect judge" (line 1) would NOT
   (A) label "the joint force" (line 14) as beautiful
   (B) be "charmed with wit" (line 6)
   (C) share the author's "spirit" (line 2)
   (D) seek "exactness of peculiar parts" (line 12)
   (E) admire the structural unity of "some well-proportioned dome" (line 15)

5. The "sleep" in line 10 probably represents
   (A) satisfaction with works that warm the mind
   (B) escape from perfect judges
   (C) boredom with witless, cold works
   (D) illness of judges with malignant intents
   (E) fatigue of the author after seeking wit

Answers and Explanations:

The poetic syntax of lines 3, 13, and especially lines 9–10 is obvious. Now, examine what the syntax means.

1. **C** To answer this question, you need to work through the poetic syntax of lines 1–10, picking up on key words. The perfect judge (line 1) will survey the whole, not seeking slight faults (line 3) and not losing "for that malignant dull delight," referring to the pleasure of finding slight faults (line 5), the pleasure of being charmed with wit (line 6). Also, note the connotative effects of "malignant."

2. **D** Again, delve into the structure of the poetic syntax. First, you can surmise from context that "lays" that do not "ebb nor flow" and are correct and regular (lines 7–8) are in contrast to a work "Where Nature moves, and rapture warms the mind" (line 4). A lay, by definition, is a type of poem. Who, then, would shun faults and keep a "quiet" tenor or direction (line 9)? Can we blame an author (line 2) for avoiding fault seekers (line 3)?

3. **D** This question requires drawing a conclusion based on restructuring the poetic syntax. If we cannot blame the author for keeping a quiet tenor, then we can conclude that he or she did sacrifice wit for technical precision.

4. **D** NOT questions can be especially tricky. One technique is to turn each answer choice into a true-false: The only true answer choice in this question is (D). A "perfect judge" would NOT seek "exactness of peculiar parts" (line 12).

5. **C** Context links sleep with a response to cold, low poems that "neither ebb nor flow" (lines 7–8), in other words, poems that are boring.

IMPORTANT CONCEPT #6: POETIC DICTION

Concept Explained:

Poetic diction refers to language that is normally associated with poetry and that has a poetic effect. The trend in modern writing is to use the diction of everyday speech; however, poets of various periods (such as the Romantics) sought a "language of poetry" with an effect that would transcend everyday speech.

The poetic diction in vogue varies with the period and the group of writers involved. Eighteenth-century writers, for example, favored *periphrasis* (substituting ornate descriptions for ordinary expression), personifications, and archaisms. The effect? An artificial, stilted form.

▼PRACTICE QUESTION▼

These lines are taken from Christina Rossetti's "A Bed of Forget-Me-Nots":

> Is LOVE so prone to change and rot
> We are fain to rear Forget-me-not
> By measure in a garden-plot?—

The central contrast in these lines makes boundaries seem

(A) inferior
(B) superior
(C) a necessary evil
(D) an unnecessary evil
(E) desirable

Explanation: About now you may be asking whether this question belongs with this quote. Yes, it does. This question demonstrates how you can use what you have learned so far about the literary elements and context clues to overcome even poetic diction used more than 150 years ago.

First, look at the sentence structure: a rhetorical question. The speaker does not expect an answer, but is using the question to make her point. Now, search for the central contrast. Obviously, she is comparing LOVE with Forget-me-nots (flowers), a metaphor. She is using growing flowers as a vehicle to describe growing LOVE. Flowers are grown within the boundaries ("by measure") in "garden-plots."

Look again at the diction used. Do you know what "fain" means? "Fain" is an archaic word labeled by some unabridged dictionaries as "poetic." How can you discover the contrast without knowing what "fain" means? You have a context clue to help you. Look at the first line: "Is LOVE so *prone* to change and rot...." In this context, "so" is an adverb showing degree. It directly points to the contrast: Is LOVE so prone (in such a condition) that we are "fain" to rear it (LOVE like flowers) within boundaries? LOVE without boundaries is contrasted to LOVE (like flowers) in boundaries. Using a rhetorical question implies that the speaker believes boundaries are inferior. A modern illustration of this sentence construction would be "Is Jerry *so afraid* of a plane crash that he is fain to drive two thousand miles to reach home?" When you use context in this case, you do not need to know what "fain" means to understand the question.

FYI: "Fain" is used often in period poetry. As a verb, it is now obsolete; as an adverb it is used with *would* (She *would fain* have come with him tonight). "Fain" as an adjective can mean "pleased" or "making do." When it means accepting less-than-desired circumstances, it is usually accompanied by the infinitive form of the verb: Is LOVE so prone to change and rot / We are fain to rear [willing to settle for rearing] Forget-me not [LOVE] / By measure in a garden-plot?—

Correct Answer: **A**

IMPORTANT CONCEPT #7: SPECIAL CONTEXTS

Concept Explained:

Historical references, dialects, and changes in definitions over time and space can all affect how well you understand a selection. Once again, however, context comes to the rescue.

1. Historical references.

You do not need to memorize literary or historical periods for the test beyond recognizing allusions that are part of our common knowledge. Some literary works might contain references and allusions that you do not recognize. Some test writers include a marginal note for readers that will explain a given reference, allusion, or use of period diction; but even without such help, many times you can use context to determine correct answers.

▼PRACTICE QUESTIONS▼

The following poem was written by Phillis Wheatley. Use context clues to answer the questions that follow.

To the Right Honourable William, Earl of Dartmouth, His Majesty's Principal Secretary of State for North America, Etc.[1]

> Hail, happy day, when, smiling like the morn,
> Fair Freedom rose New England to adorn:
> The northern clime Beneath her genial ray,
> Dartmouth, congratulates thy blissful sway:
> (5) Elate with hope her race no longer mourns,
> Each soul expands, each grateful bosom burns,
> While in thine hand with pleasure we behold
> The silken reins, and Freedom's charms unfold.
> Long lost to realms beneath the northern skies
> (10) She shines supreme, while hated Faction dies;
> Soon as appeared the goddess long desired,
> Sick at the view, she languished and expired;
> Thus from the splendors of the morning light
> The owl in sadness seeks the caves of night.
>
> (15) No more, America, in mournful strain
> Of wrongs, and grievance unredressed complain,
> No longer shalt thou dread the iron chain
> Which wanton Tyranny with lawless hand
> Had made, and with it meant to enslave the land.
>
> (20) Should you, my lord, while you peruse my song,
> Wonder from whence my love of Freedom sprung,
> Whence flow these wishes for the common good,
> By feeling hearts alone best understood,
> I, young in life, by seeming cruel fate,
> (25) Was snatched from Afric's fancied happy seat:
> What pangs excruciating must molest,
> What sorrows labour in my parents' breast?
> Steeled was that soul and by no misery moved

The word "Line" appears in the left margin aligned with line (5), (10), (15), (20), and (25) markers.

That from a father seized his babe beloved:

(30)   Such, such my case, And can I then but pray
Others may never feel tyrannic sway?

For favours past, great Sir, our thanks are due,
And thee we ask thy favours to renew,
Since in thy power, as in thy will before.

(35)   To soothe the griefs which thou didst once deplore.
May heavenly grace the sacred sanction give
To all thy works, and thou forever live
Not only on the wings of fleeting Fame,
Though praise immortal crowns the patriot's name,

(40)   But to conduct to heaven's refulgent fane,
May fiery coursers sweep the ethereal plain,
And bear thee upwards to that blessed abode;
Where, like the prophet, thou shalt find thy God.

[1]This poem was written for William, Earl of Dartmouth, who was appointed the "Principal Secretary of State" over the American colonies in 1773. He replaced Lord Hillsborough.

1. The second stanza is marked by a major
   change in
   (A) subject
   (B) rhyme scheme
   (C) rhythm
   (D) speaker
   (E) expressed auditor

2. Based on context. "The owl" in line 14 proba-
   bly represents
   (A) slavery
   (B) the speaker
   (C) the new secretary (Dartmouth) and
       increasing freedom
   (D) the former secretary (Hillsborough) and
       partisan conflict
   (E) freedom

3. The purpose of the third stanza is to
   (A) elicit the auditor's sympathy
   (B) redirect the subject to slavery issues
   (C) explain the speaker's depths of emotion
       concerning the subject
   (D) persuade the auditor to abolish slavery in
       the colonies
   (E) change the tone of the work as a whole

4. Why does the speaker repeat "Such," in line 30
   rather than complete the sentence with "Such
   was my case?"
   (A) The repetition serves to avoid an anachro-
       nism.
   (B) The amplification that follows depends
       upon an emphasis on "Such."
   (C) The repetition better suits the rhyme
       scheme.
   (D) The repetition makes "Such" become sym-
       bolic of Freedom.
   (E) The repetition rhetorically emphasizes the
       personal nature of lines 24–29.

5. For Fame to be "fleeting," yet praised to be
   "immortal" (lines 38–39) is a(n)
   (A) implicit metaphor
   (B) allegory
   (C) forensic rhetoric
   (D) oxymoron
   (E) paradox

6. The use of Freedom, Faction, Tyranny, and Fame results in which of the following effects?
   (A) It makes these ideas seem more fleeting.
   (B) It emphasizes the contrast of America's "mournful strain" line (15).
   (C) It enlarges the speaker's sense of loss.
   (D) It makes these abstract ideas seem more tangible.
   (E) It symbolizes mourning.

7. The speaker's attitude toward the poem's main auditor is best described as one of
   (A) assertive disapproval
   (B) defensive sympathy
   (C) hopeful anticipation
   (D) petulant disrespect
   (E) censorious foreboding

8. The central subject of this poem is
   (A) freedom
   (B) tyranny
   (C) slavery
   (D) Africa
   (E) faction

9. Lines 14–29 say that
   (A) the speaker's parents suffered coronary problems
   (B) the speaker was stolen from her parents
   (C) her father labored for her passage to America
   (D) the speaker's child was stolen
   (E) her entire family was seized

Answers and Explanations:

1. **E** Although there is a change in rhyme scheme in line 17, the major change is from addressing the new secretary to addressing America. She returns to addressing Dartmouth in line 20.

2. **D** Identify the pronouns and symbols: In line 10 "she" is Freedom (line 8). The goddess (Freedom) appears (line 11). In line 12 she is Faction (line 10), who is sick and dying. "Thus" (line 13), or as a result, the owl is in sadness. The owl represents Faction or the old ways of the former secretary.

3. **C** The speaker reveals firsthand knowledge of Tyranny, giving reason for her love of Freedom (lines 21, 30–31).

4. **E** There is no anachronism, and a rhetorical question follows. The couplets are not affected. To decide between D and E, determine what "such" refers to: the speaker's personal account.

5. **E** In its positive sense, praise is an element of fame, making the ideas seem somewhat contradictory.

6. **D** Describing abstract ideas as if they are concrete things (reification) makes them seem more tangible.

7. **C** The speaker is hopeful (line 5) and has a sense of anticipation (lines 32–33).

8. **A** All five answer choices are mentioned in the work. Look for relationship to determine which subject is central. Tyranny and slavery are the absence of freedom. Africa is where the speaker lost her freedom. Faction is the enemy of Freedom (first stanza).

9. **B** "I...Was snatched" (lines 24–25) "...from a father seized his babe beloved" (line 29).

2. Dialects.

Dialect is the speech of a region; *accents* are the ways words are actually pronounced. If you do much traveling, you soon realize that dialects change from one region to another. A "soda water" in West Texas is "pop" in Ohio. You can hear "y'all" in the South, "you guys" in the Midwest, and "you'uns" in the Ohio River Valley. Dialects are also influenced by such elements as nationality, ethnicity, education, and occupation. Eventually, dialects and even accents (or graphic representations of accents) become part of literature and can affect your understanding of what you are reading. Using context is very important when dealing with dialects.

This paragraph comes from Susanna Moodie's description of Grosse Isle:

> Turning to the south side of the St. Lawrence, I was not less struck with its low fertile shores, white houses, and neat churches, whose slender spires and bright tin roofs shone like silver as they caught the first rays of the sun. As far as the eye could
>
> Line reach, a line of white buildings extended along the bank, their background formed
>
> (5) by the purple hue of the dense, interminable forest. It was a scene unlike any I had ever beheld, and to which Britain contains no parallel. Mackenzie, an old Scotch dragoon, who was one of our passengers, when he rose in the morning and saw the parish of St. Thomas for the first time, exclaimed: "Weel, it beats a'! Can thae white clouts be a' houses? They look like claes hung out to drie!" There was some truth in
>
> (10) this odd comparison, and for some minutes I could scarcely convince myself that the white patches scattered so thickly over the opposite shore could be the dwellings of a busy, lively population.

A "dragoon" is a(n)

(A) sailor
(B) musket
(C) infantryman
(D) marine
(E) colonial

Mackenzie makes a comparison between

(A) houses and clouds
(B) clouds and wet clothes
(C) clouds and white patches
(D) white patches and people
(E) houses and wet clothes

Explanation: By definition, a dragoon is an infantryman. The speaker identifies him as Scotch. What is his "odd comparison?" "They look like claes hung out to drie." First, what are "They?" "Can these white clouts be a' houses?" "They" refers to houses. Now, what would "claes hung out to drie" be? Look for clues in the speaker's description. She describes the houses as "a line of white buildings" and "white patches scattered so thickly...." What would be hung out to dry? When not using electric clothes dryers, people sometimes hang their wet clothing (white sheets and white shirts) on clotheslines to dry in the wind and sun.

Correct Answers: **C, E**

3. Period vocabulary

Words change over time and space. They change in spelling and meaning, and words can even shift functions as they are used syntactically. Test selections can be taken from works written more than four hundred years ago. A lot has changed since then. For example, what does "enthusiasm" mean to you? When Samuel Johnson wrote A *Dictionary of the English Language* in 1746, he defined *enthusiasm* as "a vain belief of private revelation; a vain confidence of divine favor or communication."

You will not be expected to be fluent in period vocabulary; however, if you do encounter a word or phrase that may have changed meaning, be sure to use context to determine what the speaker means rather than what you understand the word or phrase to mean in today's culture.

▼**PRACTICE QUESTION**▼

Here is a paragraph taken from Thackeray's *Vanity Fair*.

> Has the beloved reader, in his experience of society, never heard
> similar remarks by good-natured female friends; who always wonder
> what you can see in Miss Smith that is so fascinating; or what *could*
> Line induce Major Jones to propose for that silly insignificant simpering
> (5) Miss Thompson, who has nothing but her wax-doll face to
> recommend her? What is there in a pair of pink cheeks and blue
> eyes forsooth? These dear Moralists ask....

As used in context, "forsooth" means

(A) in fact, in a persuasive tone

(B) in truth, in a sarcastic tone

(C) today, in an argumentative tone

(D) today, in an angry tone

(E) in truth, in a complimentary tone

Explanation: "Forsooth" is an archaic term meaning "in fact" or "in truth" and can be used as a grammatical absolute. Without knowing this definition, however, you can tell from the context that "today" has nothing to do with the discussion, eliminating C and D. Look at the speaker's tone. His sarcasm toward "dear Moralists" should catch your attention.

Correct Answer: **B**

ACTIVE THINKING EXERCISES FOR MEANING(S) IN CONTEXT

STEP 1. ▸FOCUS◂

Sometimes test questions will focus on relationships, such as patterns; change; contrasts; similarities; multiple themes; central contrasts, themes, and similarities; progressions; and structural parallelisms.

If you become sensitive to relationships when you first encounter a selection, often you can save time and think more clearly as you progress through the questions.

▼**PRACTICE QUESTIONS**▼

Do you see the relationship central to "Man-Woman" by Lydia H. Sigourney?

> Man's home is everywhere. On ocean's flood,
> Where the strong ship with storm-defying tether
> Doth link in stormy brotherhood
> Line Earth's utmost zones together,
> (5) Where'er the red gold glows, the spice-trees wave,
> Where the rich diamond ripens, mid the flame
> Of vertic suns that ope the stranger's grave,
> He with bronzed cheek and daring step doth rove;
> He with short pang and slight

(10)   Doth turn him from the checkered light
        Of the fair moon through his own forests dancing,
           Where music, joy, and love
              Were his young hours entrancing;
           And where ambition's thunder-claim
(15)   Points out his lot,
        Or fitful wealth allures to roam,
              There doth he make his home,
                 Repining not.

        It is not thus with Woman. The far halls
(20)   Though ruinous and lone,
        Where first her pleased ear drank a nursing mother's tone;
              The home with humble walls,
        Where breathed a parent's prayer around her bed;
           The valley where, with playmates true,
(25)   She culled the strawberry, bright with dew;
              The bower where Love her timid footsteps led;
              The hearthstone where her children grew;
              The damp soil where she cast
        The flower-seeds of her hope, and saw them bide the blast,—
(30)   Affection with unfading tint recalls,
           Lingering round the ivied walls;
        Where every rose hath in its cup a bee,
           Making fresh honey of remembered things,
        Each rose without a thorn, each bee bereft of stings.

You can physically see a balanced relationship: line 1 and line 19. You know without reading another word that this poem is about contrast: man contrasted to woman. Subject? Their views of home. Of course, you should be able to state their respective views.

Which of the following pairs does NOT express the central contrast of this poem?
(A) "music, joy, and love" (line 12); "a parent's prayer" (line 23)
(B) "He with short pang and slight" (line 9); "affection with unfading tint recalls" (line 30)
(C) "Earth's utmost zones" (line 4); "The home with humble walls" (line 22)
(D) "daring step" (line 8); "timid footsteps" (line 26)
(E) "allures to roam" (line 16); "Lingering round the ivied walls" (line 31)

Which of the following works best reflects the theme of this poem?
(A) *The Wizard of Oz*—a girl learns the value of home
(B) *Gone With the Wind*—a woman is determined to restore her home
(C) *Women: The Misunderstood Majority*—an examination of myths about women
(D) *The Husband's Message* and *The Wife's Lament*—two Old English poems calling for reunion with a missing spouse
(E) *Men Are from Mars, Women Are from Venus*—an exploration of gender-based differences

Another element to focus on in a literary work is the possibility of progression or change. Questions can ask about changes in many things, such as character or viewpoints of speakers; or they can center on a lack of change.

In Sigourney's poem, man leaves his home, "Repining not." Look at the description of woman. Do you see any progressions?

Which of the following best describes the woman's progression in the poem?
(A) Nurse → wife → parent → widow
(B) Childhood home → marital home → nursing home
(C) Infant → child → wife → mother
(D) Infant → child → field laborer
(E) Ruin → humility → love → memories

Correct Answers: **A, E, C**

A FINAL WORD ABOUT ATTAINING ▸FOCUS◂

Have you decided on your focus strategies yet for the day of the test?

Review the focus strategies used in the Active Thinking Exercises and continue practicing using the final questions (Meanings in Context) for Practice Sets A, B, and C. Finally, complete Practice Test 7. Reminder: Do not forget to look for relationships as you read.

STEP 2. MOW (MY OWN WORDS)

Looking at context to determine the meanings of words, phrases, lines, and sentences will help you paraphrase as you **MOW** a literary passage, such as "To Labor Is to Pray" by Frances S. Osgood.

> Pause not to dream of the future before us;
> Pause not to weep the wild cares that come o'er us;
> Hark how Creation's deep, musical chorus,
> Line   Unintermitting, goes up into heaven!
> (5)   Never the ocean wave falters in flowing;
> Never the little seed stops in its growing;
> More and more richly the rose heart keeps glowing,
>   Till from its nourishing stem it is riven.
>
> "Labor is worship!" the robin is singing;
> (10) "Labor is worship!" the wild bee is ringing;
> Listen! That eloquent whisper, upspringing,
>   Speaks to thy soul from out nature's great heart.
> From the dark cloud flows the life-giving shower;
> From the rough sod blows the soft-breathing flower;
> (15) From the small insect, the rich coral bower;
>   Only man, in the plan, shrinks from his part.
>
> Labor is life! 't is the still water faileth;
> Idleness ever despaireth, bewaileth;
> Keep the watch wound, or the dark rust assaileth;
> (20)   Flowers droop and die in the stillness of noon.
> Labor is glory!—the flying cloud lightens;
> Only the waving wing changes and brightens,
> Idle hearts only the dark future frightens,
>   Play the sweet keys, wouldst thou keep them in tune!
>
> (25) Labor is rest—from the sorrows that greet us;

Rest from all petty vexations that meet us;
    Rest from sin-promptings that ever entreat us;
    Rest from world-sirens that lure us to ill.
    Work,—and pure slumbers shall wait on thy pillow;
(30) Work,—thou shalt ride o'er Care's coming billow;
    Lie not down 'neath Woe's weeping willow,
      Work with a stout heart and resolute will!

    Labor is health! Lo, the husbandman reaping,
    How through his veins goes the life-current leaping!
(35) How his strong arm in its stalworth pride sweeping,
      True as sunbeam the swift sickle guides,
    Labor is wealth,—in the sea the pearl groweth;
    Rich the queen's robe from the cocoon floweth;
    From the fine acorn the strong forest bloweth;
(40)   Temple and statue the marble block hides.

    Droop not! though shame, sin, and anguish are round thee!
    Bravely fling off the cold chain that hath bound thee!
    Look to the pure heaven smiling beyond thee!
      Rest not content in thy darkness,—a clod!
(45) Work for some good, be it ever so slowly!
    Cherish some flower, be it ever so lowly!
    Labor!—all labor is noble and holy!
    Let thy great deed be thy prayer to thy God.

What is the subject? _____

In a general sense, determine the main point of each stanza:

1. _____

2. _____

3. _____

4. _____

5. _____

6. _____

What is the narrator's purpose? _____

Summarize the main idea of the entire poem (one sentence): _____

_____

▼**PRACTICE QUESTIONS**▼

Armed with this analysis, answer these questions.

1. The speaker's main purpose is best described as
   (A) persuasive
   (B) argumentative
   (C) narrative
   (D) expository
   (E) descriptive

2. The speaker supports her point in the third stanza through the use of
   (A) anecdotes
   (B) anachronisms
   (C) allusions
   (D) aphorisms
   (E) allegories

3. As used in line 4, "Unintermitting" means without
   (A) starting
   (B) interruption
   (C) currents
   (D) continual blending
   (E) an intervening agent

4. Which of the following contains a paradoxical concept?
   (A) Labor is worship (line 9).
   (B) Labor is glory (line 21).
   (C) Labor is rest (line 25).
   (D) Labor is health (line 33).
   (E) Labor is wealth (line 37).

5. Which of the following is NOT an example of poetic syntax as used in this poem?
   (A) Repetition of syntactical patterns (lines 9, 17, 25)
   (B) Placing the direct object first in a sentence (lines 23, 40)
   (C) Use of an understood subject (lines 1–3)
   (D) Inversion of normal syntactical patterns of modifiers in relation to words modified (line 38)
   (E) Inversion of the verb and its object (lines 35–36)

6. The contrasts made within this poem include
   I. dreams; reality
   II. man; nature
   III. labor, idleness
   (A) I only
   (B) II only
   (C) III only
   (D) II and III only
   (E) I, II, and III

7. The word "bower" can be a noun meaning "an anchor" or a verb meaning "to enclose." Which of the following contextual clues help to determine its meaning as used in line 15?
   I. Parallel syntactic structure with lines 13 and 14
   II. Possible omission of the verb necessary to maintain the established rhythm
   III. The need for subject-verb agreement
   (A) I only
   (B) II only
   (C) III only
   (D) I and II only
   (E) I, II, and III

8. Which of the following meanings of "clod" is LEAST applicable as used in line 44?
   (A) A lump
   (B) Something vile
   (C) A stupid fellow
   (D) A soil or clay mass
   (E) A blood clot

9 Contextually, "Idle hearts" (line 23) refers to
   (A) cowardice, as opposed to having a "heart of oak"
   (B) disagreement, as opposed to "someone after my own heart"
   (C) indifference, as opposed to caring "heart and soul"
   (D) a lack of enthusiasm, as opposed to working "heart and hand"
   (E) calmness, as opposed to "having one's heart in one's mouth"

10. Line 40 refers to
    (A) poor city planning in which structures are obscured from vision
    (B) structures enclosed by block walls
    (C) the marble floor hidden by structures built on it
    (D) a secret place containing a temple and statue
    (E) the potential hidden within unworked materials

Answers and Explanations:

1. **A** The speaker attempts to persuade her readers to take action.

2. **D** This stanza contains a series of short maxims about watches, flowers, and pianos to support her point.

3. **B** "Intermitting" is stopping and starting again at intervals. The addition of the prefix *un-* means not stopping and starting again or without interruptions.

4. **C** Generally, rest means to stop work. In this case, the speaker alludes to using work as a means to rest from sorrow, troubles (line 26), sin (line 27), and temptations (line 28).

5. **C** Lines 1–3 are written in the imperative.

6. **D** Nature is described in lines 3–15 and contrasted with man in line 16. The maxims in the third stanza contrast labor (keeping, for example, your watch wound) to the results of idleness (rust). The reader is admonished: "pause not to dream" (line 1); however, dreams are not contrasted with reality.

7. **E** Each line repeats the same syntactic structure: a preposition ("From,") followed by a verb (flows, blows, and implied or omitted verb in line 15) that agrees with its subject (shower, flower, bower).

8. **E** In this metaphor, the vehicle is "a clod" and its obvious tenor is an idle person. Clod, then, describes someone who does not or will not work. Context reveals the speaker's negative attitude toward such a person: vile, stupid, figuratively just a lump of dirt.

9. **D** Although reference is made to a frightening future, cowardice does not conform to the overall message of the poem. Contrasting lack of enthusiasm to work does.

10. **E** Content points out the concept pattern: what can be produced from nature. Cocoons produce silk for clothes (line 38); acorns grow into forests (line 39); blocks of marble are made into temples and statues.

A FINAL WORD ABOUT ▶MOWING◀

When you **MOW** any selection, determine its subject and the purpose, paraphrase each section (using context clues as necessary), and summarize the main idea.

STEP 3. BID (BREAK IT DOWN)

When you **BID** a selection for contextual meaning, you are looking at denotation, syntax, connotation, implications, and poetic syntax and diction, as well as any special contextual problems that might arise, such as dialects, historical contexts, or period vocabulary.

▼PRACTICE QUESTIONS▼

The following poem, "Snow-Flakes" by Henry Wadsworth Longfellow, was chosen for this last **BID** exercise because its meaning is a result of a powerful blending of the literary elements, particularly form, tone, use of language, and contextual meaning, as the series of practice questions will reveal.

First, **MOW** the poem, then **BID** it for contextual meaning by underlining any words, phrases, lines, or sentences that you do not understand. Return to the context of the poem to try to determine their meanings.

> Out of the bosom of the Air,
> Out of the cloud-folds of her garments shaken,
> Over the woodlands brown and bare,
> Over the harvest-fields forsaken,
> Silent and soft and slow
> Descends the snow.

Line (5)

Even as our cloudy fancies take
    Suddenly shape in some divine expression,
Even as the troubled heart doth make
(10)   In the white countenance confession,
    The troubled sky reveals
    The grief it feels.

This is the poem of the air,
    Slowly in silent syllables recorded;
(15) This is the secret of despair,
    Long in its cloudy bosom hoarded,
    Now whispered and revealed
    To wood and field.

1. The pronoun "This" in lines 13 and 15 refers to
   (A) the Air as a feminine persona
   (B) divine expressions of winter cloud forms
   (C) the falling snow and the expression of grief it symbolizes
   (D) woodland settings and the natural elements
   (E) the contrasting nature of cloudy fancies to troubled realities

2. The connotative use of "hoarded" in line 16
   (A) makes the speaker seem covetous
   (B) adds a tone of parsimoniousness
   (C) exposes the speaker's avaricious attitude
   (D) conflicts with the "divine expression" in line 8
   (E) implies both secrecy and time

3. The repetitive use of "s" in this poem is best characterized as
   (A) assonance used to emphasize meaning
   (B) alliteration used to create a mood
   (C) consonance used to punctuate the tone
   (D) consonance and alliteration used for aural appeal
   (E) dissonance used to contrast the softer tones

4. What is the effect of lack of punctuation at the ends of lines 5, 7, 9, 11, and 17?
   (A) They make the poem's rhythm faster.
   (B) They support the rhyme scheme.
   (C) They structurally reinforce the kinesthetic sense of falling.
   (D) They reflect the silence of the scene.
   (E) They have no bearing on the poem's meaning.

5. Which of the following reflects the ironic contrast of tone and its effect in lines 7–10 to lines 11–12?
   (A) Hope, then despair, creating a tone of resignation
   (B) Warmth, then coldness, creating a tone of dread
   (C) Optimism, then aggravation, creating a tone of anger
   (D) Relief, then fear, creating a tone of worry
   (E) Deliverance, then anxiety, creating a tone of apprehension

6. The speaker adds the adverb "Even" to "as" to introduce lines 7 and 9. What is the effect?
   (A) "Even" shifts the tense of the stanza.
   (B) "Even" implies cause and "as" implies effect.
   (C) "Even" adds to the tone.
   (D) "Even" emphasizes the concurrence of lines 7–10 and lines 11–12.
   (E) "Even" relates to the balance of tenor and vehicle.

7. The controlling image in this poem compares
   (A) clouds to divine expressions
   (B) snow to grief
   (C) sky to bosom
   (D) harvest-fields to silent syllables
   (E) woodlands to a troubled heart

8. As used in lines 7 and 16, "cloudy" is a(n)
   (A) understatement
   (B) overstatement
   (C) illusion
   (D) synaesthesia
   (E) pun

9. Which of the following is personified in this poem?
   (A) Woodlands
   (B) Clouds
   (C) Air
   (D) Snow
   (E) Despair

10. What is the effect of the change of syntax in the third stanza?
    (A) It highlights the beauty of the scene.
    (B) It introduces the element of fear in the speaker's tone.
    (C) It reveals the speaker's sense of awe.
    (D) It signals revealment of the speaker's main point.
    (E) It shifts attention from the vehicle to the tenor.

11. The syntactical patterns of the sentences in the first two stanzas are best described as
    (A) loose and balanced
    (B) common and periodic
    (C) balanced and periodic
    (D) parallel and loose
    (E) periodic and parallel

12. What is the overall tone of this poem?
    (A) Poignant
    (B) Embittered
    (C) Surly
    (D) Sanguine
    (E) Sardonic

Answers and Explanations:

1. **C** Taken separately, "This is the poem of the air" could refer to the descriptive elements of the poem (B and D). In conjunction with descriptive stanzas, however, it brings meaning to a figurative level (C and E). Next, look at the speaker's use of imagery to determine which one is the better of these two possible answers. How does the "air" (line 13) "whisper and reveal" (line 17) its "despair" (line 15) "To wood and field" (line 18)?

2. **E** Use of "hoarded" reinforces the concept of a revelation (line 11) of something held in secret (line 15) for a long time (line 16).

3. **D** Both initial and final consonant sounds are used to create the sound effects of this poem.

4. **C** The scene is silent; however, run-on lines pull the reader from one line down to the next. This descent reflects the figurative meaning, the slow sinking and revealing of grief and despair.

5. **A** "...divine expression" and "confession" could point to hope (A) or optimism (C); however, lines 11–12 express despair, not aggravation.

6. **D** In conjunction with "as," "even" is an adverb that structurally means simultaneity or, in this case, concurrence.

7. **B** The snow descends (line 6) like grief (line 12).

8. **E** Not all puns are meant to be humorous. The vehicle of the metaphor centers around clouds producing snow. A "cloudy fancy" or "cloudy bosom" could also refer to anxiety, unclear notions, and dark ideas.

9. **C** Air has the human characteristics of wearing garments (line 2) and having a bosom (line 16).

10. **D** "This is...This is..."—the strong syntax used in lines 13 and 15 clearly attracts attention to the point that follows.

11. **E** Lines 1–5 build to the subject and verb in line 6, just as lines 7–11 build to lines 11–12. Also, notice the parallel use of prepositional phrases, for example, in the first stanza.

12. **A** The speaker uses the falling snow metaphor as a vehicle to express his despair, which the reader vicariously can feel. The combination of expressed grief and pathos on the part of the listener creates a poignant tone. In other words, we can feel the speaker's pain.

A FINAL WORD ABOUT BIDING:

When you **BID** a literary passage, you determine

1. its meaning,
2. what form it takes,
3. whose attitude is being expressed,
4. what tone of voice is being used,
5. who the characters are and/or how the passage can be characterized,
6. what uses of language are present, and
7. what the words mean in context.

STEP 4. TT→TM (TEST TAKER TO TEST MAKER)

Learning to see patterns of thought and form in literature (and in life) is a worthwhile skill, particularly in preparing for the literature test. Also, you need to learn to identify central images. These images usually are metaphoric, although they sometimes are based on an extended simile.

In the case of the following passage from Ralph Waldo Emerson's essay on "The Poet," the central or controlling image is a metaphor.

▼PRACTICE QUESTIONS▼

You can set the stage to write a question over this controlling image by answering some questions over topic, purpose, and patterns of thought.

>   For poetry was all written before time was, and whenever we are
> so finely organized that we can penetrate into that region where the
> air is music, we hear those primal warblings and attempt to write
> Line   them down, but we lose ever and anon a word or a verse and
> (5)   substitute something of our own, and thus miswrite the poem. The
> men of more delicate ear write down these cadences more faithfully,
> and these transcripts, though imperfect, become the songs of the
> nations. For nature is as truly beautiful as it is good, or as it is
> reasonable, and must as much appear as it must be done, or be
> (10)   known. Words and deeds are quite indifferent modes of the divine
> energy. Words are also actions, and actions are a kind of words.
>
>   The sign and credentials of the poet are that he announces that
> which no man foretold. He is the true and only doctor; he knows and
> tells; he is the only teller of news, for he was present and privy to
> (15)   the appearance which he describes. He is a beholder of ideas and
> an utterer of the necessary and causal. For we do not speak now of
> men of poetical talents, or of industry and skills in meter, but of the
> true poet. I took part in a conversation the other day concerning a
> recent writer of lyrics, a man of subtle mind, whose head appeared
> (20)   to be a music-box of delicate tunes and rhythms, and whose skill and
> command of language we could not sufficiently praise. But when the
> question arose whether he was not only a lyrist but a poet, we were
> obliged to confess that he is plainly a contemporary, not an eternal

(25) man. He does not stand out of our low limitations, like a Chimborazo under the line, running up from a torrid base through all the climates of the globe, with belts of the herbage of every latitude on its high and mottled sides; but this genius is the landscape-garden of a modern house, adorned with fountains and statues, with well-bred men and women standing and sitting in the walks and terraces. We

(30) hear, through all the varied music, the ground-tone of conventional life. Our poets are men of talents who sing, and not the children of music. The argument is secondary, the finish of the verse is primary.

For it is not meters, but a meter-making argument that makes a poem,—a thought so passionate and alive that like the spirit of a

(35) plant or an animal it has an architecture of its own and adorns nature with a new thing. The thought and the form are equal in the order of time, but in the order of genesis the thought is prior to the form. The poet has a new thought; he has a whole new experience to unfold; he will tell us how it was with him, and all men will be the

(40) richer in his fortune. For the experience of each new age requires a new confession, and the world seems always waiting for its poet.

1. Chimborazo is a mountain "under the line" (line 25) near the equator. It contributes to meaning as a simile for
   (A) a true poet
   (B) a lyrist
   (C) a contemporary
   (D) nature
   (E) a doctor

2. The "argument" in line 32 is
   (A) a debate among poets
   (B) poetic meaning
   (C) defining credentials of a poet
   (D) the speaker's line of reasoning
   (E) controversy over the speaker's meaning

3. The central contrast presented in the passage can be seen to be all the following pairs EXCEPT
   (A) "primal warblings" (line 3)… "substitute" (line 5)
   (B) "a lyrist" (line 22) … "a poet" (line 22)
   (C) "poetry" (line 1) … "transcripts" (line 7)
   (D) "contemporary" (line 23) … "eternal man" (lines 23–24)
   (E) "men of talents who sing" (line 31) … "children of music" (lines 31–32)

4. The "writer of lyrics" (line 19) is described as which of the following?
   (A) A poet, eternal man, like a Chimborazo
   (B) A poet, contemporary, like a Chimborazo
   (C) A lyrist, contemporary, like a landscape garden
   (D) A lyrist, eternal man, like a landscape garden
   (E) A lyrist, contemporary, like a Chimborazo

5. The central paradox in the passage can be seen in which of the following?
   (A) "poetry was all written before time was" (line 1) versus "a poem…adorns nature with a new thing" (lines 33–36)
   (B) "words are actions"(line 11) versus "actions are a kind of words" (line 11)
   (C) "conversation" (line 18) versus "argument" (line 32)
   (D) "men of more delicate ear" (line 6) versus "men of talents who sing" (line 31)
   (E) "songs of the nations" (lines 7–8) versus "children of music" (lines 31–32)

6. Contextually, "Words and deeds are quite indifferent modes" (line 10) means
   - (A) words and deeds are both of no consequence
   - (B) it does not matter which method is used
   - (C) neither words nor deeds are particularly good
   - (D) both methods are unimportant
   - (E) both methods are only average

7. The tone of the metaphor in line 20 implies that the poetry of the writer of lyrics is
   - (A) modern as a "landscape-garden" (line 27)
   - (B) frivolous, when compared with a "region where the air is music" (lines 2–3)
   - (C) filled with jewels of "skill and command of language" (lines 20–21)
   - (D) contradictory to the "varied music" (line 30)
   - (E) capriciously above "the ground-tone of conventional life" (lines 30–31)

Answers and Explanations:

1. **A** Unlike a lyrist who "does not stand out of our low limitations" (line 24) and who "is the landscape-garden of a modern house" (lines 27–28); a poet is like a mountain. Notice the description of the poet-mountain that has "all the climates of the globe, with belts of the herbage of every latitude on its high and mottled sides." This expressive metaphor emphasizes the universal nature of true poetry and that "the world seems always waiting for its poet" (line 41).

2. **B** By definition, a poem's argument refers to the statement of its meaning.

3. **C** First, summarize the central contrast: true poetry versus mere lyrics. In context, "transcripts" are the expression of poetry.

4. **C** In lines 22–24, "lyrist" structurally corresponds to "contemporary" and "poet" to "eternal man." Also, "He does not stand out ...like a Chimborazo...but this genius is the landscape-garden of a modern house...."

5. **A** Paradox *seems* to contradict itself, yet is actually true. The concepts in B are reciprocal, in D are contrasting, in E are complementary, and in C are silly. The seeming contradiction appears in A: If all poetry was written before time was, how can a poem be a new thing? The answer, of course, is that the expression of the poem is new to the natural world.

6. **B** Based on their reciprocal nature in this context, the adjective means that the "mode" or method used is of no consequence; it does not matter.

7. **B** This tone is reinforced by the speaker's conclusion that the man in question is "plainly a contemporary, not an eternal man."

Now, examine the metaphor that predominates the work. The tenor, of course, is poetry. What vehicles are used?

In the first paragraph, poetry is compared to _____

_____

In the second paragraph, poetry is compared to _____

_____

Answers: 1. primal warbling, cadences, songs of the nations
         2. a music box and varied music

The controlling image is poetry compared to (one word): _____

To write a test question, simply write your question stem and provide your answers.

The controlling image used in the passage compares _____ with

(A) _____

(B)_____

(C) _____

(D) _____

(E) _____

Correct Answer: **E**

Finally, explain in your own words *why* your answer is correct and the others are incorrect.

A FINAL WORD ABOUT ►THINKING OUTSIDE THE BOX◄

When recognizing the seven literary elements (such as finding the meaning behind a speaker's words) becomes second nature to you, you can use them to be more discerning about the people around you and to better communicate your own meanings and purposes more effectively. Learn to understand what people mean. Then, you will have a clear understanding of where to begin when a problem calls for creative thinking outside the box of the obvious answers.

MEANING (IN CONTEXT) IN CONCLUSION

This chapter marks the end of our examination of the seven literary elements. Each has distinctive traits, yet you can see how the elements ultimately depend on one another and cannot be isolated completely from one another.

Although you have concluded the seven literary element chapters, your journey is by no means over. The time has come to see how the elements of literature can work in your own writing on the SAT by "Putting Essays on T. O. P."

PART III

PUTTING ESSAYS ON T.O.P.

Prewriting Discussion

Exercises

Putting Essays on T.O.P.

Preparing to take the literature test provides a wonderful opportunity for you to improve your writing skills for the SAT's essay requirement. This chapter contains explanations and exercises that will help you develop your interpretive, critical reading skills and the critical thinking skills you need to write a clear, effective SAT essay, using the **T**opic, **O**utline, **P**urpose method.

PREWRITING DISCUSSION

Here is a quick overview of the different types of essays.

The How-To Essay

What does it deal with? . . . . . . A process
What does it do? . . . . Explains, clarifies
Tip: Be sure of the order, i.e., steps in logical sequence.
To make it interesting: Use illustrations, description, narration.
The following would be defined as How-To Essay topics:

- How to raise tulips successfully in your region
- How to develop a better relationship with your brothers or sisters
- How to make the best pizza in town
- How to improve your grades in algebra
- How to clean your room in thirty minutes or less

The Example Essay

What does it deal with? . . Concrete examples of abstract ideas, definitions, and so forth
What does it do? . . . . Explains, clarifies
Tip: Be sure that your examples are relevant to what you are explaining.
To make it interesting: Make a connection with your readers by using specifics, if possible.
If concrete examples are used, the following would be defined as Example Essay topics:

- What is anger?
- What is the iron curtain?
- What are meteor showers?
- What is rain harvesting?
- What are "extenuating circumstances?"

Note the subtle difference between the Example Essay and the Definition Essay (described below).

The Definition Essay

What does it deal with? . . . Words, objects, abstract concepts
What does it do? . . . . Defines, explains

Tip: Be sure that you include not just synonyms, but also identify the word, object, or abstract concept as part of a *class* (love is an *emotion*) that has certain *distinguishing features* (love is an emotion that is a *warm, unselfish concern for another*).

To make it interesting: In addition to pointing out distinguishing features, define the words, objects, and abstract concepts through detail, such as examples that are easy to identify, comparison-contrast, pointing out examples that are *not* true illustrations.

If examples, synonyms, class identification, distinguishing features, and/or details are used, the following would be defined as Definition Essay topics:

- What is anger?
- What is the iron curtain?
- What are meteor showers?
- What is rain harvesting?
- What are "extenuating circumstances"?

The Comparison-Contrast Essay

What does it deal with? . . . Two or more subjects that have shared elements
What does it do? . . . . Compares, contrasts
Tip: Be sure that the subjects do have some substantial points in common.
To make it interesting: Pose questions to the reader that lead him or her to make the comparisons that make your point.

The following would be defined as Comparison-Contrast Essay topics:

- Is chocolate the best ice cream flavor?
- Will Candidate A be a better elected official than Candidate B?
- How do private day-care facilities compare to corporate employee day-care systems?
- Are women really better off than they were twenty years ago?
- The paintings of (new artist): are they a reflection of the works of Monet?

The "Why" Essay

What does it deal with? . . . Cause-and-effect relationships
What does it do? . . . . Explains, justifies
Tip: Be sure that your specified causes are accurate, true, and can be proven.
To make it interesting: Use examples that are compelling because they withstand the scrutiny of "But what if . . ." questions.

The following would be defined as Why Essay topics:

- Global warming as a cause of more powerful hurricanes
- Why Americans need to be multilingual in the twenty-first century
- The effect of video games on preschool children
- What happens to our health when fluoride is added to the public water supply?
- Why are the world's frog populations disappearing?

The Relationship Essay

What does it deal with? . . Words, objects, abstract concepts
What does it do? . . . . Classifies, analyzes

Tip: Be sure that your classification categories do not overlap—that each category is distinctive and *every* example will fit into one of the categories.

To make it interesting: Use persuasive techniques to convince the reader that your categories are valid and that you do have a point to make.

The following would be defined as Relationship Essay topics:

- The three major types of modern American grocery stores—and the end of the corner market
- The types of people who become doctors
- The modern man as one of seven categories of adventurer
- Types of exercise and the role of walking in a home exercise program
- The types of transportation in America today and the effects on global warming

The Persuasive Essay

What does it deal with? . . The writer's opinion on a subject
What does it do? . . . . Argues and/or persuades
Tip: Be sure that you gather factual proof and establish provable cause-and-effect relationships as part of your background work.

To make it interesting: When establishing inferences (inductive and deductive reasoning), cite detailed examples to help you establish your point.

The following would be defined as Persuasive Essay topics:

- UFOs: an explainable phenomenon
- The need for more cancer research
- The need for a girls' basketball team
- Has the time come for stricter water conservation?
- Do you really want year-round school?

The Descriptive Essay

What does it deal with? . . Words, objects, abstract concepts
What does it do? . . . . Describes, explains
Tip: Be sure that you do not lose the point of your essay through aimless use of descriptive adjectives.

To make it interesting: Look to imagery techniques (simile, metaphor, personification), making vivid use of words and ideas that appeal to the senses.

The following would be defined as Descriptive Essay topics. Be sure to use the description *to make a point* about:

- Prom night
- A walk in the park
- Local flooding
- Trust
- People addicted to television

The Narrative Essay

What does it deal with? . . . Events, both real and imaginary

What does it do? . . . . Narrates*, describes

Tip: Be sure that your narrative does relate an experience with some significance or that has a point.

To make it interesting: Sometimes (but not always) narratives written in the first person will draw in the reader and better create the desired effect(s).

The following would be defined as Narrative Essay topics:

- Your last shopping trip as it related to teen-age economics
- A young boy who learns a lesson about sharing with his sister
- A girl's sense of adventure and how maturity can make a difference
- The camping trip that ended in disaster due to poor planning
- A botanist who finds a new plant species in her own backyard

As you can see from this list, you have many options concerning how to focus an essay. Once you begin utilizing these options, incorporating the seven literary elements as they are appropriate to your purpose, you will begin to recognize, understand, and perhaps even appreciate their use in the writings of other essayists.

FOCUS ON THE SAT ESSAY

The type of essay you write for the SAT will probably be a persuasive essay (with an argumentative purpose). The readers who score the essays will be looking to see if you generate your own ideas, adequately defend your position, and clearly express your thinking. Persuasive essays are especially well suited to this purpose because they require you to use critical thinking skills as you take a stand on an issue.

Topic/Theme

The test will provide a topic for you by asking you to read an excerpt and respond to a related question that requires you to take a position on an issue. Your first step should be to develop from that topic a thesis sentence that clearly states your point of view.

Here is a sample essay prompt. Read it carefully.

> Let us return to Oratory, or the art of speaking well; which should never be entirely out of your thoughts, since it is so useful in every part of life, and so absolutely necessary in most. A man can make no figure without it, in Parliament, in the Church, or in the law; and even in common conversation, a man that has acquired an easy and habitual eloquence, who speaks properly and accurately, will have a great advantage over those who speak incorrectly or inelegantly.
>
> (Lord Chesterfield, 1739)
>
> For your essay: Are people more influenced by those who speak conventional or Standard English than by those whose speech is Nonstandard? Respond to this issue by writing an essay that clearly communicates your point of view. Your essay should be well organized and contain logical reasoning with detailed examples to support your position.

---

*What is the difference between a narrative essay and a short story? A narrative essay goes beyond the short story by using narrative techniques (dialogue, action sequence, descriptive elements, and so forth) and the story line itself to make a point beyond mere entertainment.

CONTENT OF YOUR THESIS SENTENCE

The thesis statement will set the tone and structure for the entire essay, so take care in writing it. What is your stand on this issue? Once you make this decision, you can work on clearly expressing your opinion.

▶FOCUS◀

SAT rules state that an essay that is not written on the topic given will receive a score of zero.

Be sure you recognize the topic before you begin writing. Also, realize that there is a difference between the topic and the slant. Sometimes the excerpt can take a slant that is different from the question, even though they are both on the same topic. Some students may find the difference in slant a little confusing as they begin to develop their thesis statements. The excerpt and the question just given, for example, are about Standard versus Nonstandard speech. Their slants, however, are *slightly* different. A persuasive (argumentative) essay in response to the excerpt alone would probably focus on "Yes, people who speak well have an advantage" or "No, they do not." In contrast, the question centers on whether people are more influenced by those who use Standard speech. A responding essay might center on "Yes, people are more influenced by the use of Standard speech" or "No, they are not."

Which slant should you use? This question is difficult to answer. A study of available sample scored essays reveals that two highest-scoring essays (6 points) responded to the slant of the question. One essay that received a high score of 5 points responded to the slant of the excerpt; however, the essay lost one point because it needed more support to the writer's argument, not because of the slant selected. (The excerpt and question were different from those given here, but similarly exhibited two different slants on the same topic.)

Based on this evidence, writing a well-developed essay, as long as it is on topic, is the first priority. If the excerpt seems a little confusing in connection with the question, realize that it may simply be a difference in the slant used.

▶FOCUS◀

Be sure your position is supportable. A vague statement of opinion, such as "I don't think Standard English is very important," is a limited perspective and cannot be supported.

STRUCTURE OF YOUR THESIS STATEMENT

The thesis sentence should contain your central point. Consequently, you have some choices to make.

Choice #1 A Do you want the sentence to serve only as a statement of your position?

Example:

> **Although past generations were highly influenced by those who used Standard speech, many people today are more impressed by the content of the message than the manner of its presentation.**

Evidence that proves the point should follow.

Choice #1 B Do you want the sentence to provide the structure for your essay?

Example:

> **Use of Standard language is a powerful influence in today's world, particularly in the fields of business and education.**

With this thesis statement, your essay should provide detailed evidence of your assertion, beginning with business, then education. If you use this structure, be sure you have enough time to deliver the evidence your thesis statement promises.

Choice #2 A Do you want the sentence to stand alone as a one-sentence paragraph?

Example:

> **Both Standard and Nonstandard English have influential rules today, depending on the listeners and the message.**

The paragraphs that follow should detail at least one specific example of circumstances in which people are influenced by Standard English and one example for Nonstandard speech.

Choice #2 B Do you want the thesis sentence to be part of an introductory (two- or three-sentence) paragraph? If so, you can place it in the beginning, middle, or end, as in the case of the following example.

> **The first step to influencing people is to communicate in a way that they understand. Some people normally use Standard English. Others do not. Consequently, both Standard and Nonstandard speech have influential roles today, depending on the listeners and the message.**

Outline

The readers will be looking for evidence of critical thinking skills in your essay. Using outline techniques will organize and enhance your critical thinking when you write a persuasive (argumentative) essay.

Outline structure

Traditionally, an outline builds on the following basic structure:

I. A main or central idea
  A. A subordinate idea that contributes to the main idea
    1. An example
      a. A detail that supports this example

If you had several days to research and write your essay, you would have more main ideas, subordinate ideas, examples, and supportive details. You have only about twenty-five minutes to compose your SAT essay. Obviously, your outline will function best as a quick prewriting tool to help you elicit and organize your ideas. Rather than using the traditional outline structure, you may want to save time by creating your own shortcut system.

Critical thinking = adequate examples and details

Begin by brainstorming a list of ideas or examples that illustrate your position. For example,

Position: Use of Standard speech is a powerful influence in today's world.

To brainstorm, begin asking questions: what? why? when? where? how?
In this case, who? News media, businesspeople, teachers....

▸FOCUS◂

You can probably list more people or fields that use Standard speech to influence others, but remember the time limit. Your outline will not be scored; you still must write the essay.

▸FOCUS◂

Students sometimes are tempted to list examples without supporting details. Details provide the insightful evidence you need to support your case and to prove your example is valid. Be sure that you have supporting details for each of your examples. Your essay will be better with one or two really well-developed illustrations than with a long list of unsupported examples. The bottom line: Your essay should contain *detailed* examples for every major point you make (an indication of critical thinking).

Thesis? _____

  Point? _____

    Example 1? _____

    Details? _____

    Example 2? _____

    Details ? _____

  Point? _____

    Example 1? _____

    Details ? _____

Critical thinking = ideas, facts, and arguments + inferences

An inference is the conclusion drawn from a set of ideas, facts, or arguments. You want to make your case with clear, logical thinking. The details provide evidence for a conclusion drawn from the facts. For example, businesspeople need to use Standard language to influence others. Why? Because in the international market, negotiations often are translated into languages such as Chinese, German, or others. The colloquialisms, slang, and idioms of Nonstandard English generally cannot be translated easily.

▸FOCUS◂

Be careful that you do not use any logical fallacies or faulty reasoning. (See the chart on page 108.) In addition, beware of jumping on the bandwagon of current trends (the readers are looking for original thinking), getting distracted onto another subject (rule #1: Stay on topic!), writing in circles (for example, "Movies make people happy because they really enjoy watching them"), or making statements that just do not make sense (such as the classic example, "If you kill yourself speeding, I'm going to wring your neck"). Also, be alert for making hasty generalizations that are based on the exceptions rather than the rules. If, for example, international business is the *only* example you can think of in which businesspeople are more influential using Standard English, you may want to hesitate before broadening the conclusion to include business in general. Finally, beware using such rash generalizations as these: Everyone knows toads cause warts, people *never* understand his writing, all people in business should use Standard English. There may be an exception to the rule. Even if you think your point is supportable, using qualifiers (such as *some* people believe toads cause warts, people *sometimes* do not understand his meaning, or often people in business can benefit from using Standard English) communicates that you are aware of exceptions and recognize that there may be more than one side to the issue.

Critical thinking = a progression of ideas

A well-written essay that demonstrates critical thinking will include a progression of ideas. Pretend that your main idea is a small stream winding its way down a hillside. At intervals, mountain springs (supporting evidence, details, examples) will add to the moving water until finally your stream of argument becomes a river that flows into the gulf waters of your conclusion. Each new idea should catch and hold your reader's attention.

As you outline your ideas, you can ensure their progression by using some of the organizational tips on pages 68 and 71. Using climactic order or deductive order, for example, naturally will result in movement of ideas, as does sequencing using causal analysis or chronology.

▸FOCUS◂

Do not just repeat the same idea, restated in different ways. Repetition is a mainstay of educational writing. Teachers restate the same ideas so that a maximum number of students will understand the idea being taught. Your SAT essay has an entirely different purpose. Each new sentence should build on the previous one by giving new information that moves the reader from point A to point B. Avoid using this type of repetition: Use of Standard language is a powerful influence in today's world. Lots of people are easily influenced by the way people speak to them.

Instead: Use of Standard language is a powerful influence in today's world. This influence can be seen in such widely diverse areas as business and education.

Progression of ideas = movement + unity

In addition to the movement of ideas already discussed, a well-written essay has unity of thought. Every sentence relates in some way to the topic of the paragraph, and every paragraph relates to your thesis statement.

Thesis statement: states the point of the entire essay.
   Paragraphs: Each paragraph as a *whole* should relate to or contribute to proving the thesis statement.
      Sentences: Each sentence should relate to the point (the topic sentence) of the individual paragraph in which it appears.
         Concluding statement: This sentence should bring the essay full circle, perhaps restating your thesis, summarizing your points, or challenging readers to reflective thought.

▸FOCUS◂

Use your outline to be sure that an example or detail does belong, for example, in the second paragraph and not in the third. A misplaced idea that is off the topic or that relates to the topic sentence of a different paragraph could stop the movement, break the unity of the essay, and destroy your progression of ideas, leaving the reader confused about where you are going and what you mean.

Purpose/Point of View

You need to adapt your use of language to suit your purpose (to establish your point of view).

Variety + coherence = interesting writing

The readers will be looking for both variety and coherence in your essay. The best way to achieve this combination is through skillful use of language.

Variety (differences) and coherence (maintaining relationships) can be achieved on three different levels in your essay:

1. Use of language = variety + coherence in thought

To achieve variety in thought, use analogies (similes, metaphors), allude to works of literature, movies, historical figures, and so forth. Discuss ironic situations, if applicable to your argument, or elements of the discussion that have been overstated or understated by others. Review the chapter on Literary Element Number Six: Use of Language for more ideas.

To achieve coherence of thought, make sure that each paragraph maintains a relationship with the previous paragraph and the thesis statement. You can use transitional words, phrases, or sentences, such as "In addition to this definitive cause…." Keep referring through a key word or phrase to your topic or position to ensure a firm connection between each paragraph and the thesis statement.

Example:

> **Use of Standard language is a powerful influence in today's world, particularly in the fields of business and education.**
>
> **A dramatic example of the degree of this influence exists in the world of international business, an arena where the gladiators swing words rather than swords and misunderstandings can mean the sudden death of the deal.**

[Paragraph continues to give specific details supporting this example.]

> **Likewise, the words of teachers and students are influential. When their speech is misunderstood, however, the results can mean not the death of a financial deal, but the birth of discussion, inquiry, debate, and learning. In the dynamic give-and-take atmosphere of today's classroom…**

[Paragraph continues to give specific details supporting this example.]

Notice that "Likewise" in the third paragraph compares to the thought in the second; "however" contrasts the second to the third paragraphs. Reference to the "death…of a…deal" seals the coherence of the two paragraphs to each other and to the thesis statement.

►FOCUS◄

Do you see the phrase "give-and-take" in the last paragraph? This phrase is a cliché. Try to avoid clichés in your essay. How else could you word this thought that would be fresh and original?

2. Use of language = variety + coherence in sentence structure

To achieve variety in sentence structure, vary the lengths of your sentences and their complexity. If a given sentence is particularly lengthy with several dependent clauses, follow it with a simple construction. Also, could a rhetorical question help make your point?

To achieve coherence in sentence structure, use parallel and balanced sentences. (See page 253). Using transitional words (for example, coordinating conjunctions, adverbs such as "similarly," and so forth) will help your sentences flow structurally from one to another and provide unity within the sentences.

3. Use of language = variety + coherence in diction

To achieve variety in diction, use synonyms, antonyms for contrasts, appropriately connotative word choices, and strong diction.

To achieve coherence in diction, maintain a somewhat formal tone throughout the essay. Do use Standard English. Avoid using sexist language, biased or emotionally slanted words, slang, colloquialisms, ornate words, or pretentious language. Try to use word choices that will prove your argument without interrupting the flow of the reader's thoughts as he or she progresses from one idea to the next. You want to gain your reader's attention through use of a compelling argument, not through shocking language.

►FOCUS◄

You do not need to memorize the thesaurus to sprinkle your writing with obscure words. At the other extreme, avoid weak diction that is vague. You want your words to capture the reader's mind and truly communicate your meaning.

PREWRITING DISCUSSION IN CONCLUSION

When you approach the SAT essay requirement, use common sense. Make your handwriting or printing legible. Try your best to use correct grammar, spelling, and punctuation; however, stay calm. The teachers who will be reading your essay know you have only limited time to plan and write your response.

The readers do expect you to compose a realistically well-written first draft that is on the topic. They will be looking for you to take a clear stand on the issue and support your position with detailed examples and ideas. Your essay should be a unified progression of ideas that demonstrates critical thinking, and it should be expressed through language that includes variety and coherence.

Obviously, formulas and models may be of little help in preparing for writing an essay that requires a responsive approach. Do not rely on formula writing that tempts you into making your writing conform to the formula rather than giving you the freedom to address the topic your own way. Learning the principles of good writing (T. O. P.) can give you such freedom of expression.

FOCUS ON PRACTICE

EXERCISE 1.

(Correct answers and essay scoring guides follow Exercise 3.)

A. Read this passage from Ben Franklin's *Autobiography* and answer the practice questions that follow.

> In truth, I found myself incorrigible with respect to Order; and now
> I am grown old, and my memory bad, I feel very sensibly the want
> of it. But, on the whole, tho' I never arrived at the perfection I had
> Line been so ambitious of obtaining, but fell far short of it, yet I was, by
> (5) the endeavour, a better and a happier man than I otherwise should
> have been if I had not attempted it; as those who aim at perfect
> writing by imitating the engraved copies, tho' they never reach the
> wish'd-for excellence of those copies, their hand is mended by the
> endeavor, and is tolerable while it continues fair and legible.
> (10) It may be well my posterity should be informed that to this little
> artifice, with the blessing of God, their ancestor ow'd the constant
> felicity of his life, down to his 79th year, in which this is written.
> What reverses may attend the remainder is in the hand of
> Providence; but, if they arrive, the reflection on past happiness
> (15) enjoy'd ought to help his bearing them with more resignation. To
> Temperance he ascribes his long-continued health, and what is still
> left to him of a good constitution; to Industry and Frugality, the early
> easiness of his circumstances and acquisition of his fortune, with all
> that knowledge that enabled him to be a useful citizen, and obtained
> (20) for him some degree of reputation among the learned; to Sincerity
> and Justice, the confidence of his country, and the honorable
> employs it conferred upon him; and to the joint influence of the
> whole mass of the virtues, even in the imperfect state he was able to
> acquire them, all that evenness of temper, and that cheerfulness in
> (25) conversation, which makes his company still sought for, and
> agreeable even to his younger acquaintance. I hope, therefore, that
> some of my descendants may follow the example and reap the
> benefit.

1. Why does the speaker label himself "incorrigible" (line 1)?
   (A) Because he lacks the courage to develop Virtue
   (B) Because he could not break a specific bad habit
   (C) Because he did not really need Order
   (D) Because, in contrast, Order is the most important Virtue
   (E) Because he refuses to acknowledge defeat

2. "Order" (line 1) refers to time management, connotative of a sense of peace and serenity; consequently, an "incorrigible" self-image concerning "Order" contains
   (A) verbal irony
   (B) sarcasm
   (C) situational irony
   (D) amplification
   (E) allusion

3. The relationship of Industry to Frugality (line 17) is mirrored in the relationship of
   (A) 24/7 to recycling
   (B) participation to observation
   (C) composing to performance
   (D) pitchers to catchers
   (E) potters to clay

4. In the second paragraph, what audience is the writer indirectly addressing?
   (A) His progeny
   (B) The virtuous ones
   (C) His ancestors
   (D) Honorable people only
   (E) Younger acquaintances

5. Why does the speaker shift from the first to third person in line 12?
   (A) To emphasize his virtues
   (B) To distance himself from his posterity
   (C) To create a more humble tone
   (D) To denote a happy and successful life
   (E) To acquaint his descendants with his lack of virtues

B. Put your essay-writing skills on T. O. P. Time limit: 25 minutes

---

Reread the first paragraph of the Benjamin Franklin selection carefully.

For your essay: Are people happier if they sometimes attempt accomplishments that may be beyond their capabilities? Respond to this issue by writing an essay that clearly communicates your point of view. Your essay should be well organized and contain logical reasoning and detailed examples to support your position.

EXERCISE 2.

Read the following account written by Lillian E. Myers and answer the practice questions that follow.

AN ENCOUNTER WITH HONEY BEES

The area where we live has received national attention because Africanized "killer" honey bees have been found here. A local man was stung severely after the sound of his lawn mower disturbed the
Line bees. In another incident, a swarm of bees stung two dogs to death
(5) and trapped the dogs' owners in the bathroom of their home until emergency workers could come to rescue them from the angry bees.

Reading in the newspaper about these bee attacks causes me to remember when I, too, had a frightening and painful encounter with honey bees.

(10) When my four brothers and I were children, our parents encouraged us to pursue personal projects. My brothers had acquired a skep of honey bees as one of our wonderful ventures. Honey bees are known as *social* bees and are considered very beneficial because they pollinate vegetable gardens, fruit trees,
(15) flowers, and many farm crops, such as clover. Some amateur beekeepers call their standard wooden hives *bee skeps*, although a "skep" is a special dome-shaped hive made of interwoven straw instead of wood. My brothers were busy with many things, and I found that I became fascinated with this new project. I was a
(20) teenager at the time, and this new interest delighted me. I was very happy that I had made friends with the bees.

One of my projects was bringing ferns and violets from the woods and planting them in the area beneath the front window of the house. The skep of bees had been conveniently located across the
(25) driveway beside my favorite flower bed. By the end of summer, I had removed several delicious combs of honey; and on an especially beautiful morning, I was about to remove another tempting honeycomb.

The beehive was a square box with a small hole at the lower front
(30) edge for the bees to gain entrance. The combs hung down into the box and were removed through the top. My beekeeping downfall was the result of the covering that prevented rain from entering the hive. This was a single sheet of roofing tin about one foot longer on each side than the size of the box. In the center on the top had been
(35) placed a large rock sufficient in weight to hold the tin in place. I had to remove the rock; the resulting sound was a shot-like blast that must have reverberated through the beehive with such a force that it startled the bees. Before I could realize what had happened, the entire colony of bees attacked me. They settled right on my head,
(40) stinging fiercely. When a bee attacks, its muscles force a stinger into the flesh to pump poison into the victim. Barbs on the stinger hold it

tightly in the flesh; the stinger is pulled from the bee's body and the bee soon dies. Of course, I began to scream.

(45) My mother heard my screams and was shocked to see the seething balloon of bees my head had become. My life was saved when God gave her the presence of mind to know what to do in this critical moment. My mother had been watering flowers nearby and quickly doused my head with a bucket of water. She continued to throw water on me with as much force as possible to dislodge the

(50) bees and managed to pull me into the house. She received a number of stings herself and cried in sympathy as she picked the stingers out of my face, neck, ears, and head. She lost count in the seventies.

I remained in shock for hours, unable to lay my head on a pillow. My eyes, nose, ears, and mouth swelled into a grotesque mask. I

(55) looked and felt terrible even weeks later with a blotchy, itchy head, face, and neck and with two black eyes.

Having miraculously survived this ordeal and the following weeks of unbelievable agony, the fact that for a long time I was nervous when I heard a buzzing sound is understandable. For many years

(60) even the buzz of an ordinary housefly would make me ill and trembling with fear.

The last of the honey was never removed from that skep of bees. The entire bee hive was hauled away. Many professional beekeepers wear hoods and gloves and, if necessary, use smoke to

(65) control angry bees.

My experience demonstrates that when sufficiently frightened, even domesticated honey bees will attack. In fact, according to recent field guide publications, the stings of domesticated bees are just as poisonous as those of Africanized bees. Experts tell us,

(70) however, that Africanized bees are "wild" honey bees. They avoid humans when possible, but will aggressively defend their hive if they are disturbed.

Honey bees are essential; we need honey bees for our agricultural crops and honey production. My experience illustrates, however, that

(75) we also need to learn how to live in harmony with bees and that care should be taken not to startle or disturb bees, whether domesticated or wild.

1. The tone of "conveniently located" in line 24 makes the writer's involvement with the bees seem

(A) naive
(B) penitent
(C) impersonal
(D) inevitable
(E) complacent

2. In line 45, the literary device used in "the seething balloon of bees" is a
   (A) metaphor
   (B) simile
   (C) metonymy
   (D) personification
   (E) symbol

3. In line 36, the "sound was a shot-like blast" performs which of these roles?
   I. Descriptive simile
   II. Alliterative illustration
   III. Onomatopoeic description
   (A) I only
   (B) II only
   (C) I and II only
   (D) II and III only
   (E) I, II, and III

4. "I remained in shock for hours" (line 53) is probably the result of all the following EXCEPT
   (A) a concussion from a violent blow
   (B) great surprise
   (C) the effects of the poison
   (D) extreme pain
   (E) the violent nature of the attack

5. "Presence of mind" in line 46 can also be paraphrased as
   (A) daydreaming
   (B) mental dignity
   (C) an anticipatory response
   (D) a flashback
   (E) quick thinking

B. Put your essay-writing skills on T. O. P. Time limit: 25 minutes.

Reread the last paragraph of the Lillian E. Myers selection carefully.

For your essay: Does society have a responsibility to protect wild species, such as African-ized honey bees, black bears, and alligators, even though they sometimes endanger people and property? Respond to this issue by writing an essay that clearly communicates your point of view. Your essay should be well organized and contain logical reasoning and detailed examples to support your position.

EXERCISE 3.

A. Read this passage from Samuel Johnson's "The Rambler, No. 4" and answer the practice questions that follow.

...for when a man had by practice gained some fluency of language, he had no further care than to retire to his closet, let loose his invention, and heat his mind with incredibilities; a book was Line thus produced without fear of criticism, without the toil of study,
(5)   without knowledge of nature, or acquaintance with life.

The task of our present writers is very different; it requires, together with that learning which is to be gained from books, that experience which can never be attained by solitary diligence, but must arise from general converse and accurate observation of the
(10)   living world. ...They are engaged in portraits of which every one knows the original, and can detect any deviation from exactness of resemblance. Other writings are safe, except from the malice of learning, but these are in danger from every common reader as the slipper ill executed was censured by a shoemaker who happened to
(15)   stop in his way at the Venus of Apelles.

But the fear of not being approved as just copiers of human manners, is not the most important concern that an author of this sort ought to have before him. These books are written chiefly to the young, the ignorant, and the idle, to whom they serve as lectures of
(20)   conduct, and introductions into life. They are the entertainment of minds unfurnished with ideas, and therefore easily susceptible of impressions; not fixed by principles, and therefore easily following the current of fancy; not informed by experience and consequently open to every false suggestion and partial account.
(25)   That the highest degree of reverence should be paid to youth, and that nothing indecent should be suffered to approach their eyes or ears are precepts extorted by sense and virtue from an ancient writer, by no means eminent for chastity of thought. The same kind, though not the same degree, of caution, is required in everything
(30)   which is laid before them, to secure them from unjust prejudices, perverse opinions, and incongruous combinations of images.

1. According to the speaker, what should be a writer's "most important concern" (line 17)?
   (A) Making the work easy to understand
   (B) Balancing entertainment with education in the writing
   (C) Making the work a proper influence on impressionable readers
   (D) Refusing to compromise thought over style
   (E) Reaching readers too idle to deal with life

2. Based upon its contextual use, "just" (line 16) conveys the idea that contemporary writers are expected to be
   (A) legally right
   (B) impartial in their descriptions of characters
   (C) meritorious in their attitudes
   (D) accurate and precise
   (E) self-righteous

3. The verbally ironic tone of "malice of learning" (lines 12–13) makes the speaker's attitude toward writers of "Other writings" seem
   (A) contemptuous
   (B) contumacious
   (C) conventional
   (D) controversial
   (E) controvertible

4. According to the speaker, the main difference between a writer who would "retire to his closet" (line 2) and "our present writers" (line 6) is
   (A) experience in life
   (B) fluency of language
   (C) natural talent
   (D) formal education
   (E) invention

5. The first and second paragraphs establish a contrast that is reflected respectively in which of these pairs of words?
   (A) Wildness...tameness
   (B) Knowledge...ignorance
   (C) Laziness...assiduousness
   (D) Loquaciousness...inarticulateness
   (E) Acceptance...criticism

B. Put your essay-writing skills on T. O. P. Time limit: 25 minutes

---

Reread the last two paragraphs of the Samuel Johnson selection carefully.

For your essay: Do the protagonists of youth fiction serve as role models for today's readers? Respond to this issue by writing an essay that clearly communicates your point of view. Your essay should be well organized and contain logical reasoning and detailed examples to support your position.

Correct Answers

Answer key to questions based on Ben Franklin's *Autobiography*:
1. **B**   2. **C**   3. **A**   4. **A**   5. **C**

Answer key to questions based on "An Encounter with Honey Bees":
1. **D**   2. **A**   3. **E**   4. **A**   5. **E**

Answer key to questions based on Samuel Johnson's "The Rambler, No. 4":
1. **C**   2. **D**   3. **A**   4. **A**   5. **C**

To Score Your Essays

Scoring for the actual SAT essay will be on a point system (6+6) with usually two graders. Use the following list to score each of your essays. Then ask a teacher (if available) to score your essays. Compare scores and discuss any differences.

Essay 1.

Directions: Check yes or no for each question.

	READER 1 (SELF)	READER 2 (TEACHER)
1. Does the essay address the topic?	Yes__No__	Yes__No__
2. Does it stay on topic?	Yes__No__	Yes__No__
3. Does the thesis statement take a stand?	Yes__No__	Yes__No__
4. Is it supportable?	Yes__No__	Yes__No__
5. Is it clearly stated?	Yes__No__	Yes__No__
6. Are there adequate examples or ideas?	Yes__No__	Yes__No__
7. Is every example supported by details	Yes__No__	Yes__No__
8. Is the reasoning free from flaws in logic?	Yes__No__	Yes__No__
9. Are the ideas original?	Yes__No__	Yes__No__
10. Is the writing free of repetitive ideas?	Yes__No__	Yes__No__
11. Is the writing free of repetitive phrasing?	Yes__No__	Yes__No__
12. Is the writing free of repetitive vocabulary?	Yes__No__	Yes__No__
13. Is the essay organized so that ideas are progressive?	Yes__No__	Yes__No__
14. Do the sentences all relate to the topic of the paragraph?	Yes__No__	Yes__No__
15. Do the paragraphs all relate to the thesis statement?	Yes__No__	Yes__No__
16. Does the essay contain variety in thought (such as analogies and allusions)?	Yes__No__	Yes__No__
17. Is there variety in sentence structure?	Yes__No__	Yes__No__
18. Is there variety in diction?	Yes__No__	Yes__No__
19. Is there coherence (maintaining relationships) between sentences and paragraphs?	Yes__No__	Yes__No__
20. Is appropriate diction used?	Yes__No__	Yes__No__

Essay 2.
Directions: Check yes or no for each question.

	READER 1 (SELF)	READER 2 (TEACHER)
1. Does the essay address the topic?	Yes__No__	Yes__No__
2. Does it stay on topic?	Yes__No__	Yes__No__
3. Does the thesis statement take a stand?	Yes__No__	Yes__No__
4. Is it supportable?	Yes__No__	Yes__No__
5. Is it clearly stated?	Yes__No__	Yes__No__
6. Are there adequate examples or ideas?	Yes__No__	Yes__No__
7. Is every example supported by details?	Yes__No__	Yes__No__
8. Is the reasoning free from flaws in logic?	Yes__No__	Yes__No__
9. Are the ideas original?	Yes__No__	Yes__No__
10. Is the writing free of repetitive ideas?	Yes__No__	Yes__No__
11. Is the writing free of repetitive phrasing?	Yes__No__	Yes__No__
12. Is the writing free of repetitive vocabulary?	Yes__No__	Yes__No__
13. Is the essay organized so that ideas are progressive?	Yes__No__	Yes__No__
14. Do the sentences all relate to the topic of the paragraph?	Yes__No__	Yes__No__
15. Do the paragraphs all relate to the thesis statement?	Yes__No__	Yes__No__
16. Does the essay contain variety in thought (such as analogies and allusions)?	Yes__No__	Yes__No__
17. Is there variety in sentence structure?	Yes__No__	Yes__No__
18. Is there variety in diction?	Yes__No__	Yes__No__
19. Is there coherence (maintaining relationships) between sentences and paragraphs?	Yes__No__	Yes__No__
20. Is appropriate diction used?	Yes__No__	Yes__No__

Essay 3.

Directions: Check yes or no for each question.

	READER 1 (SELF)	READER 2 (TEACHER)
1. Does the essay address the topic?	Yes__No__	Yes__No__
2. Does it stay on topic?	Yes__No__	Yes__No__
3. Does the thesis statement take a stand?	Yes__No__	Yes__No__
4. Is it supportable?	Yes__No__	Yes__No__
5. Is it clearly stated?	Yes__No__	Yes__No__
6. Are there adequate examples or ideas?	Yes__No__	Yes__No__
7. Is every example supported by details?	Yes__No__	Yes__No__
8. Is the reasoning free from flaws in logic?	Yes__No__	Yes__No__
9. Are the ideas original?	Yes__No__	Yes__No__
10. Is the writing free of repetitive ideas?	Yes__No__	Yes__No__
11. Is the writing free of repetitive phrasing?	Yes__No__	Yes__No__
12. Is the writing free of repetitive vocabulary?	Yes__No__	Yes__No__
13. Is the essay organized so that ideas are progressive?	Yes__No__	Yes__No__
14. Do the sentences all relate to the topic of the paragraph?	Yes__No__	Yes__No__
15. Do the paragraphs all relate to the thesis statement?	Yes__No__	Yes__No__
16. Does the essay contain variety in thought (such as analogies and allusions)?	Yes__No__	Yes__No__
17. Is there variety in sentence structure?	Yes__No__	Yes__No__
18. Is there variety in diction?	Yes__No__	Yes__No__
19. Is there coherence (maintaining relationships) between sentences and paragraphs?	Yes__No__	Yes__No__
20. Is appropriate diction used?	Yes__No__	Yes__No__

PUTTING ESSAYS ON T. O. P. IN CONCLUSION

Keep in mind that the SAT essay requirement aims at challenging you to communicate well in writing. Express your opinions clearly; back them up with evidence from literature, history, and life. What you think counts. Your ideas deserve to be heard in the best way possible.

PART IV

INTERPRETIVE SKILL PRACTICE

Diagnostic Test II:
Literature

Interpretive Skill
Practice Sets

ANSWER SHEET FOR DIAGNOSTIC TEST II

1. Ⓐ Ⓑ Ⓒ Ⓓ Ⓔ
2. Ⓐ Ⓑ Ⓒ Ⓓ Ⓔ
3. Ⓐ Ⓑ Ⓒ Ⓓ Ⓔ
4. Ⓐ Ⓑ Ⓒ Ⓓ Ⓔ
5. Ⓐ Ⓑ Ⓒ Ⓓ Ⓔ
6. Ⓐ Ⓑ Ⓒ Ⓓ Ⓔ
7. Ⓐ Ⓑ Ⓒ Ⓓ Ⓔ
8. Ⓐ Ⓑ Ⓒ Ⓓ Ⓔ
9. Ⓐ Ⓑ Ⓒ Ⓓ Ⓔ
10. Ⓐ Ⓑ Ⓒ Ⓓ Ⓔ
11. Ⓐ Ⓑ Ⓒ Ⓓ Ⓔ
12. Ⓐ Ⓑ Ⓒ Ⓓ Ⓔ
13. Ⓐ Ⓑ Ⓒ Ⓓ Ⓔ
14. Ⓐ Ⓑ Ⓒ Ⓓ Ⓔ
15. Ⓐ Ⓑ Ⓒ Ⓓ Ⓔ
16. Ⓐ Ⓑ Ⓒ Ⓓ Ⓔ
17. Ⓐ Ⓑ Ⓒ Ⓓ Ⓔ
18. Ⓐ Ⓑ Ⓒ Ⓓ Ⓔ
19. Ⓐ Ⓑ Ⓒ Ⓓ Ⓔ
20. Ⓐ Ⓑ Ⓒ Ⓓ Ⓔ

21. Ⓐ Ⓑ Ⓒ Ⓓ Ⓔ
22. Ⓐ Ⓑ Ⓒ Ⓓ Ⓔ
23. Ⓐ Ⓑ Ⓒ Ⓓ Ⓔ
24. Ⓐ Ⓑ Ⓒ Ⓓ Ⓔ
25. Ⓐ Ⓑ Ⓒ Ⓓ Ⓔ
26. Ⓐ Ⓑ Ⓒ Ⓓ Ⓔ
27. Ⓐ Ⓑ Ⓒ Ⓓ Ⓔ
28. Ⓐ Ⓑ Ⓒ Ⓓ Ⓔ
29. Ⓐ Ⓑ Ⓒ Ⓓ Ⓔ
30. Ⓐ Ⓑ Ⓒ Ⓓ Ⓔ
31. Ⓐ Ⓑ Ⓒ Ⓓ Ⓔ
32. Ⓐ Ⓑ Ⓒ Ⓓ Ⓔ
33. Ⓐ Ⓑ Ⓒ Ⓓ Ⓔ
34. Ⓐ Ⓑ Ⓒ Ⓓ Ⓔ
35. Ⓐ Ⓑ Ⓒ Ⓓ Ⓔ
36. Ⓐ Ⓑ Ⓒ Ⓓ Ⓔ
37. Ⓐ Ⓑ Ⓒ Ⓓ Ⓔ
38. Ⓐ Ⓑ Ⓒ Ⓓ Ⓔ
39. Ⓐ Ⓑ Ⓒ Ⓓ Ⓔ
40. Ⓐ Ⓑ Ⓒ Ⓓ Ⓔ

41. Ⓐ Ⓑ Ⓒ Ⓓ Ⓔ
42. Ⓐ Ⓑ Ⓒ Ⓓ Ⓔ
43. Ⓐ Ⓑ Ⓒ Ⓓ Ⓔ
44. Ⓐ Ⓑ Ⓒ Ⓓ Ⓔ
45. Ⓐ Ⓑ Ⓒ Ⓓ Ⓔ
46. Ⓐ Ⓑ Ⓒ Ⓓ Ⓔ
47. Ⓐ Ⓑ Ⓒ Ⓓ Ⓔ
48. Ⓐ Ⓑ Ⓒ Ⓓ Ⓔ
49. Ⓐ Ⓑ Ⓒ Ⓓ Ⓔ
50. Ⓐ Ⓑ Ⓒ Ⓓ Ⓔ
51. Ⓐ Ⓑ Ⓒ Ⓓ Ⓔ
52. Ⓐ Ⓑ Ⓒ Ⓓ Ⓔ
53. Ⓐ Ⓑ Ⓒ Ⓓ Ⓔ
54. Ⓐ Ⓑ Ⓒ Ⓓ Ⓔ
55. Ⓐ Ⓑ Ⓒ Ⓓ Ⓔ
56. Ⓐ Ⓑ Ⓒ Ⓓ Ⓔ
57. Ⓐ Ⓑ Ⓒ Ⓓ Ⓔ
58. Ⓐ Ⓑ Ⓒ Ⓓ Ⓔ
59. Ⓐ Ⓑ Ⓒ Ⓓ Ⓔ
60. Ⓐ Ⓑ Ⓒ Ⓓ Ⓔ

Diagnostic Test II: Literature

The purpose of this second 60-question diagnostic test is to

1. help you identify which critical reading skills based on the seven major literary elements need additional attention

2. give you additional practice in working with the structure and format of the test

3. enable you to understand the rationale behind "correct" versus "incorrect" answer choices

As with Diagnostic Test I, use the provided answer sheet to record your answers. Allow yourself one hour to complete the test.

Be sure to read all directions carefully, and do not use reference materials of any kind.

After you complete the test, use the Answer Key (see page 322) to check your answers and to determine your raw score. Then use the Analysis: Diagnostic Test II (see page 325) to help you evaluate your answer choices. Remember: This diagnostic test is intended both as a measurement instrument and as a teaching tool.

Diagnostic Test II

Directions: The following questions test your understanding of several literary selections. Read each passage or poem and the questions that follow it. Select the best answer choice for each question by blackening the matching oval on your answer sheet. **Special attention should be given to questions containing the following words: EXCEPT, LEAST, NOT.**

Questions 1–10 are based on the following poem.

Art Thou Poor, Yet Hast Thou Golden Slumbers?

Art thou poor, yet hast thou golden
    slumbers?
        O sweet content!
Art thou rich, yet is thy mind perplexed?
Line   O punishment!
(5)   Dost thou laugh to see how fools are vexed
To add to golden numbers, golden
    numbers?
    O sweet content! O sweet, O sweet
    content!
        Work apace, apace, apace, apace;
        Honest labour bears a lovely face;
(10)   Then hey nonny nonny, hey nonny nonny!

Canst drink the waters of the crispèd
    spring?
        O sweet content!
Swimm'st thou in wealth, yet sink'st in thine
    own tears?
        O punishment!
(15)   Then he that patiently want's burden bears
No burden bears, but is a king, a king!
    O sweet content! O sweet, O sweet
    content!
        Work apace, apace, apace, apace;
        Honest labour bears a lovely face;
(20)   Then hey nonny nonny, hey nonny nonny!

by Thomas Dekker

1. The speaker views poverty as
   (A) an unlikely source of happiness
   (B) the only way to find happiness
   (C) not a deterrent to happiness
   (D) an unavoidable condition
   (E) an inspiration to wealth

2. Of the devices listed, the metaphor in line 16 has the effect of
   (A) hyperbole
   (B) meiosis
   (C) fallacy
   (D) oxymoron
   (E) onomatopoeia

3. The repetition of lines 7–10 in lines 17–20 suggests that this poem may be
   (A) a folk ballad
   (B) a hymn
   (C) a nonsense verse
   (D) an aubade
   (E) a song

4. For spring waters to be "crispèd" (line 11), they would be
   (A) very cold
   (B) undulating
   (C) unpolluted
   (D) stagnant
   (E) very calm

5. Line 13 is an example of which of the following?
   I. Antithesis
   II. Paradox
   III. Antonomasia
   (A) I only
   (B) II only
   (C) III only
   (D) I and II only
   (E) I, II, and III

6. Structurally, what change occurs in line 15?
   (A) Line 15 concedes the negative aspects of his premise.
   (B) The speaker departs from the rhetorical question to summarize his point.
   (C) It reverses the poem's theme.
   (D) The speaker provides an answer to the questions posed in the first and second stanzas.
   (E) Line 15 is a restatement of lines 5–6.

7. This poem is best seen as
   (A) a condemnation of wealth
   (B) encouragement to be poor
   (C) an opinion concerning attitudes
   (D) a nonsense verse lacking deep meaning
   (E) a reproach against modern life

8. What is the tone of lines 10 and 20?
   (A) Dynamic
   (B) Endearing
   (C) Frenetic
   (D) Learned
   (E) Derisive

9. Lines 9 and 19 would indicate that the speaker is
   (A) a happy, trustworthy worker
   (B) an anxious person
   (C) naive concerning work
   (D) unrealistic in expectations
   (E) unwilling to take work seriously

10. The contrasts presented in this poem do NOT include
    (A) "poor" (line 1) and "rich" (line 3)
    (B) "slumbers" (line 1) and "perplexed" (line 3)
    (C) "labour" (line 9) and "lovely" (line 9)
    (D) "laugh" (line 5) and "vexed" (line 5)
    (E) "content" (line 2) and "punishment" (line 4)

Questions 11–16 are based on the following passage.

[a letter from an indentured female servant to her father]

Maryland, September 22nd, 1756.
Honored Father:
My being forever banished from your sight will, I hope, pardon the boldness I now take of troubling you with this. My
Line long silence has been purely owing to my
(5) undutifullness to you, and well knowing I had offended in the highest degree, put a tie to my tongue and pen, for fear I should be extinct from your good graces and add a further trouble to you. But too well
(10) knowing your care and tenderness for me, so long as I retained my duty to you, induced me once again to endeavor, if possible, to kindle up that flame again. O dear father, believe what I am going to
(15) relate, the words of truth and sincerity, and balance my former bad conduct [to] my sufferings here, and then I am sure you'll pity your distressed daughter. What we unfortunate English people suffer here is
(20) beyond the probability of you in England to conceive. Let it suffice that I, one of the unhappy number, am toiling almost day and night, and very often in horse's drudgery, with only this comfort, that "You bitch, you
(25) do not half enough!" and then tied up and whipped to that degree that you'd not serve an animal. Scarce anything but Indian corn and salt to eat, and that even begrudged…Almost naked, no shoes nor
(30) stockings to wear, and the comfort after slaving during master's pleasure, what rest we can get is to wrap ourselves up in a blanket and lie upon the ground. This is the

deplorable condition your poor Betty
(35) endures, and now I beg, if you have any
bowels of compassion left, show it by
sending me some relief. Clothing is the
principal thing wanting, which if you should
condescend to, may easily send them to me
(40) by any of the ships bound to Baltimore
Town, Patapsco River, Maryland. Give me
leave to conclude in duty to you and uncles
and aunts, and respect to all friends.

Honored Father,
your undutifull and disobedient child,
Elizabeth Sprigs

11. The speaker's attitude toward her father is one
of
(A) evasiveness
(B) contrition
(C) contention
(D) arrogance
(E) aspiration

12. The speaker's words for her father to "believe
what I am going to relate" (lines 14–15) reveal
her
(A) manipulative nature
(B) complacency toward her father's feelings
(C) resistance to her father's advice
(D) naturally obedient character
(E) change in character due to her hardships

13. What is the speaker's tone?
(A) Imposing
(B) Impartial
(C) Imploring
(D) Impregnable
(E) Impressionable

14. The main topic of the letter is
(A) a cry for help
(B) repentance for past sins
(C) informing family of the situation
(D) the unwillingness of the girl to come ome
(E) possibility of future communication

15. The "flame" (line 13) Elizabeth hopes to
rekindle is
(A) her "dutifullness"
(B) her father's care
(C) her father's anger
(D) truth and sincerity
(E) her own anger

16. Elizabeth "put a tie to my tongue and pen"
(lines 6–7). What does this phrase mean?
I. Silence due to lack of writing materials
II. Silence due to emotion
III. Silence due to guilt
IV. Silence due to illiteracy
(A) I only
(B) II only
(C) III only
(D) II and III only
(E) III and IV only

Questions 17–26 are based on the following poem.

When I Consider How My Light Is Spent[1]

When I consider how my light is spent
Ere half my days, in this dark world and
wide,
And that one talent which is death to hide
Lodged with me useless, though my soul
Line   more bent
(5) To serve therewith my Maker, and present
My true account, lest He returning chide.
"Doth God exact day-labor, light denied?"
I fondly[2] ask. But Patience, to prevent
That murmur, soon replies, "God doth not
need
(10) Either man's work or his own gifts; who best
Bear His mild yoke, they serve Him best. His
state
Is kingly. Thousands at His bidding speed
And post o'er land and ocean without rest;
They also serve who only stand and wait."

1. The poet was totally blind at about forty.
2. Imprudently

by John Milton

17. Line 9 contains a change in which of the elements?
    (A) Meter
    (B) Consonance
    (C) End rhyme
    (D) Mode
    (E) Imagery

18. The content of lines 1–8 contrasts with lines 9–14, but of the following, which is NOT a contrast?
    (A) Question and answer
    (B) Accountability and unaccountability
    (C) Resistance and acceptance
    (D) Self-interest and obedience
    (E) Impatience and patience

19. The phrase "my light is spent" (line 1), as used by the speaker, means which of these concepts?
    I. Lack of understanding
    II. The poet's blindness
    III. Personal tragedy
    (A) I only
    (B) II only
    (C) III only
    (D) I and II only
    (E) I, II, and III

20. The rhythm and number of lines in this poem make it a
    (A) couplet
    (B) ballad
    (C) limerick
    (D) sonnet
    (E) haiku

21. Patience has an attitude toward "I" (line 8) that can be described as
    (A) indifferent
    (B) edifying
    (C) angry
    (D) resentful
    (E) patronizing

22. The central theme of the poem is that
    (A) to serve God is to be obedient in all circumstances
    (B) physical handicaps can limit service to God
    (C) the best service to God is to stand and wait
    (D) blindness has robbed the speaker of being able to serve God
    (E) the speaker is among thousands who serve God

23. What does "that one talent" (line 3) represent?
    I. The natural abilities the speaker would use for God's service if the speaker were sighted
    II. The speaker's sight
    III. Hidden abilities that function despite the speaker's blindness
    (A) I only
    (B) II only
    (C) III only
    (D) I and II only
    (E) I, II, and III

24. "Light" (line 1) is in opposition to "dark" (line 2). This implies all the following opposing concepts EXCEPT
    (A) life and death
    (B) sightedness and blindness
    (C) good and evil
    (D) heaven and earth
    (E) knowledge and ignorance

25. "Day-labor" (line 7) can be paraphrased as
    (A) sighted service
    (B) work during the day
    (C) nine-to-five employment
    (D) physical work
    (E) work-for-hire

26. The indirect reference in line 3 to the "Parable of the Talents" in the Bible, in which the servant who buries his talent is cast into "outer darkness," is an example of
    (A) ambiguity
    (B) archaism
    (C) stock response
    (D) paratactic style
    (E) allusion

Questions 27–34 are based on the following passage.

"You have a tight boat, Mr. Barnstable," he said, "and a gallant-looking crew. You promise good service, sir, in time of need,
Line and that hour may not be far distant."
(5) "The sooner the better," returned the reckless sailor; "I have not had an opportunity of scaling my guns since we quitted Brest, though we passed several of the enemy's cutters coming up the Channel,
(10) with whom our bulldogs longed for a conversation. Mr. Griffith will tell you, pilot, that my little sixes can speak, on occasions, with a voice nearly as loud as the frigate's eighteens."
(15) "But not to as much purpose," observed Griffith; "'vox et præterea nihil,' as we said at the school."
"I know nothing of your Greek and Latin, Mr. Griffith," retorted the commander of
(20) the Ariel; "but if you mean that those seven brass playthings won't throw a round shot as far as any gun of their size and height above the water, or won't scatter grape and cannister with any blunderbuss in your
(25) ship, you may possibly find an opportunity that will convince you to the contrary before we part company."
"They promise well," said the pilot, who was evidently ignorant of the good
(30) understanding that existed between the two officers, and wished to conciliate all under his directions; "and I doubt not they will argue the leading points of a combat with good discretion. I see that you have
(35) christened them—I suppose for their

respective merits! They are indeed expressive names!"
"'Tis the freak of an idle moment," said Barnstable, laughing, as he glanced his
(40) eyes to the cannon, above which were painted the several quaint names of "boxer," "plumper," "grinder," "scatterer," "exterminator," and "nail-driver."
"Why have you thrown the mid-ship gun
(45) without the pale of your baptism?" asked the pilot; "or do you know it by the usual title of the 'old woman'?"
"No, no, I have no such petticoat terms on board me," cried the other; "but move
(50) more to starboard, and you will see its style painted on the cheeks of the carriage; it's a name that need not cause them to blush either."

The Pilot
by James Fenimore Cooper

27. Within the confines of the excerpt, the narrator is
    (A) intrusive
    (B) limited omniscient
    (C) naive
    (D) unreliable
    (E) a participant

28. What type of language is used by Mr. Barnstable?
    (A) Dialectal response
    (B) A high level of diction
    (C) Subordinating syntax
    (D) Poetic diction
    (E) Professional jargon

29. What is the subject of the conversation?
    (A) An argument between Griffith and Barnstable
    (B) The relative merits of ship armaments
    (C) Strategies for the upcoming battle
    (D) The intricacies of naming guns
    (E) The major components of a war vessel

30. The relationship of Barnstable and Griffith is
    (A) competitive
    (B) antagonistic
    (C) amiable
    (D) discourteous
    (E) ambivalent

31. The names of the cannons (lines 42–43) are
    (A) euphemisms
    (B) personifications
    (C) anthropomorphisms
    (D) epithets
    (E) antonomasias

32. "Our bulldogs longed for a conversation" in the second paragraph is a vehicle in a metaphor describing
    (A) hand-to-hand combat
    (B) a gun battle
    (C) a pit-bulldog fight
    (D) a pre-war conference
    (E) peace negotiations

33. Below are listed several definitions of "freaks." Which defines the use of the word in the phrase "the freak of an idle moment" in line 38?
    I. An abnormal thought
    II. Devoted to the thought
    III. A whim
    (A) I only
    (B) II only
    (C) III only
    (D) II and III only
    (E) I, II, and III

34. Based on his reaction to the exchange of words between Barnstable and Griffith, the pilot's style of leadership is based on
    (A) authoritative control
    (B) laissez-faire
    (C) group dynamics
    (D) chain of command
    (E) constant evaluation

Questions 35–42 are based on the following passage.

The lighthouse keeper said that when the wind blowed strong on to the shore, the waves ate fast into the bank, but when it
Line blowed off they took no sand away; for in
(5) the former case the wind heaped up the surface of the water next to the beach, and to preserve in equilibrium a strong undertow immediately set back again into the sea which carried with it the sand and
(10) whatever else was in the way, and left the beach hard to walk on; but in the latter case the undertow set on, and carried the sand with it, so that it was particularly difficult for shipwrecked men to get to land
(15) when the wind blowed on to the shore, but easier when it blowed off. This undertow, meeting the next surface wave on the bar which itself has made, forms part of the dam over which the latter breaks, as over
(20) an upright wall. The sea thus plays with the land holding a sandbar in its mouth awhile before it swallows it, as a cat plays with a mouse; but the fatal gripe is sure to come at last. The sea sends its rapacious east wind
(25) to rob the land, but before the former has got far with its prey, the land sends its honest west wind to recover some of its own. But, according to Lieutenant Davis, the forms, extent, and distribution of sandbars
(30) and banks are principally determined, not by winds and waves, but by tides.

. . .

I heard of a party who went off fishing back of Wellfleet some years ago, in two boats, in calm weather, who, when they
(35) had laden their boats with fish, and approached the land again, found such a swell breaking on it, though there was no wind, that they were afraid to enter it. At first they thought to pull for Provincetown,
(40) but night was coming on, and that was many miles distant. Their case seemed a desperate one. As often as they approached the shore and saw the terrible breakers that intervened, they were

(45) deterred; in short, they were thoroughly frightened. Finally, having thrown their fish overboard, those in one boat chose a favorable opportunity, and succeeded, by skill and good luck, in reaching the land,
(50) but they were unwilling to take the responsibility of telling the others when to come in and as the other helmsman was inexperienced, their boat was swamped at once, yet all managed to save themselves.

. . .

(55) The annals of this voracious beach! who could write them, unless it were a shipwrecked sailor? How many who have seen it have seen it only in the midst of danger and distress, the last strip of earth
(60) which their mortal eyes beheld. Think of the amount of suffering which a single strand has witnessed! The ancients would have represented it as a sea-monster with open jaws, more terrible than Scylla and
(65) Charybdis.

"Cape Cod"
by Henry David Thoreau

35. The imagery in the first paragraph makes the sea seem like a playful animal and the east wind like
(A) driven sand
(B) shipwrecked men
(C) a thief
(D) the undertow
(E) a friend to the land

36. The first paragraph, in its entirety,
(A) explains how beaches are formed
(B) hypothesizes the causes of shipwrecks
(C) relates the notion that wind and waves cause sandbars
(D) reinforces the important role of wind to beach formation
(E) describes the cyclical interplay of wind and wave

37. A significant factor presented in the first paragraph is that
(A) the east wind blows onto the shore
(B) the west wind blows onto the shore
(C) sandbar formation is unrelated to winds and waves
(D) winds blowing offshore carry sand away
(E) surface water is heaped up by the west wind

38. Based on context, "Scylla and Charybdis" in the last paragraph probably is a reference to
(A) a special nautical term
(B) sharks
(C) mythology
(D) marine vessels
(E) anthropology

39. What is the purpose of the anecdotal episode in the second paragraph?
(A) To illustrate the dangers of fishing
(B) To entertain the reader without a significant point
(C) To indicate the need for experience when boating
(D) To illustrate the force of the water when it hits the sandbars
(E) To sentimentalize the plight of people stranded at sea

40. The personification in the last paragraph indicates the speaker is
(A) excited about the beautiful beach
(B) contemplative of suffering
(C) disgruntled toward the shipwrecked sailors
(D) contemptuous of change
(E) high pressured in changing the reader's attitudes

41. What do the words "voracious," "danger," and "terrible" contribute to the tone of the last paragraph?
(A) Scorn
(B) Seriousness
(C) Fear
(D) Disdain
(E) Outrage

42. As used in the first paragraph, "rapacious" means
   (A) forceful and greedy
   (B) tearing and destructive
   (C) cold and unrelenting
   (D) hot and gusting
   (E) vile and odious

Questions 43–49 are based on the following passage.

A shrill sound of laughter and of amused voices—voices of men, women, and children—resounded in the street while this
Line wine game lasted. There was little
(5) roughness in the sport, and much playfulness. There was a special companionship in it, an observable inclination on the part of every one to join some other one, which led, especially
(10) among the luckier or lighter-hearted, to frolicsome embraces, drinking of healths, shaking of hands, and even joining of hands and dancing, a dozen together. When the wine was gone, and the places where it
(15) had been most abundant were raked into a gridiron-pattern by fingers, these demonstrations ceased, as suddenly as they had broken out. The man who had left his saw sticking in the firewood he was cutting,
(20) set it in motion again; the woman who had left on a door-step the little pot of hot ashes, at which she had been trying to soften the pain in her own starved fingers and toes, or in those of her child, returned
(25) to it; men with bare arms, matted locks, and cadaverous faces, who had emerged into the winter light from cellars, moved away, to descend again; and a gloom gathered on the scene that appeared more natural to
(30) it than sunshine.
   The wine was red wine, and had stained the ground of the narrow street in the suburb of Saint Antoine, in Paris, where it was spilled. It had stained many hands, too,
(35) and many faces, and many naked feet, and many wooden shoes. The hands of the man who sawed the wood, left red marks on the

billets; and the forehead of the woman who nursed her baby, was stained with the stain
(40) of the old rag she wound about her head again. Those who had been greedy with the staves of the cask, had acquired a tigerish smear about the mouth; and one tall joker so besmirched, his head more out of a long
(45) squalid bag of a nightcap than in it, scrawled upon a wall with his finger dipped in muddy wine-lees—BLOOD.
   The time was to come, when that wine too would be spilled on the street-stones, and
(50) when the stain of it would be red upon many there.

A Tale of Two Cities
by Charles Dickens

43. What does this passage describe?
   (A) A street riot
   (B) An accident
   (C) A political demonstration
   (D) A protest
   (E) A party

44. The last paragraph foreshadows that
   (A) another wine game would occur
   (B) wine will stain
   (C) some people there would kill or be killed
   (D) the people would be stained with wine again
   (E) blood stains more than wine

45. All the following characterizations can be used to describe the people on the street EXCEPT
   (A) destitute
   (B) impulsive
   (C) respited
   (D) harrowed
   (E) predictable

46. As a literary device, the man writing "BLOOD" in wine on the wall is which of the following?
    I. Foreshadowing
    II. A symbolic act
    III. Dramatic understatement
    (A) I only
    (B) II only
    (C) III only
    (D) I and II only
    (E) I, II, and III

47. Why does the speaker use the word "cadaverous" (line 26) when he could have used "pale" or "emaciated"?
    (A) It connotes that these men are like the living dead.
    (B) It identifies that this is science fiction.
    (C) It shows that they needed a break from life's drudgery.
    (D) It exaggerates the extent of the lack of color of their faces.
    (E) It emphasizes a sense of prose rhythm in the line.

48. The genre of this passage can be identified as
    (A) a character study
    (B) descriptive narrative
    (C) prose poetry
    (D) an epic drama
    (E) an epistolary novel

49. Of the list that follows, all can be used to describe the tone of lines 44–48 EXCEPT
    (A) ironic
    (B) comic
    (C) deferential
    (D) ominous
    (E) expectant

Questions 50–55 are based on the following poem.

On This Day I Complete My Thirty-sixth Year

'Tis time this heart should be unmoved,
    Since others it hath ceased to move:
Yet, though I cannot be beloved,
    Still let me love!

(5) My days are in the yellow leaf;
    The flowers and fruits of love are gone;
The worm, the canker, and the grief
    Are mine alone!

The fire that on my bosom preys
(10) Is lone as some volcanic isle;
No torch is kindled at its blaze—
    A funeral pile.

The hope, the fear, the jealous care,
    The exalted portion of the pain
(15) And power of love, I cannot share,
    But wear the chain.

But 'tis not *thus*—and 'tis not *here*—
    Such thoughts should shake my soul, nor now,
(20) Where glory decks the hero's bier,
    Or binds his brow.

                  by Lord Byron

50. Who is the speaker?
    (A) An impassioned lover
    (B) An aging paramour
    (C) A social outcast
    (D) A hermit
    (E) An unrequited lover

51. Love is characterized in the third stanza as
    (A) hostile to his needs
    (B) a fire out of control
    (C) an animal
    (D) unsatisfying
    (E) killing him

52. "The fire that on my bosom preys" is an example of
    (A) mixed metaphor
    (B) simile
    (C) caricature
    (D) *carpe diem*
    (E) apostrophe

53. The fourth stanza tells the reader that
    (A) the speaker is presently in love
    (B) love is more pain than pleasure
    (C) love is an escaped prisoner
    (D) love symbolizes unhappy emotions
    (E) the speaker plans to break free of love

54. What is the tone of the first stanza?
    (A) Demoralizing
    (B) Defiant
    (C) Temerarious
    (D) Irresolute
    (E) Exacerbated

55. Of the definitions listed, all apply to "exalted" (line 14) EXCEPT
    (A) spiritually high
    (B) magnified
    (C) dignified
    (D) physically high
    (E) extolled

Questions 56–60 are based on the following poem.

What Sugared Terms

What sugared terms, what all-persuading
   art,
What sweet mellifluous words, what
   wounding looks
Love used for his admittance to my heart!
Line Such eloquence was never read in books.
(5) He promised pleasure, rest, and endless joy,
Fruition of the fairest she alive.
His pleasure, pain; rest, trouble; joy, annoy,
Have I since found, which me of bliss
   deprive.
The Trojan horse thus have I now let in,
(10) Wherein enclosed these arméd men were
   placed—
Bright eyes, fair cheeks, sweet lips, and
   milk-white skin;
These foes my life have overthrown and
   razed.
Fair outward shows prove inwardly the
   worst:
Love looketh fair, but lovers are accurst.

                                    by R. Lynche

56. What does "she," as used in line 6, symbolize?
    (A) The woman he loves
    (B) Love
    (C) All women
    (D) Joy
    (E) His heart

57. What relationship do lines 13–14 have to the rest of the poem?
    (A) They contain a reversal in thought.
    (B) They introduce a fourth element of love's treachery.
    (C) They summarize the speaker's sense of disillusionment.
    (D) They intensify the promises of love.
    (E) They identify the object of the speaker's love.

58. "The Trojan horse" in the context of line 9 is a
    (A) magnificent animal
    (B) means of deception
    (C) military maneuver
    (D) famous beast
    (E) symbol of true love

59. "Sugared terms" (line 1) can be defined by which of these paraphrases?
    (A) Beguiling enticements
    (B) Beautiful language
    (C) Sweet negotiations
    (D) Coated stipulations
    (E) Kind words

60. Which of the descriptions that follow is the attitude of "I" toward "Love"?
    (A) Hostile antagonism
    (B) Humble contrition
    (C) Resistant pride
    (D) Optimistic anticipation
    (E) Vanquished resignation

ANSWER KEY: DIAGNOSTIC TEST II

Step 1. Score Your Test

- Use the following table to score your test.
- *Compare* your answers with the correct answers in the table:
- ✓ Place a check in the "Right" column for those questions you answered correctly.
- ✓ Place a check in the "Wrong" column for those questions you answered incorrectly.
- If you omitted answering a question, leave both columns blank.

Step 2. Analyze Your Test Results

- *Read* the portions of the "Analysis: Diagnostic Test II" (analysis follows the scoring table) that apply first to those questions you missed.
- *Scan* the rest of the analysis for those questions you answered correctly. This analysis provides the correct answers, identifies the literary element tested by each question, and briefly discusses the answer choice(s).

Step 3. Learn from Your Test Results

- *Circle* the question number on the Answer Key Table for each of the questions you answered incorrectly. Which literary elements were these questions testing?

  Obviously, due to the interrelated scope and definitions of the seven literary elements, many of the questions are actually testing more than one literary element. Consequently, these identifications serve only as a guide to pinpoint "problem" areas.
- *Review* the seven literary elements.

ANSWER KEY: DIAGNOSTIC TEST II

RIGHT	WRONG	ANSWER	1	2	3	4	5	6	7
SCORING			LITERARY ELEMENT TESTED						
		1. C			*				
		2. A						*	
		3. E		*					
		4. B							*
		5. D						*	
		6. B		*					
		7. C	*						
		8. E				*			
		9. A					*		
		10. C						*	
		11. B			*				
		12. E					*		
		13. C				*			
		14. A	*						
		15. B						*	
		16. D						*	
		17. C		*					
		18. B		*					
		19. E							*
		20. D		*					
		21. B			*				
		22. A	*						
		23. D						*	
		24. D							*
		25. A							*
		26. E						*	
		27. B			*				
		28. E						*	
		29. B	*						
		30. C					*		
		31. D						*	
		32. B						*	
		33. C							*
		34. C					*		
		35. C						*	
		36. E	*						
		37. A	*						
		38. C						*	
		39. D		*					
		40. B			*				

ANSWER KEY: DIAGNOSTIC TEST II

SCORING			LITERARY ELEMENT TESTED						
RIGHT	WRONG	ANSWER	1	2	3	4	5	6	7
		41. B				*			
		42. A							*
		43. B	*						
		44. C							*
		45. E					*		
		46. D						*	
		47. A						*	
		48. B		*					
		49. C				*			
		50. E			*				
		51. E							*
		52. A						*	
		53. A							*
		54. B				*			
		55. D							*
		56. C						*	
		57. C		*					
		58. B							*
		59. A							*
		60. E			*				

TO OBTAIN YOUR RAW SCORE:

_____ divided by 4 = _____
Total wrong   Score W

_____ minus _____ = _____
  Total right   Score W   Score R

Round Score R to the nearest whole
number for the raw score.

HOW DID YOU DO?

55–60 = Excellent
44–54 = Very Good
35–43 = Above Average
23–34 = Average
15–22 = Below Average

ANALYSIS: DIAGNOSTIC TEST II

NOTE: The scope and definition of each of the literary elements sometimes can differ among the literary critics. As a result, the rationale behind what constitutes a correct or an incorrect answer also may differ. Many of the questions in Diagnostic Test II are testing your skills in more than one literary element. Also, each answer analysis might be viewed from more than one perspective. Consequently, this analysis should be used as only a part of your study program.

1. **C** Element 3 (narrative voice) Upon first reading, the best description of the speaker's view of poverty would seem to be answer B, the only way to find happiness. But does the speaker really assert poverty to be "the only way"—or even "an unlikely source" (A) of happiness? Why are the rich "perplexed" (line 3), "vexed" (line 5), and "in…tears" (line 13) while the poor have "golden slumbers" (line 1)? The state of poverty is not the source of happiness because the speaker admits in line 15 that the poor "want's burden bears." Nevertheless, despite this "burden" placed upon him by want, the poor has contentment (lines 1–2), patience (line 15), and "Honest labour" (line 9) making the burden "No burden." The attitude of the rich who are "vexed/To add to golden numbers" makes wealth a deterrent to happiness, but the contented attitude of those who are poor makes poverty not a deterrent to happiness (C).

2. **A** Element 6 (use of language) The speaker compares the poor to a king (a metaphor) in line 16. Although the poor may be in a happier emotional state than the rich, the comparison to a king is exaggerated—hyperbole (A).

3. **E** Element 2 (form) The poem cannot be a ballad because it is not narrative; a hymn because it is not religious; a nonsense verse because it has rhythm, logic, and does not have coined words; or an aubade because it is not about early morning. The repetitive lines do, however, suggest a lyric poem meant to be sung (E).

4. **B** Element 7 (meanings in context) In the context, "crispèd" is the adjective form of the verb "crisp" that means the twisting movement associated with water that is swirling forth from a spring—undulating (B).

5. **D** Element 6 (use of language) Line 13 is a balanced sentence in which the conjunction "yet" establishes a contrast of ideas between two clauses of like grammatical construction (I). This antithesis is paradoxical (II) in that the person is swimming and sinking. Antonomasia is using a proper name for an associated idea—a figure of speech not applicable to line 13.

6. **B** Element 2 (form)

   > Stanza 1
   > Line 1 Rhetorical question
   > Line 3 Rhetorical question
   > Lines 5–6 Rhetorical question
   > Stanza 2
   > Line 11 Rhetorical question
   > Line 13 Rhetorical question
   > Line 15 "Then he…!"

   Line 15 departs from the speaker's established structure of rhetorical questions, each of which is aimed at making the point summarized in line 15: The contented ("patiently want's burden bears") poor worker is without the vexation of the rich ("No burden bears").

7. **C** Element 1 (meaning) This poem deals with attitudes. The rich are "vexed/To add to golden numbers, golden numbers" whereas the poor are contented and patient. It is this contrast in attitudes that establishes the meaning of the poem, rather than a condemnation of wealth itself or than an encouragement to be poor. The speaker has implied a generalization, however, that the named attitudes are seen in the states or conditions of wealth and poverty.

8. **E** Element 4 (tone) "Nonny" is a dialectal word that is used to call someone a simpleton—producing a derisive tone.

9. **A** Element 5 (character) This line has two possible perspectives: (1) the speaker may be personifying "Honest labour" as someone with a "lovely face" and (2) the speaker may feel that someone engaged in "Honest Labour" will have ("bear") a "lovely face"—one that is smiling and happy. Either perspective or attitude is one of a happy, trustworthy worker (A).

10. **C** Element 6 (use of language) The poor: characterized as able to slumber, laugh, and be content. This is in contrast to the rich: characterized as being perplexed, vexed, and in punishment. The speaker characterizes "Honest labour" as "lovely."

11. **B** Element 3 (narrative voice) The attitude of this poor young woman is sorrow and penitence—one of contrition. She admits the wrongful nature of her actions several times (referring to her "undu-

tifullness" and to her "former bad conduct"). She is by no means evasive either about her situation or about the hardships she must endure. Her letter shows no hint of contention or arrogance, and her only aspiration seems to be that her father will send her some clothing—a small thing in light of her deplorable situation. (Be sure to note the non-standard spelling in this selection.)

12. **E** Element 5 (character) Elizabeth, by her own admission, was undutiful and disobedient, a trouble to her father, and engaged in "bad conduct." Being beaten and starved has changed her character in the sense that she admits the wrongful nature of her former conduct toward the person she is now imploring for help (E). Although some may think she is manipulating the situation (A), the deplorable nature of her current living conditions were too harsh to justify such suspicions; this girl is really in trouble—trouble, perhaps, of her own making—but trouble nonetheless.

13. **C** Element 5 (tone) Answers B, D, and E are obviously incorrect; however, answers A and C are an opportunity for you to see how connotation can work in determining an answer choice. The reader can point to several lines in which Elizabeth implores her father for forgiveness, mercy, help; but does she not also impose upon him to send her clothes? In one sense this is true—she does place a burden upon her father to help her; however, the word impose carries with it the connotations of its other meanings, including cheating, taking advantage of others, forcing others to do what one wants—all of which this young woman is in no position to accomplish. As a result, imploring (C) is the better answer choice of the two.

14. **A** Element 1 (meaning) Considering her situation, Elizabeth would probably come home in a heartbeat if she could, making answer D improbable (and not supported by the passage). Answers A, B, C, and E are all possible; however, based on context, how can you tell which answer is best? Look at the writer's purpose: why did she write this letter? She wants her family to know that she is in trouble, that she is sorry for what she did, and that they can "easily" communicate with her. She is providing them knowledge, emotional motivation, and the means to do something—she is crying for help.

15. **B** Element 6 (use of language) "Flame" is used metaphorically in this context and is identified ("Your care and tenderness for me").

16. **D** Element 6 (use of language) The "tie to my tongue and pen" is the result of emotion ("fear") and guilt ("well knowing I had offended in the highest degree").

17. **C** Element 2 (form)
Line 9 marks a change in end-rhyme:

Line 1...spent	a	Line 9...need	c
Line 2...wide	b	Line 10...best	d
Line 3...hide	b	Line 11...state	e
Line 4...bent	a	Line 12...speed	c
Line 5...present	a	Line 13...rest	d
Line 6...chide	b	Line 14...wait	e
Line 7...denied	b		
Line 8...prevent	a		

18. **B** Element 2 (form) This two-part structure establishes several contrasts: (A) question ("Doth God exact day-labor, light denied?"— line 7) and answer ("God doth not need/Either man's work or his own gifts"—lines 9–10); (C) resistance ("my soul more bent"—line 4) and acceptance ("They also serve who only stand and wait"—line 14); (D) self-interest ("and present/My true account, lest He returning chide"—lines 5–6) and obedience ("who best/Bear His mild yoke, they serve Him best"—lines 10–11); (E) impatience ("When I consider how my light is spent/Ere half my days"—lines 1–2) and patience ("They also serve who only stand and wait" —line 14).

Answer B, however, does not establish an accurate contrast. Although the first part includes the concept of accountability, the second part states that "who best/Bear His mild yoke, they serve Him best" (lines 10–11)—another view of being accountable, NOT unaccountable.

19. **E** Element 7 (meanings in context) "Spent," as it is used here, can mean something being used up, worn out, tired out, or gone. "Light" can be symbolic of understanding (I), of vision (II), or of happiness (III).

20. **D** Element 2 (form) Sonnets are 14-line poems written in iambic pentameter.

21. **B.** Element 3 (narrative voice) Patience answers Milton's question to instruct him spiritually—edifying (B).

22. **A** Element 1 (meaning) The central idea—the theme—of the poem is a statement that summarizes the main point of the poem. What is the main point Milton is making? Whether speeding "O'er land and ocean" (line 13) or standing and waiting (line 14), whether blind or sighted, the best way to serve God is to obey Him in all circumstances (lines 10–11).

23. **D** Element 6 (use of language) "And that one talent" (line 3) represents both natural gifts and abilities and sight itself that he would use in service, but both his sight and those abilities he would accomplish with and by means of his sight are "Lodged with me useless" (line 4).

24. **D** Element 7 (meanings in context) In the context of this poem, light comes to represent Milton's life ("Ere half my days"—line 2) as contrasted to a "dark world" of death, his sight itself as contrasted to the "dark world" of blindness, good (the means "to serve therewith my Maker"—line 5) as contrasted to a dark work of evil (that does not serve), and knowledge (understanding) as contrasted to the "dark world" of ignorance. Heaven and earth, however, are not suggested in this context.

25. **A** Element 7 (meanings in context) "Day-labor" is figurative, representing work or service (labor) that requires sight (day—the time when the sighted can see with the light).

26. **E** Element 6 (use of language) This is an allusion—mentioning either directly or indirectly some well-known (literary) work, event, place, or person.

27. **B** Element 3 (narrative voice) The passage is obviously taken from a larger work; however, in this excerpt the narrator is seen as limited omniscient because the narrator gives the reader insight into the pilot's mind, but not into the thinking of any of the other characters.

28. **E** Element 6 (use of language) Barnstable uses the professional jargon (A) of a seaman: "scaling my guns," "the frigate's eighteens"—expressions indicative of a sailor who is used to high-sea battles.

29. **B** Element 1 (meaning) Barnstable, Griffith, and the man identified as "the pilot" are discussing, in terms of performance, the various types of guns used on warships. Although the pilot does divert the conversation to the names of Barnstable's cannon, the focus is upon the relative merits of ship armaments (B).

30. **C** Element 5 (character) Their conversation might support the idea that these two men are competitive (A) or even antagonistic (B), but the narrator reveals that they have a "good understanding" between them, indicating that the banter between them is good-natured and that their relationship is amiable.

31. **D** Element 6 (use of language) These "expressive names" that describe "their respective merits" are epithets (D), nouns (in this case) that emphasize the predominant characteristics of something.

32. **B** Element 6 (use of language) "Bulldogs" is an epithet-type name for guns. The "conversation" that they long for is the exchange of fire with the guns of the other ship. This metaphor comparing a gun battle (the tenor) with a dog fight (the vehicle) also contains personification of the bulldogs / guns, thus making this also an example of mixed imagery.

33. **C** Element 7 (meanings in context) The phrase "the freak of an idle moment" contains the contextual clue to the meaning of freak. Freak can mean all three of the listed definitions. It can refer to the abnormal (I) in a variety of circumstances. It can also be a name used to refer to someone devoted to something (II), especially a hobby or a movie star. In this context, however, the use of "idle moment," i.e., leisure time, indicates that these names are just whims (III).

34. **C** Element 5 (character) Although he has misread the implications of the exchange of words between Barnstable and Griffith (he does not recognize their "good understanding"), the pilot does not command the men with authoritative control (A), refrain from interference as one would who subscribes to a laissez-faire philosophy (B), refer them to one higher in command (D), or point out their errors in thinking (E). Instead he attempts to "conciliate" the two men—using human relations within group dynamics (C).

35. **C** Element 6 (use of language) The speaker presents the east wind as "rapacious," sent by the sea "to rob the land" like a thief (C).

36. **E.** Element 1 (meaning) Note that the question specifies "in its entirety":

Wind blows on shore and waves eat into bank →

Wind blows off shore and no sand taken away →

Wind heaps up surface water at beach and undertow carries away sand →

Undertow meets own surface wave and forms dam →

Wave breaks over dam → a cyclical interplay of wind and wave (E).

37. **A** Element 1 (meaning) Based on the opinion of Lieutenant Davis, the correct answer would be C if it were not for the word "unrelated" in that answer choice. Davis says that sandbar formation is "principally determined, not by winds and waves, but by tides"; he does NOT say it is unrelated. This type of question can be readily answered by using deductive reasoning. Answer A is supported by the following:

1. "…when the wind blowed strong on to the shore, the waves ate fast into the bank," and

2. "The sea sends its rapacious east wind to rob the land"; therefore,

3. the east wind blows on to shore.

38. **C** Element 6 (use of language) Context is essential to correctly answering this question: "ancients… sea-monster" (lines 62–63).

First, establish the context. The writer describes a beach (strand) where many shipwrecked sailors have died. He speculates that ancients would have called it "a sea-monster with open jaws, more terrible than Scylla and Charybdis."

The context does not support Scylla and Charybdis meaning "a special nautical term" because the comparison to a sea-monster makes them a reference to something supposedly alive. Sharks are alive and have open jaws, but the use of capitalization indicates that these are proper names. "Marine vessels" can immediately be eliminated because they are not alive and generally are not considered monsters. "Anthropology"—the study of mankind—is an obviously incorrect answer choice. The context and process of elimination leaves "mythology" as the correct answer: mythology includes ancient stories about monsters with proper names. FYI: According to mythology, Scylla was a monster off the Italian coast and Charybdis was a monster in a Sicilian whirlpool.

39. **D** Element 2 (form) The narrator is using an anecdotal episode to illustrate a point. The short narrative, itself, demonstrates a danger people encounter when fishing (A) and by means of contrast within the story demonstrates the need for experience (C); however, in the context of the entire selection in which he is discussing winds, waves, and sandbars, he uses the short narrative to illustrate just how powerful the water hitting the shore can be—answer D.

40. **B** Element 3 (narrative voice) The speaker personifies the beach as both "voracious" and as the witness of suffering—both indicative of someone whose attitude is contemplative concerning the suffering caused by this particular strand.

41. **B** Element 4 (tone) In isolation these words are indicative of elements that might cause fear (C) and perhaps outrage (E); however, in context, they project the speaker's contemplative attitude when used within rhetorical questions and figures of speech to intensify the gravity of the subject and to establish a serious tone (B).

42. **A** Element 7 (meanings in context) "Rapacious" is an adjective used to describe the act of forceful seizure and the condition of being very greedy (A).

43. **B** Element 1 (meaning) That this event is called a "wine game" eliminates answers A and D. Once the wine is gone, the people leave, conflicting with what might have been a demonstration (C). Is it a party (supported by the dancing) or is this event an accident—an unplanned happening because something has happened? The contextual clues support this latter view, especially because "these demonstrations ceased, as suddenly as they had broken out."

44. **C** Element 7 (meanings in context) The speaker states in the last paragraph that "that wine"— blood—would stain "many there." How can the stain of blood "be red" upon someone? Either by

being wounded oneself or by wounding (killing) someone else. Keeping in mind that for blood to "be spilled" refers to physical conflict/blood-shed/killing: the speaker is implying that some of the very people who had engaged in the "wine game" would eventually kill others or would perhaps be killed themselves.

45. **E** Element 5 (character) These poor people are clearly destitute (A), underfed and in rags. That they are impulsive (B) is evidenced by "these demonstrations ceased, as suddenly as they had broken out." In their miserable condition, however, they are respited (C) by this brief episode with the wine somehow spilled in the street. The harrowing (acutely distressing) nature of their situation is readily apparent, but the one thing these people are not is predictable (E).

46. **D** Element 6 (use of language) The action of the man writing "BLOOD" in wine on the wall functions as foreshadowing of coming events, as evidenced by the final paragraph of this passage, and functions as a symbolic act on several different levels, such as:

1. A symbol of the emotional intensity that the spilled wine caused—mirrored in the spilling of blood

2. A symbol of the impulsiveness with which people can react to spilled wine or to spilled blood

3. A symbol of underlying bitterness of these poor wretched people, bitterness that could be given temporary respite by a moment of abandon when wine is spilled—or by a moment of abandon when blood is spilled

47. **A** Element 6 (use of language) Several of these answer choices are applicable; therefore, you need to evaluate the best answer choice. Where do you look to make this determination? Context. Where do these men with "cadaverous" faces come from and return to? They descend again into cellars— below ground—like corpses. They are alive, but their appearance is as the dead.

48. **B** Element 2 (form) The passage consists of a narrative episode (a crowd of people on the street rejoice over wine that has been spilled, then retreat to their previous activities) that uses very descriptive language, with special attention paid to diction.

49. **C** Element 4 (tone) A man, slightly drunk with a baggy nightcap almost on his head would be a comic sight (B)—very ironic (A) in its contrast to the ominous (D) nature of the message he wrote— a message that leads the reader to expect (E) that a bloody conflict may well be ahead. The idea of yielding or submitting (C) is not an element of this act.

50. **E** Element 3 (narrative voice) The speaker's identity is revealed in the first two lines.

51. **E** Element 7 (meanings in context) Because the fire (a vehicle for love) "Is lone" and "No torch is kindled at its blaze" (line 11)—no one is caught by the sparks of his love—the love has become a self-consuming "funeral pile" (line 12)—in other words, love is killing him (E).

52. **A** Element 6 (use of language) "Fire" is a vehicle for "love"; "preys" compares fire/love to a predator, hence a mixed metaphor (two or more vehicles for the same tenor).

53. **A.** Element 7 (meanings in context) The speaker laments that he or she "cannot share" love, "But wear the chain" (lines 15–16). This implies that the speaker does have an object of affection—someone with whom he or she wants to "share" love.

54. **B** Element 4 (tone) Despite the conclusion made in the first two lines, the speaker challenges the notion by defiantly proclaiming that although love is not returned, "Still let me love!" (line 4).

55. **D** Element 7 (meanings in context) Hope, fear, jealousy, pain, power—these are all emotions, not physical attributes in this context.

56. **C** Element 6 (use of language) "She" does indeed refer to the woman the speaker loves on a *literal level*, but the key to the symbolic use is in the <u>syntax</u>: "Fruition of the fairest she alive" (line 6)—"the fairest she alive" acts as the object of the preposition "of" with "the," "fairest," and "alive" modifying "she." In normal syntactical structure, this object would require a noun, not a pronoun. What noun could be the symbolic antecedent of the pronoun in this context? The superlative "fairest...alive" points to all women: the fairest woman alive.

57. **C** Element 2 (form) In traditional sonnet form, the rhyme scheme groups this poem's thoughts:

Lines 1–4   Love tricked the speaker.

Lines 5–8   Personified Love broke his promises.

Lines 9–12   The object of his love was a Trojan horse.

Lines 13–14   Love looks fine on the outside, but is not on the inside.

The speaker is disillusioned by love—the deceptive nature of love's appearance (C).

58. **B** Element 7 (meanings in context) "Trojan horse" is a literary allusion (a use of language) to the battle over Helen of Troy in which a large wooden horse, filled with soldiers, was left as a "gift" before the enemy's gates. After the enemy brought in the horse, had a party, and fell asleep, the soldiers emerged from the horse and killed them. A "Trojan horse," in the context of this poem then, refers to such deceptions that look fine on the outside but contain an enemy within. Even without being familiar with the story of Helen of Troy, you can determine the meaning in context: The speaker has allowed in armed men (lines 9–11) that were placed in a beautiful body but who have overthrown and razed his life (line l2). The Trojan horse is a means of deception —answer B.

59. **A** Element 7 (meanings in context) "To sugar" is a process by which something that is otherwise unpleasant is covered with sugar to make it more pleasant to consume. Love, to gain "admittance to my heart" "sugared," or covered with sweetness, "terms"—referring to conditions of agreement and also referring to words. Such "sugared terms" (line l) are beguiling enticements, answer A.

60. **E** Element 3 (narrative voice) The speaker feels betrayed by "Love," but how does he react? You might expect him to be hostile (A), particularly after reading the description of what "Love" did to him, yet nowhere does he convey feelings of hostility. In contrast, he admits defeat (vanquishment) in line 12 and summarizes that "lovers" (among whom he counts himself) "are accurst" in line 14, giving voice to his resignation to the position in which "Love" has placed him.

Interpretive Skill Practice Sets

You may find that intensive practice in answering questions on each of the seven literary elements in an isolated format would be beneficial. The Interpretive Skill Practice Sets aim to give you that opportunity.

There are three Interpretive Skill Practice Sets (A, B, and C). Each set contains five literary excerpts or selections (two prose, two poetry, and one drama).

The questions are grouped in sets of five questions per literary element. You can use this intensive practice as an opportunity to practice all seven literary elements, or you may elect to practice just those literary elements that you find the most challenging.

As previously stated, the seven literary elements are very <u>interdependent</u>. As a result, labeling a particular test question as testing meaning or as testing any other single literary element should not be construed to mean that the test question is testing only one literary element. In some cases a single question might actually have at its basis perspectives from several literary elements. Also, you will find that opinions may vary greatly among literary critics and analysts concerning interpretation and assignment of the literary elements, as to their effects and uses.

Answers are on page 355.

PRACTICE SET A

Selection One

"What have you there, Sam?"

"Called at the Post-office just now, and found this here letter, as has laid there for two days," replied Mr. Weller. "It's sealed vith a vafer, and directed in round hand."

(Line)
(5)
"I don't know this hand," said Mr. Pickwick, opening the letter. "Mercy on us! what's this? It must be a jest; it—it— can't be true."

"What's the matter?" was the general inquiry.

"Nobody dead, is there?" said Wardle, alarmed at the horror in Mr. Pickwick's countenance.

(10)
Mr. Pickwick made no reply, but, pushing the letter across the table, and desiring Mr. Tupman to read it aloud, fell back in his chair with a look of vacant astonishment quite alarming to behold.

Mr. Tupman, with a trembling voice, read the letter, of which the following is a copy:—

(15)
Freeman's Court, Cornhill, August 28th, 1827.
Bardell against Pickwick

Sir,
Having been instructed by Mrs. Martha Bardell, to commence an action against you, for a breach of promise of marriage, for which the plaintiff lays her damages at fifteen hundred pounds, we beg to inform you that a writ has been issued against
(20)
you in this suit, in the Court of Common Pleas; and request to know, by return of post, the name of your attorney in London, who will accept service thereof.

We are, Sir,
Your obedient servants,
Dodson and Fogg.

(25)
Mr. Samuel Pickwick.

There was something so impressive in the mute astonishment with which each man regarded his neighbour, and every man regarded Mr. Pickwick, that all seemed afraid to speak. The silence was at length broken by Mr. Tupman.

"Dodson and Fogg," he repeated mechanically.

(30)
"Bardell and Pickwick," said Mr. Snodgrass, musing.

"Peace of mind and happiness of confiding females," murmured Mr. Winkle, with an air of abstraction.

The Posthumous Papers of the Pickwick Club
by Charles Dickens

Selection Two

Lusus animo debent aliquando dari,
Ad cogitandum melior ut redeat sibi.

—Phædrus "Fables," xiv. 5.

Line
(5)
The mind ought sometimes to be diverted, that it may return the better to thinking.

I do not know whether to call the following letter a satire upon coquettes, or a representation of their several fantastical accomplishments, or what other title to give it; but, as it is, I shall communicate it to the public. It will sufficiently explain its own
(10) intentions, so that I shall give it my reader at length, without either preface or postscript:

"MR. SPECTATOR:

"Women are armed with fans as men with swords, and sometimes do more execution with them. To the end therefore that ladies may be
(15) entire mistresses of the weapons which they bear, I have erected an academy for the training up of young women in the exercise of the fan, according to the most fashionable airs and motions that are now practised at court. The ladies who carry fans under me are drawn up twice a day in my great hall, where they are instructed in the use of
(20) their arms, and exercised by the following words of command:—Handle your fans, Unfurl your fans, Discharge your fans, Ground your fans, Recover your fans, Flutter your fans. By the right observation of these few plain words of command, a woman of a tolerable genius, who will apply herself diligently to her exercise for the space of but one half-
(25) year, shall be able to give her fan all the graces that can possibly enter into that little modish machine.

"But to the end that my readers may form to themselves a right notion of this exercise, I beg leave to explain it to them in all its parts. When my female regiment is drawn up in array, with everyone her
(30) weapon in her hand, upon my giving the word to handle their fans, each of them shakes her fan at me with a smile, then gives her right-hand woman a tap upon the shoulder, then presses her lips with the extremity of her fan, then lets her arms fall in an easy motion, and stands in readiness to receive the next word of command. All this is
(35) done with a close fan, and is generally learned in the first week...."

"Fans"
by Joseph Addison

Selection Three

Irreparableness

I have been in the meadows all the day,
And gathered there the nosegay that you see,
Singing within myself as bird or bee
When such do field-work on a morn of May.
But now I look upon my flowers, decay
Has met them in my hands, more fatally
Because more warmly clasped,—and sobs are free
To come instead of songs. What you say,
Sweet counsellors, dear friends? that I should go
Back straightway to the fields and gather more?
Another, sooth, may do it, but not I.
My heart is very tired, my strength is low,
My hands are full of blossoms plucked before,
Held dead within them till myself shall die.

by Elizabeth Barrett Browning

Selection Four

On the Grasshopper and the Cricket

The poetry of earth is never dead:
When all the birds are faint with the hot sun,
And hide in cooling trees, a voice will run
From hedge to hedge about the new-mown mead;
That is the grasshopper's—he takes the lead
In summer luxury—he has never done
With his delights; for when tired out with fun
He rests at ease beneath some pleasant weed.
The poetry of earth is ceasing never:
On a lone winter evening, when the frost
Has wrought a silence, from the stove there shrills
The cricket's song, in warmth increasing ever,
And seems to one in drowsiness half lost,
The grasshopper's among some grassy hills.

by John Keats

Selection Five

The Tragedy of Julius Caesar

(from Scene II.)

THIRD CITIZEN.
The noble Brutus is ascended: silence!

MARCUS BRUTUS.

Line   Be patient till the last.

(5)   Romans, countrymen, and lovers! hear me for my cause; and be
silent, that you may hear: believe me for mine honour; and have
respect to mine honour, that you may believe: censure me in your
wisdom; and awake your senses, that you may the better judge. If
there be any in this assembly, any dear friend of Cæsar's, to him I
(10)   say, that Brutus' love to Cæsar was no less than his. If, then, that
friend demand why Brutus rose against Cæsar, this is my answer,—
Not that I loved Cæsar less, but that I loved Rome more. Had you
rather Cæsar were living, and die all slaves, than that Cæsar were
dead, to live all free men? As Cæsar loved me, I weep for him; as he
(15)   was fortunate, I rejoice at it; as he was valiant, I honour him: but, as
he was ambitious, I slew him. There is tears for his love; joy for his
fortune; honour for his valour; and death for his ambition. Who is
here so base that would be a bondman? If any, speak; for him have
I offended. Who is here so rude that would not be a Roman? If any,
(20)   speak; for him have I offended. Who is here so vile that will not love
his country? If any, speak; for him have I offended. I pause for a
reply.

CITIZENS.
None, Brutus, none.

(25)   **MARCUS BRUTUS.**
Then none have I offended. I have done no more to Cæsar than you
shall do to Brutus. The question of his death is enroll'd in the Capitol;
his glory not extenuated, wherein he was worthy; nor his offences
enforced, for which he suffer'd death. Here comes his body,
(30)   mourn'd by Mark Antony:

Enter Antony with Cæsar's body.

who, though he had no hand in his death, shall receive the benefit of
his dying, a place in the commonwealth; as which of you shall not?
With this I depart,—that, as I slew my best lover for the good of
(35)   Rome, I have the same dagger for myself, when it shall please my
country to need my death.

CITIZENS.
Live, Brutus! live, live!

FIRST CITIZEN.
(40)   Bring him with triumph home unto his house.

SECOND CITIZEN.
Give him a statue with his ancestors.

THIRD CITIZEN.
Let him be Cæsar.

(45) FOURTH CITIZEN.
Cæsar's better parts
Shall be crown'd in Brutus.

FIRST CITIZEN.
We'll bring him to his house with shouts and clamours.

(50) MARCUS BRUTUS.
My countrymen,—

SECOND CITIZEN.
Peace, silence! Brutus speaks.

FIRST CITIZEN.
(55) Peace, ho!

MARCUS BRUTUS.
Good countrymen, let me depart alone,
And, for my sake, stay here with Antony:
Do grace to Cæsar's corpse, and grace his speech
(60) Tending to Cæsar's glories; which Mark Antony,
By our permission, is allow'd to make.
I do entreat you, not a man depart,
Save I alone, till Antony have spoke. [Exit]

FIRST CITIZEN.
(65) Stay, ho! and let us hear Mark Antony.

by William Shakespeare

QUESTIONS ABOUT MEANING

1. What is the subject of the letter in Selection One?
   (A) A breach of promise suit against Dodson and Fogg
   (B) A breach of promise suit against Samuel Pickwick
   (C) A writ of damages by Pickwick against Mrs. Martha Bardell
   (D) A writ of damages by the Court of Common Pleas against Pickwick
   (E) A breach of promise suit against Martha Bardell

2. What is the main idea of Selection Two?
   (A) Ladies should never use fans without training.
   (B) Fans are deadly weapons in the hands of ladies.
   (C) Letters to *The Spectator* are highly edited.
   (D) Ladies can be trained to use fans just as men are trained to use swords.
   (E) Fans are beautiful when used properly.

3. The main subject of the poem in Selection Three is
   (A) picking flowers
   (B) an awareness of life
   (C) dying flowers
   (D) an awareness of death
   (E) singing in the fields

4. The central concern of the poem in Selection Four is
   (A) insects
   (B) seasons of the year
   (C) nature's meaning (sounds and rhythms)
   (D) sounds of seasons
   (E) nature's cycles

5. Marcus Brutus's speech to the citizens in lines 4–22 of Selection Five deals with
   (A) justification for killing Cæsar
   (B) resistance to enemies
   (C) acquiring power and privilege
   (D) contending for the empire
   (E) political success

QUESTIONS ABOUT FORM

1. The "Mute astonishment" (line 26) of the men in Selection One is the result of
   (A) the sealed secrecy of the letter
   (B) their total trust in Pickwick's innocence
   (C) their disappointment in Pickwick's behavior
   (D) the untimely nature of the letter
   (E) the unexpected import of the letter

2. The effect of the narrator's comments about the letter in the second selection (lines 6–11) is to
   (A) prepare the readers for a shock
   (B) reveal the absurdity of the notion of training ladies to use fans
   (C) communicate that the letter is self-explanatory
   (D) present an alternative view from that of the letter
   (E) change the topic in contrast to that of the letter

3. The progression of thought in Selection Three can NOT be summarized as
   (A) from joy to sorrow to resignation
   (B) from singing to crying to silence
   (C) from work to play to death
   (D) from life to decay to death
   (E) from abandon to contemplation to conclusion

4. Lines 1–8 contrast with lines 9–14 in the fourth selection in which of the following ways?
   (A) Summer and winter
   (B) Grasshopper's voice and cricket's song
   (C) Hot and cold
   (D) Reality and unreality
   (E) Activity and inactivity

5. The dramatist in Selection Five reveals a departure in structure in line 57 by changing from
   (A) direct address to indirect statement
   (B) Brutus taking responsibility to fleeing the scene
   (C) active to passive resistance in Marcus Brutus's speech to the citizens
   (D) prose to blank verse in Marcus Brutus's speech to the citizens
   (E) the imperative to the interrogative

QUESTIONS ABOUT NARRATIVE VOICE

1. Dodson and Fogg's attitude in Selection One toward Mr. Pickwick is set forth as
   (A) impersonal and pragmatic
   (B) antagonistic and decisive
   (C) complacent and verbose
   (D) pedantic and morbid
   (E) indecisive and hypocritical

2. In order for the letter in the second selection to be "a satire upon coquettes" (lines 6–7), the writer's attitude toward ladies and their uses of fans would have to be
   (A) ironic sadness
   (B) a blend of hate and revenge
   (C) a blend of humor and censor
   (D) inspired sarcasm
   (E) a blend of defiance and resistance

3. What major change is initiated in line 11 of Selection Three?
   (A) The speaker changes attitude.
   (B) Death becomes a greater enemy than the transient nature of flowers.
   (C) A greater emphasis is placed on flowers.
   (D) The speaker becomes like the "bird or bee" of line 3.
   (E) The speaker resists a change in attitude.

4. In Selection Four, the speaker's attitude toward summer is set forth as
   (A) bitter
   (B) longing
   (C) ambivalent
   (D) curiously indifferent
   (E) antagonistic

5. In Selection Five, the attitude of the speaker toward Cæsar can be considered
   (A) contrite
   (B) complacent
   (C) melancholic
   (D) self-justifying
   (E) redoubtable

QUESTIONS ABOUT TONE

1. The speaker's tone sets forth that the three men regard the letter in Selection One as
   (A) an entertaining surprise
   (B) a curious setback
   (C) an embarrassing communication
   (D) a dangerous threat
   (E) an unexpected shock

2. The tone of the narrator's comment in Selection Two concerning the letter's form as related to purpose in line 8 ("or what other title to give it") is best mirrored by which of these paraphrases?
   (A) Who cares?
   (B) Who knows?
   (C) Is this necessary?
   (D) How rude!
   (E) Help!

3. The speaker's tone in the third selection in the last line is
   (A) resigned
   (B) parenthetical
   (C) mawkish
   (D) indignant
   (E) resentful

4. The speaker's tone in the last two lines of the fourth selection is set forth as
   (A) cavalier
   (B) calculating
   (C) dreamlike
   (D) self-demeaning
   (E) pious

5. In Selection Five, the citizens use a tone toward Marcus Brutus that is
   (A) defensive
   (B) combative
   (C) jocular
   (D) reverential
   (E) quarrelsome

QUESTIONS ABOUT CHARACTER

1. In the first selection, "alarmed at the horror in Mr. Pickwick's countenance" (lines 7–8) emphasizes Mr. Pickwick's state of
   (A) surprise
   (B) anticipation
   (C) disappointment
   (D) resentment
   (E) expectancy

2. As a character, the writer of the letter in the second selection is probably
   (A) inexperienced
   (B) unlettered
   (C) imperceptible
   (D) frivolous
   (E) imaginative

3. The speaker's friends in the third selection could be characterized as
   (A) perceptive
   (B) impertinent
   (C) obtuse
   (D) erratic
   (E) obsequious

4. According to the speaker in Selection Four, grasshoppers are personified as
   (A) hypocritical
   (B) self-delusional
   (C) fun loving
   (D) exaggerative
   (E) misdirected

5. In the fifth selection, Marcus Brutus wants the citizens to believe that he is
   (A) compassionate
   (B) patriotic
   (C) perseverant
   (D) capricious
   (E) sententious

QUESTIONS ABOUT USE OF LANGUAGE

1. The language of the letter in the first selection is expressed in
   (A) imprecise diction
   (B) a businesslike tone
   (C) highly symbolic language
   (D) an informal tone
   (E) Nonstandard English

2. The figurative use of "men with swords" (line 13) in the second selection reinforces a sense that
   (A) men should use swords like women use fans
   (B) the writer is unknowledgeable about war
   (C) women should be able to use both fans and swords
   (D) fans are weapons, too, and require training for use
   (E) men should be able to use both fans and swords

3. In the third selection, line 3 contains
   (A) an understatement
   (B) an overstatement
   (C) a simile
   (D) a metaphor
   (E) personification

4. In the fourth selection, lines 3–8 present the grasshopper as if it were a
   (A) worthless lifeform
   (B) renewable energy
   (C) playing person
   (D) mysterious thing
   (E) destructive insect

5. In the fifth selection, the question "Who is here so rude that would not be a Roman?" (line 19) is
   (A) rhetorical
   (B) sarcastic
   (C) paradoxical
   (D) an overstatement
   (E) an understatement

QUESTIONS ABOUT MEANING(S) IN CONTEXT

1. As can be presumed from the letter in Selection One, Mr. Pickwick had
   (A) never met Mrs. Martha Bardell
   (B) married Mrs. Bardell
   (C) stolen from Mrs. Bardell
   (D) a relationship with Mrs. Bardell
   (E) worked for Mrs. Bardell

2. In the second selection, the introductory quote (lines 1–5) implies that
   (A) the letter is too frivolous for use
   (B) the letter is presented as a diversion for readers
   (C) minds are wasted with useless reading
   (D) minds can be trained by diversionary thinking
   (E) the letter is presented as a work meriting serious contemplation

3. In the third selection, "more warmly clasped" (line 7) expresses which of these concepts?
   I. Cherished firmly
   II. Body heat
   III. Destructive actions
   (A) I only
   (B) II only
   (C) III only
   (D) I and II only
   (E) I, II, and III

4. In line 13 of the fourth selection, "drowsiness half lost" can be paraphrased as
   (A) a sleepless night
   (B) insomnia
   (C) dreams
   (D) incoherence
   (E) going to sleep

5. The statement in lines 14–17 of the fifth selection is set forth as
   (A) a summary of the personal actions of Marcus Brutus concerning Cæsar
   (B) a generalization about Cæsar's character
   (C) a series of excuses for Cæsar's murder
   (D) a response to ungrounded charges
   (E) the emotional ramblings of a man over the death of his friend

PRACTICE SET B

Selection One

"Goodwives," said a hard-featured dame of fifty, "I'll tell ye a piece of my mind. It would be greatly for the public behoof, if we women, being of mature age and church-members in good repute, should have the handling of such malefactresses as
Line this Hester Prynne. What think ye, gossips? If the hussy stood up for judgment before
(5) us five, that are now here in a knot together, would she come off with such a sentence as the worshipful magistrates have awarded? Marry, I trow not!"

"People say," said another, "that the Reverend Master Dimmesdale, her godly pastor, takes it very grievously to heart that such a scandal should have come upon his congregation."

(10) "The magistrates are God-fearing gentlemen, but merciful overmuch,—that is a truth," added a third autumnal matron. "At the very least, they should have put the brand of a hot iron on Hester Prynne's forehead. Madam Hester would have winced at that, I warrant me. But she,—the naughty baggage,—little will she care what they put upon the bodice of her gown! Why, look you, she may cover it with a brooch, or
(15) such like heathenish adornment, and so walk the streets as brave as ever!"

"Ah, but," interposed, more softly, a young wife, holding a child by the hand, "let her cover the mark as she will, the pang of it will be always in her heart."

The Scarlet Letter
by Nathaniel Hawthorne

Selection Two

The rational intercourse kept up by conversation is one of our principal distinctions from brutes. We should therefore endeavor to turn this peculiar talent to our advantage, and consider the organs of speech as the instruments of understanding:
Line we should be very careful not to use them as the weapons of vice, or tools of folly,
(5) and do our utmost to unlearn any trivial or ridiculous habits, which tend to lessen the value of such an inestimable prerogative. It is, indeed, imagined by some philosophers, that even birds and beasts (though without the power of articulation) perfectly understand one another by the sounds they utter; and that dogs, cats, etc., have each a particular language to themselves, like different nations. Thus it may be
(10) supposed that the nightingales of Italy have as fine an ear for their own native woodnotes as any signor or signora for an Italian air; that the boars of Westphalia gruntle as expressively through the nose as the inhabitants in High German: and that the frogs in the dykes of Holland croak as intelligibly as the natives jabber their Low Dutch. However this may be, we may consider those whose tongues hardly seem to
(15) be under the influence of reason, and do not keep up the proper conversation of human creatures, as imitating the language of different animals. Thus, for instance, the affinity between Chatterers and Monkeys, and Praters and Parrots, is too obvious not to occur at once; Grunters and Growlers may be justly compared to Hogs; Snarlers are Curs that continually show their teeth, but never bite; and the Spitfire
(20) passionate are a sort of wild cats that will not bear stroking, but will purr when they are pleased. Complainers are Screech-Owls; and Story-tellers, always repeating the same dull note, are Cuckoos. Poets that prick up their ears at their own hideous

braying are no better than Asses. Critics in general are venomous
(25) Serpents that delight in hissing, and some of them who have got by
heart a few technical terms without knowing their meaning are no
other than Magpies. I myself, who have crowed to the whole town
for near three years past, may perhaps put my readers in mind of a
Barnyard Cock; but as I must acquaint them that they will hear the
(30) last of me on this day fortnight, I hope they will then consider me as
a Swan, who is supposed to sing sweetly at his dying moments.

On Conversation
by William Cowper

Selection Three

To His Son

Three things there be that prosper all apace
And flourish, while they are asunder far;
But on a day they meet all in a place,
Line And when they meet, they one another mar.
(5) And they be these: the wood, the weed, the wag.
The wood is that that makes the gallows tree;
The weed is that that strings the hangman's bag;
The wag, my pretty knave, betokens thee.
Now mark, dear boy: while these assemble not,
(10) Green springs the tree, hemp grows, the wag is wild;
But when they meet, it makes the timber rot,
It frets the halter, and it chokes the child.
God bless the child!

by William Wordsworth

Selection Four

Worldly Place

Even in a palace, life may be led well!
So spake the imperial sage, purest of men.
Marcus Aurelius. But the stifling den
Line Of common life, where, crowded up pell-mell,
(5) Our freedom for a little bread we sell,
And drudge under some foolish master's ken
Who rates us if we peer outside our pen—
Match'd with a palace, is not this a hell?
Even in a palace! On his truth sincere,
(10) Who spoke these words, no shadow ever came;
And when my ill-school'd spirit is aflame
Some nobler, ampler stage of life to win,
I'll stop, and say: 'There were no succour here!
The aids to noble life are all within.'

by Matthew Arnold

Selection Five

Act I. Scene I

A hall in the DUKE'S palace

*Enter the DUKE of Ephesus, ÆGEON,
the Merchant of Syracuse, GAOLER, OFFICERS,
and other ATTENDANTS*

ÆGEON.   Proceed, Solinus, to procure my fall,
And by the doom of death end woes and all.

DUKE.   Merchant of Syracusa, plead no more;

Line
   I am not partial to infringe our laws.
(5) The enmity and discord which of late
   Sprung from the rancorous outrage of your duke
   To merchants, our well-dealing countrymen,
   Who, wanting guilders to redeem their lives,
   Have seal'd his rigorous statutes with their bloods,
(10) Excludes all pity from our threat'ning looks.
   For, since the mortal and intestine jars
   'Twixt thy seditious countrymen and us,
   It hath in solemn synods been decreed,
   Both by the Syracusians and ourselves,
(15) To admit no traffic to our adverse towns;
   Nay, more: if any born at Ephesus
   Be seen at any Syracusian marts and fairs;
   Again, if any Syracusian born
   Come to the bay of Ephesus—he dies,
(20) His goods confiscate to the Duke's dispose,
   Unless a thousand marks be levied,
   To quit the penalty and to ransom him.
   Thy substance, valued at the highest rate,
   Cannot amount unto a hundred marks;
(25) Therefore by law thou art condemn'd to die.

ÆGEON.   Yet this my comfort: when your words are done,
My woes end likewise with the evening sun.

*The Comedy of Errors
by William Shakespeare*

QUESTIONS ABOUT MEANING

1. The central subject of the first selection mostly concerns
   (A) sacrifice
   (B) honor
   (C) punishments
   (D) destiny
   (E) women

2. The main idea in Selection Two is that
   (A) people who do not use proper conversation are like animals
   (B) animals can talk
   (C) insults can be effective forms of communication
   (D) philosophers believe that animals communicate
   (E) animals have nationalities

3. The speaker's message in Selection Three is primarily a
   (A) description
   (B) warning
   (C) reminder
   (D) play on words
   (E) statement on nature

4. The main point of the speaker in Selection Four is that
   (A) living in a palace is the means to a well-led life
   (B) a well-led life does not depend on external conditions
   (C) working for a living is slavery
   (D) the sage was a wise man
   (E) life is lived in stages

5. What is the dramatic situation of the scene in Selection Five?
   (A) The Duke of Ephesus is afraid of the Duke of Syracuse.
   (B) A merchant has been unjustly seized and condemned to death in Syracuse.
   (C) A merchant of Syracuse wants to die.
   (D) A Syracuse merchant is to be executed because of a trade war with Ephesus.
   (E) An escaped convict is posing as a merchant from Syracuse.

QUESTIONS ABOUT FORM

1. The persuasive speech of the "hard-featured dame" in the first paragraph of Selection One is intended to
   (A) further intimidate Hester Prynne
   (B) begin a discussion among the townswomen that reveals their attitudes
   (C) summarize Hester's problem
   (D) introduce Dimmesdale's role in helping Hester
   (E) simply narrate the episode

2. Selection Two is structured in part on
   (A) cause and effect
   (B) analogy
   (C) chronological sequence
   (D) spatial sequence
   (E) induction

3. There are three parts of the poem (lines 1–4, lines 5–8, and lines 9–13) in Selection Three. Which of these sets of words most clearly reflect those parts?
   (A) Generalization; application; threat
   (B) Definition; application; warning
   (C) Generalization; explanation; warning
   (D) Warning; explanation; threat
   (E) Application; warning; threat

4. The last two lines in the poem in Selection Four provide an effect that is
   (A) an ironic twist to line one
   (B) to intensify the argument of the first stanza
   (C) to deny line one
   (D) a simplification of the argument
   (E) a resistance to the argument

5. Selection Five is structured as
   (A) couplets
   (B) a chorus
   (C) a ballad
   (D) caricature
   (E) blank verse

QUESTIONS ABOUT NARRATIVE VOICE

1. The attitude of the young wife in Selection One toward Hester, in contrast to the others, is slightly
   (A) ambivalent
   (B) sympathetic
   (C) devitalized
   (D) satirical
   (E) conciliatory

2. In Selection Two, the speaker's attitude concerning those who "do not keep up the proper conversation" (line 15) is revealed as one of
   (A) admiration
   (B) complacency
   (C) intolerance
   (D) amusement
   (E) hypocrisy

3. The change in line 8 of Selection Three from the third person "they" (line 5) to the first person "my" and second person "thee" indicates that the speaker's attitude in the poem is
   (A) didactic
   (B) hostile
   (C) impersonal
   (D) mocking
   (E) cruel

4. What is the attitude of "I" (line 13) toward Marcus Aurelius in the fourth selection?
   (A) Receptive
   (B) Ambitiously antagonistic
   (C) Blameworthy
   (D) Bravado
   (E) Bitterly disapproving

5. The attitude of the Duke toward Ægeon in Selection Five can be considered
   (A) naive
   (B) disingenuous
   (C) disillusional
   (D) stern
   (E) penitent

QUESTIONS ABOUT TONE

1. The tone of "the naughty baggage," in Selection One, makes the speaker sound
   (A) flamboyant
   (B) laconic
   (C) ostentatious
   (D) spiteful
   (E) flattering

2. When the speaker calls critics "Serpents" and "Magpies" (lines 25 and 27) in the second selection, the tone can be seen as
   (A) sarcastic
   (B) laudatory
   (C) defiant
   (D) concordant
   (E) circumspect

3. The speaker's tone in the third selection might lead the hearer to regard the boy as
   (A) gallant
   (B) a thief
   (C) mischievous
   (D) supine
   (E) incorrigible

4. The speaker's tone implies, in Selection Four, that the words of the "imperial sage" are
   (A) serious
   (B) noble
   (C) pious
   (D) pedantic
   (E) pithy

5. Ægeon's tone, in Selection Five, can be recognized as
   (A) reticent
   (B) resigned
   (C) defensive
   (D) disparaging
   (E) boisterous

QUESTIONS ABOUT CHARACTER

1. The character of the third matron in Selection One can be thought of as
   - (A) insincere
   - (B) autocratic
   - (C) inclement
   - (D) charismatic
   - (E) sophisticated

2. In Selection Two, the speaker wants his readers to think of him as
   - (A) severe
   - (B) restrictive
   - (C) lenient
   - (D) profound
   - (E) self-determined

3. In Selection Three, the direct address "dear boy" (line 9) emphasizes which of the following in the speaker's character?
   - (A) Heartlessness
   - (B) Arrogance
   - (C) Brazenness
   - (D) Austerity
   - (E) Bemusement

4. In Selection Four, the speaker reveals that he or she prioritizes
   - (A) complacency over struggle
   - (B) intrinsic values over physical wealth
   - (C) intellectual over physical strength
   - (D) sincerity over insincerity
   - (E) freedom over wealth

5. As presented in Selection Five, the Duke's decision is based on what he puts forth as
   - (A) a personal vendetta
   - (B) his position of authority
   - (C) a keen dislike of Ægeon
   - (D) resistance to authority
   - (E) national interests

QUESTIONS ABOUT USE OF LANGUAGE

1. As used in the last paragraph of the first selection, "mark" symbolizes
   - (A) her freedom
   - (B) bravery
   - (C) shame
   - (D) high fashion
   - (E) courage

2. In the second selection, the literary device used in lines 30–31 is a
   - (A) metonymy
   - (B) simile
   - (C) punch line
   - (D) digression
   - (E) metaphor

3. In the third selection, "the wood, the weed, the wag" (line 5) perform which of these roles?
   - I. Symbols of warning
   - II. An alliterative device
   - III. Dead metaphors
   - (A) I only
   - (B) II only
   - (C) I and II only
   - (D) II and III only
   - (E) I, II, and III

4. In the fourth selection, "bread" (line 5) symbolizes
   - (A) the necessities of life
   - (B) free enterprise
   - (C) entrepreneurship
   - (D) money
   - (E) resourcefulness

5. As used in line 9 of the fifth selection, "with their bloods" is
   - (A) a metaphor for dying for one's country
   - (B) confirming that they will be spared
   - (C) referring to medical use of blood
   - (D) a ritual to belong to the guilders
   - (E) figurative language for people's lives

QUESTIONS ABOUT MEANING(S) IN CONTEXT

1. In line 11 of Selection One, "autumnal" is used to mean
   (A) fall-like
   (B) colorful
   (C) elderly
   (D) cool
   (E) bitter

2. As used in the second selection, the word "instruments" (line 3) is used to mean all these concepts EXCEPT
   (A) the means to do something
   (B) tools
   (C) sound devices
   (D) formal documents
   (E) implements

3. "Frets the halter" in line 12 of the third selection can also be paraphrased as
   (A) worries the timid
   (B) wears the noose
   (C) ruffles the garment
   (D) irritates the hesitant
   (E) gnaws the animal

4. In its context, "rates" in line 7 of the fourth selection means which of these three definitions?
   I. Scolds
   II. Appraises
   III. Esteems
   (A) I only
   (B) II only
   (C) III only
   (D) I and II only
   (E) I, II, and III

5. In the fifth selection, lines 11–12 are connotative of all the following EXCEPT that
   (A) body parts are being procured
   (B) the argument is on both physical and emotional levels
   (C) hostility in this case has a sense of abruptness
   (D) the stirring up of trouble began with Syracuse
   (E) Ægeon is guilty because of his nationality

PRACTICE SET C

Selection One

A stern smile curled the Prince's lip as he spoke. Waldemar Fitzurse hastened to reply that Ivanhoe was already removed from the lists, and in the custody of his friends.

Line 'I was somewhat afflicted,' he said, 'to see the grief of the Queen of Love and
(5) Beauty, whose sovereignty of a day this event has changed into mourning. I am not a man to be moved by a woman's lament for her lover, but this same Lady Rowena suppressed her sorrow with such dignity of manner that it could only be discovered by her folded hands and her tearless eye, which trembled as it remained fixed on the lifeless form before her.'

(10) 'Who is this Lady Rowena,' said Prince John, 'of whom we have heard so much?'

'A Saxon heiress of large possessions,' replied the Prior Aymer; 'a rose of loveliness, and a jewel of wealth; the fairest among a thousand, a bundle of myrrh, and a cluster of camphire.'

'We shall cheer her sorrows,' said Prince John, 'and amend her blood, by wedding
(15) her to a Norman. She seems a minor, and must therefore be at our royal disposal in marriage. How sayst thou, De Bracy? What thinkst thou of gaining fair lands and livings, by wedding a Saxon, after the fashion of the followers of the Conqueror?'

'If the lands are to my liking, my lord,' answered De Bracy, 'it will be hard to displease me with a bride; and deeply will I hold myself bound to your Highness for a
(20) good deed, which will fulfil all promises made in favour of your servant and vassal.'

'We will not forget it,' said Prince John; 'and that we may instantly go to work, command our seneschal presently to order the attendance of the Lady Rowena and her company—that is, the rude churl her guardian, and the Saxon ox whom the Black Knight struck down in the tournament—upon this evening's banquet. De Bigot,' he
(25) added to his seneschal, 'thou wilt word this our second summons so courteously as to gratify the pride of these Saxons, and make it impossible for them again to refuse; although, by the bones of Becket, courtesy to them is casting pearls before swine.'

Ivanhoe
by Sir Walter Scott

Selection Two

That the machine has dealt art in the grand old sense a death-blow, none will deny—the evidence is too substantial: art in the grand old sense, meaning art in the sense of structural tradition, whose craft is fashioned upon the handicraft ideal,
Line ancient or modern; an art wherein this form and that form as structural parts were
(5) laboriously joined in such a way as to beautifully emphasize the manner of the joining...craft that will not see that human thought is stripping off one form and donning another, and artists are everywhere, whether catering to the leisure class of old England or ground beneath the heel of commercial abuse here in the great West, the unwilling symptoms of the inevitable, organic nature of the machine they combat,
(10) the hell-smoke of the factories they scorn to understand.

And, invincible, triumphant, the machine goes on, gathering force and knitting the material necessities of mankind ever closer into a universal automatic fabric; the engine, the motor, and the battleship, the works of art of the century!

(15)   The machine is intellect mastering the drudgery of earth that the plastic art may live; that the margin of leisure and strength by which man's life upon the earth can be made beautiful, may immeasurably widen, its function ultimately to emancipate human expression!

It is a universal educator, surely raising the level of human
(20)   intelligence, so carrying within itself the power to destroy, by its own momentum, the greed which in [William] Morris's time and still in our own time turns it to a deadly engine of enslavement. The only comfort left the poor artist, sidetracked as he is, seemingly is a mean one: the thought that the very selfishness which man's early art
(25)   idealized, now reduced to its lowest terms, is swiftly and surely destroying itself through the medium of the machine.

The artist's present plight is a sad one, but may he truthfully say that society is less well off because architecture, or even art, as it was, is dead, and printing, or the machine, lives? Every age has
(30)   done its work, produced its art with the best tools or contrivances it knew, the tools most successful in saving the most precious thing in the world—human effort...

"The Art and Craft of the Machine: Democracy and New Forms in Architecture"
Speech
by Frank Lloyd Wright

Selection Three

The Parting

Since there's no help, come let us kiss and part—
Nay, I have done, you get no more of me;
And I am glad, yea, glad with all my heart,
Line   That thus so cleanly I myself can free.
(5)   Shake hands for ever, cancel all our vows,
And when we meet at any time again,
Be it not seen in either of our brows
That we one jot of former love retain.
Now at the last gasp of Love's latest breath,
(10)   When, his pulse failing, Passion speechless lies,
When Faith is kneeling by his bed of death,
And Innocence is closing up his eyes,
Now if thou would'st, when all have given him over,
From death to life thou might'st him yet recover.

by Michael Drayton

Selection Four

On Time

Fly envious Time, till thou run out thy race,
Call on the lazy leaden-stepping hours,
Whose speed is but the heavy plummet's pace;

Line
(5)

And glut thy self with what thy womb devours,
Which is no more than what is false and vain,
And merely mortal dross;
So little is our loss,
So little is thy gain.
For when as each thing bad thou hast entombed,

(10)

And last of all, thy greedy self consumed,
Then long Eternity shall greet our bliss
With an individual kiss;
And Joy shall overtake us as a flood,
When every thing that is sincerely good

(15)

And perfectly divine,
With Truth, and Peace, and Love shall ever shine
About the supreme Throne
Of him, t' whose happy-making sight alone,
When once our heav'nly-guided soul shall climb,

(20)

Then all this earthy grossness quit,
Attired with stars, we shall for ever sit,
Triumphing over Death, and Chance, and thee, O Time.

by John Milton

Selection Five

ACT II. Scene I.

Enter ANGELO, ESCALUS, *a* JUSTICE,
PROVOST, OFFICERS *and other*
ATTENDANTS

ANGELO. We must not make a scarecrow of the law,
Setting it up to fear the birds of prey,
And let it keep one shape till custom make it
Their perch, and not their terror.

Line
(5)

ESCALUS. Ay, but yet
Let us be keen, and rather cut a little
Than fall and bruise to death. Alas! this gentleman,
Whom I would save, had a most noble father.
Let but your honour know,

(10)

Whom I believe to be most strait in virtue,
That, in the working of your own affections,
Had time coher'd with place, or place with wishing,

Or that the resolute acting of our blood
Could have attain'd th'effect of your own purpose
(15) Whether you had not sometime in your life
Err'd in this point which now you censure him,
And pull'd the law upon you.
ANGELO.   'Tis one thing to be tempted, Escalus,
Another thing to fall. I not deny
(20) The jury, passing on the prisoner's life,
May in the sworn twelve have a thief or two
Guiltier than him they try. What's open made to justice,
That justice seizes. What knows the laws
That thieves do pass on thieves? 'Tis very pregnant,
(25) The jewel that we find, we stoop and take't,
Because we see it; but what we do not see
We tread upon, and never think of it.
You may not so extenuate his offence
For I have had such faults; but rather tell me,
(30) When I, that censure him, do so offend,
Let mine own judgment pattern out my death,
And nothing come in partial. Sir, he must die.
ESCALUS.   Be it as your wisdom will.

Measure for Measure
by William Shakespeare

QUESTIONS ABOUT MEANING

1. In Selection One, the purpose of the passage is to describe a situation in which
   (A) Lady Rowena is a beautiful Norman woman
   (B) Prince John has no control over the Saxons
   (C) Lady Rowena refuses to see Prince John
   (D) a Saxon heiress is given to a Norman for marriage as a favor from Prince John
   (E) the Saxons and Normans are at war

2. The main idea of the first paragraph in Selection Two is that
   (A) art is dead
   (B) artists cater to social classes while succumbing to commercial abuse
   (C) the machine will inevitably give way to hand-crafted art
   (D) hell-smoke of factories proves the nature of the machine
   (E) the machine represents change that is resisted by artists

3. Selection Three's subject can be stated as
   (A) an angry departure
   (B) dying love
   (C) a reversal of fortunes
   (D) resisting change
   (E) love and hate

4. Of the ideas listed, which one defines the subject of Selection Four?
   (A) Time's destroying power
   (B) Eternal happiness
   (C) Eternity over Time
   (D) Time as a race
   (E) Time as a friend

5. The drama of the fifth selection can be summarized as
   (A) two brothers discussing legal theories
   (B) the Deputy defending an accused man
   (C) Escalus defending himself against false charges
   (D) an argument in which a Justice accuses the Deputy of a crime
   (E) a Justice defending an accused man to the Deputy

QUESTIONS ABOUT FORM

1. In Selection One, how does Fitzurse know that Lady Rowena was upset?
   (A) Inductive reasoning
   (B) Deductive reasoning
   (C) Process analysis
   (D) Analogy
   (E) Cause-and-effect

2. The speech in Selection Two includes elements of
   (A) chronology, problem-solving, and climax
   (B) chronology, persuasion, and spatial sequence
   (C) persuasion, criticism, and definition
   (D) deduction, climax, and narration
   (E) narration, definition, and persuasion

*3. In the Selection Three poem, what is the role of lines 13–14 to the poem as a whole?
   (A) They summarize that the speaker really no longer is in love.
   (B) They imply that the speaker is still in love.
   (C) They mourn the death of love.
   (D) They establish that death and love are synonymous.
   (E) They reinforce the speaker's determination to end the relationship.

4. In the fourth selection, line 11 contains a change in the poem's
   (A) voice
   (B) tone
   (C) subject
   (D) rhyme scheme
   (E) imagery

5. What happens as a result of the change of rhythm of "Ay, but yet" in line 5 of the fifth selection?
   (A) It breaks the monotony of the passage.
   (B) It echoes the rhythm of line 9.
   (C) It threatens the unity of the dialogue.
   (D) It emphasizes the speaker's contrasting attitude.
   (E) It reinforces Angelo's point.

* Note concerning Practice Set C, Selection Three, question 3 on form:

Your knowledge of form is tremendously valuable in these types of questions. This sonnet has an abab cdcd efef gg pattern. As previously discussed, the rhyme scheme alone is a clue: the poem is divided into four parts. Probably each part will be a progression of thought with the last couplet being perhaps a summary or perhaps a reversal. In lines 1–4 a paraphrase reveals that the speaker has been in a love relationship that is ending. The speaker's attitude? Defiant? Angry? Perhaps resentful? Lines 5–8 indicate that he does not want to let on that they were ever in love. In lines 9–12 he very dramatically personifies love, passion, faith, and innocence as they die. The reader can anticipate in the final couplet a significant point—either confirmation of the attitude he has projected so far or a reversal.

Now if thou would'st, when all have given him over,
From death to life thou might'st him yet recover.

Who is "him?" Personified love—the same love that is dying in lines 9–12. The speaker, however, says (in paraphrase), you (the person ending the relationship) can make love "recover." Now look at the answer choices. Obviously this is a reversal rather than a summary, so answer A is not correct. Answers C, D, and E also do not reflect the meaning of the couplet. But answer B—the lines imply that the speaker is still in love—can be justified, because he has given the object of his love the power to bring love back into being.

How else might the ways form contributes to meaning be questioned in this poem?

- Central contrasts, such as "death" (lines 9–12) and "life" (line 14), "cancel" (line 5) and "recover" (line 14), and so forth.
- Sequence, such as "part" (line 1) to "cancel" (line 5) to "death" (line 11) to "recover" (line 14) emphasize a progression from hopelessness to hope.

QUESTIONS ABOUT NARRATIVE VOICE

1. Prince John's view of Lady Rowena and the Saxons in Selection One can be described as the attitude of one who is
   (A) easily offended
   (B) deeply sentimental
   (C) used to a position of authority
   (D) on the defensive
   (E) willing to accommodate for the needs of others

2. The speaker views "the poor artist" (line 23 in Selection Two) with an attitude that is
   (A) directly disapproving
   (B) gently satirical
   (C) exaggerated in its criticism
   (D) unconventional in its intensity
   (E) sentimental

3. The context of the Selection Three poem reveals that the speaker ("I") is
   (A) a social outcast
   (B) an unfaithful lover
   (C) an indifferent friend
   (D) a close, personal friend
   (E) a rejected lover

4. In the Selection Four poem, the speaker's attitude toward "the supreme Throne" (line 17) is expressed in terms that are
   (A) worshipful
   (B) unrelenting
   (C) fearful
   (D) defensive
   (E) reluctant

5. In Selection Five, Angelo's attitude has qualities that make him seem
   (A) irresponsible
   (B) unyielding
   (C) ambitious
   (D) contemptuous
   (E) sentimental

QUESTIONS ABOUT TONE

1. In the first selection, De Bracy perceives Prince John's tone when offering him a Saxon bride as
   (A) congenial
   (B) condescending
   (C) facetious
   (D) amusing
   (E) defensive

2. The following statements are accurate of Selection Two EXCEPT that it cannot be said that its tone
   (A) toward artists is critical
   (B) toward artists is somewhat mocking
   (C) toward machines is antagonistic
   (D) is optimistic about machines
   (E) is defensive of machines

3. The speaker's tone in lines 1–8 of the third selection can be seen as
   (A) outraged indignation
   (B) incredulous
   (C) fascinated obsession
   (D) courteous
   (E) defensive pride

4. The speaker's tone in lines 1–2 of the fourth selection has a sound that is
   (A) bitter
   (B) lackluster
   (C) futile
   (D) cajoling
   (E) defiant

5. The tone of Angelo's conclusion in line 32 of the fifth selection has qualities that are
   (A) bitter and suspicious
   (B) infuriated and retributive
   (C) determined and authoritative
   (D) retaliatory and jaundiced
   (E) jealous and hostile

QUESTIONS ABOUT CHARACTER

1. In the second paragraph of the first selection, Lady Rowena's character is revealed as
   (A) scared and cowering in her grief
   (B) indecisive in her grief
   (C) having decorum in her grief
   (D) being complacent in her grief
   (E) being immature in her grief

2. In the second selection, artists are characterized as
   (A) complacent
   (B) unwilling to change
   (C) self-indulgent
   (D) innocent victims
   (E) nonchalant

3. "...you get no more of me" (line 2 of the third selection) makes the speaker's character seem ruled by
   (A) hurt pride
   (B) hate
   (C) hardness
   (D) an obliging nature
   (E) leniency

4. How does the speaker in the fourth selection characterize "Time?"
   (A) As gluttonous
   (B) As hypocritical
   (C) As bluffing
   (D) As mysterious
   (E) As secretive

5. In Selection Five, Escalus's words show him to be someone who
   (A) is given to flights of fancy
   (B) does not understand logical reasoning
   (C) has not fully considered the ramifications of his position
   (D) uses logical reasoning to present his case
   (E) resists authority and defies the law

QUESTIONS ABOUT USE OF LANGUAGE

1. The literary device used to refer to Lady Rowena in Selection One ("the Queen of Love and Beauty"—lines 4–5) is called a(n)
   (A) epitaph
   (B) euphemism
   (C) synecdoche
   (D) epithet
   (E) metonymy

2. In the second selection, lines 2–6 produce an effect that serves to
   (A) exaggerate the speaker's position
   (B) amplify "art in the grand old sense" (line 2)
   (C) understate the speaker's position
   (D) point out paradoxes in art
   (E) rhetorically question the "handicraft ideal" (line 4)

3. With personified Faith kneeling as Love, Passion, and Innocence die (lines 9–12 in the third selection), the effect is to
   (A) render no hope for Love's survival
   (B) emphasize the speaker's anger
   (C) mark a shift in tone
   (D) assert the power of Love
   (E) imply that the speaker still holds hope of reconciliation

4. In the fourth selection, the direct address in lines 1–10 to personified Time is an example of
   (A) irony
   (B) parody
   (C) apostrophe
   (D) cacophony
   (E) understatement

5. In Selection Five, Angelo makes his point in lines 1–4 by using a(n)
   (A) analogy
   (B) mixed metaphor
   (C) simile
   (D) allusion
   (E) allegory

QUESTIONS ABOUT MEANING(S) IN CONTEXT

1. From the context of the first selection, a "seneschal" (line 25) probably is a(n)
   (A) member of royalty
   (B) vassel
   (C) captured enemy
   (D) agent in charge of the estate
   (E) court jester

2. The "universal educator" in line 19 of the second selection is
   (A) art
   (B) human expression
   (C) idealized art
   (D) greed
   (E) the machine

*3. In the context of the third selection, how can "cleanly" (line 4) be defined?
   I. Completely
   II. In a sportsmanlike manner
   III. Morally pure
   (A) I only
   (B) II only
   (C) III only
   (D) I and II only
   (E) I, II, and III

4. In the fourth selection, "mortal dross" (line 6) probably is a reference to
   (A) spiritual life
   (B) carnal life
   (C) waste matter
   (D) time itself
   (E) worthless character

5. In the fifth selection (lines 22–23), justice seizing on someone occurs because of
   (A) opportunity
   (B) vengeance
   (C) the law only
   (D) a sense of fairness
   (E) equal rights

* Note concerning Set C, Selection Three, question 3 on Meanings of Words, Phrases, and Lines in Context:

Not only does "cleanly" refer to (I) completely, it also connotatively means in a sportsmanlike manner (II) because line 5 refers to shaking hands—an act of two opponents after a contest—and means "morally pure" (III) because, again in line 5, the speaker cancels vows.

ANSWER KEY: INTERPRETIVE SKILL PRACTICE SETS

PRACTICE SET A

QUESTIONS ABOUT MEANING
1. B 2. D 3. D 4. C 5. A

QUESTIONS ABOUT FORM
1. E 2. C 3. C 4. B 5. D

QUESTIONS ABOUT NARRATIVE VOICE
1. A 2. C 3. E 4. B 5. D

QUESTIONS ABOUT TONE
1. E 2. B 3. A 4. C 5. D

QUESTIONS ABOUT CHARACTER
1. A 2. E 3. C 4. C 5. B

QUESTIONS ABOUT USE OF LANGUAGE
1. B 2. D 3. C 4. C 5. A

QUESTIONS ABOUT MEANINGS OF WORDS, PHRASES, AND LINES IN CONTEXT
1. D 2. B 3. D 4. E 5. A

PRACTICE SET B

QUESTIONS ABOUT MEANING
1. C 2. A 3. B 4. B 5. D

QUESTIONS ABOUT FORM
1. B 2. B 3. C 4. A 5. E

QUESTIONS ABOUT NARRATIVE VOICE
1. B 2. C 3. A 4. E 5. D

QUESTIONS ABOUT TONE
1. D 2. A 3. C 4. D 5. B

QUESTIONS ABOUT CHARACTER
1. C 2. D 3. D 4. B 5. E

QUESTIONS ABOUT USE OF LANGUAGE
1. C 2. B 3. C 4. A 5. E

QUESTIONS ABOUT MEANINGS OF WORDS, PHRASES, AND LINES IN CONTEXT
1. C 2. D 3. B 4. D 5. A

PRACTICE SET C

QUESTIONS ABOUT MEANING
1. D 2. E 3. B 4. C 5. E

QUESTIONS ABOUT FORM
1. A 2. C 3. B 4. B 5. D

QUESTIONS ABOUT NARRATIVE VOICE
1. C 2. B 3. E 4. A 5. B

QUESTIONS ABOUT TONE
1. A 2. C 3. E 4. E 5. C

QUESTIONS ABOUT CHARACTER
1. C 2. B 3. A 4. A 5. D

QUESTIONS ABOUT USE OF LANGUAGE
1. D 2. B 3. E 4. C 5. A

QUESTIONS ABOUT MEANING(S) IN CONTEXT
1. D 2. E 3. E 4. B 5. A

PART V

PRACTICE TESTS

ANSWER SHEET FOR PRACTICE TEST ONE

1. (A) (B) (C) (D) (E)
2. (A) (B) (C) (D) (E)
3. (A) (B) (C) (D) (E)
4. (A) (B) (C) (D) (E)
5. (A) (B) (C) (D) (E)
6. (A) (B) (C) (D) (E)
7. (A) (B) (C) (D) (E)
8. (A) (B) (C) (D) (E)
9. (A) (B) (C) (D) (E)
10. (A) (B) (C) (D) (E)
11. (A) (B) (C) (D) (E)
12. (A) (B) (C) (D) (E)
13. (A) (B) (C) (D) (E)
14. (A) (B) (C) (D) (E)
15. (A) (B) (C) (D) (E)
16. (A) (B) (C) (D) (E)
17. (A) (B) (C) (D) (E)
18. (A) (B) (C) (D) (E)
19. (A) (B) (C) (D) (E)
20. (A) (B) (C) (D) (E)

21. (A) (B) (C) (D) (E)
22. (A) (B) (C) (D) (E)
23. (A) (B) (C) (D) (E)
24. (A) (B) (C) (D) (E)
25. (A) (B) (C) (D) (E)
26. (A) (B) (C) (D) (E)
27. (A) (B) (C) (D) (E)
28. (A) (B) (C) (D) (E)
29. (A) (B) (C) (D) (E)
30. (A) (B) (C) (D) (E)
31. (A) (B) (C) (D) (E)
32. (A) (B) (C) (D) (E)
33. (A) (B) (C) (D) (E)
34. (A) (B) (C) (D) (E)
35. (A) (B) (C) (D) (E)
36. (A) (B) (C) (D) (E)
37. (A) (B) (C) (D) (E)
38. (A) (B) (C) (D) (E)
39. (A) (B) (C) (D) (E)
40. (A) (B) (C) (D) (E)

41. (A) (B) (C) (D) (E)
42. (A) (B) (C) (D) (E)
43. (A) (B) (C) (D) (E)
44. (A) (B) (C) (D) (E)
45. (A) (B) (C) (D) (E)
46. (A) (B) (C) (D) (E)
47. (A) (B) (C) (D) (E)
48. (A) (B) (C) (D) (E)
49. (A) (B) (C) (D) (E)
50. (A) (B) (C) (D) (E)
51. (A) (B) (C) (D) (E)
52. (A) (B) (C) (D) (E)
53. (A) (B) (C) (D) (E)
54. (A) (B) (C) (D) (E)
55. (A) (B) (C) (D) (E)
56. (A) (B) (C) (D) (E)
57. (A) (B) (C) (D) (E)
58. (A) (B) (C) (D) (E)
59. (A) (B) (C) (D) (E)
60. (A) (B) (C) (D) (E)

Practice Test One

Directions: The following questions test your understanding of several literary selections. Read each passage or poem and the questions that follow it. Select the best answer choice for each question by blackening the matching oval on your answer sheet. **Special attention should be given to questions containing the following words: EXCEPT, LEAST, NOT.**

Questions 1–8 are based on the following passage.

No doubt it was having a strong effect on
him as he walked to Lowick. Fred's light
hopeful nature had perhaps never had so
Line much of a bruise as from this suggestion
(5)   that if he had been out of the way Mary
might have made a thoroughly good match.
Also he was piqued that he had been what
he called such a stupid lout as to ask that
intervention from Mr Farebrother. But it was
(10) not in a lover's nature—it was not in Fred's—
that the new anxiety raised about Mary's
feeling should not surmount every other.
Notwithstanding his trust in Mr
Farebrother's generosity, notwithstanding
(15) what Mary had said to him, Fred could not
help feeling he had a rival: it was a new
consciousness, and he objected to it
extremely, not being in the least ready to
give up Mary for her good, being ready
(20) rather to fight for her with any man
whatsoever. But the fighting with Mr
Farebrother must be of a metaphorical kind,
which was much more difficult to Fred than
the muscular. Certainly this experience was
(25) a discipline for Fred hardly less sharp than
his disappointment about his uncle's will.
The iron had not entered his soul, but he
had begun to imagine what the sharp edge
would be. It did not once occur to Fred that
(30) Mrs Garth might be mistaken about Mr
Farebrother, but he suspected that she might
be wrong about Mary. Mary had been
staying at the parsonage lately, and her
mother might know very little of what had
(35) been passing in her mind.

Middlemarch
by George Eliot

1. Lines 27–32 imply that
   (A) Fred dislikes Mary
   (B) Fred does not trust Mr. Farebrother
   (C) Fred disliked his late uncle
   (D) Mrs. Garth gossiped about Mary and Mr. Farebrother
   (E) Mary is Mr. Farebrother's sister

2. The narrator's comments in lines 15–21 make Fred seem to be
   (A) unsympathetic and jubilant
   (B) jealous and selfish
   (C) jealous and enraptured
   (D) comfortless and irritating
   (E) indulgent and forbearant

3. The phrase "metaphorical kind" (line 22) conveys the idea that the fight is
   (A) illusionary
   (B) allegorical
   (C) undisciplined
   (D) physical
   (E) mental

4. The statement in lines 25–26 that Fred was disappointed about his uncle's will is intended as
   (A) an observation concerning Fred's character
   (B) an allusion to a large cash settlement
   (C) an implication concerning Fred's financial status
   (D) an inference concerning the value of discipline
   (E) a conclusion concerning his uncle's character

5. The "bruise" in line 4 contextually denotes
   (A) injured flesh
   (B) a beating
   (C) injured feelings
   (D) verbal abuse
   (E) physical abuse

6. Lines 27–29 contain a figure of speech known as
   (A) a simile
   (B) a metaphor
   (C) alliteration
   (D) literary allusion
   (E) personification

7. As the words "light hopeful nature" (lines 2–3), "a stupid lout" (line 8), "a lover's nature" (line 10), and "a new consciousness" (lines 16–17) are used, they
   (A) imply that Fred's character is being challenged
   (B) suggest that Fred is deceitful
   (C) are bitterly ironic in tone
   (D) reinforce the metaphorical aspects of Fred's nature
   (E) indicate that Fred is not really in love

8. An accurate inference from the passage would be that Fred is
   (A) self-sacrificial
   (B) a stupid lout
   (C) a conscientious lover
   (D) a fortune seeker
   (E) somewhat egotistical

Questions 9–21 are based on the following poem.

A Bed of Forget-Me-Nots

Is love so prone to change and rot
We are fain to rear Forget-me-not
By measure in a garden-plot?—

Line I love its growth at large and free
(5)   By untrod path and unlopped tree,
Or nodding by the unpruned hedge,
Or on the water's dangerous edge
Where flags and meadowsweet blow rank
With rushes on the quaking bank.

(10) Love is not taught in learning's school,
Love is not parcelled out by rule:
Hath curb or call an answer got?—
So free must be Forget-me-not.
Give me the flame no dampness dulls,
(15) The passion of the instinctive pulse,
Love steadfast as a fixèd star,
Tender as doves with nestlings are,
More large than time, more strong than death:
This all creation travails of—
(20) She groans not for a passing breath—
This is Forget-me-not and Love.

                          by Christina Rossetti

9. The poem's main subject is concerned with the
   (A) brevity of love
   (B) nature of love
   (C) growing of Forget-me-nots
   (D) death of love
   (E) freedom of flower gardens

10. Contextually, "flags" in line 8 are
    (A) weeds
    (B) national symbols
    (C) flowers
    (D) stones
    (E) shaped gardens

11. "Rank" can have several connotative and denotative meanings. How can it be understood as used in line 8?
    I. Bad taste
    II. Bad smell
    III. Growing vigorously
    IV. In rows
    (A) I only
    (B) II only
    (C) III only
    (D) I and II only
    (E) I, II, and IV only

12. In line 12, "curb" represents which of the following?
    I. Restraint
    II. An edging or border
    III. A market
    (A) I only
    (B) II only
    (C) III only
    (D) I and II only
    (E) I, II, and III

13. What is the purpose of lines 1–3 as they relate to the rest of the poem?
    (A) They set a mocking tone for the poem.
    (B) They reveal the speaker's sense of insecurity.
    (C) They emphasize the poem's dismal tone.
    (D) They introduce the analogy that is the basis of the poem.
    (E) They reinforce the passionate nature of love.

14. The speaker compares Forget-me-nots and
    (A) flags
    (B) garden-plots
    (C) death
    (D) school
    (E) love

15. In what way do lines 4–9 relate to lines 10–21?
    (A) They are allusional.
    (B) They are metaphorical.
    (C) They reflect extreme pessimism.
    (D) They reinforce a sense of dispassionate sympathy.
    (E) They are allegorical.

16. The speaker's feeling toward love is that
    (A) love is short-lived
    (B) love can be learned
    (C) love should be unrestrained
    (D) love is weak and fragile
    (E) love is disciplined

17. The questions asked in lines 1–3 and line 12 can be considered
    (A) insolent
    (B) hostile
    (C) ambivalent
    (D) indifferent
    (E) rhetorical

18. In the context of the poem, the opposition of "untrod," "unlopped," and "unpruned" (lines 5–6) to "school," "rule," and "curb" (lines 10–12) emphasizes that
    (A) gardens can be unkempt
    (B) love is eternal
    (C) flowers are wild
    (D) love is free
    (E) love can be controlled

19. In line 16, which of these literary devices is used?
    (A) Metaphor
    (B) Simile
    (C) Personification
    (D) Understatement
    (E) Synaesthesia

20. In the first stanza, "garden-plot" (line 3) becomes for the speaker which of the representations listed below?
    (A) A figure for confinement
    (B) A symbol of beauty
    (C) A place to raise Forget-me-nots
    (D) A place of change
    (E) An imaginative place for love to exist

21. The speaker implies in lines 1–3 that we attempt to structure love to
    (A) prevent its destruction
    (B) capture its joy
    (C) measure its impact
    (D) control its effects
    (E) forget its measure

Questions 22–28 are based on the following passage.

"See! Master Coffin," cried the lieutenant, pointing out the object to his cockswain as they glided by it, "the shovel-nosed gentlemen are regaling daintily; you
(5) have neglected the Christian's duty of burying your dead."

The old seaman cast a melancholy look at the dead whale, and replied:

"If I had the creature in Boston Bay, or
(10) on the Sandy Point of Munny Moy, 'twould be the making of me! But riches and honor are for the great and the larned, and there's nothing left for poor Tom Coffin to

do, but to veer and haul on his own rolling
(15) tackle, that he may ride out the rest of the
gale of life without springing any of his old
spars."

"How now, Long Tom!" cried the officer;
"these rocks and cliffs will shipwreck you on
(20) the shoals of poetry yet; you grow
sentimental!"

"Them rocks might wrack any vessel that
struck them," said the literal cockswain;
"and as for poetry, I wants none better
(25) than the good old song of Captain Kidd;
but it's enough to raise solemn thoughts in a
Cape Poge Indian, to see an eighty-barrel
whale devoured by sharks—'tis an awful
waste of property! I've seen the death of
(30) two hundred of the creaters, though it
seems to keep the rations of poor old Tom
as short as ever."

The cockswain walked aft, while the
vessel was passing the whale, and seating
(35) himself on the taffrail, with his face resting
gloomily on his bony hand, he fastened his
eyes on the object of his solicitude, and
continued to gaze at it with melancholy
regret, while it was to be seen glistening in
(40) the sunbeams, as it rolled its glittering side
of white into the air, or the rays fell
unreflected on the black and rougher coat
of the back of the monster. In the meantime,
the navigators diligently pursued their way
(45) for the haven we have mentioned, into
which they steered with every appearance
of the fearlessness of friends, and the
exultation of conquerors.

A few eager and gratified spectators
(50) lined the edges of the small bay, and
Barnstable concluded his arrangement for
deceiving the enemy, by admonishing his
crew that they were now about to enter on
a service that would require their utmost
(55) intrepidity and sagacity.

The Pilot
by James Fenimore Cooper

22. Tom Coffin does not get rich from this whale
because
(A) he is too depressed
(B) he lacks sufficient line and tackle
(C) he is not interested in wealth
(D) he is misled by the lieutenant
(E) he is too far from a trading center

23. Tom blames his situation in part on
(A) the shovel-nosed gentleman
(B) his lack of position and education
(C) the lieutenant
(D) the whale
(E) Captain Kidd

24. Tom compares himself in lines 13–17 to
(A) fishing tackle
(B) a ship in a storm
(C) the whale
(D) a whaling ship at work
(E) Boston Bay

25. When the officer refers to "these rocks and
cliffs" (line 19), he means that
(A) dangerous land formations lie ahead
(B) the ship is about to wreck
(C) there are setbacks in Tom's life
(D) they are going to hit a whale
(E) the ship is sinking

26. The "shovel-nosed gentlemen" in lines 3–4 are
(A) the ship's crew
(B) Tom's friends
(C) sharks
(D) visiting royalty
(E) the ship's officers

27. In what tone of voice does the lieutenant say
"you have neglected the Christian's duty of
burying your dead" (lines 5–6)?
(A) Patronizing mockery
(B) Sarcastic teasing
(C) Accusatory wrath
(D) Kind insistence
(E) Aggressive hostility

28. Tom's misunderstanding (lines 22–23) of the officer's remark (lines 18–21) is ironic because
    (A) Tom did not get to salvage the whale
    (B) the boat was already shipwrecked
    (C) Tom was not really sentimental
    (D) the officer lacked insight into Tom's meaning
    (E) Tom, himself, had been speaking metaphorically

Questions 29–37 are based on the following poem.

Come Down, O Maid

"Come down, O maid, from yonder
   mountain height.
What pleasure lives in height (the shepherd
   sang),
In height and cold, the splendor of the hills?
But cease to move so near the heavens and
Line   cease
(5) To glide a sunbeam by the blasted pine,
To sit a star upon the sparkling spire;
And come, for Love is of the valley, come,
For Love is of the valley, come thou down
And find him; by the happy threshold, he,
(10) Or hand in hand with Plenty in the maize,
Or red with spirted purple of the vats,
Or foxlike in the vine; nor cares to walk
With Death and Morning on the Silver
   Horns,
Nor wilt thou snare him in the white ravine,
(15) Nor find him dropped upon the firths of ice,
That huddling slant in furrow-cloven falls
To roll the torrent out of dusky doors.
But follow; let the torrent dance thee down
To find him in the valley; let the wild
(20) Lean-headed eagles yelp alone, and leave
The monstrous ledges there to slope, and
   spill
Their thousand wreaths of dangling water-
   smoke,
That like a broken purpose waste in air.
So waste not thou, but come; for all the
   vales
(25) Await thee; azure pillars of the hearth
Arise to thee; the children call, and I
Thy shepherd pipe, and sweet is every
   sound,

Sweeter thy voice, but every sound is sweet;
Myriads of rivulets hurrying thro' the lawn,
(30) The moan of doves in immemorial elms,
And murmuring of innumerable bees."

          by Alfred, Lord Tennyson

29. The genre of this poem is called
    (A) a pastoral love lyric
    (B) a pastoral love epic
    (C) a didactic narrative
    (D) a dramatic monologue
    (E) a pastoral elegy

30. The poem is written in
    (A) ballad stanza
    (B) blank verse
    (C) couplets
    (D) forced rhyme
    (E) sonnet form

31. The speaker in the poem can be identified through context as
    (A) a young girl
    (B) the mountain
    (C) a shepherd
    (D) the hills
    (E) Love

32. Which of the following is NOT personified in the poem?
    (A) Love
    (B) Plenty
    (C) Silver Horns
    (D) Death
    (E) Morning

33. The tone of the speaker's question in lines 2–3 in the context of the poem is
    (A) condemning
    (B) didactic
    (C) impetuous
    (D) explosive
    (E) conciliatory

34. Lines 7–19 refer to love figuratively, making it appear as
    (A) a friend of death
    (B) only a visitor to the mountain
    (C) an angry force in the mountain
    (D) someone living happily in the valley
    (E) the victim of the mountain

35. The speaker sees the "mountain height" (line 1) and the "valley" (line 7) as symbolic of all the following concepts EXCEPT
    (A) lack of love and love
    (B) unhappiness and happiness
    (C) death and life
    (D) day and night
    (E) cold and warmth

36. In this poem, what is the role of the mountain?
    I. A symbol of aloofness
    II. A metaphor of snowy climates
    III. The abstract image of the maid
    (A) I only
    (B) II only
    (C) III only
    (D) I and III only
    (E) I, II, and III

37. The poem's meaning is discerned through several elements of opposition; however, which of the following pairs of words does NOT correctly reflect these elements?
    (A) "height" (line 1) and "down" (line 8)
    (B) "maid" (line 1) and "height" (line 2)
    (C) "blasted" (line 5) and "Plenty" (line 10)
    (D) "white" (line 14) and "red" (line 11)
    (E) "eagles" (line 20) and "children" (line 26)

Questions 38–42 are based on the following passage.

Dream delivers us to dream, and there is no end to illusion. Life is a train of moods like a string of beads, and as we pass
(Line) through them they prove to be many-
(5) colored lenses which paint the world their own hue, and each shows only what lies in its focus. From the mountain you see the mountain. We animate what we can, and we see only what we animate. Nature and
(10) books belong to the eyes that see them. It depends on the mood of the man whether he shall see the sunset or the fine poem. There are always sunsets, and there is always genius; but only a few hours so
(15) serene that we can relish nature or criticism. The more or less depends on structure or temperament. Temperament is the iron wire on which the beads are strung. Of what use

is fortune or talent to a cold and defective
(20) nature? Who cares what sensibility or discrimination a man has at some time shown, if he falls asleep in his chair? or if he laugh and giggle? or if he apologize? or is infected with egotism? or thinks of his
(25) dollar?

"Experience"
by Ralph Waldo Emerson

38. The speaker's use of language in this passage projects a tone that is
    (A) hostile
    (B) placating
    (C) contemplative
    (D) antagonistic
    (E) arrogant

39. In this passage, a string of beads is a figuratively used
    (A) symbol of illusions
    (B) vehicle to explain the relationship of temperament to moods
    (C) vehicle to illustrate temperament's role in dreams
    (D) literary allusion
    (E) reference to the events of life

40. According to the passage, how we see the world is determined by
    (A) our dreams
    (B) nature
    (C) books
    (D) criticism
    (E) our moods

41. According to the passage, which of the following gives value to fortunes or talent?
    (A) Dreams
    (B) Moods
    (C) Nature
    (D) Animations
    (E) Temperament

42. The speaker's use of rhetorical questions emphasizes
    (A) the importance of a defective nature
    (B) his own sense of disillusionment
    (C) the importance of temperament
    (D) the dreamlike quality of life
    (E) his argumentative tone

Questions 43–53 are based on the following poem.

Devoid of Reason

Devoid of reason, thrall to foolish ire,
I walk and chase a savage fairy still,
Now near the flood, straight on the
   mounting hill,
Now midst the woods of youth, and vain
Line   desire.
(5) For leash I bear a cord of careful grief;
For brach I lead an overforward mind;
My hounds are thoughts, and rage
   despairing blind,
Pain, cruelty, and care without relief.
But they, perceiving that my swift pursuit
(10) My flying fairy cannot overtake,
With open mouths their prey on me do
   make,
Like hungry hounds that lately lost their suit,
And full of fury on their master feed,
To hasten on my hapless death with speed.

by Thomas Lodge

43. Using the more specific word "hounds" (line 7) rather than the more general word "dogs" has which of these effects?
(A) Emphasizes that they hunt prey
(B) Illustrates the speaker's sense of drama
(C) Varies the tone of the poem
(D) Symbolizes all predators
(E) Reinforces a sense of grief

44. The hounds in the poem are best set forth as
(A) a savage fairy
(B) the speaker's angry thoughts
(C) the speaker's troubled thoughts
(D) death
(E) reason

45. The meaning of "an overforward mind" (line 6) can be seen in the paraphrase
(A) mentally unstable
(B) a mind ahead of its time
(C) precocious
(D) overactive thoughts
(E) politically active

46. The phrase "thrall to foolish ire" (line 1), as used in the poem, is mirrored by which of these phrases?
(A) Seeking fool's gold
(B) A slave to rash anger
(C) Desiring vengeance
(D) Escaped from an asylum
(E) A man too angry to think clearly

47. The central argument of the poem is that
(A) the speaker is insane
(B) the speaker is a sportsman
(C) an angry enemy is killing the speaker
(D) anger is self-destructive
(E) anger is therapeutic

48. By considering the poem in its entirety, the reader should view the speaker's attitude toward the fairy as
(A) frenzied
(B) insolent
(C) reverential
(D) derisive
(E) laudable

49. The role of lines 13–14 in terms of the rest of the poem can be summarized by which of these statements?
(A) They intensify the speaker's sense of justice.
(B) They summarize the irony of the speaker's situation.
(C) They signal a departure from the subject.
(D) They intensify the falsity of the speaker's words.
(E) They threaten the position of the fairy established in lines 2 and 10.

50. Lines 13–14 contain which of the following phonic devices?
(A) Echo rhyme
(B) Eye rhyme
(C) Imperfect rhyme
(D) Onomatopoeia
(E) Alliteration

51. Lines 9–10 are pivotal to the meaning of the poem because which of the following happens?
   (A) Anger is made more intense.
   (B) The speaker's position changes from attacker to victim.
   (C) The hounds become real.
   (D) The speaker's position changes from fear to anger.
   (E) The fairy is caught.

52. The meaning of the poem is structurally contrasted between lines 1–8 and lines 9–14. This contrast is NOT seen in the words
   (A) "chase" (line 2) and "cannot overtake" (line 10)
   (B) "I lead" (line 6) and "they, perceiving" (line 9)
   (C) "foolish ire" (line 1) and "hapless death" (line 14)
   (D) "savage fairy" (line 2) and "hungry hounds" (line 12)
   (E) "flood" (line 3) and "speed" (line 14)

53. The hounds' attack in lines 9–14 is symbolically ironic because
   (A) the hounds are not really dogs
   (B) dogs do not really chase fairies
   (C) hunting dogs seldom turn on their masters
   (D) the speaker has already confessed to his lack of reason
   (E) the speaker's own angry thoughts are destroying him

Questions 54–60 are based on the following passage.

Mrs Moorland was a very good woman, and wished to see her children every thing they ought to be; but her time was so much occupied in lying-in and teaching the little
(5) ones, that her elder daughters were inevitably left to shift for themselves; and it was not very wonderful that Catherine, who had by nature nothing heroic about her, should prefer cricket, base ball, riding on
(10) horseback, and running about the country at the age of fourteen, to books—or at least books of information—for, provided that nothing like useful knowledge could be gained from them, provided they were all
(15) story and no reflection, she had never any objection to books at all. But from fifteen to seventeen she was in training for a heroine; she read all such works as heroines must read to supply their memories with those
(20) quotations which are so serviceable and so soothing in the vicissitudes of their eventful lives.

From Pope, she learnt to censure those who
'bear about the mockery of woe.'
(25) From Gray, that
'Many a flower is born to blush unseen.
'And waste its fragrance on the desert air.'

From Thompson, that
—'It is a delightful task
(30) 'To teach the young idea how to shoot.'

And from Shakespeare she gained a great store of information—amongst the rest, that
—'Trifles light as air,
(35) 'Are, to the jealous, confirmation strong,
'As proofs of Holy Writ.'

That
'The poor beetle, which we tread upon,
'In corporal sufferance feels a pang as great
(40) 'As when a giant dies.'

And that a young woman in love always looks
—'like Patience on a monument
'Smiling at Grief.'

Northanger Abbey
Jane Austen

54. That Mrs. Moorland's time "was so much occu-
pied in lying-in and teaching the little ones"
(lines 3–5) supports the idea that
(A) education was reserved for male children
(B) she is rearing many children
(C) she was reclusive
(D) she avoided adult company
(E) that children were seen and not heard

55. As used in lines 6–7, "not very wonderful"
means
(A) awesome
(B) to be wondered at
(C) to be expected
(D) terrible
(E) the object of wonder

56. The metaphor in lines 29–30 implies thinking
with
(A) accuracy
(B) speed
(C) youthful vigor
(D) education
(E) delight

57. As described in this passage in lines 7–16,
Catherine is
(A) a scholar
(B) morose
(C) perfunctory
(D) a tomboy
(E) quarrelsome

58. According to the passage, before the age of
fifteen, Catherine chose books that were
(A) "how-to" books
(B) shallow stories
(C) self-help
(D) romances
(E) heroic

59. In its context, who are "those who 'bear about
the mockery of woe'" (lines 23–24)?
 I. People who insult those in grief
 II. People who pretend to be suffering mis-
fortune
 III. People who express grief through
laughter
(A) I only
(B) II only
(C) III only
(D) I and III only
(E) I, II, and III

60. Shakespeare's simile in lines 37–40 is a use of
language called the
(A) symbol
(B) rhetorical question
(C) parody
(D) meiosis
(E) hyperbole

ANSWER KEY: PRACTICE TEST ONE

1. D	7. A	13. D	19. B	25. C	31. C	37. B	43. A	49. B	55. C
2. B	8. E	14. E	20. A	26. C	32. C	38. C	44. B	50. E	56. A
3. E	9. B	15. B	21. A	27. B	33. E	39. B	45. D	51. B	57. D
4. A	10. C	16. C	22. E	28. E	34. D	40. E	46. B	52. E	58. B
5. C	11. C	17. E	23. B	29. A	35. D	41. E	47. D	53. E	59. B
6. B	12. D	18. D	24. B	30. B	36. A	42. C	48. A	54. B	60. E

TO OBTAIN YOUR RAW SCORE:

_____ divided by 4 = _____
Total wrong   Score W

_____ minus _____ = _____
Total right   Score W   Score R

Round Score R to the nearest whole
number for the raw score.

HOW DID YOU DO?

55–60 = Excellent
44–54 = Very Good
35–43 = Above Average
23–34 = Average
15–22 = Below Average

EXPLANATIONS: PRACTICE TEST ONE

NOTE: Most practice tests cannot duplicate the content and conditions of the actual Literature Test. Also, the scope and definitions of the literary elements can differ among literary critics; therefore, the rationale behind what constitutes a correct or an incorrect answer choice may vary. Each of these practice tests, however, gives you an opportunity to analyze selections, think critically, and develop your test-taking skills so you can do your personal best on the SAT Subject Test in Literature.

1. **D** Although Fred might no longer trust Mr. Farebrother (line 15), lines 29–32 indicate that Mrs. Garth said things about Mary and Mr. Farebrother that may or may not be true, in other words, gossip.

2. **B** He felt he had a rival (jealous); he would not give her up for her good (selfish).

3. **E** A contrast is made: If the fight is not muscular (physical), it must be mental.

4. **A** The context of this entire selection concerns Fred's character or nature, not his money.

5. **C** Fred's feelings are the context: they are hurt or injured.

6. **B** A knife in the back, a blade in the heart: these are classic metaphors that compare emotional pain caused by others to the pain of a knife blade.

7. **A** Context eliminates B, C, and D. Does Fred *really* love Mary? Perhaps not, but he thinks he is "in love" enough to fight for her (E). His "light hopeful nature," however, is being challenged with feelings of jealousy, insecurity, and pain.

8. **E** Context contradicts or does not support answer choices A—D. Although not directly stated, the overall tone of the passage indicates that Fred's pride is hurt, implying that he is somewhat egotistical.

9. **B** The entire poem is an extended analogy, comparing love and Forget-me-nots (line 21). In this comparison, love's brevity (line 1), death (line 18), and freedom (line 11) are mentioned, but taken together as a whole, the subject is the nature of love.

10. **C** You may not know that the iris flower is called a flag; however, context eliminates B, D, and E. In company with Forget-me-nots, meadowsweet, and rushes, flags are flowers, not weeds.

11. **C** Again, context provides the answer. A bad taste or smell would ruin the beauty described. To grow "in rows" (IV) contradicts growing free.

12. **D** A curb borders a flower bed, restraining growth.

13. **D** By eliminating the obviously incorrect answers, D and E remain. Although the speaker is passionate about her subject, this rhetorical question does not address the passion of love. It does, however, establish the comparison of growing love to raising Forget-me-nots.

14. **E** Note lines 1–3, 10–14, and 21: "Love is not taught…, not parcelled out by rule:… So free must be Forget-me-not."

15. **B** Lines 4–9 describe Forget-me-nots, lines 10–21, love. Line 13 is pivotal to the metaphoric or implied comparison of love to Forget-me-nots.

16. **C** Notice lines 10–11: The speaker believes love is not taught and is not subject to rules; both love and Forget-me-nots should grow "free" without restraints.

17. **E** These questions are rhetorical by definition. The speaker is making a point, not expecting an answer.

18. **D** The central contrast is restraint (lines 10–12) versus unrestraint (lines 5–6) of flowers and love. The emphasis of this contrast supports the speaker's view that love is and should be free of restraints.

19. **B** A simile makes a comparison using "like" or "as."

20. **A** She loves "its growth at large and free" (line 4), not "By measure" (line 3).

Note: Technically, the speaker says that Forget-me-nots should be unrestrained like love is unrestrained, making love (an abstract concept) the vehicle and flowers (a concrete thing) the tenor. Usually the concrete expression is used to describe an abstract idea. This reversal is a way to strengthen her argument, an assumption that love naturally should be unrestrained.

21. **A** In line 1, "Change and rot" indicate destruction, so we raise flowers (or figuratively love) in a garden-plot (or restrained environment).

22. **E** That if he were in Boston Bay, he would get rich from the whale (lines 8–10) implies that he is too far from a port.

23. **B** He claims "riches and honor are for the great and the larned," not for him (lines 11–12).

24. **B** A ship has tackle or rigging and spars (to support the sails). The "gale of life" compares his life to a storm.

25. **C** The officer continues Tom's analogy, calling his troubles "rocks and cliffs."

26. **C** Lines 27–29 identify the "shovel-nosed gentlemen" as sharks.

27. **B** Context does not support that the officer is patronizing, wrathful, kind, or hostile. He is teasing Tom in lines 18–21, and personification of the sharks ("shovel-nosed gentlemen") sets a sarcastic tone.

28. **E** The officer's teasing is based on Tom's own use of figurative language in lines 12–17. For Tom to suddenly become "literal" is ironic.

29. **A** This poem does not tell a story (C), is not an elegy or lament over someone's death (E), and obviously is not part of an epic. You might be tempted with answer choice D, but the shepherd (line 27) and subject (love) make it a pastoral love lyric.

30. **B** Blank verse is written in iambic pentameter, with no rhyme scheme.

31. **C** Line 2 identifies the speaker as "the shepherd."

32. **C** Love (line 8) goes "hand in hand with Plenty" (line 10), but does not walk / with Death and Morning (lines 12–13). Where do they walk? "on the Silver Horns" (line 13)

33. **E** The shepherd tries to win over the Maid, echoing "come" in lines 1, 7, and 8.

34. **D** Love is "of the valley" (line 8) and "happy" (line 9).

35. **D** The "mountain height" symbolizes lack of love, because "Love is of the valley" (line 8). It also represents unhappiness because "What pleasure lives in height?" (line 2), implying that the valley symbolizes pleasure or happiness. Line 13 places Death and Morning (a pun: mourning) on the mountain, which represents cold (lines 3 and 15). The sunbeam does "glide… by the blasted pine" on the mountain; however, the valley does not represent the night (D).

36. **A** No comparison (metaphor) is being made, and the mountain is where the maid dwells, not an image of her. The mountain is a traditional symbol representing aloofness: cold.

37. **B** Establishing the central contrast will help you: the contrast of mountains (representing cold, aloofness, death) and the valley (warmth, love, and life). In this poem, the maid is currently on the mountain height.

38. **C** To be contemplative is to look at a subject (idea or thing) intently. The speaker is intently thinking about the role of mood and temperament on our perceptions.

39. **B** The beads are moods (lines 2–3), and the beads (moods) are strung on the iron wire of temperament (lines 17–18).

40. **E** We pass through moods/beads, which "prove to be many-colored lenses which paint the world their own hue" (lines 4–5).

41. **E** Lines 18–20 establish the relationship of temperament (for example, "a cold and defective nature") to the use or value of fortune or talent.

42. **C** The questions in lines 17–23 all relate to man's nature or temperament and its implied effects.

43. **A** The hounds turn the speaker into prey (line 11). Generally, hounds are hunting dogs.

44. **B** Line 7 directly expresses the metaphor. He compares his thoughts to hounds.

45. **D** At first glance, "Devoid of reason" (line 1) supports answer choice A. However, a forward mind is bold, eager, moving ahead. To be overforward would be to have thoughts that race ahead. Note: a "brach" is an archaic word for female hound. Context should lead you to the correct answer, however, without knowing the definition of "brach."

46. **B** Although E fits the poem's general meaning, B contains the synonyms for each word in the phrase.

47. **D** The subject? The speaker's anger. His point? His own angry thoughts, like hounds, are consuming him (line 13).

48. **A** He walks and chases the "savage fairy" (line 2). Later, the metaphor shifts to the hound image in lines 6–7, but his attitude remains constant: he is frenzied almost to the point of insanity to overtake the "flying fairy" (line 10), "Devoid of reason."

49. **B** The concluding couplet of a sonnet often serves to summarize. The irony? He is "master" of his own angry thoughts, yet they are killing him.

50. **E** The repetition of "f" and "h" is alliterative.

51. **B** From lines 1 to 6, the speaker chases, bears, and leads. When he admits he cannot overtake his fairy, he becomes the victim of his angry thoughts (hounds).

52. **E** Neither "flood" nor "speed" relate to the change from attacker in lines 1–8 to victim in lines 9–14.

53. **E** The speaker's condition is an example of situational irony, in which his very own thoughts have become "hungry hounds" that feed on their master.

54. **B** Plural "little ones" (at least two) and plural elder daughters (at least two) in line 5: she has at least four children.

55. **C** One meaning of "wonderful" is "surprising." For something to be "not very surprising" is to be what is expected.

56. **A** To teach someone to shoot is to train the person to take careful, accurate aim.

57. **D** She prefers engaging in activities that traditionally are done by boys, rather than spending her time reading (lines 8–11).

58. **B** Lines 10–16 indicate she would read books of "all story and no reflection."

59. **B** A mocking is an imitation, by definition, often false or vain.

60. **E** Hyperbole is an overstatement or exaggeration: A beetle feels as much pain as when a giant dies.

ANSWER SHEET FOR PRACTICE TEST TWO

1. Ⓐ Ⓑ Ⓒ Ⓓ Ⓔ
2. Ⓐ Ⓑ Ⓒ Ⓓ Ⓔ
3. Ⓐ Ⓑ Ⓒ Ⓓ Ⓔ
4. Ⓐ Ⓑ Ⓒ Ⓓ Ⓔ
5. Ⓐ Ⓑ Ⓒ Ⓓ Ⓔ
6. Ⓐ Ⓑ Ⓒ Ⓓ Ⓔ
7. Ⓐ Ⓑ Ⓒ Ⓓ Ⓔ
8. Ⓐ Ⓑ Ⓒ Ⓓ Ⓔ
9. Ⓐ Ⓑ Ⓒ Ⓓ Ⓔ
10. Ⓐ Ⓑ Ⓒ Ⓓ Ⓔ
11. Ⓐ Ⓑ Ⓒ Ⓓ Ⓔ
12. Ⓐ Ⓑ Ⓒ Ⓓ Ⓔ
13. Ⓐ Ⓑ Ⓒ Ⓓ Ⓔ
14. Ⓐ Ⓑ Ⓒ Ⓓ Ⓔ
15. Ⓐ Ⓑ Ⓒ Ⓓ Ⓔ
16. Ⓐ Ⓑ Ⓒ Ⓓ Ⓔ
17. Ⓐ Ⓑ Ⓒ Ⓓ Ⓔ
18. Ⓐ Ⓑ Ⓒ Ⓓ Ⓔ
19. Ⓐ Ⓑ Ⓒ Ⓓ Ⓔ
20. Ⓐ Ⓑ Ⓒ Ⓓ Ⓔ

21. Ⓐ Ⓑ Ⓒ Ⓓ Ⓔ
22. Ⓐ Ⓑ Ⓒ Ⓓ Ⓔ
23. Ⓐ Ⓑ Ⓒ Ⓓ Ⓔ
24. Ⓐ Ⓑ Ⓒ Ⓓ Ⓔ
25. Ⓐ Ⓑ Ⓒ Ⓓ Ⓔ
26. Ⓐ Ⓑ Ⓒ Ⓓ Ⓔ
27. Ⓐ Ⓑ Ⓒ Ⓓ Ⓔ
28. Ⓐ Ⓑ Ⓒ Ⓓ Ⓔ
29. Ⓐ Ⓑ Ⓒ Ⓓ Ⓔ
30. Ⓐ Ⓑ Ⓒ Ⓓ Ⓔ
31. Ⓐ Ⓑ Ⓒ Ⓓ Ⓔ
32. Ⓐ Ⓑ Ⓒ Ⓓ Ⓔ
33. Ⓐ Ⓑ Ⓒ Ⓓ Ⓔ
34. Ⓐ Ⓑ Ⓒ Ⓓ Ⓔ
35. Ⓐ Ⓑ Ⓒ Ⓓ Ⓔ
36. Ⓐ Ⓑ Ⓒ Ⓓ Ⓔ
37. Ⓐ Ⓑ Ⓒ Ⓓ Ⓔ
38. Ⓐ Ⓑ Ⓒ Ⓓ Ⓔ
39. Ⓐ Ⓑ Ⓒ Ⓓ Ⓔ
40. Ⓐ Ⓑ Ⓒ Ⓓ Ⓔ

41. Ⓐ Ⓑ Ⓒ Ⓓ Ⓔ
42. Ⓐ Ⓑ Ⓒ Ⓓ Ⓔ
43. Ⓐ Ⓑ Ⓒ Ⓓ Ⓔ
44. Ⓐ Ⓑ Ⓒ Ⓓ Ⓔ
45. Ⓐ Ⓑ Ⓒ Ⓓ Ⓔ
46. Ⓐ Ⓑ Ⓒ Ⓓ Ⓔ
47. Ⓐ Ⓑ Ⓒ Ⓓ Ⓔ
48. Ⓐ Ⓑ Ⓒ Ⓓ Ⓔ
49. Ⓐ Ⓑ Ⓒ Ⓓ Ⓔ
50. Ⓐ Ⓑ Ⓒ Ⓓ Ⓔ
51. Ⓐ Ⓑ Ⓒ Ⓓ Ⓔ
52. Ⓐ Ⓑ Ⓒ Ⓓ Ⓔ
53. Ⓐ Ⓑ Ⓒ Ⓓ Ⓔ
54. Ⓐ Ⓑ Ⓒ Ⓓ Ⓔ
55. Ⓐ Ⓑ Ⓒ Ⓓ Ⓔ
56. Ⓐ Ⓑ Ⓒ Ⓓ Ⓔ
57. Ⓐ Ⓑ Ⓒ Ⓓ Ⓔ
58. Ⓐ Ⓑ Ⓒ Ⓓ Ⓔ
59. Ⓐ Ⓑ Ⓒ Ⓓ Ⓔ
60. Ⓐ Ⓑ Ⓒ Ⓓ Ⓔ

Practice Test Two

Directions: The following questions test your understanding of several literary selections. Read each passage or poem and the questions that follow it. Select the best answer choice for each question by blackening the matching oval on your answer sheet. **Special attention should be given to questions containing the following words: EXCEPT, LEAST, NOT.**

Questions 1–12 are based on the following poem.

The Spring

Now that the winter's gone, the earth hath
  lost
Her snow-white robes, and now no more
  the frost
Candies the grass, or casts an icy cream
Line Upon the silver lake or crystal stream;
(5) But the warm sun thaws the benumbèd
  earth,
And makes it tender; gives a sacred birth
To the dead swallow; wakes in hollow tree
The drowsy cuckoo and the humble-bee.
Now do a choir of chirping minstrels bring
(10) In triumph to the world the youthful spring.
The valleys, hills, and woods in rich array
Welcome the coming of the longed-for May.
Now all things smile, only my love doth
  lour;
Nor hath the scalding noonday sun the
  power
(15) To melt that marble ice, which still doth hold
Her heart congealed, and makes her pity
  cold.
The ox, which lately did for shelter fly
Into the stall, doth now securely lie
In open fields; and love no more is made
(20) By the fireside, but in the cooler shade
Amyntas now doth with his Chloris sleep
Under a sycamore, and all things keep
Time with the season; only she doth carry
June in her eyes, in her heart January.

            by Thomas Carew

1. The relationship between "my love" in line 13 and the "earth" in line 1 can be seen in the relationship of
   (A) "grass" (line 3) and "fields" (line 19)
   (B) "ice" (line 15) and "congealed" (line 16)
   (C) "May" (line 12) and "June" (line 24)
   (D) "hollow tree" (line 7) and "shelter" (line 17)
   (E) "cold" (line 16) and "warm" (line 5)

2. Given the context of the poem, the ox most likely went to shelter in lines 17–19 because it
   (A) was startled by the bee in line 8
   (B) was avoiding the "scalding noonday sun" (line 14)
   (C) was fleeing winter storms
   (D) was seeking "cooler shade" (line 20)
   (E) was afraid of the cold-hearted lover

3. In the final line, the incongruity that "she doth carry June in her eyes, in her heart January" implies that
   (A) her looks are deceptive
   (B) she suffers from poor vision
   (C) she really does enjoy spring
   (D) her actions cover a warm personality
   (E) she dislikes cold weather

4. In its context, "smile" (line 13) makes nature seem
   (A) repugnant and loathsome
   (B) jubilant and responsive
   (C) aesthetic and unrestrained
   (D) wary and deliberate
   (E) impetuous and audacious

5. In the context of the poem as a whole, the speaker has an attitude toward "my love" (line 13) that is projecting
   (A) critical discrimination
   (B) cautious prudence
   (C) undaunted daring
   (D) angry impatience
   (E) apprehensive trepidation

6. In lines 14–16, what literary device is used to describe the coldness of her heart?
   (A) Allegory
   (B) Hyperbole
   (C) Caricature
   (D) Simile
   (E) Interior monologue

7. The synaesthesia of "melt that marble ice" appeals to which of the following senses?
   (A) Thermal, tactile, and visual
   (B) Thermal, aural, and kinesthetic
   (C) Gustatory, thermal, and tactile
   (D) Kinesthetic, olfactory, and visual
   (E) Tactile, visual, and gustatory

8. The poem contains a contrast that can be seen in all the following pairs EXCEPT
   (A) "snow-white robes"…"no more the frost" (line 2)
   (B) "the warm sun"…"the benumbèd earth" (line 5)
   (C) "makes"…"gives" (line 6)
   (D) "dead"…"wakes" (line 7)
   (E) "smile"…"lour" (line 13)

9. The poem can be called
   (A) a pastoral sonnet
   (B) a celebration of spring
   (C) an ode to spring
   (D) a comparison and contrast of the seasons
   (E) an expression of frustration by a daunted lover

10. "Dead" (line 7) contextually means all the following EXCEPT
    (A) barren
    (B) unproductive
    (C) cold
    (D) unfruitful
    (E) unerring

11. As used in this poem, June and January (line 24) figuratively represent all the following EXCEPT
    (A) elements of personality
    (B) months of the year
    (C) warmth and coldness
    (D) change and resistance to change
    (E) new growth and dormancy

12. "Candies" in line 3 means
    (A) to preserve
    (B) to sweeten
    (C) to cover
    (D) to crystallize
    (E) to congeal

Questions 13–23 are based on the following passage.

"Are you mad, old man?" demanded Sir Edmund Andros, in loud and harsh tones. "How dare you stay the march of King
Line James's Governor?"
(5)   "I have stayed the march of a King himself, ere now," replied the gray figure, with stern composure. "I am here, Sir Governor, because the cry of an oppressed people hath disturbed me in my secret
(10) place; and beseeching this favor earnestly of the Lord, it was vouchsafed me to appear once again on earth, in the good old cause of his saints. And what speak ye of James? There is no longer a Popish tyrant
(15) on the throne of England, and by tomorrow noon, his name shall be a byword in this very street, where ye would make it a word of terror. Back, thou that wast a Governor, back! With this night thy power is ended—
(20) to-morrow, the prison!—back, lest I foretell the scaffold!"
       The people had been drawing nearer and nearer, and drinking in the words of their champion, who spoke in accents long
(25) disused, like one unaccustomed to converse, except with the dead of many years ago. But his voice stirred their souls. They confronted the soldiers, not wholly without arms, and ready to convert the very stones
(30) of the street into deadly weapons. Sir

Edmund Andros looked at the old man; then he cast his hard and cruel eye over the multitude, and beheld them burning that lurid wrath, so difficult to kindle or to (35) quench; and again he fixed his gaze on the aged form, which stood obscurely in an open space, where neither friend nor foe had thrust himself. What were his thoughts, he uttered no word which might discover. (40) But whether the oppressor were overawed by the Gray Champion's look, or perceived his peril in the threatening attitude of the people, it is certain that he gave back, and ordered his soldiers to commence a slow (45) and guarded retreat. Before another sunset, the Governor, and all that rode so proudly with him, were prisoners, and long ere it was known that James had abdicated, King William was proclaimed throughout New (50) England.

"The Gray Champion"
by Nathaniel Hawthorne

13. The tone of "'I have stayed the march of a King himself, ere now'" (lines 5–6) makes the Gray Champion seem
(A) audacious and in rapport
(B) unyielding and conniving
(C) propitious and conducive
(D) challenging and defiant
(E) indulgent and acquiescent

14. Contextually, "stay" in line 3 is a way of saying
(A) to hinder
(B) to wait
(C) to quell
(D) to await
(E) to endure

15. Another way of saying "drinking in" (line 23) is
(A) imbibing liquid
(B) absorbing mentally
(C) swallowing hard
(D) swallowing liquor
(E) toasting

16. Sir Edmund Andros's character in this passage seems as one who is
(A) a cynic
(B) a benefactor
(C) unmercifully cruel
(D) compassionately natured
(E) sympathetic

17. The identity of the Gray Champion can be surmised from this passage to be
(A) a respected townsman
(B) well known in the area
(C) used to public speaking
(D) too old to fight in the battle
(E) a mysterious figure

18. Below is a list of statements concerning the passage. All are supported by the context EXCEPT that the
(A) narrative is at a point of climax
(B) main character is the Gray Champion
(C) villain is Sir Edmund Andros
(D) tone is comical
(E) tone is patriotic

19. Which of these literary devices is used in lines 14–12?
(A) Rhetorical question
(B) Sarcasm
(C) Foreshadowing
(D) Satire
(E) Paradox

20. In lines 13–21, the Gray Champion implies that
(A) the Governor will escape
(B) the current king should be respected
(C) he is afraid
(D) he can influence future events
(E) retreat is his only option

21. The Gray Champion's tone in lines 13–21 is
(A) stolid
(B) placid
(C) nonchalant
(D) indulgent
(E) threatening

22. Of what significance are the words "ere" (line 6), "ye" (lines 13, 17), "thou" (line 18), and "wast" (line 18)?
    (A) They indicate the time and place of the origin of the speaker.
    (B) They satirize the usual language of the period.
    (C) They imply that the speaker is unbalanced.
    (D) They are the same diction used by the townspeople.
    (E) They suggest that the Gray Champion is German.

23. In line 34, "so difficult to kindle" implies that
    (A) the people do not really care
    (B) the people were incited against their natures
    (C) the people have endured much cruelty
    (D) the people will not continue to be angry
    (E) the people are really on Sir Edmund's side

Questions 24–32 are based on the following poem.

Poems from the Passionate Pilgrim

Fair is my love, but not so fair as fickle;
Mild as a dove, but neither true nor trusty;
Brighter than glass, and yet, as glass is, brittle;
Line Softer than wax, and yet, as iron, rusty:
(5)   A lily pale, with damask dye to grace her,
      None fairer, nor none falser to deface her.
Her lips to mine how often hath she joined,
Between each kiss her oaths of true love swearing!
How many tales to please me hath she coined,
(10) Dreading my love, the loss thereof still fearing!
      Yet in the midst of all her pure protestings,
      Her faith, her oaths, her tears, and all were jestings.
She burnt with love, as straw with fire flameth,
She burnt out love, as soon as straw out-burneth;
(15) She framed the love, and yet she foiled the framing,
She bade love last, and yet she fell a-turning.
Was this a lover, or a lecher whether?
Bad in the best, though excellent in neither.

by William Shakespeare

24. Line 15 is structured as elements
    (A) that understate the case
    (B) in antithesis
    (C) that overstate the case
    (D) of a narrative poem
    (E) of a riddle

25. Which of the following literary devices is used in line 1?
    (A) Alliteration
    (B) Apostrophe
    (C) Catastrophe
    (D) Forced rhyme
    (E) Metaphor

26. This poem's meaning includes a central contrast that is reinforced by all the following pairs EXCEPT
    (A) "Fair"…"fickle" (line 1)
    (B) "fairer"…"falser" (line 6)
    (C) "lips"…"joined" (line 7)
    (D) "burnt with love"…"burnt out love" (lines 13–14)
    (E) "lover"…"lecher" (line 17)

27. "She foiled the framing" (line 15) deals with
    (A) the speaker's falsifying of love's evidence
    (B) destruction of property
    (C) painted picture frames
    (D) allegorical figures of fine art
    (E) her thwarting of the very love she devised

28. The relationship of her dread of the speaker's love to her fear of losing it in line 10 is an example of a(n)
    (A) litote
    (B) paradox
    (C) oxymoron
    (D) malapropism
    (E) induction

29. Which of the following is the best description of the overall structural development of the theme in this poem?
    (A) The poem is a narrative epic.
    (B) The speaker compares, then contrasts, and finally praises his lover.
    (C) The speaker develops a series of compliments and criticisms.
    (D) The poem is a trilogy of love lyrics.
    (E) The speaker and his lover engage in dialogue.

30. In line 12, "all were jestings" projects an attitude of
    (A) disillusionment
    (B) congeniality
    (C) intimacy
    (D) devotion
    (E) isolation

31. Which of the answers listed identifies the literary device used to describe the speaker's lover in lines 2–4 and 13?
    (A) Simile
    (B) Metaphor
    (C) Personification
    (D) Synecdoche
    (E) Metonymy

32. The literary device used in lines 10 and 15–16 is
    (A) cacophony
    (B) dissonance
    (C) symbolism
    (D) mock heroism
    (E) irony

Questions 33–42 are based on the following passage.

'...Your sister is an amiable creature; but yours is the character of decision and firmness, I see. If you value her conduct or happiness, infuse as much of your own spirit
Line into her, as you can. But this, no doubt, you
(5) have been always doing. It is the worst evil of too yielding and indecisive a character, that no influence over it can be depended on.—You are never sure of a good impression being durable. Every body may
(10) impression being durable. Every body may sway it; let those who would be happy be firm.—Here is a nut,' said he, catching one down from an upper bough. 'To exemplify,— a beautiful glossy nut, which, blessed with
(15) original strength, has outlived all the storms of autumn. Not a puncture, not a weak spot any where.—This nut,' he continued, with playful solemnity,—'while so many of its brethren have fallen and been trodden
(20) under foot, is still in possession of all the happiness that a hazel-nut can be supposed capable of.' Then, returning to his former earnest tone: 'My first wish for all, whom I am interested in, is that they should be firm.
(25) If Louisa Musgrove would be beautiful and happy in her November of life, she will cherish all her present powers of mind.'

Persuasion
by Jane Austen

33. The speaker's tone can be considered
    (A) outraged
    (B) inhibited
    (C) inquisitive
    (D) didactic
    (E) masterful

34. As used in the passage, November
    (A) is simply a month of the year
    (B) renders the speaker's point moot
    (C) refers to an appointment to be made
    (D) symbolizes old age
    (E) is a vehicle for firmness

35. The speaker uses a nut as
    (A) a simile
    (B) an example of a weak character
    (C) a midday snack
    (D) a vehicle to explain a firm character
    (E) an expression of insult

36. Based on contextual clues, the reader can conclude that the auditor's sister
    (A) resists change
    (B) is a younger sister
    (C) lacks resolve
    (D) is unbalanced
    (E) is much older than the auditor

37. The speaker dislikes a "too yielding and indecisive" character (line 7) because
    (A) he was once betrayed
    (B) such a person is not reliable
    (C) such a character does not leave a good
    impression
    (D) such a person grows old early
    (E) he is too judgmental

38. Why does the speaker use the phrase "its
brethren" (lines 18–19) rather than "the other
nuts?"
    (A) It implies that nuts are part of a family.
    (B) It conveys that nuts provide a serious
    analogy.
    (C) It echoes his point concerning the
    auditor's sister.
    (D) It symbolizes the hazel-nut family.
    (E) It establishes personification within the
    analogy.

39. What is the subject of the speaker's advice?
    (A) Character building
    (B) Horticulture
    (C) Raising hazel-nuts
    (D) Sibling relationships
    (E) Respect

40. The second sentence (lines 3–5) indicates that
    (A) the sister is unhappy
    (B) the auditor has influence over her sister
    (C) the sister misbehaves
    (D) the auditor is weak-natured
    (E) the speaker has never met the sister

41. In line 18, "playful solemnity" is a(n)
    (A) verbal irony
    (B) paradox
    (C) oxymoron
    (D) dramatic irony
    (E) sarcasm

42. In what type of language is the speaker's
advice given?
    (A) Poetic diction
    (B) Prose rhythms
    (C) Comparison and contrast structure
    (D) Unusual syntax
    (E) Highly personalized and metaphoric lan-
    guage

Questions 43–51 are based on the following poem.

Somewhere or Other

Somewhere or other there must surely be
  The face not seen, the voice not heard,
The heart that not yet—never yet—ah me!
  Made answer to my word.

Line

(5) Somewhere or other, may be near or far;
  Past land and sea, clean out of sight;
Beyond the wandering moon, beyond the
  star
That tracks her night by night.

Somewhere or other, may be far or near;
(10) With just a wall, a hedge, between;
With just the last leaves of the dying year
  Fallen on a turf grown green.

by Christina Rossetti

43. The use of "—never yet—ah me!" in line 3
    (A) renders the speaker's emotion more
    intense
    (B) illustrates the speaker's lack of commu-
    nicative skills
    (C) suggests that someone is listening
    (D) implies that no one is really there
    (E) introduces a new thought

44. The speaker's feelings toward "The face" in
line 2 project a sense of
    (A) hostility
    (B) longing
    (C) incredulity
    (D) anxiety
    (E) authority

45. As used in this poem, the "heart" (line 3)
serves as
    (A) the main point of an argument
    (B) the center of emotions
    (C) an organ that pumps blood
    (D) courage
    (E) memorization

46. Of the following representative pairs of words, which mirrors the contrast between the second and third stanzas?
    (A) reliable ...unreliable
    (B) uncertain ...certain
    (C) attainable ...unattainable
    (D) distant ...close
    (E) desolate ...inviting

47. In its context, "tracks" (line 8) implies that the star
    (A) marks the sky at night
    (B) is a sportsman
    (C) is hunting
    (D) is seeking the speaker's love
    (E) leads the way

48. What is the result of the use of "grown green" in line 12?
    (A) It contrasts life against the death in line ll.
    (B) It summarizes the meaning of the poem.
    (C) It emphasizes the speaker's hopelessness.
    (D) It suggests that the turf lacks proper care.
    (E) It combines a sense of freedom with care.

49. In the poem, the "face...voice...heart" (lines 2–3) is
    I. a synecdoche representing an unknown person
    II. a metaphor for lost people
    III. a symbol of being alone
    (A) I only
    (B) II only
    (C) III only
    (D) II and III only
    (E) I, II, and III

50. The poem's theme deals with
    (A) roaming to far places
    (B) the importance of a home
    (C) strangers in strange places
    (D) reconciliation with an estranged person
    (E) the existence of a person that the speaker has never met

51. What is the consequence of "near or far" (line 5) and "far or near" (line 9)?
    (A) The reversal interrupts the rhyme scheme.
    (B) The diction places emphasis on the metrical patterns.
    (C) The reversal implies confusion of the speaker.
    (D) The syntactical arrangement places emphasis on "far" in the second stanza and on "near" in the third stanza.
    (E) The syntactical arrangement places emphasis on "near" in the second stanza and on "far" in the third stanza.

Questions 52–60 are based on the following passage.

...Our day of dependence, our long apprenticeship to the learning of other lands, draws to a close. The millions that
Line around us are rushing into life cannot
(5) always be fed on the sere remains of foreign harvest. Events, actions arise that must be sung, that will sing themselves. Who can doubt that poetry will revive and lead in a new age, as the star in the
(10) constellation Harp, which now flames in our zenith, astronomers announce, shall one day be the pole star for a thousand years?

    In this hope I accept the topic which not only usage but the nature of our association
(15) seem to prescribe to this day—the American Scholar. Year by year we come up hither to read one more chapter of his biography. Let us inquire what light new days and events have thrown on his character and his hopes
(20) .... The state of society is one in which the members have suffered amputation from the trunk and strut about so many walking monsters—a good finger, a neck, a stomach, an elbow, but never a man.

(25)   Man is thus metamorphosed into a thing, into many things. The planter, who is man sent out into the field to gather food, is seldom cheered by any idea of the true dignity of his ministry. He sees his bushel
(30) and his cart, and nothing beyond, and sinks into the farmer, instead of man on the farm.

The tradesman scarcely ever gives an ideal worth to his work but is ridden by the routine of his craft, and the soul is subject to
(35) dollars. The priest becomes a form; the attorney a statute-book; the mechanic a machine; the sailor a rope of the ship.

In this distribution of functions the scholar is the delegated intellect. In the right state
(40) he is *Man Thinking*. In the degenerate state, when the victim of society, he tends to become a mere thinker, or still worse, the parrot of other men's thinking.

"The American Scholar"
by Ralph Waldo Emerson

52. The focus of the first paragraph is that
   (A) America is dependent on foreign scholarship
   (B) poetry is like a star
   (C) there is a population explosion
   (D) Harp will be the next pole star
   (E) America must engage in intellectual pursuits

53. By figuratively using "metamorphosed" in line 25, the speaker
   (A) renders the argument a philosophically macabre issue
   (B) emphasizes the mundane aspects of the issue
   (C) suggests that the change is an element of science fiction
   (D) shows a lack of respect for society
   (E) puts aside the previous discussion of amputation

54. "Poetry will revive" (lines 8–9) indirectly reveals that in the speaker's opinion
   (A) poetry is a person
   (B) poetry is universally dead
   (C) poetry is like a star
   (D) American poetry is loved by millions
   (E) American poetry is not being written or read

55. The metaphor used in the last paragraph is found in the phrase
   (A) "the degenerate state"
   (B) "the parrot of other men's thinking"
   (C) "when the victim of society"
   (D) "distribution of functions"
   (E) "to become a mere thinker"

56. A significant effect of the phrase "man sent out into the field to gather food" (lines 26–27) over the word "planter" is that
   (A) thing rather than man is emphasized
   (B) he becomes more like the farmer
   (C) man rather than thing is emphasized
   (D) true dignity is lost through a cause-and-effect relationship
   (E) planting becomes a philosophical experience

57. In the second paragraph, the speaker would have the reader believe that Americans have become
   (A) too specialized and labeled
   (B) American Scholars
   (C) representatives of the association
   (D) characterized and hopeful
   (E) eager to encounter "new days and events"

58. In the context of line 5, "sere" can be seen as
   (A) withered
   (B) sparse
   (C) unhealthy
   (D) contaminated
   (E) rotted

59. In the context of the passage, what does the speaker identify as being the cause of the degenerated state of man?
   (A) The American Scholar
   (B) The trunk
   (C) Society
   (D) Foreign scholars
   (E) Harp

60. An implication produced by the use of the word "apprenticeship" (line 2) is that
   (A) American Scholars have been experiencing a period of learning from foreign men's thinking
   (B) the speaker advocates sending students abroad to study
   (C) the speaker advocates stopping the practice of sending students abroad to study
   (D) we still have much to learn from foreign men's thinking
   (E) our degree of dependence on foreign learning must expand to include the oncoming millions

ANSWER KEY: PRACTICE TEST TWO

1. E	7. A	13. D	19. C	25. A	31. A	37. B	43. A	49. A	55. B
2. C	8. C	14. A	20. D	26. C	32. E	38. E	44. B	50. E	56. C
3. A	9. E	15. B	21. E	27. E	33. D	39. A	45. B	51. D	57. A
4. B	10. E	16. C	22. A	28. B	34. D	40. B	46. D	52. E	58. A
5. D	11. B	17. E	23. C	29. C	35. D	41. C	47. C	53. A	59. C
6. B	12. C	18. D	24. B	30. A	36. C	42. E	48. A	54. E	60. A

TO OBTAIN YOUR RAW SCORE:

_____ divided by 4 = _____
Total wrong   Score W

_____ minus _____ = _____
Total right   Score W   Score R

Round Score R to the nearest whole
number for the raw score.

HOW DID YOU DO?

55–60 = Excellent
44–54 = Very Good
35–43 = Above Average
23–34 = Average
15–22 = Below Average

EXPLANATIONS: PRACTICE TEST TWO

NOTE: Most practice tests cannot duplicate the content and conditions of the actual Literature test. Also, the scope and definitions of the literary elements can differ among literary critics; therefore, the rationale behind what constitutes a correct or an incorrect answer choice may vary. Each of these practice tests, however, gives you an opportunity to analyze selections, think critically, and develop your test-taking skills so you can do your personal best on the SAT Subject Test in Literature.

1. **E** This relationship is the central contrast of the poem. The earth is now warm, but the speaker's love cannot be melted, even by the sun (lines 14–15).

2. **C** A before-and-after relationship is established in line 1: "winter's gone." Before May, the ox would seek shelter from storms. Upon May's arrival, it would "lie / In open fields" (lines 18–19).

3. **A** June represents summer warmth. Eyes can represent a wide range of ideas, including "windows to the soul," "flirting eyes," and "giving him the eye" as an expression of invitation. January represents the winter cold. Traditionally, the heart is the seat of emotion or true feelings. She is warm toward him with her eyes, but emotionally she is cold.

4. **B** His love frowns ("lours"), but nature smiles, characteristic of someone jubilant and responsive.

5. **D** The tone of lines 14–16 is angry and impatient.

6. **B** How cold is her heart? It is congealed, as cold as marble ice: exaggerated imagery.

7. **A** This phrase appeals to three senses: melt (thermal), marble (visual and tactile), ice (visual and thermal).

8. **C** The central contrast is warm, spring-summer, awakening, happy versus cold, winter, sleeping, unhappy. In context of line 6, "makes…gives" are both part of spring.

9. **E** The comparison and contrast of the seasons is the vehicle the speaker uses to express his frustration.

10. **E** Nature making the transition from a dead, cold winter to warm spring when nature reproduces does not involve the concept of making or not making an error.

11. **B** The key to this question is "figuratively." June and January are months of the year *literally*.

12. **C** Frost would cover grass.

13. **D** Be sure to consider entire answer choices. He does respond in an unyielding manner (B), but he is not conniving. In context with lines 3–4, his response to "How dare you…?" seems *both* challenging and defiant.

14. **A** Even if you are unfamiliar with the word "stay," simply substitute each answer choice in the sentence to see which one fits the context: "How dare you *hinder* the march…?"

15. **B** Again, substitute and check the context: "The people had been…absorbing mentally the words of their champion."

16. **C** He is "loud and harsh" (line 2) with "hard and cruel" expressions (line 32).

17. **E** He came from a "secret place" (lines 3–10) with "accents long disused" (lines 24–25)—mysterious.

18. **D** Obviously, there is no comedy in this selection.

19. **C** Lines 45–50 confirm the Gray Champion's predictions came true; line 19 foreshadows the future.

20. **D** "—back, lest I foretell the scaffold!" (line 20) implies that he believes that if he predicts the Governor's execution, it will happen.

21. **E** He threatens his enemy with the scaffold.

22. **A** These archaic words would be spoken in a time long ago in a place where English was spoken.

23. **C** The people were oppressed and crying (line 8), but it took the words of the Gray Champion to stir their souls (line 27) and bring them to seek stones for weapons (lines 24–28). They obviously have endured much cruelty to reach this degree of "lurid wrath" (line 34).

24. **B** The line balances contrasting terms with parallel grammatical structure.

25. **A** This line contains repetition of initial "f" sounds.

26. **C** The central contrast is expressed in line 1. His love is fair, but also fickle (to a greater degree). Line 7 expounds upon her fair side only.

27. **E** To foil is to thwart or stop the success of something. To frame is to devise or make, in this case, love.

28. **B** Her emotions are self-contradictory, a paradox.

29. **C** Line 1 "Fair,…but…fickle": The same pattern is used in lines 2, 3, 4, 5–6. Lines 7–8 compliment, 9–10 criticize. Versions of this pattern continue to the end of the work.

30. **A** The speaker realizes the truth and is no longer under the illusion that her expressions of love are true.

31. **A** A comparison using "like" or "as" is a simile.

32. **E** Her situation is ironic: She destroys the love she desires or, rather, does not want to lose.

33. **D** He gives her a little lesson in character, complete with an illustration.

34. **D** Months and time of year often represent stages and times of life in songs and literature.

35. **D** He is contrasting the value of "the character of decision and firmness" (lines 2–3) to the "evil of …indecisive character" (lines 6–7). The nut, he says, does not have a weak spot (lines 16–17).

36. **C** He contrasts the sister as "amiable," but the auditor as firm (lines 1–3), implying that the sister lacks resolve.

37. **B** "Every body may sway it,…" (lines 10–11), in other words, unreliable.

38. **E** One effect of personification in an analogy is to help the listener make a psychological connection to the thing being personified and thereby personally apply the point being explained.

39. **A** Lines 2–3 provides the subject: "the character of decision and firmness,…"

40. **B** The speaker makes an assumption that the auditor has the power to "infuse" her "spirit" into her sister.

41. **C** To be both playful and solemn is self-contradictory.

42. **E** The nut illustration is a metaphor, and his remarks are aimed at influencing the auditor personally.

43. **A** You do not need to know the literary term "aposiopesis," but you should be able to recognize that when a speaker emotionally stops or hesitates mid-sentence, generally the effect is to make that emotion seem more intense.

44. **B** Notice in lines 1–2: "there must surely be / The face…." She has a sense of longing.

45. **B** For a heart to make "answer to my word" fits the traditional image of one heart speaking to another: emotions.

46. **D** The main contrast is distance: Stanza 2 speaks of a distant place, "Past land and sea"; stanza 3 speaks of a near one, "With just a wall, a hedge, between."

47. **C** The star follows the moon like a hunter tracks game.

48. **A** Answer choices B, D, and E are obviously unsupported by context. At first glance, lines 11–12 could project hopelessness; however, "just" in line 11 minimizes the importance of the dead leaves.

49. **A** No comparison is at work in these lines, and although we might assume the speaker is alone, there is no direct evidence.

50. **E** The theme is established in the first stanza: "The face not seen…."

51. **D** Go to context to select between answer choices D and E. Lines 6–8 deal with a faraway place; lines 10–13, a near place.

52. **E** Establish the subject: the American Scholar (lines 15–16). In relation to that subject, the apprenticeship (line 2) must relate to scholarship. That the foreign scholarship is coming to a close implies that Americans must no longer rely on the scholarship of others, but pursue their own.

53. **A** The speaker seems to want shock value. He begins by an amputation analogy, using "metamorphosed," (a verb connotative of nonhuman, scientific topics) as a transition into a paragraph that amplifies his point.

54. **E** To revive, poetry must be unconscious, unused, unhealthy, or dead (in this case, unused or not being read).

55. **B** He compares the scholar to a parrot, one who mindlessly repeats what is said by others.

56. **C** The effect is expressed directly in lines 25–31: labels, such as "planter" or "farmer," turn man "into a thing."

57. **A** The dismembered man analogy introduces the idea of specialization and labels. He amplifies this idea with examples in the third and fourth paragraphs.

58. **A** By definition, "sere" means "withered."

59. **C** He is "the victim of society" (line 41).

60. **A** For the apprenticeship to draw "to a close" (line 3), American Scholars must have been in apprenticeship (learning or training) from the thinking of foreign scholars.

ANSWER SHEET FOR PRACTICE TEST THREE

1. Ⓐ Ⓑ Ⓒ Ⓓ Ⓔ
2. Ⓐ Ⓑ Ⓒ Ⓓ Ⓔ
3. Ⓐ Ⓑ Ⓒ Ⓓ Ⓔ
4. Ⓐ Ⓑ Ⓒ Ⓓ Ⓔ
5. Ⓐ Ⓑ Ⓒ Ⓓ Ⓔ
6. Ⓐ Ⓑ Ⓒ Ⓓ Ⓔ
7. Ⓐ Ⓑ Ⓒ Ⓓ Ⓔ
8. Ⓐ Ⓑ Ⓒ Ⓓ Ⓔ
9. Ⓐ Ⓑ Ⓒ Ⓓ Ⓔ
10. Ⓐ Ⓑ Ⓒ Ⓓ Ⓔ
11. Ⓐ Ⓑ Ⓒ Ⓓ Ⓔ
12. Ⓐ Ⓑ Ⓒ Ⓓ Ⓔ
13. Ⓐ Ⓑ Ⓒ Ⓓ Ⓔ
14. Ⓐ Ⓑ Ⓒ Ⓓ Ⓔ
15. Ⓐ Ⓑ Ⓒ Ⓓ Ⓔ
16. Ⓐ Ⓑ Ⓒ Ⓓ Ⓔ
17. Ⓐ Ⓑ Ⓒ Ⓓ Ⓔ
18. Ⓐ Ⓑ Ⓒ Ⓓ Ⓔ
19. Ⓐ Ⓑ Ⓒ Ⓓ Ⓔ
20. Ⓐ Ⓑ Ⓒ Ⓓ Ⓔ

21. Ⓐ Ⓑ Ⓒ Ⓓ Ⓔ
22. Ⓐ Ⓑ Ⓒ Ⓓ Ⓔ
23. Ⓐ Ⓑ Ⓒ Ⓓ Ⓔ
24. Ⓐ Ⓑ Ⓒ Ⓓ Ⓔ
25. Ⓐ Ⓑ Ⓒ Ⓓ Ⓔ
26. Ⓐ Ⓑ Ⓒ Ⓓ Ⓔ
27. Ⓐ Ⓑ Ⓒ Ⓓ Ⓔ
28. Ⓐ Ⓑ Ⓒ Ⓓ Ⓔ
29. Ⓐ Ⓑ Ⓒ Ⓓ Ⓔ
30. Ⓐ Ⓑ Ⓒ Ⓓ Ⓔ
31. Ⓐ Ⓑ Ⓒ Ⓓ Ⓔ
32. Ⓐ Ⓑ Ⓒ Ⓓ Ⓔ
33. Ⓐ Ⓑ Ⓒ Ⓓ Ⓔ
34. Ⓐ Ⓑ Ⓒ Ⓓ Ⓔ
35. Ⓐ Ⓑ Ⓒ Ⓓ Ⓔ
36. Ⓐ Ⓑ Ⓒ Ⓓ Ⓔ
37. Ⓐ Ⓑ Ⓒ Ⓓ Ⓔ
38. Ⓐ Ⓑ Ⓒ Ⓓ Ⓔ
39. Ⓐ Ⓑ Ⓒ Ⓓ Ⓔ
40. Ⓐ Ⓑ Ⓒ Ⓓ Ⓔ

41. Ⓐ Ⓑ Ⓒ Ⓓ Ⓔ
42. Ⓐ Ⓑ Ⓒ Ⓓ Ⓔ
43. Ⓐ Ⓑ Ⓒ Ⓓ Ⓔ
44. Ⓐ Ⓑ Ⓒ Ⓓ Ⓔ
45. Ⓐ Ⓑ Ⓒ Ⓓ Ⓔ
46. Ⓐ Ⓑ Ⓒ Ⓓ Ⓔ
47. Ⓐ Ⓑ Ⓒ Ⓓ Ⓔ
48. Ⓐ Ⓑ Ⓒ Ⓓ Ⓔ
49. Ⓐ Ⓑ Ⓒ Ⓓ Ⓔ
50. Ⓐ Ⓑ Ⓒ Ⓓ Ⓔ
51. Ⓐ Ⓑ Ⓒ Ⓓ Ⓔ
52. Ⓐ Ⓑ Ⓒ Ⓓ Ⓔ
53. Ⓐ Ⓑ Ⓒ Ⓓ Ⓔ
54. Ⓐ Ⓑ Ⓒ Ⓓ Ⓔ
55. Ⓐ Ⓑ Ⓒ Ⓓ Ⓔ
56. Ⓐ Ⓑ Ⓒ Ⓓ Ⓔ
57. Ⓐ Ⓑ Ⓒ Ⓓ Ⓔ
58. Ⓐ Ⓑ Ⓒ Ⓓ Ⓔ
59. Ⓐ Ⓑ Ⓒ Ⓓ Ⓔ
60. Ⓐ Ⓑ Ⓒ Ⓓ Ⓔ

Practice Test Three

Time allowed: One hour

Directions: The following questions test your understanding of several literary selections. Read each passage or poem and the questions that follow it. Select the best answer choice for each question by blackening the matching oval on your answer sheet. **Special attention should be given to questions containing the following words: EXCEPT, LEAST, NOT.**

Questions 1–10 are based on the following speech.

Speech delivered to the Women's State Temperance Society convention in Rochester, New York in 1853

We have been obliged to preach woman's rights because many, instead of listening to what we had to say on temp-
Line erance, have questioned the right of a
(5) woman to speak on any subject. In courts of justice and legislative assemblies, if the right of the speaker to be there is questioned, all business waits until that point is settled. Now, it is not settled in the mass of minds
(10) that woman has any rights on this footstool, and much less a right to stand on an even pedestal with man, look him in the face as an equal, and rebuke the sins of her day and generation. Let it be clearly under-
(15) stood, then, that we are a woman's rights society; that we believe it is woman's duty to speak whenever she feels the impression to do so; that it is her right to be present in all the councils of church and state. The fact
(20) that our agents are women settles the question of our character on this point.

Again, in discussing the question of temperance, all lecturers, from the beginning, have made mention of the
(25) drunkards' wives and children, of widows' groans and orphans' tears. Shall these classes of sufferers be introduced but as themes for rhetorical flourish, as pathetic touches of the speaker's eloquence? Shall
(30) we passively shed tears over their condition, or by giving them their rights, bravely open to them the doors of escape from a wretched and degraded life? Is it not legitimate in this to discuss the social degradation, the legal
(35) disabilities of the drunkard's wife? If in showing her wrongs, we prove the right of all womankind to the elective franchise; to a fair representation in the government; to the right in criminal cases to be tried by peers of
(40) her own choosing—shall it be said that we transcend the bounds of our subject?...

by Elizabeth Cady Stanton

1. The phrase "passively shed tears" (line 30) is a paradox that can also be seen in which of the phrases listed below?
   (A) Excitedly exclaimed approval
   (B) Passionately cried out
   (C) Shockingly revealed the truth
   (D) Aggressively withdrew himself
   (E) Stressfully explained herself

2. In this selection, the speaker's tone includes qualities that are
   (A) frustrated and intense
   (B) genuinely hopeful
   (C) compromising and complacent
   (D) reluctantly hopeful
   (E) disdainfully reticent

3. As used in its context, "obliged to preach woman's rights" (lines 1–2) would lead the reader to believe that
   (A) the Temperance Society's primary goal was to preach "woman's rights"
   (B) the women were being forced to abandon the temperance issue
   (C) the Temperance Society was ineffective in suffrage issues
   (D) the women were turning to religion to communicate their suffrage and temperance issues
   (E) the women were forced to "woman's rights" in order to be heard on the temperance issue

4. The opposing sides of the issue are connotatively represented by all the following EXCEPT
   (A) passiveness…bravery
   (B) wrong…right
   (C) confusion…clarity
   (D) deception…sincerity
   (E) degradation…fair representation

5. Of the statements listed below, which mirrors the relationship between the first paragraph and the second paragraph?
   (A) The Temperance Society is "a woman's rights society"; it advocates women owning property.
   (B) Lack of "woman's rights" impedes the fight against drunkenness; granting "woman's rights" could be a boon to the women and children suffering from husbands and fathers who are drunkards.
   (C) Women are the agents of the Temperance Society; lecturers can participate through eloquence.
   (D) Women have a duty to speak concerning pressing social issues; drunkards' wives live wretched and degraded lives.
   (E) Most people do not believe women have rights to free speech; most people deplore drunkenness.

6. In the second paragraph, the speaker would have the reader believe that some lecturers are
   (A) imprudent
   (B) discreet
   (C) quiescent
   (D) insincere
   (E) emotional

7. The connotations of the phrase "transcend the bounds of our subject" (line 41)
   (A) emphasize that the struggle for "woman's rights" is beyond the scope of the temperance issue
   (B) demonstrate that men often do hold women in subjection
   (C) contrast that, if an examination of woman's suffering proves the need for "woman's rights," then such discussion is germane to the subject
   (D) contrast the baseness of the subject of drunkenness to the loftiness of the subject of temperance
   (E) facilitate a shift in tone in the argument, from outrage to lofty self-confidence

8. What is the organizational pattern the speaker uses to persuade her audience?
   (A) Metaphorical reasoning
   (B) Process analysis
   (C) Inductive/deductive reasoning
   (D) Spondaic stress
   (E) Metrical scan

9. In line 32, the speaker uses the phrase "the doors of escape" as a(n)
   (A) simile for woman's legal rights
   (B) epithet for woman's legal rights
   (C) euphemism for woman's legal rights
   (D) anachronism for the Women's Rights Movement
   (E) hyperbole for woman's rights

10. "Footstool" and "pedestal" (lines 10–12), as used in this passage, represent
    (A) the aesthetic distance between man and woman
    (B) a denouement to establish a final point
    (C) synaesthesia of sound and sight
    (D) the speaker's platform
    (E) an elevation of tone to heighten the argument

Questions 11–23 are based on the following poem.

Wood-notes

Whoso walks in solitude
And inhabiteth the wood,
Choosing light, wave, rock and bird
Before the money-loving herd,
(5) Into that forester shall pass,
From these companions, power and grace.
Clean shall he be, without, within,
From the old adhering sin;
All ill dissolving in the light
(10) Of his triumphant piercing sight:
Not vain, sour, nor frivolous;
Nor mad, athirst, nor garrulous;
Grave chaste, contented tho' retired,
And of all other men desired,
(15) On him the light of star and moon
Shall fall with pure radiance down;
All constellations of the sky
Shall shed their virtue thro' his eye.
Him Nature giveth for defence
(20) His formidable innocence;
The mountain sap, the shells, the sea,
All spheres, all stones, his helpers be;
He shall meet the speeding year
Without wailing, without fear;
(25) He shall be happy in his love,
Like to like shall joyful prove;
He shall be happy while he woos,
Muse-born, a daughter of the Muse.
But if with gold she bind her hair
(30) And deck her breast with diamond,
Take off thine eyes, thy heart forbear,
Tho' thou lie alone on the ground!

by Ralph Waldo Emerson

11. The subject of the poem deals with
(A) the benefits of living close to nature
(B) wilderness survivals
(C) becoming a hermit
(D) resisting temptations
(E) nature watching

12. Which of the phrases listed below mirrors the paradox seen in the phrase "formidable innocence" (line 20)?
(A) Innovative mistake
(B) Paralyzing fearfulness
(C) Defective fortifications
(D) Legalized permissiveness
(E) Innocuous dreadfulness

13. In lines 9–10, which of the following sound devices is used?
(A) Dissonance
(B) Onomatopoeia
(C) Assonance
(D) Cacophony
(E) Caesura

14. What is the main idea of lines 29–32?
(A) A rejection of wealth
(B) An admonition to reject natural physical beauty
(C) A rejection of the earth's treasure
(D) An admonition to reject a mate who has different values
(E) An admonition to reject all love

15. Based on the context of the rhyme scheme, the writer of this poem probably intends all the following pairs of words to correspond EXCEPT
(A) "solitude" (line 1) and "wood" (line 2)
(B) "bird" (line 3) and "herd" (line 4)
(C) "moon" (line 15) and "down" (line 16)
(D) "innocence" (line 20) and "sea" (line 21)
(E) "love" (line 25) and "prove" (line 26)

16. Line 29 contains a change in
(A) rhythm
(B) rhyme scheme
(C) voice
(D) verse form
(E) dialect

17. "Walks in solitude" in line 1 contrasts with "money-loving herd" in line 4. This contrast
    (A) emphasizes the individualism of the forester
    (B) emphasizes the loneliness of the forester
    (C) echoes the theme of line 22
    (D) suggests points of comparison
    (E) symbolizes the problems people face with loneliness

18. In the context of the poem, the forester's character is shown to be one of
    (A) a malcontent
    (B) fearful only of death
    (C) higher moral character
    (D) unnatural qualities
    (E) irresponsible behavior

19. The consequences of shortening words in lines 13, 18, and 32 are
    (A) allusional
    (B) metrical
    (C) symbolic
    (D) rhetorical
    (E) metaphoric

20. The natural elements are portrayed as
    (A) hostile to the forester
    (B) ambivalent to the herd
    (C) compassionate to the daughter of the Muse
    (D) challenges to the forester
    (E) friends to the forester

21. The opposing ideas within the poem are NOT seen in
    (A) individualism...conformity
    (B) courage...fear
    (C) innocence...sinfulness
    (D) justice...injustice
    (E) happiness...unhappiness

22. In the context of the entire poem, the forester (line 5) contrasts to the herd (line 4) and projects which of these ideas?
    I. The natural man vs. the artificial man
    II. An indictment against contrived literary forms
    III. A statement of the forester's mistake in judgment
    IV. An indictment against exchanging true values for monetary gain
    (A) I only
    (B) II only
    (C) I, III, and IV only
    (D) I, II, and IV only
    (E) I, II, III, and IV

23. In this poem, the "daughter of the Muse" (line 28) "with gold" in her hair (line 29) is which of these literary uses?
    I. A representative of vanity
    II. A characterization of artificiality
    III. A symbol of contrived literary forms
    (A) I only
    (B) II only
    (C) III only
    (D) I and III only
    (E) I, II, and III

Questions 24–33 are based on the following passage.

    And lest some should persuade ye, Lords and Commons, that these arguments of learned men's discouragement at this your
Line Order are mere flourishes, and not real, I
(5) could recount what I have seen and heard in other countries where this kind of inqui- sition tyrannizes; when I have sat among their learned men, for that honor I had, and been counted happy to be born in such a
(10) place of philosophic freedom as they supposed England was, while themselves did nothing but bemoan the servile condition into which learning amongst them was brought; that this was it which had damped
(15) the glory of Italian wits; that nothing had been there written now these many years but flattery and fustian. There it was that I found and visited the famous Galileo,

grown old, a prisoner to the Inquisition for
(20) thinking in astronomy otherwise than the
Franciscan and Dominican licensers thought.
And though I knew that England then was
groaning loudest under the prelatical yoke,
(25) nevertheless I took it as a pledge of future
happiness that other nations were so
persuaded of her liberty.

"Areopagitica"
by John Milton

24. What is the central topic of the passage?
(A) Intellectual freedom
(B) Animosity among countries
(C) Italy's justice system
(D) English literature
(E) Italian licensers

25. The organizational pattern used most by the
writer of this passage is best decribed as
(A) cause and effect
(B) comparison and contrast
(C) definition
(D) process analysis
(E) analysis and classification

26. What is the speaker's purpose?
(A) Argumentation
(B) Information
(C) Entertainment
(D) Description
(E) Persuasion

27. Contextual clues show that "Galileo" (line 18)
refers to a(n)
(A) poet and philosopher of the Order
(B) rebel against intellectual dictatorship
(C) English astronomer
(D) symbol of the Inquisition
(E) Franciscan licenser

28. The main reason for the irony in the admiration held by other countries for the speaker's
country is that
(A) England truly had more intellectual freedoms
(B) the other countries did not really know
England
(C) England was less philosophically free than
the other countries
(D) the other countries enjoyed hidden freedoms
(E) both England and the other countries
were partners in the Order

29. According to the speaker, repression of learn-
ing in Italy resulted in writing that was
(A) strong and forthright
(B) defensive and satirical
(C) insincere and pretentious
(D) shocking and cynical
(E) humble and direct

30. Lines 1–4 put forth the idea that
(A) supporters of the Order contend that the
opposition is just putting on a show
(B) the Order was not really issued
(C) there are no supporters for the Order
(D) there is real general support for the Order
(E) the opposition to the Order lacks sincerity

31. The "prelatical yoke" (line 24) contributes to
meaning as a
(A) simile for causing a loud noise
(B) gently satirical view of the Order
(C) mocking description of ecclesiastical
groups
(D) personification of the Order
(E) metaphor for ecclesiastical rules govern-
ing intellectual matters

32. The final statement of the passage is presented
for which of these intents?
(A) A change in attitude of the speaker
(B) A statement of the speaker's optimism
(C) A statement of the speaker's sense of for-
lornness
(D) A challenge to other countries
(E) An example of ungrounded pessimism

33. Use of the word "servile" in line 12 is connotative that
    (A) learning had become submissive to others' dictates
    (B) all philosophic freedoms were gone
    (C) the Order was a slave to philosophy
    (D) England was not a slave-state
    (E) Italy had conquered philosophic freedom

Questions 34–44 are based on the following poem.

The Flower

Once in a golden hour
  I cast to earth a seed.
Up there came a flower,
  The people said, a weed.

(5) To and fro they went
  Thro' my garden-bower,
And muttering discontent
  Cursed me and my flower.

Then it grew so tall
(10) It wore a crown of light,
But thieves from o'er the wall
  Stole the seed by night.

Sow'd it far and wide
  By every town and tower,
(15) Till all the people cried,
  'Splendid is the flower.'

Read my little fable:
  He that runs may read.
Most can raise the flowers now,
(20) For all have got the seed.

And some are pretty enough,
  And some are poor indeed;
And now again the people
  Call it but a weed.

      by Alfred, Lord Tennyson

34. The main theme of the "fable" (line 17) is
    (A) the problems gardeners face with thieves
    (B) a statement concerning dishonesty
    (C) the intense beauty inherent in some plant forms
    (D) how human nature affects perceptions of value
    (E) the probability that something beautiful will be stolen

35. In this poem, the word "runs" (line 18) means which of the definitions listed below?
    I. Moves swiftly or rapidly
    II. Thinks quickly without hindrance
    III. Meditates
    IV. Melts and flows
    (A) I only
    (B) II only
    (C) IV only
    (D) I, II, and III only
    (E) II and III only

36. In its context, "read" (line 18) means which of the definitions listed below?
    I. Utter aloud
    II. Learn true meaning
    III. Foretell
    IV. Record or show
    (A) I only
    (B) II only
    (C) IV only
    (D) I, III, and IV only
    (E) I, II, and IV only

37. In this poem, the progression of "weed" (line 4) to "flower" (line 16) to "weed" (line 24) represents the
    (A) lack of horticultural knowledge of the people
    (B) admiration with which the speaker looks at the flower
    (C) ironic nature of the people's attitude
    (D) despair with which the speaker views the people
    (E) hostility of the people toward the speaker

38. The hour was "golden" in line 1 because
    (A) the sun was shining
    (B) the seed became a splendid flower
    (C) the flower was yellow
    (D) the seed was yellow
    (E) the seed was gold

39. Contextually, "wore a crown of light" (line 10) makes the flower seem
    (A) regal and beautiful
    (B) prolific
    (C) lanky and leggy
    (D) top-heavy and weighted down
    (E) fragile and airy

40. Line 17 contains a change in
    (A) rhyme scheme
    (B) imagery
    (C) tone
    (D) speaker
    (E) voice

41. Of the pairs of words listed below, which mirrors the contrast of the development of "the flower" in this poem?
    (A) Turnips…turnip greens
    (B) Lawn…crabgrass
    (C) Queen Anne's Lace…ragweed
    (D) Roses…thorns
    (E) Grapes…vine

42. The phrase "Cursed me and my flower" (line 8) highlights the people's
    (A) limited vocabularies
    (B) judgmental natures
    (C) acceptance of the situation
    (D) deferential attitude
    (E) diabolical plan

43. The speaker wants the reader to view the fable as
    (A) just a clever story
    (B) an amusing anecdote
    (C) aimed at children
    (D) a tall tale
    (E) an important lesson in life

44. The speaker undergoes a change in attitude toward "my flower" in lines 1–4 and 9–12 in contrast to the description in lines 21–24 because
    (A) the speaker also considers the flower a weed
    (B) the flower will never be a weed to the speaker
    (C) the speaker is no longer emotionally attached to the flower
    (D) the flower really was a weed all along
    (E) the people's perception has not influenced the perception of the speaker

Questions 45–52 are based on the following passage.

'Who is it, then, Mr Kenneth?' I repeated impatiently.

'Hindley Earnshaw! Your old friend
Line Hindley—' he replied. 'And my wicked
(5) gossip; though he's been too wild for me this long while. There! I said we should draw water—But cheer up! He died true to his character, drunk as a lord—Poor lad; I'm sorry, too. One can't help missing an old
(10) companion; though he had the worst tricks with him that ever man imagined, and has done me many a rascally turn—He's barely twenty-seven, it seems; that's your own age; who would have thought you were born in
(15) one year?'

I confess this blow was greater to me than the shock of Mrs Linton's death: ancient associations lingered round my heart; I sat down in the porch, and wept as
(20) for a blood relation, desiring Kenneth to get another servant to introduce him to the master.

I could not hinder myself from pondering on the question—'Had he had fair play?'
(25) Whatever I did, that idea would bother me: it was so tiresomely pertinacious that I resolved on requesting leave to go to Wuthering Heights, and assist in the last duties to the dead. Mr Linton was extremely
(30) reluctant to consent, but I pleaded eloquently for the friendless condition in which he lay; and I said my old master and foster-brother had a claim on my services as strong as his own. Besides, I reminded him
(35) that the child, Hareton, was his wife's nephew, and, in the absence of nearer kin, he ought to act as its guardian; and he ought to and must inquire how the property was left, and look over the concerns of his
(40) brother-in-law.

Wuthering Heights
by Emily Brontë

45. Which of the literary devices listed below is used in lines 7–8 to characterize Hindley?
    (A) Metaphor
    (B) Personification
    (C) Paradox
    (D) Simile
    (E) Amplification

46. The speaker implies that the request to go to Wuthering Heights was really for the purpose of
    (A) determining the circumstances of Hindley's death
    (B) mourning the dead
    (C) playing the spy for Mr. Linton
    (D) establishing property rights
    (E) leaving Mr. Linton's employment

47. Mr. Kenneth's relationship to Hindley Earnshaw can be seen to include all the following EXCEPT
    (A) Kenneth and Hindley were friends
    (B) Hindley deceived Kenneth
    (C) Kenneth views Hindley as an alcoholic
    (D) Kenneth views Hindley as very young
    (E) Kenneth and Hindley hated one another

48. The last paragraph supports the idea that Hareton is
    (A) the speaker's son
    (B) the speaker's half-brother
    (C) Mr. Kenneth's son
    (D) Mrs. Linton's nephew
    (E) Hindley Earnshaw's nephew

49. Which of the following is NOT a meaning of the phrase "tiresomely pertinacious" as it is used in line 26?
    (A) Unyielding
    (B) Perverse
    (C) Obstinate
    (D) Determined
    (E) Stubborn

50. The speaker's argument to Mr. Linton can best be identified as
    (A) a type of inductive reasoning
    (B) fanciful and unfounded
    (C) an appeal to his sense of duty
    (D) an appeal to his sense of retribution
    (E) half-hearted and dutiful

51. The phrase "draw water" (line 7) is possibly a slang expression meaning to
    (A) bring water from a well
    (B) prepare refreshments
    (C) cry
    (D) prepare bath water
    (E) drain a flooded area

52. The best definition of "gossip" as it is used in line 5 is
    (A) a foster-parent
    (B) a close friend
    (C) a person who chatters
    (D) a person who repeats idle talk
    (E) a person who repeats rumors about others

Questions 53–60 are based on the following poem.

My Lute, Be as Thou Wast

My lute, be as thou wast when thou didst grow
With thy green mother in some shady grove,
When immelodious winds but made thee move,
Line And birds on thee their ramage did bestow.
(5) Sith that dear voice which did thy sounds approve,
Which used in such harmonious strains to flow,
Is reft from earth to tune those spheres above,
What art thou but a harbinger of woe?
Thy pleasing notes be pleasing notes no more,
(10) But orphan wailings to the fainting ear;
Each stop a sigh, each sound draws forth a tear,
Be therefore silent as in woods before,
Or if that any hand to touch thee deign,
Like widowed turtle, still her loss complain.

by William Drummond

53. "My lute" in line 1 is an example of the poet's use of
    (A) simile
    (B) metaphor
    (C) personification
    (D) apostrophe
    (E) litote

54. The poem presents
    (A) the speaker's passionate love of music
    (B) a contrast of the natural to the unnatural
    (C) the speaker mourning the death of a loved one
    (D) a youth speaking to his music teacher
    (E) an individual addressing music

55. The change in rhyme scheme of lines 5–8 as contrasted to lines 1–4 is echoed in the
    (A) change in tone of lines 5–8
    (B) change in rhythm
    (C) revelation of a reversal in tone in line 9
    (D) renewed sense of optimism in line 9
    (E) revelation of meaning in lines 5–8

56. The lute's "green mother" (line 2) is a figurative reference to a
    (A) tree
    (B) grove
    (C) wind
    (D) bird
    (E) singer

57. By using the context of the poem, "widowed turtle" in line 14 can be viewed as
    (A) a reptile, known for withdrawing into its hard shell
    (B) a turtleback, known in archaeology as a stone implement
    (C) a turtledove, known for devotion to its mate
    (D) turtlehead herb, known for the shape of its corolla
    (E) turtle peg, known for its use in harpooning sea turtles

58. The lute's music seems to represent which of the following for the speaker?
    (A) A musical instrument
    (B) Reflections of the speaker's mood
    (C) A friend and companion
    (D) Light and harmony
    (E) Nature

59. The speaker views the lute with feelings that can be described as
    (A) shocked
    (B) condescending
    (C) dispassionate
    (D) fearless
    (E) antagonistic

60. Of the following, which is the LEAST acccurate statement concerning the poem?
    (A) It is a sonnet.
    (B) Lines 9–10 contain a metaphor.
    (C) Line 2 contains personification.
    (D) The phrase "orphan wailings" (line 10) refers to children of the speaker.
    (E) "Ramage" (line 4) contrasts with "harmonious" (line 6).

ANSWER KEY: PRACTICE TEST THREE

1. **D**	7. **C**	13. **C**	19. **B**	25. **B**	31. **E**	37. **C**	43. **E**	49. **B**	55. **E**
2. **A**	8. **C**	14. **D**	20. **E**	26. **A**	32. **B**	38. **B**	44. **C**	50. **C**	56. **A**
3. **E**	9. **B**	15. **D**	21. **D**	27. **B**	33. **A**	39. **A**	45. **D**	51. **C**	57. **C**
4. **C**	10. **D**	16. **B**	22. **D**	28. **C**	34. **D**	40. **A**	46. **A**	52. **B**	58. **B**
5. **B**	11. **A**	17. **A**	23. **E**	29. **C**	35. **E**	41. **C**	47. **E**	53. **D**	59. **E**
6. **D**	12. **E**	18. **C**	24. **A**	30. **A**	36. **B**	42. **B**	48. **D**	54. **C**	60. **D**

TO OBTAIN YOUR RAW SCORE:

_____ divided by 4 = _____

Total wrong   Score W

_____ minus _____ = _____

Total right   Score W   Score R

Round Score R to the nearest whole
number for the raw score.

HOW DID YOU DO?

55–60 = Excellent
44–54 = Very Good
35–43 = Above Average
23–34 = Average
15–22 = Below Average

EXPLANATIONS: PRACTICE TEST THREE

NOTE: Most practice tests cannot duplicate the content and conditions of the actual Literature test. Also, the scope and definitions of the literary elements can differ among literary critics; therefore, the rationale behind what constitutes a correct or an incorrect answer choice may vary. Each of these practice tests, however, gives you an opportunity to analyze selections, think critically, and develop your test-taking skills so you can do your personal best on the SAT Subject Test in Literature.

1. **D** Generally, tears are the expression of deep emotion, in contrast to a passive attitude. Aggression is an attack, an expression of hostility in contrast to withdrawal, or backing away from a hostile attack.

2. **A** Frustration is evident in "...many, instead of listening to what we had to say on temperance, have questioned the right of a woman to speak on any subject" (lines 2–5). The speaker's response is intense: "Let it be clearly understood..." (lines 14–15).

3. **E** To be obliged is to be forced. Many would not listen to their thoughts on temperance because they were women.

4. **C** What are the opposing sides of the issue? Woman's right to be heard and to vote versus repression of those rights. Notice that the temperance issue

serves largely as a motivator. The speaker mocks those who "passively shed tears" (line 30) in favor of those who "bravely open to their doors of escape" (lines 31–32). To shed tears "passively" hints at deception, as opposed to the forthrightness of "Let it be clearly understood...." The wrong of degradation and the right of fair representation (C and E) are obviously reflected in this speech. Confusion and clarity, however, are not an issue.

5. **B** Answer choices A and C are obviously incorrect, D and E are too narrow, but B reflects the opposing sides of the issue as they relate to the motivator (temperance).

6. **D** The speaker accuses lecturers of using temperance as "themes for rhetorical flourish" and "pathetic touches of the speaker's eloquence" (lines 28–29).

7. **C** The speaker clearly uses the contrast of temperance and woman's rights as two different issues as a means to provide the basis for a cause-and-effect relationship: attaining rights will attain temperance and a better life for women and children.

8. **C** Premise 1: Lines 5–8. Premise 2: Lines 8–14. Conclusion: Lines 14–21. Also, in the second paragraph, notice the use of rhetorical questions to inductively build a case that she has not (by implication) transcended the subject of temperance by demanding woman's rights.

9. **B** An epithet describes a characteristic of a person or thing. In this case, women's legal rights are doors of escape for some women.

10. **D** Symbolically, the speaker is talking about the distance between man and woman (A), but not from an aesthetic perspective. The footstool/pedestal analogy deals with the speaker's platform, not in the literal sense, but as principles or policies that govern the rights of speakers.

11. **A** Notice lines 1 and 5–6: The speaker asserts that living alone in the woods will result in "power and grace."

12. **E** For innocence to be formidable, it would elicit dread or fear. For dreadfulness to be innocuous, it would be harmless.

13. **C** The vowel "i" is repeated, an example of assonance.

14. **D** Whether a figurative mate ("a daughter of the Muse"—line 28) or literal, if she is "Like to like" (line 26) and shares the values described in lines 1–24, fine. If not, the speaker prefers being alone (line 32).

15. **D** Here is a quick way to look at rhyme scheme: When the rhymes are in couplets, generally lines 1–2 will rhyme, 3–4 will rhyme, and so forth. Scan the answer choices for the pair that begins with an even line number.

16. **B** Lines 29 and 31 rhyme, making a change in rhyme scheme.

17. **A** A herd, when referring to people rather than animals, is negatively connotative, showing contempt, making the solitude of the forester more desirable.

18. **C** He is not a money-lover (line 4), he has power, grace, is clean from sin (lines 6–7), and so forth.

19. **B** Shortening words, called "apocope," generally is to help sustain the established rhythm.

20. **E** They give him "power and grace" (line 6) and innocence (line 20).

21. **D** First, establish the opposing ideas: a natural life versus one of artificiality. All the answer choices fit these ideas except justice and injustice.

22. **D** The first choice is the central contrast of the poem. The muse in line 28 supports II and line 4 supports IV. Answer choice III contradicts the main point.

23. **E** The advice by the speaker to reject her means she has not met the "Like to like" test in line 26. Why? Unlike the forester, she is vain and artificial. Also, a Muse is a classic symbol of inspired literature. To be decorated and adorned with gold, in this context, would be contrived.

24. **A** Lines 2–4, "arguments of learned men's discouragement at this your Order," in conjunction with his statement concerning England's "prelatical yoke" (line 24) reveal the central topic.

25. **B** He compares the lack of intellectual freedom in both England and other countries and contrasts the view other countries hold of England's intellectual freedom.

26. **A** We can assume that the speaker does eventually try to persuade his readers to take an action (E). In this small passage, he simply is arguing his point to convince readers that England was suffering under the "prelatical yoke."

27. **B** He is a "prisoner...for thinking" (lines 19–20), implying that the Inquisition, an intellectual dictatorship, arrested him as one who rebelled against their ideas.

28. **C** Lines 22–23 tells us that "...England then was groaning loudest...."

29. **C** In line 17, "flattery" is insincere and "fustian" is pretentious.

30. **A** The opposition (supporters of the Order) called arguments against the Order "mere flourishes."

31. **E** A yoke is traditionally used metaphorically to refer to difficult rules or oppressive laws placed on people who often have no way to resist.

32. **B** The speaker optimistically sees "future happiness."

33. **A** Servitude is connotative of submission.

34. **D** All five answer choices are correct, but which one best states the theme? Notice the portrayal of the people as they make full circle in their perception of the flower's worth.

35. **E** Context does not support I or IV. Lines 17–18 introduce the speaker's conclusion or summary point, which he wants his reader to understand and contemplate.

36. **B** Again, "read," and "runs" both relate in meaning to the speaker introducing the point he wants his readers to understand.

37. **C** How ironic that people would downgrade as a weed what they do not have, steal it, and call it "Splendid" until everyone has it, then downgrade it again!

38. **B** Figuratively, "a golden hour" traditionally refers to a time of happiness or flourishing. Why was it golden? Because the seed became a splendid flower.

39. **A** A crown symbolizing royalty and light (as from the sun) is beautiful.

40. **A** The ABAB rhyme scheme is broken.

41. **C** Those who love its delicate white flowers call this plant in the carrot family "Queen Anne's Lace." Those who hate it growing wild call it "ragweed."

42. **B** A character study, this poem reveals how quickly people change in their judgments, depending on how the situation affects them personally.

43. **E** According to the speaker, understanding this little lesson of life is important, hence the admonition in lines 17–18.

44. **C** Once the flower made the moment golden, but now "some are pretty enough, / and some are poor indeed." His interest no longer centers on the flower, itself, but rather on the lesson taught by the experience.

45. **D** "...drunk as a lord" is a comparison using "as."

46. **A** Answer choices B, C, and D refer to reasons used to gain permission to go. The real reason is stated in lines 23–29: The speaker suspects murder.

47. **E** Answer choice (A) can be found in lines 3–5, (B) in lines 11–12, (C) in line 8, and (D) in lines 12–13; however, the passage does not support E.

48. **D** Line 35, "Hareton, was his [Mr. Linton's] wife's nephew."

49. **B** The speaker could not stop the desire to investigate Earnshaw's death. This desire was not perverse.

50. **C** Lines 37–38: "...he ought to...; and he ought to and must....": These words imply a sense of duty.

51. **C** People generally cry over a death.

52. **B** Although Earnshaw may have chattered or repeated idle talk and rumors, context supports that he viewed him as a friend.

53. **D** Apostrophe is direct address to an auditor.

54. **C** Addressing his lute is the vehicle the speaker uses to mourn "that dear voice" (line 5) that "Is reft from earth" (line 7).

55. **E** The speaker uses lines 5–8 to reveal the death of "that dear voice." The rhyme scheme is ABBA BABA CDDE FF.

56. **A** Lutes of Drummond's day were generally made of wood.

57. **C** Traditionally, a turtle in poetry refers to the turtledove. Even if you are unaware of this meaning, context should show that the speaker is explaining devotion for his lost mate. A turtledove is symbolic of such devotion.

58. **B** While his love was alive, the lute was "harmonious" (line 6); now it is a "harbinger of woe" (line 8).

59. **E** He wants the lute to be silent, as before it was made (lines 1–2, 12).

60. **D** A sonnet is fourteen lines in iambic pentameter (A). He compares the music to orphan wailings (B). A tree is personified as a "mother" (C). Birds chirp or warble, implying unstructured sounds; the lute's strains were harmonious, structured, controlled (E). There is no context to support that the speaker has any children (D). The "orphan wailings" are what the "pleasing notes" in line 9 have become.

ANSWER SHEET FOR PRACTICE TEST FOUR

1. Ⓐ Ⓑ Ⓒ Ⓓ Ⓔ
2. Ⓐ Ⓑ Ⓒ Ⓓ Ⓔ
3. Ⓐ Ⓑ Ⓒ Ⓓ Ⓔ
4. Ⓐ Ⓑ Ⓒ Ⓓ Ⓔ
5. Ⓐ Ⓑ Ⓒ Ⓓ Ⓔ
6. Ⓐ Ⓑ Ⓒ Ⓓ Ⓔ
7. Ⓐ Ⓑ Ⓒ Ⓓ Ⓔ
8. Ⓐ Ⓑ Ⓒ Ⓓ Ⓔ
9. Ⓐ Ⓑ Ⓒ Ⓓ Ⓔ
10. Ⓐ Ⓑ Ⓒ Ⓓ Ⓔ
11. Ⓐ Ⓑ Ⓒ Ⓓ Ⓔ
12. Ⓐ Ⓑ Ⓒ Ⓓ Ⓔ
13. Ⓐ Ⓑ Ⓒ Ⓓ Ⓔ
14. Ⓐ Ⓑ Ⓒ Ⓓ Ⓔ
15. Ⓐ Ⓑ Ⓒ Ⓓ Ⓔ
16. Ⓐ Ⓑ Ⓒ Ⓓ Ⓔ
17. Ⓐ Ⓑ Ⓒ Ⓓ Ⓔ
18. Ⓐ Ⓑ Ⓒ Ⓓ Ⓔ
19. Ⓐ Ⓑ Ⓒ Ⓓ Ⓔ
20. Ⓐ Ⓑ Ⓒ Ⓓ Ⓔ

21. Ⓐ Ⓑ Ⓒ Ⓓ Ⓔ
22. Ⓐ Ⓑ Ⓒ Ⓓ Ⓔ
23. Ⓐ Ⓑ Ⓒ Ⓓ Ⓔ
24. Ⓐ Ⓑ Ⓒ Ⓓ Ⓔ
25. Ⓐ Ⓑ Ⓒ Ⓓ Ⓔ
26. Ⓐ Ⓑ Ⓒ Ⓓ Ⓔ
27. Ⓐ Ⓑ Ⓒ Ⓓ Ⓔ
28. Ⓐ Ⓑ Ⓒ Ⓓ Ⓔ
29. Ⓐ Ⓑ Ⓒ Ⓓ Ⓔ
30. Ⓐ Ⓑ Ⓒ Ⓓ Ⓔ
31. Ⓐ Ⓑ Ⓒ Ⓓ Ⓔ
32. Ⓐ Ⓑ Ⓒ Ⓓ Ⓔ
33. Ⓐ Ⓑ Ⓒ Ⓓ Ⓔ
34. Ⓐ Ⓑ Ⓒ Ⓓ Ⓔ
35. Ⓐ Ⓑ Ⓒ Ⓓ Ⓔ
36. Ⓐ Ⓑ Ⓒ Ⓓ Ⓔ
37. Ⓐ Ⓑ Ⓒ Ⓓ Ⓔ
38. Ⓐ Ⓑ Ⓒ Ⓓ Ⓔ
39. Ⓐ Ⓑ Ⓒ Ⓓ Ⓔ
40. Ⓐ Ⓑ Ⓒ Ⓓ Ⓔ

41. Ⓐ Ⓑ Ⓒ Ⓓ Ⓔ
42. Ⓐ Ⓑ Ⓒ Ⓓ Ⓔ
43. Ⓐ Ⓑ Ⓒ Ⓓ Ⓔ
44. Ⓐ Ⓑ Ⓒ Ⓓ Ⓔ
45. Ⓐ Ⓑ Ⓒ Ⓓ Ⓔ
46. Ⓐ Ⓑ Ⓒ Ⓓ Ⓔ
47. Ⓐ Ⓑ Ⓒ Ⓓ Ⓔ
48. Ⓐ Ⓑ Ⓒ Ⓓ Ⓔ
49. Ⓐ Ⓑ Ⓒ Ⓓ Ⓔ
50. Ⓐ Ⓑ Ⓒ Ⓓ Ⓔ
51. Ⓐ Ⓑ Ⓒ Ⓓ Ⓔ
52. Ⓐ Ⓑ Ⓒ Ⓓ Ⓔ
53. Ⓐ Ⓑ Ⓒ Ⓓ Ⓔ
54. Ⓐ Ⓑ Ⓒ Ⓓ Ⓔ
55. Ⓐ Ⓑ Ⓒ Ⓓ Ⓔ
56. Ⓐ Ⓑ Ⓒ Ⓓ Ⓔ
57. Ⓐ Ⓑ Ⓒ Ⓓ Ⓔ
58. Ⓐ Ⓑ Ⓒ Ⓓ Ⓔ
59. Ⓐ Ⓑ Ⓒ Ⓓ Ⓔ
60. Ⓐ Ⓑ Ⓒ Ⓓ Ⓔ

Practice Test Four

Time allowed: One hour

Directions: The following questions test your understanding of several literary selections. Read each passage or poem and the questions that follow it. Select the best answer choice for each question by blackening the matching oval on your answer sheet. **Special attention should be given to questions containing the following words: EXCEPT, LEAST, NOT.**

Questions 1–7 are based on the following passage.

Mr. And Mrs. Hackit, from the neighbouring farm, are Mrs. Patten's guests this evening; so is Mr. Pilgrim, the doctor from
Line the nearest market-town, who, though
(5) occasionally affecting aristocratic airs, and giving late dinners with enigmatic side-dishes and poisonous port, is never so comfortable as when he is relaxing his professional legs in one of those excellent
(10) farmhouses where the mice are sleek and the mistress sickly. And he is at this moment in clover.

For the flickering of Mrs. Patten's bright fire is reflected in her bright copper tea-
(15) kettle, the home-made muffins glisten with an inviting succulence, and Mrs. Patten's niece, a single lady of fifty, who has refused the most ineligible offers out of devotion to her aged aunt, is pouring the rich cream
(20) into the fragrant tea with a discreet liberality.

Reader! *did* you ever taste such a cup of tea as Miss Gibbs is this moment handing to Mr. Pilgrim? Do you know the dulcet
(25) strength, the animating blandness of tea sufficiently blended with real farmhouse cream? No—most likely you are a miserable town-bred reader, who think of cream as a thinnish white fluid, delivered in infinitesimal
(30) pennyworths down area steps; or perhaps, from a presentiment of calves' brains, you refrain from any lacteal addition, and rasp

your tongue with unmitigated bohea. You have a vague idea of a milch cow as
(35) probably a white-plaster animal standing in a butterman's window, and you know nothing of the sweet history of genuine cream, such as Miss Gibbs's: how it was this morning in the udders of the large sleek
(40) beasts, as they stood lowing a patient entreaty under the milking-shed; how it fell with a pleasant rhythm into Betty's pail, sending a delicious incense into the cool air; how it was carried into that temple of moist
(45) cleanliness, the dairy, where it quietly separated itself from the meaner elements of milk, and lay in mellowed whiteness, ready for the skimming-dish which transferred it to Miss Gibbs's glass cream-jug.
(50) If I am right in my conjecture, you are unacquainted with the highest possibilities of tea: and Mr. Pilgrim, who is holding that cup in his hands, has an idea beyond you.

Amos Barton
by George Eliot

1. The narrator of this account can best be described as
   (A) unintrusive and fallible
   (B) intrusive and unconscious
   (C) self-effacing in the first person
   (D) self-effacing in the third person
   (E) intrusive and self-conscious

2. What is the effect of the narrator's condescending attitude toward the reader in the last paragraph?
   (A) It antagonizes the reader.
   (B) It creates hyperbole through descriptive contrast.
   (C) It diminishes the value of the subject.
   (D) It creates an ironic epiphany.
   (E) It makes a paradoxical contrast.

3. That Mr. Pilgrim is "in clover" (line 12) means that he is
   (A) animalistic
   (B) happy
   (C) hedonistic
   (D) a farmer
   (E) affecting airs

4. That Miss Gibbs "refused the most ineligible offers" implies that
   (A) she is a woman of high standards
   (B) her aunt's regard was important to her
   (C) no suitors offered her a better situation
   (D) she prefers being single
   (E) no one ever courted her

5. What is the effect of the narrator addressing the "Reader!" in line 22?
   (A) It draws attention away from Miss Gibbs.
   (B) It makes the narrator seem less credible.
   (C) It establishes a relationship between reader and narrator.
   (D) It diminishes the role of the narrator.
   (E) It introduces the subject.

6. In context, "unmitigated bohea" (line 33) is
   (A) a foreign liquor
   (B) black tea without milk
   (C) tea thinned with milk
   (D) green tea
   (E) black coffee

7. Which of the following pairs of words are used as metaphors in this passage?
   (A) "poisonous port" (line 7)… "mice" (line 10)
   (B) "rich cream" (line 19)… "fragrant tea" (line 20)
   (C) "cream" (line 27)… "brains" (line 31)
   (D) "beasts" (line 40)… "pail" (line 42)
   (E) "incense" (line 43)… "temple" (line 44)

Questions 8–21 are based on the following poem.

The Art of Poetry

A poem, where we all perfections find,
Is not the work of a fantastic mind;
There must be care, and time, and skill, and pains;
Line Not the first heat of inexperienced brains.
(5) Yet sometimes artless poets, when the rage
Of a warm fancy does their minds engage,
Puffed with vain pride, presume they understand,
And boldly take the trumpet in their hand:
Their fustian muse each accident confounds;
(10) Nor can she fly, but rise by leaps and bounds,
Till, their small stock of learning quickly spent,
Their poem dies for want of nourishment.
In vain mankind the hot-brained fool decries,
No branding censures can unveil his eyes;
(15) With impudence the laurel they invade,
Resolved to like the monsters they have made.
Virgil, compared to them, is flat and dry;
And Homer understood not poetry:
Against their merit if this age rebel,
(20) To future times for justice they appeal.
But waiting till mankind shall do them right,
And bring their works triumphantly to light,
Neglected heaps we in bye-corners lay,
Where they become to worms and moths a prey.

by John Dryden

8. The topic of this poem is
   (A) writers of artless poetry
   (B) inspired monsters
   (C) writers of artful poetry
   (D) how to compose artful poetry
   (E) the works of Homer and Virgil

9. Concerning "artless poets" (line 5), the speaker conveys an attitude that is
   (A) exultant
   (B) convivial
   (C) beguilingly larkish
   (D) tediously practical
   (E) bitterly disapproving

10. A "fantastic mind" (line 2), in contrast to line 3, is in reference to
   (A) capricious thinking
   (B) wonderfully talented thinking
   (C) genius
   (D) creativity
   (E) imagination

11. "And Homer understood not poetry" (line 18) is an expression that reveals the artless poets'
   (A) submissive humility
   (B) chagrined countenance
   (C) pompous arrogance
   (D) groveling servility
   (E) dignified venerability

12. Which of these statements best conveys a reaction of artless poets to criticism of their poetry?
   (A) They look to Virgil and Homer to prove them correct.
   (B) They accept criticism and use it to improve.
   (C) They refuse any unjustly received rewards.
   (D) They claim that a coming age will prove them correct.
   (E) They discontinue writing and leave their poems in neglected heaps.

13. That the works of artless poets become "neglected" and moth-eaten (lines 23–24) in the future can be seen as
   (A) tragic
   (B) ironic
   (C) surprising
   (D) sentimental
   (E) melodramatic

14. The poem is described in lines 11–12 in terms of a
   (A) bird in flight
   (B) depository of learning
   (C) starving, living thing
   (D) monster to be killed
   (E) proud overseer

15. The speaker's tone in lines 17–18 can be considered
   (A) sarcastic
   (B) uncensorious
   (C) magnanimous
   (D) roguish
   (E) reverential

16. Which of the following phrases identifies the meaning of "laurel" as used in line 15?
   I. Honors and awards for poetry
   II. Fame as artful poets
   III. Plants about which poems are written
   (A) I only
   (B) II only
   (C) III only
   (D) I and II only
   (E) I, II, and III

17. The main contrast of the poem is best reflected by which of these pairs of phrases?
   (A) "the work of a fantastic mind" (line 2) and "a warm fancy" (line 6)
   (B) "Puffed with vain pride" (line 7) and "dies for want" (line 12)
   (C) "care, and time, and skill, and pains" (line 3) and "small stock of learning" (line 11)
   (D) "With impudence" (line 15) and "to worms and moths a prey" (line 24)
   (E) "this age rebel" (line 19) and "to worms and moths a prey" (line 24)

18. The "fustian muse" (line 9), as used in context, represents
   (A) inspired thinking
   (B) beautiful poetry
   (C) a monster
   (D) pompous thoughts
   (E) skill in writing

19. "Nor can she fly, but rise by leaps and bounds" (line 10) serves to emphasize
    (A) that writing requires a muse
    (B) the inconsistent quality of artless poetry
    (C) the experiences gained in writing poetry
    (D) that writing poetry requires time
    (E) that poems lift the reader's thoughts

20. Which of the following statements best reflects the speaker's attitude toward writing poetry?
    (A) Writing poetry takes work.
    (B) Many different styles are necessary.
    (C) Artless poets can learn and grow.
    (D) Poems outlive their writers.
    (E) Even artless poets can contribute to the art of poetry.

21. The speaker implies that artless poets are
    (A) hardworking but untalented
    (B) careful and humble
    (C) disrespectful but talented
    (D) cautious and resolved
    (E) lazy and proud

Questions 22–28 are based on the following passage.

The sea, vast and wild as it is, bears thus the waste and wrecks of human art to its remotest shore. There is no telling what it
Line may not vomit up. It lets nothing lie; not
(5) even the giant clams which cling to its bottom. It is still heaving up the tow-cloth of the *Franklin*, and perhaps a piece of some old pirate's ship, wrecked more than a hundred years ago, comes ashore today.
(10) Some years since, when a vessel was wrecked here which had nutmegs in her cargo, they were strewn all along the beach, and for a considerable time were not spoiled by the salt water. Soon
(15) afterward, a fisherman caught a cod which was full of them. Why, then, might not the Spice Islanders shake their nutmeg trees into the ocean, and let all nations who stand in need of them pick them up? However, after
(20) a year, I found that the nutmegs from the *Franklin* had become soft.

You might make a curious list of articles which fishes have swallowed—sailors' open clasp-knives, and bright tin snuffboxes, not
(25) knowing what was in them—and jugs, and jewels, and Jonah. The other day I came across the following scrap in a newspaper.

A RELIGIOUS FISH—A short time ago, mine host Stewart, of the Denton Hotel,
(30) purchased a rock-fish, weighing about sixty pounds. On opening it he found in it a certificate of membership of the M.E. Church, which we read as follows:

Methodist E. Church	Member
(35) Founded A. D. 1784	
Quarterly Ticket	18
	Minister

For our light affliction, which is but for a moment, worketh for us a far more
(40) exceeding *and* eternal weight of glory.
—2 Cor. 4:17.
    O what are all my sufferings here,
    If, Lord, thou count me meet
    With that enraptured host t' appear,
(45)   And worship at thy feet.

The paper was, of course, in a crumpled and wet condition, but on exposing it to the sun, and ironing the kinks out of it, it became quite legible.

Denton [Maryland] Journal
"Cape Cod"
by Henry David Thoreau

22. The *"Franklin"* probably refers to
    (A) a man
    (B) a fish
    (C) a shore
    (D) a cargo
    (E) a boat

23. "Jonah," as used in line 26, is a(n)
    (A) metaphor
    (B) allusion
    (C) simile
    (D) aphorism
    (E) antithesis

24. Of the literary devices listed below, which is used in lines 25–26 to describe items found in fishes?
    (A) Slanted rhyme
    (B) Alliteration
    (C) Apostrophe
    (D) Dead metaphor
    (E) Eye rhyme

25. As used in line 22, "curious" can be considered as also meaning
    (A) accurate
    (B) fastidious
    (C) strange
    (D) prying
    (E) desirous to know

26. A possible reason that the certificate of membership was newsworthy is that
    (A) it was still legible after being eaten by a fish
    (B) it was so old
    (C) it was from a shipwreck
    (D) it contained no names or addresses
    (E) it contained a poem in the certificate

27. In line 43, "meet" can NOT be considered to mean
    (A) encountered
    (B) suitable
    (C) qualified
    (D) adapted
    (E) fit

28. In lines 24–25, "not knowing what was in them" might lead one to believe that
    (A) fish lack intelligence
    (B) snuff attracts fish
    (C) the fish were attracted by the brightness
    (D) snuff is poisonous to fish
    (E) the snuff harmed the fish

Questions 29–42 are based on the following poem.

The Light of Other Days

Oft in the stilly night
   Ere slumber's chain has bound me,
Fond Memory brings the light
Line   Of other days around me:
(5)   The smiles, the tears
     Of boyhood's years,
   The words of love then spoken;
     The eyes that shone,
     Now dimm'd and gone,
(10) The cheerful hearts now broken!
Thus in the stilly night
   Ere slumber's chain has bound me,
Sad Memory brings the light
   Of other days around me.
(15) When I remember all
   The friends so link'd together
I've seen around me fall
   Like leaves in wintry weather,
     I feel like one
(20)   Who treads alone
   Some banquet-hall deserted,
     Whose lights are fled
     Whose garlands dead,
   And all but he departed!
(25) Thus in the stilly night
   Ere slumber's chain has bound me,
Sad Memory brings the light
   Of other days around me.

by Thomas Moore

29. Which of the following is the LEAST applicable definition of "stilly" as it is used in this poem?
    (A) Simple
    (B) Still
    (C) Calm
    (D) Silent
    (E) Quiet

30. "Light" (line 3), in the context of this poem, is connotative of all the following EXCEPT
    (A) a previous time
    (B) understanding
    (C) remembrances
    (D) awareness
    (E) radiation

31. In line 2, sleep is made to appear as a
    (A) weak link
    (B) towing device
    (C) golden necklace
    (D) captor
    (E) thief

32. The speaker uses "Thus" in lines 11 and 25 rather than "Oft" as in line 1. What is the effect?
    (A) It shifts the tense of the stanza.
    (B) "Oft" implies frequence, whereas "Thus" implies infrequency.
    (C) "Thus" establishes a cause-and-effect relationship.
    (D) "Thus" emphasizes the tone.
    (E) "Thus" signals a restatement of the theme.

33. Of the pairs of words listed below, which best reflects the contrast of lines 5–8 to lines 9–10?
    (A) "eyes" (line 8) and "hearts" (line 10)
    (B) "tears" (line 5) and "broken" (line 10)
    (C) "night" (line 1) and "light" (line 13)
    (D) "love" (line 7) and "cheerful" (line 10)
    (E) "Fond Memory" (line 3) and "Sad Memory" (line 13)

34. The speaker in the poem is best described as someone who is feeling
    (A) nostalgic and happy
    (B) lonely and abandoned
    (C) warm and caring
    (D) wistful and peaceful
    (E) angry and bitter

35. The relationship between "friends" in lines 15–18 and "I" in lines 19–24 is also seen in which of the following pairs?
    (A) "fall" (line 17) and "dead" (line 23)
    (B) "wintry" (line 18) and "deserted" (line 21)
    (C) "remember" (line 15) and "feel" (line 19)
    (D) "link'd together" (line 16) and "alone" (line 20)
    (E) "leaves" (line 18) and "lights" (line 22)

36. Of the literary devices listed below, which is used to describe the friends in lines 15–18?
    (A) Simile
    (B) Illusion
    (C) Personification
    (D) Understatement
    (E) Overstatement

37. This poem can best be seen as presenting the thoughts of someone
    (A) who is becoming fearful of death
    (B) whose friends and family are gone
    (C) whose life is just beginning
    (D) who has not adjusted to feelings of guilt
    (E) who is in love

38. Contextually, moving from "boyhood's years" (line 6) to "wintry weather" (line 18) to "departed" (line 24) reflects a change from the
    (A) abstract to the concrete
    (B) sad to the happy
    (C) past to the future
    (D) spoken to the unspoken
    (E) real to the unreal

39. The poem's overall subject is
    (A) youth
    (B) memories
    (C) old age
    (D) death
    (E) sleep

40. Line 19 is notable for introducing which of the following?
    (A) The rhyme scheme changes from that of the first stanza.
    (B) Personification is used to depict the speaker's life.
    (C) Light becomes a symbol for vision.
    (D) The speaker examines his present condition.
    (E) The speaker refuses to be comforted by Memory.

41. What is the effect of the simile as used in lines 19–24?
    (A) It highlights the events missing in the speaker's life.
    (B) It contrasts the role of "Memory" in line 27.
    (C) It introduces the element of fear into the speaker's tone.
    (D) It depicts the speaker's boyhood years.
    (E) It emphasizes the speaker's sense of loneliness.

42. The "banquet-hall" in line 21 is contextually referring to
    (A) a place to eat
    (B) a gathering place
    (C) the speaker's life
    (D) the place where the speaker once met people
    (E) the speaker's old home

Questions 43–47 are based on the following passage.

This outward mutability indicated, and did
not more than fairly express, the various
properties of her inner life. Her nature
Line appeared to possess depth, too, as well as
(5)   variety; but—or else Hester's fears deceived
her—it lacked reference and adaptation to
the world into which she was born. The
child could not be made amenable to rules.
In giving her existence, a great law had
(10) been broken; and the result was a being,
whose elements were perhaps beautiful and
brilliant, but all in disorder; or with an order
peculiar to themselves, amidst which the
point of variety and arrangement was
(15) difficult or impossible to be discovered.
Hester could only account for the child's
character—and even then, most vaguely and
imperfectly—by recalling what she herself
had been, during that momentous period
(20) while Pearl was imbibing her soul from the
spiritual world, and her bodily frame from
its material of earth. The mother's
impassioned state had been the medium
through which were transmitted to the
(25) unborn infant the rays of its moral life; and,

however white and clear originally, they
had taken the deep stains of crimson and
gold, the fiery lustre, the black shadow, and
the untempered light, of the intervening
(30) substance. Above all, the warfare of
Hester's spirit, at that epoch, was
perpetuated in Pearl. She could recognize
her wild, desperate, defiant mood, the
flightiness of her temper, and even some of
(35) the very cloud-shapes of gloom and
despondency that had brooded in her
heart. They were now illuminated by the
morning radiance of a young child's
disposition, but, later in the day of earthly
(40) existence, might be prolific of the storm and
whirlwind.

The Scarlet Letter
by Nathaniel Hawthorne

43. The speaker presents Pearl's character as
    (A) dull and insipid
    (B) intelligent, but willful
    (C) underdeveloped, but skillful
    (D) temperamental, but loving
    (E) guilty and morose

44. The passage supports the idea that
    (A) Hester and Pearl were nothing alike
    (B) Pearl was much calmer in nature than Hester
    (C) Hester feels guilt over Pearl's character
    (D) Hester and Pearl hate one another
    (E) Pearl is deeply attached to Hester

45. The phrase "later in the day of earthly existence" (lines 39–40) can be thought of as
    (A) childhood
    (B) death
    (C) old age
    (D) adulthood
    (E) infancy

46. In the last sentence, "storm and whirlwind" are used as vehicles in a metaphor describing
    (A) the epoch of Pearl's birth
    (B) Hester's character mirrored in Pearl
    (C) dispositions in general
    (D) Pearl's physical appearance
    (E) a radiant personality

47. In line 20, "imbibing" is best seen as meaning
    (A) taking in, as fluid
    (B) drinking
    (C) taking in, as spiritual
    (D) soaking into
    (E) concealing

Questions 48–52 are based on the following poem.

Answer

Sound, sound the clarion, fill the fife!
　To all the sensual world proclaim,
One crowded hour of glorious life
　Is worth an age without a name.

　　　　　by Sir Walter Scott

48. The poem exhibits elements that are
    (A) apologetic
    (B) apathetic
    (C) aphoristic
    (D) apocalyptic
    (E) aposiopetic

49. Of the devices listed below, which is used to draw the hearer's attention in line 1?
    (A) Alliteration, echoism, and spondaic foot
    (B) Triple rhyme
    (C) Echoism and pun
    (D) Alliteration, enjambement, and echoism
    (E) Imperfect rhyme

50. Of the following phrases, which best conveys the theme of the poem?
    (A) A glorious life of anonymity
    (B) Quality of life over quantity
    (C) A celebration in the sensual world
    (D) Longevity over reputation
    (E) Responsibilities

51. The contrasting theme of the poem could be expressed as
    I. "Crowded"…"worth"
    II. "Glorious"…"without a name"
    III. "Hour"…"age"
    (A) I only
    (B) II only
    (C) I and II only
    (D) II and III only
    (E) I, II, and III

52. In line 4, the "name" connotes
    (A) a royal title
    (B) a concept or denomination
    (C) a good reputation or honor
    (D) a representative
    (E) an appellation

Questions 53–60 are based on the following passage.

Act I. Scene 1

Narvarre. The King's park

Enter the King, Berowne, Longaville, *and* Dumain

KING.　Let fame, that all hunt after in their lives,
　　　　Live regist'red upon our brazen tombs,
　　　　And then grace us in the disgrace of death;
　　　　When, spite of cormorant devouring Time,
(5)　　 Th' endeavour of this present breath may buy
　　　　That honour which shall bate his scythe's keen edge,
　　　　And make us heirs of all eternity.
　　　　Therefore, brave conquerors—for so you are
　　　　That war against your own affections
(10)　　And the huge army of the world's desires—
　　　　Our late edict shall strongly stand in force:
　　　　Navarre shall be the wonder of the world;
　　　　Our court shall be a little Academe,
　　　　Still and contemplative in living art.
(15)　　You three, Berowne, Dumain, and Longaville,
　　　　Have sworn for three years' term to live with me
　　　　My fellow-scholars, and to keep those statutes
　　　　That are recorded in this schedule here.
　　　　Your oaths are pass'd; and now subscribe your names,

(20) That his own hand may strike his
      honour down
      That violates the smallest branch
      herein.
      If you are arm'd to do as sworn to
      do,
      Subscribe to your deep oaths, and
      keep it too.

LONGAVILLE. I am resolv'd; 'tis but a three
            years' fast.
(25) The mind shall banquet, though the
      body pine.
      Fat paunches have lean pates; and
      dainty bits
      Make rich the ribs, but bankrupt
      quite the wits.

                    "Love's Labour's Lost"
                    by William Shakespeare

53. The situation of this drama is that
    (A) the king is planning a military battle
    (B) three men request the king's help
    (C) the king is about to die and plans his final
        hours
    (D) Time has cut into the heart of Navarre
    (E) the king enlists three men to three years
        of study

54. The king's motivation, as described in lines
    1–7, is
    (A) to establish his reputation beyond his
        death
    (B) to prevent his own death
    (C) to reestablish his rule in Navarre
    (D) to entrap his three friends
    (E) to conquer "the huge army of the world's
        desires" (line 10)

55. The metaphor in lines 8–10 suggests that the
    "statutes" in line 17
    (A) are laws of Navarre
    (B) are part of a peace negotiation
    (C) concern physical rules
    (D) are part of a military code
    (E) resemble a battle plan for soldiers

56. In this scene, there is a symbolic conflict
    between
    (A) youth and age
    (B) women and men
    (C) peace and war
    (D) life and death
    (E) learning and ignorance

57. The king's words reveal that he is
    (A) a coward
    (B) anticipating war
    (C) a war hero
    (D) new to scholarship
    (E) an idealistic man

58. As used in the passage, the contrasts of
    "banquet...pine" (line 25), "Fat...lean" (line
    26), and "rich...bankrupt" (line 27) are
    designed to
    (A) diminish the importance of the statute
    (B) mirror the king's search for immortality
    (C) emphasize the incompatibility of learning
        and sumptuous living
    (D) impact the grace found in death
    (E) imply that Time does not really devour

59. As presented in the drama, the elements in
    line 27 ("Make rich the ribs, but bankrupt
    quite the wits") are in
    (A) corroboration
    (B) trisyllabical form
    (C) antithesis
    (D) a tragic flaw
    (E) a cotangent

60. In the paradoxical relationship of "grace . . .
    in the disgrace of death" (line 3), the grace is
    the result of
    (A) posthumous celebrity
    (B) the hunt for fame
    (C) human greed
    (D) death itself
    (E) life itself

ANSWER KEY: PRACTICE TEST FOUR

1. E	7. E	13. B	19. B	25. C	31. D	37. B	43. B	49. A	55. C
2. B	8. A	14. C	20. A	26. A	32. C	38. C	44. C	50. B	56. D
3. B	9. E	15. A	21. E	27. A	33. E	39. B	45. D	51. D	57. E
4. C	10. A	16. D	22. E	28. C	34. B	40. D	46. B	52. C	58. C
5. C	11. C	17. C	23. B	29. A	35. D	41. E	47. C	53. E	59. C
6. B	12. D	18. D	24. B	30. E	36. A	42. C	48. C	54. A	60. A

TO OBTAIN YOUR RAW SCORE:

_____ divided by 4 = _____
Total wrong   Score W

_____ minus _____ = _____
Total right   Score W   Score R

Round Score R to the nearest whole
number for the raw score.

HOW DID YOU DO?

55–60 = Excellent
44–54 = Very Good
35–43 = Above Average
23–34 = Average
15–22 = Below Average

EXPLANATIONS: PRACTICE TEST FOUR

NOTE: Most practice tests cannot duplicate the content and conditions of the actual Literature test. Also, the scope and definitions of the literary elements can differ among literary critics; therefore, the rationale behind what constitutes a correct or an incorrect answer choice may vary. Each of these practice tests, however, gives you an opportunity to analyze selections, think critically, and develop your test-taking skills so you can do your personal best on the SAT Subject Test in Literature.

1. **E** The speaker's expressed opinions make him intrusive; directly addressing the reader makes him self-conscious.

2. **B** Such a superior attitude over tea and milk creates hyperbole disproportionate to the subject. The nature of the subject makes his insulting tone more comical than antagonizing (A). There are no diminishing (C) or paradoxical (E) elements to his descriptions, and although his descriptions hint at an experience of epiphany, his condescending attitude ruins such a moment for the reader.

3. **B** To be "in clover" means the fields are producing and you are experiencing prosperous living. Such colloquial phrases vary by region. For example, in Texas a desirable circumstance is "walking in tall cotton."

4. **C** The addition of "most ineligible," carries several implications. Publicly, she is devoted to her aunt. She refused most ineligible offers. What made them ineligible? Were there any eligible offers? Would she have refused an eligible offer in favor of her aunt?

5. **C** Whether for good or bad, when the narrator directly addresses the reader, a relationship is established.

6. **B** Do you know what a "bohea" is? You should know that "unmitigated" means that something has not been lessened or softened. Next, look at context. The subject is cream in tea. If "you refrain from any lacteal addition," then you drink "unmitigated bohea," black tea without milk.

7. **E** The narrator explains his metaphor for you in lines 44–45: "that temple of moist cleanliness, the dairy," where, of course, the warm milk sends "incense into the cool air."

8. **A** Line 5 reveals the topic: "artless poets" whose poems die (line 12) as "monsters" (line 16).

9. **E** He sees such poets as proud (line 7), unlearned (line 11), and impudent (line 15).

10. **A** By definition, a "fantastic mind" is capricious. Also, a contrast is established with careful, skillful thinking on one side and fanciful thinking on the other.

11. **C** You should be familiar with the names Virgil and Homer, but even if you are not, context tells you that the speaker is holding them in contrast to artless poets. Consequently, they must represent true poets. To criticize their work would be pompous and arrogant.

12. **D** Read lines 19–20: They "appeal" to "future times" to "do them right" (line 21).

13. **B** Artless poets believe the future will prove them correct, but does this future point ever arrive? Instead, their works are in "Neglected heaps" (line 23), an ironic situation.

14. **C** Associating learning and thinking with food (nourishment) is an example of traditional imagery ("food for thought"). For a poem to die "for want of nourishment" relates to such imagery and makes the poem seem like a living, or in this case, starving-to-death thing.

15. **A** These artless poets ironically consider themselves better than Virgil and Homer. Such undeserved praise is said with critical intent, sarcasm.

16. **D** Context points to honor and fame in the future (lines 20–23). Plants are not involved.

17. **C** Define the central contrast: artless poets and their works versus true poets and poetry. Line 3 describes what is necessary for a perfect poem (line 1), in contrast to the quickly exhausted "small stock of learning" (line 11) of the artless poem.

18. **D** A fustian work is inflated or pompous.

19. **B** Artless poets do not sustain their work at high levels of expression, but inconsistently go up and down in thought and probably form.

20. **A** The speaker's position is stated in lines 1–3: Poetry takes "care, and time, and skill, and pains."

21. **E** They are unwilling to expend the care, time, skill, and pain necessary (line 3): and they are proud (line 7).

22. **E** A ship could have a tow-cloth (line 6) and a cargo (lines 10–12, 21–22), and could be wrecked at sea.

23. **B** You should be familiar with the account of Jonah and the whale, a well-known biblical allusion.

24. **B** Repetition of the initial "j" sound is an example of alliteration.

25. **C** How strange for a fish to swallow an open knife! "Curious" also means "strange" in this context.

26. **A** Context shows the speaker's fascination with how long nutmegs were not spoiled by the water. Consistently, he points out that the paper is still legible. Also, note that the paper tells when the church was founded, but not when the words were written.

27. **A** Substituting each choice in the line will reveal the correct answer in context with line 43: "encountered" does not make sense used in line 43.

28. **C** The fish are not after the contents; therefore, the fact that the boxes were "bright tin" (line 24) implies they are attracted by the brightness.

29. **A** Again, substitute each choice in context and you will find that "simple" does not fit the meaning of the line.

30. **E** In conjunction with "Fond Memory," radiation is too literal in meaning.

31. **D** Of the five answer choices, only a captor would bind another with chains.

32. **C** "Thus" can mean "in this or that manner" or "therefore."

33. **E** Establish the contrast. (Notice the colon in line 4.) In lines 5–8 the speaker describes "Fond Memory." Lines 9–10 shift to the negative, and line 11 shifts to "thus" as the cause for Memory being labeled "Sad" (line 13).

34. **B** Obviously, he is not happy, warm, or peaceful. Is he angry and bitter (E)? Perhaps, however, lines 19–24 clearly describe a lonely, abandoned person.

35. **D** Answer choice D reflects the speaker's central point: I had friends (link'd together); now they are gone and I am alone.

36. **A** His friends "fall / Like leaves," an example of simile.

37. **B** The situation of the speaker is revealed in lines 19–24: He is alone "And all but he departed!"

38. **C** Reference to the winter season is traditionally figurative of old age. Line 24 expresses his lonely condition, but also hints at or foreshadows his inevitable future.

39. **B** The subject appears in lines 3, 13, and 27: "Fond Memory."

40. **D** The speaker deals mostly with his memory to this point. He now reveals how all these memories of the past and his current condition affect him today.

41. **E** (A) is a correct answer choice on a literal level. He is missing eating and laughing at banquets with his friends. However, the question asks the effect of the simile. How lonely it sounds to be the last one left when the party is over! Remember: Look for the *best* answer choice.

42. **C** Examine the simile: In the banquet-hall of his life, he once dined with friends. Now, his friends are gone and he is alone in life.

43. **B** He calls her "brilliant" (line 12), but not amenable to rules (line 8).

44. **C** Hester is afraid (line 5), confesses "a great law had been broken" in having Pearl (lines 9–10) and is aware that her own "warfare" was "perpetuated" in her daughter (lines 30–32). These elements imply the basis for guilt: The flaws in Pearl's character are Hester's fault.

45. **D** The contrast to "the now… morning radiance of a young child's disposition" eliminates A and E, and logically death (B) would not be a correct answer choice. Again, look at the contrast: childhood now versus "storm and whirlwind" later. A character of storm and whirlwind is more likely in adulthood than in old age.

46. **B** The answer is found in the context of lines 22–23: "The mother's impassioned state" was passed to her unborn infant.

47. **C** What was she imbibing? "…her soul from the spiritual world"

48. **C** Aphorism is a concise statement that makes a point.

49. **A** Repetition of initial "s" and "f" is alliteration; repetition of "sound" is echoism; two strong, stressed syllables ("sound, sound") is a spondee.

50. **B** The theme is quality ("a glorious life" versus "life without a name") over quantity ("One crowded hour" versus "an age").

51. **D** The theme is found in the contrast of line 3 to 4. The speaker prefers a short, glorious life to one that is long, but without glory.

52. **C** This name is in contrast "to a glorious life."

53. **E** The situation is expressed in lines 16–17: fellow-scholars vow a three-year term.

54. **A** "Let fame …Live regist'red upon our brazen tombs…" (lines 1–2). The king wants his headstone to tell future generations of his deeds.

55. **C** They are going to "war against …affections / And… the world's desires." Such a battle would require them to agree to rules of conduct. Included is a three-year fast (line 24).

56. **D** Time is viewed as one that devours (line 4) in death, but the king seeks to become "heirs of all eternity" or life through fame.

57. **E** Ideals are ideas considered goal-worthy, even if impractical. To be idealistic is to live a life based on ideals.

58. **C** Again, these contrasts reflect the two sides of the king's figurative war between mind and body.

59. **C** A balance of contrasts: you can have food without learning or learning without food.

60. **A** "Let fame …Live regist'rd upon our brazen tombs" (lines 1–2). To grace someone is to honor him or her, in this case, after death.

ANSWER SHEET FOR PRACTICE TEST FIVE

1. Ⓐ Ⓑ Ⓒ Ⓓ Ⓔ
2. Ⓐ Ⓑ Ⓒ Ⓓ Ⓔ
3. Ⓐ Ⓑ Ⓒ Ⓓ Ⓔ
4. Ⓐ Ⓑ Ⓒ Ⓓ Ⓔ
5. Ⓐ Ⓑ Ⓒ Ⓓ Ⓔ
6. Ⓐ Ⓑ Ⓒ Ⓓ Ⓔ
7. Ⓐ Ⓑ Ⓒ Ⓓ Ⓔ
8. Ⓐ Ⓑ Ⓒ Ⓓ Ⓔ
9. Ⓐ Ⓑ Ⓒ Ⓓ Ⓔ
10. Ⓐ Ⓑ Ⓒ Ⓓ Ⓔ
11. Ⓐ Ⓑ Ⓒ Ⓓ Ⓔ
12. Ⓐ Ⓑ Ⓒ Ⓓ Ⓔ
13. Ⓐ Ⓑ Ⓒ Ⓓ Ⓔ
14. Ⓐ Ⓑ Ⓒ Ⓓ Ⓔ
15. Ⓐ Ⓑ Ⓒ Ⓓ Ⓔ
16. Ⓐ Ⓑ Ⓒ Ⓓ Ⓔ
17. Ⓐ Ⓑ Ⓒ Ⓓ Ⓔ
18. Ⓐ Ⓑ Ⓒ Ⓓ Ⓔ
19. Ⓐ Ⓑ Ⓒ Ⓓ Ⓔ
20. Ⓐ Ⓑ Ⓒ Ⓓ Ⓔ

21. Ⓐ Ⓑ Ⓒ Ⓓ Ⓔ
22. Ⓐ Ⓑ Ⓒ Ⓓ Ⓔ
23. Ⓐ Ⓑ Ⓒ Ⓓ Ⓔ
24. Ⓐ Ⓑ Ⓒ Ⓓ Ⓔ
25. Ⓐ Ⓑ Ⓒ Ⓓ Ⓔ
26. Ⓐ Ⓑ Ⓒ Ⓓ Ⓔ
27. Ⓐ Ⓑ Ⓒ Ⓓ Ⓔ
28. Ⓐ Ⓑ Ⓒ Ⓓ Ⓔ
29. Ⓐ Ⓑ Ⓒ Ⓓ Ⓔ
30. Ⓐ Ⓑ Ⓒ Ⓓ Ⓔ
31. Ⓐ Ⓑ Ⓒ Ⓓ Ⓔ
32. Ⓐ Ⓑ Ⓒ Ⓓ Ⓔ
33. Ⓐ Ⓑ Ⓒ Ⓓ Ⓔ
34. Ⓐ Ⓑ Ⓒ Ⓓ Ⓔ
35. Ⓐ Ⓑ Ⓒ Ⓓ Ⓔ
36. Ⓐ Ⓑ Ⓒ Ⓓ Ⓔ
37. Ⓐ Ⓑ Ⓒ Ⓓ Ⓔ
38. Ⓐ Ⓑ Ⓒ Ⓓ Ⓔ
39. Ⓐ Ⓑ Ⓒ Ⓓ Ⓔ
40. Ⓐ Ⓑ Ⓒ Ⓓ Ⓔ

41. Ⓐ Ⓑ Ⓒ Ⓓ Ⓔ
42. Ⓐ Ⓑ Ⓒ Ⓓ Ⓔ
43. Ⓐ Ⓑ Ⓒ Ⓓ Ⓔ
44. Ⓐ Ⓑ Ⓒ Ⓓ Ⓔ
45. Ⓐ Ⓑ Ⓒ Ⓓ Ⓔ
46. Ⓐ Ⓑ Ⓒ Ⓓ Ⓔ
47. Ⓐ Ⓑ Ⓒ Ⓓ Ⓔ
48. Ⓐ Ⓑ Ⓒ Ⓓ Ⓔ
49. Ⓐ Ⓑ Ⓒ Ⓓ Ⓔ
50. Ⓐ Ⓑ Ⓒ Ⓓ Ⓔ
51. Ⓐ Ⓑ Ⓒ Ⓓ Ⓔ
52. Ⓐ Ⓑ Ⓒ Ⓓ Ⓔ
53. Ⓐ Ⓑ Ⓒ Ⓓ Ⓔ
54. Ⓐ Ⓑ Ⓒ Ⓓ Ⓔ
55. Ⓐ Ⓑ Ⓒ Ⓓ Ⓔ
56. Ⓐ Ⓑ Ⓒ Ⓓ Ⓔ
57. Ⓐ Ⓑ Ⓒ Ⓓ Ⓔ
58. Ⓐ Ⓑ Ⓒ Ⓓ Ⓔ
59. Ⓐ Ⓑ Ⓒ Ⓓ Ⓔ
60. Ⓐ Ⓑ Ⓒ Ⓓ Ⓔ

Practice Test Five

Directions: The following questions test your understanding of several literary selections. Read each passage or poem and the questions that follow it. Select the best answer choice for each question by blackening the matching oval on your answer sheet. **Special attention should be given to questions containing the following words: EXCEPT, LEAST, NOT.**

Questions 1–8 are based on the following passage.

'Could Colonel Forster repeat the
particulars of Lydia's note to his wife?'
'He brought it with him for us to see.'
Line   Jane then took it from her pocket-book,
(5)   and gave it to Elizabeth. There were the
contents:

MY DEAR HARRIET,

You will laugh when you know where I am
gone, and I cannot help laughing myself at
(10)   your surprise tomorrow morning, as soon as
I am missed. I am going to Gretna Green,
and if you cannot guess with who, I shall
think you a simpleton, for there is but one
man in the world I love, so think it no harm
(15)   to be off. You need not send them word at
Longbourn of my going, if you do not like
it, for it will make the surprise the greater,
when I write to them, and sign my name
Lydia Wickham. What a good joke it will
(20)   be! I can hardly write for laughing. Pray
make my excuses to Pratt, for not keeping
my engagement, and dancing with him to
night. Tell him I hope he will excuse me
when he knows all, and tell him I will dance
(25)   with him at the next ball we meet, with
great pleasure. I shall send for my clothes
when I get to Longbourn; but I wish you
would tell Sally to mend a great slit in my
working muslin gown, before they are
(30)   packed up. Good bye. Give my love to
Colonel Forster, I hope you will drink to our
good journey.

Your affectionate friend,
LYDIA BENNET.

(35)   'Oh! thoughtless, thoughtless Lydia!'
cried Elizabeth when she had finished it.
'What a letter is this, to be written at such a
moment. But at least it shews, that she was
serious in the object of her journey.
(40)   Whatever he might afterwards persuade
her to, it was not on her side a scheme of
infamy. My poor father! how he must have
felt it!'
'I never saw any one so shocked. He
(45)   could not speak a word for full ten minutes.
My mother was taken ill immediately, and
the whole house in such confusion!'
'Oh! Jane,' cried Elizabeth, 'was there a
servant belonging to it, who did not know
(50)   the whole story before the end of the day?'

Pride and Prejudice
by Jane Austen

1. Lydia Bennet's letter indicates that she
   (A) is priggish and pedantry in her attitude
       toward her family
   (B) is going on vacation to Gretna Green
   (C) is eloping with Pratt
   (D) is in love with Pratt
   (E) is eloping with Wickham

2. Of the following, all are correct concerning
   the letter EXCEPT that
   (A) it reveals that Lydia has planned the trip
       well in advance
   (B) its tone is giddy and excited
   (C) it reveals that Lydia's plans were not gen-
       erally known
   (D) its purpose is to announce a surprise
   (E) it was addressed to Mrs. Forster

417

3. Elizabeth's remarks concerning the letter's contents indicate that
   (A) Lydia is not really in love
   (B) Wickham does love Lydia
   (C) Wickham may not intend to marry Lydia
   (D) the family will take the news well
   (E) Wickham's intentions are sincere

4. Elizabeth's response to the letter shows that she
   (A) disapproves of Lydia's conduct
   (B) is jealous of Lydia's happiness
   (C) does not understand what has happened
   (D) is very happy for Lydia
   (E) wishes that she, too, could elope

5. The expression "a scheme of infamy" (lines 41–42) means
   (A) a respectable idea
   (B) a shameful plan of action
   (C) a well-planned course of action
   (D) an ill-advised idea
   (E) a concise statement of intents and purposes

6. Under the circumstances of the letter, for Lydia to promise Pratt a dance at the next ball reveals that her feelings are
   (A) shy and coy
   (B) embarrassed and resentful
   (C) humble and introspective
   (D) flippant and insolent
   (E) direct and pragmatic

7. The words "simpleton" (line 13), "joke" (line 19), and "laughing" (line 20) show that Lydia
   (A) is a congenial person
   (B) has an inappropriate attitude
   (C) regards her family as emotionally unstable
   (D) has a keen sense of perception
   (E) suspects that the family knew of her plan

8. Elizabeth's question in lines 48–50 reveals that
   (A) she wants to find someone who can tell her more
   (B) such a servant should be dismissed
   (C) she wishes Lydia's action could be kept secret
   (D) the servants are generally unaware of such happenings
   (E) Lydia took care that no servants would learn of her plan

Questions 9–15 are based on the following poem.

May

I feel a newer life in every gale;
    The winds that fan the flowers,
And with their welcome breathings fill the sail,
Line   Tell of serener hours—
(5)   Of hours that glide unfelt away
    Beneath the sky of May.

The spirit of the gentle south-wind calls
    From his blue throne of air,
And where his whispering voice in music falls,
(10)   Beauty is budding there;
The bright ones of the valley break
    Their slumbers, and awake.
The waving verdure rolls along the plain,
    And the wide forest weaves,
(15) To welcome back its playful mates again,
    A canopy of leaves;
And from its darkening shadow floats
    A gush of trembling notes.

Fairer and brighter spreads the reign of May;
(20)   The tresses of the woods
With the light dallying of the west-wind play;
    And the full-brimming floods,
    As gladly to their goal they run,
    Hail the returning sun.

                by James Gates Percival

9. The "bright ones of the valley" (line 11) probably are
   (A) gifted children
   (B) sunbeams
   (C) flowers
   (D) gems
   (E) reflective windows

10. The word "verdure" places an emphasis on which of the following?
    (A) Movement
    (B) Multicolor
    (C) Windy conditions
    (D) Green color
    (E) Flatness

11. "The tresses of the woods" (line 20) is an example of which of these literary devices?
    (A) Antithesis
    (B) Simile
    (C) Metonymy
    (D) Synecdoche
    (E) Personification

12. The end-rhyme used in lines 20 and 22 is an example of
    (A) rime riche
    (B) eye rhyme
    (C) echo verse
    (D) forced rhyme
    (E) feminine rhyme

13. The "playful mates" in line 15 are probably
    I. migrating birds
    II. the south (line 7) and west (line 21) winds
    III. children on summer vacation
    (A) I only
    (B) II only
    (C) III only
    (D) I and II only
    (E) I, II, and III

14. The central imagery of this poem is based on
    (A) sound
    (B) movement
    (C) color
    (D) light
    (E) darkness

15. In line 8, "his blue throne of air" serves as which of the following?
    (A) Hyperbole
    (B) Euphemism
    (C) Personification
    (D) Ambiguity
    (E) Plurisignation

Questions 16–24 are based on the following passage.

In the very olden time, there lived a semi-
barbaric king, whose ideas, though
somewhat polished and sharpened by the
Line progressiveness of distant Latin neighbors,
(5) were still large, florid, and untrammelled, as
became the half of him which was barbaric.

He was a man of exuberant fancy, and,
withal, of an authority so irresistible that, at
his will, he turned his varied fancies into
(10) facts. He was greatly given to self-
communing, and when he and himself
agreed upon anything, the thing was done.
When every member of his domestic and
political systems moved smoothly in its
(15) appointed course, his nature was bland and
genial; but whenever there was a little hitch,
and some of his orbs got out of their orbits,
he was blander and more genial still, for
nothing pleased him so much as to make
(20) the crooked straight, and crush down
uneven places.

Among the borrowed notions by which
his barbarism had become semified was
that of the public arena, in which, by
(25) exhibitions of manly and beastly valor; the
minds of his subjects were refined and
cultured.

But even here the exuberant and barbaric
fancy asserted itself. The arena of the king
(30) was built, not to give the people an
opportunity of hearing the rhapsodies of
dying gladiators, nor to enable them to
view the inevitable conclusion of a conflict
between religious opinions and hungry
(35) jaws, but for purposes far better adapted to
widen and develop the mental energies of
the people. This vast amphitheatre, with its
encircling galleries, its mysterious vaults,
and its unseen passages, was an agent of
(40) poetic justice, in which crime was punished,
or virtue rewarded, by the decrees of an
impartial and incorruptible chance.

When a subject was accused of a crime
of sufficient importance to interest the king,
(45) public notice was given that on an
appointed day the fate of the accused
person would be decided in the king's
arena—a structure which well deserved its
name; for, although its form and plan were
(50) borrowed from afar, its purpose emanated
solely from the brain of this man, who,
every barleycorn a king, knew no tradition
to which he owed more allegiance than

pleased his fancy, and who ingrafted on
(55) every adopted form of human thought and
action the rich growth of his barbaric
idealism.

The Lady or the Tiger?
by Frank Stockton

16. The words "large, florid, and untrammelled"
(lines 5) are characteristic of which of the following personality traits?
    I. Unrestrained
    II. Traitorous
    III. Restrained
    IV. Abstruse
    (A) I only
    (B) II only
    (C) III only
    (D) I and IV only
    (E) II and IV only

17. As used in the passage, "self-communing"
(lines 10–11) can be recognized as
    (A) schizophrenia
    (B) consulting with counselors
    (C) relying on the thinking of others
    (D) counterintelligence
    (E) introspection

18. Which of the answers below can be considered
the vehicle used to describe problems in the
king's life?
    (A) Pinballs
    (B) Electrons
    (C) Solar system
    (D) Molecules
    (E) Eyes

19. From where did the king get the idea of the
public arena?
    (A) Self-communing
    (B) Distant Latin neighbors
    (C) Nature
    (D) Planetary signs
    (E) Domestic and political systems

20. Within the last paragraph, the king is characterized by the speaker as
    (A) lonely
    (B) dull
    (C) reliable
    (D) morally motivated
    (E) self-confident

21. The words "barbaric idealism" (lines 56–57), as
seen as a paradox, compares with which of the
following?
    (A) Savage beasts
    (B) Gentle children
    (C) Respectful dignitaries
    (D) Honor among thieves
    (E) Life among enemies

22. Historically, "a conflict between religious opinions and hungry jaws" (lines 33–35) can be
exemplified by
    (A) theological debates
    (B) throwing Christians to the lions
    (C) theological criticisms
    (D) the Salem witch trials
    (E) resistance to civil authority

23. As used in line 40, "poetic justice" is used ironically because
    (A) although impartial, chance is in antithesis
to true justice
    (B) justice requires no agent
    (C) justice was the subject of the king's poetry
    (D) the amphitheatre is being personified
    (E) crime usually is rewarded and virtue pun-
ished

24. As given in line 52, the phrase "every barleycorn a king" can best be thought of as
    (A) a king over an agricultural society
    (B) a king in every respect
    (C) commoners given royal status
    (D) a society that worships grain
    (E) a humorous personification for a drunken
king

Questions 25–30 are based on the following poem.

Ah! Sun-flower

Ah, sun-flower! weary of time,
Who countest the steps of the Sun;
Seeking after that sweet golden clime,
Where the traveller's journey is done;

(5) Where the Youth pined away with desire,
And the pale Virgin shrouded in snow,
Arise from their graves, and aspire
Where my sun-flower wishes to go.

by William Blake

25. In the poem, "snow" (line 6) is which of the following?
    I. A symbol of purity
    II. A personified dress
    III. The agent of cold and preservation
    (A) I only
    (B) II only
    (C) III only
    (D) I and III
    (E) I, II, and III

26. Which of the following best expresses the theme developed throughout the poem?
    (A) "Seeking" (line 3) and "arise" (line 7)
    (B) "countest" (line 2) and "pined" (line 5)
    (C) "journey" (line 4) and "sun-flower" (line 8)
    (D) "traveller's" (line 4) and "Youth" (line 5)
    (E) "golden" (line 3) and "pale" (line 6)

27. The word "aspire" (line 7), in context, means which of the following?
    I. Exhale
    II. Desire
    III. Ascend
    IV. Seek
    (A) I only
    (B) II only
    (C) III only
    (D) IV only
    (E) I, II, and III only

28. The sun-flower is described in lines 1–4 in terms of
    (A) a devitalized life form
    (B) ambitious for fame and glory
    (C) able to fulfill its wishes
    (D) bound to the earth
    (E) seeking warmer weather

29. The sun-flower, as defined in the poem, is best seen as
    (A) a symbol of warmth
    (B) a vigorous winter flower
    (C) representing man's journey through life
    (D) a metaphor for beauty
    (E) a weed

30. A conclusion supported by the poem's context is that when the "journey is done"
    (A) the sun-flower's travels will begin
    (B) the sun will find the "sweet golden clime" (line 3)
    (C) counting the sun's steps will cause the sunflower to die
    (D) wishing will turn to desire
    (E) time will no longer be a factor

Questions 31–40 are based on the following passage.

Whether heroic verse ought to be admitted into serious plays is not now to be disputed: it is already in possession of the stage; and, I dare confidently affirm that
(5) very few tragedies, in this age, shall be received without it. All the arguments which are formed against it can amount to no more than this—that it is not so near conversation as prose; and therefore not so
(10) natural. But it is very clear to all who understand poetry that serious plays ought not to imitate conversation too nearly. If nothing were to be raised above that level the foundation of poetry would be destroyed.
(15) And if you once admit of a latitude, that thoughts may be exalted, and that images and actions may be raised above the life, and described in measure without rhyme, that leads you insensibly from your own
(20) principles to mine: you are already so far onward of your way that you have forsaken

the imitation of ordinary converse; you are gone beyond it; and to continue where you are is to lodge in the open field, betwixt
(25) two inns. You have lost that which you call natural, and have not acquired the last perfection of art. But it was only custom which cozened us so long: we thought, because Shakespeare and Fletcher went no
(30) farther, that there the pillars of poetry were to be erected; that, because they excellently described passion without rhyme, therefore rhyme was not capable of describing it. But time has now convinced most men of that
(35) error. It is indeed so difficult to write verse that the adversaries of it have a good plea against many who undertake that task without being formed by art or nature for it.

"Of Heroic Plays"
by John Dryden

31. Heroic verse is described in lines 1–4 in terms of
(A) an orphan art form
(B) a conquering force
(C) something incapable of sustaining interest
(D) someone greedy of dramatic presentation
(E) something resistant to change

32. Lines 4–6 suggest that
(A) heroic verse is infrequently used
(B) tragedies do not contain heroic verse
(C) people do not want heroic verse in tragedy
(D) audiences and critics expect tragedies to have heroic verse
(E) most tragedies without heroic verse are received

33. Heroic verse is defined as
(A) 14-line poems in iambic pentameter
(B) unrhymed lines in iambic pentameter
(C) a form of parody
(D) comic verse
(E) rhymed couplets in iambic pentameter

34. As revealed in the passage, some argue that prose is
(A) more natural than heroic verse
(B) more desirable than heroic verse
(C) the mainstay of tragedy
(D) too imitative of conversation
(E) too exalted

35. The speaker's attitude implies that
(A) not all tragedies are tragic
(B) poetry is a higher level of communication than prose
(C) prose is a higher level of communication than poetry
(D) unrhymed prose of exalted images is best
(E) tragedy should imitate natural conversation

36. Lines 31–33 might be called an error in reasoning because the statement is
(A) based on the false assumption that Shakespeare and Fletcher "excellently described passion without rhyme"
(B) an overstatement
(C) a faulty generalization
(D) an understatement
(E) describing a construct that is structurally impossible

37. As presented by the speaker, a conclusion might be reached that the tragedies of Shakespeare and Fletcher
(A) are in heroic verse
(B) are rhymed
(C) used no poetic images
(D) used the exalted language of poetry, but without rhyme
(E) do not use the exalted language of poetry

38. According to the speaker, "the last perfection of art" (lines 26–27) is acquired through
(A) rhyme
(B) rhythm
(C) prose
(D) drama
(E) tragedy

39. The inference of the last sentence is that the speaker
    (A) will entertain no arguments against verse in drama
    (B) views verse as a simple matter to include in drama
    (C) highly respects prose writers
    (D) believes writing verse is a universal skill
    (E) would prefer no verse to poorly written verse

40. Being lodged "in the open field, betwixt two inns" (lines 24–25) metaphorically describes
    (A) conversational prose without rhyme
    (B) conversational prose with rhythm
    (C) images too exalted for conversation, but without the rhyme of poetry
    (D) no rhyme or poetic images
    (E) no poetic images, but rhymed lines

Questions 41–46 are based on the following poem.

Popular

Popular, Popular, Unpopular!
'You're no Poet'—the critics cried!
'Why?' said the Poet. 'You're unpopular!'
Line Then they cried at the turn of the tide—
(5) 'You're no Poet!' 'Why?'—'You're popular!'
Pop-gun, Popular and Unpopular!

by Alfred, Lord Tennyson

41. Of the literary devices listed below, which is used to set the tone of the speaker's message in the poem as a whole?
    (A) Simile
    (B) Metaphor
    (C) Personification
    (D) Alliteration
    (E) Apostrophe

42. In the last line, the speaker's meaning is accentuated by the use of
    (A) rhyme
    (B) onomatopoeia
    (C) mixed figures
    (D) genteel comedy
    (E) rhythm

43. Which of the following maxims best summarizes the speaker's meaning?
    (A) What goes around comes around.
    (B) A bird in hand is worth two in the bush.
    (C) A stitch in time saves nine.
    (D) Pride goes before a fall.
    (E) He is between a rock and a hard place.

44. The main situation in the poem can be described as that of
    (A) an unpopular poet
    (B) a popular poet
    (C) a problem of perceptions
    (D) poor poetry
    (E) a problem of talent

45. The label "critics" (line 2) refers to people who
    (A) analyze and review literary works
    (B) hate poetry
    (C) love poetry
    (D) deliberately avoid reading popular poetry
    (E) personally dislike poets

46. The effect of "Pop-gun" in the last line serves to
    (A) imply danger from critics
    (B) emphasize the erratic nature of popularity
    (C) vilify critics
    (D) threaten those who criticize the work
    (E) change the tone of the poem

Questions 47–54 are based on the following passage.

I need not speak of the voyage home but may add a few remarks as to arctic work, on points not generally understood. The
Line incentive of the earliest northern voyages
(5) was commercial, the desire of the northern European nations to find a navigable northern route to the fabled wealth of the East. When the impracticability of such a route was proven, the adventurous spirit of
(10) Anglo-Saxon and Teuton found in the mystery, the danger, the excitement, which crystalized under the name North Pole, a worthy antagonist for their fearless blood. The result of their efforts has been to add
(15) millions to the world's wealth, to demonstrate some of the most important

scientific propositions, and to develop some
of the most splendid examples of manly
courage and heroism that adorn the human
(20) record.

Let me call your attention to that flag, that
tattered and torn and patched flag you see
hanging over the mantel there. That is the
flag from which I have taken pieces for
(25) deposit in the cairns I built. You will notice
that three pieces are gone. One is in the
cairn at the "farthest north," 87.6 degrees;
a second piece I placed in a cairn I built on
one of the twin peaks of Columbia, Cape
(30) Columbia; and the third in the cairn on the
northern point of Jesup Land....

In view of the fact that the work has
defined the most northern land in the world,
and has fixed the northern limit of the
(35) world's largest island, was that work a
useless expenditure of time, effort, and
money? Neither the club nor I think so. The
money was theirs, the time and effort mine.

"Arctic Exploration"
by Robert E. Peary

47. The speaker's purpose is best described as
    (A) persuasive
    (B) argumentative
    (C) prescriptive
    (D) informative
    (E) descriptive

48. As used by the speaker, the LEAST accurate
    understanding of "blood" (line 13) is
    (A) parental heritage
    (B) temperament
    (C) life fluid
    (D) race
    (E) disposition

49. The North Pole is described in lines 11–13 in
    terms of
    (A) a suitable opponent
    (B) a villain
    (C) a friend to man
    (D) the personification of an Anglo-Saxon or
        Teuton
    (E) a coward

50. By stating "The money was theirs, the time and
    effort mine" in the last line, the speaker is
    (A) suggesting that he is dissatisfied with the
        arrangement
    (B) referring to the inequitable aspects of the
        journey
    (C) indicating that the money was inadequate
        for the journey
    (D) stressing the more romantic elements of
        an expedition
    (E) suggesting that he views the responsibility
        for expenditures as an equitable
        dichotomy

51. The speaker does NOT credit the Anglo-Saxon
    and Teuton explorers with advances in
    (A) bloodline research
    (B) economics
    (C) science
    (D) humanity
    (E) exploration

52. A "cairn" (lines 25–27) is
    (A) a cavern or cave
    (B) an ice cave
    (C) a cliff
    (D) a landmark
    (E) a flag holder

53. Probably, the flag
    (A) was desecrated by the explorers
    (B) is an antique from the Anglo-Saxons
    (C) is worn and torn from the hardships of
        the expedition
    (D) represents the speaker's family crest
    (E) is no longer of any value due to its condi-
        tion

54. Of the following definitions, "crystalized" (as it
    is used in line 12) means
    (A) coated with sugar
    (B) coated with something else to give a false
        appearance
    (C) caused to form crystals
    (D) was given a definite form
    (E) assumed a crystalline form

Questions 55–60 are based on the following poem.

The Scholar

My days among the Dead are past;
Around me I behold,
Where'er these casual eyes are cast,
Line The mighty minds of old:
(5) My never-failing friends are they,
With whom I converse day by day.

With them I take delight in weal
And seek relief in woe;
And while I understand and feel
(10) How much to them I owe,
My cheeks have often been bedew'd
With tears of thoughtful gratitude.

My thoughts are with the Dead; with them
I live in long-past years,
(15) Their virtues love, their faults condemn,
Partake their hopes and fears,
And from their lessons seek and find
Instruction with an humble mind.

My hopes are with the Dead; anon
(20) My place with them will be,
And I with them shall travel on
Through all Futurity;
Yet leaving here a name, I trust,
That will not perish in the dust.

by Robert Southey

55. The subject of this poem is
(A) dying young
(B) past scholars
(C) resisting death
(D) famous past scholars
(E) education

56. The speaker can best be labeled as someone who
(A) is dead
(B) is a past student
(C) is a scholar
(D) is unlearned
(E) is a future scholar

57. What is the speaker's attitude toward "the Dead" (line 1) as revealed in the central theme of the poem?
(A) Deferential, but not worshipful
(B) Ungrateful
(C) Antagonistic
(D) Humble, but not responsive
(E) Shortsighted

58. What effect is produced by the last two lines of the poem?
(A) They make the speaker seem vain.
(B) They intensify the pessimistic tone.
(C) They reinforce the continuous nature of scholarship.
(D) They indicate that scholarship is rare.
(E) They stress the sincere nature of scholars.

59. The third and fourth stanzas establish a contrast that is reflected in which of these pairs of words?
(A) Dead…alive
(B) Seek…travel
(C) Humble…hope
(D) Past and present…future
(E) Instruction…name

60. Based upon its contextual use, the word "live" (line 14) conveys which of these statements summarizing the speaker's position?
   I. The speaker has forgotten the lives of the Dead.
   II. The speaker intellectually feeds on past knowledge.
   III. The speaker's mind dwells on the past.
(A) I only
(B) II only
(C) III only
(D) II and III only
(E) I, II, and III

ANSWER KEY: PRACTICE TEST FIVE

1. E	7. B	13. D	19. B	25. A	31. B	37. D	43. E	49. A	55. B
2. A	8. C	14. B	20. E	26. A	32. D	38. A	44. C	50. E	56. C
3. C	9. C	15. C	21. D	27. C	33. E	39. E	45. A	51. A	57. A
4. A	10. D	16. A	22. B	28. D	34. A	40. C	46. B	52. D	58. C
5. B	11. E	17. E	23. A	29. C	35. B	41. D	47. D	53. C	59. D
6. D	12. B	18. C	24. B	30. E	36. C	42. B	48. C	54. D	60. D

TO OBTAIN YOUR RAW SCORE:

_____ divided by 4 = _____
Total wrong   Score W

_____ minus _____ = _____
Total right   Score W   Score R

Round Score R to the nearest whole
number for the raw score.

HOW DID YOU DO?

55–60 = Excellent
44–54 = Very Good
35–43 = Above Average
23–34 = Average
15–22 = Below Average

EXPLANATIONS: PRACTICE TEST FIVE

Note: Most practice tests cannot duplicate the content and conditions of the actual Literature test. Also, the scope and definitions of the literary elements can differ among literary critics; therefore, the rationale behind what constitutes a correct or an incorrect answer choice may vary. Each of these practice tests, however, gives you an opportunity to analyze selections, think critically, and develop your test-taking skills so you can do your personal best on the SAT Subject Test in Literature.

1. **E** Lydia Bennet (lines 18–19) believes she will become Lydia Wickham.

2. **A** She did not take any clothes with her and had planned to dance that evening, circumstances that imply a hasty decision.

3. **C** Emphasis on "she" in line 38 and her reference to "a scheme of infamy" reveal that Elizabeth questions Wickham's intentions.

4. **A** She calls Lydia "thoughtless" (line 35).

5. **B** By definition, infamy includes elements of disgrace. Negative connotations of "scheme" reinforce that the plan is shameful.

6. **D** She expects to be a married woman in a very structured society. To expect her family to convey such a message shows disregard for others (insolence) and a disrespectful (flippant) attitude.

7. **B** By calling Harriet a simpleton and considering her shocking "surprise" a joke, Lydia's diction or choice of words in her letter further communicate her inappropriate attitude.

8. **C** The tone reveals her feelings: "Oh! Jane," she cries. To even bring up the subject of servants knowing what happened reveals her distress.

9. **C** This line relates to line 10: "Beauty is budding there"; flowers are "The bright ones" that awaken from a winter's sleep.

10. **D** "Verdure" refers to the beautiful green colors of growth.

11. **E** To have hair forming tresses (curls or braids) generally is a human characteristic, but in this case it is given to the woods, a nonhuman.

12. **B** "Woods" and "floods" *look* like a rhyme, regardless of pronunciation.

13. **D** Birds play in the leaves (line 16). The south and west winds are normally associated with summer. Children are not mentioned.

14. **B** Although elements of all five answer choices can be found in this poem, winds (movement) provide the connecting thread from stanza to stanza. Stanza 1: the gales bring in newer life; 2: the south-wind calls; 3: waving green growth welcomes birds; and 4: the west-wind plays.

15. **C** Sitting on a throne is a human characteristic.

16. **A** None of these words relates to being a traitor, restrained, and/or abstruse; however, ideas that are "large" or bigger than those of others, "florid" or ornate, and "untrammeled" or unlimited in freedom are unrestrained.

17. **E** By definition, self-communion is thinking of or to oneself, involving elements of introspection. Context supports this idea in lines 11–12, "when he and himself agreed upon anything...."

18. **C** Line 17 reveals that at times "some of his orbs got out of their orbits...."

19. **B** The idea was borrowed (line 22), probably from "distant Latin neighbors" (line 4).

20. **E** He was "every barleycorn a king" and had the confidence in his own opinion to insert ("ingraft," a variant spelling of "engraft") his own sense of idealism on the thoughts and actions of others.

21. **D** Look for the contradiction: Barbarians are savages, yet have ideals? Thieves steal, yet have honor?

22. **B** This historical allusion traditionally can be found in American and British literature and refers to a time when people were thrown into arenas or dens of lions because of their religion.

23. **A** True justice requires discernment of guilt or innocence. It cannot be determined by chance.

24. **B** Barleycorn is a grain of barley, a cereal grass used to make malt and to thicken soup. Figuratively, the speaker means he is a king in even the smallest areas.

25. **A** Context reveals a contrast. The Youth in line 5 "pined away with desire"; the Virgin is "shrouded in snow," a traditional symbol of purity.

26. **A** What is the theme? The sun-flower seeks "that golden chime," but is bound to earth. The Youth and Virgin arise and go.

27. **C** The word could mean all four definitions; however, context points to "ascend": They ascend where the sun-flower can only wish to go.

28. **D** The sun-flower is "weary of time," never leaving its earthbound pattern of following the Sun.

29. **C** Until the point of death (line 7), man's journey through life is earthbound, like the sun-flower.

30. **E** The sun-flower is weary of time, implying that those who find the "golden clime" at the end of their journey are no longer concerned with time.

31. **B** That heroic verse is "in possession" hints at a time when it was not. Consequently, it has taken possession at some point.

32. **D** Without heroic verse, the speaker asserts, few tragedies will "be received" or accepted.

33. **E** You should know that heroic verse consists of rhymed couplets in iambic pentameter.

34. **A** The speaker says in lines 8–9 that prose is more "near conversation" and "natural."

35. **B** His attitude is revealed in lines 12–14: If nothing can go above the imitation of conversation (prose), then "the foundation of poetry would be destroyed."

36. **C** Other writers might describe passion well with rhyme.

37. **D** The "pillars of poetry" were erected with Shakespeare and Fletcher, but without rhyme.

38. **A** Images are raised (lines 16–17), implying use of poetic language beyond "ordinary converse" (line 22), losing the imitation of natural conversation (lines 25–26). What, in context, could be the perfection of poetic language? Rhyme.

39. **E** He sees poorly written verse as a "good plea" used by the "adversaries of it."

40. **C** Inn #1: You have lost the natural (conversation); Inn #2: You have not acquired perfection (rhyme).

41. **D** The irony of the poet's situation causes an explosive tone to his response. This tone is projected by the alliterative repetition of "p."

42. **B** "Pop-gun," a word that sounds like its meaning, is a use of onomatopoeia and continues the alliteration of the work.

43. **E** A summary of the speaker's point: He is criticized whether he is popular or unpopular.

44. **C** What is a "Poet"? How does popularity or the lack of popularity affect the merits of a poet's work? The insights or perception gained from answers to these questions would stop the critics' contradictory judgments.

45. **A** By definition in this context, a critic is one who analyzes and reviews literary works.

46. **B** A pop-gun is a toy; it would not imply danger (A), vilify (C), or threaten (D) anyone. The poem's tone is consistent; however, a gun that uses air to blow harmless corks or pellets is erratic. Also, it reflects the speaker's opinion of the critics.

47. **D** Although the question in the last paragraph hints at argument, the passage is mostly informative.

48. **C** The context is the Anglo-Saxon and Teuton explorers. The mention of their "adventurous spirit" would place emphasis on the figurative, not literal. Heritage, temperament, race, and disposition can be "fearless."

49. **A** A "worthy antagonist" is somewhat synonymous with "a suitable opponent."

50. **E** He aligns himself with the club (lines 35–38) against any who would question the expenditures; a partnership is implied.

51. **A** He does credit them with advances in economics (lines 14–15), science (lines 16–17), humanity, and exploration (lines 17—20).

52. **D** By definition, a cairn is a pile of stones used as a landmark.

53. **C** The flag went with him on his expeditions (lines 23–25).

54. **D** Mystery, danger, and excitement are abstracts. The North Pole is a place, symbolically giving these abstracts a definite form.

55. **B** Past scholars are the speaker's friends (stanza 1) to whom he is grateful (stanza 2), from whom he learns (stanza 3), and with whom he believes he will spend eternity (stanza 4).

56. **C** The speaker is a student of the past, a type of scholar.

57. **A** He obviously respects them; however, notice in line 15 that he does not hesitate to condemn their faults.

58. **C** Today's scholars learn from yesterday's scholars and become the teachers of tomorrow's scholars.

59. **D** "I live in long-past years" (line 14) and "find / Instruction" (line 17–18) in the present, but "I with them shall travel… Futurity" (lines 21–22).

60. **D** He "Partake[s] their hopes and fears" (line 16) and studies them "with an humble mind" (line 18).

ANSWER SHEET FOR PRACTICE TEST SIX

1. Ⓐ Ⓑ Ⓒ Ⓓ Ⓔ
2. Ⓐ Ⓑ Ⓒ Ⓓ Ⓔ
3. Ⓐ Ⓑ Ⓒ Ⓓ Ⓔ
4. Ⓐ Ⓑ Ⓒ Ⓓ Ⓔ
5. Ⓐ Ⓑ Ⓒ Ⓓ Ⓔ
6. Ⓐ Ⓑ Ⓒ Ⓓ Ⓔ
7. Ⓐ Ⓑ Ⓒ Ⓓ Ⓔ
8. Ⓐ Ⓑ Ⓒ Ⓓ Ⓔ
9. Ⓐ Ⓑ Ⓒ Ⓓ Ⓔ
10. Ⓐ Ⓑ Ⓒ Ⓓ Ⓔ
11. Ⓐ Ⓑ Ⓒ Ⓓ Ⓔ
12. Ⓐ Ⓑ Ⓒ Ⓓ Ⓔ
13. Ⓐ Ⓑ Ⓒ Ⓓ Ⓔ
14. Ⓐ Ⓑ Ⓒ Ⓓ Ⓔ
15. Ⓐ Ⓑ Ⓒ Ⓓ Ⓔ
16. Ⓐ Ⓑ Ⓒ Ⓓ Ⓔ
17. Ⓐ Ⓑ Ⓒ Ⓓ Ⓔ
18. Ⓐ Ⓑ Ⓒ Ⓓ Ⓔ
19. Ⓐ Ⓑ Ⓒ Ⓓ Ⓔ
20. Ⓐ Ⓑ Ⓒ Ⓓ Ⓔ

21. Ⓐ Ⓑ Ⓒ Ⓓ Ⓔ
22. Ⓐ Ⓑ Ⓒ Ⓓ Ⓔ
23. Ⓐ Ⓑ Ⓒ Ⓓ Ⓔ
24. Ⓐ Ⓑ Ⓒ Ⓓ Ⓔ
25. Ⓐ Ⓑ Ⓒ Ⓓ Ⓔ
26. Ⓐ Ⓑ Ⓒ Ⓓ Ⓔ
27. Ⓐ Ⓑ Ⓒ Ⓓ Ⓔ
28. Ⓐ Ⓑ Ⓒ Ⓓ Ⓔ
29. Ⓐ Ⓑ Ⓒ Ⓓ Ⓔ
30. Ⓐ Ⓑ Ⓒ Ⓓ Ⓔ
31. Ⓐ Ⓑ Ⓒ Ⓓ Ⓔ
32. Ⓐ Ⓑ Ⓒ Ⓓ Ⓔ
33. Ⓐ Ⓑ Ⓒ Ⓓ Ⓔ
34. Ⓐ Ⓑ Ⓒ Ⓓ Ⓔ
35. Ⓐ Ⓑ Ⓒ Ⓓ Ⓔ
36. Ⓐ Ⓑ Ⓒ Ⓓ Ⓔ
37. Ⓐ Ⓑ Ⓒ Ⓓ Ⓔ
38. Ⓐ Ⓑ Ⓒ Ⓓ Ⓔ
39. Ⓐ Ⓑ Ⓒ Ⓓ Ⓔ
40. Ⓐ Ⓑ Ⓒ Ⓓ Ⓔ

41. Ⓐ Ⓑ Ⓒ Ⓓ Ⓔ
42. Ⓐ Ⓑ Ⓒ Ⓓ Ⓔ
43. Ⓐ Ⓑ Ⓒ Ⓓ Ⓔ
44. Ⓐ Ⓑ Ⓒ Ⓓ Ⓔ
45. Ⓐ Ⓑ Ⓒ Ⓓ Ⓔ
46. Ⓐ Ⓑ Ⓒ Ⓓ Ⓔ
47. Ⓐ Ⓑ Ⓒ Ⓓ Ⓔ
48. Ⓐ Ⓑ Ⓒ Ⓓ Ⓔ
49. Ⓐ Ⓑ Ⓒ Ⓓ Ⓔ
50. Ⓐ Ⓑ Ⓒ Ⓓ Ⓔ
51. Ⓐ Ⓑ Ⓒ Ⓓ Ⓔ
52. Ⓐ Ⓑ Ⓒ Ⓓ Ⓔ
53. Ⓐ Ⓑ Ⓒ Ⓓ Ⓔ
54. Ⓐ Ⓑ Ⓒ Ⓓ Ⓔ
55. Ⓐ Ⓑ Ⓒ Ⓓ Ⓔ
56. Ⓐ Ⓑ Ⓒ Ⓓ Ⓔ
57. Ⓐ Ⓑ Ⓒ Ⓓ Ⓔ
58. Ⓐ Ⓑ Ⓒ Ⓓ Ⓔ
59. Ⓐ Ⓑ Ⓒ Ⓓ Ⓔ
60. Ⓐ Ⓑ Ⓒ Ⓓ Ⓔ

Practice Test Six

Time allowed: One hour

> Directions: The following questions test your understanding of several literary selections. Read each passage or poem and the questions that follow it. Select the best answer choice for each question by blackening the matching oval on your answer sheet. **Special attention should be given to questions containing the following words: EXCEPT, LEAST, NOT.**

Questions 1–11 are based on the following passage.

'Talking of scandal,' returned Mr
Fellowes, 'have you heard the last story
about Barton? Nisbett was telling me the
Line other day that he dines alone with the
(5) Countess at six, while Mrs Barton is in the
kitchen acting as cook.'

'Rather an apocryphal authority, Nisbett,'
said Mr Ely.

'Ah,' said Mr Cleves, with good-natured
(10) humour twinkling in his eyes, 'depend upon
it, that is a corrupt version. The original text
is, that they all dined together with six—
meaning six children—and that Mrs Barton
is an excellent cook.'

(15) 'I wish dining alone together may be the
worst of that sad business,' said the Rev.
Archibald Duke, in a tone implying that his
wish was a strong figure of speech.

'Well,' said Mr Fellowes, filling his glass
(20) and looking jocose, 'Barton is certainly
either the greatest gull in existence, or he
has some cunning secret,—some philtre or
other to make himself charming in the eyes
of a fair lady. It isn't all of us that can make
(25) conquests when our ugliness is past its
bloom.'

'The lady seemed to have made a
conquest of him at the very outset,' said Mr
Ely. 'I was immensely amused one night at
(30) Granby's when he was telling us her story
about her husband's adventures. He said,
"When she told me the tale, I felt I don't

know how,—I felt it from the crown of my
head to the sole of my feet".'

(35) Mr Ely gave these words dramatically,
imitating the Rev. Amos's fervour and
symbolic action, and every one laughed
except Mr Duke, whose after-dinner view of
things was not apt to be jovial. He said,—

(40) 'I think some of us ought to remonstrate
with Mr Barton on the scandal he is
causing. He is not only imperilling his own
soul, but the souls of his flock.'

'Depend upon it,' said Mr Cleves, 'there
(45) is some simple explanation of the whole
affair, if we only happened to know it.
Barton has always impressed me as a right-
minded man, who has the knack of doing
himself injustice by his manner.'

(50) 'Now I never liked Barton,' said Mr
Fellowes. 'He's not a gentleman....'

Amos Barton
by George Eliot

1. In lines 1–3, Mr. Fellowes's choice of words
   (A) suggests that Barton was the subject of previous scandals
   (B) introduces gossip to their conversation
   (C) marks the beginning of a joke
   (D) renders what he says as unbelievable
   (E) weakens his credibility

2. Mr. Ely characterizes Nisbett as
   (A) a credible witness
   (B) psychologically unbalanced
   (C) someone not to be believed
   (D) learned and authoritative
   (E) a lawyer

431

3. Which of the following could be considered synonymous with "corrupt" as used in line 11?
   (A) Rotten
   (B) Evil
   (C) Taking bribes
   (D) Foreign admixtures
   (E) Containing alterations

4. The main difference in meaning between the two versions of the story concerning Barton centers on
   (A) Mrs. Barton's cooking
   (B) whether the Countess was actually there
   (C) greed and corruption
   (D) the prepositions "at" and "with"
   (E) dining in the kitchen

5. "Six," as used in line 5, refers to
   (A) children
   (B) time
   (C) a date
   (D) dinner guests
   (E) age

6. The "figure of speech" (line 18) implied by Duke's tone can be seen as which of these uses?
   (A) Personification of dining
   (B) "Sad business" representing Duke
   (C) "Dining alone together" representing many other bad circumstances
   (D) Apostrophe to Barton
   (E) Rhetorical question for Barton

7. Mr. Fellowes's tone in lines 19–21 can be considered
   (A) humorous
   (B) sad
   (C) angry
   (D) unrelenting
   (E) suspicious

8. Fellowes characterizes Barton in lines 21–22 as either
   (A) guilty or innocent
   (B) naive or clever
   (C) easily deceived or a deviser of a secret plan
   (D) a fraud or possessor of a love charm
   (E) athletic or witty

9. Lines 42–43 contain inferences that Mr. Barton
   (A) is a shepherd
   (B) is a sheep farmer
   (C) does not care about scandal
   (D) resists constructive criticism
   (E) is in a position of leadership

10. The tone of "Now *I* never liked Barton" (line 50) conveys an attitude that is
    (A) overbearing and judgmental
    (B) humorous and charming
    (C) expectant and excited
    (D) respectful and placating
    (E) suspicious and resentful

11. The expression used in lines 33–34 is an example of which of the following?
    (A) Cliché
    (B) Pun
    (C) Satire
    (D) Contradiction
    (E) Witticism

Questions 12–30 are based on the following poem.

The Hurricane

Happy the man who, safe on shore,
   Now trims, at home, his evening fire;
Unmov'd he hears the tempests roar,
Line   That on the tufted groves expire:
(5) Alas! on us they doubly fall,
   Our feeble barque must bear them all.

Now to their haunts the birds retreat,
   The squirrel seeks his hollow tree,
Wolves in their shaded caverns meet,
(10) All, all are blest but wretched we—
Foredoomed a stranger to repose,
No rest the unsettled ocean knows

While o'er the dark abyss we roam,
   Perhaps, with last departing gleam,
(15) We saw the sun descend in gloom,
   No more to see his morning beam;
But buried low, by far too deep,
On coral beds, unpitied, sleep!

> But what a strange, uncoasted strand
> (20)   Is that, where fate permits no day—
> No charts have we to mark that land,
>   No compass to direct that way—
> What Pilot shall explore that realm,
> What new Columbus take the helm!

* * *

> (25) The barque, accustomed to obey,
>   No more the trembling pilots guide:
> Alone she gropes her trackless way,
>   While mountains burst on either side—
> Thus, skill and science both must fall;
> (30) And ruin is the lot of all.

by Philip Freneau

12. The effect of the use of a pause in line 10 is
    (A) to emphasize a sense of contrast
    (B) to imply that animals are of major importance
    (C) to echo the "all" in line 6
    (D) to continue the established meter
    (E) to resume the stress begun in line 5

13. The attitude of the speaker toward the man on shore (line 1) reflects the speaker's
    (A) good humor
    (B) anger
    (C) respect
    (D) sympathy
    (E) fear

14. Why do "Wolves in their shaded caverns meet" (line 9)?
    (A) They are escaping the man on shore.
    (B) They are haunted by the birds and squirrels.
    (C) They are strangers to the land.
    (D) They are seeking shelter from the storm.
    (E) They are being tracked by the barque.

15. The most appropriate descriptive adjective to convey the speaker's tone and meaning concerning the "strange, uncoasted strand" (line 19) is
    (A) exotic
    (B) unfamiliar
    (C) mysterious
    (D) beautiful
    (E) friendly

16. The relationship established in the paradoxical phrase "uncoasted strand" (line 19) is reflected in which of the following phrases?
    (A) Childless mother
    (B) Rainless desert
    (C) Frosted cake
    (D) Mirrored wall
    (E) Uncontrolled anger

17. As used in line 24, "Columbus" represents
    (A) explorers
    (B) weathercasters
    (C) the man on shore
    (D) the dead
    (E) the living

18. Of the following statements, which one best summarizes the effect of "Unmov'd" in line 3?
    (A) It stresses the man on shore's sense of safety.
    (B) It emphasizes the speaker's stubborn attitude.
    (C) It projects the turbulent nature of the storm.
    (D) It echoes the violence of the hurricane.
    (E) It contrasts with the evening fire in line 2.

19. Of the following pairs of words, which pair LEAST effectively illustrates the contrast in content developed within the first two stanzas of the poem?
    (A) "Safe" (line 1)…"Foredoomed" (line 11)
    (B) "hears" (line 3)…"bear" (line 6)
    (C) "barque" (line 6)…"ocean" (line 12)
    (D) "repose" (line 11)…"unsettled" (line 12)
    (E) "happy" (line 1)…"wretched" (line 10)

20. In line 4, the phrase "on the tufted groves expire" reveals the man on shore's
    (A) position of danger
    (B) impending death
    (C) need to escape
    (D) sheltered position
    (E) resistance to escape

21. In line 11, "a stranger" would probably be identified as
    (A) one who is unfamiliar to the speaker
    (B) one who is unaccustomed to rest
    (C) one who is a guest of the speaker
    (D) one who is a visitor on the ship
    (E) one who is a foreigner on the shore

22. An implication of "Foredoomed" (line 11) most likely is that the speaker
    (A) is antagonistic toward strangers
    (B) wants strangers to remain in repose
    (C) believes that repose is only for strangers
    (D) is resistant concerning accepting the outcome of the storm
    (E) believes that his turbulent end is inevitable

23. In line 15, which of the following changes occurs?
    (A) The sun is obscured by fog.
    (B) A shift to personification enlivens the scene.
    (C) A change to past tense of the verb introduces the concept of death.
    (D) Use of first person plural emphasizes the reader's sense of danger.
    (E) Introduction of imperfect rhyme emphasizes danger.

24. What is a "barque" (line 6)?
    (A) A sailor
    (B) A man on shore
    (C) A pilot
    (D) A storm
    (E) A sailing vessel

25. Of the following statements, which one best summarizes the main idea of the concluding couplet (lines 29–30)?
    (A) Skill and science could prevent their loss.
    (B) The ship is a product of science.
    (C) Skill and science caused the ship's destruction.
    (D) Mankind cannot overcome nature.
    (E) Some may escape the ruin of the storm.

26. The "mountains" in line 28 can be thought of as all the following EXCEPT
    (A) the destruction of safety and security as they burst
    (B) symbols of stability in an explosive situation
    (C) a vehicle in a metaphor describing the water
    (D) ironic representations of places of safe haven
    (E) a vehicle in a simile describing the distant land

27. The word "Perhaps" (line 14) creates an effect that serves to
    (A) suggest that the storm may pass soon
    (B) stress the uncertainty that many will die
    (C) symbolize the hope of the storm's passing
    (D) establish a pattern of alliteration
    (E) suggest some may not have seen the sunset

28. From a contextual perspective, "abyss" (line 13) can mean all the following EXCEPT
    (A) the center of an escutcheon
    (B) a great gulf of water
    (C) immeasurable amounts
    (D) the immensity of depth
    (E) the ocean depths

29. Line 27 refers to the barque figuratively as a
    (A) ship out of control
    (B) vagrant caught in a storm
    (C) social outcast
    (D) pilot lost at sea
    (E) lost, blind woman feeling her way

30. In line 21, "that land" might be seen as which of the concepts listed below?
    I. A distant safe haven
    II. Death
    III. The bottom of the sea
    (A) I only
    (B) II only
    (C) III only
    (D) II and III only
    (E) I, II, and III

Questions 31–38 are based on the following passage.

Hasty Pudding
[corn meal mush] A Poem, in Three Cantos

Omne tulit punctum qui miscuit utile dulci
["He has gained all approval who has
mixed the useful with the sweet"—HORACE]
*He makes a good breakfast who mixes
pudding with molasses.*

PREFACE

A simplicity in diet, whether it be
considered with reference to the happiness
of individuals or the prosperity of a nation,
Line is of more consequence than we are apt to
(5) imagine. In recommending so important an
object to the rational part of mankind, I
wish it were in my power to do it in such a
manner as would be likely to gain their
attention. I am sensible that it is one of
(10) those subjects in which example has
infinitely more power than the most
convincing arguments or the highest charms
of poetry. Goldsmith's *Deserted Village*,
though possessing these two advantages in
(15) a greater degree than any other work of
the kind, has not prevented villages in
England from being deserted. The apparent
interest of the rich individuals, who form the
taste as well as the laws in that country, has
(20) been against him; and with that interest it
has been vain to contend.

The vicious habits which in this little piece
I endeavor to combat, seem to me not so
difficult to cure. No class of people has any
(25) *interest* in supporting them; unless it be the
interest which certain families may feel in
vying with each other in sumptuous
entertainments. There may indeed be some
instances of depraved appetites, which no
(30) arguments will conquer; but these must be
rare. There are very few persons but what
would always prefer a plain dish for
themselves, and would prefer it likewise for
their guests, if there were no risk of
(35) reputation in the case. This difficulty can
only be removed by example; and the

example should proceed from those whose
situation enables them to take the lead in
forming the manners of a nation. Persons of
(40) this description in America, I should hope,
are neither above nor below the influence
of truth and reason, when conveyed in
language suited to the subject.

Whether the manner I have chosen to
(45) address my arguments to them be such as
to promise any success is what I cannot
decide. But I certainly had hopes of doing
some good, or I should not have taken the
pains of putting so many rimes together. The
(50) example of domestic virtues has doubtless a
great effect. I only wish to rank *simplicity of
diet* among the virtues. In that case I should
hope it will be cherished and more
esteemed by others than it is at present.

by Joel Barlow

31. The speaker probably intends "diet" (line 1) to
convey which of the following meanings?
  I. A regulated manner of living
  II. Eating habits
  III. Daily fare
  (A) I only
  (B) II only
  (C) II and III only
  (D) I and III only
  (E) I, II, and III

32. The speaker's purpose includes
  (A) informing
  (B) persuading
  (C) hypothesizing
  (D) instructing
  (E) describing

33. According to the speaker, Goldsmith's *Deserted
Village* (line 13)
  (A) prevented England's villages from being
  deserted
  (B) is the best poem ever written
  (C) is a convincing argument and charming
  poetry
  (D) overcame English laws
  (E) provides a powerful example of his
  premise

34. In the context of line 21, "vain" means
    (A) having no genuine value
    (B) conceited
    (C) lacking in sense
    (D) trivial
    (E) ineffective

35. The second paragraph puts forth that
    (A) most people prefer simplicity in diet
    (B) the argument will be difficult to execute
    (C) not enough people are willing to take the lead
    (D) truth and reason have been abandoned
    (E) the language is not suitable to the subject

36. The speaker considers simplicity of diet to be
    (A) unattainable
    (B) without interest
    (C) a virtue
    (D) a risk to reputation
    (E) below the influence of truth and reason

37. The speaker's view includes that
    (A) vicious habits cannot be broken
    (B) depraved appetites prevent the general assimilation of virtue
    (C) most people prefer elegant dishes
    (D) leaders should set a good example
    (E) "rimes" (line 49) are of best influence in this case

38. In line 45, "them" should be identified as
    (A) people of depraved appetites
    (B) American social leaders
    (C) families competing in sumptuous entertainments
    (D) English landed gentry
    (E) lawyers

Questions 39–46 are based on the following poem.

CANTO I

Ye Alps audacious, through the heavens
  that rise,
To cramp the day and hide me from the
  skies;
Ye Gallic flags, that o'er their heights
  unfurled,
Bear death to kings, and freedom to the
  world.

Line
(5) I sing not you. A softer theme I choose,
A virgin theme, unconscious of the muse,
But fruitful, rich, well suited to inspire
The purest frenzy of poetic fire.
    Despise it not, ye bards to terror steeled,
(10) Who hurl your thunders round the epic
  field;
Nor ye who strain your midnight throats to
  sing
Joys that the vineyard and the stillhouse
  bring;
Or on some distant fair your notes employ,
And speak of raptures that you ne'er enjoy.
(15) I sing the sweets I know, the charms I feel,
My morning incense, and my evening meal,
The sweets of Hasty Pudding. Come, dear
  bowl,
Glide o'er my palate, and inspire my soul.
The milk beside thee, smoking from the kine,
(20) Its substance mingled, married in with thine,
Shall cool and temper thy superior heat,
And save the pains of blowing while I eat.
    Oh! could the smooth, the emblematic
  song
Flow like thy genial juices o'er my tongue,
(25) Could those mild morsels in my numbers
  chime,
And, as they roll in substance, roll in rime,
No more thy awkward unpoetic name
Should shun the muse, or prejudice thy
  fame:
But rising grateful to the accustomed ear,
(30) All bards should catch it, and all realms
  revere!

                    "Hasty Pudding"
                    by Joel Barlow

39. The subject of the poem is based on
    (A) the importance of writing poetry
    (B) a patriotic theme
    (C) extolling the virtues of eating a hot cereal
    (D) advice to other poets to write about mundane subjects
    (E) writing epic poetry

40. As used in line 22, "pains" can be thought of as
    (A) great care or effort
    (B) torture
    (C) a hurting sensation
    (D) penalty
    (E) hunger pains

41. Which of the definitions below is the definition of "the kine" as used in line 19?
    (A) A friendly person
    (B) Sugar maple trees
    (C) Cows
    (D) The cookstove
    (E) Lanterns

42. The speaker claims to eat Hasty Pudding
    (A) for breakfast and dinner
    (B) only on special days
    (C) within the confines of poetic verse
    (D) at a "distant fair" (line 13)
    (E) only with "sweets" (line 15)

43. In the first stanza, the speaker contends that Hasty Pudding is
    (A) a well-known patriotic subject
    (B) loftier than the Alps
    (C) a theme akin to odes, mountains, and flags
    (D) not as inspiring as patriotic themes
    (E) a subject that is new to poetry

44. Of the following devices listed, which is used in lines 17–18?
    (A) Apostrophe
    (B) Alliteration
    (C) Simile
    (D) Metaphor
    (E) Aposiopesis

45. In lines 23–26, the speaker uses elements of syntactical parallelism to
    (A) establish a pattern of onomatopoeia
    (B) reinforce the alliterative pattern of the previous stanza
    (C) enhance the simile comparing the writing process and eating
    (D) negate anticipated antagonism toward the simplicity of the subject
    (E) point out his sense of urgency in the matter

46. The song is "emblematic" (line 23) in that the poet wants the poem
    (A) to be filled with moralistic mottoes
    (B) and the process of writing it to represent the Hasty Pudding experience
    (C) to reflect a lofty theme and patriotic tone
    (D) and the process of writing it to incorporate elements of established symbols
    (E) to become accepted as part of the main body of symbolic literature

Questions 47–53 are based on the following passage.

I had been now thirteen days on shore, and had been eleven times on board the ship; in which time I had brought away all
Line that one pair of hands could well be
(5) supposed capable to bring, though I believe verily, had the calm weather held, I should have brought away the whole ship, piece by piece. But preparing the twelfth time to go on board, I found the wind began to
(10) rise; however, at low water I went on board, and though I thought I had rummaged the cabin so effectually, as that nothing more could be found, yet I discovered a locker with drawers in it, in
(15) one of which I found two or three razors and one pair of large scissors, with some ten or a dozen of good knives and forks; in another I found about thirty-six pounds value in money, some European coin, some
(20) Brazil, some pieces of eight, some gold, some silver.
    I smiled to myself at the sight of this money. "O drug!" said I aloud, "what art thou good for? Thou art not worth to me,
(25) no, not the taking off of the ground; one of those knives is worth all this heap; I have no manner of use for thee; e'en remain where thou art and go to the bottom as a creature whose life is not worth saving."
(30) However, upon second thoughts, I took it away, and wrapping all this in a piece of canvas, I began to think of making another raft; but while I was preparing this, I found the sky overcast, and the wind began to
(35) rise, and in a quarter of an hour it blew a

fresh gale from the shore; it presently
occurred to me that it was in vain to
pretend to make a raft with the wind offshore, and that it was my business to be
(40) gone before the tide of flood began,
otherwise I might not be able to reach the
shore at all. Accordingly I let myself down
into the water and swam across the
channel, which lay between the ship and
(45) the sands, and even that with difficulty
enough, partly with the weight of the things
I had about me, and partly the roughness
of the water, for the wind rose very hastily,
and before it was quite high water, it blew
(50) a storm.

    But I was gotten home to my little tent,
where I lay with all my wealth about me
very secure. It blew very hard all that night,
and in the morning, when I looked out,
(55) behold, no more ship was to be seen; I was
a little surprised, but recovered myself with
this satisfactory reflection, viz., that I had
lost no time, nor abated no diligence to get
everything out of her that could be useful to
(60) me, and that indeed there was little left in
her that I was able to bring away if I had
had more time.

               Robinson Crusoe
               by Daniel Defoe

47. The circumstances described in the passage
support the idea that the speaker has
(A) the nature of a petty thief
(B) an ineptitude toward his circumstances
(C) been part of a salvage crew
(D) innate survival skills
(E) a plan for an immediate rescue

48. The use of figurative language in the second
paragraph (lines 22–29) includes all the fol-
lowing EXCEPT
(A) elements of mixed figures
(B) metaphor
(C) simile
(D) personification
(E) understatement

49. The phrase "vain to pretend" (lines 37–38)
might also be worded as
(A) conceited actions to take
(B) trivial to allege
(C) useless to plan
(D) lacking in sense to put in a claim
(E) unimportant to feign

50. In line 39, "my business" refers to the
speaker's
(A) salvaging operation
(B) anxiety or concern
(C) power of interference over the ship
(D) matter or affair
(E) policy

51. "Viz." (line 57) means
(A) in other words
(B) for example
(C) namely
(D) about
(E) equal to

52. Which of the following attitudes does the nar-
rator exhibit toward the storm?
(A) Shock and despair
(B) Gripping fear
(C) Unsubmissive resistance
(D) Calm composure
(E) Self-satisfied defiance

53. The speaker's "second thoughts" in line 30
serve to indicate his
(A) anticipation of a change in circumstances
(B) indecisive character
(C) deeply insightful nature
(D) overwhelming sense of greed
(E) tendency toward elements of a split per-
sonality

Questions 54–60 are based on the following poem.

My Life—to Discontent a Prey

My life—to Discontent a prey—
    Is in the sere and yellow leaf.
'Tis vain for happiness to pray:
Line   No solace brings my heart relief.
(5) My pulse is weak, my spirit low;
    I cannot think, I cannot write.
I strive to spin a verse—but lo!
    My rhymes are very rarely right.

I sit within my lowly cell,
(10)   And strive to court the comic Muse;
But how can Poesy excel,
    With such a row from yonder mews?
In accents passionately high
    The carter chides the stubborn horse;
(15) And shouts a 'Gee!' or yells a 'Hi!'
    In tones objectionably hoarse.

In vain for Poesy I wait;
    No comic Muse my call obeys.
My brains are loaded with a weight
(20)   That mocks the laurels and the bays.
I wish my brains could only be
    Inspired with industry anew;
And labour like the busy bee,
    In strains no Genius ever knew.

(25) Although I strive with all my might,
    Alas, my efforts all are vain!
I've no *afflatus* —not a mite;
    I cannot work the comic vein.
The Tragic Muse may hear my pleas,
(30)   And waft me to a purer clime.
Melpomene! assist me, please,
    To somewhat higher heights to climb.

by Henry S. Leigh

54. The rhymes used throughout the poem are remarkable because they are mostly
    (A) synonyms
    (B) homonyms
    (C) similes
    (D) redundant
    (E) transitional

55. Throughout the poem, the speaker characterizes himself as NOT
    (A) moody
    (B) troubled
    (C) conceited
    (D) argumentative
    (E) inspired

56. In the context of the entire poem "the sere and yellow leaf" (line 2) represents
    (A) the poet's preference for tragic poetry
    (B) the condition of the poet's attitude
    (C) the time of year
    (D) the poet's preference for comic poetry
    (E) the end of life

57. The poem emphasizes
    (A) the isolation of the poet
    (B) the poet's genius
    (C) mythology
    (D) the poet's reliance on the Muses for his verse
    (E) the quietness needed for writing poetry

58. In relation to the rest of the poem, the last four lines include
    (A) a change of rhythm
    (B) the speaker's discontent replaced by tragedy
    (C) a mood shift from futile to hopeful
    (D) change of rhyme scheme
    (E) a mood shift from despairing to self-reliant

59. Personified "Discontent" in line 1
    (A) shows the speaker's anger
    (B) serves as a friend
    (C) emphasizes a desire to change
    (D) serves to victimize the speaker
    (E) comforts the speaker

60. The speaker can be described as all the following EXCEPT
    (A) discouraged
    (B) self-reliant
    (C) wanting to write comic poetry
    (D) dependent
    (E) wanting the Muses to get to work

ANSWER KEY: PRACTICE TEST SIX

1. A	7. A	13. E	19. C	25. D	31. E
2. C	8. D	14. D	20. D	26. E	32. B
3. E	9. E	15. B	21. B	27. E	33. C
4. D	10. A	16. A	22. E	28. A	34. E
5. B	11. A	17. A	23. C	29. E	35. A
6. C	12. A	18. A	24. E	30. D	36. C

37. D	43. E	49. C	55. E
38. B	44. A	50. B	56. B
39. C	45. C	51. C	57. D
40. A	46. B	52. D	58. C
41. C	47. D	53. A	59. D
42. A	48. E	54. B	60. B

TO OBTAIN YOUR RAW SCORE:

_____ divided by 4 = _____
Total wrong   Score W

_____ minus _____ = _____
  Total right   Score W   Score R

Round Score R to the nearest whole
number for the raw score.

HOW DID YOU DO?

55–60 = Excellent
44–54 = Very Good
35–43 = Above Average
23–34 = Average
15–22 = Below Average

EXPLANATIONS: PRACTICE TEST SIX

NOTE: Most practice tests cannot duplicate the content and conditions of the actual Literature test. Also, the scope and definitions of the literary elements can differ among literary critics; therefore, the rationale behind what constitutes a correct or an incorrect answer choice may vary. Each of these practice tests, however, gives you an opportunity to analyze selections, think critically, and develop your test-taking skills so you can do your personal best on the SAT Subject Test in Literature.

1. **A** Line 2: "the last story" implies previous stories.

2. **C** Line 7: "an apocryphal authority" would be false by definition.

3. **E** The corrupt version of a story would not be accurate.

4. **D** "At" six would refer to the hour; "with" six refers to the number of children there. The other answer choices are not central to the contrast.

5. **B** See the explanation above.

6. **C** An oxymoron, this expression represents the confused story about dining as part of a larger scandal.

7. **A** To be jocose is to be joking.

8. **D** His amplification in lines 22–24 explains his meaning. A gull is a cheat or trickster, and a philter is a love potion or charm.

9. **E** "Flock" is a traditional, biblical symbol for the members of the church. Figuratively, the leader is the pastor or shepherd.

10. **A** Mr. Fellowes begins the gossip about Barton in the first paragraph and does not accept the kinder sentiments toward Barton that Cleves expresses in lines 44–46. The emphasis on "I" also makes him seem overbearing and judgmental.

11. **A** This cliché is still in use: from the top of my head to the bottom of my feet.

12. **A** Birds, squirrels, and wolves have places to go for shelter ("All, all"), but the speaker does not.

13. **E** The description of the happy, safe man on shore further emphasizes the fear felt by the man on the ship.

14. **D** The tempests are roaring (line 3); a hurricane is coming.

15. **B** At first, this description may seem mysterious, but context reveals the place to be the bottom of the sea, where there are no charts. It is unfamiliar.

16. **A** A strand is a shoreline; a coast is the land next to the sea. How can a shoreline not have a coast? How can a mother not have a child?

17. **A** In antonomasia, a proper name represents an idea. In this case, Columbus represents explorers.

18. **A** "Unmov'd" refers to his lack of need to move to a place of safety and to his calm state of mind.

19. **C** Lines 1–4 describe man in safety; lines 5–12 describe man and animal in danger. Answer choices A, B, D, and E reflect this contrast.

20. **D** The dangerous storm expires, ceases, or terminates on shore.

21. **B** To be a "stranger to repose" would be not to know rest.

22. **E** To be "Foredoomed" is a reference to predestination; in this case to be doomed to destruction is inevitable.

23. **C** The use of past tense for their last sunset foreshadows death, further emphasizing his sense of hopelessness.

24. **E** By definition, a barque is a ship or sailing vessel.

25. **D** Despite the skill of the sailors or the scientific principle used to design a seaworthy vessel, nature is stronger.

26. **E** No simile (a comparison using "like" or "as") appears in the last stanza.

27. **E** "Perhaps" can mean "by chance" or "possibly" and modifies the verb.

28. **A** An escutcheon is a shield with a family's coat of arms on it.

29. **E** To grope is to feel your way blindly; trackless is to be without a path or rail.

30. **D** In this land, there is "no day" (line 20), nor are there charts or compass directions. In other words, this refers to death at the bottom of the sea.

31. **E** Lines 1–5 reveal the context to be greater than just eating habits; he connects diet with individual happiness and national prosperity.

32. **B** Lines 44–54 reveal that the speaker wishes to change his readers' minds and, by implication, their habits.

33. **C** Goldsmith's poem possesses "these two advantages" (line 14) listed in lines 12–14.

34. **E** Goldsmith's poem could not overcome those against him: to be "vain to contend" is to be useless to fight against.

35. **A** Notice lines 31–32: only a "few persons but what would always prefer a plain dish."

36. **C** His point is directly expressed in lines 51–52: "I…rank *simplicity of diet* among the virtues."

37. **D** Lines 35–39 deal with leadership; some people should set an example.

38. **B** The pronoun's antecedent is found in lines 39–40: "Persons of this description." What description? "those whose situation enables them to take the lead" (lines 37–38).

39. **C** Lines 15–17 state the subject: Hasty Pudding, eaten in a bowl with milk.

40. **A** The speaker uses milk to cool his hot mush to "save the pain of blowing," to save the effort.

41. **C** Context: Milk comes "smoking" or warm from the cow.

42. **A** Line 16 reveals that he eats it morning and evening.

43. **E** The subject is "A virgin theme, unconscious of the muse" (line 6).

44. **A** The speaker directly addresses a bowl of cereal, an example of apostrophe.

45. **C** "…could the song / Flow like thy…juices…, Could those…moral… chime, / and, as they roll in substance, roll in rime…." He wants the poem to reflect the smoothness and flow of the mush.

46. **B** An emblem symbolically represents something.

47. **D** He salvaged items needed for survival.

48. **E** The speaker may exaggerate the worthlessness of money, but he does not understate it.

49. **C** Substitute each phrase in the sentence to find the best choice: "it was [useless to plan] to make a raft."

50. **B** He is anxious that "the tide of flood" would strand him from shore.

51. **C** By definition, "Viz." means "namely."

52. **D** Although a "little surprised" (line 56), he was calm and satisfied with his situation.

53. **A** When survival gear is his primary need, why would he gather and take to shore money unless he anticipates possible rescue?

54. **B** Homonyms are words that sound the same, but have different meanings and often different spellings.

55. **E** He seeks the comic Muse (line 10), but "In vain" (line 17).

56. **B** He wants to write comic Posey, but cannot. He is so discontented that "My life…," he says, "Is in the sere [dried up] and yellow leaf." On a deeper level, note that he considers writing tragic poems. (lines 29–30). In that case, the leaf could represent the serious elements in his life as a basis for tragic poems.

57. **D** Note lines 10, 18, and 29–32 in which he courts, waits on, and makes pleas to muses.

58. **C** The speaker has become hopeful because "The Tragic Muse *may* hear my pleas…" (emphasis added).

59. **D** He does not want his life to be like dried leaves, but rather he wants to be happy (line 3). Notice, however, that he sees himself as Discontent's "prey," in other words, a victim.

60. **B** He is discouraged (line 6) because he wants to write "Poesy" (lines 9–10), but he is dependent on muses of mythology, calling on them to help him (lines 29–32). He is not self-reliant.

ANSWER SHEET FOR PRACTICE TEST SEVEN

1. Ⓐ Ⓑ Ⓒ Ⓓ Ⓔ
2. Ⓐ Ⓑ Ⓒ Ⓓ Ⓔ
3. Ⓐ Ⓑ Ⓒ Ⓓ Ⓔ
4. Ⓐ Ⓑ Ⓒ Ⓓ Ⓔ
5. Ⓐ Ⓑ Ⓒ Ⓓ Ⓔ
6. Ⓐ Ⓑ Ⓒ Ⓓ Ⓔ
7. Ⓐ Ⓑ Ⓒ Ⓓ Ⓔ
8. Ⓐ Ⓑ Ⓒ Ⓓ Ⓔ
9. Ⓐ Ⓑ Ⓒ Ⓓ Ⓔ
10. Ⓐ Ⓑ Ⓒ Ⓓ Ⓔ
11. Ⓐ Ⓑ Ⓒ Ⓓ Ⓔ
12. Ⓐ Ⓑ Ⓒ Ⓓ Ⓔ
13. Ⓐ Ⓑ Ⓒ Ⓓ Ⓔ
14. Ⓐ Ⓑ Ⓒ Ⓓ Ⓔ
15. Ⓐ Ⓑ Ⓒ Ⓓ Ⓔ
16. Ⓐ Ⓑ Ⓒ Ⓓ Ⓔ
17. Ⓐ Ⓑ Ⓒ Ⓓ Ⓔ
18. Ⓐ Ⓑ Ⓒ Ⓓ Ⓔ
19. Ⓐ Ⓑ Ⓒ Ⓓ Ⓔ
20. Ⓐ Ⓑ Ⓒ Ⓓ Ⓔ

21. Ⓐ Ⓑ Ⓒ Ⓓ Ⓔ
22. Ⓐ Ⓑ Ⓒ Ⓓ Ⓔ
23. Ⓐ Ⓑ Ⓒ Ⓓ Ⓔ
24. Ⓐ Ⓑ Ⓒ Ⓓ Ⓔ
25. Ⓐ Ⓑ Ⓒ Ⓓ Ⓔ
26. Ⓐ Ⓑ Ⓒ Ⓓ Ⓔ
27. Ⓐ Ⓑ Ⓒ Ⓓ Ⓔ
28. Ⓐ Ⓑ Ⓒ Ⓓ Ⓔ
29. Ⓐ Ⓑ Ⓒ Ⓓ Ⓔ
30. Ⓐ Ⓑ Ⓒ Ⓓ Ⓔ
31. Ⓐ Ⓑ Ⓒ Ⓓ Ⓔ
32. Ⓐ Ⓑ Ⓒ Ⓓ Ⓔ
33. Ⓐ Ⓑ Ⓒ Ⓓ Ⓔ
34. Ⓐ Ⓑ Ⓒ Ⓓ Ⓔ
35. Ⓐ Ⓑ Ⓒ Ⓓ Ⓔ
36. Ⓐ Ⓑ Ⓒ Ⓓ Ⓔ
37. Ⓐ Ⓑ Ⓒ Ⓓ Ⓔ
38. Ⓐ Ⓑ Ⓒ Ⓓ Ⓔ
39. Ⓐ Ⓑ Ⓒ Ⓓ Ⓔ
40. Ⓐ Ⓑ Ⓒ Ⓓ Ⓔ

41. Ⓐ Ⓑ Ⓒ Ⓓ Ⓔ
42. Ⓐ Ⓑ Ⓒ Ⓓ Ⓔ
43. Ⓐ Ⓑ Ⓒ Ⓓ Ⓔ
44. Ⓐ Ⓑ Ⓒ Ⓓ Ⓔ
45. Ⓐ Ⓑ Ⓒ Ⓓ Ⓔ
46. Ⓐ Ⓑ Ⓒ Ⓓ Ⓔ
47. Ⓐ Ⓑ Ⓒ Ⓓ Ⓔ
48. Ⓐ Ⓑ Ⓒ Ⓓ Ⓔ
49. Ⓐ Ⓑ Ⓒ Ⓓ Ⓔ
50. Ⓐ Ⓑ Ⓒ Ⓓ Ⓔ
51. Ⓐ Ⓑ Ⓒ Ⓓ Ⓔ
52. Ⓐ Ⓑ Ⓒ Ⓓ Ⓔ
53. Ⓐ Ⓑ Ⓒ Ⓓ Ⓔ
54. Ⓐ Ⓑ Ⓒ Ⓓ Ⓔ
55. Ⓐ Ⓑ Ⓒ Ⓓ Ⓔ
56. Ⓐ Ⓑ Ⓒ Ⓓ Ⓔ
57. Ⓐ Ⓑ Ⓒ Ⓓ Ⓔ
58. Ⓐ Ⓑ Ⓒ Ⓓ Ⓔ
59. Ⓐ Ⓑ Ⓒ Ⓓ Ⓔ
60. Ⓐ Ⓑ Ⓒ Ⓓ Ⓔ

Practice Test Seven

Time allowed: One hour

Directions: The following questions test your understanding of several literary selections. Read each passage or poem and the questions that follow it. Select the best answer choice for each question by blackening the matching oval on your answer sheet. **Special attention should be given to questions containing the following words: EXCEPT, LEAST, NOT.**

Questions 1–6 are based on the following passage.

I do not think that we ever knew his real
name. Our ignorance of it certainly never
gave us any social inconvenience, for at
Line Sandy Bar in 1854 most men were
(5) christened anew. Sometimes these
appellatives were derived from some
distinctiveness of dress, as in the case of
"Dungaree Jack"; or from some peculiarity
of habit, as shown in "Saleratus Bill," so
(10) called from an undue proportion of that
chemical in his daily bread; or from some
unlucky slip, as exhibited in "The Iron
Pirate," a mild, inoffensive man, who
earned that baleful title by his unfortunate
(15) mispronunciation of the term "iron pyrites."
Perhaps this may have been the beginning
of a rude heraldry; but I am constrained to
think that it was because a man's real name
in that day rested solely upon his own
(20) unsupported statement. "Call yourself
Clifford, do you?" said Boston, addressing
a timid new-comer with infinite scorn; "hell
is full of such Cliffords!" He then introduced
the unfortunate man, whose name
(25) happened to be really Clifford, as "Jay-bird
Charley,"—an unhallowed inspiration of the
moment, that clung to him ever after.

"Tennessee's Partner"
by Bret Harte

1. The narrator's comments concerning "Saleratus Bill" reveal that he
   (A) especially enjoyed bread
   (B) used large amounts of yeast
   (C) earned a high salary
   (D) made bread that was sour
   (E) used large amounts of baking soda

2. Lines 5–11 contain elements of all the following EXCEPT
   (A) cause and effect
   (B) amplification
   (C) example
   (D) metonymy
   (E) personification

3. The LEAST accurate description of "a rude heraldry," as used in line 17, is
   (A) a barbarous devising of family lineage
   (B) a discourteous announcement
   (C) a robust harbinger of official status
   (D) a vulgar granting of nomenclature
   (E) an inaccurate genealogical lineage

4. That "The Iron Pirate" was named mispronouncing "iron pyrites" might indicate that
   (A) Sandy Bar was a shipping port
   (B) Sandy Bar was a mining town
   (C) the man really was a pirate
   (D) the man was known as a thief
   (E) the man was born in Sandy Bar

5. In line 22, "with infinite scorn" emphasizes Boston's
   (A) sense of indignation
   (B) anger at injustice
   (C) insolence
   (D) resistance of authority
   (E) quiescence

6. The statement made in lines 1–5 can be described as
   (A) a statement of reality regarding the situation
   (B) an opinion held by the narrator only
   (C) a controversial premise to an argument
   (D) a contention in a debate
   (E) a feeble excuse for inexcusable conduct

Questions 7–16 are based on the following poem.

The Sonnet
II

Scorn not the sonnet; Critic, you have frown'd,
   Mindless of its just honours; with this key
   Shakespeare unlock'd his heart; the melody
Of this small lute gave ease to Petrarch's wound;
(5) A thousand times this pipe did Tasso sound;
   With it Camöens sooth'd an exile's grief;
   The Sonnet glitter'd a gay myrtle leaf
Amid the cypress with which Dante crown'd
His visionary brow: a glow-worm lamp,
(10) It cheer'd mild Spenser, call'd from Faery-land
To struggle through dark ways; and, when a damp
   Fell round the path of Milton, in his hand
The Thing became a trumpet; whence he blew
Soul-animating strains—alas, too few!

by William Wordsworth

7. In the poem in its entirety, the speaker reveals an attitude toward "Critic" (line 1) that can be considered
   (A) angry and belligerent
   (B) reproachful and retaliatory
   (C) censorious and didactic
   (D) provocative and probing
   (E) class-conscious and authoritative

8. From the context, "Camöens" (line 6) probably refers to a
   (A) political prisoner
   (B) poet
   (C) revolutionary
   (D) critic
   (E) sonnet

9. The speaker's use of "alas, too few!" in the last line produces which of the effects listed below?
   (A) It summarizes that not enough poets write sonnets.
   (B) It contends that more critics should appreciate the sonnet.
   (C) It sets forth an element of quantity over quality.
   (D) It heightens the sense of nostalgia and melancholy of the sonnet.
   (E) It shifts emphasis to a yearning for Milton to have written more sonnets.

10. The phrase "a gay myrtle leaf/Amid the cypress" (lines 7–8) figuratively means that
    (A) Dante wrote sonnets about nature
    (B) myrtle leaves are pretty in cypress arrangements
    (C) the sonnet provided a contrast among Dante's works about death
    (D) myrtle leaves and cypress were used to foretell the future
    (E) Dante favored sonnets over more serious poetic forms

11. In this poem, the vehicles "key" (line 2), "lute" (line 4), and "trumpet" (line 13) emphasize
    (A) the weaknesses of Shakespeare, Petrarch, and Milton
    (B) the means by which poets achieve their ends
    (C) the ways sonnets can be used musically
    (D) the emotional release, solace, and stimulus that the sonnet provides
    (E) the contrast to Tasso, Camöens, and Dante

12. That Tasso wrote a thousand sonnets (line 5) may be a(n)
    (A) simile
    (B) hyperbole
    (C) irony
    (D) allusion
    (E) metonymy

13. The effect of the syntactical placement of "in his hand" in line 12 is to
    (A) emphasize Milton's skill
    (B) make "The Thing" (line 13) of greater importance
    (C) put aside the theme of the poem
    (D) recognize the balance of subject and execution
    (E) attract greater attention to the poem over the poet

14. In the last line, "alas, too few!" is said in a tone that is
    (A) nonchalant
    (B) zealous
    (C) wistful
    (D) ambitious
    (E) incendiary

15. In line 9, "a glow-worm lamp" is a metaphoric reference to
    (A) a critic
    (B) Spenser
    (C) a sonnet
    (D) Faery-land
    (E) Dante

16. In line 14, the speaker uses the word "Soul-animating" for the purpose of
    (A) making the sonnet into a higher literary form
    (B) varying the rhythm
    (C) suggesting that Milton had died
    (D) establishing an alliterative relationship with "strains"
    (E) symbolizing death

Questions 17–26 are based on the following passage.

So much for Industry, my Friends, and Attention to one's own Business; but to these we must add *Frugality*, if we would
Line make our *Industry* more certainly successful.
(5) A Man may, if he knows not how to save as he gets, *keep his Nose all his life to the Grindstone*, and die not worth a *Groat* at last. *A fat Kitchen makes a lean Will*, as Poor Richard says; and,

(10) Many Estates are spent in the Getting,
      Since Women for Tea forsook Spinning and Knitting,
      And Men for Punch forsook Hewing and Splitting.

If you would be wealthy, says he, in another *Almanack, think of Saving as well*
(15) *as of Getting*: The Indies have not make Spain rich, because her Outgoes are greater than her Incomes. Away then with your expensive Follies, and you will not have so much Cause to complain of hard
(20) Times, heavy Taxes, and chargeable Families; for, as Poor Dick says,

      Women and Wine, Game and Deceit,
      Make the Wealth small, and Wants great.

(25) And farther, *What maintains one Vice, would bring up two Children*. You may think perhaps, That a *little* Tea, or a *little* Punch now and then, Diet a *little* more costly, Clothes a *little* finer, and a *little*
(30) Entertainment now and then, can be no great Matter; but remember what Poor Richard says, *Many a Little makes a Mickle*; and farther, *Beware of little Expences; a small Leak will sink a great Ship*; and
(35) again, *Who Dainties love, shall Beggars prove*; and moreover, *Fools make Feasts, and wise Men eat them*.

"Poor Richard Improved"
by Benjamin Franklin

17. The speaker is most concerned with which of the following topics?
    (A) Economy and temperance
    (B) Occupation and commerce
    (C) Socials and hospitality
    (D) Taxes and wages
    (E) Food and drink

18. Which of the following pieces of advice can be best understood literally but not figuratively?
    (A) "A fat Kitchen makes a lean Will." (line 8)
    (B) "If you would be wealthy…think of Saving as well as of Getting." (lines 13–15)
    (C) "What maintains one Vice, would bring up two Children." (lines 25–26)
    (D) "A small Leak will sink a great Ship." (line 34)
    (E) "Who Dainties love, shall Beggars prove." (lines 35–36)

19. A "Groat" (line 7) can be thought of as
    (A) a small farm animal
    (B) a portion of fabric
    (C) a portion of rum cut with water
    (D) a trivial amount
    (E) a painful cry

20. Which of the following adjectives can be used to describe Poor Richard's advice?
    (A) Dialectal
    (B) Episodic
    (C) Aphoristic
    (D) Epistolary
    (E) Satiric

21. Use of the term "Poor Dick" (line 21) contributes to the sense that
    (A) the speaker feels sorry for Dick
    (B) Dick is actually not wealthy
    (C) Dick did not follow his own advice
    (D) the speaker is being sarcastic
    (E) the speaker feels comfortable in quoting him

22. In the selection, "Nose…to the Grindstone" (lines 6–7) is a saying that expresses which of the following ideas?
    I. Working at close range to a millstone
    II. Staying at hard, steady labor
    III. Unremitting self-requirement in work and duty
    (A) I only
    (B) III only
    (C) I and II only
    (D) II and III only
    (E) I and III only

23. The "fat Kitchen" (line 8) is actually
    (A) a heavyset cook
    (B) an oversized kitchen
    (C) extravagance in the food budget
    (D) a diet too rich in animal fat
    (E) a greasy kitchen

24. As supported by the context of the passage, "lean Will" (line 8) alludes to
    (A) undernourishment
    (B) poor diet
    (C) a dwindling estate to inherit
    (D) a life-threatening illness
    (E) hard labor

25. "Many a Little makes a Mickle" (line 32) might be restated as which of the following expressions?
    (A) Gain a little, lose a little
    (B) Sew on the bottom what you took off the top
    (C) It all adds up to trouble
    (D) One step forward and two steps back
    (E) Pennies add up to dollars

26. "Away then" in line 17 has a tone that is
    (A) bombastic
    (B) desiderative
    (C) obsequious
    (D) authoritative
    (E) disparaging

Questions 27–32 are based on the following passage.

I used to see packs of half-wild dogs
haunting the lonely beach on the south
shore of Staten Island, in New York Bay, for
Line the sake of the carrion there cast up; and I
(5) remember that once, when for a long time I
had heard a furious barking in the tall grass
of the marsh, a pack of half a dozen large
dogs burst forth on to the beach, pursuing a
little one which ran straight to me for
(10) protection, and I afforded it with some
stones, though at some risk to myself; but
the next day the little one was the first to
bark at me. Under these circumstances I
could not but remember the words of the
(15) poet:

Blow, blow, thou winter wind
Thou art not so unkind
    As *his* ingratitude;
Thy tooth is not so keen,
(20) Because thou art not seen,
    Although thy breath be rude.
Freeze, freeze, thou bitter sky,
Thou dost not bite so nigh
    As benefits forgot;
(25) Though thou the waters warp,
Thy sting is not so sharp
    As friend remembered not.

Cape Cod
by Henry David Thoreau

27. The overall theme of this passage is
(A) a defense for an unwise action
(B) a musing upon an ironic situation
(C) an angry accusation against disloyalty
(D) a revelation of poor judgment
(E) an attempt at appearing confident

28. In the passage, what is the literary role of the little dog?
I. A vehicle in an analogy
II. A symbol of ingratitude
III. A character representing a type of person
(A) I only
(B) II only
(C) I and III only
(D) II and III only
(E) I, II, and III

29. Because of the events and circumstances of the episode, the speaker's attitude toward the little dog becomes
(A) betrayed and hurt
(B) hostile and angry
(C) confused and ambivalent
(D) sympathetic and concerned
(E) determined and aggressive

30. The incident at New York Bay brings the poem to the speaker's mind because
(A) the speaker is feeling sentimental and lonely
(B) the poem describes the weather at the bay
(C) the speaker is reminiscing about a former friend
(D) the poem describes the cruelty of an unrequited friendship
(E) the speaker was stimulated intellectually by the fear of the event

31. In the poem, the speaker seems to view the natural elements as
(A) dangerous threats
(B) symbols of deception
(C) understandable harshness
(D) unexplainable phenomena
(E) unrelenting challengers

32. In the second stanza of the poem, the "bitter sky" is an example of
(A) alliteration
(B) paradox
(C) irony
(D) synaesthesia
(E) digression

Questions 33–38 are based on the following passage.

She heeded nothing of what I said; but
when she had tasted the water and drawn
breath, she went on thus—
Line 'I tell you I could not forget it; and I took
(5) my revenge: for you to be adopted by your
uncle, and placed in a state of ease and
comfort, was what I could not endure. I
wrote to him; I said I was sorry for his
disappointment, but Jane Eyre was dead:
(10) she had died of typhus fever at Lowood.
Now act as you please: write and

contradict my assertion—expose my
falsehood as soon as you like. You were
born, I think, to be my torment: my last
(15) hour is racked by the recollection of a deed
which, but for you, I should never have
been tempted to commit.'

'If you could be persuaded to think no
more of it, aunt, and to regard me with
(20) kindness and forgiveness—'

'You have a very bad disposition,' said
she, 'and one to this day I feel it impossible
to understand: how for nine years you
could be patient and quiescent under any
(25) treatment, and in the tenth break out all fire
and violence, I can never comprehend.'

'My disposition is not so bad as you
think. I am passionate, but not vindictive.
Many a time, as a little child, I should have
(30) been glad to love you if you would have let
me: and I long earnestly to be reconciled to
you now: kiss me, aunt.'

I approached my cheek to her lips: she
would not touch it. She said I oppressed her
(35) by leaning over the bed, and again
demanded water. As I laid her down—for I
raised her and supported her on my arm
while she drank—I covered her ice-cold and
clammy hand with mine: the feeble fingers
(40) shrank from my touch—the glazing eyes
shunned my gaze.

'Love me, then, or hate me, as you will,' I
said at last, 'you have my full and free
forgiveness: ask now for God's and be at
(45) peace.'

Jane Eyre
by Charlotte Brontë

33. The element of conflict in this passage
revolves around
(A) two women angry over past wrongs
(B) a woman struggling against death
(C) two people both wanting child custody
(D) a woman and her conscience
(E) a mother and her daughter

34. The woman probably complained that Jane
"oppressed her by leaning over the bed" (lines
34–35) because she
(A) really felt ill
(B) was communicating her continued hatred
(C) was protecting Jane from contagion
(D) needed fresh air and space
(E) wanted to intensify Jane's sense of guilt

35. After the woman's admission concerning the
adoption, why would Jane behave as she does?
(A) She never really wanted to be adopted.
(B) She is anticipating developing a new relationship.
(C) She is building on the bond of their old
relationship.
(D) The woman is very ill and Jane truly forgives her.
(E) Jane is pretending forgiveness to achieve
family status.

36. The tone of lines 11–13 can be considered
(A) reconcilable
(B) propitious
(C) audacious
(D) collaborative
(E) synergetic

37. As evidenced in the second paragraph, the
woman's attitude is best summarized by which
of these statements?
(A) She blames the uncle for abandoning
Jane.
(B) She blames Jane for the wrong she did to
Jane.
(C) She is truly sorry and accepts full responsi-
bility.
(D) She is released from her tormented guilt.
(E) She assumes that Jane will forgive her.

38. Of the following list of literary devices, which
one is used in lines 25–26 to describe Jane's
personality?
(A) Simile
(B) Personification
(C) Synecdoche
(D) Metonymy
(E) Metaphor

Questions 39–45 are based on the following poem.

A Winter Piece

From frozen climes, and endless tracts of
    snow,
From streams which northern winds forbid
    to flow,
What present shall the muse to *Dorset*
    bring,
Line Or how, so near the pole, attempt to sing.
(5) The hoary winter here conceals from sight
All pleasing objects which to verse invite.
The hills and dales, and the delightful
    woods,
The flow'ry plains, and silver-streaming
    floods,
By snow disguis'd, in bright confusion ly,
(10) And with one dazzling waste fatigue the
    eye.

No gentle breathing breez prepares the
    spring,
No birds within the desert region sing,
The ships, unmov'd, the boist'rous winds
    defy,
While rattling chariots o'er the ocean fly.
(15) The vast *Leviathan* wants room to play,
And spout his waters in the face of day.
The starving wolves along the main sea
    prowl,
And to the moon in icy valleys howl.
O'er many a shining league the level main
(20) Here spreads itself into a glassy plain:
There solid billows of enormous size,
Alps of green ice, in wild disorder rise.

by Ambrose Philips

39. The speaker alludes to which of the following as the occasion for this poem?
    (A) A letter home from a boy to Dorset
    (B) A poet speaking to "the muse" (line 3)
    (C) A poet examining the winter landscape for inspiration
    (D) Dorset inviting a writer to describe a blizzard
    (E) An individual learning to sing about nature

40. The readers can presume in lines 3–7 that
    (A) the speaker is inspired by the "frozen climes" (line 1)
    (B) Copenhagen is a center for poetic activity
    (C) the speaker is expecting a gift to be sent
    (D) ideas for writing poetry are influenced by geographic location
    (E) the speaker is seeking a gift to purchase

41. All the pairs listed below reflect the main contrast developed in the poem EXCEPT
    (A) "frozen" (line 1)…"flow" (line 2)
    (B) "winds" (line 2)…"sing" (line 4)
    (C) "conceals"…"sight" (line 5)
    (D) "forbid" (line 2)…"invite" (line 6)
    (E) "confusion" (line 9)…"delightful" (line 7)

42. As used in line 10, the literary role of "waste" is as a(n)
    (A) allusion to well-lit areas
    (B) ironic allusion
    (C) symbol of man's problems
    (D) hyperbole
    (E) play on words

43. Why is there a lack of "room to play" (line 15)?
    (A) Frozen water
    (B) Severe wind
    (C) Encroaching civilization
    (D) Severe drought
    (E) Snowdrifts

44. The "glassy plain" (line 20) is an example of which of these literary devices?
    (A) Antithesis
    (B) Personification
    (C) Metaphor
    (D) Synecdoche
    (E) Metonymy

45. The use of "rattling" in line 14 is a phonic device known as
    (A) oxymoron
    (B) onomatopoeia
    (C) alliteration
    (D) euphony
    (E) low style

Questions 46–52 are based on the following passage.

In order to gain a clear and just idea of the design and end of government, let us suppose a small number of persons settled in
Line some sequestered part of the earth,
(5) unconnected with the rest; they will then represent the first peopling of any country, or of the world. In this state of natural liberty, society will be their first thought. A thousand motives will excite them thereto;
(10) the strength of one man is so unequal to his wants, and his mind so unfitted for perpetual solitude, that he is soon obliged to seek assistance and relief of another, who in his turn requires the same. Four or five united
(15) would be able to raise a tolerable dwelling in the midst of a wilderness, but one man might labor out the common period of life without accomplishing any thing; when he had felled his timber he could not remove it,
(20) nor erect it after it was removed; hunger in the mean time would urge him to quit his work, and every different want would call him a different way. Disease, nay even misfortune, would be death; for though
(25) neither might be mortal, yet either would disable him from living, and reduce him to a state in which he might rather be said to perish than to die.

Thus necessity, like a gravitating power,
(30) would soon form our newly arrived emigrants into society, the reciprocal blessings of which would supersede, and render the obligations of law and government unnecessary while they
(35) remained perfectly just to each other; but as nothing but Heaven is impregnable to vice, it will unavoidably happen that in proportion as they surmount the first difficulties of emigration, which bound them together in a
(40) common cause, they will begin to relax in their duty and attachment to each other: and this remissness will point out the necessity of establishing some form of government to supply the defect of moral virtue.

Common Sense
by Thomas Paine

46. The first sentence is presumably
(A) an opinion asserted through lack of experience
(B) establishing a cause-and-effect relationship
(C) a statement of fantasy
(D) the speaker's summary statement
(E) establishing structure of an analogous model

47. According to the speaker, society is mostly a result of
(A) disease
(B) hunger
(C) necessity
(D) vice
(E) duty

48. In the last paragraph, the speaker wants the reader to believe that
(A) laws are reciprocal blessings
(B) law and government are products of virtue
(C) government is based on common causes
(D) overcoming difficulties gives place to vice
(E) establishing government binds people together

49. The speaker distinguishes "to perish" from "to die" (lines 27–28) to emphasize
(A) the inevitability of death for men who are alone
(B) the disabilities that result from living alone
(C) the demoralizing effects of loneliness
(D) the destructiveness of disease and accident
(E) the ironic situation misfortune places upon a man who is alone

50. In the final paragraph, gravity is used as a vehicle in a simile to explain
(A) why men form societies
(B) the reciprocal blessings of societies
(C) the obligations of law and government
(D) why laws are necessary
(E) defects of moral virtue

51. The "assistance and relief" discussed in line 13 are the result of
(A) a need for structure
(B) excitement over change
(C) natural liberty
(D) law and government
(E) wants and loneliness

52. As used in line 25, "mortal" indicates
    (A) fatal or causing death
    (B) of this world
    (C) causing death of the soul
    (D) affecting with fear of death
    (E) implacable

Questions 53–60 are based on the following passage.

Act I
Scene, an Apartment at Charlotte's
CHARLOTTE *and* LETITIA *discovered*

LETITIA.   And so, Charlotte, you really
    think the pocket-hoop unbecoming.

CHARLOTTE.   No, I don't say so. It may
(5)   be very becoming to saunter round the
    house of a rainy day; to visit my
    grand-mamma, or to go to Quakers'
    meeting: but to swim in a minuet, with
    the eyes of fifty well-dressed beaux
(10)   upon me, to trip it in the Mall, or walk
    on the battery, give me the luxurious,
    jaunty, flowing, bell-hoop. It would
    have delighted you to have seen me
    the last evening, my charming girl! I
    was dangling o'er the battery with
(15)   Billy Dimple; a knot of young fellows
    were upon the platform; as I passed
    them I faltered with one of the most
    bewitching false steps you ever saw,
    and then recovered myself with such a
(20)   pretty confusion, flirting my hoop to
    discover a jet black shoe and brilliant
    buckle...how my little heart thrilled to
    hear the confused raptures of—
    "Demme, Jack, what a delicate foot!"
(25)   "Ha! General, what a well-turned—"

LETITIA. Fie! fie! Charlotte [*stopping her
    mouth*], I protest you are quite a
    libertine.

CHARLOTTE.   Why, my dear little prude,
(30)   are we not all such libertines? Do you
    think, when I sat tortured two hours
    under the hands of my friseur, and an
    hour more at my toilet, that I had any
    thoughts of my Aunt Susan, or my
(35)   cousin Betsey? though they are both
    allowed to be critical judges of dress.

LETITIA.   Why, who should we dress to
    please, but those who are judges of its
    merit?

(40) CHARLOTTE.   Why, a creature who does
    not know *Buffon* from *Soufflé*—Man!—
    my Letitia—Man! for whom we dress,
    walk, dance, talk, lisp, languish, and
    smile. Does not the grave Spectator
(45)   assure us that even our much
    bepraised diffidence, modesty, and
    blushes are all directed to make
    ourselves good wives and mothers as
    fast as we can? Why, I'll undertake
(50)   with one flirt of this hoop to bring
    more beaux to my feet in one week
    than the grave Maria, and her
    sentimental circle, can do, by sighing
    sentiment till their hairs are grey.

(55) LETITIA.   Well, I won't argue with you;
    you always out-talk me: let us change
    the subject. I hear that Mr. Dimple
    and Maria are soon to be married.

CHARLOTTE.   You hear true. I was
(60)   consulted in the choice of the wedding
    clothes. She is to be married in a
    delicate white satin, and has a
    monstrous pretty brocaded lutestring
    for the second day....

The Contrast
by Royall Tyler

53. The girls' conversation consists of
    (A) a didactic tone
    (B) metaphoric constructions
    (C) casual language
    (D) poetic diction
    (E) highly structured syntax

54. In line 63, "monstrous pretty" is an example of which of the following literary devices?
    (A) Hyperbole
    (B) Apostrophe
    (C) Simile
    (D) Oxymoron
    (E) Alliteration

55. The context reveals that seemingly the "Spectator" (line 44) refers to a(n)
    (A) bodyguard
    (B) accepted authority on conduct
    (C) nanny
    (D) religious leader
    (E) overseer

56. Charlotte (lines 14–18) probably
    (A) accidentally fell
    (B) was at a wild, drunken party
    (C) was surprised by the boys' admiration
    (D) is defensive of her conduct
    (E) deliberately tripped

57. The word "swim" (line 7) connotatively suggests
    (A) too large clothing
    (B) moving through water
    (C) to be in a flood
    (D) smooth motions
    (E) covered with liquid

58. A "libertine" (line 28), as used in this context, is someone who is
    (A) morally unrestrained
    (B) a freedman
    (C) a skeptic
    (D) politically involved
    (E) a member of a sect

59. Maria is characterized by Charlotte as
    (A) headstrong
    (B) lacking in social skills
    (C) emotional
    (D) older
    (E) argumentative

60. From her comments, Charlotte indicates that she
    (A) has a fiance
    (B) is as sentimental as Maria
    (C) resents Letitia's attitude
    (D) concurs with the "Spectator"
    (E) was insulted by Letitia's protest

ANSWER KEY: PRACTICE TEST SEVEN

1. E	7. C	13. A	19. D	25. E	31. C	37. B	43. A	49. E	55. B
2. E	8. B	14. C	20. C	26. D	32. D	38. E	44. C	50. A	56. E
3. E	9. E	15. C	21. E	27. B	33. D	39. C	45. B	51. E	57. D
4. B	10. C	16. D	22. D	28. E	34. B	40. D	46. E	52. A	58. A
5. C	11. D	17. A	23. C	29. A	35. D	41. B	47. C	53. C	59. C
6. A	12. B	18. B	24. C	30. D	36. C	42. E	48. D	54. D	60. D

TO OBTAIN YOUR RAW SCORE:

_____ divided by 4 = _____
Total wrong   Score W

_____ minus _____ = _____
Total right   Score W   Score R

Round Score R to the nearest whole
number for the raw score.

HOW DID YOU DO?

55–60 = Excellent
44–54 = Very Good
35–43 = Above Average
23–34 = Average
15–22 = Below Average

EXPLANATIONS: PRACTICE TEST SEVEN

NOTE: Most practice tests cannot duplicate the content and conditions of the actual Literature test. Also, the scope and definitions of the literary elements can differ among literary critics; therefore, the rationale behind what constitutes a correct or an incorrect answer choice may vary. Each of these practice tests, however, gives you an opportunity to analyze selections, think critically, and develop your test-taking skills so you can do your personal best on the SAT Subject Test in Literature.

1. **E** Saleratus is baking soda, an ingredient used in biscuits.

2. **E** Human qualities are not given to any nonhuman in this passage.

3. **E** To be rude is not necessarily to be inaccurate.

4. **B** Iron pyrite is a mineral found in mines.

5. **C** Clifford was timid and a newcomer. Lines 16–19 indicate that the men did not trust one another, even to believe their names. The bullylike behavior toward the newcomer, combined with distrust, projects an insolent attitude.

6. **A** The speaker is simply explaining the situation as it existed in 1854 in Sandy Bar.

7. **C** First, he reproves the Critic in line 1; then he teaches him his error through citing many examples of famous poets who wrote sonnets. The sonnet was a key to Shakespeare, a lute to Petrarch, a pipe to Tasso, soothing to Camões, a leaf to Dante, a lamp to Spenser, and a trumpet to Milton.

8. **B** Context tells you that all the men's names in this poem refer to poets.

9. **E** The "damp" around Milton alludes to his blindness, a sadly emotional allusion that, in combination with describing his sonnets as "soul-animating," projects a tone of yearning.

10. **C** Even if you are unfamiliar with Dante's work, you can look at context to answer this question. The sonnet is compared to a "gay myrtle leaf." The figurative language used eliminates the literal nature of answer choices A and B. There are no hints in context that Dante foretold the future (D) or favored sonnets (E). However, the gay myrtle leaf (sonnet) "glitter'd …amid the cypress"—a contrast.

11. **D** The sonnet provides emotional release (an opened heart), musical solace to a wounded nature, and stimulus for soul-animating poems.

12. **B** This line could be an exaggeration, although some poets are very prolific.

13. **A** Would the sonnet become a trumpet in anyone else's hand? The implication is that it would not, emphasizing Milton's skill.

14. **C** A wistful tone includes vague yearnings. The speaker wishes Milton had written more sonnets.

15. **C** The poem's movement depends on a series of vehicles explaining the sonnet. The sonnet is a key, lute, pipe, gay myrtle leaf, glow-worm lamp, and trumpet.

16. **D** The "s" is repeated, creating alliteration.

17. **A** Economy or frugality (line 3); temperance (lines 27–37): Notice that what normally is viewed as showing self-restraint or temperance ("a little tea"), Poor Richard views as too much, using verbal irony to be sarcastic.

18. **B** This advice is best taken literally. In contrast, a "fat Kitchen" represents high expenses, "two Children" represent any obligation or necessity that requires money to maintain, the Leak in the Ship represents when money is lost and lives are ruined as a result, and Dainties represent anything overpriced and/or unneeded.

19. **D** A groat is a small amount.

20. **C** He uses a series of concise statements intended to make his point. FYI: [Poor] Richard Saunders was Franklin's pseudonym.

21. **E** Using a nickname projects a sense of familiarity in this context.

22. **D** This line is a traditional saying relating to perseverance in work.

23. **C** The speaker's point in line 8 is that buying costly ingredients and foods will drain the food budget until there is not enough money to buy food at all.

24. **C** Also, a "lean Will" is a play on words (pun) referring to an inheritance wasted by extravagance.

25. **E** "Mickle" means "much." Add up many small amounts and you will have a comparatively large amount.

26. **D** The entire selection has the tone of one who has authority based on confidence that he is right. Also, "Away then…" is a command such as used by people in positions of authority.

27. **B** He perhaps used poor judgment in confronting a pack of dogs (A and D) and he seems to feel the dog was disloyal, but he projects no anger (C). The situation, however, is ironic, and quoting a poem that reflects that irony reveals the speaker's contemplative mood.

28. **E** The poem serves to pull what would have otherwise been just an anecdote into what is now an analogy in which the dog, a symbol of ingratitude, represents friends "remembered not."

29. **A** Context eliminates B, C, and E. When defending the dog, the speaker probably felt concern for its safety and sympathetic to its situation, but those feelings changed when the dog barked at him.

30. **D** The concept of ingratitude and the feelings of hurt it elicits are found in both the incident and the poem.

31. **C** The speaker understands harshness in nature (lines 17, 24, 26), but not in friends.

32. **D** Bitter is gustatory (taste); the sky is visual: a blend of senses.

33. **D** Context eliminates answer choices B, C, and E. Are both women angry? No (lines 42–45). The dying woman is struggling with her conscience (lines 14–17).

34. **B** She also shrank from Jane's touch (lines 37–40).

35. **D** The last paragraph reveals Jane's response; she forgives her.

36. **C** Daring Jane to reveal her "falsehood" is audacious.

37. **B** Her attitude reflects a classic abuser who blames the victim for his or her own wrongdoing.

38. **E** She describes Jane's personality in the tenth year as "fire and violence," an implied comparison.

39. **C** Lines 3–6 reveal his intent to write a poem, but the winter snow is concealing the usual objects of poetry (lines 7–10).

40. **D** The speaker is "so near the pole"—a factor in nature and his poetry.

41. **B** What is the contrast? Winter (line 5) versus spring (line 11). In winter, things are frozen, concealed, forbidding, and confused. In spring, they flow, are in sight, are inviting, and are delightful.

42. **E** "Waste" can refer to the "dazzling" all-white snow blanketing the scene and to the loss of the inspiring scene beneath it.

43. **A** *Leviathan* is a biblical allusion to a sea creature mentioned in the book of Job and commonly used in literature to represent a large size and/or such a large animal as a whale. Even without being familiar with this allusion, the context of line 16 places the *Leviathan* playing in water.

44. **C** The "main" (line 19) can refer to the sea or be short for "mainland." Context supports the sea. Regardless, "glassy plain" compares the main to glass, a metaphor.

45. **B** The word "rattling" sounds like its meaning (onomatopoeia).

46. **E** He is describing the design and ultimate purpose of government. How does he structure the description? He establishes a model or example that can be used for comparison and discussion.

47. **C** Lines 29–30 establish the cause-and-effect relationship: Necessity becomes "like a gravitating power."

48. **D** Lines 38–44: "as they surmount…difficulties…they will…relax in their duty…and [need] government to supply… moral virtue."

49. **E** Disease and misfortune may not kill him directly, but the reduced physical condition that results might stop him from attaining food and shelter, in which case he would "perish."

50. **A** The answer appears in lines 29–30: "necessity, like a gravitating power" is the reason emigrants form into a society.

51. **E** Man seeks "assistance and relief" because of "wants" (line 11) and "solitude" (line 12).

52. **A** As part of the ironic situation being described, "mortal" would refer to causing death.

53. **C** The girls, particularly Charlotte, are speaking as friends in a revealing, casual tone.

54. **D** The two words ("monstrous pretty") are self-contradictory, in other words, an oxymoron.

55. **B** This literary allusion is clearly a reference to a respected authority on the need for women to become good wives and mothers. FYI: *The Spectator* was a daily periodical written by Richard Steele and Joseph Addison in the early 1700s.

56. **E** Her accident was a "bewitching false step," implying her intent.

57. **D** One can swim in a dance, connotative of smooth movements.

58. **A** The language and references used reveal that this play is depicting a period of formal society and conservative moral judgments. As such, for Charlotte to flirt openly, exposing her ankle to view, would be a morally unrestrained act.

59. **C** She calls Maria "grave" (line 52) and contrasts Maria's sentimental attitudes to her own flirting.

60. **D** She attempts to use *The Spectator* to prove her point in lines 44–49.

INDEX

A

absolute, 251
abstract language, 248
accent, 270
active voice, 136
allegorical meaning, 51
allegory, 214
alliteration, 31, 40, 169
allusion, 216
amplification, 226
anachronism, 227
analogy, 30, 71, 210
analysis and classification, 71
anapestic foot, 81
anastrophe, 265
anecdote, 48
antagonist, 199
anthropomorphism, 216
antihero(ine), 199
antithesis, 233
antonomasia, 223
aphorism, 257
apophasis, 227
apostrophe, 233
argument, 239
argumentation, 35
argumentative purpose, 49
aside, 105, 200
assonance, 31, 170
atmosphere, 154
attitude, 179
aubade, 60
autobiography, 72

B

balanced sentence, 253
ballad, 99
ballad stanza, 93
basic terms, 8
biblical allusion, 218
biography, 72
blank verse, 92

C

cacophony, 170
caesura, 84
carpe diem, 58
cause and effect, 71
central theme, 30
character (the), 199
character development, 196
characterization, 179, 186

character sketch, 199
choleric humour, 192
chorus, 134
chronological sequence, 68
cliché, 257
climactic order, 68
climactic sentence, 52
climate, 181
climax, 74, 104
College Board, 3
colloquial expressions, 237
comedy, 76, 102
common sentence, 252
comparison/contrast, 71
complement, 251
complication, 74, 103, 105
compound rhyme, 87
conceit, 214
conclusion, 35
concrete language, 248
concrete poetry, 102
confidant, 32, 200
conflict, 74, 103
conjunction, 256
connectives, 251
connotation, 261
consonance, 170
context, 10
controlling image, 212
conventional motifs and themes, 58
correspondence, 91
couplets, 34, 42, 92
crisis, 104
criticism, 73
cumulative sentence, 252

D

dactylic foot, 81
dead metaphor, 214
deductive order, 68
deductive reasoning, 71
definition, 71
denotation, 247, 261
dénouement, 74, 97, 104
description, 35, 71
descriptive purpose, 47
dialect, 236, 270
diaries, 72
diction, 31, 233, 236, 251
discovery, 104
dissonance, 170
division, 71

459

NOTES

NOTES

NOTES

NOTES

NOTES